A HISTORY OF
GREEK PHILOSOPHY

VOLUME II

A HISTORY OF
GREEK PHILOSOPHY

BY

W.K.C.GUTHRIE

F.B.A.

*Master of Downing College and
Laurence Professor of Ancient Philosophy in the
University of Cambridge*

VOLUME II

THE PRESOCRATIC TRADITION FROM
PARMENIDES TO DEMOCRITUS

CAMBRIDGE
AT THE UNIVERSITY PRESS
1969

PUBLISHED BY
THE SYNDICS OF THE CAMBRIDGE UNIVERSITY PRESS
Bentley House, 200 Euston Road, London, N.W. 1
American Branch: 32 East 57th Street, New York, N.Y. 10022
West African Office: P.O. Box 33, Ibadan, Nigeria

Standard Book Number: 521 05160 6
Library of Congress Catalogue Card Number: 62-52735

First published 1965
Reprinted 1969

First printed in Great Britain at the University Printing House, Cambridge
Reprinted in Great Britain by Alden & Mowbray Ltd.
at the Alden Press, Oxford

CONTENTS

Contents

Contents

Contents

Contents

Contents

The device on the cover is from a coin of Clazomenae, the birthplace of Anaxagoras, of Roman Imperial date. It shows the philosopher holding a globe, recalling perhaps the saying attributed to him that the study of the heavens and the whole universe is what makes life worth while (see p. 269 n. 2).

PREFACE

The phrase 'Presocratic tradition' is chosen for the title of this volume, rather than 'Presocratic philosophers', in acknowledgment of the fact that not all those included are Presocratic in the literal sense. (The main purpose of chapter VI is to bring home this point.) We shall continue to follow a line or family of philosophers who were interested in the same things and could meet on common ground to fight their intellectual battles, each trying to correct or refine on the views of the others on the same subject. Many of them were known in antiquity as the physical or natural philosophers, and I considered using this description in the title; but natural philosophy can hardly be stretched to cover the True Way of Parmenides or the paradoxes of Zeno, and their common interest can best be described as an investigation into the nature of reality and its relation to sensible phenomena. Man was not excluded from their surveys, but in both his individual and his social aspects was treated rather as an appendage to evolutionary theories of cosmogony. So far as modern terms are applicable, they dealt in physical and social anthropology rather than in ethics or politics. Others meanwhile were making man the centre of their study, and with his cosmic setting as background only, were laying the foundations of European moral and political theory. Since the two types of thinker were contemporaneous, and acquainted with each others' work, there could be no impenetrable barriers between them, and so we find Democritus, a *physikos* if ever there was one, also writing on ethical and political matters, though his expounders (perhaps wisely) concentrated on the atomic theory of the real world as his main achievement. Conversely the humanists made full use of current scientific theories as a basis for their teaching on the nature and behaviour of man. Yet on the whole they pursued fundamentally different aims, the 'Presocratics' seeking the advancement of knowledge for its own sake, and the Sophists and Socrates trying in different ways to discover and pursue the best life. Italian philosophers like the Pythagoreans and Empedocles also, it is true, preached a way of life, but it was one which could only be attained through an understanding of the cosmos, and its essentially religious character had nothing in common with the sceptical outlook of the Sophists. The fact that Empedocles was one of the leading politicians of his city finds little reflexion in his poems. The humanism which was developing side by side with the continuance of metaphysical and early scientific theory in the fifth century is here put aside, to be taken up in the next volume.

I am grateful to the reviewers of volume I both for the generous welcome which they gave it, and also for some highly pertinent criticisms. One of these touches on a point which has exercised me considerably, namely the order of exposition. I have kept to a chronological order of philosophers, dealing with each as a complete individual before passing to the next. There is much to be said for the method which my critic (and doubtless others) would prefer, of dividing by topics, following each separate problem or group of problems—the *physis* of things, the source of motion, cosmogony, the origins of life —as it was developed by successive thinkers throughout the period. The difficulty about this method is that none of the problems are in fact separate. The conclusions of these men about the ultimate constitution of things, the cause of motion or the nature of the soul were intimately connected and affected their pronouncements on every other topic as well. Each presents us with a system marvellously coherent down to its smallest details. It is indeed easy to see how a man's ideas on the 'first principles' of matter can affect what he has to say about cosmogony, cosmology and astronomy;[1] but some may think that at least minor topics like magnetism or the sterility of mules (which seems to have exercised a disproportionate fascination over our philosophers or those who reported them) could have been separated from the large metaphysical or cosmic speculations, a procedure which would have undoubted advantages for those who wish to refer quickly or conveniently to a compendium of ancient views on this or that aspect of natural science. Yet even that is not so.

This has not been my sole motive. In honesty I must confess that

---

[1] The critic who has provoked these remarks, Stephen Toulmin, has noted in his *Architecture of Matter* (p. 296) how this is happening now, no less than it did at the very beginning of science.

Preface

I am more interested in people than in theories, in philosophers than in philosophy. This, I hope, does not mean paying less attention to the development of ideas, but it does mean a preference for presenting the bearers of these ideas as individual characters, which, I should claim, even the unsatisfactory nature of our information permits us to see that they were. Their philosophies are the outcome of contrasting temperaments (as, perhaps, are all philosophies), and it is this human interest which I have tried above all things to bring out. In no one is it more vividly displayed than in Empedocles, and for that reason I have said a little more on this topic in introducing him (pp. 122 f.). As a second best for those readers whose interest lies primarily in the other direction, I have provided a fairly extensive table of contents, and also tried to make the index a means of finding out, as quickly as possible, the kind of information on the development of separate topics which would have been more easily available had the book been written the other way round. For this reason I have chosen to draw it up myself, and must bear the responsibility for any shortcomings in it.

We cannot remind ourselves too often of the difference between philosophy as it was understood in the period here treated, and as it is most often understood today, at least in our own country. This we may briefly do with the aid of two definitions, a modern and an ancient. The first was uttered in 1960: 'There is now a fair measure of agreement among philosophers that theirs is what is technically called a second-order subject. They do not set out to describe, or even to explain, the world, still less to change it. Their concern is only with the way in which we speak about the world. Philosophy, it has been said, is talk about talk.' Set beside this a pronouncement of the first century B.C.: 'Philosophy, to interpret the word, is nothing else but the pursuit of wisdom; and wisdom, as the old philosophers defined it, consists in a knowledge of things divine and human, and of the causes by which these things are maintained.'[1]

Books have usually been referred to in the notes by short titles, and articles by periodical, date and page only. Full particulars of books,

[1] A. J. Ayer, *Philosophy and Language* (inaugural lecture 1960, reprinted in *Clarity is not Enough*, ed. H. D. Lewis, 1963, p. 403); and Cicero, *De officiis*, 2. 2. 5.

and titles of articles, will be found in the bibliography. The standard collection of Greek texts relating to Presocratic philosophy is that of Diels, re-edited by Kranz (abbreviated DK; see bibliography, p. 508), to which reference is constantly made in the following pages. Under each philosopher the texts are divided into two sections. The first (A) contains *testimonia*, that is, accounts in later Greek authorities of the philosopher's life and doctrines, or paraphrases of his writings; in the second (B) are collected what in the opinion of the editors are genuine quotations from the philosopher himself. In this book the number of a 'B' passage is normally preceded by 'fr.' (fragment), while for the others the letter 'A' is retained.

The present volume owes many improvements to Sir Desmond Lee, Mr F. H. Sandbach, Dr G. S. Kirk and Dr G. E. R. Lloyd, who between them have read the whole in typescript. I have not, however, in every case adopted their suggestions, and the responsibility for any misjudgments is wholly mine. The index of passages has been compiled by Mr John Bowman. It is inevitable that mention of other scholars should most frequently occur in cases of disagreement, and I am acutely aware of how often I have mentioned the names of writers to whose works I am deeply indebted, only to express a criticism or difference of opinion. I hope they will accept this acknowledgment that these brief references by no means represent my appreciation of all that I have learned from them. I also noticed on reading the proofs that I have been quite inconsistent in referring to living authors by their titles or by plain surname, and I trust that these purely accidental variations will cause no offence.

DOWNING COLLEGE   W. K. C. G.
CAMBRIDGE

NOTE ON THE SOURCES

The meagreness of our inheritance of original works of the Greek philosophers is commented on in Volume I (24f.). For the Presocratics in particular we depend on excerpts, summaries and comments made by later writers. The problems to which this gives rise have always been recognized, and adequate accounts of the nature of the sources are available in several works, of which the best and most accessible is that of G. S. Kirk in KR, 1–7. (Others will be found in Ueberweg–Praechter, 10–26, Zeller, *Outlines*, 4–8, Burnet, *EGP*, 31–8.) In view of this I am making no attempt at a general appraisal at the beginning, but shall rather deal with particular source-problems as they arise over individual thinkers. (For the all-important Aristotle see especially Volume I, pp. 41–3.) But a certain amount must be briefly repeated here in order to make intelligible such references as will be necessary to 'Aët.', 'the *Placita*', 'Plut. *Strom.*' or 'Stob. *Ecl.*'

Theophrastus the pupil of Aristotle wrote a general history of earlier philosophy and special works on some individual Presocratics. Only extracts survive, though they include the greater part of the book *On Sensation*. These works of Theophrastus formed the main foundation for what is known as the doxographical tradition, which took different forms: 'opinions' arranged according to subjects, biographies, or somewhat artificial 'successions' (διαδοχαί) of philosophers regarded as master and pupil.

The classification of the doxographical material was undertaken in the monumental work of Hermann Diels, *Doxographi Graeci* (Berlin, 1879), to which all subsequent researchers into Presocratic philosophy owe an incalculable debt. The collections of the works of the early thinkers were known as δόξαι ('opinions', hence 'doxography') or τὰ ἀρέσκοντα (Latinized as *Placita*). There are two such collections or summaries extant, the *Epitome* falsely claimed as Plutarch's, and the *Physical Extracts* (φυσικαὶ ἐκλογαί) appearing in the *Anthology* or *Florilegium* of 'Stobaeus' (John of Stobi, probably fifth century A.D.). From a reference in the Christian bishop Theodoret (first half of fifth

xvii

century) it is known that both of these go back to a certain Aëtius, and the two are printed by Diels in parallel columns as the *Placita* of Aëtius. Aëtius himself, who is otherwise unknown, was probably of the second century A.D.

Between Theophrastus and Aëtius was a Stoic summary, of the first century B.C. at the latest, which can be detected behind doxographical accounts in Varro and Cicero, and was named by Diels the *Vetusta Placita*.

The doxographies in Hippolytus's *Refutation of all Heresies*, and the pseudo-Plutarchean *Stromateis* ('Miscellanies') preserved in Eusebius, appear to be independent of Aëtius.

The *Lives of the Philosophers* by Diogenes Laertius (probably third century A.D.) exists entire, and contains matter from various Hellenistic sources of uneven value.

To sum up, our information about the Presocratic philosophers depends first of all on extracts or quotations from their works which range from one brief sentence in the case of Anaximander (and of Anaximenes perhaps not even that) to practically the whole of the *True Way* of Parmenides. Secondly we have occasional mention and discussion of Presocratic thought in Plato, and a more systematic exposition and criticism in Aristotle. Finally there is the post-Aristotelian information which (with a few exceptions which will be mentioned in discussing the sources for particular philosophers) depends on brief, and sometimes garbled, epitomes of the work of Theophrastus, the distortions frequently taking the form of adaptation to Stoic thought. To see through this veil to the mind of archaic Greece is the primary task of Presocratic scholarship. Whether it is worth while no one had a better right to say than Hermann Diels, who at the end of his life declared, in a posthumously published lecture: 'I count myself fortunate in that it has been vouchsafed to me to dedicate the best part of my powers to the Presocratics.'[1]

For further details readers are referred to the account of Kirk mentioned above. In addition, an appraisal of the historical work of Theophrastus, which does him more justice than earlier accounts, is to be found in C. H. Kahn, *Anaximander*, 17–24.

[1] 'Ich schätze mich glücklich, dass es mir vergönnt war, den besten Teil meiner Kraft den Vorsokratikern widmen zu können' (*Neue Jahrbb. f. d. klass. Altertum*, 1923, 75).

LIST OF ABBREVIATIONS

In general, the titles of works cited in the text have not been so abbreviated as to be difficult of elucidation. Some periodicals, however, and a few books cited repeatedly, are referred to as follows:

PERIODICALS

AJA	*American Journal of Archaeology.*
AJP	*American Journal of Philology.*
CP	*Classical Philology.*
CQ	*Classical Quarterly.*
CR	*Classical Review.*
HSCP	*Harvard Studies in Classical Philology.*
JHS	*Journal of Hellenic Studies.*
PQ	*Philosophical Quarterly.*
REG	*Revue des Études Grecques.*
TAPA	*Transactions of the American Philological Association.*

OTHER WORKS

ACP	H. Cherniss, *Aristotle's Criticism of Presocratic Philosophy.*
CAH	*Cambridge Ancient History.*
DK	Diels–Kranz, *Fragmente der Vorsokratiker.*
EGP	J. Burnet, *Early Greek Philosophy.*
HCF	G. S. Kirk, *Heraclitus: the Cosmic Fragments.*
KR	G. S. Kirk and J. E. Raven, *The Presocratic Philosophers.*
LSJ	Liddell–Scott–Jones, *A Greek–English Lexicon*, 9th ed.
OCD	*Oxford Classical Dictionary.*
RE	*Realencyclopädie des klassischen Altertums*, ed. Wissowa, Kroll *et al.*
TEGP	W. Jaeger, *Theology of the Early Greek Philosophers.*
ZN	E. Zeller, *Die Philosophie der Griechen*, ed. W. Nestle.

I

THE ELEATICS

A. PARMENIDES

(1) *Date and life*

Presocratic philosophy is divided into two halves by the name of Parmenides. His exceptional powers of reasoning brought speculation about the origin and constitution of the universe to a halt, and caused it to make a fresh start on different lines. Consequently his chronological position relative to other early philosophers is comparatively easy to determine. Whether or not he directly attacked Heraclitus,[1] had Heraclitus known of Parmenides it is incredible that he would not have denounced him along with Xenophanes and others. Even if ignorance of an Elean on the part of an Ephesian is no sure evidence of date, philosophically Heraclitus must be regarded as pre-Parmenidean, whereas Empedocles, Anaxagoras, Leucippus and Democritus are equally certainly post-Parmenidean.

His approximate date is given by Plato in his dialogue *Parmenides*, when he describes a meeting between Parmenides and Socrates (127a–c):

Zeno and Parmenides once came to Athens for the Great Panathenaea. Parmenides was well advanced in years, about sixty-five, quite grey-haired, and of distinguished appearance, and Zeno was nearly forty....Socrates at the time was very young.

It would seem from this that Parmenides was forty or more years older than Socrates, who could hardly be described as 'very young' unless he was under twenty-five. Since Socrates was born in 470/69, this puts the birth of Parmenides at approximately 515–10.

It is true that Diogenes Laertius (9.23) gives his *floruit* as the 69th Olympiad (504–1), which is in conflict with this. Burnet however justly draws attention in this connexion to the mechanical methods of

---

[1] See vol. I, 408 n. 2 and pp. 23 ff., 32 below.

I

Apollodorus on whom Diogenes relied. It is likely that, as with Xenophanes, his point of reference was the foundation of Elea, the supposed *floruit* of Xenophanes being assumed as the birth-year of his 'pupil'. Birth and *floruit* are calculated at forty-year intervals. Similarly Parmenides's own pupil Zeno is said to have 'flourished' ten Olympiads later. As Burnet says, one can attach little importance to such combinations. Plato on the other hand, whether or not the meeting between Socrates and Parmenides is historical, had no reason to give such exact information about their ages unless he knew it to be correct.[1]

It is impossible to say at what age Parmenides wrote his philosophical poem. In fr. 1.24 he makes the goddess address him as κοῦρε (literally 'youth' or 'young man'). This however indicates no more than his relationship to her as disciple or recipient of her oracle. In the *Birds* of Aristophanes Peisthetairus, who is certainly not a young man, is addressed by the teller of oracles in the same way.[2]

By a tradition going back to Plato's nephew Speusippus, Parmenides was said to have been a legislator to whom Elea owed some at least of its laws.[3] Theophrastus, and after him later writers, make him a pupil of Xenophanes, though Aristotle did not commit himself, but reported only that this was 'said to be' the case (*Metaph.* 986 b 22). It is quite possibly true. Parmenides was much younger, but would have been about forty when the long-lived Xenophanes died. Both lived in Magna Graecia, and the influence of Xenophanes's conception of unity on Parmenides is clear, whether it came from his writings or from personal contact.[4]

The only other reported fact about his life is that he was at some

---

[1] Burnet, *EGP*, 169f.; KR, 263f. See also *Theaet.* 183e, *Soph.* 217c. Different views have been taken: see, e.g., ZN, 681–3 (note); Ueberweg–Praechter, 81f.; Mansfeld, *Offenbarung*, 207.

[2] θέσπιε κοῦρε, *Av.* 977. See W. J. Verdenius, *Mnemos.* 1947, 285 (anticipated by Nestle, ZN, 728).

[3] D.L. 9.23, quoting Speusippus 'in the first book *On Philosophers*'. Plutarch (*Adv. Col.* 1126a) adds that the citizens were made to swear annually to abide by the laws of Parmenides. A vaguer reference is in Strabo 6.1, p. 252. (DK, A 1 and 12.) There is no good reason to doubt this political activity on the part of Parmenides as of other Presocratic philosophers, but the cautionary remarks of Jaeger (*Aristotle*, Eng. tr. app. 2, 454, n. 1) should be noted. E. L. Minar (*AJP*, 1949, 41–55) suspects a connexion between Parmenides's political views and social position and his philosophical conceptions of being and seeming.

[4] That Aristotle's own statement should have arisen solely from the casual remark of Plato at *Soph.* 242d, which makes no mention of the relationship between the two men, seems to me highly unlikely, though others have thought differently. (See KR 265.)

time a Pythagorean. This is related circumstantially by Diogenes (1.21):

Though he was a pupil of Xenophanes he did not follow him. He also associated with Ameinias son of Diochaites, the Pythagorean, a poor man but of fine character, and it was rather Ameinias whose disciple he became. When he died, Parmenides built a shrine for him, being himself a man of noble birth and wealth, and it was Ameinias, not Xenophanes, who converted him to the quiet life.

The otherwise unknown Ameinias is not likely to have been an invention, and the shrine (ἡρῷον) with its inscription would be a monument of some permanence and doubtless itself the authority for the fact. Proclus (*in Parm.* 1, p. 619.4, DK, A 4) says simply that Parmenides and his pupil Zeno were 'both not only Eleans but also members of the Pythagorean school, as Nicomachus has recorded'. That Parmenides was at one time an adherent of Pythagoreanism finds some confirmation in his own work, but he certainly broke away from it, as from all other previous philosophical systems.

(2) *Writings*

He wrote in the hexameter metre of Homer and Hesiod, and the poem was preserved until a late date. It was available in its entirety to Simplicius, who quotes it at length for reasons which he states (*Phys.* 144.26):

The lines of Parmenides on the One Being are not many, and I should like to append them to this commentary both as confirmation of what I say and because of the rarity of the book.[1]

There follows a quotation of fifty-three lines, after which he adds: 'These then are the lines of Parmenides about the One Being.' One may assume that on this supremely important topic he has given the relevant passage complete. Altogether we now possess 154 lines, unevenly distributed. After a prologue of thirty-two lines, the poem is in two parts, dealing respectively with truth and seeming. Diels

---

[1] Diels (*Lehrgedicht*, 26) remarks that Simplicius's copy was excellent, and was probably in the library of the Academy, though Proclus used a different MS. He adds, without quoting evidence, that Aristotle's copy was not so good as Theophrastus's. Fr. 16 may be an example of what he had in mind, but the explanation is probably that Theophrastus was the more careful and less impromptu excerptor.

estimated that about nine-tenths of the first part has survived, whereas of the second there are only small scraps amounting to perhaps one-tenth. Fortunately the first part is by far the most important, and Simplicius showed his good sense in ensuring that it at least should go down to posterity in Parmenides's own words.

The style of the poem is variable. Of the central 'Way of Truth', in which he tries to expound the novel and paradoxical doctrine of the unity of Being and its consequences, the remark of Proclus that it is 'more like prose than poetry' is if anything an understatement. As he develops his strictly logical argument, Parmenides is hampered at every turn, and far more than Lucretius, by the *patrii sermonis egestas*. One can feel the struggle to convey philosophical concepts for which the expression does not yet exist, and some lines are scarcely amenable to translation at all. The prologue on the other hand is full of mythical imagery, and steeped in a religious fervour which it would be unwise to ignore. The fragments of the 'Way of Seeming' also show signs of a gift for poetic expression.[1]

(3) *A central problem*

The poem of Parmenides raises peculiar problems, and it will be as well to approach the text with the chief of these already in mind. In the prologue he receives from a goddess the promise that she will reveal to him two sorts of information: first the truth about reality, then the opinions of mortals, which are unambiguously said to be false. 'Nevertheless these too shalt thou learn' (fr. 1.31). In conformity with this, the first part of the poem deduces the nature of reality from premises asserted to be wholly true, and leads among other things to the conclusion that the world as perceived by the senses is unreal. At this point (fr. 8.50) the goddess solemnly declares that she ceases to speak the truth, and the remainder of the instruction will be 'deceitful'; yet she will impart it all 'that no judgment of men may outstrip thee'. Then follows the second part of the poem consisting of a cosmology

---

[1] To J. Beaufret, the line νυκτιφαὲς περὶ γαῖαν ἀλώμενον ἀλλότριον φῶς was 'un des plus beaux vers de la langue grecque' (*Le Poème de P.*, 8). It at least indicates, as Diels pointed out, that Parmenides had a sense of humour and was not above making a pun. See p. 66 below. Adverse criticisms of his style in antiquity are collected by Diels, *Lehrgedicht*, 5 ff.

on traditional lines. Starting from the assumption of a pair of opposites, 'fire' and 'night' or light and darkness, it proceeds as a narrative of an evolutionary process in time. The 'true way', on the other hand, had asserted that reality was, and must be, a unity in the strictest sense and that any change in it was impossible: there is no before or after, and the exposition unfolds as a timeless series of logical deductions.

Here is the crux. Why should Parmenides take the trouble to narrate a detailed cosmogony when he has already proved that opposites cannot exist and there can be no cosmogony because plurality and change are inadmissible conceptions? Has it in his eyes no merit or validity whatsoever, so that his purpose in composing it is only to show it up, together with all such attempts at cosmogony, for the hollow shams that they are? If so, the further question arises: what is it? Some have thought it to be based on a particular cosmic system of which he disapproved, for instance that of Heraclitus or the Pythagoreans.[1] Others have suggested, following up the goddess's own words about the 'opinions of mortals' in general, that it is partly or wholly intended as a synthesis of what the ordinary man believed about the world; others again that it is an original production, indeed the best that Parmenides could devise, but still intended to show that even the most plausible account of the origin and nature of the sensible world is utterly false. These critics point to the motive expressed by the goddess, 'that no judgment of mortals may outstrip (or get the better of) thee'.

An alternative is to suppose that Parmenides is doing his best for the sensible world, perhaps on practical grounds, by giving as coherent an account of it as he can, saying in effect: I have told you the truth, so that if I go on to speak about the world in which we apparently live you will know it is unreal and not be taken in. But after all, this is how it does appear to us; however misleading our senses may be, we must eat and drink and talk, avoid putting our hand in the fire or falling over a precipice, live in short as if their information were genuine. Being ourselves mortals we must come to terms with this

---

[1] Specific criticisms of earlier thinkers in Parmenides, with the possible exception of Heraclitus, are not obvious. The efforts of K. Reich to identify Anaximander's ἄπειρον with non-being, and to find a reference to Pythagorean doctrines of rebirth in the παλίντροπος κέλευθος of fr. 6.9, cannot be said to be successful. On the latter see H. Schwabl, *Anz. f. d. Altertumswiss* 1956, 146f. Some have seen criticism of Anaximenes in fr. 4, but cf. p. 32 below.

deceitful show, and I can at least help you to understand it better than other people.

These are the most baffling problems which Parmenides presents: the nature of the 'Way of Seeming' and the relation between it and the 'Way of Truth'. Yet the essence of his remarkable achievement lies, as might be expected, within the Way of Truth itself.

(4) *The prologue*[1]

Contrasting Parmenides and Heraclitus, Cornford wrote (*Plato and Parm.* 29): 'Heraclitus is the prophet of a *Logos* which could only be expressed in seeming contradictions; Parmenides is the prophet of a logic which will tolerate no semblance of contradiction.' In this description both are called prophets. Applied to a logician the term may sound contradictory, yet it is true that Parmenides was at one with Heraclitus in claiming a prophetic or apocalyptic authority for his teaching. He wrote in epic verse, evidently agreeing with Xenophanes that this medium must not be left to the retailers of scandalous myths. To live up to his reputation as a teacher, the poet must prove himself able to write the truth, not malicious fables. But to a Greek the gift of poetry meant that he was not writing unaided. Other poets had their Muse. Homer begins by invoking his, and Hesiod tells in circumstantial detail how the Muses came and taught him his song as he pastured his flock beneath Helicon in his native Boeotia. This was not metaphor, but reflected a genuine belief in an inspiration whereby the poet is granted deeper insight into the truth than other men. Heraclitus, writing in prose, had solemnly claimed to be uttering a truth that

---

[1] Some may think the following account of the prologue is superficial and ignores difficulties of detail. A full treatment will be found in J. Mansfeld, *Offenbarung des Parmenides*, ch. 4. To treat it at such length is impossible here, and in any case a reading of Mansfeld, as of some other scholars, has made me doubt whether in fact the attempt to press all the details of Parmenides's mysterious journey and force them into literal consistence is legitimate. Certainly some of Mansfeld's interpretations are highly speculative, e.g. the idea that εἰδώς in *v.* 3 implies that Parmenides has already received his revelation from the goddess and therefore is on his way *back* (on which Mansfeld bases a great deal), or the claim to see a connexion between the λάϊνος οὐδός of *v.* 12 and the 'solid wall' of the universe in A37. His book is a thorough and independent piece of work, and a treasury of the results of previous scholarship, for which a reader may be confidently referred to it. It is indispensable to a serious student of Parmenides, especially perhaps for its concern to determine what in later terminology are the logical forms of the arguments which he was already capable of using. But each must go his own way. The approach here is different, and I have not attempted to note all the places in which I have thought differently from Mansfeld.

endures for ever. When in the introductory lines of his poem Parmenides announces that what he has to say was revealed to him by a goddess after a magical journey through the gates of Day and Night, he is making a similar claim in the poet's traditional manner.

The prologue, which we owe in the main not to Simplicius but to Sextus, may be translated as follows:[1]

The mares that carry me as far as my heart ever aspires sped me on, when they had brought and set me on the far-famed road of the god [i.e. the Sun], which bears the man of knowledge over all cities. On that road was I borne,

v. 1. φέρουσι. The present suggests habit: Parmenides is a shaman-like figure for whom such spiritual journeys are a regular experience (Morrison, *JHS*, 1955, 59). For the opt. ἱκάνοι, cf. *Il.* 4.263 πιέειν ὅτε θυμὸς ἀνώγοι, etc. (Kühner–Gerth, II, 2.452).

v. 2. πολύφημον may just possibly mean something like 'sagacious' (Jaeger), a transferred epithet. Fränkel (*Wege u. Formen*, 159, n. 4) denies that it ever means 'famous', saying that φήμη is rather 'Kunde, bedeutungvolles, wirksames Wort'. He is followed by Verdenius, *Parm.* 12. LSJ on the other hand quote Pindar, *Isthm.* 8.64 θρῆνος π. as an instance where π. is equivalent to πολύφατος, famous. Either sense would be possible there as here. See also Mansfeld, *Offenbarung*, 229, n. 1.

v. 3. δαίμονος. So Sextus, and there is no reason to alter to δαίμονες with Stein, Wilamowitz and DK. Others take δαίμονος as fem., referring to the goddess who is introduced at *v*. 22. Several scholars have recognized that Parmenides sees himself as travelling through the sky in the Sun's chariot, as is indeed sufficiently obvious. Like Phaethon he has the Sun's daughters as guides and charioteers (*vv*. 9, 24), the axle is blazing (*v*. 7), the starting-point is the house of Night (*v*. 9; see esp. Bowra, *CP*, 1937, 103 f.). It is all the more strange that so few have made the identification given above. (Sextus in his paraphrase gives the masc. article to δαίμονος, though one cannot be certain what god he had in mind.) As Fränkel noted, the relative pronoun could go equally well with ὁδόν or δαίμονος (*op. cit.* 160). I do not know why Parmenides made the steeds mares (they are masc. in Pindar, *Ol.* 7.71), but this need not affect the identification.

κατὰ πάντ' ἄστη. These words have caused much unnecessary trouble and emendation. Burnet and Jaeger took them to mean that Parmenides's way led *through* all cities, which caused Burnet to suppose, somewhat prosaically, that he was a kind of itinerant sophist, and Jaeger to alter the text as inconsistent with *v*. 27 (see Burnet, *EGP*, 172, n. 1; Jaeger, *Paideia*, I, 177, n. 1). But the poet is consistent throughout. He is crossing the sky in the Sun's own chariot, and this path, since it traverses the whole world, naturally carries him 'over all cities', while at the same time it is 'far from the footsteps of men'. The phrase is Homeric; cf. *Il.* 4.276 νέφος...ἐρχόμενον κατὰ πόντον ὑπὸ Ζεφύροιο ἰωῆς and 19.92 f. οὐ γὰρ ἐπ' οὔδει...ἀλλ'...κατ' ἀνδρῶν κράατα. (The text of the Thurii tablet, Orph. fr. 47.3 Kern, sometimes quoted in this connexion, is too uncertain for it to be added to the evidence.) Similarly, Phaethon was carried 'terras per omnes' (Lucr. 5.398).

εἰδότα φῶτα. The word εἰδώς certainly carried overtones of mystical religion, of which some scholars have made much; but to be εἰδώς is a fitting privilege for one following the track of the Sun, who knows everything because he πάντ' ἐφορᾷ καὶ πάντ' ἐπακούει (*Od.* 11.109; *Il.* 3.277).

for by it the wise steeds took me, straining at the chariot, and the maidens led the way. And the blazing axle in the axle-boxes made the sockets sing,

[1] Fr. 1, Sext. *Math.* 7.111. From now on, the exposition will take the form of a translation of the poem with commentary. The translation bristles with difficulties and alternative possibilities. These will be considered, and the choice of rendering defended, in notes. More general questions of interpretation will be treated in the text.

driven on both sides by the two whirling wheels, as the daughters of the Sun, having left the house of Night, hastened to bring me to the light, throwing back the veils from their heads with their hands.

v. 4. The meaning of πολύφραστοι is not certain. The most recent discussion is that of A. Francotte in *Phronesis*, 1958. He suggests that it means 'eloquent'. The horses, like those of Achilles, have the gift of speech. (Cf. p. 10, n. 2 below.) I have hesitated to adopt this translation out of a feeling that it would be an extraordinarily abrupt way of introducing and leaving such an important idea. But it may be right.

v. 6. The reading χνοίησιν ἵει (Diels) is not absolutely certain. See DK *ad loc.*
σύριγγος ἀϋτήν. Commonly translated 'the sound of a pipe' (though not by KR, 266). But σῦριγξ must surely bear the same meaning as in *v.* 19 below, viz. the socket of an ἄξων (in this case the opening in the wheel-nave into which it fitted). Cf. Aesch. *Th.* 205 σύριγγες ἔκλαγξαν, *Suppl.* 181 οὐ σιγῶσιν.

v. 7. αἰθόμενος. Taken by Burnet, DK and others to mean 'glowing' with heat engendered by the speed (δοιοῖς γὰρ κτλ.). But, as Bowra has pointed out (*CP*, 1937, 104), this is a mistranslation: the word means 'blazing'. It has therefore no predicative force here, but is an epithet appropriate to the Sun's fiery chariot. γάρ links with the main verb.
δινωτοῖσιν. Perhaps, as in Homer, 'turned', 'rounded', with no reference to motion.

v. 8. σπερχοίατο. Iterative. Cf. *v.* 1 ἱκάνοι and Fränkel, *op. cit.* 159. As Vos pointed out (see now Mansfeld, *Offenbarung*, 238f.), this sentence could mean: 'As the daughters of the Sun, having left the house of Night, hastened to escort me.' This need not however imply the remarkable idea that the mares made the first part of the journey on their own, without drivers.

v. 10. Some see symbolic significance in the casting back of the veils, and Bowra 'a detail indicative of almost indecent haste, which surely comes from some old story'. But it may be no more than a vague Homeric echo: the prologue is full of such. Nausicaa and her maidens play ball ἀπὸ κρήδεμνα βαλοῦσαι (*Od.* 6.100), and the mourning Hecuba ἀπὸ λιπαρὴν ἔρριψε καλύπτρην (*Il.* 22.406).

There are the gates of the paths of Night and Day, set between a lintel and a threshold of stone. They themselves, high in the sky, are blocked with great doors, of which avenging Justice holds the alternate keys. Her the maidens beguiled with soft words, and skilfully persuaded her to push back swiftly for them the bolted bar from the gates. The doors flew back and revealed the wide opening between their leaves, swinging in turn in their sockets the bronze-bound pivots made fast with dowels and rivets. Straight through them the maidens kept the chariot and horses on the highway.

v. 14. ἀμοιβούς by itself need only mean that the 'keys' alternately open and shut the gates, or alternatively that they cross one another. In epic Greek κληῖδες were either bars put across the leaves of a door to shut it (e.g. *Il.* 12.455) or hooks with which the bar could be reached from the outside in order to move it (as in *Od.* 21.47). The present phrase can hardly be unconnected in sense with the ὀχῆες ἐπημοιβοί of *Il.* 12.455f., and the κληῖς may be identical with the ὀχεύς removed by Dike in *v.* 16. ἔχει would then bear the meaning 'has charge of', as the Horae have charge of the gates of heaven in Homer (*Il.* 5.749).

On Greek locks and bolts see Diels, *Lehrgedicht*, 116ff.; E. Pottier in Daremberg–Saglio, III, 603ff., and for further reff. W. R. Pritchett, *Hesperia*, 1956, 179 n. and 234. In Parmenides's account the γόμφοι and περόναι may perform a different function, but it seems in accordance with recent archaeological evidence to suppose that they were the means of fastening the bronze caps to the pivots. See Robinson and Graham, *Olynthus*, 8 (1938), 253–4; Robinson, *ibid.* 10 (1940), 295. In spite of the technical nature of the description, I am inclined to think that to raise the question why keys are spoken of in the plural is rather like asking why St Peter has the keys (rather than key) of heaven. See, however, Mansfeld, *Offenbarung*, 240.

πολυχάλκους. Bronze-bound rather than brazen: the pivots were usually of wood, the lower end being shod with a bronze cap (Robinson and Graham, *loc. cit.*; Pritchett, *loc. cit.* 235).

And the goddess welcomed me graciously, took my right hand in hers, and addressed me with these words:

Young man, who comest to my house companioned by immortal charioteers with the steeds that bear thee, I greet thee. No evil lot has sent thee to travel this road—and verily it is far from the footsteps of men—but Right and Justice. It is meet for thee to learn all things, both the unshaken heart of well-rounded truth and also what seems to mortals, in which is no true conviction. Nevertheless these things too shalt thou learn, namely that what seems had assuredly to exist, being indeed everything.

v. 28. That Θέμις brought him to the goddess means that his journey is something permitted or sanctioned.

v. 29. εὐκυκλέος (a ἅπαξ λεγόμενον) is the reading of Simplicius. εὐφεγγέος Proclus, εὐπειθέος Sext., Clem. Alex., Plut., D.L. The last was the accepted reading until Diels vindicated εὐκυκλέος (*Lehrgedicht*, 55–6). In *Phronesis*, 1958, 21ff., G. J. Jameson argued for εὐπειθέος, but cf. Vlastos in *Gnomon*, 1959, 194, n. 4.

vv. 31–2 have caused much difficulty and been interpreted in many ways. The translation above follows that of Owen in *CQ*, 1960, 88f., where the most usual earlier version is discussed. Many renderings are given by Nestle in ZN, 733, n. 1.

v. 32. Diels's notion of putting an apostrophe after the last letter of δοκίμως and supposing elision of αι, making it the infin. of δοκιμόω or δοκίμωμι for δοκιμάζω, carried little conviction and was dropped by Kranz. See Kranz, *SB Preuss. Ak.* 1916, 1170, and now the objections of Owen, *loc. cit.* 87 and W. R. Chalmers in *Phronesis*, 1960, 7.

περῶντα is kept by Kranz in DK, but the reading περ ὄντα is much better attested in the text of Simplicius, and I have followed Owen in retaining it. But, as he says, 'no major point of interpretation now hangs on it'.

The important feature of Owen's translation is that ὡς τὰ δοκοῦντα κτλ. are not a comment of the goddess, but summarize the content of the opinions of mortals which she has promised to relate. Once this is seen, the difficulties of the clause largely disappear. For Mansfeld's interpretation see *Offenbarung*, 128, 156ff. He does not discuss Owen's, though otherwise giving a very full and useful summary of alternative translations.

The essential features of the prologue are these. Parmenides is privileged above other mortals. Like a more fortunate Phaethon, he is borne through the sky in the sun-chariot with the Sun's daughters to drive him. The journey is not narrated stage by stage, but the key-points are brought out in an impressionistic manner. It is a journey from Night to Day. Where these meet is a formidable barrier, the importance of which is emphasized by dwelling on the details of its construction, a gate guarded by the figure of Justice. None may pass without her permission, that is, unless his passage is sanctioned by right and by divine consent.

The Eleatics

Once through the gate, the road leads straight to the house of an unnamed goddess, probably not immediately since Parmenides speaks of continuing straight along the carriage-way (ἁμαξιτός); but we cannot say how far, for he wastes no time over inessentials, but simply throws a spotlight on the critical points in the journey. The goddess confirms his right to be there, and promises to teach him 'all things', both the truth and what is falsely believed by mortals.

This narrative plainly gives to what follows it the character of a divine revelation, but to determine how seriously Parmenides believed in this is not easy.[1] The mythical elements of the prologue are for the most part traditional. Much of the phraseology is borrowed from Homer and Hesiod.[2] The goddess who instructs the poet corresponds to the Muse of the epic writers, who may also be addressed as 'goddess', as in the opening line of the *Iliad*: 'Sing, goddess, of the wrath.' When at the beginning of the catalogue of ships Homer invokes the Muses to aid him, he adds (*Il.* 2.485): 'for you are goddesses, and are present and know all things'. Hesiod was taught his song by the Muses as he pastured his sheep under Helicon, and it is noteworthy that they said to him (*Theog.* 27f.): 'We know how to say many false things resembling true, and we know how to utter the truth when we wish.' Parmenides was under the influence of an old tradition, though he turned it to novel ends, when he told of the goddess saying that she would teach him both the truth and what seems true but is not. There are also hints that he was acquainted with the Orphic poems,[3] but

---

[1] On the character of the prologue see especially Nestle in ZN, 726–9; Bowra, *CP*, 1937, 97–112; Fränkel, *Wege u. Formen*, 158–73; Diels, *Lehrgedicht*; Kranz, *SB Preuss. Ak.* 1916, 1158–76.

[2] Cf. e.g. *v.* 5 with *Il.* 2.390, *Od.* 6.261, 24.225; *v.* 15 with Hes. *Th.* 90, *Od.* 16.286–7, 19.5–6; *v.* 25 with *Il.* 18.385; *v.* 27 with *Il.* 6.202, *Od.* 9.119. E. A. Havelock even argues, in *HSCP*, 1958, that the journey of Odysseus is the primary model, and that this *Odyssey* motif is continued in the philosophical parts of the poem. Naturally he agrees that the horses and chariot belong to a different set of associations (the πολύφραστοι ἵπποι of *v.* 4 are the horses of Achilles, a suggestion first made by Diels), but this does not seem to him so big an exception as it may to others. Parallels with the *Odyssey* are also drawn by Mansfeld, *Offenbarung*, 230.

[3] Notably in the reference to Δίκη πολύποινος. Cf. Orph. fr. 158. Diels and others have quoted ps.-Dem. 25.11 (Orph. fr. 23) as a parallel proving that the Orphic verse is ancient. See on this point Gruppe, *Rhaps. Theog.* 708; Dieterich *Kl. Schr.* 412f.; Kern, *De theogoniis*, 52. Later in the poem the contemptuous dismissal of mortals at fr. 6.4ff. looks like a reminiscence of Orph. fr. 233. Both in Parmenides and the Orphic writer the railing at mortals is primarily directed against their ignorance. Hence εἰδότα φῶτα in *v.* 3 probably carries its overtones of religious initiation. (For exx. see Bowra, 109.) One may compare also the *light* which is granted to Eleusinian initiates in the next world and is one of their chief joys (Ar. *Frogs*, 455f.).

all these echoes are on a verbal level and demonstrate no more than that Parmenides was steeped in the tradition of older and contemporary poetry. (Bowra quotes similar images in Pindar, Bacchylides, Simonides and others.) There is for instance no hint in his teaching that he subscribed to the characteristic Orphic doctrines. The general character of the prologue points rather to the (of course not unrelated) 'shamanistic' strain in early Greek religious thought, represented by semi-legendary figures like Aithalides, Aristeas, Abaris, Epimenides and Hermotimus. Of Aithalides it was said that he had from Hermes the gift that his *psyche* could travel now in Hades and now above the earth (Pherecydes, fr. 8 DK). Aristeas made similar magical journeys and could appear in two places at once (Hdt. 4.13 ff.), and the soul of Hermotimus was accustomed to leave his body lying and wander alone in search of knowledge (Pliny, *N.H.* 7.174). Epimenides while his body slept encountered the goddesses Truth and Justice (Epim. fr. 1 DK *ad fin.*), which brings his experience close to that of Parmenides.

What is here described reads like a similar spiritual journey 'above the earth' with knowledge as its goal. The resemblance of such a journey to those of the shamans of Siberia and elsewhere was noted long ago by Diels, and the increase in comparative material since his time has only strengthened the resemblance.[1] They too can project their souls on spiritual journeys, sometimes through the sky, during which they acquire superhuman knowledge.

In this religious and apocalyptic tradition Parmenides has chosen to set the implacable logic which occupied the heart of his poem. He was a native of South Italy, where mystical religion was at home, and almost

---

[1] Diels, *Lehrgedicht*, 14 f., referring to Radloff, *Aus Sibirien*, II, 3 ff. Parmenides's vision is again related to shaman-poetry by K. Meuli in *Hermes*, 1935, 171 f. In *Gks and Irrational*, ch. 5, Dodds makes out a case for actual historical contact, through trade and colonization, between the Greeks and the shamanistic cultures centred in Siberia.

On shamanistic journeys in general see Norah K. Chadwick's *Poetry and Prophecy*, of which the last chapter ('The Spiritual Journeys of the Shamans') emphasizes their universality. Note also that among the principal themes are journeys 'to the bright Heavens above' as well as to the underworld, and that 'in these expeditions the men generally require the help of supernatural beings, especially supernatural women'. (Cf. the Heliades.) W. Burkert (*Weisheit u. Wiss.* 130) brings forward evidence for his belief that 'shamanistic practices seem to have been still current in S. Italy of the 6th century B.C.' Perhaps, however, Eliade's work on *Shamanism* (since 1964 available in a revised English edition) should caution us against too free a use of the term with reference to Greek practice or belief. See the section on shamanistic ideologies and techniques among the Indo-Europeans (pp. 375 ff.).

certainly a Pythagorean; and Pythagoras was believed to have been a reincarnation of both Aithalides and Hermotimus (D.L. 8.4–5; DK 14.8). One cannot doubt that the prologue describes a genuine experience. As a mere literary device nothing could be more unsuited to the main content of the poem, which would have been much better conveyed in the plain prose of an Anaximenes or an Anaxagoras. Clearly, however, Parmenides was not a rationalist of the Ionian type, and it is extraordinarily difficult, at the immense spiritual distance from which we contemplate his remains, to know how much weight should be given to the non-rational element in his writings. Like other figures of archaic Greece, he achieved an outstanding intellectual advance within a framework of almost primitive irrationality. How far had he freed himself from it? Bowra points out (*op. cit.* 98) that whereas his predecessors had believed in the reality of the mythical apparatus (e.g. Epimenides believed his converse with gods in the Dictaean Cave to be a literal fact), 'Parmenides is plainly allegorizing'. The gates and the paths of Night and Day are conflated from Hesiod and the *Odyssey*,[1] but for him the journey through the gates from Night to Day represents a progress from ignorance to the knowledge or truth which awaits him on the other side. The road (ὁδός) is a widespread poetical image, but for Parmenides, who carries it right through the poem, it is allegorized as a 'road of inquiry'. The right path (κέλευθος) follows truth, to go wrong is to follow 'an indiscernible track' (ἀταρπός). Thus he 'used certain ideas and images which were familiar to his time, but he used them for a new purpose, and especially he narrowed their application to his own sphere of the search for knowledge' (*ibid.* 112).

Yet while agreeing with Bowra that Parmenides's use of allegory must have been conscious and deliberate, we must not forget the extent to which, even in those passages which display it, the ground had been prepared in the pre-philosophical past. The spiritual odyssey of the shaman had always been a search for knowledge. The equation 'road or journey = quest for knowledge = lay or narrative conveying the results of that quest' was not his own, but already present in the

---

[1] Hes. *Th.* 748 speaks of Night and Day greeting each other as they cross the great bronze threshold, the one entering as the other emerges. Parm. 1.11 is modelled verbally on *Od.* 10.86 ἐγγὺς γὰρ Νυκτός τε καὶ Ἥματός εἰσι κέλευθοι.

shamanistic practices of which his poem contains distinct though far-off echoes.[1]

This religious ancestry, and the extent to which it was a living force for Parmenides, must then be borne in mind throughout, but not exaggerated. He put his philosophy in the mouth of a goddess, through a prologue containing elements taken from earlier religious poetry and in some cases traceable to a shamanistic origin; but he is not to be summed up as 'a psychologically unstable person who has received a call to the religious life'.[2] A few quotations from Bowra's article probably bring us as near to the truth as we can get. Parmenides 'writes not as a mere logician but as one who has had a very special experience similar to that of those who have consorted with the gods'. He 'regarded the search for truth as something akin to the experience of mystics, and he wrote of it with symbols taken from religion because he felt that it was itself a religious activity'. At the same time the prologue is not to be explained solely by its origins: 'Parmenides is plainly allegorizing. The allegory may of course be based on something akin to a mystical experience, but it is none the less an allegory. ...Parmenides is not giving the literal record of a spiritual adventure but clothing his search for truth in allegorical dress.' If these statements seem to display some inconsistency, it is probably an inconsistency inherent in the philosopher's own mind, in the tension between an inherited and still valid pattern of thought and his own revolutionary intellectual vigour.[3]

(5) *Two ways of inquiry: one true, the other impossible*

(Fr. 2) Come now, I will tell (and do thou lay up my word when thou hast heard it) the only ways of inquiry that are to be thought of. The one, that it is and that it is impossible for it not to be, is the path of Persuasion (for

---

[1] This has been shown by Meuli, *op. cit.* 172f.

[2] Dodds's definition of a shaman, *Gks and Irrational*, 140.

[3] The words of so sensitive a critic as Hermann Fränkel are also worth quoting. Parmenides is a philosopher, and in a philosophical text, he says, one is inclined to suppose that the subject speaks for itself, independently of the language, which is rather accidental. 'Yet' (I translate) 'much elementary misunderstanding results, and much of the best, most individual and alive in the doctrine itself is lost, until we make up our minds to read the work as an epic poem of the epoch at which it was written, and by means of the language to grasp the actual historical phenomenon' (*Wege und Formen*, 157). 'For the archaic period, word and thought, speech and its subject are one, and this is true in a special sense for Parmenides' (*ibid.* 158).

she attends on Truth). The other, that it is not, and that it must necessarily not be, that I declare is a wholly indiscernible track; for thou couldst not know what is not—that is impossible—nor declare it, (fr. 3) for it is the same thing that can be thought and can be.

2.5. ἡ δ' ὡς οὐκ ἔστιν τε καὶ ὡς χρεών ἐστι μὴ εἶναι. Kranz (*SB Preuss. Ak.* 1916, 1173) takes οὐκ ἔστιν to mean 'it does occur that something is not', i.e. there is, besides what is, a non-existent. This he thinks is shown by 6.1, which he translates, following Diels: 'One must say and think that ⟨only⟩ that which is, is: for there is being, but there is not not-being (*das Nichtseiende*).' So understood this first false way brings with it becoming and perishing, loco-motion, and change. It is the way of the generality of men. The second false way mentioned in fr. 6 is the way of the Heracliteans. This interpretation seems worth mentioning, but is im-probable. Apart from the translation of 6.1 (for which see next note), Kranz does not in his article translate the second half of 1.5. It is of course translated without comment in DK ('dass NICHT IST *ist*, und dass Nichtsein erforderlich ist'), but taken as a whole his rendering seems forced and unnatural.

The translation of fr. 3 follows Zeller and Burnet. The infinitive has its original dative force, and the meaning is literally 'the same thing is for thinking and for being', an exactly parallel construction to εἶσι νοῆσαι in 2.2. This justifies also the rendering of 6.1 as 'It is necessary that what is for speaking and thinking should be', i.e. 'What can be spoken and thought about must be'. See Burnet, *EGP*, 173, n. 2. I still think this the most probable translation, even if Burnet's specific argument that the bare infinitive could not be the subject of a sentence is not conclusive. (On that point see Heidel, *Proc. Am. Ac.* 1913, 720, and Verdenius, *Parm.* 34f.) It does not (like Hölscher's version criticized by Mansfeld, *Offenbarung*, 63) involve the incongruity of taking νοεῖν as passive and εἶναι as active (if it is right to speak in these terms when εἶναι is not a transitive verb). Mansfeld's preferred translation ('Denn Denken und Sein sind dasselbe') turns out to mean much the same. It does not, he says, imply (as one would suppose) the identity of Thought and Being, but only that 'the object of thought is at the same time the subject of being' (*op. cit.* 67); or as he puts it on p. 101, with what seems to me doubtful logic: 'Das Seiende ist der einzige Gegenstand des Denkens, das einzig Denkbare. *Deshalb* sind Sein und Denken identisch.' (My italics.)

The subject of the verb 'is' is not expressly named. It has most commonly been taken to be 'what is', i.e. Parmenides is uttering a logical tautology: what is, is. So for instance Diels and Cornford. Burnet construed it as body or corporeality: 'The assertion that *it is* amounts just to this, that the universe is a *plenum*.' This conclusion is, as Raven justly remarks, 'at least premature'. Verdenius suggested 'all that exists, the total of things', again perhaps prematurely.[1] Others have thought it wrong to look for any subject. 'At this early stage in his poem Parmenides's premise ἔστι (*it is*) has no definite subject at all.' So Raven and Fränkel suggested that the verb *is* 'is primarily used by Parmenides as a so-called impersonal, somewhat like "it

---

[1] In a later note (*Mnemos.* 1962, 237) he has revised his opinion in favour of the suggestion that the subject is ἀληθείη, in the sense not of a logical category but of 'the true nature of things'. He invites us to compare frr. 8.51 and 1.29.

rains", "raining takes place"'. To this Professor Owen has pertin-
ently objected that something more definite must be intended 'because
Parmenides goes on to prove various characteristics of the subject of
his ἔστι'. Owen's own solution is that 'what is declared to exist is
simply what can be talked or thought about', and is actually mentioned,
not here in fr. 2, but in fr. 6.1: 'What can be spoken and thought about
must be.'[1]

Thus the serious choice of subject lies between 'what is' and 'what
can be talked and thought about'. In one way it does not seem serious,
for Parmenides in any case identifies the two, and according to Owen
himself, 'no one will deny that, as the argument goes, τὸ ἐόν [what is]
is a correct description of the subject'. His objection to taking it as the
unexpressed subject itself is the logical one that 'it turns the *is* into a
mere tautology, and the *is not* correspondingly into a flat contradiction,
whereas Parmenides thinks it necessary to *argue* for *is* and against *is
not*'. He does not assume it from the start.

In saying that something *is*, Parmenides undoubtedly had in mind
what can be talked and thought about, since he explicitly identifies the
two. That then is a correct description of the subject, as also is 'what
is'. Nevertheless it does not seem quite fair to scholars such as Cornford, who suppose that in fr. 2 he is saying simply 'what is, is', to
object either that they are unaware that a tautology is incapable of
proof, or that they accuse Parmenides of failing to see this simple point.

The history of Greek thought up to his time may allow a different
view, for the polemical character of the poem is unquestioned. Later
he argues with devastating precision that once one has said that something *is*, one is debarred from saying that it *was* or *will be*, of attributing
to it an origin or a dissolution in time, or any alteration or motion
whatsoever. But this was just what the Milesians had done. They supposed that the world had not always existed in its present cosmic state.
They derived it from one substance, which they asserted to have changed
or moved in various ways—becoming hotter or colder, drier or wetter,

---

[1] See his article 'Eleatic Questions' in *CQ*, 1960. References for the other views mentioned
above will be found there, except Burnet's (*EGP*, 178 f.). Patin and Calogero also supposed
that ἔστιν had no particular subject. The fullest review of opinions is in Mansfeld, *Offenbarung*,
45–55. He himself thinks that the propositional logic which Parmenides is using makes it unnecessary to look for a subject (p. 58). His discussion makes no mention of Owen.

rarer or denser—in order to produce the present world-order. (Cf. Parmenides, 8.40–1.) Of course if it had been said to them, 'What is, *is*, is it not?', they must have agreed at once. In refuting their contentions, Parmenides is not so much *proving* the tautology as showing that earlier thinkers, as well as the ordinary run of mankind, had never formulated it explicitly, and so had evaded its implications. It is perhaps the first, but certainly not the last time that a philosopher has thought it necessary to start from a tautology for the same reasons.[1]

In the long extract known as fr. 8, he starts by saying 'It is' (that is, on the Dielsian interpretation, stating the tautology that what is, is), and then goes on to state and demonstrate, not the statement that 'it is', but certain 'marks' (σήματα) along this way; that is, certain attributes which whatever *is* must possess. It must be everlasting, indivisible, motionless, etc., although hitherto people had carelessly said that what is can come into being, divide itself, move, and perish. Even here in fr. 2 it seems too much to say that 'It is' is proved or argued for. It is stated and said to be true. For the sake of completeness Parmenides then mentions its contrary (though, as Owen and others agree, there is no suggestion that anyone ever takes this way), and briefly dismisses it as inconceivable. In this and fr. 8, taken together, he says to his fellow-men in effect: 'What is, is. You call this a tautology, and so do I, but you do not think clearly enough to see what that admission leads to. If you give to *is* its full and proper force, you are precluded from saying that what is suffers any process of becoming or perishing, change or movement.'

To repeat, this is no denial of the claim that what *is*, according to Parmenides, is what can be spoken and thought of: he says so himself. But the argument that no one thinks it necessary to *argue* for a tautology does not rule out the possibility that if the subject were expressed in 2.3, it would run: 'What is, is, and cannot not-be.' Moreover in the same century Gorgias thought it possible to argue for a logical contradiction: he 'proved' that what is is not (οὐδὲ τὸ ὂν ἔστιν). If this could be done, then surely at the same stage of thought, or slightly

---

[1] 'Trivialities and platitudes deserve emphatic affirmation when, as often in philosophy, they are explicitly or implicitly denied, or forgotten, or overlooked' (J. R. Bambrough, *Proc. Arist. Soc.* 1960–1, 215).

earlier, it could seem both possible and necessary to argue the tautology.[1]

The significance of this will be brought out in fr. 8. Meanwhile he dismisses the statement 'It is not' as impossible. For him it is sufficient justification of this to say that the subject of such a statement could never enter our minds, for what is not can neither be recognized nor pointed out to another. He could hardly have been expected to reckon with the frivolities of late fifth-century sophistry. The Sophists seized on the forms of Eleatic logic to make all knowledge seem absurd, as Gorgias was doing with his defence of the thesis 'It is not'. Parodying the title *On Nature or the Existent* commonly given to works of the natural philosophers, he produced a treatise *On the Non-existent or on Nature*, in which he argued three theses: (*a*) that nothing exists, (*b*) that if anything existed we could have no knowledge of it, (*c*) that if anyone knew it he could not communicate his knowledge.

Fr. 3 is usually translated as above: 'It is the same thing that can be thought and can be.' Similarly, 6.1: 'What can be spoken and thought of must be (i.e. exist).'[2] To find any other English equivalent is difficult, but this only emphasizes the inadequacy of translation and the truth that language and thought are inseparable. As translated, the statements seem simply mistaken. It is obviously possible to speak and think of objects that do not exist, like the unicorns, centaurs and present King of France beloved of the twentieth-century philosopher.

It is true that on this point philosophy has advanced, but for the historian the matter is not closed by saying that Parmenides was mistaken. His 'mistake' opens the way to an understanding of the rather different conceptions of mental processes and speech held by the ancient Greeks.[3] The verb translated *think of* (*noein*) could not, in and before his time, convey the notion of imagining something non-existent, for

[1] Gorg. fr. 3; DK, 11, 280.11 ff. See also Reinhardt, *Parm.* 36.

[2] For Mansfeld's version see note on translation. He denies the accepted view that fr. 3 follows directly on fr. 2 and suggests (p. 82) a conjectural line which, if it stood between them, would yield the logic that he favours.

[3] K. von Fritz has made the point that a study of the history of Greek philosophical and scientific terms offers a unique opportunity for an inquiry into the connexions between philosophical and pre-philosophical thought. This is because the Greeks developed their philosophical terminology entirely within their own language, not from foreign sources like ourselves. Their terms are therefore either words directly taken over from common speech or adaptations of such words (*CP*, 1943, 79).

it connoted primarily an act of immediate recognition. In Homer it may mean little more than seeing; at any rate it is directly connected with the sense of vision, as in *Il.* 15.422: 'When Hector saw with his eyes (ἐνόησεν ὀφθαλμοῖσιν) his cousin fallen in the dust.' More precisely, it is used when through the sight of a concrete object a character suddenly realizes the full meaning of a situation. Aphrodite appeared to Helen disguised as an old woman: only when Helen pierced the disguise and recognized that she was dealing with a goddess is the verb *noein* used (*Il.* 3.396). It may thus mean the substitution of a true for a false impression, not considered as a process of reasoning, but as a sudden illumination, a seeing with the mind.[1] Similarly it may mean the visualization of things distant in time or space. (Cf. Parm. 4.1.) The faculty of doing this (*noos* or *nous*) may be paralysed or put out of action by physical force or strong emotion, but never in Homer, and only very rarely in other surviving literature before Parmenides, can it be deceived.[2]

This peculiar status of the *noos* is emphasized by the belief in it as something external to the other faculties, not dependent like them on bodily organs, and more than human. A character in the *Helena* of Euripides says (1014 ff.): 'The *nous* of the dead is not indeed alive, yet it has an immortal intelligence (or faculty of knowing, γνώμη) when it has plunged into the immortal *aither*.' More directly, in another line of the same poet (fr. 1018): 'The *nous* in each of us is god.' When rational thought had progressed much further than in Parmenides's

---

[1] For further examples and analysis of νόος and νοεῖν in Homer, see von Fritz, *CP*, 1943, 79–83. What is said here owes much to his excellent article and those which followed it on the use of the words in Presocratic philosophy, in *CP*, 1945, 223–42, and 1946, 12–34. (Cf. vol. 1, 426, n. 1.) His conclusion for Homer is that all the meanings found there 'can be derived from one original and fundamental concept, which may be defined as the realisation of a situation'. The relationship to sight was well expressed by Sainte-Beuve in his *Cahiers*: 'Homère dit *noeo* — je vois, je conçois. Voir et concevoir, c'est la même chose, ce n'est plus la sensation, c'est déjà la pensée, la perception.'

[2] Von Fritz (*CP*, 1945, 226) finds three passages in Hesiod where the νόος is not merely dulled but deceived. They are *Theog.* 537; *Erga*, 323 and 373. But *Theog.* 537 is a reference to the famous story of Prometheus and Zeus. Prometheus divided the portions Διὸς νόον ἐξαπαφίσκων, 'trying (or thinking) to deceive the νόος of Zeus'; whereas, as everyone knows, Zeus's νόος was not deceived. In *Erga*, 323, it is κέρδος that deceives the νόος. This is very close in sense to the passages in Homer where the νόος is, in von F.'s words, dulled or blunted by emotion. The only clear indication that deception can occur is *Erga*, 373, which warns against allowing a lascivious woman to deceive one's νόος. These three passages do however illustrate how 'the transition from a dulled to a deceived νόος is very easy' (von F., *CP*, 1945, 226).

time, Aristotle himself, for all his intellectual maturity and acute analysis of mental faculties and activities, felt bound to concede infallibility to *nous*, and to make a sharp distinction between its activity and the processes of discursive reasoning. In the *Posterior Analytics* he writes: 'Of the thinking states by which we grasp truth, some are unfailingly true, others admit of error—opinion, for instance, and calculation—whereas scientific knowing and *nous* are always true.' It even retains its mysterious and ambiguous status as 'that which alone comes into us from outside and is divine', and although Aristotle is contemptuous of religious doctrines of immortality and reincarnation, he admits that the *psyche* may perhaps survive the dissolution of the living man—'not all of it, but the *nous*'.[1] Its proper function is to grasp universal truths immediately and intuitively, as in the inductive leap, and so to assure the primary premises or principles on which deductive argument is based.

It was, then, a general Greek belief that human powers of cognition included a faculty of immediate apprehension of the true nature of an object or situation, comparable to, but going deeper than, the immediate apprehension of superficial qualities by the senses. 'In Greek philosophy itself...*nous* is never the merely *siccum lumen*, the clear, cold light which *we* are sometimes in the habit of calling reason.'[2] It is this faculty that Parmenides names when he says that whatever is apprehended by it must be.

There remains the impossibility of speaking about, or mentioning, what is not. This too was by no means an absurd contention for the earliest Greek pioneer of logical thought. At the end of fr. 2 the verb

---

[1] *An. post.* 100b5, Oxford trans.; *Gen. an.* 736b27; *Metaph.* 1070a25. In the last passage Jaeger (Oxford Text, 1957), alone of editors, brackets the relevant words as 'postea addita ut videtur'. He gives no reason, but in case any reader shares the suspicion, he may be referred instead to *De an.* 413b25, where Aristotle says that νοῦς 'appears to be a different class of *psyche*, and this alone can be separated as the eternal from the perishable'. There is no need to adduce the obscure doctrine of the division of νοῦς into active and passive in *De an.* 3.5, but there too we are told that one species at least of νοῦς is separate and eternal (430a23).

[2] James Adam, *Cambridge Praelections*, 33. Those thinkers who contrast the inadequacy of human comprehension as compared with divine do not use the words νοῦς, νοεῖν in this connexion. Cf. Heraclitus, frr. 78, 79, 83; Alcmaeon, fr. 1; Xenophanes, fr. 34; vol. I, pp. 344, 396f., 413. The nearest to it is when Xenophanes says that God is not like man in νόημα. Parmenides himself is the first to speak, in his contempt for the mass of mortals, of their πλακτὸν νόον (6.6). That someone should do this some time was inevitable, but the expression must have carried a flavour of paradox or oxymoron, like ἄσκοπον ὄμμα in 7.4.

is *phraʒein*, which, though often translated 'say' or 'tell', meant in the epic language which Parmenides is using, and frequently later, to show or point out. At 6. 1 he uses *legein*, the ordinary word for *say*, *speak of*, or *mean* (Fr. *vouloir dire*). There are however indications that this word too had a history (perhaps connected with the magical identification of name and object) which made it difficult for a Greek to see how one could logically speak of what was not. 'To say nothing' in Greek does not mean to be silent: it is the regular expression for talking nonsense, uttering what does not correspond with reality. The difficulty of the problem here raised by Parmenides's uncompromising and elementary logic may be judged from the fact that Plato much later had to devote a considerable amount of attention to resolving it, in such language as:

It seems to follow necessarily that to speak of what is not 'something' is to speak of nothing at all. Must we not even refuse to allow that in such a case a person is *saying* something though he may be speaking of nothing? Must we not assert that he is not even saying anything when he sets about uttering the sounds 'a thing that is not'?[1]

All previous thinkers had taken the physical world as a datum and interested themselves in questions of its origin, the kind of basic stuff that might underlie its variegated appearance, and the mechanical processes by which it was produced. Parmenides refused to accept this datum, or any datum. Like an ancient Descartes, he asked himself what, if anything, it was impossible not to believe; and to him the answer was *est*: something exists. If we accept Owen's persuasive interpretation of fr. 2, not even this was the ultimate premise. That was, like Descartes's, *cogito*; but the first inference was not *cogito ergo sum*, but *cogito, ergo est quod cogito*.

(6) *The true way and the false*

(Fr. 6) What can be spoken and thought of must be, for it is possible for it to be, but impossible for nothing to be. This I bid thee consider, for this way of inquiry is the first from which I ⟨hold thee back⟩.

---

[1] *Soph.* 237e, trans. Cornford. Cornford comments (PTK, 205): 'It is hard to translate the above argument because the phrase λέγειν τι is used in two ways, (1) to "speak of something" that your words refer to; and (2) "to express a meaning" or say something significant as opposed to "saying nothing" or "talking nonsense" (οὐδὲν λέγειν). But the ambiguity does not vitiate the argument.'

For the relics in Parmenides's thought of the universal folk-belief uniting thing and name, cf. Diels, *Lehrgedicht*, 85.

But also from this one, on which mortals, knowing nothing, wander two-headed; for helplessness in their own breasts guides their erring mind. They are borne along, both deaf and blind, mazed, hordes with no judgment, who believe that to be and not to be are the same and not the same, and the path of everything is one that turns back upon itself.

(Fr. 7)   For this shall never prevail, that things that are not are, but do thou keep thy thought from this way of inquiry; and let not habit born of much experience force thee along this way, to ply a heedless eye and sounding ear and a tongue, but judge by reason (*logos*) the much-contested refutation spoken by me.

6.1. The construction is the same as in fr. 2.1 and fr. 3. So Burnet, *EGP*, 174, n. 1, who points out that Simplicius supports the rendering. Kranz (*SB Preuss. Ak.* 1916, 1173, and in DK) translates differently: 'It is necessary to say and to think that *only* what is [das Seiende] is.' Either translation represents what was for Parmenides a truth, as does that which takes τό as a pronoun. (So Mansfeld, *Offenbarung*, 81: 'Man muss folgendes sagen und denken: nur *das Seiende* ist.' Italics are his.)

6.1–2. S. Tugwell (*CQ*, 1964, 36f.) claims that to give ἔστι its potential sense here and in 2.2 is to separate that sense from the existential to an anachronistic extent. He therefore translates: 'What exists to be referred to or thought about must exist; for it is there to exist, nothing is not there to exist.' The point is a difficult one. The potential use of ἔστι goes back to Homer, so that to translate it as potential here can hardly be called an anachronism. The argument against it should surely be the novel insistence of Parmenides that εἶναι always carries an existential significance. Yet he cannot speak about the one Being at all without using ordinary language in a way which a strict application of his own criteria would disallow. (It is easy to pick out examples in fr. 8.) At the same time, since his conscious insistence on the existential force of εἶναι is undoubted, Tugwell's translation is suggestive and may represent something that was in his mind. But if so, let no one continue to claim that Parmenides was incapable of arguing a tautology!

6.3. The last word of the line has fallen out of the MSS. of Simplicius, but was restored as εἴργω by Diels on the basis of 7.2.

6.4. βροτοὶ εἰδότες οὐδέν. Cf. vol. 1, 398.

6.5. πλάττονται. For the form (= πλάζονται) see Diels, *Lehrgedicht*, 72.

6.5ff. Cf. Orph. fr. 233 Kern (μηδαμὰ μηδὲν εἰδότες κτλ.). More generally Diels (*op. cit.* 68) compares Hes. *Th.* 26, Epimenides, fr. 1, and the Hebrew prophets. ἄκριτα may have special relevance for Parmenides: they cannot make the κρίσις between being and not being (fr. 8.15; see Mansfeld, *Offenbarung*, 87).

6.8. For οὐ not μή cf. 8.40.

6.9. πάντων could be masc.: 'the path of all of them (*sc.* mortals) turns back upon itself'. See KR, 272, n. 1. Owen in *CQ*, 1960, 91, evidently takes it so.

7.1. δαμῇ, 'This shall never be proved', Burnet; 'nec unquam hoc cogatur, esse', etc., Stein. (An unusual construction in Latin, but cf. Cic., *Epp. ad Brut.* 2.7.4.) When the line is quoted by Plato (*Soph.* 237a), the MSS. have οὐδαμῇ or οὐ δαμῇ. At Ar. *Metaph.* 1089a4 they differ. In Simplicius, who quotes it in three places, τοῦτο δαμῇ is best attested. (See Ross on Ar. *loc. cit.*) Probably it is correct, but no parallel usage of δαμάζω can be quoted. W. Borgeaud (*Mus. Helv.* 1955, 277) has suggested that Parmenides wrote δαμ' ῇ, οὐ...δαμά being in tmesis.

These two quotations, which we owe to different authorities, probably form one continuous passage of the poem. In the first three lines the thought is uncomfortably condensed, but Parmenides is apparently arguing that the object of speech and thought must exist because *prima facie* it can exist; it cannot therefore be nothing, since 'nothing' *cannot* exist; but if it is something, it exists. Having then, in the proof of the existence of the object of speech and thought, brought in the statement that 'nothing' cannot exist, the goddess takes the opportunity to point out that *this* way (which one must take *ad sensum* to be the way of thinking that 'nothing' *can* exist) is the first to be avoided. It is the one mentioned in fr. 2 as the second of two conceivable ways, and then dismissed as impossible to follow.

Ostensibly, however, she goes on immediately to mention a third way, which like the second is to be avoided. Now as Cornford pointed out (*CQ*, 1933, 99), it is not expressly stated in fr. 2 that the two ways there mentioned exhaust the possibilities of 'ways that alone can be thought of'; and he concluded that the goddess meant to announce three ways there, a fact which is only concealed by the fragmentary nature of the text. Nevertheless, fr. 2 conveys a strong impression that the two ways *are* exclusive of others, and perhaps we can allow that Parmenides did speak of an initial duality without thereby doing damage to the logical structure of the poem. The 'third way' is, after all, not independent of the other two, but an illegitimate fusion of them both. For Parmenides of all people there is no third possibility distinct both from 'it is' and 'it is not'. The condemnation of mortals in fr. 6 rests on their belief that 'to be and not to be are the same and not the same'. The statement rejected in fr. 7, 'that things that are not are', is only a rephrasing of this: it is 'not the Way of Not-being, but the mortal belief just mentioned, i.e. that what-is-not can be by becoming or change' (Cornford, *loc. cit.* 100, n. 3). The correctness of this is shown by the following lines with their reference to eyes, ears and tongue; and yet the belief that 'it is possible for nothing to exist' (the first false way, warned against in fr. 6) could hardly be distinguished as an entirely separate 'way' from one described by the words 'that things that are not are'.

Nevertheless there are in fact three ways, one right and two wrong: (1) belief that 'It is', i.e. something exists and the word *is* must be applied to it with all its force; (2) denial that 'It is', or assertion that there is nothing; (3) haphazard confusion between 'is' and 'is not'.

Of the second way we hear no more, since none have been tempted to follow it. The third way incorporates the opinions of mortals, mentioned in the prologue as offering no true conviction. It is said to result from habit and the use of the senses, and includes the belief that 'what is not is' and that 'to be and not to be are the same and not the same'.[1]

It needs no argument that men believe that 'to be and not to be are *not* the same': no one in his senses would deny it. But, says Parmenides, they also think that 'what is not is' and that 'to be and not to be *are* the same'. When he goes on to deduce the consequences of the statement 'What is, is', it becomes clear that in condemning this behaviour he means to deny the belief in any change, motion, becoming or perishing of what is, a belief which results naturally from the use of eyes, ears and other sense-organs. Its logical refutation will come in fr. 8.

It is a much-disputed historical question whether this criticism is aimed partly or solely at Heraclitus. There is no external evidence to help: we can only say it is possible, but not certain, that Parmenides had read the other's work. If he had, there is no doubt that it would have outraged his logical mind. The view of Bernays that Heraclitus is the sole object of criticism was vigorously defended by Kranz, who went so far as to regard it as one of 'the cornerstones of the history of the Presocratics'.[2] In the same year Reinhardt was denying it outright, and von Fritz has declared that 'Reinhardt has proved conclusively that Parmenides does not refer to Heraclitus in the famous passage on the error of the "two-headed mortals"'.

We are hardly within the province of 'conclusive proof', but a few observations may be made. First, Parmenides's language (or the language of the goddess) makes it clear that the stricture is directed

---

[1] Mansfeld (*Offenbarung*, 31 and 34) apparently thinks it is the belief of mortals in *their own* existence that is in question. He does not argue the point, and it is surely very unlikely.

[2] Bernays, *Ges. Abh.* 1, 62, n. 1; Kranz, *SB Preuss. Ak.* 1916, 1174: 'Dieses bleiben die Ecksteine der Geschichte der Vorsokratiker: Heraklit zitiert und bekämpft Pythagoras, Xenophanes und Hekataios, nicht Parmenides: dieser aber zitiert und bekämpft Heraklit.' In a later article (*Hermes*, 1934, 117f.), it is not so much Heraclitus himself as his followers ('die Anhänger Heraklits') whom Kranz supposes to have been the objects of attack. He cites as an example the Heraclitizing Hippocratic treatise *De victu*. Since however he himself assumes a gap of only about ten years between the work of Heraclitus and Parmenides, putting Heraclitus's after 490 and Parmenides's after 480, there was not much time for the Ἡρακλείτειοι (first mentioned by Plato) or οἱ φάσκοντες ἡρακλειτίƺειν (Ar. *Metaph.* 1010a11) to have got going, let alone become widely known. For references to other scholars on both sides of the controversy, see Mansfeld, *Offenbarung*, 1, nn. 1 and 2.

against all and sundry, not confined to a particular philosopher. It can only be a question of whether Heraclitus was in his mind as an outstanding representative of the 'hordes with no judgment'. The source of their error is reliance on eye and ear, and Heraclitus had said that he gave preference to the objects of sight and hearing (fr. 55), which is not contradicted by his assertion that eyes and ears are bad witnesses if the *psyche* is barbarian (fr. 107). He saw truth in the *Logos*, and Parmenides too uses this word in 7.5, perhaps, as Kranz thought, to oppose a true *logos* to the other's false one. Again, though 'to be and not to be are the same and not the same' can describe the state of mind of the ordinary man, its phraseology recalls nothing so much as the paradoxes in which Heraclitus and no one else showed such delight.[1] Even if he did not say 'we are and are not' (fr. 49a, deemed spurious by Gigon and Kirk), statements like 'wishes and does not wish' (32), 'by differing it agrees' (51), 'in changing it rests' (84a), 'living and dead, waking and asleep, young and old are the same' (88) display the quintessence of that imbecility which Parmenides here deplores. No one but Heraclitus made such statements, and moreover the doctrine of the identity of opposites in fr. 88 is made to depend on the fact of change from one to the other; and change in Parmenides's view implied the being of what is not. Much more than the ordinary man, Heraclitus made the whole world depend on a continuous process of change and struggle. He above all others was at the opposite pole from the philosophy of motionless being. It is in the light of all this and more that one must see the use of the word 'backward-turning' in 6.9, which some have thought an unmistakable reference to the 'backward-turning adjustment' of Heraclitus fr. 51. (See vol. 1, 439, n. 3.) To place such reliance on a single word is unwise, but also perhaps unnecessary. Where no single phrase brings conviction, the cumulative effect may be considerable.

There are, then, strong hints in his language that for Parmenides Heraclitus was the arch-offender, no doubt because, while other men were inarticulately confused, he did not shrink from making the contradiction explicit yet still upheld it. But the criticism applies to

---

[1] Cf. Ar. *Metaph.* 1005 b 23 ἀδύνατον γὰρ ὁντινοῦν ταὐτὸν ὑπολαμβάνειν εἶναι καὶ μὴ εἶναι, καθάπερ τινὲς οἴονται λέγειν Ἡράκλειτον.

all 'ignorant mortals', whether philosophers or not. Its point is that what is, is, and cannot ever not be. To maintain this is to go against *all* common belief, according to which there is such a thing as *genesis*, the process of coming into being. This process demands that the same thing at one time is not and at another time is; also that it is at one time the same and at another not the same. Thus men imagine things as passing back and forth between being and not being, a course of thought which 'turns back upon itself'.

Moreover in condemning this way the goddess warns Parmenides against being forced along it by 'habit born of experience', which again does not sound as if she had in mind solely the doctrine of one enigmatic and individual philosopher. What she is in fact enjoining on him appears in the next lines: it is *not to trust the senses*,[1] but instead to *judge by reason*. Here for the first time sense and reason are contrasted, and we are told that the senses deceive and that reason alone is to be trusted. It is a decisive moment in the history of European philosophy, which can never be the same again. Whether or not Parmenides believed the one reality to be material is a minor question which in any case admits of no answer, but we cannot agree with Burnet (*EGP*, 182) that 'Parmenides is not, as some have said, the father of idealism; on the contrary, all materialism depends on his view of reality'.

Burnet refers to the fact that Parmenides, while still belonging to an age before the word *asomaton*—incorporeal—had been invented, relentlessly pursues monism to its ultimate logical conclusion, and so infers his one reality to have been 'a spherical, motionless, *corporeal* plenum'. But let us think in Greek, remembering that even when a later philosopher like Plato wished to refer to the two kinds of being which we should naturally call corporeal and incorporeal, he did not normally use the terms *somatikon* and *asomaton*: even when coined they remained comparatively rare. He spoke of perceptible (*aistheton*) and intelligible (*noeton*). *Aistheton* can safely be identified with the bodily wherever it occurs, and similarly *noeton* not only means 'intelligible' but also and everywhere denotes the bodiless and immaterial. The essential point is therefore that Parmenides was the first to draw the

---

[1] Eye and ear at least. It is probably true (see Mansfeld, *Offenbarung*, 43) that the tongue is introduced here as the organ of speech rather than taste.

distinction between *aistheton* and *noeton*—between the data of eyes and ears on the one hand and of *logos* on the other—and to say that the latter was real and true and the former unreal. Material and non-material are concepts which he would scarcely have understood: what matters is that in his view reality cannot be seen or heard, felt or tasted, but only inferred by a process of dialectical reasoning such as he was the first to employ. Considering how much the distinction between intelligible and sensible meant to Plato, and how he exalted the intelligible at the expense of the sensible, the conclusion can hardly be avoided that the way to his particular form of idealism was first opened by Parmenides. It was not without reason that he referred to him as 'a reverend and aweful figure'.

(7) *The only true way: the marks of 'what is'*

(a) *It is eternal, neither coming into being nor perishing*

(Fr. 8, *vv.* 1–21) One way alone is yet left to tell of, namely that 'It is'. On this way are marks in plenty that since it exists it is unborn and imperishable, whole, unique, immovable and without end. (5) It *was* not in the past, nor yet *shall* it be, since it now *is*, all together, one and continuous.

(6) For what birth of it wilt thou seek? How and from what did it grow? I shall not allow thee to say or think 'from what is not', for it is not to be said or thought that 'it is not'. (9) And what need would have prompted it to grow later or sooner, beginning from nothing? Thus it must either fully be or else not be.

(12) Nor will the force of evidence suffer anything besides itself to arise from what is not. Therefore Justice does not relax with her fetters and allow it to come into being or perish, but holds it fast. (16) The verdict on this lies here: It is or it is not. But this verdict has already been given, as it had to be, that the one path should be left alone as unthinkable, unnamed, for it is no true path, and that the other exists and is real. (19) How could what is afterwards perish? And how could it come into being? (20) For if it came into being, it *is* not, nor yet if it is going to be at some future time. Thus becoming is extinguished, and perishing not to be heard of.

v. 1. μῦθος ὁδοῖο (objective gen.), which Simplicius gives, is a striking but not impossible phrase, and much more probable than the θυμὸς ὁδοῖο of Sextus.

v. 4. Reading οὖλον μουνογενές τε, which has much better authority than the feeble ἐστι γὰρ οὐλομελές τε of Kranz (in DK but not the choice of Diels). See C. H. Kahn, *Anaximander*, 157, n. 1 for the meaning of the suffix -γενής.

v. 4. ἠδ' ἀτέλεστον. This if correct (and no other reading is attested) means without end in time, everlasting, as Simplicius assumed. Owen (*CQ*, 1960, 101f.) would substitute ἠδὲ τέλειον (which is true of τὸ ἐόν in another sense) on the grounds: (i) that ἀτέλεστον simply repeats ἀνώλεθρον, (ii) that it is not elsewhere found with this sense: in Homer it means unaccomplished or unfulfilled, (iii) that the present list of attributes is a programme of what is to be argued in detail, and something is wanted to correspond to the argument that it is οὐκ ἀτελεύτητον (*v.* 32) or τετελεσμένον (*v.* 42). This may be right. On the other hand one may say that Parmenides's addiction to Homeric clichés, particularly at the ends of lines, might have tempted him into the repetition, and to giving the word ἀτέλεστον a new twist. In this case I think his own employment of epic language is a more likely explanation than Owen's conjecture that the orthodox Homeric clausula crept in as the result of copyists' errors. As to point (i), I do not see that redundancy is in itself an objection, when Owen himself describes οὖλον μουνογενές in *v.* 5 as 'the exact equivalent' of ἓν συνεχές in *v.* 6.

vv. 12–13. I have translated as above only after much hesitation. The alternative (if the reading is sound) is to take αὐτό to refer to 'what is': '...allow anything to come into being, beside what is, from what is not'. So Cornford, *Plato and Parm.* 37, followed by KR, 274f. and others. This is a little more difficult to get out of the Greek, though it is doubtless possible that αὐτό should be used with no grammatical antecedent to stand for 'what we are talking about all the time'. (Cf. Gadamer in *Festschr. Reinhardt*, 67, n. 4: 'das regierende Wort des Ganzen'.) The same thing is stated in other words in *vv.* 36–7: 'Nothing else either is or will be besides that which is.' On this interpretation, what Parmenides is giving here is an argument for the uniqueness and wholeness of the one being, and my main reason for not adopting it is that this seems an intrusion into the arguments against its birth and destruction which otherwise fill the whole of this section. Its wholeness (continuity, indivisibility) is argued in *vv.* 22–5, and entails its uniqueness, which also emerges from arguments like those in 44–9, as well as being asserted in 36–7.

Karsten, and later Reinhardt (*Parm.* 42), cut the knot by reading τοῦ for μή, on which see text. Most recent commentators have refused to take this bold step, though many agree that an unwanted (and unmetrical) μή has crept in in *v.* 33.

v. 14. χαλάσασα πέδησιν, with the same sense as the accusative, has a suspicious ring. One is disposed to agree with Diels that it 'lässt sich nicht erklären', in spite of Kranz's claim that it is parallel to a Homeric expression like ἔγχεσιν ἀλλήλων ἀλεώμεθα (*Il.* 6.226), where in fact Monro and Allen (*O.C.T.*) prefer the reading ἔγχεα. The reading of Simplicius is πέδησιν, which Diels (*Lehrgedicht*, 78, 153) takes as the acc. of a noun of action: 'relaxes her fettering'.

v. 16. κέκριται, i.e. in fr. 2.

v. 19. Translated above is ἔπειτ' ἀπόλοιτο ἐόν (Karsten, Stein, Kranz, KR). The MSS. of Simplicius have one letter different, making ἔπειτα πέλοι τὸ ἐόν, which was retained by Diels, Reinhardt, Burnet, Cornford. 'How could what is be going to be in the future?' (Cornford). A reference to perishing, balancing that to coming-into-being in the second half of the line, seems the more probable.

We now embark on the central theme of Parmenides's doctrine, the deductions to be drawn from the simple statement *esti*: 'It is' or 'Something exists'. The word had been used hitherto to cover much the same variety of meaning as the English verb 'to be'. It meant what we more usually express by the word 'exist', though one may compare the biblical 'Before Abraham was, I am', and the noun 'a being' meaning an existing thing or creature. It also expressed, like its English counterpart, predication or relationship—'is white', 'is greater than' —though it should be noted that in non-existential sentences the copula was frequently omitted: in Greek 'Socrates wise' (ὁ Σωκράτης σοφός) is a complete sentence. No grammatical or semantic work had yet been done to distinguish between different senses of the same word, and there was still a general tendency, which we have remarked before (vol. 1, 85, 86), to assume that a single word had only one 'proper' meaning. This proper meaning Parmenides assumes to be the existential, and on that assumption draws certain conclusions which undermine the universally accepted conception of the real world. The necessary characteristics of reality are briefly listed in *vv.* 3–6 of fr. 8: it is eternal, unmoving, one and continuous, and past and future are meaningless for it. In the following lines these features are substantiated one by one.

The main weight of the passage so far translated is directed at proving that 'what is' cannot have come into existence at some past time, nor can it cease to be in the future. It must be admitted that the argument against becoming would appear better balanced if one had the boldness to excise, as Reinhardt insisted on doing, the negative from *v.* 12. This would give a symmetrical refutation of the coming-to-be of what is, namely that it could not have come to be either from what is not (7–9) or from what is (12 ff.). The paraphrase by Gorgias which Reinhardt quotes is not indeed conclusive evidence against the negative. It runs:

What is cannot have come into being. If it did, it came either from what is or what is not. But it did not come from what is, since if it is existent it did not come to be but already is; nor from what is not, for the non-existent cannot generate anything.

This makes the two halves of the argument symmetrical, but the last clause looks like a rewording of *v.* 12 in its accepted form, and indeed affords some support for the translation given above as against that of Cornford.[1] If one would wish the negative away, it is because it scarcely seems consistent with the dialectical power elsewhere displayed by Parmenides that he should first rebut the generation of what is out of what is not by the vigorous assertion that 'what is not' cannot even be mentioned, and then follow this with an unnecessary and much feebler argument that 'what is not' can generate nothing but itself. The reason may be that Parmenides enjoys casting in the teeth of the cosmogonists something that they themselves had all accepted as

[1] Gorg. fr. 3 DK, *ap.* Sext. *Math.* 7.71. See also notes to translation on previous page.

obvious. *Ex nihilo nihil fit* was an axiom of Greek thought, as Aristotle remarked. 'Generation from the non-existent is impossible; in this opinion all the natural philosophers concur' (*Phys.* 187a34).

If however *v.* 12 does begin the argument that 'what is cannot originate from what is', it continues satisfactorily. The decision is implicit in what has gone before: the only alternatives are to be and not to be, and the latter has been rejected. Hence being can only be thought of in the present. Whatever the reading and meaning of *v.* 12, this must be the argument of the following lines. As Simplicius interprets, after quoting the passage (*Phys.* 78.24): 'This he clearly demonstrates about true being, that it is not generated; neither from something existing, for no existing thing preceded it, nor from the non-existent, for the non-existent is nothing.'

The imperishability of what is is not so explicitly argued, but follows clearly enough from the exclusive alternatives 'it is' and 'it is not' and the absolute rejection of the latter; for to suppose that what is can perish is to suppose that at some future time it will be possible to say of it 'it is not'. This serves also as an additional argument against its generation, since the denial that 'it is' cannot be entertained for past time any more than future. In fact past and future have no meaning in or for reality (*v.* 5), which adds force to the subsidiary argument of *vv.* 9 and 10: even supposing that something could come from nothing, what could cause this to happen at any particular time rather than another?

Here is a second major intellectual achievement, comparable both intrinsically and in its influence on later philosophy to the distinction between sensible and intelligible, namely the distinction between time and eternity, the recognition of *eternal* as a separate category from *everlasting*. To conceive of something as merely everlasting is to set it in time. One says that just as it is now, so it was thousands of years ago and will be in the future. But for the eternal 'was' and 'will be' have no meaning, and the time-sequence is abolished. Thus Plato taught that the physical universe was as old as time (it 'has been and is and shall be perpetually through all time'), but it is not eternal (ἀΐδιος). It lives through days and nights, months and years, and all these are parts of time, and 'was' and 'shall be' are forms of time that have come to be; and we are wrong to transfer them unthinkingly to eternal being. We say that it was and is and shall be; but 'is' alone really belongs to it.... That which is for ever in the same state immovably cannot be becoming older or younger by the lapse of time, nor can it ever become so; neither can it now have been, nor will it be in the future.[1]

For all Plato's greater maturity of thought and resources of expression, it is difficult to overestimate his debt to the man who first had the intellectual vision to say of 'what is': 'It was not in the past, nor yet shall it be, since it now is all together.'

The eternity (in the sense of imperishability) of the one reality had of course been asserted by the Milesians. Anaximander applied to his *apeiron* the epithets deathless, imperishable, ageless. At the same time he claimed that there arose in it, by 'separation', the nucleus from which the world grew. What Parmenides points out is that if reality is eternal and is one, then it could never have become the starting-point (*arche*) of a manifold world. But its eternity and its unity must be accepted. Just as 'what is', had it been generated, would have had to come out of what is not, so would any other being; and this is impossible. Hence the real is not only eternal but unique. This does away with any idea of a living and growing universe, such as both Milesians and Pythagoreans had described. The time element in the world of men's imagination is emphasized, in contrast with reality, in fr. 19: 'Thus in appearance these things come into being and now are, and having matured will come to an end in the future; and for them men have assigned a name to distinguish each one.' If something is, there can be nothing surrounding it (περιέχον), no reservoir of fresh substance on which it can feed, like the *apeiron* around the *gonimon* of Anaximander or the 'infinite breath' surrounding the 'seed' of the Pythagorean cosmos. Even more patently illusory is the multiplicity of existing things in which the ordinary unthinking man believes. All alike are confounded by the simple dilemma here propounded by Parmenides, which Aristotle has sum-

---

[1] *Tim.* 38c2–3, 37e–38a (trans. Cornford). Fränkel's argument that Parmenides's words do not express the same distinction has not convinced me (*Wege u. Formen*, 191, n. 1). In particular the addition of ποτε in *v.* 5 seems rather to emphasize the negation of past and future than to qualify it in any way.

marized with brevity and clarity: 'What is does not come into being, for it is already; and nothing could come into being from what is not.'[1]

(b) It is continuous and indivisible

(8.22–5) Nor is it divisible, since it all equally is. It does not exist more fully in one direction, which would prevent it from holding together, nor more weakly in another, but all is full of what is. Therefore it is all continuous, for what is is close to what is.

With the argument in these lines must be connected fr. 4, whose exact position in the poem is uncertain:

But look at things which, though distant, are securely present to the mind; for thou shalt not cut off for thyself what is from contact with what is, neither as scattering in order, in every direction and manner, nor drawing together.

8.22. I have followed Owen's proposal to accent ἔστιν and regard ὁμοῖον as adverbial (*CQ*, 1960, 92f.). This fits better with the sense of the next line, but it will be obvious that on many points I do not follow Owen's interpretation. In particular he seems to regard the recognition of any implicit reference in Parmenides to earlier cosmologists as an accusation of 'resting his argument' on their assumptions, or as '*saddling* it with a subject from earlier cosmology', and so inconsistent with his greatness as 'a radical and conscious pioneer' (*ibid.* 93, 95). This may be fair criticism of some parts of Cornford's interpretation, but is not a reason for excluding practically any allusion to the cosmologists from the Way of Truth. It is just his pushing of their premises to a logical conclusion which allows him to make a clean break with them and shows what a radical pioneer he was.

4.1. KR construe βεβαίως with λεῦσσε: 'Look steadfastly', but the word-order seems against this. So also Vlastos, whose version of the line is an individual one: 'See securely with the mind things absent as though they were present.' (*TAPA*, 1946, 72f.) Hölscher has argued for ὁμῶς (not ὅμως), to be taken closely with λεῦσσε (*Hermes*, 1956, 385ff.; for the translation see also Mansfeld, *Offenbarung*, 212).

4.2. ἀποτμήξει. ἀποτμήξεις Brandis. The arbitrary alteration seems unwarranted, but the force of the middle (if that is what it is) is not obvious. Cornford and KR simply translate 'cut off'. Diels (*Lehrgedicht*, 64) said that the middle is used to show that it is not a literal cutting-off but takes place within the mind. He compares the difference between ὁρίζειν and ὁρίζεσθαι.

An alternative is to regard it as 3rd sing. active. So Diels later (in DK) and Reinhardt (*Parm.* 49, n. 2), with νόος as subject; also Zeller, for whom it was 'probably impersonal' (ZN, 692, n. 2). Gomperz imported κενεόν as subject! Other versions of 4.1 and 2, worth mentioning but dubious, are those of Schottlaender in *Hermes*, 1927, 435f., and J. Bollack, *REG*, 1957, 56–71. The latter supposes ἔχεσθαι to mean 'keep away from', like the Homeric ἐχώμεθα δηϊότητος.

The extraordinary difficulties that have been perceived in this fragment (for which see de Santillana, *Prologue to P.* 22; with his own translation I heartily disagree) seem largely artificial. Mansfeld supposes that the fragment belongs to the Way of Seeming (*Offenbarung*, 208). His arguments are: (1) from the plural participles in *v.* 1. This seems to me to force more than its

---

[1] *Phys.* 191a30 οὔτε γὰρ τὸ ὂν γίγνεσθαι — εἶναι γὰρ ἤδη — ἔκ τε μὴ ὄντος οὐδὲν ἂν γενέσθαι. Cf. 185a3 οὐ γὰρ ἔτι ἀρχή ἐστιν, εἰ ἓν μόνον καὶ οὕτως ἕν ἐστιν. ἡ γὰρ ἀρχὴ τινὸς ἢ τινῶν.

author intended into a purely general passage. (2) In *v.* 2, the articles before ἐόν and ἐόντος point to at least two ὄντα. On the contrary, the command not to separate what is from what is (i.e. itself) emphasizes its unity. (3) κόσμος cannot refer to the intelligible world. Precisely: that is why Being cannot be scattered through it (if one renders it 'world'), or according to it (if 'order' is the better translation). (4) πάντη πάντως is a type of phrase which does not occur again in the Way of Truth but several times in the Seeming. This may be so, but does it prove anything? In denying that truth is in the opinions of mortals, Parmenides is very likely to deny it in their own phraseology.

The evidence that Parmenides, in his criticisms of earlier thought, had Heraclitus especially in mind, is cumulative. It is relevant therefore to compare the denial in fr. 4 of any scattering or drawing together, and the assertion that things absent are to the mind present, with Heraclitus's statement as given by Plutarch (fr. 91): 'It scatters and again draws together, it approaches and goes away.' The indivisibility of reality in 8.22 may also remind us of Heraclitus's description of his method at the beginning of his work (fr. 1): 'Dividing each thing and showing how it is.'[1]

Fr. 4 begins by exalting the capacity of mind, or insight (evidently as contrasted with the senses), to make far-off things present. The ground for this was already prepared, in that the function of the *noos* as early as Homer included the summoning-up of things distant in space or time,[2] but for Parmenides the omnipresence which the mind perceives is an objective reality. The senses suggest that some things are here, some there, and that they move away from or draw towards each other, just as Heraclitus had said (indeed he spoke of them doing both at once), and this separation and conjunction had been held to account for the natural order (*cosmos*). In truth there can be no *cosmos*, for order implies the arrangement of more than one unit, and reality is a single, continuous whole. If we follow the goddess's advice to ignore the senses and judge by reason, we shall see that being can never be separated from itself.

The lines 8.22–5 argue for the indivisibility and continuity of being, both of which were mentioned in the preliminary list of *vv.* 5–6. Since the sole choice lies between 'It is' and 'It is not', there are no degrees in being: 'It must either fully be or else not be' (*v.* 11). Up to now,

---

[1] A surprising number of scholars see a reference to Anaximenes here. This seems far-fetched.

[2] Cf. von Fritz in *CP*, 1943, 91. He cites *Il.* 15.80ff., which describe the *noos* of a much-travelled man 'darting swiftly' over the lands he has seen.

the only form of being conceivable had been corporeal being. Hence when Parmenides for the first time makes explicit (in order to show up its logical absurdity) the idea of degrees of being, these have to be understood as degrees of density, which makes the language of these lines more intelligible. The lack of homogeneity which would result from 'what is' existing more or less might cause it to fall apart and be divided. Strict adherence to the premise that 'it is' forbids this: 'All is (equally) full of what is', an undifferentiated continuum.

By this argument too any cosmogony of the Milesian type, from a single *arche*, is dismissed as impossible. If Anaximander's *apeiron* were really a unity, without internal distinctions, then no internal distinctions could have appeared in it. For a cosmos to emerge, there must have been some unevenness of texture, some lack of homogeneity or equilibrium in it to start with. The condensation and rarefaction of Anaximenes's world-process are similarly ruled out.

In the claim that what exists is indivisible and continuous, with no interstices between separate bits of being, 'for what is is close to what is', we have Parmenides's denial of the void. This had been a feature particularly of the Pythagorean world-system. It separated the units out of which the world was built, and which were thought of at the same time as arithmetical units, geometrical points, and physical particles. In its physical manifestation, as that which separated the smallest particles, the Pythagoreans identified it with air, that air which the cosmos breathed in from the surrounding infinite in order to separate the bodies within it.[1] It is evident that earlier and contemporary thinkers were still far from grasping the notion of empty space or vacuum. Parmenides faced them with it, and showed that on their own monistic premises it was an impossible conception. Since being was still imagined as something physical and tangible, empty space could only be found where being was not. But where being is not, there can only be non-being, i.e. empty space is non-existent. So great and lasting was the impact of this revolutionary thought that when Leucippus and Democritus wished later to affirm the existence of space they could only do so in the form of an audacious paradox—

[1] See the description of Pythagorean cosmogony in vol. I, 278 ff.

33

'What is not exists, just as much as what is'—explaining that by 'what is' they meant body, and by 'what is not' void.[1]

(c) *It is motionless, and lies complete within* peirata

(8.26–33) But unmoved, in the grip of mighty bonds, it *is* without beginning or ceasing, since coming into being and perishing have been driven afar off and true conviction has rejected them. (29) Remaining the same in the same place it rests by itself and so remains firmly where it is; for powerful Necessity holds it in the bonds of a chain that hems it in all round, (32) because it is not allowed that what is should be incomplete; for it is not lacking, but by not being it would lack everything.

vv. 29–30. The variants in expression (recorded by DK *ad loc.*) do not affect the sense.

v. 33. A much-disputed line. Simplicius read ἔστι γὰρ οὐκ ἐπιδευές· μὴ ἐὸν δ' ἂν παντὸς ἐδεῖτο, which is unmetrical. The question is whether the metre is to be restored by expunging the negative. So Bergk, Zeller, Diels, and British scholars generally (Burnet, Cornford doubtfully, KR; but not Owen, *CQ*, 1960, 86, n. 5). Cornford renders 'If it were (imperfect?), it would be in need of everything'. Friedländer on the other hand kept μή by reading ἐπιδεές (trisyllabic) for ἐπιδευές (DK, 11, 423), and it is also retained by Fränkel (*Wege u. Formen*, 192f.), Solmsen (*Gnomon*, 1931, 479, n. 1), Gadamer (*Festschr. Reinhardt*, 63ff.), Verdenius (*Parm.* 77).

I take my stand on two points: if ἐόν were predicative, it could not refer right back to ἀτελεύτητον, but only to ἐπιδεές; but secondly this choice is unnecessary because in fact Parmenides would not use his key-word ἐόν in this emphatic position as a mere copula. On this ground μή should be retained, though the train of thought remains difficult.

In these and the following lines the diction reaches a height of epic and religious solemnity. The endings of two of them are taken straight

[1] Democr. fr. 156, p. 392, n. 3 below. Cf. Arist. *Metaph.* 985b 4ff. It is now, I suppose, necessary to defend this well-established interpretation of *vv.* 22–5 against Owen's contention that the reference to continuity is wholly temporal (*CQ*, 1960, 97). οὐδὲ διαιρετόν ἐστιν clearly introduces a fresh point: it is not dependent on the abolition of γένεσις καὶ ὄλεθρος in the previous section. The truth of πᾶν ἐστιν ὁμοῖον admittedly rests on the conclusion in *v.* 11 ἢ πάμπαν πελέναι χρεών ἐστιν ἢ οὐχί, which meant that there is no temporal process of generation such as would allow of 'what is' coming into existence bit by bit. But once established, this has a further legitimate consequence, that at any given moment (or rather in the continuous present which is all that Parmenidean logic allows) 'what is' exists fully, not in varying degrees; and from this the conclusion may be drawn that it is continuous and 'in contact with itself' not in respect of temporal succession but actually. τῇ in *v.* 23 cannot have a temporal reference. The earlier mention of συνεχές in *v.* 6 is taken by Owen to be occasioned by the denial of past and future in the previous line, and its meaning determined by the following question: 'For what birth of it wilt thou seek?' But *vv.* 3–6 simply enumerate all the characteristics of τὸ ἐόν, which are then dealt with one by one from *v.* 6 onwards. τίνα γὰρ γένναν κτλ. begins the proof of the first characteristic (ἀγένητον): it has nothing to do with συνεχές.

Solmsen (*Arist.'s System*, 4) says that although the statement πᾶν ἔμπλεόν ἐστιν ἐόντος seems to deny empty intervals, and was so understood by some of Parmenides's followers, 'yet to accept it in this sense involves an unwarranted translation of Parmenides's rigidly ontological thought into conceptions of a more physical or spatial nature'. This seems to me to be itself a translation of Parmenides's thought into inapplicable modern terms. On the denial of void in Parmenides, see further p. 36, n. 1 below.

from Homer. One of these, telling how 'Fate fettered' reality and made it motionless (*v.* 37), could not fail to recall to a reader the dramatic moment when 'Fate fettered' Hector to stand still (μεῖναι) outside the walls of Troy when the rest of the Trojans had fled like deer within the city, and so to meet Achilles and his death. Other words and phrases also keep the poetry on the same high plane.[1] For reality to be imperfect would be contrary to right ordinance (*themis*). Necessity and Fate, Ananke and Moira, were in Parmenides's day mighty personal beings, of whom Ananke appears also in the second part of the poem. Just as here she holds the one being in the bonds of a *peirar*, and her companion Moira fetters it to be unmoved (*vv.* 37–8 below), so in the world as it appears to mortals she herself 'fetters' or compels the heaven to hold the *peirata* of the stars (10.6). Whatever the relation between the two worlds of reality and seeming, the language of each is designed to remind us of the other; and the Ananke who controls the sky and the stars is the same cosmic goddess who in Plato's *Republic* holds the spindle on which all the circles of the stars revolve. This cosmic Ananke appears again in an Orphic theogony known to the Neoplatonists, where she is 'stretched out over the whole cosmos, reaching to its limits (*perata*)'.[2] The religious intensity of the passage, and its

---

[1] The two Homeric endings are ἀμφὶς ἐέργει (*v.* 31) and Μοῖρ' ἐπέδησεν (*v.* 37). So *Il.* 13.706 and 22.5. ἀτελεύτητον occurs in *Il.* 4.175 (ἀτελευτήτῳ ἐπὶ ἔργῳ), and in 1.527 Zeus says that what he has confirmed with his nod will not be ἀτελεύτητον. This is as much as to say that it τετελεσμένον ἔσται (cf. Parm. 8.42), which occurs commonly in Homer with the meaning 'accomplished', 'completed'. The precedents are sufficient warrant for translating ἀτελεύτητον here 'imperfect', 'incomplete', rather than 'infinite'.

The phrase μεγάλων ἐν πείρασι δεσμῶν (*v.* 26) has a solemn and exalted ring. δεσμοί (δεσμά) and πείρατα are brought together in *H. Hymn Ap.* 129 οὐδ' ἔτι δεσμά σ' ἔρυκε λύοντο δὲ πείρατα πάντα, where they are practically synonymous; which invites a comparison between *Il.* 14.200f. πείρατα γαίης 'Ωκεανόν τε and the unknown poet quoted by Porphyry: 'Ωκεανὸς τῷ πᾶσα περίρρυτος ἐνδέδεται χθών. (Schol. *ad Il.* 18.490, quot. Onians, *Origins of European Thought*, 316.) Cf. also *Od.* 12.179 ἐκ δ' αὐτοῦ πείρατ' ἀνῆπτον, of the companions of Odysseus binding him to the mast. Similar language to *v.* 26 also appears in Hesiod's description of the serpent which πείρασιν ἐν μεγάλοις παγχρύσεα μῆλα φυλάσσει (*Th.* 335). Here πείρατα are coils. Theognis (140) says that men are held fast in the πείρατ' ἀμηχανίης.

[2] Plato, *Rep.* 616c, 617b; Orph. fr. 54 Kern. On the date of the Orphic theogonies, and the various elements in them, see Guthrie, *Orph. and Gk. Rel.* 73 ff. It is of course the date of a particular component that is of importance, rather than the date of compilation. Diels and Kern thought it obvious that the compiler of the Hieronymian version was at this point dependent on Plato: 'sin vero Platoni Orphica ante oculos obversata esse credas, idem efficias quod volumus, imitatorem antiqui carminis Orphici esse Hieronymum' (Kern, *De theogg.* 33). That Plato *was* acquainted with the Orphic theogonies appears from his references to them, e.g. *Philebus*, 66c, where he quotes a line verbatim.

allusion to the traditional functions of Ananke, must not be set aside any more than the fact that the whole exposition is a revelation from a goddess.

To turn to the argument, Parmenides here asserts with all the force of language at his command that reality is totally immovable. This is the explanation promised by the occurrence of the same characteristic (ἀτρεμές) in the preliminary list (v. 4). Yet it may be asked how Parmenides thinks he has proved, or here proves, that reality is unmoved in the sense of staying in the same place (v. 29). The banishment of becoming and perishing substantiates only the impossibility of beginning or ceasing. According to Fränkel, absence of *kinesis* ('motion') in Greek includes changelessness, but even if this is correct (on which point see vol. 1, 382), what is needed is the converse: a demonstration that changelessness includes absence of locomotion. On the other hand Parmenides has just shown, in the immediately preceding lines, that reality is one and indivisible, homogeneous and continuous, and 'all is full of being'. So his reason is not far to seek. If all that exists is a single continuous plenum, there is nowhere for it to move as a whole, nor has it any parts which could change places internally.[1]

The complete immobility of the real, the impossibility of *kinesis* in any sense of the word, is for Parmenides the climax of his message. Hence no doubt the compelling grandeur of his language at this point.

[1] This obvious explanation was generally accepted until Fränkel propounded his alternative view. He argues that locomotion is a kind of change, and all change involves the illegitimate concept of coming-to-be and passing-away. But this is to import much that Parmenides does not say, nor is the involvement of coming-to-be and destruction in any act of locomotion at all obvious without explanation. The argument is certainly one which Parmenides could have put forward on his own premises: the movement of anything implies that it goes to where it 'was not' before, and that it 'is not' now where it formerly was; and since 'is not' is unthinkable, motion in space is also inconceivable. But if this is what he wished us to understand at this point, he has left a great deal to his reader's imagination.

Two English scholars, G. S. Kirk and M. C. Stokes, have recently put forward a view based on Fränkel's (*Phronesis*, 1960, 1–4). They claim that the explanation by the plenitude of being finds no support in the fragments of Parmenides and attribute it to a superficial reading of Plato, *Theaet.* 180e3–4, a passage which I have not thought it necessary to introduce in support of the hitherto accepted interpretation. In their view the argument from the absence of void was first put forward by Melissus. I disagree with this, just as I do not agree that it is a 'bad' argument against motion (Matson, *CQ*, 1963, 29).

Owen, strangely to my mind, exactly reverses the order of Parmenides's reasoning: 'the conclusion is drawn that, since there cannot be movement, there cannot be room for movement' (*CQ*, 1960, 99, with reference to v. 42).

Solemn rhetoric and the introduction of the great goddess Ananke have their part in persuading us no less than logic, for, as other fifth-century poets sang, 'The might of Ananke is invincible', and no charm or spell can prevail against her.[1] He has also deliberately called up in our minds the image of Xenophanes's pantheistic god, who 'always remains in the same place, not moving at all', only adding a little to the emphasis of the language.[2] Parmenides's thought was stimulated by this spherical cosmic divinity, which neither moved from place to place nor was subject to generation and destruction; but his logic advanced the concept of motion and change still further and denied it validity in all its forms. After him the way was paved for the all-embracing concept of *kinesis* which we find in Aristotle, with its four-fold division into locomotion, growth and diminution, qualitative alteration, and generation and destruction.[3]

These lines also introduce a notion that was clearly of great importance for Parmenides, that of a *peirar* or *peiras* (pl. *peirata*). These are epic and poetic forms of a word which in its prose form *peras* is already familiar, especially in the account of Pythagoreanism. Its contrary *apeiron* we first met as the *arche* of Anaximander. The *apeiron* is the unbounded or indefinite, and *peras* is usually translated 'limit'. In Parmenides *peiras* falls again and again on our ears with the force of a blow. Reality is in the *peirata* of great bonds (*v. 26*): Ananke holds it in the bonds of a *peiras* (*v. 31*): there is an ultimate *peiras* (*v. 42*): it lies within its *peirata* (*v. 49*). Even in the world as it appears to erring mortals, Ananke constrains the heavens to hold the *peirata* of the stars (10.7).

The reversal of dative and genitive between *vv.* 26 and 31 suggests that *peirata* and *desmoi* (bonds) are interchangeable, and this is consistent with the use of *peirar* in Homer and the epic tradition.[4] The

---

[1] Aesch. *P.V.* 105; Eur. *Alc.* 965 ff. Cf. *Hel.* 514, and Maass, *Orpheus*, 268 ff.

[2] Xenoph. fr. 26.1: αἰεὶ δ' ἐν ταὐτῷ μίμνει κινούμενος οὐδέν. Parm. 8.29–30: ταὐτόν τ' ἐν ταὐτῷ τε μένον καθ' ἑαυτό τε κεῖται χοὔτως ἔμπεδον αὖθι μένει. Fränkel's suggestion of reading μενεῖ (future) is an unhappy one (*Wege u. Formen*, 191); the repetition μένον...μένει has its own effectiveness.

[3] Cf. again vol. I, 382.

[4] For a fuller account, not without some speculative elements, see Onians, *Origins of Eur. Thought*, 310 ff. There are of course more general uses of the word in Homer, as ὑμῆς ἐπὶ πείρασι γαίης in *Od.* 9.284, and more mysterious conjunctions with ὀλέθρου (plus ἐφῆπται in *Il.* 12.79), ὀϊζύος, ἔριδος, νίκης; but none is inconsistent with a derivation from the concrete sense.

divine infant Apollo, says the Homeric hymn in his honour, soon burst his swaddling bands: 'No longer did the bonds hold thee back, and all the *peirata* were loosed.' When the companions of Odysseus bound him to the mast, that he might listen to the Sirens in safety, they fastened the *peirata* around it. In Hesiod *peirata* are the coils of the serpent within which it guards the golden apples of the Hesperides. The constant notion is that of *encirclement*: so again Oceanus, imagined as a circular river girdling the earth, is called its *peirar* in the *Iliad*, and a later poet says that by flowing round the earth it *binds* it.[1] Progress from a concrete to an abstract sense being more likely than the reverse, we may take it that *peirar* first meant a material bond, a rope or chain. Of course in the fifth century *peras* was in common use with no other meaning than 'limit', whether in a spatial, temporal or more abstract sense; but Parmenides is writing in the epic tradition, as one steeped in the language and thought of Homer and Hesiod, and the point may prove to have some importance.

The argument for confining all reality within *peirata* seems to be this. What is *apeiron* is essentially unfinished, incomplete, never a perfect whole however much of it one may include. But reality cannot be incomplete. That would mean that to some extent it 'was not', but, as we know, one cannot qualify not-being as 'to some extent' or 'in some respect': the only choice is between *is* and *is not*. 'Is lacking' is equivalent to 'is not', hence if it *were not* it would be lacking altogether. In some such way one may perhaps explain the difficult lines 32–3.

In this short passage Parmenides has further advanced his intellectual revolution on two fronts. The denial of change and motion condemns all human experience as illusory and once again excludes the possibility of any cosmogony; and the insistence that reality is totally confined within *peirata* destroys specifically the basis of Anaximander's system.

To appreciate the tremendous impact of Parmenides it is necessary to anticipate by an occasional forward glance at his great successor Plato. In addition to points already noted, a comparison of Plato's descriptions of 'what really exists' with those of Parmenides leaves no doubt about the historical origin of some elements in his thought. Two examples will suffice. At *Phaedo* 78 d we read concerning 'each thing

[1] For reff. and Greek texts see p. 35, n. 1 above.

in itself which is, the existent (τὸ ὄν)', that 'being of one form it remains by itself, constant and the same, and never admits of any alteration in any respect whatsoever'. This unchanging reality a man may only grasp in full clarity with his mind (65 c, e), 'not employing sight in his thinking nor dragging in any other sense along with his reasoning', for sight and hearing hold no truth for men (65 b). Then there is the *Timaeus* (27 d):

In my opinion we must first of all make the following distinction: what is it that always is and has no becoming, and what on the other hand becomes continually and never is? The one comprehensible by the mind with reasoning, the other conjectured by opinion with irrational sensation, coming to be and passing away, but never really *being*.

The metaphysical concept of immutable being, and the epistemological contention that knowledge is only explicable as a contact of the mind with an actual, stable and non-sensible object of knowledge, are cornerstones of Platonism. Although it does not go the whole way with Parmenides, yet without him both its metaphysic and its theory of knowledge might have been very different.

(d) Recapitulation: coming-into-being, locomotion and alteration are names without content

(8.34–41) What can be thought [apprehended] and the thought that 'it is' are the same; for without that which is, in which [i.e. in dependence on, or in respect of which] it is expressed [or revealed], thou shalt not find thought. Nothing exists or can exist apart from what is, since Fate has fettered it so as to be whole and unmoved. Therefore all things must be a name which mortals have laid down [or agreed upon] believing them to be true [real]: coming into being and perishing, being and not being, change of place and alteration of bright colour.

v. 34. This line has been understood in a variety of ways, and it must be admitted that various interpretations are possible. The above translation assumes ἔστι (so accented) before νόημα and takes οὕνεκεν as equivalent to ὅτι. So Zeller, Heidel, Gomperz, Fränkel, Kranz, Calogero, Cornford, von Fritz, KR. (For earlier versions see ZN, 694, n. 1.) It also takes ἔστι νοεῖν to be parallel in construction to νοεῖν ἔστιν in fr. 3 and εἰσι νοῆσαι in 2.2. Others (Diels, von Fritz, Verdenius, Vlastos) have believed that both here and in fr. 3 the infin. is the subject: 'Thought is the same....'

There is also an alternative rendering of οὕνεκεν as 'that for the sake of which' or 'that because of which', the purpose or foundation of thought. So Diels, and see Hölscher in *Hermes*, 1956, 390ff. This was the interpretation of Simplicius (*Phys.* 87.17): ἕνεκα γὰρ τοῦ νοητοῦ, ταὐτὸν δὲ εἰπεῖν τοῦ ὄντος, ἐστι τὸ νοεῖν τέλος ὂν αὐτοῦ. Von Fritz gives οὕνεκεν the same grammatical force, but notes that in early Greek it generally signifies causality or logical consequence rather than purpose, and renders: 'νοεῖν and the cause or condition of νοεῖν are the same' (*CP*, 1945, 238). Both this sense and the sense of ὅτι are well supported in early Greek including Homer. The word could however be taken as Simplicius took it without disturbing the rendering of the first half of the line given here: 'What can be thought is the same as that which is the cause or condition of thought', i.e. (as Simplicius adds) τὸ ὄν.

There are thus, apart from minor differences, two main lines of interpretation. One (of which Vlastos is the chief modern advocate; see *Gnomon*, 1953, 168) involves the identity of thought and being; according to the other (which is followed here) the line repeats what has been said already in fr. 2.6–8 and fr. 3, namely that it is impossible to think (νοεῖν) what is not: there is no thought without an existing object. In Mansfeld's translation (*Offenbarung*, 65) the sequence of thought does not seem to me altogether clear.

v. 35. For a different rendering of πεφατισμένον, based on his conception of the formal logic employed by Parmenides, see Mansfeld, *op. cit.* 85.

v. 36. The text is probably corrupt, since Simplicius quotes it in two versions, one of which (οὐδὲν γὰρ ἔστιν ἢ ἔσται, *Phys.* 86.31) lacks a syllable metrically, whereas the other (οὐδ' εἰ χρόνος ἔστιν ἢ ἔσται, 146.9) leaves a conditional clause hanging in the air. Preller's ἢ before ἔστιν, adopted by DK, is the simplest cure, though it leaves the intrusion of χρόνος difficult to explain. (οὐδὲν χρέος Stein.) I cannot make Parmenidean sense out of Coxon's οὐδὲ χρόνος, 'There is not and will not be any Time outside Being' (*CQ*, 1934, 138), and I have little fear that the reading of Simplicius 86.31 strays far from the meaning.

v. 37. Μοῖρ' ἐπέδησεν. Borrowed from Homer (p. 35, n. 1 above).

v. 38. The line quoted by Plato at *Theaet.* 180e as οἷον ἀκίνητον τελέθει τῷ παντὶ ὄνομ' εἶναι is commonly taken (e.g. by DK) as an inaccurately memorized version of this one. But it is twice quoted in the same form by Simplicius (*Phys.* 29.18 and 143.10) without reference to the *Theaetetus*, and is therefore more likely to be a separate fragment, whether or not Cornford was right in his view of its meaning and place in the poem (*Plato's Theory of Knowledge*, 94, n. 1).

A variant reading is ὀνόμασται (a form repeated at 9.1), which is accepted by Woodbury (*HSCP*, 1963, 145–60). This gives the translation: 'With reference to it (i.e. τὸ ὄν) are all the names given that mortal men have instituted.' It may be right, but, as my discussion will show, I do not think the objections to the generally received reading are as strong as Woodbury makes out.

v. 40. εἶναί τε καὶ οὐχί. Parmenides presumably does not wish to say that εἶναι is a mere name. His expression is far from perfect (since it is strictly parallel to γίγνεσθαί τε καὶ ὄλλυσθαι *both* of which are unreal), but what he must intend to deny is the co-existence of being and not-being. (So now Mansfeld, *Offenbarung*, 142.)

These eight lines are usually, and rightly, regarded as a recapitulation of the main conclusions already reached about the nature of reality, followed by a full and explicit statement, also largely but not entirely recapitulation, of their annihilating effect on all that is customarily thought real. They may be paraphrased thus. All thought must have a real object. One cannot apprehend (know, recognize: the verb is still *noein*) something in the mind without an apprehension of its existence (cf. 2.7–8), for thought depends on 'what is'—a real object —for its fulfilment, unfolding or expression. This real object is unique, whole and unmoved. It follows that coming into being and perishing (which involve the conjunction of being with not being), movement in space, and change of quality are all unreal. Contrary to the firm belief of those who utter these 'names', they are mere words standing for nothing real. This is repeated at the end of the second part of the poem, where the goddess, having described a physical, pluralized cosmos, concludes (fr. 19):

Thus according to appearance these things have arisen and now are, and as they have grown will end in time to come; and men have laid down a distinguishing name for each of them.

For Parmenides there is no contradiction in the idea that the erring faculties of mortals should coin names which correspond to no reality, although it is impossible 'to think or utter that which is not'. When men's mouths produce the terminology of change, they are literally 'saying nothing' (οὐδὲν λέγουσι), nor can they be said to *noein* what is not; there is no act of *noein* at all. Of English words, *noein* in this context seems to signify 'meaning' as much as any other. Since mortals *name* the other things which are not real, it might be supposed that they must *think* about them; but what they utter is mere names without content, meaningless words. It implies no recognition or grasping, since it is only a naming of unreal things. To see a logical difficulty here, Plato had to stand on Parmenides's shoulders and employ resources of thought and language which were scarcely at his disposal.

The question of appearing and seeming without being, and of things being spoken yet not being true—all this is still full of perplexity as it has always been in the past. It is terribly difficult to see in what terms you can say or think that falsehoods have a real existence, without being caught in contradiction when you open your mouth (*Soph.* 236 e).

The question whether names were 'natural' or 'conventional', a strange one to us, became lively in the late fifth century. Like many of the puzzles which the Sophists enjoyed, it had its roots in Parmenides. His own answer is explicit. The names given to things in the world of experience cannot be 'in nature'; not simply, as one might think, because they were mere conventional labels attached to things which might just as well be called something else (as it is a matter of where a man was born whether he calls a particular substance *wood* or *bois*); but because there is no real object at all for them to be attached to.

The limitations imposed by his pioneer situation provide also the most likely answer to those who argue that he consciously and deliberately identified thought with being, and hence what thinks with what is: his one reality anticipates Aristotle's god in being engaged in purely intellectual activity: 'Eleatic Being is mind' (Vlastos). Apart from fr. 8.34 and fr. 3, which have here been translated differently, Vlastos relies on the indirect argument that the thought which knows can hardly be denied existence. Hence it must be at least a part of being (for being is unique), and since being is 'all alike' it cannot be a part of being without being the whole of it.[1] Fortunately we possess practically the whole of the Way of Truth, and can say with some confidence that Parmenides nowhere states this train of thought; and it is dangerous to put arguments into his mouth, even if from our point of view they are an inescapable consequence of what he does say. It should suffice to remark that in attempting to explain his theory of human knowledge, both Vlastos and others rely heavily on fr. 16 as expressing his own sincerely held view. But fr. 16 speaks of a 'mixture' of elements in the human frame and obviously belongs to the Way of Seeming. The mixture must be composed (as is generally agreed) of the two primary contraries of the cosmology described in this part of the poem, namely fire or light (the rare) and night or darkness (the dense): of these 'that which prevails is thought' (16.4; see on this fr. pp. 67 f. below). The critics may be right in supposing that Parmenides meant this seriously as an explanation of how mortal minds can err; that is scarcely something that could be accounted for on the assumption of one unchanging reality. At any rate it is not so accounted for, and Parmenides does not seem to have regarded the plurality involved as fatal to the validity of his explanation. Yet it is a more violent contradiction of the unity of being than we need assume here, if we suppose him to have acquiesced in the idea that it is possible to think about 'what is' without advancing to the rather sophisticated conclusion that 'what is' must itself be thinking. He was not that kind of idealist.[2]

---

[1] *Gnomon*, 1953, 168.

[2] Cornford is on this point a better guide. Cf. *Plato and Parm.* 34, n. 1: 'He nowhere suggests that his One Being thinks, and no Greek of his date or for long afterwards would have seen anything but nonsense in the statement that "A exists" means the same as "A thinks"....Parmenides certainly held that there can be no thought without an object that is; but nothing in the poem supports the interpretation that thinking is the same thing as its object.' Mr G. Jameson has acutely pointed out the error of confusing an explicit statement that thought and its object are identical with the primitive inability to distinguish between the two (*Phronesis*, 1958, 22 f.). Cf. also Owen, *CQ*, 1960, 95, n. 5.

Eleatic Being and Mind

The one new point in this summary is the denial that what is can change colour. The example of colour no doubt stands for qualitative change in general, and it is introduced along with generation and perishing, being and not being, without further comment. Such alteration would indeed be immediately recognized in his time as a special case of becoming. There was as yet no awareness of a distinction between substance and quality. Either therefore one may say that the same thing (the coloured object) is and is not (i.e. is white and not white, no difference being felt between the predicative and existential uses of the verb; this is the ambiguity that was afterwards exploited by the Sophists) or, what more probably represents the early fifth-century outlook, the same thing (i.e. the colour white) *is* when the object is characterized by it, and *is not* (disappears) when the object changes colour. On either supposition, if alteration takes place the same thing is not and is, or is other than what is—more obviously so than in change of place— so that its impossibility would not seem to be in need of separate demonstration.[1]

(e) *It is 'like a round ball'*

(8.42–9) But since there is a furthest limit, it is complete on every side, like the mass of a well-rounded ball, equal every way from the centre; for it may not be at all greater or smaller in this direction or in that; for neither is there what is not, which might stop it from reaching its like, nor is it possible that what is should be here more, and here less, than what is, since it is all inviolate; for equal on all sides to itself, it meets its limits uniformly.

v. 43. σφαίρης, 'ball' rather than 'sphere'. The word is more likely to have the concrete sense that it bears in Homer, where Nausicaa and her maidens play with a σφαίρη (*Od.* 6.100), than the later, more general application of it to anything spherical in shape. (Cf. G. Jameson, *Phronesis*, 1958, 15, n. 3.) Whether or not Parmenides thought of 'what is' as extended, the point is not settled by the argument that he only *compares* it to a sphere, as distinct from calling it spherical. The comparison to a ball, so far as it goes, suggests that it *is* spherical. (Owen agrees, *CQ*, 1960, 95.)

v. 44. ἰσοπαλές. This is the earliest extant use of this word, which elsewhere in the fifth century means 'equally matched' of opposing forces in battle (Hdt. 1.82.4), of equal strength (Hdt. 5.49.8), equal in numbers (with πλήθει, Thuc. 4.94), or simply equal (Thuc. 2.39 κινδύνους). It does not

---

[1] Especially when we consider that the contemporary Greek words for 'altered' and 'to alter' were ἀλλοῖος and ἀλλοιοῦν. In Homer ἀλλοῖος can be a synonym for ἄλλος, as in *Od.* 16.181f. ἀλλοῖός μοι, ξεῖνε, φάνης...ἄλλα δὲ εἵματ' ἔχεις, and in *Il.* 4.258 ἠμὲν ἐνὶ πολέμῳ ἠδ' ἀλλοίῳ ἐπὶ ἔργῳ the use of ἄλλος would not alter the sense. Since therefore Parmenides has already shown that there cannot be ἄλλο πάρεξ τοῦ ἐόντος, there is no more to be said.

On colour as representing change in general, cf. the illuminating note of Fränkel, *Wege u. Formen*, 206, n. 2.

seem to have the specialized sense of equally balanced, poised, or *gleichgewichtig*, which some translators give it here.

v. 46. Reading οὐκ ἐόν with the Aldine ed. and DK. The MSS. of Simplicius have οὔτε ἐόν or οὔτε ὄν. On the Aldine version Diels commented 'recte' in his own ed. of Simplicius (1882), but by 1897 he had changed his mind and tentatively proposed an otherwise lost word οὔτεον (not two words as printed by DK and Cornford) = οὔτι = οὐδέν: 'for neither is there a nothing' (Diels, *Lehrgedicht*, 90f.).

v. 49. ὁμῶς ἐν πείρασι κύρει may mean 'It lies (is, finds itself) evenly within its limits'. On the whole I think that to regard the words as equivalent, by tmesis, to ἐγκύρει πείρασι corresponds more to known usage than to suppose κύρω to be used absolutely for 'be', 'be situated'. The doctrine is unaffected.

In these few lines the conjunction 'for' occurs three times, and 'since' twice: a striking example of what is apparent throughout the poem, the ordering of its contents in the guise of a formal deductive argument. The originality of this procedure, and the intellectual power required to initiate it, may easily escape us from their familiarity in later writing. While giving them due acknowledgment, we need not assume that this great pioneer was capable at one bound of unfolding a lengthy argument according to strict rules of inference. Sometimes a clause made dependent on another through a 'for' or a 'since' is little more than a repetition in different words; sometimes it expresses the conclusion in a religious or metaphorical form. Thus at *v.* 29 reality remains firmly in the same place, *for* Ananke holds it in the bonds of a *peiras*; and in *v.* 48 it hardly adds a cogent reason for the uniformity of being to say 'since it is all inviolate'. (The adjective, *asylon*, whence comes our noun *asylum*, signifies protection from violent attack or robbery.)

Parmenides does not hesitate to repeat himself, as indeed, considering the novelty and difficulty of his doctrine, he was wise to do. Here we have in essentials the statement of *vv.* 23 and 24 over again, that what is cannot be in greater or less degree in one direction or another. The expression is varied slightly, but with Parmenides's conception of reality, 'greater or smaller' means the same. In the earlier passage it followed that it 'held together' and was a continuous plenum. Here it is said that there are no intervals of not-being to separate portions of homogeneous being.

The crux of the passage lies in the question how to interpret the reference to spherical shape and the spatial language of 'equal every way from the centre'. Are the 'furthest limit', and the limits which it 'meets uniformly' (or alternatively 'within which it rests'), limits of spatial extension? How, in short, did Parmenides conceive of his one true being? As purely conceptual, or as occupying space?

Certain things about it are beyond doubt. It is grasped by intellectual insight, not by the senses. It is immutable and timeless, neither changing in quality nor moving in space. It is unique, completely homogeneous, and indivisible. All this shows plainly that it is not a body filling space with its physical bulk as, say, the earth does.

From these certainties some have concluded that the *peirata* on which such repeated emphasis is laid, and which hold reality so firmly in the grip of their bonds, have nothing to do with spatial limits but are used figuratively to signify the *invariancy* of the one being. The reference to a chain that 'hems it in' or 'constricts it all round' is purely metaphorical, even though (which makes this position a little difficult) it is brought in as the immediate explanation of why reality, like the god of Xenophanes, remains always in the same place. On the same argument *vv.* 42–3 do not say, as they seem to, that 'what is' has boundaries and is spherical, but only that it is spatially, as it has been said to be temporally, *invariant*. Effectively, space has been abolished, as time was abolished by the denial of past and future. Reality is compared to a sphere simply 'because there is nothing true of it at one point or in one direction which is not true elsewhere. Its uniformity is like the perfect balance of a ball about its centre.'[1]

I believe that the linking of *peirata*, encircling bonds or limits, with spatial contexts has more significance than this. The temporal situation is different, in fact diametrically contrary. If 'what is' is to exist completely at every moment, and never for one moment not to exist in any sense or to any extent, then it must have no temporal limits; and the idea of a reality without temporal limits was not strange to Parmenides,

[1] This, if I understand him rightly, is the position taken up by Owen in his masterly article in *CQ*, 1960, from which the last sentence is quoted. But I see Parmenides through such different spectacles that I am seriously afraid of misrepresenting him. In any case the force of his argument can only be appreciated at length and in his own words. He justly calls attention to the insurmountable difficulty of expression which confronted Parmenides 'The very proof which rules out all variation in time and space has to use language which implies temporal and spatial distinctions. It has to say that what exists is continuous...; and that it remains the same; and that it is uniform in all directions. Just as Parmenides can only prove the unintelligibility of οὐκ ἔστιν by himself denying the existence of certain states of affairs, so he can only show the vacuousness of temporal and spatial distinctions by a proof which employs them' (p. 100).

having already been mooted by a thinker to whom he owed much, Xenophanes. If on the other hand it had no spatial limits, then according to the ideas of the time it would *never* exist completely. As he says in *vv.* 29 ff.: 'It remains firmly where it is, for Ananke holds it in the bonds of a *peiras* that confines it all round, *because* what is must not be incomplete.' Similarly in *vv.* 42–3, '*Since* there is a furthest limit, it is *complete* on every side, like a round ball'.

The difficulty of a modern interpreter is that he feels himself confronted with only two alternatives: either something goes on for ever indefinitely, or where it stops there must be something else, or at the least empty space, beyond it; whereas for Parmenides there is only 'what is' and nothing else, not even empty space, for that is 'what is not'. How then can what is lie within *peirata*, except in the metaphorical sense of being invariant? It appears for instance to Owen that if we take the sphericity of reality seriously, we must suppose Parmenides to be using the argument from continuity, which in *vv.* 22–5 was used to prove that there is *no* part of reality that borders on nothing, 'to prove that reality does border on nothing in all directions at an equal distance from a centre'.

This would have seemed strange nonsense to Parmenides. It depends on a Euclidean conception of space as infinite which had not yet penetrated the Western consciousness.[1] The question: 'If all that exists is finite and spherical, what lies beyond it?' is one which he had no impulse to ask himself. (It was first raised by Melissus; see p. 107 below.) If, anachronistically, we ask it for him, we must reply that there is neither something (for all existence is contained within it) nor nothing (for nothing does not exist and cannot even be imagined). The All of Parmenides is more like the curved and finite Einsteinian space than the Euclidean conception which still dominates our ordinary thinking.[2] Plato speaks of 'your thinkers like Melissus and Parmenides who assert that everything is one and stands still within its own boundaries *because it has no room in which it moves*' (*Theaet.* 180e).

[1] See Cornford, *The Invention of Space* (1936).
[2] In this connexion cf. especially von Weizsacker's remarks on Einstein's conception of space in *The Relevance of Science*, 145, especially the sentence: 'Beyond a certain limit there may neither be other galaxies nor will there be empty space but there might be the very same galaxies as on this side of the limit.'

Can All that Exists be Finite?

It was a typically Hellenic idea, fraught with momentous and some would say dire consequences for science, that a special uniqueness and perfection attached to *roundness*, including spherical shape in solid bodies and circularity in surfaces or motion. What impressed the Greek was the way in which a single line or surface turned back upon itself completely, so that, as Heraclitus said (fr. 103), 'Beginning and end are common', and could be assumed at any point on it. To Alcmaeon this had a mysterious connexion with human life.[1] Xenophanes had already connected it with divinity, and it was most commonly summed up in the epithet 'perfect' or 'complete' (*teleion*). The perfection of the circle and sphere was basic to the cosmologies of Plato and Aristotle, from which was born the whole progeny of stellar spheres which haunted the world down to and beyond the time of Copernicus, so that even he was too much under its spell to see that his own hypothesis had turned it into useless lumber.

The cosmos, said Plato, is spherical because the sphere is 'the most perfect and self-consistent (or uniform) of shapes'. Nothing went out or came into it from anywhere, 'since there was nothing' (*Tim.* 33b, c). No one but Parmenides himself had the logical stubbornness to reject the testimony of his own eyesight completely and deny every form of motion, but both Plato and Aristotle deferred to him so far as to emphasize the fact that the sphere is the only shape whose motion (revolution) can occur without requiring any space outside it. Aristotle also, in applying the term 'perfect' to the sphere, defines it as meaning 'that outside which there is nothing', in contrast to the *apeiron*, of which however much you may take, there is always something left outside; and he calls the sphere the primary figure because it 'corresponds to unity', being bounded by one continuous surface. The perfection and 'wholeness' of a circle are similarly connected with its unity as a line.

Above all, for both Plato and Aristotle there was nothing whatso-

[1] See vol. 1, 351 ff. Parmenides himself had a circle in mind when he wrote (fr. 5): 'It is all one (lit. "common") to me whence I begin, for thither I shall come back again.' The position of this fragment in the poem, and hence its precise application, are quite uncertain; but although we know it only from one mention in Proclus, it seems a little drastic to question its genuineness as Jameson does (*Phronesis*, 1958, 20f.). Most probably it refers to the description of the one Being in the Way of Truth: starting from any of the σήματα (8.2), the goddess can arrive at any of the others (Mansfeld, *Offenbarung*, 106).

ever outside the spherical cosmos, and this excluded empty space (or 'nothing' in the Parmenidean sense) as well as matter. Aristotle is quite explicit: 'There is neither place nor void nor time outside the heaven.'[1]

We may cite Plato and Aristotle on this point without fear of anachronism. In the first place, all that needs to be shown is the bare possibility of conceiving the whole of reality as spherical without asking the question whether or not it 'borders on nothing'. Secondly, the language of Plato in many places makes it clear that in teaching the perfection and completeness, the uniformity and self-sufficiency of the sphere he was directly under the sway of Parmenides. He had indeed advanced, but the advance consisted in the ability to separate the noetic world of pure, intelligible form from every spatial association. At each step he had either to satisfy the conditions laid down by Parmenides or justify his departure from them.

What then was in the mind of Parmenides? It may be helpful to recall his well-attested acquaintance with Pythagorean thought. According to the Pythagoreans there was void both inside and outside the cosmos. Internally it is what keeps things apart; externally it is the 'infinite breath' which the cosmos draws in for its nourishment and growth.[2] The process of cosmogony consisted in general terms of the imposition of limit on this unlimited. This scheme of things Parmenides denied point by point. Internally there is nothing that keeps things apart, since reality is one and continuous: 'what is is close to what is'. Nor is there anything outside, whether it be called void or breath. That assumption was only justified so long as the universe was supposed to need an external source on which to draw, that is, so long as it was incomplete. But 'it is not allowed that what is should be incomplete, for it is not lacking'. There is no unlimited (*apeiron*); the *peirata* embrace all that is; and this 'unlimited' which Parmenides has abolished was at the same time physical matter, empty space, and time or duration. To do away with it was an audacious stroke, aimed it

---

[1] Ar. *Phys.* 207a7; *De caelo*, 286b10ff.; *Metaph.* 1016b16; *De caelo*, 279a11ff.

[2] Ar. *Phys.* 213b22: 'The Pythagoreans also said that void exists, and that it enters the universe from the infinite breath, the universe being supposed to breathe in the actual void, which keeps different kinds of things apart'; and again in his *On the Pythagoreans*, bk. 1 (*ap.* Stob.: see DK, vol. 1, 460.3): 'The universe is unique, and from the infinite it draws in time, breath, and void which distinguishes the places of separate things.' For further details see vol. 1, 280.

would seem primarily at the Pythagoreans, but also a lever wherewith to overthrow every normal person's conception of reality. It is no wonder that he hammered it home with the fourfold repetition of *peiras*, backed up with the insistence on bonds and fetters imposed by divine authority.

Now we know, chiefly from the repeated criticisms of Aristotle, that the Pythagoreans, excited by the discovery of the part played by mathematical laws of proportion and harmony in the ordering of the cosmos, and guided by impulses religious as well as scientific, declared outright that 'things are numbers'. 'Granted that spatial magnitude consists of these elements [*sc.* limited and unlimited, odd and even, the elements of number], how could some bodies be heavy and some light?' 'When they construct physical bodies out of number...they appear to be talking about some other universe and other bodies, not those that we perceive.' 'From the monad and the unlimited spring numbers, from numbers points, from points lines, out of which surfaces are formed, out of surfaces solid figures, *and from these, perceptible bodies.*'[1] In this last leap, from the geometrical solid to physical nature, they betrayed the primitivism still lurking in their thought, and it was on this that Parmenides pounced. The cosmos, which like most of us they believed to be real, was for them a sphere, containing other spheres within it, all of them revolving, and all containing visible and tangible body, composed of fire, water, air and earth. Parmenides retained the geometrical basis of all this, but denied the illegitimate leap from the intelligible geometrical figure to the moving and perceptible world. His reality is the spherical solid of the geometer, now for the first time separated from its physical manifestations, an object of thought, not sense. It is one, continuous, homogeneous, motionless, timeless, finished and complete. Extended in space? No more and no less than the figures of which Euclid supplies definitions at the beginning of the various books of the *Elements*.

[1] Ar. *Metaph.* 990a12, 1090a32, Alex. Polyhist. *ap.* D.L. 8.25. This aspect of Pythagoreanism has been treated in vol. 1, 229ff.

No interpretation of Parmenides today can be entirely novel, and in the present section it will be obvious to an informed reader how much I owe to Cornford and Mr J. E. Raven. Nevertheless the account given here is the result of an attempt to rethink the problem in the light of the fragments and other ancient sources, and I have therefore confined myself to this general acknowledgment of their work.

The Eleatics

(8) *The false way of what seems to mortals*

(8.50–61) Here I cease the trustworthy account and thought concerning truth. From this point learn the opinions of mortals, listening to the deceitful pattern of my words. They made up their minds to name two forms, (54) of which it is not right to name one (it is in this that they have gone astray); and they adjudged them contrary in form and assigned marks apart from each other: on the one hand flaming heavenly Fire, very rare and light, in every direction the same as itself but not the same as the other; and also that other, separate, the very opposite, blind Night, a dense and heavy form. This whole likely-seeming ordering I tell thee, that no judgment of mortals may outrun thee.

v. 51. δόξας. Cornford (*CQ*, 1933, 100) notes how the range of this word exceeds that of any corresponding English one, including (1) what seems real, by appearing to the senses; (2) what seems true, beliefs; (3) what seems right, or is decided, as in the legislative formula ἔδοξε τῷ δήμῳ.

v. 52. κόσμον ἐπέων. A phrase borrowed from earlier poetry. Cf. Solon, 2.2, κόσμον ἐπέων ᾠδὴν ἀντ' ἀγορῆς θέμενος and κόσμον ἀοιδῆς in the Orphic verse quoted by Plato, *Phil.* 66c; also Democr. fr. 21 ῞Ομηρος... ἐπέων κόσμον ἐτεκτήνατο παντοίων (Diels, *Lehrgedicht*, 92). I am doubtful about de Santillana's interpretation of these words (*Prologue to P.*, 10). It seems to give an unnatural emphasis to κόσμον at the expense of ἐπέων, and I believe ἀπατηλόν does mean deceitful.

v. 54. τῶν μίαν οὐ χρεών ἐστιν. Zeller translated 'one of which should not be named', i.e. the other exists and may be named: 'von denen in Wahrheit freilich nur dem einen Wirklichkeit zukommt' (ZN, 701), and Nestle retained this. See ZN, 703, n. 2 for its defence and a summary of some other renderings. So also Burnet, Gilbert, Kranz, Albertelli, Vlastos. Reinhardt (*Parm.* 70) also says that the error of mortals is to name two forms instead of one only, but gives this a peculiar twist; this does *not* mean, he says, that one of them is nearer to true being than the other. Nestle with some justification calls his interpretation far-fetched and capricious.

Cornford (*CQ*, 1933, 108f.; *P. and P.* 46) preferred to render 'of which it is not right to name (so much as) one'. He repeated Diels's objection (*Lehrgedicht*, 93) that Zeller's version would require τὴν ἑτέρην for μίαν. I do not find this objection compelling. Parmenides's expression is often odd, nor is there anything very strange (certainly nothing obscure) in the phrase μίαν τῶν δύο, especially if he felt the need of emphasis. Cornford's translation on the other hand would more naturally be represented by οὐδὲ μίαν and that of Simplicius and KR by μίαν μόνην. In spite of Ar. *Thesm.* 549, I still feel that on Cornford's interpretation Parmenides's expression would be misleading, but I may be wrong. Cf. Long, *Phronesis*, 1963, 98.

Simplicius (*Phys.* 31.8) supposed that the error of mortals lay in failing to see that it is impossible to posit one of a pair of physical opposites without the other. The Greek therefore means 'of which it is not right to name *only* one'. Some modern scholars have followed him, e.g. Coxon writes (*CQ*, 1934, 142): 'We see now why Parmenides deliberately assumed two first principles instead of one. Out of a single element nothing can come but itself, since, in the absence of anything else, it must always be completely uniform.' KR too translate: 'of which they must not name one only', and remark that this is the difference between objects of reason and objects of sense: according to reason only one of a pair of opposites can be accepted; according to sense it is impossible to accept one without the other. Similarly Diès and Raven, *P. and E.* 39. Verdenius (*Parm.* 61–3) also says that two forms, not one only, must be named, but argues that this condemnation comes not from the goddess but from mortals themselves.

Fränkel's interpretation will be given in the text. See also the review of previous opinion in Mansfeld, *Offenbarung*, 123–7.

v. 55. σήματ' ἔθεντο recalls the σήματ' ἔασι of *v.* 2. The 'signs or tokens that exist' are contrasted with those that men have arbitrarily assumed. Another reminder of true being, for whatever purpose, seems intended in ἑωυτῷ πάντοσε τωὐτόν (*v.* 57). Cf. ταὐτόν *v.* 29 and οἱ γὰρ πάντοθεν ἶσον *v.* 49.

v. 57. This line as quoted three times by Simplicius (*Phys.* 30, 39, 180) contains three adjectives, ἤπιον ἀραιόν ἐλαφρον, which together make the line too long. It is usual to delete ἀραιόν (ἤπιον ὂν μέγ' [ἀραιὸν] ἐλαφρόν DK), but Verdenius (*Mnemos.* 1947, 25–7) has argued persuasively for its retention and the omission of ἤπιον. Of his four arguments note particularly the parallelism with the two epithets applied to Night, which is declared to be the direct contrary of Fire, and the part played by τὸ ἀραιόν in Parmenides's cosmology (A 37, 43, 53). This passage as Simplicius had it was interspersed with scholia written 'as if by Parmenides himself' (*Phys.* 31.3 ff.).

v. 59. ἀδαής, as Fränkel pointed out (*Wege u. Formen*, 182, n. 4), is regularly active in sense (unknowing, insensitive, apathetic), not passive (unknowable or invisible).

v. 60. ἐοικότα. Cornford (*P. and P.* 46, n. 2) aptly compares Xenoph. fr. 35, ἐοικότα τοῖς ἐτύμοισι and Hes. *Th.* 27, ἐτύμοισιν ὁμοῖα. The latter is particularly relevant, for in putting himself under the instruction of a divine teacher who claims to tell both truth and falsehood Parmenides must have had in mind the Muses of his predecessor who 'know how to tell many false things like to the true, and how to tell the truth when we wish'. The phrase of Hesiod goes back to Homer (*Od.* 19.203). I do not see how Verdenius can know that to have the meaning probable, plausible, or only apparent which it has in Plato, ἐοικότα would at this earlier period need to be followed by a dative. In this line, surely, the goddess announces the nature of the subject-matter of the second part of the poem in the same way as it is summed up at the end (fr. 19): 'Thus *according to appearance* (κατὰ δόξαν) these things have arisen and now are.' Similarly, Mansfeld's claim (*Offenbarung*, 146) to see significance in the absence of ἐτύμοισι seems to me captious.

Imperturbably pursuing her argument, the goddess now declares that she has said all that can be said about what truly exists. She has described a reality to which none but a disembodied mind could confine its attention, something utterly different from the world in which each one of us, including Parmenides, supposes himself to live, and which none of us can ignore if he is to continue living. Henceforward Parmenides, the uniquely privileged mortal who has journeyed through the gates of the paths of Night and Day, will know our world for the deceitful show that it is. Nevertheless it is possible to understand and interpret it either well or badly, for appearances do not present a chaotic confusion; indeed our daily life depends on their regularity, and a cursory inspection of our surroundings confirms it. They suggest a detailed process of ordering or systematization (διάκοσμον), and Parmenides must master its principles so that his own understanding of it is better than anyone else's. It is possible to improve on previous cosmogonies.

The realm of truth is rather like the mathematical model or world-image of the modern physicist with its relationship to the physical world reversed. For some physicists, at least, the model is 'merely an intellectual structure. To a certain extent it is arbitrary.' 'The world-image is due to our imagination and is of a provisional and changeable character.'[1] This world-image contains only mathematical magnitudes, which are perfectly definable but never observable, in contrast to the physical world which may be observed but never precisely measured or defined. Reverse the relationships, call the physicist's model reality and the physical world a construction of the human intellect and imagination, and we shall approach very closely to the Parmenidean ontology. It was an astonishing achievement. Planck had the work of generations of exact scientists behind him when he wrote that 'a clear and consistent distinction between the magnitudes of the world of the senses and the similarly-designated magnitudes of the world-image is indispensable'. When we reflect that the need for an analogous distinction was grasped by one man early in the fifth century B.C., even though the ontological status of the two worlds was reversed, we may begin to appreciate something of the extraordinary quality of the few pioneer minds of classical Greece.

This is the difference between the man who has had the truth divinely revealed to him and the crowd of mortals who 'knowing nothing, wander two-headed'. They confuse being and not-being, deluding themselves that 'things that are not are'. He has the distinction ever present in his mind. For him therefore it is legitimate to go on from reality to study the world of seeming. Once the goddess has revealed the truth (and she could not have done so more clearly and emphatically), such study will not mislead him as to its status. Of the motive for it she says only: 'that no judgment of mortals may outrun thee'. His account of appearances will excel those of others.[2] To ask 'But if it is unreal, what is the point of trying to give an account of it at all?' is to put a question that is not likely to have occurred to him. Men must obviously come to terms with appearances, and for all the

---

[1] Max Planck, *The Philosophy of Physics*, 50 and 68.

[2] The translation of the clause is clear, but contrary conclusions have been drawn from it. Owen thinks that, since the aim is only to be armed against witless mortals, 'no ontological claims have been made and the cosmology need be no more than a dialectical device', which is what he believes it to be (*CQ*, 1960, 85). Long (*Phronesis*, 1963, 105 f.) accepts Owen's interpretation but emphasizes the didactic purpose of such a device. Verdenius on the other hand claims that this line provides 'convincing proof of the positive value which Parmenides attached also to the second part' (*Parm.* 48). So also Kranz: 'Dieses System wird von der Göttin als etwas Neues verkündet, und Parmenides war es *so wertvoll*, dass er sie aussprechen lässt: nie wird ein Mensch ein besseres finden' (*SB Berlin*, 1916, 1171 f.).

divine favour which he enjoys, Parmenides is not a god. This is not to water down his logic. There is all the difference in the world between living and thinking as if the phenomena were real and studying phenomena in the full consciousness of the impassable gulf that separates them from reality.[1]

'From solid figures come sensible bodies.' There lay the fatal error on which Parmenides put his finger, in the supposition that there could be a transition in nature from the intellectual world of mathematical form to the world of physical bodies and change, and that both worlds are on the same level of reality. In that guise it was an error of the Pythagoreans, and it is scarcely rash to infer that it was reflexion on their mathematical conception of physics that led him to his great discovery.[2] But the discovery was of course equally fatal to any cosmological theory, religious or scientific, which started from the dictum universally accepted by early Greek thinkers and ascribed by them to their ancient poet and religious teacher Musaeus: 'All things came into being out of one, and are resolved into one' (D.L. 1.3). From unity nothing but unity can be derived. The first step in describing the evolution of a cosmos, with all its ordered variety, must be to name 'two forms';[3] but since reality has been proved to be one, this

---

[1] At first glance a reader may be reminded of the cosmic illusion of Maya in Indian thought. It too can be described as 'the imposition of a multiple and mutable unreality upon a sole and unique immutable Real' (Sri Aurobindo in S. Radhakrishnan and C. A. Moore, *A Source Book in Indian Philosophy*, p. 595; see his whole section, 'The Power of Illusion, Maya', pp. 589–97), and more particularly as 'the realm of the phenomenal pairs of opposites' (H. Zimmer, *Philosophies of India*, 440). In fact, however, India and Parmenides are poles apart. Parmenides makes and tests his hard-and-fast distinctions by sheer intellectual reasoning (*logos*), which is for him the sole purveyor of truth. In Brahmanism, not only the senses but 'thought, the intellect itself, must be transcended if true reality is to be attained. Logic is...an imperfect, inadequate instrument for the final insight' (Zimmer, 380). If any Greek thinker were to be brought into comparison with Indian ideas, it might rather be Heraclitus. Sankhya and Yoga, at any rate, speak of 'the identity of apparently incompatible elements, representing a union of things which on the logical level exclude each other'. There is 'a constant transformation of things into their antitheses—antagonism being but the screen of a cryptic identity. Behind the screen the contending forces are in harmony' (Zimmer, 313).

But in truth the motives and methods of the Indian schools, and the theological and mystical background of their thought, are so utterly different from those of the Greeks that there is little profit in the comparison.

[2] Yet K. Reich, *Parm. und die Pythagoreer* (Hermes, 1954), contains some far-fetched notions, particularly the suggestion of a link between fr. 6, *vv.* 8–9, and the doctrine of reincarnation.

[3] I cannot follow A. A. Long's argument about an 'abstract' use of μορφή (*Phronesis*, 1963, 101). At least to substitute anything like 'shapeliness' for 'shape' or 'form' in Aesch. *P.V.* 212, which he cites, would turn it into nonsense.

immediately shows up the illusory character of such a world. With this final warning the goddess proceeds to her account of the origin and present arrangement of phenomena.

This phrase from *v.* 54 ('of which it is not right to name one') neatly illustrates the difficulty which Parmenides had in using the language at his disposal to express himself clearly, for it has been seriously understood as meaning (*a*) that *two* forms should be named (i.e. not one *only*), (*b*) that one should not be named and the other should, (*c*) that *none* should be named (i.e. not *even* one). An attractive interpretation is that of H. Fränkel. Of two forms, one should not be named. This does not mean that one of the two forms *about to be described* is illegitimate and the other consequently legitimate, i.e. that Light exists though Night does not, for Light is not to be identified with the one being of the Way of Truth, even if there turns out to be a certain analogy between them. It means simply that men name two forms when it is right to name only one, to wit *being*, or 'what is'. This is in fact neither of the two that mortals do name, which have not yet been given their titles or characteristics. The initial mistake lies in naming two forms *at all*.[1] I should like to believe that Fränkel's explanation is correct, but cannot rule out the alternative that if one accepts the world of appearances then it is necessary to posit two ultimate forms to account for its genesis. On this interpretation Parmenides is claiming that it is illogical to suppose simultaneously (*a*) that there is a world containing many different things, (*b*) that this plurality arose from a single *arché*. This convicts all (and they were not only philosophers) who had supposed that 'all things arose from one',[2] and that the opposites (which they did posit) were derivative.

[1] Fränkel, *Wege u. Formen*, 180. In this way F. retains the mention of one form while seeking a way out of the difficulty raised by Diels and Cornford that this would require τὴν ἑτέρην for μίαν: 'Aber ἑτέρην würde bedeuten, dass zwar die eine Gestalt gestrichen werden müsse, die andere aber, das Licht, so wie sie angesetzt wird richtig sei. Nun ist bisher nichts über das Wesen und den Namen der beiden Gestalten ausgesagt; nur ihre Zweizahl wurde festgestellt.'

The interpretations of other scholars are given in more detail in the notes on the translation. Mansfeld has recently put forward a new one, on which he bases far-reaching conclusions: τῶν μίαν means 'die Einheit der duo' (*Offenbarung*, 129, 130, n. 2), as it were τῶν τὴν ἑνότητα. I cannot see that this is a possible translation, nor agree that it is what Simplicius says at *Phys.* 31.7.

[2] Cf. vol. I, 69. In this way, as Deichgräber and Mansfeld have pointed out (see *Offenbarung*, 140 and 145), Parmenides has some claim to be regarded as the discoverer of the concept of an irreducible element which was developed by Empedocles.

The Two Forms. Aristotle's Interpretation

So far we have been dealing, for the first time, with a section of a philosopher's work of which the greater part has survived, and have been freed from the irksome necessity of extracting his thought to a large extent from second-hand accounts and criticisms. What has been said up to this point about the ways of truth and seeming and their relation to each other is what seems most probable from a reading of his own words.[1] It is interesting nevertheless to see that it is close to the interpretation of Aristotle. His general attitude to Parmenides was one of condescension: he was certainly mistaken, and his mistakes arose from trying to indulge in abstract argument before the principles of logic had been sufficiently well developed: the faults common to him and his school (Aristotle thought) were inexperience and lack of practice in the techniques of reasoning which they were trying to use. At the same time Aristotle singles out Parmenides as more intelligent and profound than the others. He 'saw further' (*Metaph.* 986b27); 'Parmenides must be thought to have spoken better than Melissus' (*Phys.* 207a15); the premises of both Parmenides and Melissus were false, and their arguments invalid, 'but Melissus's account is cruder and presents no difficulty' (*ibid.* 185a9).

Aristotle saw as clearly as any modern critic that only the doctrine of 'one being' contained the truth for Parmenides, and that the physical world of plurality and change was simply false.

'Convinced that, beside what is, what is not is nothing, of necessity he supposed that one thing exists, namely what is, and nothing else' (*Metaph.* 986b28).

'Some earlier philosophers, e.g. Melissus and Parmenides, flatly denied generation and destruction, maintaining that nothing which is either comes into being or perishes; it only seems to us as if this happens' (*De caelo* 298b14).

'They say that no existing thing either comes into being or perishes because what comes into being must originate either from what exists or from what does not, and both are impossible: what is does not become (for it already is), and nothing could come to be from what is not' (*Phys.* 191a27).

[1] Of course not all will agree. The status of the 'way of seeming' is a highly controversial topic, so much so that to discuss the various theories of it put forward in the nineteenth and twentieth centuries would not only be intolerably long but inevitably cloud the issue. A view rather similar to the one put forward here is given by Mugler in *L'Ant. Class.* 1958, 80.

Again, in a criticism of Plato:

'But if there is to be an absolute Being and an absolute Unity, it is extremely difficult to see how there will be anything else besides; how, I mean, existing things can be more than one. What is other than what is does not exist, so that the argument of Parmenides will necessarily apply, that everything that exists is one, namely "what is"' (*Metaph.* 1001 a 29).

Yet in his work *On Coming-to-be and Perishing* he makes statements like these:

'Those who start with two things, as Parmenides did with fire and earth, make the intermediates mixtures of these' (330b 13) and 'Parmenides says there are two things, what is and what is not, which he calls fire and earth' (318b 6).

The link between these contradictory statements, as he sees it, he gives in the continuation of a passage from the *Metaphysics* already quoted (986b 31). Parmenides, he says, necessarily believed that one thing and one thing only exists,

but being compelled to follow appearances, and supposing that what existed was one by definition[1] but more than one according to sensation, he restores two causes and two principles, hot and cold, meaning fire and earth. Of these he ranks the hot with what is[2] and the cold with what is not.

Aristotle's interpretation of Parmenides was, then, first, that reality is one, unchanging and eternal; secondly, that the account described as 'the beliefs of mortals' is an attempt to bring system and coherence into the world of appearances after an initial insistence that it is unreal; and thirdly, that this account is his own. No ancient critic, indeed, makes any suggestion that it might be either a synthesis of existing ideas (whether common-sense or philosophical) or a repetition of a particular scheme such as the Pythagorean. Aristotle also makes a fourth point. Both here and in the work *On Coming-to-be and Perishing* (318b6, quoted above) he sees, probably in a part of the 'way of

---

[1] κατὰ τὸν λόγον. λόγος does multiple duty in Greek and cannot be adequately represented by a single English equivalent. (Cf. vol. 1, 420ff.) In Aristotle, 'definition' was a frequent meaning, and may have been uppermost in his mind here. But the introduction of the word suggests also, as he no doubt intended, Parmenides's own use of it, as in 7.5 κρῖναι λόγῳ. The only legitimate procedure is to judge by *logos* (deductive reasoning), and the contrast of it here with αἴσθησις brings out the inability of sensation to make contact with the truth.

[2] τάττειν κατά does not imply identity but only analogy. Mansfeld (*Offenbarung*, 138) compares *Pol.* 1310b32 ἡ βασιλεία τέτακται κατὰ τὴν ἀριστοκρατίαν.

seeming' now lost,[1] an affinity between one of the two contrary first principles and 'what is' and between the other and 'what is not'. This seems to be an attempt to bridge the gulf between the two parts of the poem, though what the connexion is, and whether he is correct in assuming that Parmenides made it, is as yet by no means clear. This will need further investigation, but the other three points accord well with the impression given by the extant verses of Parmenides himself.

(9) *Cosmogony and cosmology*

(Fr. 9)   Then since all things have been named Light and Night, and the names appropriate to their powers assigned to these and those, everything is full alike of Light and obscure Night, both equal, since there is nothing that shares in neither.

These lines are perhaps not perspicuous at first sight. Light (or fire) and Night (or darkness) are each self-identical (8.57–9), and between them they include the whole range of perceptible contrary qualities: Light carries with it hot, rare, light (as opposed to heavy), etc., and Night cold, dense, heavy, etc. Thus everything in the physical world is ranged under one or other of these two, since everything consists of a combination of opposites: the moment a primary pair is posited (instead of the one being which truth demands), it pervades the whole world, since every physical object must be characterized by an opposite or opposites. ('Nothing shares in neither.') The names assigned to the various powers (i.e. qualities) signify no more than so many manifestations of the basic pair Light and Night.

This explanation is not far from Fränkel's (*Wege u. Formen*, 180f.). It gives a clear and coherent argument, which is not easily obtained from a translation of the final words as 'neither has any part in the other' (Cornford) or 'neither has any share of nothingness' (KR); also Mansfeld, *Offenbarung*, 156: 'Keines von beiden Anteil hat an Nichts.' Fränkel shows also that his version gives to μετεῖναι its most usual and natural meaning.

v. 2. δυνάμεις. Qualities were regularly thought of at this time as active powers, from their effect on the senses or the physical state of a body, as 'the hot' can heat it, 'the heavy' can make it sink. See further Cornford, *P. and P.* 47 with n. 2.

v. 4. ἴσων. I see no reason for denying that this refers to equality of quantity or extent as Bignone thought. Fränkel is emphatic that it does not, and translates it by 'gleichwertig'. So also Coxon, *CQ*, 1934, 141, 'equal in status'. But one may compare the Pythagorean commentaries quoted in D.L. 8.26, ἰσόμοιρά τ' εἶναι ἐν τῷ κόσμῳ φῶς καὶ σκότος, which in turn recall Sophocles's γῆς ἰσόμοιρ' ἀήρ (*El.* 87), on which Jebb says: 'Air coextensive with earth, having a μοῖρα, a domain in space, equal to that of earth.' This he supports by reference to Hes. *Th.* 126f.

> Γαῖα δέ τοι πρῶτον μὲν ἐγείνατο ἶσον ἑαυτῇ
> Οὐρανὸν ἀστεροένθ' ἵνα μιν περὶ πάντα καλύπτοι.

Of the section dealing with the origin and structure of the cosmos we have only a few brief fragments, which cannot, even with the aid of secondary sources, yield anything like a complete picture. It begins with the 'two forms', which are not Parmenides's own invention, but,

---

[1] Cherniss, here as on most points, recommends an attitude less favourable to Aristotle than that adopted in this book. See *ACP*, 48, n. 192.

as the goddess says, what mortals have already decided to posit. We shall expect them therefore to reflect current views on the primary opposites. Fr. 9 makes it clear that each of these is, as it were, the heading of a list, the two lists making up between them all sensible qualities and things ('Everything is called Light and Night'), ranged in pairs of contraries. The fragments themselves give rare and dense (recalling Anaximenes), light and heavy (8.57 and 59), male and female, right and left (frr. 12.5 and 17), and of these the last two pairs, as well as light and darkness themselves, appear in the similarly parallel Pythagorean list of contraries given by Aristotle.[1] The intelligible items in that list (unity, limit, odd and their contraries) naturally do not appear, since Parmenides is confining himself to the sensible world and has demonstrated the impossibility of bringing the two together.

Aristotle and the doxography add the pairs hot and cold (though it is scarcely an addition to say that fire is hot), and soft and hard, and mention earth as an alternative to Night or darkness in contrast with Fire.[2] Peripatetic language also classified the Parmenidean contraries as active and passive respectively. Theophrastus spoke of 'two principles, fire and earth, one serving as matter, the other as cause and maker' (A7). Aristotle would doubtless have said the same. When in the *Metaphysics* (986b34) he speaks of Parmenides as positing 'hot and cold, meaning fire and earth', he calls these 'causes and principles', and one may assume that in relation to his own scheme of causation he would class the one as efficient (ποιοῦν) and the other as material cause (or πάσχον).

Both the equation of darkness with earth and the division into active and passive are commonly regarded as anachronisms on the part of Aristotle and his followers, but they are no more than a restatement in their own terms of a very old belief common to the philosophy and mythology of the period before Parmenides. It goes back to the idea

---

[1] *Metaph.* 986a22. See vol. 1, 245, and cf. Cornford, *P. and P.* 47.

[2] Ar. *Metaph.* 986b34, *GC*, 330b14; Theophr. *De sensu*, 3 (A46), *Phys. Op.* fr. 8 (A7); schol. *ap.* Simpl. *Phys.* 31.3. The explicit identification of darkness with earth need not have been a Peripatetic importation: cf. Alex. *ap.* Simpl. 38.23 καὶ ὀνομάζει τὸ μὲν πῦρ φῶς τὴν δὲ γῆν σκότος. πῦρ and φῶς are equated in the poem itself, so it is possible that the other equation occurred in the large portion which is lost. Cf. also ZN, 702. On the other hand the language of Ar. *Metaph.* 986b34 and Simpl. 25.16 seems to throw some doubt.

LA CITE DE DIEU EDITION FRANCAISE ABREGEE "
(2 dollars)

Je promets de rendre à
Pierre Bellemare la totalité
des livres en dépôt chez moi
(concernant les Études classiques)
et tous ceux qui apparaissent
sur la liste d'achat jointe à la
promesse d'achat   / prix de vente :
                                  $325.⁰⁰ (can.)

Exporter Guthrie

History of Greek Philosophy
Cambridge 2 vols

of Earth-mother and Sky-father, according to which (as generally in early physiology) the mother provides only the material and a place in which the new life can grow, and the father is the agent which animates it. He might do this through his fertilizing rain, but even so he was called Aither (Eur. fr. 839), and the active element was heat rather than moisture. This is reflected in a famous passage of Plato's *Republic* (509b), and again when characters in Aeschylus (*Cho.* 984) and Sophocles (fr. 1017 N.) call the sun 'Father'. The myth related by Aristophanes in Plato's *Symposium* (190b), that men are offspring of the Sun and women of the Earth, follows the general pattern of Greek thought in emphasizing the relation of the sexes to the two cosmic bodies.

This notion, appearing in various picturesque forms of myth, recurs in the philosophers both before and after Parmenides. Anaximander explained the origin of life by the action of the hot and dry at the circumference of the cosmos, or more concretely of the sun, on the cold and moist at the centre (i.e. the nascent earth, surrounded by *aer*, darkness). The fifth-century zoogony in Diodorus gives a detailed picture of how life started in moist places under the action of heat. Empedocles spoke of fire raising up men and women out of the earth (and cf. pp. 189, 206 below), Anaxagoras (in the inadequate sketch of Diogenes) of animals born from the moist, the hot and the earthy, and his pupil Archelaus of their birth from the earth 'when it had become hot'. 'Fire is the universal moving force' affirmed the writer of the Hippocratic *De victu*. Aristotle truly said that, because the male generates in another, the female in herself, 'therefore in the universe also men regard the earth as of a feminine nature and the sky and sun as procreators and fathers'.[1]

It is hardly rash to assume, with Aristotle and Theophrastus, that when Parmenides was constructing a cosmogony according to the opinions of mortals, and began with two opposed principles Fire (heat, light) and Darkness (cold, earth), he thought of Fire and its correlatives as the active element, and its contrary as the passive. It would no doubt be possible, if we had the complete poem, to range a whole series of

[1] Anaximander A 11 (vol. I, 101 f.) and cf. A 10 and 27; Diod. 1.7; Emped. fr. 62; Anaxagoras and Archelaus A I (D.L. 1.9, 2.17); *De victu*, 3, VI, p. 472 Littré; Arist. *Gen. an.* 716a15.

subordinate qualities, or aspects of these, in parallel columns according to this criterion.[1]

(Fr. 11)   How earth and sun and moon and *aither* common to all and the Milky Way and highest Olympus and the hot force of the stars started to come into being.

(Fr. 10)   And thou shalt know the nature of the *aither* and all the constellations in it and the destructive acts of the sun's pure shining torch, and whence they arose; and thou shalt learn the acts of the round-eyed moon and her nature. Thou shalt know too the surrounding sky, whence it sprang and how Necessity compelled it to hold the limits of the stars.

This order for the two fragments seems probable in view of the way Simplicius introduces fr. 11 (*De caelo*, 559.20: Π. δὲ περὶ τῶν αἰσθητῶν ἄρξασθαί φησι λέγειν), which suggested to Diels that fr. 11 is the general introduction to the sense-world and fr. 10 introduces the special cosmogony and cosmology.

10.1 and 5. Heinimann (*Nomos u. Physis*, 90) thought φύσις was used here in the much rarer sense of γένεσις. He points to v. 3 καὶ ὁππόθεν ἐξεγένοντο and v. 6 ἔνθεν ἔφυ as evidence. In fact their separate mention tells strongly against the notion, which is in any case unlikely.

11.2. Some of the Pythagoreans divided the sky into Olympus (sphere of the fixed stars), cosmos (region of the planets, sun and moon) and Ouranos (sublunary). See Philolaus, A 16.

These scraps of introduction to cosmogony and cosmology show that Parmenides described celestial phenomena in detail. But he went further. After quoting fr. 11 Simplicius adds (*De caelo*, 559.26; DK, B 11): 'And he[2] related the evolution of things that come into being and perish down to the parts of animals', and Plutarch says (*Adv. Col.* 1114b; DK, B 10) that Parmenides 'composed a cosmic system and, mingling the elements Light and dark, out of and by means of these produced all phenomena. He has much to say about earth and sky and sun and moon, and recounts the origin of mankind.' There was also a theogony, so that Plato could refer casually to 'the ancient stories of the gods which Hesiod and Parmenides relate', and Cicero mentions that it contained certain deified abstractions on Hesiodic lines—War, Discord, Love—of which Love alone occurs in an extant fragment.[3]

[1] To attempt this on the extant evidence raises a curious and interesting little problem, which I have relegated to an appendix (pp. 77–80 below).

[2] The MSS. vary between παραδίδωσι and παραδεδώκασι. In the latter case it refers to Parmenides and Melissus together.

[3] Plato, *Symp.* 195c; Cic. *N.D.* 1.11.28. Plato's Agathon seems to know his Parmenides when, in protest against the assaults said by these poets to have been committed by the gods against each other, he asserts that they must have been the work of Ananke, not Eros. In Parm. fr. 13, Eros is the firstborn child of the goddess one of whose names is Ananke. Mansfeld (*Offen-*

This part of the poem must have been of considerable length, and we have scarcely any quotations from it. Fortunately, although it may contain some novel features, it is in its author's eyes a deliberate concession to human weakness: his contribution to philosophy lay elsewhere.

Frr. 12 and 13. After quoting the last eleven lines of fr. 8 Simplicius writes (*Phys.* 39.12):

'A little later, having spoken of the two elements, he introduces the creative power thus (fr. 12.1–3):

"The narrower [*sc.* bands, see below] were filled with unmixed Fire, those next to them with Night, but a due portion of flame is injected. And in the middle of these is the goddess who steers all things."

This goddess he also makes responsible for producing the gods, saying (fr. 13):

"First of all gods she devised Eros" and so on.'

Fr. 12, which Simplicius elsewhere quotes entire, continued with lines (4–6) showing that the goddess mentioned is in one aspect Aphrodite goddess of love:

For she it is who has charge of all the concerns of loathed birth and of union, sending female to mingle with male, and again conversely male to female.

It is appropriate therefore that Eros should be her firstborn. Aristotle classes Parmenides, along with Hesiod, among those who 'put love or desire among things as a first cause (*arche*)' (*Metaph.* 984b24).

The only other information about cosmology comes from a condensed and disordered paraphrase of Aëtius which may be translated thus (2.7.1, A37):

For Parmenides says that there are circular bands wound round one upon the other, one made of the rare, the other of the dense;[1] and others between these mixed of light and darkness. What surrounds them all is solid like a wall. Beneath it is a fiery band, and what is in the very middle of them all is solid, around which again is a fiery band. The most central of the mixed

barung, 166f.) has the (to me) extremely strange idea that the other gods whom the goddess 'devised' are her *thoughts*. Cicero also says that Parmenides affirmed the divinity of the outermost heaven, which is only in conformity with general belief.

[1] Or alternatively: 'lying around, made alternately of the rare and the dense' (Fränkel, *Wege u. Formen*, 183).

bands is for them all the ⟨origin⟩ and ⟨cause⟩[1] of motion and becoming, which he also calls steering goddess and keyholder[2] and Justice and Necessity. The air has been separated off from the earth, vaporized by its more violent condensation, and the sun and the circle of the Milky Way are exhalations of fire. The moon is a mixture of both earth and fire. The *aither* lies around above all else, and beneath it is ranged that fiery part which we call heaven, beneath which are the regions (? bodies: the Greek has no noun) around the earth.

It is impossible to reconstruct a detailed cosmic order from this garbled and confused summary,[3] but in conjunction with fr. 12 it may throw some light on the relation of Parmenides's cosmology to those of others, and the relation between the two parts of his poem. The word *stephanai*, here translated 'circular bands' and meaning literally crowns or garlands, is perhaps a reminiscence of Hesiod, who speaks of 'the shining stars with which the heaven is garlanded',[4] but it recalls also Anaximander's rings or circles of fire surrounded by darkness or mist (vol. 1, 90, 93). Fr. 12 confirms Aëtius to the extent that in Parmenides's system some were of pure fire, others of fire and darkness mixed, and that a supreme goddess, who in the old Ionic phrase 'steers all things', occupies a central position.[5] Besides being the goddess of sexual union and birth, she was Ananke (Necessity), who in fr. 10

[1] The text is corrupt here. ἀρχήν and αἰτίαν are inserted by DK, though Diels emended differently in Dox. 335. But the corruption may go deeper. As Morrison remarks (*JHS*, 1955, 61) it is odd to have the goddess described as a στεφάνη.

[2] The MSS. of Stobaeus have κληροῦχον, 'holder of the lots'. This may be right. Burnet (*EGP*, 190, n. 3) was reminded of the κλῆροι in Plato's myth of Er (*Rep.* 617e), though there it is in fact not Ananke herself, but Lachesis her daughter, who has them in her lap. But all edd. have accepted the slight emendation to κληδοῦχον on the grounds that in the prologue (1.14) Justice 'holds the keys'. There is much to be said for this.

[3] So at least I still think, but for a magnificent attempt to do so the reader may be referred to J. S. Morrison's article in *JHS*, 1955. Mansfeld (*Offenbarung*, 163 f.) supposes that the rings represent a stage in cosmogony, so that it is wrong to expect them to correspond with the existing astronomical system.

[4] *Th.* 382, ἄστρα τε λαμπετόωντα τά τ' οὐρανὸς ἐστεφάνωται.

[5] Fränkel (*Wege u. Formen*, 185) says that ἐν μέσῳ τούτων means *between* these (i.e. between Fire and Night). He compares Plato, *Symp.* 202e, where Eros is ἐν μέσῳ θνητοῦ τε καὶ ἀθανάτου. Where *rings* are concerned, the expression is ambiguous, but I think that 'in the middle of them' is the more likely rendering. So also Diels, *Lehrgedicht*, 107. (Mansfeld follows Fränkel, *Offenbarung*, 164.)

Fränkel also believes that fr. 12 is the sole basis for the account in Aëtius, and that Theophrastus (from whom Aëtius condensed it) misunderstood the lines. F. Solmsen (*Gnomon*, 1931, 481) calls this 'as good as certain'. But I agree with Vlastos who, in connexion with a different fragment, speaks of Theophrastus as having presumably a full text of the poem (*TAPA*, 1946, 67, n. 13). Do Fränkel and Solmsen mean, then, that the poem contained no more about the στεφάναι than is in fr. 12? This cannot be true, since the fragment has only a fem. article and adjective with no noun.

determines the limits of the stars. In this cosmic role she appears nearly a century later in the myth of Er in Plato's *Republic*, where again we must imagine her seated in the centre of the universe, and her control of the movements of the heavenly bodies is symbolized by a spindle which she turns in her lap. The eight whorls of this spindle represent the courses of the fixed stars, sun, moon and planets. They vary in colour and brightness and thus bear a general resemblance to the circular bands of Parmenides, one inside the other, some fiery, some dark and some mixed. The descriptions of Plato and Parmenides are in a common tradition, and the only possible tradition is the Pythagorean. The Pythagorean elements in the Platonic vision are well known. They include the musical 'harmony' or scale of notes produced by the varying distances and speeds of the planetary spheres, and the doctrine of the cycle of lives. Does this tradition throw further light on the nature and identity of the goddess?

We have records of two Pythagorean cosmological systems, one geocentric and one not. When Philolaus replaced the earth with a fire at the centre of the universe, making the earth into a planet, he called this central fire, among other names, 'Mother of the gods' and 'Hearth of the whole.' (In Greek *Hestia*, meaning hearth, was a goddess, for the hearth had strong religious associations.) That is, he had to transfer to the new cosmogonic centre the titles commonly given to the earth ('cosmogonic', since for a Pythagorean the living cosmos grew from the centre, the central point being its 'seed', the warm source of life). 'Earth the Mother,' wrote Euripides (fr. 944), 'but the wise call thee Hestia, seated in the sky.' Hestia is again identified with the earth in Plato's *Phaedrus* (247a). The essential connexions of the name are central position (as in a Greek house) and life-giving warmth. Those Pythagoreans who retained the geocentric scheme, and for whom therefore the central fire was a fire at the centre of the earth, described it as a creative power, a function also ascribed by Empedocles to the hot centre of the earth:

They speak of fire at the centre as the creative power which animates the whole earth from the centre and warms that part of it which has grown cold.[1]

[1] Simplicius. The evidence for this para. will be found in the section on Pythagorean cosmology in vol. 1 (282 ff.).

In view of all this, it looks as if Parmenides, in putting together a cosmology which is to take account of extant views but improve upon them, has chosen for his central directing goddess the divine, generative fire in the centre, or the depths, of the earth. This, to his probably Pythagorean-trained mind, was the *daimon* who was so widely worshipped under the name of Earth herself, Mother of all life. In Hesiod she gave birth not only to the mountains and the sea, but also to the starry heaven. In Aeschylus, as here in Parmenides, she is 'one form with many names', and his Prometheus calls her Themis, which brings her close to the Justice of Parmenides. The association between Earth and Justice appears again in the *Choephori*. Like prophecy, the dispensation of justice is within the province of most chthonian powers.[1] This supposition is in no way contradicted by the fact that for Parmenides the elements Fire and Earth were contraries, opposed as the active to the passive. It is not the cold and earthy element which is divine and life-producing, but the element of fire in the earth, which 'warms the cold part of it'. So in Empedocles all life arose out of the earth, but only because 'many fires burn beneath it'. It is the fire which 'sent them up'.[2]

One or two details of the fragmentary account of the natural world remain to be mentioned. Parmenides has been credited with ascribing spherical shape to the earth, and though legitimate doubts have been expressed, it is probable that he did. The evidence is in two sentences of Diogenes. At 9.21 he says: 'He was the first to declare that the earth is spherical and is situated at the centre.' In placing it at the centre he was anticipated by Anaximander and some of the Pythagoreans, if

---

[1] E.g. Hades, Aesch. *Suppl.* 230f. Other passages referred to above are Hes. *Th.* 126ff.; Aesch. *P.V.* 209f., *Cho.* 148.

[2] Emp. frr. 52 and 62. Cf. vol. I, 292, where I wrote, with no thought of Parmenides, of 'the generative power of the earth, in which the activating principle was always heat'; also p. 59 above. Wilamowitz drew attention to the dual aspect of the earth in Greek thought, corresponding to the two words γῆ and χθών. χθών refers in origin to the cold, dead depths; the earth only became γῆ when she had been fructified by heat (*Glaube*, 1.210).

Here is perhaps the answer to an objection which has been made to the Aristotelian characterization of Parmenides's fire as the activating power, namely that in this capacity it would be superfluous, since the activating power is the goddess (ZN, 705). Fire is a manifestation of the goddess's activity.

The view that the *daimon* of Parmenides corresponds to the central fire of the Pythagoreans, though here thought out afresh, is not new. See, e.g., ZN, 717f. In the note on p. 718 Nestle mentions some alternative theories. De Santillana (*Prologue to P.* 7f.) puts her on the ecliptic pole.

not more generally. Anaximander's argument that the earth remains at the centre without support on account of its 'equilibrium' is also attributed to him, as well as to Democritus (Aët. in A 44). The second statement is at 8.48: 'We are told that Pythagoras was the first to call...the earth round, though Theophrastus says it was Parmenides and Zeno that it was Hesiod.' The vagueness of this has aroused very natural suspicions, but at least the attribution to Parmenides goes back through the Hellenistic age to Theophrastus, who resisted the tendency to give the credit for this discovery, as for many others, to Pythagoras.[1]

Several discoveries are attributed by our sources to both Parmenides and Pythagoras, and it is likely that in describing the physical world he would follow his Pythagorean teachers on many points. Within the realm of becoming, his one all-important point of difference with them did not apply. Both are said to have perceived the identity of the Morning and Evening Stars (a fact which Greek astronomers must have learned very early from their Babylonian neighbours), and to have divided the earth into zones. The latter is more likely to have been the work of a later Pythagorean, if, as has been suggested in the previous volume (294), the sphericity of the earth was a later discovery. It must however be admitted that the evidence for these attributions is insufficient, and Posidonius had obtained from somewhere the information that the zoning of Parmenides was peculiar in that he made the torrid zone twice as broad as that between the tropics, overflowing into the temperate zones (A 44 a).

He used the word 'water-rooted' of the earth,[2] not, presumably, reviving the view of Thales that it floated on water, but perhaps

---

[1] The above remarks are more positive in tone than those at vol. 1, 294. I have been impressed by the arguments of Kahn (*Anaximander*, 115–18), which seem to me to have the advantage over Morrison's in *JHS*, 1955, 64. An earlier sceptic was Heidel, *Frame of Greek Maps*, 70–2. What is said at D.L. 8.48 is surely good evidence that the statement at 9.21 also depends on Theophrastus, and that therefore the ambiguous στρογγύλην in the latter passage must be the equivalent of σφαιροειδῆ. On the other hand the uncritical Diogenes also accepted the statement that Anaximander called the earth spherical (2.1), which is contradicted by other ancient evidence and denounced by Kahn himself as 'a Hellenistic confusion' (*op. cit.* 56). One cannot say that the case for Parmenides is proved. If it is accepted, it is a strange freak of history that so fundamental a discovery should have been made by one for whom the whole physical world was an unreal show.

[2] ὑδατόριζον fr. 15 a. The υ would be lengthened for the dactylic verse, as in Emped. fr. 21.11.

referring to the rivers of the underworld which are mentioned in the *Odyssey* (10.513 f.) and whose courses Plato describes in detail in the myth of the *Phaedo*. His alleged statements that the earth was made of compacted air and the stars of compressed fire are reminiscent of Ionian ideas, though whether he himself used their familiar word 'felting', which appears in the doxography, cannot of course be known in the absence of his own verses. The Milky Way is a mixture of dense and rare (which is said to account for its colour), or alternatively a 'breathing of fire', and the sun and moon have been detached from it, one from the rare and hot part and the other from the dense and cold.[1]

The moon is described in two extant verses: (fr. 14) 'A night-shining, foreign light wandering round the earth' and (fr. 15) 'Always looking towards the rays of the sun'. In the first he puns on a phrase in Homer, where a word similar to that used here for 'light' means 'man', the whole phrase simply meaning 'a foreigner'.[2] These lines are probably the authority for the statement that Parmenides recognized that the moon was illuminated by the sun. Fr. 14, however, does not imply this. Fr. 15 might be thought to do so, and the doxography as represented by Aëtius gives him credit for the assertion. However, our faith in this is weakened when the same authority elsewhere declares that Thales first made the discovery, and that Pythagoras, Parmenides, Empedocles, Anaxagoras and Metrodorus followed him; and against it we have the more impressive authority of Plato, who in the *Cratylus* clearly gives the credit to Anaxagoras. It might be thought to receive some support from the assertion that Parmenides derived the sun from the hot, and the moon from the cold and dense part of the Milky Way, were it not that the same authority in another place says that he called the moon fiery. There is unfortunately no check on the accuracy of these incautious statements.[3]

---

[1] For this and the preceding paragraph see the *Strom.* in A 22 and Aët. in A 37, 39, 40a, 41, 43, 43 a.

[2] ἀλλότριος φώς, *Il.* 5.214, *Od.* 18.219, etc.; ἀλλότριον φῶς Parmenides. The line was imitated by Empedocles: fr. 45 κυκλοτερὲς περὶ γαῖαν ἑλίσσεται ἀλλότριον φῶς. (We need not linger over Tannery's suggestion that a Neopythagorean, wishing to refer to *the Master* the discovery which gives *Anaxagoras* his greatest title to fame, interpolated a modification of *Parmenides* into *Empedocles*.)

[3] Aët. in A 42, Plato, *Crat.* 409 a–b.

Parmenides: Cosmology: Theory of Knowledge

(10) Theory of knowledge: the soul

Theophr. *De sensu*, 1 ff. (A46): 'The majority of beliefs about sensation, and the most widely held, fall into two classes. Some effect it by similarity, others by the contrary, by similarity Parmenides, Empedocles and Plato, and by the contrary Anaxagoras and Heraclitus. Parmenides gives no general explanation, but only says that there are two elements and knowledge corresponds to the preponderant one. Thought varies according to whether the hot or the cold prevails, but that which is due to the hot is better and purer, though even then it requires a certain balance. "For", he writes (fr. 16), "as is at any moment the mixture of the straying limbs, so is the mind in men; for what thinks is the same for each and every man, the substance of the limbs. What preponderates is thought." He speaks of sensation and thought as the same. Hence memory and forgetfulness too are due to these two elements through their mixture. But whether or not it will be possible to think, and what will be the arrangement, if they are equal in the mixture, he does not go on to explain. Nevertheless that he does attribute sensation to the opposite itself is clear from his statement that a corpse has no awareness of light and heat and sound because the fire has deserted it, but does perceive their contraries like cold and silence. In general, everything that exists has some awareness.'

The translation of fr. 16 follows the text in Theophrastus, except that if his ἑκάστοτ᾽ for Aristotle's ἕκαστος is read, Stephanus's κρᾶσις must be substituted for the κρᾶσιν of the MSS. With Aristotle's text (*Metaph.* 1009b 22) the translation is 'as each man has the mixture of his straying limbs'. Mansfeld (*Offenbarung*, 175–85) retains the κρᾶσιν of the MSS. of Theophrastus and supposes that the subject is the goddess. This involves taking ἔχει κρᾶσιν as the equivalent of κεράννυσι (pp. 181f.), for which I do not find his parallels altogether convincing. (E.g. Semon. fr. 1, τέλος μὲν Ζεὺς ἔχει κτλ., hardly seems relevant.)

The next sentence has been translated in various ways, e.g. with ὅπερ as object of φρονέει, but the above version is offered as being the most natural translation of the Greek as well as giving a satisfactory connexion of thought between the first and second clauses.

μέλεα, lit. 'limbs', i.e. the body, for which no collective word was yet in common use. Some have thought that the word was intended to have a more general sense here, meaning either the opposites hot and cold themselves or something between the two universal 'Forms' (light and darkness) and the parts of the human frame. See Rostagni, *V. di Pit.* 109, n. 1; Verdenius, *Parm.* 6–7. Empedocles speaks of the μέλεα of the whole sphere. This would of course give excellent sense in the context of Theophrastus's remarks.

In *v.* 4, πλέον could mean either 'more' or 'full'. (See Schwabl, *Anz. f. d. Altertumswiss.* 1956, 136, no. 12 and 148, no. 30.) Mansfeld (*op. cit.* 189–94) chooses 'full', thus making Theophrastus's whole interpretation rest on a mistranslation. He argues that a human body *always* contains more Night than Fire. There can be no question of Fire and Night prevailing *in turn*, and this would damage the logical connexion of thought in the passage. But even if this is so, does the κρᾶσις μελέων necessarily imply that one thinks with the whole body? Could not fire prevail in that part which is doing the thinking? According to one doxographic report the ψυχή is formed of fire and earth and occupies the breast. Parmenides is fairly certain to have come down on one side or the other in the contemporary controversy over whether the organ of thought was in the breast or the head. (See further p. 69 below.) But this is really a topic on which we are too ill informed for certainty.

The quotation from Parmenides, in conjunction with the account of Theophrastus, gives a fairly intelligible theory of sensation and knowledge, even though much of the detail is omitted.[1] In emphasizing the mutability and inconstancy of human perceptions he is following earlier poetic tradition, with echoes of Homer and Archilochus.[2] Perception and understanding have entirely physical causes, and their clarity or otherwise depends on the condition of the body. Preponderance of fire or light in the perceiving subject brings about better and clearer perception, and since like is known by like, this means the perception of more light and less darkness. So far the statement bears out Aristotle's impression that there is an analogy between fire or light in the Way of Seeming and truth or being in the real world.

However, it must not be forgotten that all this takes place in the deceitful world of seeming.

It would be wrong to jump to the conclusion that this preponderance provides also the physical formula for the knowledge of Being. No such formula could be given without translating Being into terms of Becoming. ...The mortal frame, *qua* mortal, cannot think Being. Yet the 'knowing man' can and does think it....To resolve the paradox is impossible, for it is only the epistemological counterpart of the ontological dualism of Being and Becoming.[3]

So long as the human body is regarded as a compound of the opposites, light and dark or heat and cold and their correlatives (which is how

[1] For detailed discussion of the theory see Verdenius, *Parm.* 6ff.; Vlastos in *TAPA*, 1946, 66–77; Fränkel, *Wege u. Formen*, 173–9; Vlastos in *Gnomon*, 1959, 193–5.

[2] Archil., fr. 68 Diehl; Homer, *Od.* 18.136–7. See Fränkel, *op. cit.* 174. The lines from the *Odyssey* surely do *not* mean 'Dass Zeus den Tag sendet und damit das Denken bestimmt' (as Mansfeld renders them, *Offenbarung*, 184).

[3] Vlastos, *TAPA*, 1946, 71 f. He continues however: 'But though this dualism is never broken down, it is nevertheless mediated.' His solution is that true judgment of Being has for its basis not merely 'more' light, but all light. As death is all darkness, there can be imagined an opposite state of all light. 'The mind's power to think Being must imply just such a power to divest itself completely of the darkness in the frame, merge itself wholly with the light, and thus be as changeless as the light.' So immovable a thought 'would think light as pure Being'. He compares the allegory of the prologue, where the knowing man is carried beyond 'this dark world' into the realm of light. 'Translated into physical terms,' he continues, 'this can only mean that though the quest for truth begins with a mere preponderance of light, it can only be completed in a state of mind which is free from any darkness whatever.' I cannot attach any meaning to the phrase 'translated into physical terms' as applied to the prologue, for it already speaks in physical terms. What Professor Vlastos seems to want to do is to translate the *knowledge of Being*, as expressed in the Way of Truth, into physical terms; and if we do that, we are false to the essence of Parmenides's teaching.

every contemporary natural philosopher would regard it), what is described is in the eyes of Parmenides a deceitful counterpart of the truth which imposes itself on mortal minds. The relationship between this counterfeit world and Being will be further considered in the next section.

Considered on its merits as a physical theory (and there can be no doubt that Parmenides intended it to be taken seriously on its own level), the account offers as a point of interest the attribution of some measure of perception even to corpses. It is probable however that most thinkers of the time believed that sensation and thought were a matter of degree, and were present in rudimentary forms in all natural substances. This was inherent in the early hylozoistic outlook (vol. 1, 142f.), and with the statement that according to Parmenides 'everything that exists has some awareness' we may compare Empedocles, a practically contemporary philosopher also in the Italian tradition, who wrote that 'everything has thought and its due portion of insight' (fr. 110.10). The sensitivity of corpses is however extremely limited, because the *warmth* of life has left them. The idea may have arisen from a Pythagorean background, for, as we read in the Pythagorean commentaries excerpted by Alexander,[1] 'all things live which partake of heat (hence plants also are living things), but not all have soul, which is a detached part of *aither*, both hot and cold'. Heat is the condition of life, and, because of the preponderance of heat in him, man is related to the gods, which is the reason why they take care of him.

On the nature of the soul (*psyche*) there are only a few scraps of indirect information, not altogether consistent. It is said to be fiery, as one would expect, but also to be made of fire and earth, and located in the breast. This ought perhaps to be taken with the statement that Parmenides, Empedocles and Democritus identified mind and *psyche*, and according to them no living creature is utterly without reason.[2] That men and animals as a whole are compounded of fire and earth, with fire as the lively and cognitive part, was an old and widespread belief. In Hesiod the first woman was created out of mud by the god

---

[1] *Ap.* D.L. 8.25–6. For Alexander see vol. 1, 201, n. 3.
[2] See Aëtius and Macrobius in Parmenides A45. In speaking of the location of the soul or mind, Aëtius employs as usual the Stoic term ἡγεμονικόν.

of fire, and in the creation-myth of Plato's *Protagoras* the gods fashioned men out of a mixture of earth and fire. The Prometheus-story points in the same direction, replacing the notion of life-giving fire in the bosom of Mother Earth herself, which was given a more philosophical expression by Empedocles. Since the purely fiery part is reason, and every living creature possesses some quota of warmth, rationality may have been thought to be only a question of degree. Then when philosophers attempted to rationalize the accepted beliefs, and could still only do so on the material plane, it would be natural that some of them should treat the living body as a unity of mingled fire and earth rather than divide it into two separate entities, body and soul. This however, so far as concerns Parmenides, must remain speculative, for it would be unwise to rely too much on the casual utterance of a writer like Macrobius.

Simplicius says of the goddess mentioned in frr. 12 and 13 that she 'sends souls now from the visible to the unseen, and again the other way'. This has sometimes been taken to refer to a doctrine of immortality and palingenesis: there is an upper, aetherial realm, and the unseen is the earth; birth is a descent and death the return to a higher life.[1] Once again we are dealing with a tiny and ambiguous scrap of evidence, but more probably the reference is to the goddess's power over ordinary birth (mentioned in fr. 12) and death. At one time she is assisting life out of the invisibility of nonentity (or perhaps the darkness of the womb, either of a human mother or of the earth whence all life originated), and later she sends the soul down to Hades, whose name itself means 'the unseen'.[2]

---

[1] Simpl. *Phys.* 39.18, quoted by DK with fr. 13. Gigon, for instance (*Ursprung*, 281), translates τὸ ἐμφανές as 'light', and sees here the standard Parmenidean opposition of Light and Darkness. The earth is made of Darkness, therefore 'the Light' is a supra-terrestrial realm. He then connects Simplicius's statement with that of D.L. 9.22 that 'men were first born from the sun', where several scholars have thought it right to emend ἡλίου (sun) to ἰλύος (mud). The origin of men from the sun thus becomes a modification (*eine offensichtliche Umgestaltung*) of the Pythagorean belief that the abode of souls is in the stars. There is nothing inherently improbable in supposing that Parmenides followed Pythagorean religious beliefs in the Way of Seeming, but the translation of ἐμφανές as 'light' is dubious, and it is impossible that in the writings of a Platonist like Simplicius τὸ ἐμφανές should stand for the heavenly realm. For any Platonist, τὸ ἐμφανές is the visible and phenomenal as opposed to τὸ ἀειδές, the upper realm of true Being, invisible because it *transcends* the limits of vision and is accessible only to reason.

[2] I find Mansfeld's suggestion (*Offenbarung*, 168–74) improbable, that ἐμφανές and ἀειδές are the elements fire and night, and Simplicius's sentence is simply his paraphrase of fr. 16. The unusual

(11) *Being and seeming*

One view of the Way of Seeming[1] is that it is 'wholly dialectical' in intent. That is to say, Parmenides wishes to provide his reader with the best possible account of the world as it appears to mortals, not because that account is in any way nearer to reality than others: the arguments of the Way of Truth have proved it to be totally unreal. His motive, expressed in the words 'that no judgment of mortals may outstrip thee', is only that no one may be able to produce a more plausible description and explanation of the natural world which might shake belief in its unreality. For this purpose nothing but the best would do, and in fact even his own story, which he took great pains to make as persuasive as possible and yet had already proved to be false, did not succeed in its aim: on the whole, men continued to believe that phenomena had some reality at least.

According to this argument, Parmenides wrote a cosmology as convincing and watertight as he could *in order to* make people accept his proof that it was non-existent. But if a man wishes not simply to assign to cosmology its proper subordinate place, but to destroy its whole foundation, it seems an unlikely and unwise procedure to construct the most persuasive account possible—even if he has argued beforehand that it is based on false logic.[2] Accordingly a different approach will be made here.

In attacking the problem of the relation between truth and opinion, being and seeming (on which something has been said already), one is immediately struck by certain correspondences between names and expressions in the different parts of the poem which are evidently

sense of πέμπειν which this requires he defends by reference to fr. 12. 5, but it only has that sense there if one accepts his peculiar version of that fragment as well. πέμπουσ' ἄρσενι θῆλυ means what it says: 'sending the female to the male'. According to Mansfeld (*op. cit.* 165) 'male' and 'female' *also* stand for fire and night, and the sentence has no reference to sex or birth!

[1] G. E. L. Owen's in *CQ*, 1960.

[2] In the course of a friendly discussion on the point, Professor Owen cited the *Principia Mathematica* of Russell and Whitehead as a partial parallel. He added: 'Russell and Whitehead, of course, wanted to save mathematics and so strove to make the logical foundations secure. Parmenides wanted to put an end to cosmology and so strove to show that it rested on false foundations. Otherwise the analogy between his treatment of cosmology and their treatment of mathematics is close enough for the purpose.' To my mind, this fundamental difference of aim renders the comparison useless.

intentional. In the Way of Seeming everything starts from the two primary opposites Fire (or Light) and Night. In the prologue the poet's journey is from the house of Night to the Light, guided by the Sun-maidens: an obvious allegory of the progress from ignorance to knowledge or from falsehood to truth. This lends support to the Aristotelian view that within the Way of Seeming Light was in some way closer to Being than Night. Further support has just been found in Theophrastus's account of the theory of knowledge in the Way of Seeming. Preponderance of fire in the bodily composition leads to 'better and purer' knowledge. Since like is known by like, nearer apprehension of reality must be attained when there is something closer to reality in the thinking subject. Fire is the nearest to Being in the phenomenal world, hence its predominance brings the mortal mind as close as it can come, without divine revelation, to the perception of Being.

Correspondences also occur in the mention of deities. Justice appears in all three parts. In the prologue she is keyholder of the gates of the ways of Night and Day, and she and her cognate Themis, so Parmenides is assured, have sponsored his journey through them. In the Way of Truth she sees to it that there is no becoming or perishing of what is, and in the Way of Seeming Justice is one of the names of the goddess who 'directs all things'. In view of this, one may suppose that her command of the passage between Night and Day in the prologue is linked with her control over the admixture of Night and Light in the Way of Seeming.

Ananke (Necessity) is another name for the all-directing goddess. As such she *fetters* the heaven to hold the *peirata* of the stars. In the Way of Truth Fate *fettered* 'what is' to be whole and unmoved, and Justice had fetters with which she prevented 'what is' from suffering birth or decay. In the same section mighty Ananke herself keeps 'what is' in the bonds of a *peiras*. Because Being has a final *peiras* it is said to be spherical: in the Way of Seeming the *peirata* of the stars are held by the spherical heaven which goes round the world, encompassing all the circular bands. Others too believed the universe to be spherical, but for Parmenides its spherical shape must have had special significance, when the only way that he could describe the realm of intelligible Being was by comparing it to 'the mass of a well-rounded ball'.

The interlocking of the language is done with deliberate care. To cite another example, the subject-matter of truth is distinguished from that of seeming as being from becoming. The true function of Ananke is to sustain the being of 'what is'. This simply means (since divine agency has only metaphorical application to the one Being) that Being necessarily *is*: changeless, timeless, indivisible etc. But as it falsely seems to mortals, she maintains Becoming, and her power to do this appears as the power of fire, warmth or light, which are therefore part of her nature. Becoming is in the apparent world the counterfeit of Being in the real. If (*per impossibile*) becoming should cease, and the perceptible cosmos turn dead and cold, its motionlessness would not be that of Being but at the opposite pole. It would resemble the state of corpses, which 'through lack of fire have no feeling of light, heat or sound but only of their contraries like cold and silence'. Fire, then, the necessary agent of becoming, is the nearest in the phenomenal world to Being in the real. This analogy of Fire with Being seems to be emphasized in a deliberate echo when one compares the language describing the self-identity of Being in 8.29, 'the same in the same place it remains by itself', with that applied to Fire in 8.57, 'in every direction the same as itself'.[1]

What are we to make of all this? First, it is no detraction from the extraordinary consistency of Parmenides's thought to say that one cannot read his poem without feeling that he is constantly struggling against the sheer inadequacy of the available language. Simplicius the Neoplatonist says that he calls the second part of his poem deceptive 'not as being false in an absolute sense', and although this is probably wrong, it is worth remembering that if Parmenides had wanted to say it, it would have been beyond his power to do so. When he wrote: 'The verdict lies here: is it or is it not?', he was to a great extent the prisoner of language. Anyone asked that now would reply, 'In what sense are you using the verb "to be"? In the sense of existing, or being this or that, or what?' Such questions were not admissible for Parmenides. Not only did the word have only one sense for him, but he

---

[1] I do not agree that the simple phrase κατ' αὐτό, applied to Night, is necessarily the equivalent of this description of Fire (Mansfeld, *Offenbarung*, 133 ff.). It only emphasizes the separateness of the two opposites, and need not conflict with Aristotle's assessment of their respective analogies to ὄν and μὴ ὄν.

considered all others guilty of illogicality for not having recognized this truth.

Next, in assessing Parmenides, it is impossible to avoid comparison with Plato, who in spite of his greater maturity of thought and expression based himself firmly on the logic of his Eleatic predecessor. In a passage from the *Timaeus* already quoted he draws as sharply as Parmenides ever did the distinction between being and becoming, what can be thought about and what only seems.

The first distinction to be made is this: what is it that always is, and never becomes; and what becomes everlastingly but never *is*? The one comprehensible by intellection with reasoned argument, being always consistent, the other believed by opinion with unreasoning sensation, coming into being and perishing but never truly *being* (27 d–28 a).

Again in the *Republic* (477 b):

Then opinion and knowledge are directed towards different *objects*, each according to its own function.
Yes.
And the natural object of knowledge is what is.

A little later, when he is comparing the relation of the eye to sunlight with that of the mind to truth, his language becomes strikingly Parmenidean (508 d):

When the soul comes to rest on an object *illuminated* by truth and *Being*, it understands and knows and appears to have *nous*; but when it regards what is *mixed with darkness*, that is, what comes to be and perishes, it has only *opinion* and its sight is dimmed: its beliefs shift up and down and it is like something without *nous*.

Here we have the equation of truth and being with light and the statement that what becomes and perishes is mixed with darkness. Opinion is dim-sighted and shifts up and down, as in Parmenides the mortals who rely on opinion are blind, and are borne along on a path that turns back on itself; and only 'what is' can be the object of *nous*.

Plato's solution was to abandon the exclusive antithesis between what is and what is not, and to classify the sensible world as a third ontological category, 'wallowing between not-being and pure being' (*Rep.* 479 d). Cognition is correspondingly threefold: opinion or belief is a mental state between knowledge and ignorance. Knowledge, which to deserve the name must be certain and permanent, can only have changeless Being as its object: the absolutely non-existent can obviously not be known at all: concerning the world of appearances, of which our senses make us aware as a congeries of changing, appearing and disappearing objects, we hold beliefs or opinions as changeable as the objects themselves. In the *Sophist* such arguments are directed against Parmenides by name:

In self-defence we must question the argument of our father Parmenides and force the conclusion that what is not, in some respect *is*, and conversely that what *is*, in a way is not (241 d).

For Parmenides there was no third way. To suppose a category 'between what is and what is not' was expressly contrary to the divinely revealed *logos*. What follows is false. But it is, as the word 'seeming' suggests, a phantom or image of reality (Plato would call it an *eikon*),[1] and of that phantom some aspects bear more resemblance to reality than others. If there were no resemblance, it is difficult to see how it could 'deceive'. This is not to weaken Parmenides's logic by introducing any degrees of reality. The phenomenal world is of the nature of a hallucination or dream. Everything in a dream is equally unreal, but anyone who has dreamed knows that some dream-elements are more *like* reality than others. One day we say: 'Last night I dreamed about the house I lived in as a boy. It was extraordinarily vivid, and every detail was just as it used to be.' Another time: 'I dreamed about the house I lived in as a boy. At least that is what it was in my dream, though I see now that it wasn't very like it.' The conclusion commonly drawn from the goddess's words at 8.50ff., that there is no relation or resemblance between Being and its counterfeit, is wrong, and it is not un-Parmenidean to say that some parts of the latter remind one of Being more than others.

What Parmenides has not succeeded in establishing is any logical relationship between the truth and its counterfeit, or any logical status for the world of seeming. If it 'is not', why do we imagine it

---

[1] And the goddess herself says that it is ἐοικότα πάντα (8.60). *Sophist*, 239 c ff. considers the question: what is an εἴδωλον, and in what sense can it be said to be real?

and what is the difference between illusion and blank nothingness?
That is precisely the problem which he bequeathed to Plato, and which
Plato thought he had solved by substituting a trichotomy—being, non-
being, and becoming: knowledge, ignorance, and belief—for the
Eleatic dichotomy.[1] As for Parmenides, we can only end as we began,
with a reminder of the deeply religious and mystical character of the
prologue. He is mortal like others, living in the world of seeming, but
by divine favour he has been granted knowledge of true Being. His
journey in the sun-chariot from darkness to light was more than a
series of steps in deductive reasoning, though it was that as well. It
afforded a glimpse of the eternal, a release from the bondage of earthly
existence. Such release, such *ekstasis*, had been attained by psychologically gifted seers before him, but to transform this recognized
religious experience into a philosophical revolution was the achievement of none but Parmenides.[2] The attributes of Being, as revealed by
the goddess, follow a strict deductive order. In his spiritual preparation
for this unique experience he owed much to the Pythagoreans, for they
too had combined mystical religion with the recognition of intelligible,
mathematical truth; but their insight fell short of revealing the impassable logical gulf separating that world of timeless truth from the
shifting panorama of physical objects and events. It is hardly a criticism
of Parmenides to say that in the very moment of a discovery which
changed the whole face of philosophy there was not also revealed to
him a means of accounting for the false semblance of reality exhibited
to mortals by the world of appearances, nor of bringing the two worlds
into any logical relationship again without contravening the new and
austere canons of thought which he himself had just laid down. His
permanent contribution to thought was to assert that what is, is, and
can be thought about, and what is not, is not, and cannot be thought
about; and to state and abide by the consequences of those assertions.

---

[1] Of Reinhardt's *Parmenides* von Fritz writes (*CP*, 1945, 237) that he has 'shown conclusively
that the second part is neither a description of the actual beliefs and opinions of the "two-headed
mortals"...nor an attempt to give a better system of the world of mere belief than most people
have, but that it is fundamentally an attempt to *show how there can be* a world of belief side by side
with truth *and how it originates*' (my italics). But this is just what Parmenides did not do, nor,
so far as I can see, could he even attempt it on the premises which he adopts and sticks to so
consistently and courageously.

[2] This point has been well put by E. Topitsch in *SB Wien*, 1959, 7.

Parmenides: Summing-up

The immediate effect was shock, but the further advance of philosophy depended on the explicit assertion of those statements and their absorption, by whatever means, into a wider synthesis.

APPENDIX

The Opposites in Parmenides

As has been pointed out on p. 58, the qualities associated with Fire and Night respectively form a *systoichia* on the lines of the Pythagorean one, except that it is confined to sensible properties. It is tempting therefore to try to reconstruct such a parallel table, bearing in mind that it is intended by Parmenides as a rationalization of existing beliefs. Analogy with the general tenour of Greek thought would suggest the following:[1]

Active	*Passive*
fire	night
bright	dark
sky	earth
hot	cold
dry	moist
rare	dense
light	heavy
right	left
male	female
soft	hard

This conjectural table corresponds, where they overlap, to the Pythagorean, in which brightness, right and male are together opposed to darkness, left and female. It agrees with current Greek ideas in ranging dense, cold and heavy on the passive side and rare, hot and light on the active, for this suits any account which, like Anaximander's

[1] Dry and moist are not in our authorities but can hardly have been missing. I have placed soft and hard according to the note found by Simplicius in his copy of the poem, but in view of the statement in A37 that Parmenides believed the outermost shell of the cosmos to be hard and solid, with fire immediately below it, I feel some doubt about this. The pair occupied an ambiguous position among the opposites in Greek thought, owing to the varied effects of heat, which on the one hand dries out moisture, and on the other hand liquefies hard substances. Thus *De victu* (ch. 9) describes the hard parts of the body, like bone, as formed by the agency of fire in solidifying by driving out the water. On the other side is the common association of heat with the abundant blood, moisture and pliancy (ὑγρότης) of youthful bodies, and cold with the dryness and brittleness of age. (See also pp. 188 f. below.)

77

or the myths, derives life from the moist and solid earth when acted upon by the hotter, rarer element fire. The alignment of the opposites is most clearly seen in Hippolytus's account of Anaxagoras (A 42):

The *dense, moist, dark* and *cold*, and all *heavy* bodies came together to the centre, solidified, and formed the earth; but the opposites of these, the *hot*, the *bright*, the *dry* and the *light* projected themselves to the further parts of the *aither*.

Above all, the columns as here given would agree with all Greek thought in assigning the superior and active power to the male element, the inferior and passive role to the female. Here however comes the problem, for this is just what Parmenides does not appear to do. He does indeed (and for this we have his own words) associate male with right and female with left hand (fr. 17), thus far confirming the expectation that he could not have been so un-Greek as to have given the superior place to the female. But our informants say that in his physiology men are preponderantly cold and dense, women preponderantly warm and rare. The testimonies are these.

Arist. *De part. an.* 648a25 (A 52): 'Some say fish are warmer than land-creatures, so that their natural heat counterbalances the cold of their environment, and bloodless animals warmer than those with blood, and females than males; e.g. Parmenides and certain others say that women are hotter than men, arguing that the menstrual flow is due to the heat and the abundance of blood. Empedocles however says the opposite.'

Aët. 5.7.1-2 (DK, 31 A 81 and 28 A 53). 'According to Empedocles distinction of sex depends on heat and cold, wherefore he says that when living creatures arose out of the earth, the first males appeared in the south and east, and the females in the northerly parts. Parmenides says the contrary: those in the north were males (for the male partakes more of density), and those in the south females in accordance with their rarefied texture.'

It seems unlikely that these sources are mistaken, especially as they take the trouble to point out that Empedocles took a contrary view.[1] Aristotle also adds the circumstantial detail about the menses, though

---

[1] This would raise another small puzzle if we were to trust Censorinus (Emped. A 81) when he says that Empedocles, like Parmenides, supposed male and female embryos to be engendered in the right- and left-hand sides of the womb respectively; for it would then be even more strange that the two should be at odds over the relation of male and female to heat and cold. But Aristotle appears to distinguish Empedocles from those who connect difference of sex with position in the womb (*GA*, 765a4).

it is just possible that this might come from the 'certain others' and not from Parmenides. Yet this evidence makes it very difficult to construct a consistent list of opposites for Parmenides. If it is to contain the pair male and female at all, it seems we must put male on the negative side of 'invisible Night', and female on the side of Fire. But if we do this, then fr. 17 compels us to put right hand also with Night and left hand with Fire, contrary to the Pythagorean (and, one would have thought, any other Greek) scheme.

Probably male and female were not pure opposites in his system, but 'mixtures of them', as Aristotle says air and water were (*Gen. et corr.* 330b 14). There is a suggestion of this in the use of the comparative by Aëtius. But it is difficult to believe in any explanation by a Greek which makes the male colder and denser—and so presumably darker, heavier and generally more passive and negative—than the female. Nor does it suit the statement of Parmenides himself that males are formed on the right-hand side and females on the left. Right belongs in the same column as brightness or fire, the column of superior qualities. That is where the Pythagoreans put it, along with goodness, so that, as Simplicius said (*De caelo* 386.20): 'They called right good and left bad.'

The truth may be that whereas in cosmology broad schematic accounts were still the rule, with primary opposites playing traditional roles, in a subject like embryology a considerable amount of elementary observation was taking place, and a more empirical outlook allowed for greater variety of opinion about the role of the opposites. *De victu* (ch. 34, VI, 512 Littré) subscribes to the common view that in general males are hotter and drier than females (though this varies also with age, ch. 33), but attributes this not to any original genetic principle but (*a*) to the way of life led by each, and (*b*) to the 'purgation of the hot' undergone monthly by females. Here we see an author drawing from the same phenomenon (the menses) a conclusion opposite to that which Aristotle ascribes to Parmenides. In the same passage Aristotle records the belief of some that fish are warmer than land-creatures because they need more natural heat to counteract the cold of their environment. It is easy to see here also that a contrary conclusion could, and commonly would, be drawn from the same observations.

Again, the cosmologists, as we have noted, regularly associated thick with cold and rare with heat; but at least for Aristotle, when it came to physiology it was possible to equate thick and hot. There is, he says (*Gen. an.* 765 a 34 ff.), something to be said for connecting distinction of sex with hot and cold, right and left; for the right-hand parts of the body *are* hotter than the left, and concocted sperm is hotter, and also thickened (συνεστός); and it is thickened sperm that has the higher generative power (*sc.* and is therefore capable of producing the superior male sex).

B. ZENO

(1) *Date and life*

Zeno of Elea, a pupil of Parmenides, defended his master's paradoxical thesis by the device, not of arguing directly in its favour, but of showing up its contrary as absurd. In the course of this exposition of the contradictions which, as it seemed to him, were inherent in the notions of plurality and motion, he produced a series of arguments on which logicians and mathematicians have sharpened their wits from his day to our own.

Plato, in a passage already quoted in connexion with Parmenides (p. 1 above), says that he was some twenty-five years younger than his teacher. Probably therefore he was born about 490. Apollodorus put his *floruit* at 464–1, following his own mechanical procedure of making the disciple forty years younger than the master. Others mention the Olympiads of 468–5 and 456–3. The differences are not great, and the safest course is to follow Plato.[1]

Little is known of his life. He is said to have been a particularly loyal citizen of his native Elea, 'preferring it to the arrogance of Athens', whither he refused to migrate.[2] Presumably therefore he spent most of his life in S. Italy, though a sojourn in Athens is attested not only by Plato but by a remark in Plutarch's *Life of Pericles* (ch. 4; and cf. 5) that Pericles heard lectures by him. The Platonic *Alcibiades*

---

[1] For the datings of Apollod. (*ap.* D.L. 9.29), Euseb. and the Suda see DK, A 1–3. If Plato's story is true, that Zeno wrote his masterpiece at an early age, this may have helped to push back his *floruit* in the eyes of later antiquity.

[2] οὐκ ἐπιδημήσας πώμαλα πρὸς αὐτούς, D.L. 9.28. The words need not imply that he never even visited Athens.

also says (*Alc. I*, 119a) that Callias son of Calliades was taught by Zeno for a fee of 100 minae, and this can hardly have taken place elsewhere than in Athens. Stories were current in later antiquity of his resistance to a tyrant and heroic behaviour under torture, but both the name of the tyrant and the details of the story vary.

(2) *Writings and method*

Zeno wrote in prose. Plato speaks as if he were known for one work only, and Simplicius employs similar terms. The Suda appears to mention four: *Disputations, Against the philosophers, On nature* (if these two are not one title), and an examination of the work of Empedocles. The first three could easily have been names given in Alexandrian times to a single work, and it is rather dubious whether Zeno could have written a work on Empedocles, which is only attributed to him by this one late source.[1] One of the logical puzzles, the 'millet seed', is given by Simplicius in the form of a question put by Zeno to the Sophist Protagoras. He must therefore have known it either simply as an anecdote or from a dialogue in which Zeno and Protagoras were speakers. However, none of the surviving quotations from Zeno sounds as if he wrote dialogues himself, and it is unlikely that anyone before Aristotle should have put himself into a dialogue. The story as Simplicius gives it cannot come directly from his work, though it may of course have been based on something in it.[2] Most of our knowledge of the contents of the work comes from Aristotle and his Neoplatonic commentators. To the latter we owe a number of direct quotations, but on the question whether they still possessed the entire treatise opinions have varied considerably.[3]

[1] Zeller (ZN, 745 n.) thought it impossible that the book on Empedocles should be genuine, but his reasons are not compelling. Gaye (*J. Phil.* 1908, 114) supposes Empedocles to have been a somewhat older contemporary of Zeno, and concludes that the work was polemic. His suggestion that the fourth of the extant arguments against motion is directed particularly against Empedocles is highly conjectural.

Lee (*Z. of E.* 8) thinks the title πρὸς τοὺς φιλοσόφους may be genuine, and provides some evidence that Zeno regarded the Pythagoreans as his chief opponents. Cf. vol. 1, 204; Burnet, *EGP*, 312 (but also ZN, 438). Heidel on the other hand (*AJP*, 1940, 22) thought it 'most improbable' that the title was Zeno's, ' if we date the work about 465'. He does not say why.

[2] Cf. Burnet, *EGP*, 312; Lee, *Z. of E.* 110; Alfieri, *Atomos Idea*, 42, n. 1. The argument itself is mentioned as Zeno's by Aristotle, *Phys.* 250a19.

[3] Tannery in 1885 thought Simplicius 'ne possédait qu'un résumé', but Heidel, usually a somewhat sceptical scholar, asserted without argument in 1940 that 'Simplicius still had the original

Zeno's treatise was divided into several arguments (*logoi*), each containing a number of *hypotheses*. These were so called because they opened with a conditional sentence, the object being to show that *on this hypothesis* impossible and contradictory conclusions are inescapable.[1] In Plato's *Parmenides*, for instance, Socrates quotes the first *hypothesis* of the first *logos* as follows: 'If existing things are many, they must be like and unlike.'

In all probability he confined himself to this dialectical refutation of Parmenides's opponents, and did not bother his head about any description of the illusory world of nature corresponding to the second part of Parmenides's poem. One or two late sources refer to him some vague statements about the cosmos and man, but these are of no interest and probably wrongly attributed.[2]

The method adopted by Zeno was something new, as Aristotle recognized when he called him the inventor, or pioneer, of dialectic.[3] By 'dialectic' Aristotle meant a definite technique, to which he devotes a whole treatise, the *Topics*. It is the art of arguing, not from premises that are necessary, self-evident or previously demonstrated (which are all that a philosopher may use in his search for positive truth), but from beliefs commonly accepted or accepted by other thinkers, with the object of exposing them if they are false or in-

text in hand'. Two years later Fränkel, writing in the same periodical, remarked that none of the commentators seems to have used Zeno's book at first hand for his exposition of the argument. Taylor pronounced it uncertain whether they did or not. Lee thinks that at *Phys.* 140.27 Simplicius 'definitely claims to have had access to an original work of Zeno', although he quotes only from the arguments against plurality and not from those against motion. The inference from his words is not certain. From *Phys.* 138–9 Zeller concluded that although Alexander and Porphyry did not have the complete work, Simplicius himself must have had it because he describes its contents in detail as well as quoting a passage. He admits however that 99.17f. is evidence that Simplicius himself had doubts about the completeness of his own copy, and surely its incompleteness is confirmed on p. 140, where he conjectures that an argument attributed by Porphyry to Parmenides should in fact be credited to Zeno 'There is nothing like it in the Parmenidean writings,' he says, 'and most of our information refers the dilemma based on dichotomy to Zeno.' However, we may say with confidence that he had at the least a comprehensive series of verbatim extracts dealing with the arguments against plurality.

[1] For Plato's ὑποθέσεις Simplicius uses the word ἐπιχειρήματα. Proclus (DK, A15) said that there were 40 *logoi* in all, but his information is unconfirmed and probably second-hand.

[2] D.L. 9.29 and Stobaeus (Aët. 1.7.23, 27 and 28, *Dox.* 303). See on this ZN, 746, n. 1. The Stobaeus passage, by an obvious error (perhaps textual), includes under the heading 'Melissus and Zeno' ideas peculiar to Empedocles.

[3] εὑρετὴν διαλεκτικῆς D.L. 9.25, from Aristotle's dialogue the *Sophist* (cf. 8.57); ἀρχηγόν Sext. *Math.* 7.7.

adequate (*Top.* 1.1). In the *Rhetoric* (1355 a 29–36) he says that only rhetoric and dialectic draw contrary conclusions from identical premises, not to make people believe both, but in order to lay bare the real state of affairs and find the way out when someone is arguing unfairly. Thus Zeno, to take one example, argued from the premise 'there are many existing things' that these things must be both finite and infinite in number, his object being to make plain the truth (discovered by Parmenides) that reality is a unity. This extraction of contradictories is also referred to by Plato, who in the *Phaedrus* (261 d) calls him the Eleatic Palamedes, who can make the same things appear like and unlike, one and many, at rest and in motion. (The hero Palamedes was renowned for cunning and inventiveness.)[1]

(3) *History of interpretation*

Most of the arguments of Zeno of which we have knowledge may be divided into two sets, directed respectively against the ideas of *plurality* and *motion*. In addition there is one brief argument raising a difficulty about the existence of *place*, and finally the 'millet seed' ('If a single grain makes no sound in falling, how can a bushel make a sound?'), whose pedigree we have seen to be not above suspicion. It would seem obvious therefore that he is, as Plato said, a faithful disciple of Parmenides, who had taught him that reality was one, indivisible and motionless, and empty space non-existent and unthinkable.

This was the accepted opinion until, in the latter part of the nineteenth century, the Frenchman Paul Tannery put forward the view that Zeno had no wish to deny the possibility of motion, but only to affirm its incompatibility with a belief in plurality. Aristotle (who is practically our sole source for this set of arguments) misunderstood him and underestimated the subtlety of his thought. His real aim was to refute a Pythagorean thesis that solid bodies, surfaces and lines are pluralities, i.e. pluralities of points, considered as infinitesimal magnitudes. Tannery was followed by V. Brochard and G. Noël, and this French interpretation (represented also by Bayle and Milhaud) made a great impression, especially on philosophers and mathematicians, who

---

[1] On Zeno and dialectic see also Lee, *Z. of E.* 113 ff.

now began to see in Zeno an intellectual giant who had changed the face of mathematics and logic. This estimate of him was given most striking expression by the Germans H. Hasse and H. Scholz, and notably upheld in England by Lord Russell, who characterized the four arguments on motion as 'immeasurably subtle and profound'.[1]

The point of view attributed to Zeno by Tannery was certainly an astonishing one for a follower of Parmenides. Van der Waerden (*op. cit.* below, 143) has pointed out that it credits him with the following train of thought: 'On the hypothesis of plurality motion is impossible. Since however motion evidently can occur, plurality must be rejected.' Zeller never accepted Tannery's view, and a vigorous reaction against it was started by the Italian G. Calogero in 1932, and given fresh impetus by van der Waerden in 1940. These scholars insisted that any interpretation of Zeno must start from his Eleatic background (which is assured by Plato), and denied that our information yields any evidence of a polemic against infinitesimals or against the Pythagoreans.

In England Cornford, and after him Sir Desmond Lee, while seeing Zeno as primarily an upholder of the Eleatic thesis of the unity of being, endorsed Tannery's opinion so far as to argue that the critics of Parmenides whom he set out to refute were the Pythagoreans. Cornford in particular developed his theory of Pythagorean 'number-atomism' as the target of Zeno's attacks. Raven, while critical of the 'number-atomism' hypothesis, had no wish to deny their anti-Pythagorean purport, though he thought them couched in terms which could apply to other pluralist theories too. The difficulty felt by Lee, and clearly expressed by A. E. Taylor, in supposing Zeno to be attacking only the general assumptions of plurality and motion common to all mankind, is this: he is admittedly arguing from his opponents' premises, yet the premises he takes are much too specific, e.g. that magnitudes are infinitely divisible and at the same time made up of (indivisible) elements. 'To make sense of these arguments', concludes Lee, 'we must suppose them to have been directed against a system in which certain definite confusions were made.'

Against this it is certainly arguable that the dialectical nature of

---

[1] Not that he agreed with Tannery's interpretation of the purpose of the paradoxes. See *Knowledge of the External World*, 174.

Zeno's *logoi* implies no more than that he started from the simple premises 'there is plurality' and 'there is motion', both of which are asserted not only by the ordinary man but by all opponents of Eleaticism. This is the line recently taken, against Cornford and Lee, by N. B. Booth in a vigorous development of the views of Calogero and van der Waerden. In particular he deprecates as anachronistic the modern tendency to accuse Aristotle of failing to understand Zeno on the ground that Zeno could not have made the elementary logical blunders of which Aristotle supposes him guilty. Zeno's arguments, he thinks, may have been provoked partly by the Pythagoreans, but they are directed against the whole idea of motion, plurality and place, not against specifically Pythagorean theories of them. This was also the opinion of W. A. Heidel, who cited the remark of Philoponus that those who speak of plurality rely on its self-evidence: there *are* horses, men and other creatures and objects. This, he says, is common sense, not philosophy, nor are the Pythagoreans likely to have indulged in the kind of ridicule of Parmenides of which Plato makes Zeno speak.[1] About the same time as Booth, G. E. L. Owen also came out strongly for the view that the anti-Pythagorean interpretation is a myth. There is, he considers, inadequate evidence for the state of Pythagorean mathematics in Zeno's time, and if it was what it is usually supposed to be, Zeno's arguments would not be directed primarily at it.

Bibliographical note

Since Zeno in the present work must be only an incident in a long story, and will be treated mainly from the historical point of view, it may be as well to collect here a list of the principal discussions of him, which (besides giving the necessary references for the views of those just mentioned) will assist any who wish to follow up his relevance for present-day thought.

For Tannery, Brochard, Noël and Russell see the references in Booth, article (i) below, nn. 2 and 3, or H. D. P. Lee, 124–5.

[1] 'The word κωμῳδεῖν suggests a rather gross type of derision, though it was not necessarily quite so arbitrary and irresponsible as in the *Nubes*' (Fränkel, *AJP*, 1942, 203, n. 91). Nestle (ZN, 747, n. 2) plausibly suggested that Zeno might have had in mind the parody of Eleatic reasoning produced by Gorgias, and called by him 'On the Non-existent or on Nature'.

ZN, 741–65.

R. K. Gaye, On Aristotle, *Phys.* Z, IX, 239 b 33–240 a 18 (Zeno's fourth argument against motion), *J. Phil.* (1908), 95–116.

F. Cajori, The History of Zeno's Arguments on Motion, *Amer. Math. Monthly* (1915).

H. Hasse and H. Scholz, *Die Grundlagenkrisis der griech. Mathematik* (Berlin, 1928).

G. Calogero, *Studi sull' Eleatismo* (Rome, 1932).

A. E. Taylor, Appendix A to translation of Plato's *Parmenides* (Oxford, 1934), 112–23.

W. D. Ross, Aristotle's *Physics* (Oxford, 1936), introd. 71–85.

H. D. P. Lee, *Zeno of Elea* (Cambridge, 1936).

F. M. Cornford, *Plato and Parmenides* (Kegan Paul, 1939), ch. 3 (Zeno and Pythagorean atomism).

W. A. Heidel, The Pythagoreans and Greek Mathematics, *AJP* (1940), 1–33.

J. O. Wisdom, Why Achilles does not fail to catch the tortoise, *Mind* (1941), 58–73. (Also A. D. Ritchie, same title, *Mind* (1946), 310.)

H. Fränkel, Zeno of Elea's attacks on plurality, *AJP* (1942), 1–25 and 193–206. (German version, revised, in *Wege u. Formen* (1955), 198–236.)

A. Ushenko, Zeno's Paradoxes, *Mind* (1946), 151–65.

J. E. Raven, *Pythagoreans and Eleatics* (Cambridge, 1948), ch. 5 (Zeno of Elea).

J. Mau, *Zum Problem des Infinitesimalen bei den antiken Atomisten* (Berlin, 1954), 8–19.

N. B. Booth (i) Zeno's Paradoxes, *JHS* (1957), II, 187–201; (ii) Were Zeno's arguments directed against the Pythagoreans?, *Phronesis* (1957), 90–103; (iii) Were Zeno's arguments a reply to attacks upon Parmenides?, *Phronesis* (1957), 1–9.

G. E. L. Owen, Zeno and the Mathematicians, *Proc. Aristot. Soc.* (1957–8), 199–222.

W. Kullmann, Zeno und die Lehre des Parmenides, *Hermes* (1958), 157–72.

R. E. Siegel, The Paradoxes of Zeno: some similarities between ancient Greek and modern thought, *Janus* (1959), 24–47.

Vlastos's review of KR in *Philos. Rev.* (1959), 532–5.

P. J. Bicknell, The Fourth Paradox of Zeno, *Acta Classica* (Cape Town, 1961), 39–45.

V. C. Chappell, Time and Zeno's Arrow, *Journ. of Philos.* (1962), 197–213.

J. O. Nelson, Zeno's Paradoxes on Motion, *Rev. of Metaph.* (1963), 486–90.

Zeno in Plato's Parmenides

S. Quan, The Solution of the Achilles Paradox, *Rev. of Metaph.* (1963), 473–85.

M. Schramm, *Die Bedeutung der Bewegungslehre des Aristoteles für seine beide Lösungen der zenonischen Paradoxie* (Frankfurt-a.-M., 1962), is criticized, so far as the second refutation is concerned, by Merlan in *Isis* (1963), 299.

(4) General purpose

The general nature and purpose of Zeno's arguments are clearly stated by Plato. When all allowance is made for the conventional freedoms of dialogue, he remains a source too close to the original to be ignored. Whether or not the discussion between Parmenides, Zeno and Socrates is historical, Zeno came to Athens during the manhood of Socrates, and it is unlikely that Socrates missed the opportunity of making his acquaintance. Plato's authority for speaking of Zeno, both as talker and writer, is first-class.

His story is that, when Parmenides and Zeno were in Athens for the Great Panathenaea, Zeno read his treatise to a small group including Socrates. Afterwards, Socrates asked him to read over again the first hypothesis of the first argument. He then repeated it in his own words so that Zeno could confirm that he had understood it correctly, and continued:[1]

I see, Parmenides, that Zeno's intention is to associate himself with you by means of his treatise no less intimately than by his personal attachment. In a way, his book states the same position as your own; only by varying the form he tries to delude us into thinking that his thesis is a different one.[2] You assert... that the All is one... Zeno, for his part, asserts that it is not a plurality; each expresses himself in such a way that your arguments seem to have nothing in common, though really they come to very much the same thing....

Yes, Socrates, Zeno replied; but you have not quite seen the real character of my book.... The book makes no pretence of disguising from the public the fact that it was written with the purpose you describe.... The book is in fact a sort of defence of Parmenides' argument against those who try to make fun of it by showing that his supposition, that there is a One, leads to many absurdities and contradictions. This book, then, is a retort against those

[1] *Parm.* 128a, trans. Cornford.
[2] This deception seems to have succeeded with some of Zeno's modern interpreters.

who assert a plurality. It pays them back in their own coin with something to spare, and aims at showing that, on a thorough examination, their own supposition that there is a plurality leads to even more absurd consequences than the hypothesis of the One. It was written in that controversial spirit in my young days; and someone copied it surreptitiously, so that I had not even the chance to consider whether it should see the light or not.

The setting may be fictional, and perhaps also the story of the un-authorized publication, though it is no evidence against it that as Zeno tells it it seems a little inconsistent with his present behaviour in reading it aloud to an admiring audience. Both alike are elements in Plato's story, and it would be logical to play off one against the other only if one were in the story and the other an independently attested fact. But whatever we think of the incidents, we must believe what Plato says about the content of Zeno's book,[1] and start from his statement that its general purpose was to defend Parmenides's thesis by showing up greater absurdities in its contrary. There must have been many who 'tried to make fun' of it in the way he describes.

(5) *Plurality* (Lee, 1–11)[2]

Zeno said, according to Themistius (Lee, 1), that unity and indivisi-bility inevitably go together. In Lee, 2 (Simplicius), we have his proof that reality is both one and indivisible. Plurality is a self-contradictory notion because (*a*) it demands a number of (indivisible) units: 'plurality *is* a collection of units' (Eudemus in Lee, 6; DK, A21); (*b*) it implies that reality is divisible. If so, however, it must be infinitely divisible, for it must be a magnitude, and any magnitude is divisible into parts which are still magnitudes and so themselves divisible, however small. But if this is the case, there is nothing that can be called a unit, for any-thing that one takes as such can still be divided and so is not unitary.

---

[1] 'Unreservedly', as Fränkel rightly says (*AJP*, 1942, 203; *Wege u. Formen*, 233). But he himself seems to go rather far in 'conjecture or imagination' when he describes Zeno as a 'con-jurer', speaks of his 'swift legerdemain' and says it is 'next to impossible to distinguish the lighter aspects of his art from the deep significance of his ideas'. While well aware of their profundity, he nevertheless 'often playfully, lustily, and defiantly deceives and mystifies the reader'. Fränkel quotes Brochard's description of one aspect of the paradoxes as 'une plaisanterie innocente'. At the risk of being thought lacking in humour, I confess I cannot see Zeno in this light.

[2] The references are to the passages given in Lee's *Zeno of Elea*, a convenient collection which is rather fuller than that in DK.

Hence, since plurality is a plurality of units, there can be no plurality either.

In Lee, 4 (DK, A 21), Aristotle criticizes Zeno by saying that on his own principles if the one itself is indivisible it must be nothing. Apparently Zeno argued that what does not increase a thing when added to it nor decrease it when subtracted from it has no magnitude, and what has no magnitude does not exist; but a point, which is the only indivisible unit, must have this character. This must have been aimed at people who claimed that the things in the world were made up of a plurality of units having the characteristic of geometrical points; not, that is, merely the ordinary man who unthinkingly accepts the multiplicity of nature, but the Pythagoreans with their confusion between geometrical and corporeal entities (for which see vol. 1, 236 ff., 266).

Simplicius adds from Eudemus (Lee, 5; DK, A 16) that Zeno was credited with saying that if anyone could explain to him the nature of the unit (that is, evidently, of the units of which they believed the multiple world to consist), he would be able to admit plurality.

A further argument was that things comprising a plurality would be both infinitely large and infinitely small (Lee, 9 and 10; DK, frr. 1 and 2):

(*a*) Infinitely large. If a thing has size and depth, one part of it must be separate from another. [Obviously the parts cannot occupy the same space.] Now one part of it must be the outer surface, which limits it, and lies beyond the inner part. If it is merely a geometrical surface (i.e. with no depth), it is not a part of a solid body at all, in fact it is nothing, and the object has no limiting surface; but if it has depth (i.e. is a solid body itself), then it too must have an outer part or surface and an inner part, and so on *ad infinitum*.[1]

(*b*) The only alternative is that the parts of each thing have no magnitude: but an infinite number of parts of no magnitude can never add up to a magnitude.

Three remarks may be made on this. First, Fränkel points out that, since each succeeding 'skin' of an object would be thinner than the last, its total extension would not be infinite but would converge to a certain sum.

---

[1] I follow Fränkel's explanation in *AJP*, 1942, 193 ff. (In referring to Fränkel's work I shall omit the pagination of the revised German version. All the passages I shall cite are identical in both.)

While the construction may go on indefinitely, and the object may continue to stretch out and increase, yet, at any stage of the operation, the thing could be put into a crate which is larger than it is or can ever become (*AJP*, 1942, 196).

So a modern mathematician would reason, and Fränkel thinks that Zeno so reasoned too. He would therefore translate *apeiron* in the phrase 'so large as to be *apeira* in magnitude' by 'unlimited' (i.e. having no definite limit) as distinct from 'infinite'. This considerably weakens the force of the antithesis ('so great as to be *apeira* in size and so small as to have no size at all') and is unlikely. He cites Anaximander, for whom, as he rightly says, the word had both meanings. This is very different from using one to the exclusion of the other. For that he can only quote Aristotle, a more sophisticated logician than either Anaximander or Zeno. Either Zeno himself (which is more likely) did not distinguish the senses, or he used the ambiguous term dialectically because he knew his opponents to be incapable of grasping that what goes on increasing indefinitely need not be actually infinite in size. The second point is that Zeno commits himself to the statement: 'Only that which has magnitude exists', which Aristotle interpreted as being a body.[1] This applies to the units from which his opponents have to construct their plurality of physical objects, but not, one would suppose, to the one being of Parmenides which he believes in. However, the purely dialectical nature of Zeno's reasoning (which all ancient authorities assert and the existing arguments confirm) puts the historian at a disadvantage which cannot be wholly overcome. He shows that accepted notions of plurality rest on premises which make them absurd, but nowhere positively states the character of the unity in which he himself believes. Thirdly, this argument refutes (even if not exclusively) the Pythagorean doctrine that solid, three-dimensional bodies have their origin in two-dimensional planes.

Finally we have a complementary argument (Lee, 11; DK, fr. 3) that if there is a plurality, it must contain both a finite and an infinite number of components: finite, because they must be neither more nor less than they are; infinite, because if they are separate at all, then how-

[1] And having magnitude was interpreted by Aristotle as being corporeal: *Metaph.* 1001b10 ὡς δηλονότι ὄντος μεγέθους τοῦ ὄντος, καὶ εἰ μέγεθος, σωματικόν.

ever close together they are, there will always be others between them, and yet others between those, *ad infinitum*. This is another application of the hypothesis of infinite divisibility. Fränkel compares the reasoning of Plato's *Parm.* 165 a–b: In any object, if one picks on one point as the beginning, and another as the centre, there will always be a beginning of the beginning, and a smaller part in the centre of the centre and so on.

All the above arguments against plurality apply to any sort of plurality, but in choosing the form of attack that he did, Zeno must have had an eye on the Pythagoreans of a generation before the 'fluxion' method of producing figures and bodies from points. (See vol. 1, 262 ff.) These had as yet formulated no clear distinction between a geometrical point and a minimum magnitude, and Zeno faced them with the dilemma: if the units from which they constructed the world had no magnitude, then nothing with magnitude could be produced from them; if they had, then the infinite divisibility of any quantum led them to absurdities.

(6) *Motion: the paradoxes* (Lee, 17–36)

Late authorities (Lee, 17–18; DK, fr. 4) give a general argument of Zeno's against motion, to the effect that if anything moves, it must move either in the place where it is or in the place where it is not. The latter is impossible (nothing can act or be acted upon where it isn't), and where a thing *is*, it must be at rest. This, however, is very similar to the paradox of the flying arrow (no. 3 below), and may be only a condensation of it.[1] The arguments against motion, as given by Aristotle in his *Physics* (239 b 9 ff.) and amplified by the Greek commentators, are four. These constitute the famous paradoxes of Zeno on which the attention of philosophers and mathematicians has chiefly been focused.

(1) *The dichotomy* (Lee, 19–25; DK, A 25). Motion is impossible

---

[1] It is given briefly by D.L. and expanded by Epiphanius (Lee, 18). Its full form was probably that quoted several times by Sextus from Diodorus Cronus (a Megarian of the end of the fourth cent. B.C.), but in one instance (*Math.* 10.87) also as a familiar, or current, *logos*. See Sext. *Pyrrh. hyp.* 2.245, 3.71 (Lee, p. 64); without attribution 2.242. That it was only a condensed statement of the 'arrow' was suggested by A. E. Taylor in his translation of the *Parmenides*, 116.

because an object moving between any two points *A* and *B* must always cover half the distance before it gets to the end. But before covering half the distance it must cover the half of the half, and so *ad infinitum*. Thus to traverse any distance at all it must cover an infinite number of points, which is impossible in any finite time.

At 233a21 Aristotle criticizes this argument by pointing out that 'infinite' has two senses: to be infinite in divisibility is not the same as to·be infinite in extent. Any continuum is infinitely divisible, and this applies to time as well as to space. Hence it is perfectly possible to traverse in a finite time a space which is infinite in divisibility, though not in extent. Later in the *Physics* however, at 263a11, he returns to the point and admits that although this is a sufficient argument *ad hominem* against Zeno, it does not fully and satisfactorily account for the facts.

If [he says] one leaves out of account the distance and the question whether it is possible to traverse an infinite number of distances in a finite time, and asks the same questions about time itself (for time contains an infinite number of divisions), this solution will no longer be adequate.

This second attack on the problem shows that Aristotle was not un-aware of its deeper significance, and this awareness, together with his claim that the earlier answer was sufficient for Zeno, makes it improb-able that (as some recent writers have claimed) Zeno himself saw all the implications and Aristotle simply failed to catch his meaning.[1] Aristotle's own solution involves recourse to the distinction between potential and actual (one of his own major contributions to thought): 'In a continuum there is an infinite number of halves, but only potenti-ally, not actually' (263a28).

(2) *Achilles and the tortoise* (Lee, 26 and 27; DK, A26).[2] The fleet-footed Achilles will never overtake a tortoise if he gives it any start at all. To do so, he must first reach the point from which it started, but by that time the tortoise will have moved further. When he has covered

---

[1] See Ross's ed. of the *Physics*, introd. p. 73.

[2] Called 'the Achilles' by Aristotle, who says simply that he will not overtake 'the slowest'. That his rival was a tortoise we know from the commentators, and Plutarch (*Comm. not.* 1082e) says that the Stoics matched the tortoise against 'the swift horse of Adrastus'. (The quotation is metrical.) No doubt later employers of the paradox embroidered it with different stories.

that further distance the tortoise will again have moved on, and so on. As in the dichotomy, Achilles will have to pass through an infinite number of points to catch up the tortoise, and this is assumed to be impossible. Aristotle treats this argument as essentially the same as the dichotomy, and vulnerable to the same criticism. The only difference is that the dichotomy involved successive division into equal halves, whereas this involves division into decreasing portions corresponding to the relative speeds of the runners.

(3) *The flying arrow* (Lee, 28–34; DK, A27). The two previous arguments depended on the assumption that a spatial length could not be reduced to minimal units but was infinitely divisible. This one, on the other hand, is only effective on the premise that time consists of indivisible minimal instants.

The text of the paradox in Aristotle is obscure in detail, and is probably corrupt and incomplete, but its general tenour is plain enough and a restoration is possible with the aid of fuller statements in the Greek commentators. Zeno seems to have argued that an arrow which appears to be flying is really stationary because everything that occupies a space equal to itself must be at rest in that space, and at any given instant of its flight (literally, every 'now') an arrow can only occupy a space equal to itself; therefore at every instant of its flight it is motionless.

After stating this argument, Aristotle disposes of it by denying that time is composed of separate moments. Earlier in the *Physics* he had argued more fully that it is meaningless to talk of either motion or rest as taking place in a 'now'.[1] It is true that if we try to describe the state of the arrow at one instant only, we cannot say that it is either in motion or at rest, for an instant (in the sense of an indivisible and durationless unit of time corresponding to a point in geometrical space) is not a reality but a mental construct.[2]

---

[1] As regards motion his argument runs like this (234a 24ff.). Motion may be slower or faster. Now suppose that in a given 'now' something traverses the distance *A–B*. In the same 'now' something moving more slowly will traverse a shorter distance *A–C*, which means that the more rapidly moving object will traverse that distance in less than a 'now'. This is absurd, for there is *ex hypothesi* no time shorter than a 'now'.

[2] Cf. the argument at 238b36ff. that there can be no first or last instant of movement or rest. (I owe something here to an excellent unpublished paper on the paradoxes by Mr F. G. Beetham.)

(4) *The stadium* (Lee, 35 and 36; DK, A28).[1] In the stadium are three rows, each containing an equal number of equal-sized objects or bodies,[2] arranged initially as follows:

```
          A A A A
        B B B B→
            ←C C C C
```

The *A*'s are stationary, the *B*'s and *C*'s begin to move in opposite directions at the same time and with equal velocity, until all three rows are opposite each other.

```
          A A A A
          B B B B
          C C C C
```

The leading *B* has now passed two *A*'s while the leading *C* has passed four *B*'s. Now, says Zeno, bodies moving with equal velocity must take the same time to pass an equal number of bodies of the same size. Therefore (since *A*'s, *B*'s and *C*'s are all equal), $4A = 2A$, or alternatively half a given time is equal to the whole. The conclusion, like that of the other arguments, was a reiteration of Parmenides's thesis that motion is unreal.

This argument ignores the obvious fact that some of the bodies involved are moving and some are at rest, and that, says Aristotle, was Zeno's mistake: 'The fallacy lies in assuming that a body takes an

---

[1] Commonly so called because Aristotle speaks of the bodies involved as moving ἐν τῷ σταδίῳ. But there is no mention of Zeno having called them runners or chariots (as he might have done for the sake of colour and vividness; cf. Achilles and the tortoise), and mention of the stadium in connexion with such colourless entities as ὄγκοι seems to have little point. KR call this paradox 'the moving rows' and no. 1 'the stadium', because in one place (*Top.* 160b8) Aristotle, apparently referring to the dichotomy, speaks of 'the argument of Zeno that it is impossible to move or traverse the stadium'. This however, in view of the traditional attachment of the title to the 4th argument, is a little confusing.

[2] ὄγκοι: the essential meaning of the word is something that has bulk. Eudemus in his account called them cubes.

equal time to pass with equal velocity a body that is in motion and a body of equal size at rest' (240a1). This judgment of Aristotle is the most controversial point in modern interpretations of Zeno. Since Tannery it has been commonly thought that he could not possibly have been guilty of such an elementary logical howler. Zeller however (who argues against Tannery in a footnote) thought it rash to assume that because the fallacy is obvious at sight to the least philosophical of us now, it would not be taken seriously by Zeno. The error of assuming that the space traversed by a body is measured by the size of the body it passes, whether the latter is stationary or in motion, 'might well escape the first man to reflect on the laws of motion in this universal way, and all the more easily if, like Zeno, he set out with the conviction that his examination of them would lead to contradictions' (ZN, 762). This view has been revived by N. B. Booth, who writes (*JHS*, 1957, II, 194): 'There is no evidence to support the view that Zeno never made blunders which seem elementary to us now; this is a dogma of modern thinkers, who fail to take into account either the numerous other blunders of the Eleatic philosophers or the limitations of the times.'[1]

Those who believe that in this matter Zeno must have been wronged by Aristotle defend him on the ground that he was arguing against opponents who denied the infinite divisibility of matter. If the *onkoi* (bodies) represent indivisible minima, then his argument is valid, and moreover the arguments fall neatly into two pairs, the first two arguing on the assumption of infinite divisibility and the last two on the contrary assumption (applied first to time and then to space).[2] We say that be-

---

[1] Even nowadays some things have to be said which sound surprisingly elementary. One would have thought the time long past when it had to be pointed out that a body can only be said to move in relation to another body; but the following was thought worth writing by Frege in 1891, and was translated and republished in *Synthese*, 1961, 350–1:

'All these discussions (i.e. discussions about men walking backwards on the decks of moving ships, etc.) can be solved by the insight that the expression "*a* moves" is incomplete and has to be replaced by the expression "*a* moves in relation to *b*". The propositions "*a* moves in relation to *b*" and "*a* does not move in relation to *c*" do not necessarily contradict each other. Also our physicists will agree that one can never observe the motion of a body as such, but only its motion in relation to another body.... Why then was so little attention paid to it by the physicists? The incomplete expression "*a* moves" is so convenient and it is sanctioned by its usage in ordinary language which is also very often employed in physics.'

[2] Tannery, Brochard and others attached much importance to this point too, that the arguments are arranged according to a consistent logical scheme; and this in its turn is denied by Zeller and Booth, who say with some justification that Aristotle provides no evidence for it.

cause the *C*'s are also moving, the first *B* can pass two *C*'s in the time in which it passes one stationary *A*. But if so, there must be a period in which it passes one *C*, and in that period it will pass half an *A*. Common sense would say that is exactly what it does; but the opponents whom Zeno has in mind cannot say so, because for them each *A* is an indivisible minimum passed in an indivisible instant of time.[1]

Such an argument, as Raven says, would certainly be useful against the Pythagoreans who were still confusing indivisible arithmetical units with the points in infinitely divisible geometrical magnitudes, and tacitly assuming (as Zeno assumed for dialectical purposes) that everything that exists has some physical size. Indeed if he intended it, it considerably strengthens the case of those who believe that in formulating his arguments he had the Pythagoreans chiefly in mind. It is of course possible that Aristotle misrepresented Zeno's thought; but unfortunately we are in his hands and those of his commentators, since we have no information from any other source. And they give no hint that any such further argument occurred, at least explicitly, in his book. There is no evidence for it, and since they had the whole book and we have only what they choose to tell us, we are in a weak position to dispute the point with them. Moreover the considerations adduced by Zeller and Booth have some weight.[2]

(7) *Place* (Lee, 13–16; DK, A 24)

Still following his plan of assisting Parmenides not by positive arguments in favour of his theses but by showing their contraries to be impossible and absurd, Zeno disposes of the notion of place or space[3]

---

[1] For this explanation see Ross, *Physics*, introd. 81 f.; Owen, *Proc. Ar. Soc.* 1957–8, 209; KR, 296 f.

[2] If the use of the word ὄγκος has any relevance to the discussion, I think it helps to tip the balance in the same direction. In this I differ from Lee (p. 104), who regards it as an ambiguous word which might well be applied to the confused Pythagorean notion of a unit-point-atom. On the contrary, the word seems deliberately chosen to avoid ambiguity and insist that the bodies concerned have *bulk*, and are not therefore infinitesimal. So also Booth, *Phronesis*, 1957, 91: that the ὄγκοι are indivisible units 'is not stated in the Greek and it is most unlikely that Zeno could have used *oncos* in the very particular technical sense which is required of it by those who maintain this theory'.

[3] The word used, τόπος, is ambiguous between space and place, two conceptions which were not at this time clearly separated in the Greek mind. This argument is also mentioned, with reference to an imitation of it by Gorgias, in [Ar.] *MXG*, 979 b 25. See also Cornford, *P. and P.* 148 f.

in addition of those of plurality and motion. Like his other arguments this one too is made possible by the peculiar philosophical situation in his time. No one, that is, had yet conceived the idea of incorporeal being, although both Heraclitus and Parmenides had in their different ways brought thought to a stage where it needed such a conception if it was not to be at the mercy of paradox and absurdity. The argument, which again we owe in the first place to Aristotle, is simple. Everything that exists exists in a place (or occupies a space). Therefore if place exists, it also exists in a place, and so on *ad infinitum*. This is absurd, therefore place does not exist.

(8) *Sensation: the millet seed* (Lee, 37 and 38; DK, A29)

Although there is some doubt about the exact form in which Zeno put forward this argument (see p. 81 with n. 2 above), it is vouched for by Aristotle as in essence his own.[1] It seems to be an extension into a different field of his attack on infinitesimals, which here serves the additional Parmenidean purpose of discrediting sensation. Either a thing has magnitude or it has not. Similarly, either a thing makes a sound or it does not. If the interlocutor replies in the affirmative to his question 'Does a single seed make a sound in falling?', he pursues the matter by asking whether half a seed makes a sound, and so on. To the negative reply he rejoins that since a sum of zeros is still zero, there will be no such thing as sound. In this way support is given to the exhortation of Parmenides (fr. 7) that we should not trust the senses.

(9) *Zeno and Parmenides*

It has rightly been pointed out that Zeno's arguments against motion are themselves arguments against plurality no less than those which attack it directly.[2] Nevertheless this is not necessary as evidence that he was all the time conducting a 'defence of Parmenides' as Plato

---

[1] Against Zafiropoulo's attempt to deny Zeno's authorship of this argument see Mau, *Problem des Infinitesimalen*, 18.

[2] E.g. Ross, *Physics*, 72: 'The apparent fact of motion, involving the occupation of different places at different times, is a *prima facie* evidence of plurality, and therefore Zeno tries to deprive pluralism of this support by proving the non-existence of motion.' Owen (*Proc. Ar. Soc.* 1957–8, 201) aims at showing that the arguments against motion play an essential part in the attack on plurality. Cf. also Fränkel in *AJP*, 1942, 14.

makes him claim to do. The immobility of what is is explicitly asserted in Parmenides's poem, separately from the other thesis of its unity. In 8.26 and 38 the epithet 'immobile' is applied to it, and in *vv.* 29 f. we learned that 'remaining the same in the same place it rests by itself and so remains firmly where it is'.

Fränkel sums up well the effect of the arguments against motion in these words (*AJP*, 1942, 14):

Motion is impossible because it cannot in any plausible way penetrate the continua of time, space, and mass. To analyse and justify motion, we must first of all differentiate within the continua. But if we do set up a multiple continuum and try to make motion operate in it, one of two things will happen. Either motion will be smothered and brought to a ridiculous stand-still among the too numerous and too fanciful elements of the artificial medium; or motion will wreck the articulate continuum by splitting the units out of which we constructed it. The experiments drastically bear out the fact that a continuum does not yield to differentiation and plurality. It is homogeneous.

He then quotes from Parmenides 8.22 and 25: 'Nor is it divisible, since it all equally is....[1] Therefore it is all continuous.' Similarly 8.5 and 6 proclaim that it 'now is, all together, one and continuous'.

Zeno in fr. 3 (Lee, 11, pp. 90 f. above) says that 'if there are many things, they will be infinite in number, for there will always be others between them, and again others between these'. Fränkel (*AJP*, 1942, 4) finds this assertion 'rather startling', because 'nowhere does Eleaticism deny that two things can be in direct contact'. This is a strange comment, when we consider that by Eleatic logic two things cannot even exist. The origin of this argument is also presumably to be found in Parmenides 8.22–5: 'Nor is it divisible...but all is full of what is. Therefore it is all continuous, for *what is is close to what is.*' With this go closely *vv.* 45–8:

For it may not be at all greater or smaller in this direction or in that; for neither is there what is not, which might stop it from reaching its like, nor is it possible that what is should be here more, and here less, than what is.

---

[1] Or as Fränkel would render it, perhaps more accurately: 'Nor is it capable of differentiation, since it is all homogeneous' (*ibid.* n. 36). For ὁμοῖον see note on p. 31 above.

Again (4.2) 'Thou shalt not cut off for thyself[1] what is from contact with what is'. It is assumed that any two things must be separated if they are to be two and not one. As Aristotle said (*Phys.* 263a23), once we bisect a continuum (mentally or otherwise), we make two points out of what was one before, for the point at which it is bisected becomes the end of one half and the beginning of the other; and how can this happen unless by conceiving the two as separate? But then what separates them, being a third thing, must itself be separated from them by something else, and so on. Parmenides's procedure had been to deny the divisibility of being by saying that, if it were divided, what separates its parts must be either what is or what is not. It cannot be what is not (i.e. emptiness), for that by definition does not exist, nor can it be what is, for nothing exists besides what is. ('The force of evidence will not suffer anything besides itself to come into being', 8.12–13.) Reality being one is continuous, and this depends on its being always in contact with itself. Hence the Eleatic argues that if reality is many, it is *not* continuous and its components are *not* in contact. There must be something between them.

Another buttress to the Parmenidean edifice is provided by Zeno's additional proof, by infinite regress, of the non-existence of place or space. Since this was a consequence of the continuity of the one being as described by Parmenides (p. 33 above), its continuity and unity here receive further support. A further close connexion between master and pupil has been pointed out by Fränkel in a comparison between the presupposition of the 'arrow' paradox and the Parmenidean description of motion. In the paradox, the impossibility of motion depends on supposing it to be of a discontinuous or cinematographic[2] character, imagining it in terms of giving up one position in favour of another, 'or, in short, of an "exchange of position"' (*AJP*, 1942, 9). This was exactly the phrase used by Parmenides in relegating motion to the realm of empty names which mortals use, believing them to be realities.[3]

---

[1] Or 'cut off in thy mind'. See p. 31, n. on 4.2 above.

[2] This useful descriptive term goes back to Bergson. (See Russell, *Knowledge of the External World*, 179.)

[3] τόπον ἀλλάσσειν 8.41. As Fränkel notes, Parmenides uses the broad term τόπος for lack of a special word for position.

Another possible echo occurs to me. In reporting the arrow paradox, Aristotle employs the expression ὅταν ᾖ κατὰ τὸ ἴσον, and κατὰ τὸ ἴσον ἑαυτῷ occurs three times in Simplicius's account.

Finally we have just seen, in the 'millet seed' argument, support for Parmenides's condemnation of the senses.

(10) *Conclusion*

To conclude, Zeno was a single-minded and enthusiastic disciple of Parmenides, who brought his remarkable intellectual powers to bear on one thing only, accurately described by Plato as 'the defence of the *logos* of Parmenides'. All his arguments are aimed at making men accept the unpalatable truth that reality is one, indivisible, and motionless, by the dialectical method of showing up absurdities in the contrary hypothesis. Incidentally to this overriding purpose he developed the dialectical method of argument itself, and pointed out logical difficulties in the conceptions of plurality, motion, time and space which, in the words of A. E. Taylor, 'led to a reconstruction of mathematical fundamental concepts which began in the age of Plato and has barely been completed in our own'. His opponents include all who believe that rabbits run and time passes—all, that is, who follow the dictates of common sense; but the form of his arguments suggests that among contemporary philosophers he, like his master, had in mind, mainly if not exclusively, the teaching of Pythagoras and his followers which had taken such deep root in the soil of his native Italy.

Note on certain Chinese paradoxes

Needham in his *Science and Civilisation in China* (II, 190f.) quotes a list of Chinese paradoxes which were under discussion about 320 B.C. He notes that one or two are strikingly similar to Zeno's, though, as he says, it is hard to believe in any transmission or influence. Such are:

'If a stick one foot long is cut in half every day, it will still have something left after 10,000 generations.'

'There are times when a flying arrow is neither in motion nor at rest.'

In the sense required ('occupying a place equal to itself') the phrase is unusual and has given some trouble to translators. If, as is probable, it goes back to Zeno, it may be an adaptation of Parm. 8.49 οἱ γὰρ πάντοθεν ἴσον, ὁμῶς ἐν πείρασι κύρει. Here the fact that it is equal to itself is taken as evidence that it lies between certain limits from which it cannot move. Zeno expands this argument, and removes the formal truism that a thing is equal to itself, by making it κατὰ τὸ ἴσον; that is, in accordance with, or in line with, what is equal to itself, viz. its πείρατα.

Needham remarks that the second of these is 'startlingly similar to Zeno', but I wonder if it is not even more subtle. All Eleaticism depends on the uncompromising 'either–or'. There is no hint in Zeno of a state which is neither motion nor rest. The cut stick on the other hand makes exactly a point of Zeno's. (It is also worth comparing the quotations from the Mohist Canon at III, 92.) Others in the list remind one more of Heraclitus, e.g. 'The sun at noon is the sun declining, the creature born is the creature dying'.

C. MELISSUS

(1) *Introductory*

The only known facts about the public life of Melissus the philosopher, son of Ithagenes, are surprising but well authenticated. He was a Samian statesman and admiral who took advantage of a tactical error on the part of Pericles to inflict a resounding defeat on the Athenian fleet, thereby temporarily relieving the blockade which it was conducting against his native island. This was recorded by Aristotle, and the battle, which is mentioned by Thucydides, took place in 441 B.C.[1] His maturity therefore coincided with the full tide of the Periclean age and its intellectual ferment in Athens and elsewhere. He was a contemporary of Empedocles, Anaxagoras and Herodotus and probably somewhat older than the atomists Leucippus and Democritus, though in our ignorance we cannot rule out on chronological grounds the view, to which some have inclined, that the atomists were an influence on his work rather than *vice versa*. His writings contain hints of polemic against all these thinkers, but in the absence of external data their relationship to him has been a matter of much dispute.[2]

Although a Samian, his acceptance and defence of the main tenets of Parmenides (the unity, eternity and immobility of reality, and the

[1] Arist. *ap.* Plut. *Per.* 26. He seems to have inflicted two reverses on the Athenians, and (to be strict) all that Plutarch explicitly attributes to Aristotle is the statement that he 'also defeated Pericles himself in a sea-battle' (i.e. in addition to the engagement of 441, in which he seized an opportunity offered by Pericles's absence). But Aristotle was doubtless the source of both stories, which will have come from his *Constitution of Samos*. Cf. also Plut. *Them.* 2, *Adv. Col.* 1126b, and D.L. 9.24.

[2] The earliest reference to Melissus by name is in the Hippocratic treatise *De natura hominis* (ch. 1, VI. 34 Littré), which is probably of the late fifth century and was attributed by Aristotle (*Hist. anim.* 512 b 12) to Hippocrates's son-in-law Polybus. (See Kahn, *Anaximander*, 126.)

rejection of the senses) put him philosophically among the Eleatics; and we may perhaps see here, with Burnet, 'the effect of the increased facility of intercourse between East and West which was secured by the supremacy of Athens' (*EGP*, 321). The doxographers call him a pupil of Parmenides, but this they would do in any case on the strength of his teaching, and we cannot say when, if at all, the two men met. There are some useful, though sharply critical, references to him in Aristotle, and Simplicius quotes important verbatim extracts from his book *On Nature or What Is*.[1] The treatise *On Melissus, Xenophanes, Gorgias* (*MXG*, for which see vol. 1, 367–70) reproduces the content of the known fragments reasonably accurately, but adds nothing save the point that there can be no mixture in the one reality (pp. 115 f. below). Melissus appears to have confined himself to discussion of reality and the folly of trusting the senses, without adding any description of the 'seeming' world corresponding to the second part of Parmenides's poem. Simplicius, who clearly possessed the works of both philosophers, writes: 'Melissus simply says that there is no becoming at all, whereas Parmenides says that there is in seeming though not in truth.'[2]

(2) *The nature of reality*

For all his acceptance of the main tenets of Eleaticism, Melissus had a mind of his own. On the one hand he produces some fresh arguments in favour of the Parmenidean description of reality, and on the other he endows it with other characteristics, one at least of which is in direct contradiction to his master. It is reasonable to attribute some of these changes to the fact that he had to meet new conceptions which were being put forward by other philosophers since Parmenides composed his poem, and this possibility will be considered in its place. Like

[1] It is often said that these titles were only given to fifth-century works by Alexandrian scholars, but this is disproved by the title maliciously given by Melissus's contemporary Gorgias to his reversal of Eleatic reasoning: *On the Non-existent or on Nature*. That this was a direct allusion to Melissus is doubted by Nestle (*RE*, xv, i, 531) on the grounds that the parody is directed against Parmenides himself. It of course attacks the whole Eleatic position, and in any case according to Simplicius Parmenides and Melissus gave their works the same title (*De caelo*, 556.25). Simplicius himself had no doubts: ὁ Μ. καὶ τὴν ἐπιγραφὴν οὕτως ἐποιήσατο τοῦ συγγράμματος (*Phys.* 70.16, cf. *De caelo*, 557.10).

[2] Simpl. *De caelo*, 556.12. The misguided attempt of Reinhardt (*Parm.* 71 f.) to discover a 'second part' in Melissus has been justly criticized by Nestle, ZN, 774 n.

Zeno he wrote in prose, and exhibits none of the religious exaltation which overflows from the prologue into the main poem of Parmenides with its solemn pronouncements about the actions of Dike, Ananke and Moira. His preference is for explicit, pedestrian, and sometimes wearisomely repetitive argumentation.

(a) Reality has the characteristics stated by Parmenides and others consistent with them

Melissus follows Parmenides in holding that reality is one and undivided, ungenerated and everlasting, homogeneous, motionless and not subject to growth or change; and that in consequence the senses cannot witness to the truth. But a difference between the two men appears at once in their expression of a fundamental property of reality: its eternity. 'It was not nor shall it be, since it now is', said Parmenides (8.5); but Melissus, as if deliberately, brings this back to the plane of common sense by writing (fr. 2), 'It is and always was and always shall be'. The easily comprehensible notion of everlastingness replaces the more profound one of timelessness. The impossibility of becoming he demonstrates on purely Parmenidean lines (fr. 1):

For if it came into being, before it came into being there must have been nothing; if there were nothing, nothing would ever come into being out of nothing.

Elsewhere also he either repeats or develops arguments of Parmenides, for example in fr. 7.2–3, which is a not unfair specimen of his verbosity. He is arguing that what is cannot perish or grow or alter:

For if it were to undergo any of these things, it would no longer be. For if it changed, what is would of necessity not be homogeneous, but what formerly was must perish, and what is not must come to be. If then it were to alter by a single hair in ten thousand years, in the fulness of time it will perish entirely. Nor is it possible for it to be rearranged, for the previously existing order does not perish, nor the order which is not come to be. And when nothing is added nor perishes nor is altered, how could it still exist if the order were changed? For if something became different, it would at the same time have its order changed.

It seems unnecessary to argue against change of order (*kosmos*) when reality is one and without parts. But according to *MXG*,

Melissus felt that to assure the unity of reality, he must defend it against the idea that it was 'one by mixture'. Evidently he was already aware of pluralist reactions against Parmenides like that of Empedocles. (See pp. 115f. below.) The picturesque addition about alteration of a single hair in ten thousand years was perhaps motivated by the thought that, if change is admitted at all, then Heraclitus had shown that it must be continuous even if imperceptible (vol. 1, 451f.).

Parmenides had been content to attribute the immobility of what is to the mighty bonds of Ananke (pp. 34f. above). Melissus demonstrates it explicitly from the absence of void, which also is stated and argued (fr. 7.7):

Nor is there any void, for void is nothing, and nothing cannot be. Nor does it [*sc.* what is] move, for it has no place to which it can withdraw, but is full. If there were void, it would withdraw to the void; but since there is no void, it has nowhere to withdraw to.

This open rebuttal of the void by name (*kenon* = emptiness or what is empty) is not to be found in Parmenides, whereas Melissus gives it considerable prominence, so that it has even been possible for scholars to argue that he was the first to make use of the idea. (See p. 36, n. 1 above.) This new emphasis may have a bearing on his relation to the atomists, who accepted void as an essential feature of their cosmogony.

From the absence of void Melissus points out that what is can contain no variations of density and rarity, as Anaximenes and those who followed him believed (7.8):

And there cannot be dense and rare, for it is impossible that what is rare should be as full as what is dense, but the rare is emptier than the dense. The decision to be made about full and not full is this: if a thing has room for something else, and takes it in, it is not full; but if it does not have room to take it in, it is full. Now it must be full if there is no void, and if it is full it does not move.

The sudden switch back to the question of motion, which had been settled earlier in the fragment, is typical of the irritating form of Melissus's argumentation. In the disproof of degrees of density and rarity he is developing a hint of Parmenides (8.23f.):

It does not exist more fully in one direction, which would prevent it from holding together (*or* being continuous), nor more weakly in another, but all is full of what is.

The indivisibility of what is, which Parmenides (8.22) had rested simply, and perhaps a little cryptically, on the statement that 'it all equally is', Melissus deduces from its immobility (fr. 10):

For if what is is divided, it moves; but if it moved, it would no longer be.

This rather curious argument shows that he has in mind only the division of reality as an accomplished fact. That it might be theoretically divisible (as in fact any magnitude must be), without ever being actually divided, is something that he does not consider.

In his denial of plurality, and hence of all sensible objects and qualities, he also adopts a more elaborate line of argument (fr. 8.2–6). As examples he cites the four elements, earth, water, air and fire (another pointer to Empedocles), metals, colours, hot and cold, hard and soft, living and dead.[1] Men believe that these exist, and that change occurs from one to the other, so that, for example, hard iron is worn away by contact with the finger, water changes to earth and stone, and 'we see and hear aright'. This is false because, if these things existed, then it follows from criteria of existence already established that (8.2)

each must be such as it appeared to us at first, and not change nor become different, but each must always be as it is.

But (8.4–6)

all seem to us to become different and to change from their appearance at any particular time. Evidently then we did not see aright nor do those many things rightly seem to be, for they would not change if they were real, but each would be such as it seemed; for nothing is stronger than that which truly exists.[2] But if it changes, what is has perished and what is not has come into being. Thus if there were many things, they would have to be such as the One is.

The conclusion, which Melissus set at both the beginning and the end of this section, is his own, and constitutes a rather neat *reductio ad absurdum* of plurality, particularly in view of two characteristics of his one reality which still remain to be considered. It may be added that those who see in the pluralism of the atomists an acceptance of this

---

[1] Here he probably has Anaxagoras in mind. Cf. p. 286, n. 1 below.

[2] Or 'existing truth (= reality)', τοῦ ἐόντος ἀληθινοῦ. According to the physicists whose views are collectively opposed here, physical properties occur in pairs of conflicting opposites, and change occurs when and where one opposite proves stronger than another; for example, a rise in temperature is expressed in terms of hot overcoming cold.

challenge ('Very well then, let us assume many things that *are* just like your One') have perhaps scarcely paid enough attention to these further properties.

(b) *Reality is infinite*

Parmenides had laid great emphasis on the finite character of the real, claiming that this was essential to its wholeness and perfection and buttressing it with solemn religious sanctions. I have tried to show how at his stage of thought it was possible to combine this with the conviction that nothing, not even empty space, existed outside it.[1] It is here that Melissus makes a radical departure from his master. What is, he says, has no bounds or limits (*perata*), but is in fact *apeiron*, infinite. He does not argue against Parmenides, so we do not know how he would have met the point that limits were necessary for its completeness; but he recognizes the difficulty of imagining anything as bounded if it is not bounded by *something*. So far as his own words go, we meet this only at a later stage, when he is arguing, not for the infinity of what is, but from its infinity, as an established premise, to its unity.

He inferred its unity from its infinity on the argument 'if it were not one, it would come up against [*or* be limited by] something else' (fr. 5, Simpl.).

Again (fr. 6):

To be infinite, it must be one; for if there were two, they could not be infinite but would have limits in relation to [*or* be limited by] one another.

It is true that Melissus had other excellent arguments, inherited from Parmenides, for the unity of reality; but, as we see, he did rest it also on its infinity, and this he attempted to prove, unfortunately for our good opinion of him, in ways which show him to have been still capable of a rather primitive confusion of thought. Aristotle indeed comes to his rescue here with the information that he had one good argument. Simplicius does not quote it, nor have we it in Melissus's own words at all, and in fact Aristotle does not name Melissus as its author. Nevertheless it is too similar to the arguments already quoted to have come from anyone else, and it is interesting that we should owe it to Aristotle, who had such a low opinion of Melissus that he called

[1] Parm. 8.26–33, 42–4: see pp. 38, 46–9 above.

him 'more naïve' than Parmenides and his arguments 'crude and offering no difficulty', and dismissed him with the crushing remark: 'One absurdity is granted and the rest follows; that is simple enough.' (*Metaph.* 986b26, *Phys.* 185a10.) What Aristotle says is:

They say that the All is one, unmoved and infinite; for a limit would bring it up against the void.[1]

This of course is the objection that naturally occurs to a modern reader confronted with Parmenides's statement that the total sum of existence is bounded and spherical in shape.

But Melissus also proved the infinity of reality at greater length in a more questionable way. Having shown by Parmenidean arguments that what is can never have come into being, he continued (fr. 2):

Since then it did not become, it is and always was and always will be, and has neither beginning nor end but is infinite. For if it came to be, it would have a beginning (having come into being, it must have become at some time) and an end (for having come to be, it would at some time have ceased);[2] but

---

[1] *GC*, 325a14. The subject of the paragraph is 'some of the earlier philosophers' who 'hold that what is is necessarily one and unmoved'.

The possibility must be allowed that although the explanatory clause can refer to the property of infinity alone, this sentence may be no more than a rough rewording of Melissus's own frr. 5 and 6, in which the infinity of the real is assumed, and its unity deduced therefrom on the ground that plurality would involve limits and so be incompatible with infinity. I prefer however to take the more charitable view that Aristotle has preserved here a sound argument of Melissus's against finitude, in spite of the fact that Melissus adduces an illogical one as well.

[2] The translation here follows DK. There is some doubt whether γινόμενον or γενόμενον represents what Melissus wrote. γινόμενον occurs in the full quotation each time Simplicius gives it (*Phys.* 29.24–5 and 109.20–3). But in the latter place he repeats it followed by ὄν in the second parenthesis (which if correct would necessitate the translation given above), and in his exegesis he repeats the word as γενόμενον. Spengel (*Eudemi frr.* 18) restored γενόμενον in the main quotation and Diels followed him. γινόμενον makes possible, though not necessary, the translation of Burnet (*EGP*, 322): 'it would have ceased to come into being at some time or another'. So also KR, 299: 'it would at some time have stopped coming into being'. Kahn (*Festschr. Kapp*, 23) and Cherniss (*ACP*, 70) translate similarly. Ross (*Physics*, 472) thinks the meaning is: 'it must have had a (spatial) beginning (i.e. a part which came first into being) and a (spatial) end (i.e. a part which came last into being)'. Although Melissus did believe this, the presence of ποτε makes it impossible that he should be saying so here.

In any case 'to have an end' (temporally) must surely mean to cease to be. I take the sentence to be an expansion of Parm. 8.27 ἔστιν ἄναρχον ἄπαυστον. That whatever has come into being will also cease to be—that γένεσις involves ὄλεθρος—as Aristotle later believed, might have seemed obvious to Melissus on Parmenidean grounds. These parentheses are intended to supply a reason why '*it always was and always will be*'.

In the first sentence DK's text is that of Simpl. 29.22. At 109.20 he has ἔστι δέ, ἀεὶ ἦν, i.e. 'since it did not come into being, but *is*, it always was and always will be...'. This makes excellent sense and is preferred by Loenen, *Parm. Mel. Gorg.* 145.

since it neither began nor ended, it always was and always will be and has no beginning nor end; for it is impossible for anything to exist for ever unless it exists as a whole.[1]

From this fragment alone, one might suppose Melissus to be simply making the obvious point that what has no beginning nor end is infinite in temporal duration. We have seen, however (vol. i, 86, 337), that earlier Greek thinkers experienced difficulty in separating the various senses in which something could be said to be infinite or unlimited (*apeiron*), and Melissus was no exception. His thought must have been something like this, though the steps in the argument were doubtless not taken consciously: 'Reality is ungenerated, therefore it has no beginning nor end; what has no beginning nor end is infinite (*apeiron*, without *perata* or limits), and what has no limits is spatially as well as temporally unlimited, since limits in space are *perata* just as much as those in time.' A brief aside of Aristotle's makes it easier to see how the matter presented itself (*Phys.* 186a11–14). If something has a beginning, he says, Melissus thought of it as 'in every case a beginning of the thing, not of the time', i.e. the beginning in his view attached itself to the object generated rather than the time of generation. The generation of, say, an animal starts of course at a particular time, but it also starts at a particular point in space, with a microscopic part of what grows into the large creature that it finally becomes. If, then, a thing has no beginning, it has no starting-point in space, i.e. no boundary.[2]

---

[1] The last clause is a restatement of the argument against coming-to-be. This is a *process*, which must occupy time, and during that time the thing which is in process of coming to be must partly be and partly not be, which for a Parmenidean is impossible. 'It is or it is not': there is no alternative. Cf. Parm. 8.11 ἢ πάμπαν πελέναι χρεών ἐστιν ἢ οὐχί.

Cherniss takes the meaning to be 'unless it is everything'. For his view of the fr. see *ACP*, 67–71, and cf. Verdenius in *Mnemosyne*, 1948, 8–10. Cherniss compares fr. 3, supposing that πᾶν εἶναι is the same as τὸ μέγεθος ἄπειρον εἶναι (p. 70, n. 287). If this is what Melissus meant, he is tacitly correcting the reasoning of Parmenides, for whom if reality was to contain everything, it had to be finite or completed (τετελεσμένον, οὐκ ἀτελεύτητον): if it had no end it would be 'lacking' (fr. 8.32, 42).

[2] D. E. Gershenson and D. A. Greenberg have suggested a different interpretation of Ar. *Phys.* 186a10–16 (*Phronesis*, 1961, 7–9). Their attribution of the words εἶτα καὶ τοῦτο ἄτοπον to Melissus's own argument is persuasive, but their view is weakened by the assumption that 'everyone' allows that time has no beginning, or that this was 'the commonly accepted view'. Time (χρόνος), according to Greek ideas, could very well have a beginning, cf. vol. i, 338f. On the whole I believe with all other scholars that εἶτα καὶ τοῦτο ἄτοπον is a comment on Melissus by Aristotle himself.

Aristotle also made his criticism in logical form, accusing Melissus of the illegitimate conversion of a universal affirmative proposition. Two of his several statements of this criticism are these:

Such is the argument of Melissus that the All is infinite. He takes as his premise that the All is ungenerated (for nothing can be generated from nothing), and that everything that is generated has a beginning. If then the All was not generated, it has no beginning, so that it is infinite. But this does not necessarily follow. It is not true that if everything generated has a beginning, everything that has a beginning is generated, any more than if everyone in a fever is hot, everyone who is hot has fever.

The argument of Melissus also depends on this [i.e. illegitimate conversion]; for he claims that if what is generated has a beginning, what is ungenerated has no beginning, so that if the universe is ungenerated it is also infinite. This is not true, for the sequence is the other way round.[1]

There is no flaw in arguing that what is ungenerated has no *temporal* beginning, and in censuring Melissus Aristotle must be using the word 'infinite' in the most general sense, including spatial infinity. That he was justified in attributing this extension to Melissus appears from two further direct quotations in Simplicius. For the conversion we have fr. 4:

Nothing which has a beginning and an end is either everlasting or infinite,

where the use of the word *apeiron* as well as 'everlasting' (ἀΐδιον) shows that more than temporal infinity is intended. Finally in fr. 3 Melissus is even more explicit:

But just as it is for ever, so it must be infinite in magnitude.

I would emphasize that different interpretations of Melissus's views on this point are possible. (See in particular that of Cherniss referred to in n. 1 to p. 108 above.) What is undoubted is that he contradicted Parmenides by holding that reality is infinite in magnitude, and achieved an intellectual advance by raising the question: if reality is both one and finite, what are its limits? What does it border on? Not on the void, for that is non-existent; nor on something else, for then there must be more than one reality.[2]

---

[1] *Soph. el.* 167b13 and 181a27. Other statements are at 168b35–40 and *Phys.* 186a10–13.

[2] I must confess that I can make no sense of Loenen's assertion (*Parm. Mel. Gorg.* 157f.) that 'magnitude' is to be understood 'in a qualitative sense', so that the terms μέγας and μέγεθος in Melissus 'refer to greatness or perfection'.

(c) Reality has no body

We come now to one of the most difficult of all Melissus's pronouncements. Simplicius writes:

That he means reality to be incorporeal he declares in the words: 'If it exists it must be one, and being one it must have no body. If it had thickness, it would have parts, and would no longer be one.'[1]

It seems then that Melissus asks us to reconcile the following statements:

(1) Reality is infinite in magnitude.
(2) There is no emptiness in it but it is 'full'.
(3) It has no body.

It is not surprising that to some scholars this has seemed impossible.[2]

The dilemma is generally put in the form: Is reality corporeal or incorporeal? That is, Melissus's sentence 'It must have no body (*soma*)' is taken as meaning that it is incorporeal in the full sense which that word carries today. This is not necessarily true. One of the plainest lessons of Presocratic thought is that the notion of incorporeal existence was not achieved by a single step, but was a gradual process. Aristotle, for whom it was an accomplished fact, rightly uses the

---

[1] Simpl. *Phys.* 109.34 (and cf. 114.19), Melissus fr. 9. At the beginning of the quotation the MSS. of Simplicius are divided between εἰ μὲν οὖν εἴη (EF) and εἰ μὲν ὂν εἴη (D). Diels printed the latter in his ed. of Simplicius, but DK have the former. I do not think the variation affects the sense sufficiently to be of use in deciding the question whether these words refer, as some have thought, not to the Eleatic One Being but to each of a plurality of units such as was believed in by those whom Zeno attacked (pp. 88–91 above). This theory, according to which Simplicius completely misunderstood Melissus in spite of having his book complete, seems to me highly improbable and I shall not refer to it again. Burnet (*EGP*, 327f.) follows Zeller (ZN, 770, n. 2) in favouring it, and it is put succinctly by Nestle in *RE*, xv, i, 531. It is no argument in favour of it that Aristotle (*Metaph.* 986b18) said of Melissus that, in contrast to Parmenides, he ἔοικε τοῦ κατὰ τὴν ὕλην ἑνὸς ἅπτεσθαι. Aristotle's ὕλη is not σῶμα, as Zeller himself concedes. Melissus's reality does indeed resemble Aristotelian prime matter in more than one way, e.g. in being at the same time ἄπειρον (wherein it chiefly differs from what is κατὰ τὸν λόγον) and imperceptible to the senses.

[2] The most important recent discussions are those of H. Gomperz, *Hermes*, 1932, 157ff.; Raven, *Pyth. and El.* ch. 6; Vlastos, *Gnomon*, 1953, 34–5; Booth, *AJP*, 1958, 61–5. Booth's conclusion is a cautious *non liquet*. All the others in some way modify the earlier view of Zeller, Burnet and Nestle. Vlastos's normally acute reasoning is here fatally weakened by his argument that the combination of the incorporeality of Being with its infinity is possible for Melissus simply 'because the infinity in question is that of beginningless and endless duration, not that of unlimited spatial extension'. This is irreconcilable with the phrase ἄπειρον τὸ μέγεθος in fr. 3, which Vlastos mentions without any comment. Even apart from the meaning of this phrase, the form of the sentence (ὥσπερ...οὕτω καί) makes it clear that a new point is being introduced, not a mere repetition of ἔστιν ἀεί.

adjective *asomaton* (bodiless) in comparative and superlative forms when speaking about his predecessors. In choosing their primary substance, or considering the composition of the soul, they inclined towards what was 'more incorporeal', or nearer to incorporeality, by reason of fine texture, lightness or mobility. Thus fire is 'the most incorporeal' of the elements, air is 'more incorporeal' than water.[1]

In his important article on the word *asomaton*, H. Gomperz reminds us that in its earliest contexts (that is, in Homer) *soma* meant a corpse. It was rapidly extended to apply to the body of a living human being or animal, and this remained its practically universal significance in classical literature. When in philosophical contexts, and probably not before the late fifth century,[2] it was extended to include physical body in general, it was still confined (as Gomperz notes) to that which possessed two essential properties of organic bodies: perceptibility to the senses (especially touch and sight) and inclusion within definite spatial boundaries. An entity can therefore be described as 'not having a *soma*' if it is intangible and invisible and has no boundaries (is *apeiron*), characteristics that we know already to belong to the Being of Melissus. It is also understandable that to have a *soma* involves having parts and being divisible, and on this ground too an Eleatic would have to deny the somatic character of the real.

The denial of 'thickness' (*pachos*) is more difficult to grasp. One must agree with Theodor Gomperz (*Gr. Th.* 1, 190) that Melissus was not simply denying a third dimension to reality and reducing it to a two-dimensional plane. He was in fact in a rather tight corner. He still wished to uphold the main Eleatic thesis of the unity, imperceptibility, indivisibility etc. of reality, but being aware of certain difficulties in the first statement of it by Parmenides, and also in all probability of the penetrating arguments of Zeno, he was forced to introduce refinements

---

[1] For examples see H. Gomperz, *Hermes*, 1932, 167, n. 1. Raven (*P. and E.* 89–92) has some sensible things to say against over-simplification of this question.

[2] Apart from the present passage (and it is by no means certain that Being was inanimate for Melissus), I doubt if there is any occurrence of σῶμα relating to inanimate objects in the fifth century except in Gorgias's parody of Eleatic reasoning (fr. 3, DK, 11, 281) and perhaps, if it is genuine, Philolaus fr. 12. In Gorg. fr. 11 (*ibid.* 290.17) λόγος is personified. For Diogenes of Apollonia ἀήρ, which he called an ἀθάνατον σῶμα, was both animate and intelligent. In tragedy (where it is frequent), Thucydides, and other non-philosophical literature σῶμα is always the body of a man or animal. I suggest that in Melissus fr. 9 the translation of DK should run 'so darf es keinen Leib besitzen', not 'Körper'.

into what was already a highly paradoxical doctrine. Parmenides had spoken of 'what is' as bounded like a sphere, with centre and circumference. Was not this to introduce parts into it and endanger its unity and indivisibility? Zeno had argued that whatever exists must have magnitude *and thickness* (*pachos*), with one part alongside another. He was attacking the champions of plurality, but the argument could all too easily be turned against the Parmenidean One. Such dilemmas remained unavoidable until the concept of fully incorporeal, non-spatial existence was entertained, and that was not yet. Aristotle throws some light on the situation as he looks back on the Eleatics from the Platonic point of view. For him reality was divided into the realm of physical nature and the higher realm of intelligible and eternal entities, incorporeal and beyond the confines of space and time. They were the objects of different studies, *physike* and first philosophy or *theologike*. The Eleatic conception was still monistic; their arguments had deprived reality of sensible qualities without lifting it out of the spatial order. Therefore Aristotle writes of Parmenides and Melissus in *De caelo* (298 b 21):

They however, being unaware of the existence of anything beyond the substance of sensible objects, and perceiving for the first time that unchangeable entities were demanded if knowledge and wisdom were to be possible, transferred to sensible objects the description of the higher.

In other words, the Eleatics were trying to give to reality the intelligibility and eternal changelessness of a Platonic or Aristotelian pure form without its transcendence. In doing so, they naturally brought philosophy to a very difficult stage at which it could not, and did not, rest. *Pachos*, which one might translate '*palpable* density', evidently suggested to Melissus both the composite and the sensible, and so was ruled out as an attribute of the one Being. Being is 'full', and infinitely extended in space, but the notion of density or rarity cannot be applied to it: 'there cannot be dense and rare' (fr. 7.8). Scholars who have tried to confine Melissus within later thought-categories, making him answer questions like 'is it corporeal or incorporeal?', have felt bound to reject one or other of his statements on the grounds that taken together they are self-contradictory and unintelligible. I should claim that self-contradiction and unintelligibility have not quite been reached, though they are not far off. Certainly thought could go no further in this direction. It had to make a fresh start, but not without taking the Eleatics into account. The directions in which it will now go are largely determined by the Eleatic experiment. It was in the interests of intellectual progress that monism should be carried to its extreme before it was abandoned.

(d) Reality feels no pain

In the list of attributes, mostly negative, of 'what is', after saying that it is everlasting, infinite, one and homogeneous, that it neither perishes nor grows nor changes, Melissus adds surprisingly that it feels neither pain nor grief.[1] Later in the fragment he expands this:

Nor does it feel pain. It could not be entire if it were in pain, for a thing in pain could not be for ever, nor has it the same power as what is healthy. Nor would it be all alike if it were in pain, for it would feel pain by the addition or subtraction of something, and would no longer be alike. Nor could what is healthy feel pain, for then what is and is healthy would perish, and what is not would come to be. And the same argument applies to grief as to pain.

The arguments adduce nothing new. Pain is incompatible with completeness and with the rule that reality must not undergo addition, subtraction or destruction. The interesting thing is that Melissus should think the point worth mentioning at all. Zeller wrote that the denial of pain to reality need not mean that he ascribes to it an unbroken sensation of wellbeing or bliss, 'so long as it remains unproven that he ascribed to it any sensation at all'. This is unreasonably sceptical. To say of something that it 'feels neither pain nor pleasure', or any other pair of contrary sensations, might indeed be a mode of denying it any feeling at all; but to mention the absence of pain alone would be a strange way for anyone to describe something completely insensitive. Others have gone to the opposite extreme and seen in the words an element of mysticism, or even the origin of the ontological proof of the existence of God.[2]

---

[1] Fr. 7.2 οὔτε ἀλγεῖ οὔτε ἀνιᾶται. The first verb is used primarily of physical pain but also in the fifth century of mental distress, the second one only of the latter. In Hdt. 4. 68 ἀλγεῖ is used of illness (cf. French *souffrant*), and Loenen (*Parm. Mel. Gorg.* 157, n. 60) follows Covotti in taking it so here. In view of the contrast with ὑγιές this is quite probably correct.

[2] For Zeller's view and a consensus of previous opinions, see ZN, 777, n. 2, 774, n. 1 *fin.* More recent critics have taken little notice of the clause.

Without going as far as this, we may take the words as a timely reminder that in the normal belief of early Greek thought the ultimately real is alive and divine. It was so for the Milesians, the Pythagoreans and Heraclitus. It was so for Xenophanes, to whose one unmoving god Eleatic thought owed much of its inspiration. If we look ahead to the immediate successors of the Eleatics, who conscientiously retained as much of their thought as was consistent with 'saving the phenomena', we find the sphere of Empedocles '*rejoicing* in its circular stillness' and 'a sacred mind darting through the whole cosmos'. For Anaxagoras Mind, 'alone and by itself', controlled the cosmic processes. There is no evidence that any philosopher entertained the concept of lifeless matter before the atomists Leucippus and Democritus, and for all except Parmenides and Zeno there is positive evidence that reality was alive.[1] With these two there is at least nothing to suggest that they were exceptions, and taking into account the theology of Parmenides's teacher Xenophanes, and the reference to freedom from pain in his follower Melissus, it is more likely than not that he too took for granted that reality was alive. The almost casual way in which Melissus introduces this particular characteristic alongside the known properties of Eleatic Being strongly suggests that the assumption naturally underlying it could simply be taken for granted. So far as they go, these considerations perhaps support those scholars who would identify being and thought in Parmenides, for the life of 'what is' could hardly be manifested in any other activity but thinking (*noein*). But on this it is scarcely possible to dogmatize.[2] Against those who speak of mysticism and proofs of the existence of God, it is necessary to point out that, even if Parmenides and Melissus retained, almost automatically, this legacy from earlier thought, their remains show that it was of little importance to them.

[1] Aëtius does in fact say that for Parmenides 'the motionless and finite spherical' was god, and for Melissus and Zeno 'the One and the All' (DK, 28, A 31 and 30, A 13). His summary list of the gods of all philosophers (*Dox.* 301–3) does not inspire confidence, but there may have been *some* basis for his statements. Olympiodorus also speaks of Melissus's belief in the divinity of the one reality, but his language betrays considerable confusion. (DK, A 13: he calls it the ἀρχὴ πάντων τῶν ὄντων.)

[2] See pp. 41 f. above and cf. the activity of Xenophanes's god (fr. 25) νόου φρενί. The arguments against their particular line of thought remain valid.

(3) *Relation to other philosophers*

The reaction against Eleatic paradox was not long in coming. In the second half of the fifth century Empedocles, Anaxagoras, and the atomists Leucippus and Democritus all sought in different ways to circumvent the logic of Parmenides and by pluralistic theories restore reality to the everyday sensible world. Melissus remained an Eleatic, but he was a contemporary of these others, and the external data are too scanty to determine the relative chronology of their work. Some however have seen indications in the fragments themselves that Melissus was aware of the arguments of the pluralists.

In fr. 7.8 he is pretty clearly tilting at an Ionian predecessor, Anaximenes, and his contemporary follower Diogenes of Apollonia, when he denies variations of dense and rare, and again in 8.3 when he mentions the opinion that earth and stones come from water. There are no obvious signs of an interest in Pythagoreanism, though Raven thinks it 'tenable' that the objection voiced by Melissus against the finite character of the Parmenidean One (that if it is finite and spherical there must be something outside it) was not his own but had its origin in Pythagorean criticism.[1]

In fr. 10 Melissus denies the partition of reality, and according to *MXG* he also denied that it could be a mixture. Both denials follow from its unity and immobility, and the fact that he thought it worth while both to state and argue them separately is attributed by Zeller to a desire to refute Empedocles, who tried to escape the Eleatic objections to generation and destruction by reducing them to processes of mixture and separation of indestructible elements. Zeller might have gone further. For instance fr. 7.3 points in the same direction:

Nor is it possible for it to be rearranged, for the previously existing order (*kosmos*) does not perish, nor the order which is not come to be.[2]

---

[1] *P. and E.* 79–82. The second of his three arguments, that the objection was raised by a Pythagorean (Archytas) at a later date, is a dubious ally. The other two are circumstantial, and Raven himself is the first to admit that the suggestion is incapable of proof.

Those who believe that fr. 9 was written in criticism of the units composing a plurality (p. 110, n. 1 above) believe it to be aimed at the Pythagoreans (Burnet, *EGP*, 327).

[2] Loenen (*Parm. Mel. Gorg.* 160) takes μετακοσμεῖσθαι (like μέγεθος) in a 'qualitative' sense. With the sentence about κόσμος following, this is very unlikely, and not made likelier by quoting the words of LSJ 'rearrange: hence, *modify*'. In the only remotely contemporary reference which they give, namely Hipp. *Fract.* 2, the word unmistakably means, as Littré translates, *ils s'arrangeraient autrement*. The writer of *MXG* had no doubt of the meaning of the verb when he para-

Empedocles spoke of the elements as 'at one time coming together by the agency of Love into one *kosmos*, and at another scattering apart', 'unceasingly changing places', and 'running through one another'.[1] The language of Empedocles may also have occasioned the curiously elaborate arguments which Melissus put forward against the notion of mixture. It is true that we have not his own words here, but according to the report of *MXG* he defined 'unity in the sense of mixture'[2] as occurring when 'there are many things moving into one another'. It could be of two sorts, by combination (σύνθεσις) or by 'a kind of superposition (ἐπιπρόσθησις) brought about by overlapping (or interlacing, ἐπάλλαξις)'. Neither case is compatible with transformation into a true unity,[3] since the elements retain their distinctive identities and could be separated again.

Again, it is believed with good reason that Empedocles was the first to specify the four elements earth, water, air and fire as the ultimate components of the universe; and in his denial of physical substances and qualities in fr. 8 Melissus leads off with just these four. Little doubt can be left that he was aware of this attempt to evade Eleatic logic by a resort to pluralism, and did his best to defeat it.

In the arguments of fr. 8 against the sensible world some have seen an attack on Anaxagoras, but they seem to have no more specific target than the general tendency of mankind to believe their senses.[4]

phrased (974a20) οὔτε μετακοσμούμενον θέσει οὔτε ἑτεροιούμενον εἴδει. Diller (*Hermes*, 1941, 365), without even considering Empedocles, sees here a polemic against the atomism of Leucippus. This seems perverse.

[1] Frr. 26.5, 17.6, 17.34.

[2] With ἐν ἐκ πλειόνων (*MXG*, 974a24) cf. Emped. fr. 26.8 ἓν ἐκ πλεόνων μεμάθηκε φύεσθαι. The accuracy of *MXG* where covered by the surviving frr. justifies trust in it when at one point it goes beyond them.

It is possible that Melissus was attacking pluralism on a wider front. Apelt (*Jbb. f. Philol.* 1886, 739f.) suggested with some plausibility that in using the words σύνθεσις, ἐπιπρόσθησις and ἐπάλλαξις he may have had atomistic modes of combination in mind. Apelt also points out that the fact that only mechanical mixture had been conceived of by Melissus's time, not chemical (which appears first in Aristotle, cf. *GC*, I. 10), played into his hands: no mixture could produce a true unity.

[3] Apelt's translation of ὧν οὐδέτερον συμβαίνειν (*op. cit.* 742, cf. Bonitz, *Ind. Ar.* 713a10). Others translate 'neither happens', attributing to Melissus an un-Eleatic appeal to experience. If this is correct, he presumably made use of it as a sufficient *argumentum ad homines*.

[4] 'The language seems more applicable to him than anyone else', Burnet, *EGP*, 328. Raven too thinks this suggestion probable, KR, 305, 364. Nestle however (ZN, 774 n.) found 'insufficient ground' for Burnet's suggestion, and Loenen (*Parm. Mel. Gorg.* 169f.) agrees that Melissus's target here is *communis opinio*.

Burnet also suggests that when Melissus says that 'what is' οὔτε ἀλγεῖ οὔτε ἀνιᾶται this perhaps

Finally there are the atomists. In this connexion much has been made of the conclusion expressed by Melissus in fr. 8: 'If there were many things, they would have to be such as the One is.' It is commonly held that the atomism of Leucippus and Democritus was a response to this challenge:[1] there *were* many things with the properties of the Eleatic One—indestructibility, homogeneity, indivisibility, lack of internal change—though they were microscopic in size and innumerable. They were however subject to motion in space (for in spite of the Eleatics there was such a thing as empty space), and this brought about their collision and mutual entanglement out of which the universe with all its apparent variety was built up. Except for the reference to Melissus this is, roughly, Aristotle's account of the atomic theory, and there is no reason to doubt it.

Obviously, however, such a theory might have been already produced in answer to Parmenides and Zeno, and to Zeller the argument used by Melissus against motion, that it presupposes void and void cannot exist because what exists is full, was clear evidence of an acquaintance with atomic doctrine, which therefore must have preceded his own. Nestle followed him in supposing Melissus to be conducting a defence of Eleaticism against the atomists. The sequence would then be this. Before Parmenides the notion of a true void had not been grasped: the Pythagoreans for instance confused it with air. The arguments of Parmenides made such loose thinking impossible for the future, but concentrating as he did on the attributes of reality, it was only by implication that he denied the void. He does not mention it, but only says that what is is continuous and all is full of what is (fr. 8.23–5, pp. 31–4 above). The atomists saw the implications, brought them into the open and denied them. Consequently Melissus had to be equally explicit, mentioning void or emptiness by name and denying its existence.

It must be admitted that the sentence 'if there were many, they would have to be such as the One is' by no means proves that Melissus came first and the atomists took up his challenge. In the context of its argument it follows from one thing only: the immutability of what

refers to Anaxagoras's theory that perception was ἀεὶ μετὰ λύπης and involved πόνος. See Theophr. *De sensu* 29 (DK, 59, A92), Arist. *EN*, 1154b7, *EGP*, 326 (p. 318 below). This seems even more dubious.

[1] See, e.g., *EGP*, 335; KR, 306, 406, and p. 392 below.

exists. Even if we were right, he says, in supposing that the four elements, metals, living and dead, black and white, etc., had reality, our senses must yet be liars when they show us these phenomena as *changing*: if they were real, they would have to remain always the same. Then follows the sentence in question, in which he evidently has primarily, and perhaps for the moment solely, in mind the *immutability* of the One. If however one takes the sentence by itself and gives it its full universal content ('such as the One is *in every respect*') then it is not true that each atom fulfils the requirements, for the One is infinite in size and has no 'body' (i.e. limited and tangible bulk). The atoms are small and in the aggregate tangible.[1] It remains a possibility that the atomists may have been indebted to Melissus for the concept of the infinity of reality, although they applied it not to the individual 'ones' or atoms but to their aggregate and the space in which they moved. In both the Ionian and the Eleatic traditions it was probably a universal notion, consciously or unconsciously entertained, that the whole sum of existence was contained within a spherical boundary, with no need felt to ask the question whether anything lay beyond it. This may even be true of Anaximander. (See vol. 1, 85.) Yet if predecessors are necessary, infinite void could equally well have been developed by the atomists from Pythagorean ideas.

To conclude, certainty is difficult to attain when we depend entirely on internal evidence, and that in a fragmentary state. Even this however enables one to say with confidence that Melissus was already acquainted with the poems of Empedocles, though it is not sufficient to give a decisive answer to the question of priority between him and Anaxagoras or the atomists. All were alive and active during the same period. Ancient authorities were divided on whether Leucippus came from Miletus or Elea. If the former, the Samian admiral may well have known him. Whether he did, and whether he read the books of Leucippus's fellow-atomist from Abdera, we cannot hope to know at this distance of time. For the history of thought the important thing is that Melissus was firmly in the Eleatic tradition, whereas the atomists were post-Eleatic in the sense that they consciously reacted against Parmenidean doctrine.

[1] Calogero (*Studi sull'Eleat.* 83, n. 1) also sees no necessity to suppose that Melissus's sentence foreshadows atomism, and Lee (*Z. of E.* 113) calls it 'the famous fragment on atomism'.

II

IONIANS AND ELEATICS:
THE RISE AND FALL OF MONISM

Our next concern will be with the advocates of pluralistic systems, since the one remaining monist, Diogenes of Apollonia, wrote after them and with knowledge of their work. It may be worth pausing first to look briefly back on the development of monism.

Otto Gilbert, in an interesting article published in 1909, argued for a much closer relationship between Ionian and Eleatic monism than is usually conceded. Externally there is a remarkable geographical inter-locking: Xenophanes from Colophon, a near neighbour of Miletus, migrated to the West and probably taught Parmenides, and Melissus the 'Eleatic' came from Samos. Philosophically, Gilbert saw a strong affinity in fundamentals, ranging both schools on the same side against the common view of reality as a casual aggregate of independent things or substances. Both believed in an ultimate, ungenerated unity. This One was for the Ionians everlasting, divine, and co-extensive—indeed identical—with the world and all that existed. In the words of Diogenes, the last representative of this tradition (fr. 2): 'My opinion is, in sum, that all existing things are differentiated from the same thing and are the same thing', and this is the view attributed by Aristotle to the earlier philosophers in the same tradition, when he represents them (*Metaph.* 983 b 8) as positing 'that from which all existing things are, out of which they first come to be and into which they are resolved in the end, the substance persisting but changing in its affections'.

These thinkers, then, shared with their Eleatic critics the fundamental tenets that reality was one, ungenerated and everlasting, and in all probability alive and divine.[1] They did not, like the 'flowing philo-sophers' on whom Plato poured so much scorn, abolish the stability of Being for an endless flux of Becoming. They combined both Being and

[1] That the One was divine both to Ionians and Eleatics is taken as certain by Gilbert, and cf. p. 114 above.

Becoming, permanence and change, unity and plurality, identity and difference in a single system. So much is true of the Milesians. Heraclitus is a unique and complex case, but in spite of the *logos*-fire, his doctrines that strife was the condition of existence, opposites identical, and everything in continuous motion and change, were a powerful influence undermining Being in favour of Becoming. Xenophanes made the first move towards a stricter notion of unity which excluded altogether the possibility that the cosmos could have been generated. In Gilbert's belief his cosmic deity anticipated the Eleatic one by excluding any form of motion whatsoever. I have given reasons for doubting this (vol. 1, 382), but certainly he prepared the way for the transition from Ionian to Eleatic monism by his insistence that the one god who is the sum of all that exists is ungenerated and cannot move from place to place.

The achievement of Parmenides was to demonstrate by logical argument that Being and Becoming were mutually exclusive. The choice must be made, and its outcome was not in doubt: something must exist. 'It is'; therefore 'becoming and perishing have been driven afar off'. If Being excludes Becoming, and Being is one, all plurality is banished to the realm of deceptive appearance. The spherical shape of the one existent Parmenides retained from Xenophanes. The Eleatics (in words of Apelt which have been sufficiently confirmed in the previous pages) present us with 'the exaltation of the bare mathematical form of the world into its essential character', while at the same time 'it must be recognized that neither Melissus nor the other Eleatics succeeded in their underlying intention of completely freeing the abstract mathematical form from the conception of the material which filled it'.

The culmination of this train of thought was to deprive sense-perception of any contact with reality, and to demand acceptance of the paradoxical notion that nothing existed save a single undifferentiated entity—spherical (Parmenides) or of infinite magnitude (Melissus)—which filled all space (though their way of expressing this was that empty space did not exist), yet was intangible and invisible and only to be grasped by the intellect. For philosophy to rest there was impossible. Diogenes fell back on a reaction to earlier Ionian ideas which ignored the genuine advances in thought initiated by Parmenides. For those who could not emulate this ostrich-like procedure, there were only two courses open:

(i) Remaining, as the Eleatics had done, on a single plane of reality, to abandon monism for a plurality of ultimate physical elements, all equally real and everlasting, and construct a perceptible cosmos out of them. This evaded, without refuting, some of the logic of Parmenides, but respected it to the maximum consistent with preserving and explaining the sensible world.

(ii) To admit two grades of reality: the fully existent which was eternal, unchanging and intelligible as Parmenides had said, and the shifting world of the senses which could only be the subject of opinion, not of knowledge or intellection. Though not deserving the name of Being, it was yet not completely non-existent, but constituted a third class, not recognized by Parmenides, the world of Becoming, intermediate between Being and Non-being. In this way of escape from the Parmenidean dilemma lay much of the inspiration of Plato's thought.

III

EMPEDOCLES

A. INTRODUCTION[1]

The study of the Presocratic philosophers has a twofold interest. First, there are certain broad lines of development to be discerned. One may trace, for instance, the progress from a purely hylozoistic outlook to the emergence of a motive element separate from, and acting on, the rest, carrying with it the gradual separation of the spiritual from the material and a growing awareness of supersensible reality. From a different angle one may treat this purely as the problem of motion, investigating the causes leading to, and the consequences flowing from, Parmenides's bold denial of its possibility. Another leading motif is the change of emphasis from matter to form, or from a qualitative to a quantitative view of the world, in which the Pythagoreans played the leading role with their insistence on mathematical pattern as the essential element. On the subjective side there is an awakening sensitiveness to the limitations of human knowledge and in particular the inadequacy of the physical instruments of perception. With this goes the widening rift between reason and the senses and varying estimates of the trust to be placed in the latter. Alternatively one may concentrate on the methods of early philosophy and investigate its progress in logical thinking, to which the Eleatics had so much to contribute.

Secondly, however, the men themselves, as soon as they can be seen at all through the mists of tradition, stand out as strongly marked personalities each with an individuality and motives all his own. It is this, as much as the development of philosophy to which they contributed, that gives the subject its perennial attraction. It would be historically false, as well as less interesting, to consider them simply as links in a chain of intellectual progress. That is why it is best, without

[1] All the texts in the section of DK relating to Empedocles, both *testimonia* and fragments, are translated into Italian in Bignone's study *Empedocle*.

losing sight of themes and problems, to order a history of the period not *problemgeschichtlich* but under the names of its outstanding men.

To no one do these observations apply with such force as to Empedocles. He is indeed unique, one of the most complex and colourful figures of antiquity, about whom the judgment of critics has at all times been correspondingly diverse. Philosophically, he had paid serious attention to Parmenides and endeavoured to rescue the natural world from Eleatic denial. Yet he was deeply moved by a mystical view of the human soul in which he passionately believed, now groaning over its cruel fate as a fallen spirit, now triumphing in the assurance of his own imminent release from earthly woes and return to the joys of heaven. Critics are fond of quoting as Renan's the remark that he was 'un Newton doublé d'un Cagliostro', but this is hardly just either to Empedocles or to Renan.[1] When all allowance has been made for legend, he appears at once as philosopher, mystic, poet, political reformer and physician, with something of the magician about him and a corresponding touch of arrogance and showmanship, although sometimes, in relating the sins which involved him in the miseries of earthly life, he may seem to show an anguished humility. It is no wonder that many critics have tended to pick out one or another side of his character and dismiss the rest as unimportant or unhistorical. But if the combination seems improbable, we need a scholar like Kranz to remind us (however obvious it may sound) that 'we are in a quite different age from our own', the age which Nietzsche called the tragic, and others have called the lyric or romantic age of Greece. This is the significance of Empedocles: one of the most remarkable individuals of any period,

---

[1] Diels used the phrase to support his theory of two distinct periods in Empedocles's life, claiming that it was impossible to be both at once. It might be fairer to compare the religious side of Empedocles with Newton's own interest in alchemy and the prophecies of Daniel: he has been called 'the first modern scientist and the last of the mages' (Andrade, *Sir I. Newton*, 133).

In fact however Renan found in Empedocles much that appealed to his own spirit of rationalism and liberalism, and few have praised him more highly. 'Empédocle', he wrote, 'ne cède à aucun de ces génies extraordinaires de la philosophie grecque anté-socratique, qui furent les vrais fondateurs de la science et de l'explication mécanique de l'univers.' There follow details of his scientific achievements, and only then does he add: 'Par d'autres côtés, ce Newton paraît doublé d'un Cagliostro', and mention his love of show and claims to miraculous powers.

In the 1870's Acragas had by no means forgotten its hero: 'Le parti libéral de Girgenti vit à la lettre d'Empédocle. Son image se voit à chaque pas; son nom est prodigué aux lieux publics à l'égal de celui de Garibaldi; à peine y eut-il un discours où sa gloire ne fût rappelée' (*Mélanges d'hist. et de voyages*, 103 f.).

he is yet one who could scarcely be imagined in any other society but his own, the world of the Western Greeks in the early fifth century B.C. 'So individualisiert sich seine Zeit in Empedokles.'[1]

A central problem in the interpretation of his remains arises from the fact that he wrote two poems, generally considered utterly different in character. One was given the title *On Nature*, which links it with the work of those who were trying to explain the natural world, according to their lights, on scientific and rational grounds. The other, called *Purifications*, is religious in content and purpose. It describes the pilgrimage of the spirit, banished by its own fault from the realms of the blessed to which it properly belongs, and doomed to undergo a cycle of incarnations in all manner of forms of earthly life; and it reveals the nature of the primal impurity and the means of expiation and return to the bliss of immortality.

Many have seen glaring inconsistencies between these two poems. At the least they are thought to reveal a wholly different spirit and intention, and many and various explanations have been proposed for this. They have been assigned to different periods of his life: when he wrote the second his beliefs and outlook had changed. Thus Bidez painted a romantic picture of the *Purifications* as written by a young man at the height of his powers and flushed with success in politics, medicine and the arts, addressing his fellow-citizens with the pride and assurance of an acknowledged and popular leader. Later, sobered by exile (there is some evidence that he was banished), he turned in solitude to the study of natural science, having presumably seen the folly of his earlier pretensions to magical or quasi-magical powers. Diels was equally convinced that the doctrines of *On Nature*, which he saw as 'wholly materialistic and atheistic', could not have been held at the same time as those of the *Purifications*; but he completely reversed their relationship. The *Purifications* is a later retractation, when the loneliness of exile had converted its author to a mystical faith. The language of Otto Kern is even more picturesque: Empedocles 'experienced his Damascus' when in South Italy he came in contact with mystagogues

---

[1] Hölderlin, *Grund zum Empedokles*. (The text of this is printed in Kranz's *Empedokles*, 315–26.) The words remain true even though no scholar would today accept Hölderlin's characterization of the period.

of the Orphic religious sect. Both these views depend solely on psychological probability, for there is no external evidence of the relative dates.[1]

Another view is that the two poems can well have been contemporary, but that Empedocles had, as it were, 'a religious view for Sundays and a scientific one for weekdays'. 'As a rule theology and natural science exist side by side in his mind quite independently.'[2] Scholars speak of 'watertight compartments' between science and faith in thinkers of this type.[3] Similar views are still held. 'Any attempt to synthesize his religious and scientific opinions', writes Dodds, 'is precisely what we miss in him.' Vlastos is unequivocal: from his own point of view as well as ours, the two pictures of reality presented by Empedocles 'remain not only heterogeneous but contradictory at crucial points; they admit of no rational, or, for that matter, even imaginative harmony.'[4]

Such critics sometimes adduce as parallels modern scientists who may be sincere believers in the Christian faith but make little attempt to bring their religious beliefs into intellectual harmony with what they have learned in the laboratory. Yet the idea of the conflict between science and religion, or of the religious-minded scientist who must forget what he knows in order to retain his beliefs, finds its place more easily in the nineteenth or twentieth century A.D. than in the lyric age of Greece. The surprising statement of Burnet, that 'all through this period there seems to have been a gulf between men's religious beliefs, if they had any, and their cosmological views', finds little support in the literature of the time. Indeed it is here above all, in the union of rational thought with mystical exaltation, that Empedocles sums up and

[1] No chronological conclusions can be based on the fact that Plutarch (*De exil.* 607 c, quoted by DK with fr. 115) introduces a quotation from the *Purifications* with the words ἐν ἀρχῇ τῆς φιλοσοφίας, though to say this is not to agree with the improbable conjecture of Bignone (*Emped.* 488) that Plutarch meant 'at the beginning of *Greek* philosophy'. Fr. 131 may contain a reference, in the *Purifications*, to the poem *On Nature*, thus showing the latter to have been written first. See Reinhardt in *CP*, 1950, 172–4.

The views outlined above are to be found in Bidez's *Biog. d' Empéd.*, Diel's article in *SBB*, 1898, and Kern, *Rel. d. Gr.* II, 146.

[2] Rohde, *Psyche*, 379. Cf. by contrast Cornford, *Princ. Sap.* 109. Yet Rohde's explanation of how this could be is interesting (pp. 382–4), and somewhat modifies his own earlier statement.

[3] 'Des cloisons étanches', Delatte, *Conceptions de l'enthousiasme*, 25. For reff. to some earlier 'separatists' see ZN, 1007–9.

[4] Dodds, *Greeks and Irrational*, 146; Vlastos, *PQ*, 1952, 120.

personifies the spirit of his age and race. Apollo was Greek and Dionysus was Greek. It was Greek to say with Pindar, Herodotus and the tragedians that man must know himself mortal and not seek to vie with the gods; and it was Greek to say of a dead man 'God shalt thou be instead of mortal'. We have perhaps been too long accustomed to equating 'Greek' with 'classical'. In admiring the exact proportions, the pure, formal beauty of the Parthenon (which we see without the garish colours that once adorned it), we think of its builders as the people of 'Nothing too much'; forgetting perhaps that the very place where these words were written up was also the scene of the nocturnal *orgia* of Bacchus where all restraint was abandoned in the emotional purgation of *ekstasis* and *enthusiasmos*—'outside oneself' and 'god in us'. The Hellenic mind has its romantic as well as its classical aspect, and both reach a climax without incongruity in the genius of this remarkable Sicilian.

All this must find justification in the detailed study which follows. There are two kinds of inconsistencies, those that must have been obvious to the writer himself and those that strike a scholar as he looks back from the intellectual level of a different civilization with quite other beliefs. Only those of the first kind could necessitate the chronological hypotheses of a Bidez or a Diels. It was the achievement in particular of E. Bignone in his book *Empedocle* to show that no such inconsistencies exist.[1] Those of the second sort seem glaring at first, but an imaginative effort, based on knowledge, to recapture the spirit of the age in which the poems were written may soften even these. If they do not completely disappear, it will not be surprising. There are several obstacles to a completely rational explanation of all Empedocles's ideas. The first is the fragmentary state of his remains. Next, since he was poet and mystic as much as philosopher, his system was probably not completely consistent by the canons of rationalism; moreover the doxographers, on whom we depend to fill the gaps, were prosaic individuals who would inevitably distort the poetic elements. Finally,

---

[1] For some other scholars who have taken a similar view, see the references given by Verdenius in *Mnemosyne*, 1948, p. 10, n. 9. Perhaps the contribution which showed the most insight until recently is that of Diès in *Le Cycle Mystique*, pt. 2, ch. 3. Now, however, we have a thoughtful and largely successful attack on the problem by C. H. Kahn in *Arch. f. Gesch. d. Phil.* 1960.

he himself acknowledged more than once the inadequacy of human faculties to fathom all the secrets of nature.[1]

Apart from actual inconsistencies of thought, some see in the poems vital differences of temper, mood and purpose. These impressions must always remain too subjective to be of much value. Thus Kranz, who has revived the view of Bidez, finds that the poem *On Nature* 'bears in itself the fire of youth'.[2] This evidently did not seem so to Diels, and it is in fact rather strange to find more 'fire' in this poem than in the *Purifications*. For Jaeger, 'as soon as the first lines of the *Katharmoi* [*Purifications*] strike our ear, we find ourselves in a realm where a completely different, mystico-theological style and type of thought prevail'.[3] Yet *On Nature* offers us passages like this:

Ye gods, hallow my lips and draw a pure stream from them, and thou, O much-wooed, white-armed maiden Muse, in so far as it is lawful for us creatures of a day to hear, escort me, driving from the house of Piety the chariot obedient to the reins,

and teaches of Love and Strife as the two forces universally operative in nature, saying of the one that it is 'she by whom men think kindly thoughts and do peaceful acts, calling her by the names of Joy and Aphrodite', and of the other that when all the elements have been merged by Love into a single sphere which is divine, then 'great Strife is nurtured in its limbs and leaps to its privileges as the time is fulfilled which is fixed for them in turn by a broad oath'.[4]

Is a 'mystico-theological' style lacking here? When intangibles like this are introduced, rational discussion must fail, and agreement be despaired of.

Above all it must never be forgotten that very few of the quotations are explicitly assigned by our sources to one poem or the other. Most of the distribution has been done by modern editors on the basis of

[1] There have been worse comments on Empedocles than that of Clara Millerd: 'The important thing in understanding him is to stop thinking at the right moment' (*On the Interpr. of E.*, 21).

[2] *Hermes*, 1912, 20. Cf. *Hermes*, 1935, 111–19. Kranz still upheld the priority of the *Purifications* in his book *Empedokles* (1949), and Reinhardt renewed the attack on it in *CP*, 1950, 172–7.

[3] *TEGP*, 133.

[4] Frr. 3.1–5, 17.23–4, 30, cf. p. 247, n. 3 below. Not only did a late writer (Menander or Genethlios, DK, A23) call the cosmologies of Parmenides and Empedocles 'hymns of nature', but Empedocles himself in the π. φύσεως speaks of his πόρος ὕμνων (fr. 35.1).

their preconceptions of the content appropriate to each, so that it is not unfair to say that they have to some extent reconstructed the poems for themselves.[1]

B. DATE AND LIFE

Although the years of Empedocles's birth and death cannot be determined with certainty, the general opinion is well founded that they must have been approximately 492–32.[2] That he lived to the age of sixty has the authority of Aristotle. Apollodorus put his *floruit* in Ol. 84 = 444–1, but as he also records that he visited Thurii 'just after its foundation' in 445–4, it appears that he is making that his datum and applying his rule-of-thumb that Empedocles was forty at the time. He was already politically active in the sixties, and Aristotle's statement that he was younger than Anaxagoras is narrowed by Theophrastus to 'not much younger'. There are grounds for dating Anaxagoras's birth at about 500.[3]

Being some 20–25 years younger than Parmenides, Empedocles could easily have been his pupil as later sources say. He evidently wrote before Melissus (pp. 115 f. above), but there is nothing in his work or Anaxagoras's to suggest that either knew of the other, and it is doubtful which had the priority.[4] Among his approximate con-

---

[1] This is an important point, for which see H. S. Long, *AJP*, 1949, 144f. Long notes that '24 of the 153 fragments can be apportioned between the two works with something approaching certainty'.

[2] So Zeller, ZN, 941 n. He was followed by Jacoby, *Apollod. Chron.* 271 ff.; Wellmann, *RE*, v, 2508; Diels, *SBB*, 1884, 344, n. 2; Kranz, *Hermes*, 1912, 20; Bignone, *Emped.* 296, n. 1; Burnet, *EGP*, 198, n. 2; Wilamowitz, *SBB*, 1929, 653 ('in the nineties'); Millerd, *Emped.* 5. There are no dissentients, though some are naturally more cautious. KR (321) draw only the tentative conclusion that his *floruit* must have been around the middle of the century.

[3] Died aged 60, Ar. *ap.* D.L. 8.52 and 74. For Apollodorus see *ibid.* See also Ar. *Metaph.* 984a11 and Theophr. *ap.* Simpl. *Phys.* 25.19 (DK, A7). The testimony of Eusebius (A8–10) is of far less weight. For Anaxagoras see p. 322 below.

[4] There is no agreement over the meaning of Aristotle's words at *Metaph.* 984a11 that Anaxagoras was τῇ μὲν ἡλικίᾳ πρότερος τοῖς δ' ἔργοις ὕστερος. The last words have been taken to mean (*a*) that he wrote later, (*b*) that his philosophy was inferior, (*c*) that it was superior (Breier and Bonitz: see the latter *ad loc.*). (*b*) was preferred by Alexander, though he admits that in other places Aristotle rates Anaxagoras's work the higher. Ross *ad loc.* thinks Alexander 'probably correct', although the literal sense of ὕστερος is 'quite possible'. Kahn (*Anaximander*, 163–5) has argued strongly for Alexander's interpretation. He thinks the chronological priority of Empedocles's work ruled out because at 984b15 Aristotle introduces the νοῦς of Anaxagoras as if it were the first appearance of a motive cause in philosophy, while Empedocles was the first to conceive it as double. I do not think we can draw such definite chronological conclusions from Aristotle's words, particularly as Anaxagoras was in fact the first to make a clean break between

temporaries were Protagoras the Sophist of Abdera, and at Athens Pericles and Sophocles, Socrates and Euripides. To some it seems almost incredible that a figure like Empedocles could have lived in the heyday of Greek rationalism, enlightenment and scepticism. 'We seem', wrote Freeman the historian of Sicily, 'to see a man of some former age, or else a man of some age as yet far distant, brought from his own world to act along with Pericles and Ephialtes in doing the practical work of the fifth century before Christ.' To Bignone too he seemed to belong to another world, the spiritual kin of Epimenides and Pherecydes, Pythagoras and Onomacritus, men 'wrapped by legend in a kind of penumbra of hieratic Oriental wisdom'.[1] But the atmosphere of his native Sicily bred such characters more easily than that of Athens. Only with his younger follower Gorgias of Leontini did the spirit of scepticism make itself felt in a Sicilian, and Gorgias was no stranger to the intellectual circles of mainland Greece.

Anyone who goes to Acragas, the great city that looks down from its height on the yellow river—so Empedocles himself described it, and Virgil's epithet *arduus* is carefully chosen—must feel pleasure that so vivid and dramatic a character was born and lived in so appropriate a setting. From the acropolis the ground falls steeply away, then sweeps up again into a long ridge, itself descending on the seaward side

---

motive cause and matter, whereas Empedocles, in Aristotle's view, involved it in the 'mixture' in an unsatisfactory way: αὕτη δ᾽ [*sc.* ἡ φιλία] ἀρχὴ καὶ ὡς κινοῦσα...καὶ ὡς ὕλη· μόριον γὰρ τοῦ μίγματος. It might have served Kahn's argument better to quote Plato's attribution to Anaxagoras of the statement that the moon gets its light from the sun as something ὃ ἐκεῖνος νεωστὶ ἔλεγεν (*Crat.* 409a). Since this and the eclipse of the sun by the moon were also known to Empedocles (pp. 196f. below), Plato's remark might seem to indicate the priority of Anaxagoras.

As an instance of non-chronological priority Kahn quotes Theophrastus *ap.* Simpl. *Phys.* 26.8 Πλάτων τῇ μὲν δόξῃ καὶ τῇ δυνάμει πρότερος τοῖς δὲ χρόνοις ὕστερος. This had already been quoted in a judicious note by Zeller (ZN, 1261, n. 2), who nevertheless concludes that Aristotle's words in themselves are not decisive, but that a comparison of doctrine suggests the priority of Empedocles. With this I agree. Even the one point which Zeller cites as tending in the other direction, namely that the constitution of matter in Anaxagoras might seem less advanced than that in Empedocles or the atomists, cannot seriously affect anyone who has appreciated the subtlety and ingenuity of the Anaxagorean theory. On the other hand the direct dependence of Empedocles on Parmenides for his premises, which he sometimes repeats in Parmenides's own words, is striking. To consider Empedocles before Anaxagoras is certainly the logical order. (Zeller's discussion of this question on pp. 1261–4 is still worth reading.) This is not to say that any of the fragments of Anaxagoras can show him to have been dependent on Empedocles. Gigon (who favours the same view as Kahn) has criticized this claim effectively in *Philologus*, 91, pp. 2f.

[1] E. A. Freeman, *Hist. of Sicily*, ii, 342; Bignone, *Emped.* 5f.

in sheer cliffs of considerable height yet much lower than the summit on which we are perched. On this ridge, in full view below us, stands the magnificent line of six great Doric temples, one of them the largest in the Greek world save only that of Artemis at Ephesus. Religion must have played a prominent part in the life of the Acragantines. Beyond the temples lies the sea, and 'seeing with the mind' (as Empedocles bids us) what is beyond reach of our eyes, we are aware of the opposite coast of Africa, whose swarthy inhabitants shared Sicily with the Greeks then and for many centuries later, and whose proximity accounts for much in the fiery and unstable character of Sicily and the Sicilians. 'Their cities teem with a mixture of peoples, and they change easily from one form of constitution to another.'[1]

The island was a home of chthonian cults, in which the affinity of man to his god takes a prominent place. (Cf. vol. 1, 197f.) With its fertile soil, it was 'sacred to Demeter and Kore', and claimed that 'these goddesses appeared first of all in the island, which was the first to bring forth grain on account of the goodness of the soil'. At Enna in the centre of the island was shown the spot where Pluto had risen up to carry off Kore–Persephone to the underworld, and the torches which the distracted Demeter carried in her search were lit at the fires of Etna.[2] In this cult the island claimed priority even over the Eleusinian mysteries and Athens. It was moreover open to the influence of Orphic and Pythagorean communities in South Italy, and it seemed appropriate to Pindar, in warning the tyrant of Acragas of the dangers of success, to mention the doctrine of transmigration as well as of punishments and rewards in the hereafter.[3]

In Empedocles's boyhood Acragas was at the height of its fame and power under the rule of the tyrant Theron (488–72). He must have been only a few years old when Theron with his son-in-law Gelon of Syracuse defeated the Carthaginians at Himera on the same day (so Herodotus says) as that other victory of Hellenism over barbarians at

---

[1] These words which Thucydides puts into Alcibiades's mouth (6.17.2), though aimed at furthering his own plans, are true enough. If πολιτῶν (E), rather than the πολιτειῶν of the other MSS., is what Thuc. wrote, the meaning is 'They are always changing their citizens and receiving new ones'.

[2] Diodorus 5.2–5. Pindar (*Nem.* 1.13) says the island was the gift of Zeus to Persephone.

[3] Pind. *Ol.* 2.56ff. Bowra, and cf. the remarks on Thurii, pp. 131 f. below.

Salamis. The wealth and vigour of the city were advertised in Greece itself by a series of victories at the great games, for its horses were famous; but culture was not forgotten and the tyrant was an active patron of music, poetry and medicine.

Within a year after Theron's death the tyranny, in the person of his unworthy son Thrasydaeus, was overthrown, and Acragas became a no less vigorous and prosperous democracy (Diod. 11.53). In this political transformation Empedocles played a leading part. He himself came of a wealthy and aristocratic family. His grandfather had won a horse-race at Olympia, and his father Meton seems to have been instrumental in preventing a return of tyranny (D.L. 8.51, 72). Following in his footsteps Empedocles became a champion of democracy, and dissolved an oligarchic organization known as the Thousand (*ibid.* 66). He is said to have persuaded the Acragantines to abandon party strife and cultivate political equality, and for his own part to have refused the offer of a kingship. But his democratic ideals, and perhaps also his methods (for some of the stories collected by Diogenes, even if legendary, suggest at least a reputation for impetuosity), made enemies. These took advantage of his absence abroad to oppose his return, and he died an exile in the Peloponnese.[1]

His visit to Thurii is attested by a contemporary, Glaucus of Rhegium.[2] This city, founded on a Panhellenic basis under Athenian auspices, attracted many famous men, and it is interesting, as Kranz remarks, to think that there Empedocles could have met intellectual leaders from all parts of Hellas, men like Protagoras, Herodotus, and the town-planner Hippodamus. Perhaps more important in relation to his teaching is the fact that his travels should have taken him to a

---

[1] This at least is the most probable of a number of versions of his death (D.L. 8.67). The story of his leap into Etna, *deus immortalis haberi dum cupit* (Horace, *A.P.* 464), only to be betrayed by his sandal, perhaps goes back to Heraclides Ponticus (D.L. 8.69, Heracl. fr. 85 Wehrli), as does another more favourable to the divine status to which he in fact laid claim in fr. 112. After a sacrifice he disappeared, and a servant told how in the middle of the night he had heard a great voice call 'Empedocles', and seen an unearthly light; whereupon his disciple Pausanias ordered that divine honours should be paid to him (D.L. 8.67, Heracl. 86 W.).

The offer of kingship is reported by D.L. (8.63) from Aristotle, and the authority of Xanthus, whom Aristotle is quoting, takes it back to Empedocles's lifetime. On the historicity of this and the story of the dowries (D.L. 8.73), see Bignone, *Emped.* 78 and 82, n. 1.

[2] Cited by Apollodorus (D.L. 8.52). More precisely, Glaucus was said to have been contemporary with Democritus (*ibid.* 9.38).

centre of Pythagorean and Orphic influence. Croton, the 'capital' of the Pythagoreans, under a Pythagorean general conquered Sybaris, on the site of which Thurii was founded (vol. 1, 176); and four of the Orphic tablets, assuring the dead initiate that he has put off mortality and become an immortal god, were found in Thurian graves.

It was said that during his stay in the Peloponnese he spent some time at Olympia, and that his *Purifications* was recited there by a rhapsode named Cleomenes.[1]

C. PERSONALITY: HEALER AND WONDER-WORKER

Of his personal character something has already been said. There are no contemporary accounts, but those of later writers agree well with the impression gained from his poems. Timaeus remarked (D.L. 8.66) that his political egalitarianism seemed in strange contrast to the egotism and boastfulness revealed in his poems. With that went a certain *panache*, a love of colour and pageantry. He liked to walk about with a grave expression, wearing a purple robe with a golden girdle, a Delphic wreath, shoes of bronze, and a luxuriant growth of hair, and attended by a train of boys. In his own poems he speaks of himself as honoured and revered by men and women, among whom he moves garlanded with ribbons and fresh foliage.[2]

Among the gifts which, he says, men and women implored of him was 'to hear the word of healing for all sorts of diseases' (fr. 112.9–10), and to his pupil he promises to impart knowledge of 'all drugs that exist for ills and old age' (111.1). His work is pervaded by a keen interest in the organs of the body and their functions, and later writers mention him as a doctor and the founder of the Sicilian medical school. Its most famous representative, Philistion the contemporary of Plato, followed Empedoclean doctrine in more than one respect.[3] At this time medicine was not separated either from philosophy on the one hand

---

[1] D.L. 8.66 and 63, Athen. 14.620d (DK, A12). E. Mensching (*Favorin*, 93) points out that if the recitation of Olympia is a fact, the *Purifications* will belong to Empedocles's later years, since this was a customary way of making a new work known.

[2] Favorinus *ap.* D.L. 8.73, Aelian in DK, A18, Emped. fr. 112.

[3] Satyrus *ap.* D.L. 8.58, Pliny and Galen in DK, A3. For Philistion see Wellmann, *Frr. d. gr. Ärzte*, 1, 69f. As to regarding Empedocles as the actual founder of a medical school, caution is enjoined by G. E. R. Lloyd in *Phronesis*, 1963, 121. But cf. pp. 216f. below.

or from religion and even magic on the other. 'Some', says Empedocles in the fragment just quoted, 'come in search of oracles, others to hear the word of healing...', reminding us that Apollo and Asclepius had the title *Iatromantis*, a single compound word meaning 'physician-seer' (Aesch. *Suppl.* 263, *Eum.* 62). The author of *De vetere medicina* castigates Empedocles, from the point of view of the more empirical Ionian school, for being of the philosophic type who believe that to cure diseases one must understand nature as a whole. But another Hippocratic treatise, *De victu*, adopted much the same amalgam of scientific and religious considerations as he did.[1]

Although therefore Empedocles may have made serious contributions to physiology and medical theory, these are not to be rigidly separated from his fame as a wonder-worker which has brought to the lips of many modern critics the word 'charlatan'. He promises his pupil not only remedies against ills and old age, but in the same passage the power to raise the dead, as well as to control the winds and make or banish rain. Some stories told of his prowess will illustrate his reputation and the difficulty of assessing it. Diogenes (8.70) had read that the nearby city of Selinus had suffered an epidemic caused by pollution of their river. Empedocles by diverting two neighbouring streams into it cleared its waters and stopped the plague. This is a perfectly credible story, in harmony with his evident interest in the application of science and technology to the amelioration of human conditions. That the plague at Selinus was historical is confirmed by contemporary coins.[2] Yet because the story ends by saying that the Selinuntines in their

[1] *VM*, 20, I. 620 Littré (DK, A71). For *De victu* see the remarks and translation in Bignone, *Emped.* 652 ff., esp. bk. IV (659 ff.).
[2] Head, *Hist. Num.* 167 f., and more fully in *Coins of Ancient Sicily*, 83 f.; B.M. Guide to Greek Coins nos. 52 and 53 on pp. 28 f. and pl. 16. One coin shows on the obverse Apollo, with Artemis, shooting an arrow from his bow (as symbol of pestilence, cf. *Il.* 1.43–52); on the reverse the river-god Selinus sacrificing before an altar of Asclepius (identified by a cock). The other has (obv.) Heracles fighting a bull, and (rev.) another river-god Hypsas sacrificing at a serpent-entwined altar, with a marsh-bird and celery-leaf (emblem of Selinus). 'These coins thus supplement each other, and in their curious fulness of detail form a most illuminating commentary on the dry statement of the ancient biographies of Empedocles' (Head). W. Fuchs (*Mitt. des Deutsch. Arch. Inst., Röm. Abt.* 1956, 115) suggests that the new temple was dedicated to Hera Telaia after the city had been purified by Empedocles, in 466. (Some scholars doubt the existence of a cult of Asclepius in Sicily as early as this. Head in the second edition of his *Hist. Num.* 1911, replaced his name by that of 'Apollo (?) the healer', but reverted to Asclepius in the B.M. Guide. The cock certainly suggests Asclepius rather than Apollo, but for our present interests the point is immaterial.)

gratitude honoured Empedocles as a god,[1] some scholars dismiss it as an invention arising solely from his own claim to divine status.

He was also reputed to have kept a woman alive for thirty days without breath or pulse. It is natural to connect this with his claim to revive the dead, and its source, Heraclides (see D.L. 8.61), was certainly capable of fancy; but some have defended the tale as that of a cataleptic. Another butt for sceptics is the story, as told by Timaeus (D.L. 8.60), that when the etesian winds were damaging the crops he had bags made of asses' skins and stretched out on high points to catch the winds. Catching the wind in bags is a magician's trick well known from the story of Aeolus in the *Odyssey*, and the story is suspected of having grown out of his own claim in fr. 111 to control them. If however what he erected was a screen or windbreak the device becomes a practical one, and many have earned a reputation for magic by being a little ahead of their contemporaries in invention and initiative. Plutarch indeed says simply that Empedocles walled up a gorge through which unhealthy winds were blowing.[2] His study of nature seems to have had the ulterior aim of controlling her, which he shares with modern scientists more than with most Greek thought, even though at the time it was inevitable that in the means employed no distinction should be made between the natural and the magical. He is fond of explaining natural phenomena by analogy with human arts and crafts, speaking in his poems of the mixing of paints (fr. 23) and of dyeing (fr. 93), comparing the motion of the blood to that of water in a clepsydra (fr. 100) and the hot springs of volcanic Sicily to artificial heating systems (Seneca in A68).

D. WRITINGS

The only writings of Empedocles of which we have any knowledge are the poem on nature and the *Purifications*, though others were more

---

[1] προσκυνεῖν καὶ προσεύχεσθαι ὡς θεῷ. This perhaps goes further than the familiar θεὸς δ' ὡς τίετο δήμῳ of Homer, but the spontaneous paying of divine honours to a man as σωτήρ, though rare in the classical period, is not unknown (*e.g.* Dion and Lysander, Plut. *Dion*, 46, *Lys.* 18).

[2] Plut. *De curios.* 515c, DK, A14. This you may call, according to choice, a transparent rationalization of an earlier legend or the historical basis on which the legend was erected. Caution is enjoined by the remarks of Nilsson on the use of hides in weather-magic (*Gr. Feste*, 6). On all three stories see ZN, 943 n., Bignone *Emped.* 72, n. 2.

or less plausibly ascribed to him.[1] He had a reputation as an orator and teacher of rhetoric (Aristotle called him the inventor of the art, D.L. 8.57), and Gorgias, also a Sicilian, was his pupil;[2] but unlike his fellow-islanders Corax and Tisias he is not credited with any treatises on the subject. No doubt he taught by example rather than precept, for both his career and some of his poetry support the ancient verdict that he was an outstanding orator.

Diogenes (8.77) says that the poem on nature and the *Purifications* together amounted to 5000 lines. This number should probably be smaller, as it is likely that the first was contained in two books (rolls), and the latter in one.[3] Even so, and although we possess more of the text of Empedocles than of any other Presocratic philosopher, the surviving portion is very small, amounting to no more than 450 lines in all.

He wrote in the epic tradition, keeping the hexametric metre and to some extent the language. But his style has a marked individuality, and gives the impression that he is not, like Parmenides in the main part of his work, forcing hard, dry logic into an alien mould, but using a medium that comes naturally to him as the best vehicle for his thought. In the extensive use of similes he follows Homer, but the similes themselves are practically all drawn from the sphere of human

[1] Aristotle in the π. ποιητῶν mentioned a poem on the expedition of Xerxes, a prooimion to Apollo (both of which were said to have been burned by Empedocles's sister), and tragedies. Of the tragedies, Hieronymus of Rhodes said he knew 43, Neanthes 7, while Heraclides Lembos declared them spurious. See D.L. 8.57–8. A medical work in 600 lines is recorded by D.L. (8.77; cf. the Suda, DK, A2). Diogenes also credits him with epigrams, the genuineness of which was defended by Diels, *SBB*, 1884, 362, n. 1.

[2] For authorities see Burnet, *EGP*, 201, n. 2 and Classen in *Proc. African Class. Assocs.* 1959, 37 with notes.

[3] The evidence is very dubious. The Suda (A2) says that the π. φύσεως was in two books amounting to about 2000 lines. Tzetzes however (on fr. 134) speaks of a third book on nature. There is no hint that the Καθαρμοί ran to more than one book, and for this 3000 lines would be an impossible length. Diels therefore (in *SBB*, 1898, 396ff.) wished to emend the text of D.L. to make a total of 3000 for both poems (πάντα τρισχίλια for πεντακισχίλια). He argued that the third book was a myth, Tzetzes's quotation being in fact from the Καθαρμοί. Many scholars followed him, but Bignone (*Emped.* 106, n. 4, 632–4) thought the error more likely to lie in the Suda, and accepted the combined total of 5000 lines, with three books for the π. φύσεως.
  Neither the Suda (c. A.D. 1000) nor Tzetzes (twelfth century) is a particularly reliable source. As for Diogenes, DK (1, 282 n.) say that the source of his figures is Lobon, a man best known for his forgeries. So it seems we must remain in the dark about the precise length of the poems. I do not know the basis of Kranz's remark (*Emped.* 26) that the Καθαρμοί may have amounted to no more than 500 lines.

contrivance (in addition to those mentioned at the end of the last section we have baking, cheesemaking, a wheel, a lantern, the alloying of metals) and employed to illustrate general laws.[1] Effective use is made of condensed or telescoped similes achieved by the transferred use of a word in a short phrase: he speaks of the harbours of love, the shore of life, the melting-pots of earth; life is drawn off with a sword and water cut from a fountain; Aphrodite unites with pegs or dowels of love; we wear a garment of flesh.[2] The poetic effect is only heightened when we know that such phrases can be an imaginative expression of what was to Empedocles a fact, the unity of all living organisms. For him it is more than metaphor when he speaks of the ear as growing a sprout of flesh, of olives bearing eggs, of the sea as the sweat of the earth, of arms as branches. The underlying thought becomes explicit in a quotation preserved by Aristotle (fr. 82) in which Empedocles says that hair, leaves, feathers and scales are 'the same'. So too since the first men and women grew out of the earth they are called 'shoots from the realm of night'. Plutarch showed himself a perceptive critic when he wrote (*Qu. conv.* 683e, see fr. 148): 'It is not his habit to decorate his subject-matter, for the sake of fine writing, with pretty epithets like bright colours, but rather to make each one the expression of a particular essence or potency.'

He was impressed with the difficulties of composition with such a complex theme on his hands, and self-consciously explains his chosen method. This involved an elaborate interweaving of arguments by going back on his tracks, putting things in a different way, repeating lines and half-lines in new contexts. So we have fr. 24, of which the most probable translation is something like: 'fitting the heads of my tale into one another, not to traverse a sole and single path'.[3] At 35.1, using a metaphor from irrigation, he announces: 'But now I shall return again to the path of song which I set forth before, channelling off discourse from discourse, thus...', and again at 17.15: 'As I said before when making known the limits of my discourse...', followed

---

[1] On Empedocles's use of simile see especially Snell, *Disc. of Mind*, 213 ff. and pp. 476–9 of Solmsen's interesting article *Nature as Craftsman* in *JHI*, 1963.

[2] Frr. 98.3, 20.5, 96.1, 138, 143, 87, 126. On the σαρκῶν χιτών see also p. 254, n. 1 below.

[3] Cf. Bignone, *Emped.* 418, who however seems to extract rather much from the words. With κορυφαὶ μύθων cf. λόγων κορυφαί in Pind. *Ol.* 7.69, *Pyth.* 3.80.

by a repetition of the first two lines of the fragment. 'It is good', he assures us (fr. 25), 'to say even twice what has to be said', and one of his devices is to recall what he has said in one connexion by repeating a line or half-line in a different context. Similar repetitions occur in Homer, but Empedocles gives new point to the ancient literary practice.[1]

A difference between the two poems appears in the fact that *On Nature* is addressed by name to a single person, his favourite pupil Pausanias: 'Listen Pausanias, son of wise Anchitus' (fr. 1). This puts it in an old tradition of admonitory poetry, of which the best known examples are Hesiod's *Works and Days*, addressed to his brother, and the elegiacs of Theognis written for the instruction of Cyrnus. Empedocles goes further than these. In fr. 111, in which he promises that his pupil will learn the cures for all diseases, have power over the weather and even conquer death, he states emphatically: 'For thee alone will I do this'; and he even enjoins secrecy, 'in the Pythagorean manner' as a speaker in Plutarch says when quoting fr. 5: '...to keep within thy dumb heart.' The seriousness of such an injunction, as with the Pythagoreans, is hard to assess: Kranz concluded that Pausanias only gave the poem to the world after his master's death.

The *Purifications*, on the other hand, are almost shouted from the rooftops. They begin (fr. 112):

Friends, who dwell in the great city looking down on yellow Acragas, on the heights of the citadel, intent on fine works, honoured refuge of strangers, unacquainted with want, I give you greeting!

and adjurations in the plural are scattered through the fragments, contrasting with the second person singular of the other poem. It is interesting that the personal and confidential form of address is employed for what we should regard as the more scientific part of his writings, whereas the rules for a religious life and the doctrine of the *daimon*, imprisoned in a series of mortal bodies until it finally wins purification and freedom, are proclaimed openly to the citizens of Acragas. This is in keeping with what we know of Pythagorean tradition, which contains hints that mathematical discoveries were

[1] Cf. Bignone, *Emped.* 220f., 602f., with examples listed 602, nn. 3 and 4; J. Souilhé, *Arch. de Philos.* 1932, 340.

more jealously guarded than the doctrine of transmigration. (Cf. vol. 1, 149, 153.) It should however be clear by now that any attempt to differentiate between *On Nature* and the *Purifications* as respectively a scientific and a religious poem is an over-simplification. Nor must it ever be forgotten how few of the fragments can be assigned with certainty to one poem or the other (pp. 127 f. above).

E. ESCAPE FROM PARMENIDES: THE FOUR ROOTS

The poem on nature contains several deliberate echoes of Parmenides. Most of these are used to emphasize points of agreement, though in one instance his words are recalled only to be denied. In speaking of an ultimate plurality, which will make a physical world possible, Empedocles commands his disciple (17.26): 'Hear thou the *un*deceiving order of my discourse', an obvious echo of Parmenides 8.52.[1] He is no believer in the infallibility of the senses. They are feeble instruments, but so is the mind (*nous*), and man can scarcely hope for certainty.

(Fr. 2) Narrow are the powers that are spread through the body, and many the miseries that burst in, blunting thought.[2] Men behold in their span but a little part of life,[3] then swift to die are carried off and fly away like smoke, persuaded of one thing only, that which each has chanced on as they are driven every way; yet each boasts that he has found the whole. So little are these things to be seen or heard by men, or grasped by the understanding. Thou then, since thou hast turned aside to this place,[4] shalt learn no further than mortal wit can reach.

---

[1] κόσμον ἐμῶν ἐπέων ἀπατηλὸν ἀκούων Parmenides.

συ δ' ἄκουε λόγου στόλον οὐκ ἀπατηλόν Empedocles.

[2] This line is repeated with small variation at 110.7.

[3] Text doubtful. I have translated δ' ἐν ζωῆσι βίου with DK. The MSS. of Sextus have δὲ ζωῆσι βίου. ζωῆς ἀβίου Scaliger, Burnet, Bignone. ζωῆς ἰδίου Diels.

[4] The force of these words, presumably addressed to Pausanias, is not obvious: Diels wished to take them literally as a reference to the fact that Pausanias is sharing Empedocles's exile. Rohde offers an entirely different (and it must be admitted, unlikely) suggestion (*Psyche*, Eng. tr. 406, n. 96): he believes the words are addressed to Empedocles himself by the ψυχοπομποὶ δυνάμεις which are mentioned by Porphyry in connexion with fr. 120, and mean 'since you have strayed to this earth from the soul's proper abode'. The sense may be quite unexciting—'since you have left others and come to me for instruction'—and the choice of words prompted by the echo of a Homeric ending δεῦρο λιάσθης (*Il.* 22.12). But Rohde's sense (with the correction that the words are addressed by Empedocles himself to Pausanias) gives the best connexion with the following clause: 'Since you have come down to earth, you cannot go beyond a mortal's understanding.' On the verb see H. Fränkel in *Antidoron*, 275–7. He translates: 'Du hast dich von dem Schwarm der gewöhnlichen Menschen abgesondert.'

This is reminiscent of the way in which Alcmaeon and Heraclitus recognized the limitations of human thought (vol. 1, 344, 413). In spite of it, Parmenides's outright condemnation of the senses is countered by the claim that all alike are aids to knowledge and none is to be preferred.

(Fr. 3.9) Come now, observe with all thy powers how each thing is clear, neither holding sight in greater trust compared with hearing, nor noisy hearing above what the tongue makes plain, nor withhold trust from any of the other limbs [organs, parts of the body], by whatever way there is a channel to understanding, but grasp each thing in the way in which it is clear.[1]

More commonly however the language of Parmenides is recalled to show how far Empedocles is prepared to go with him. He accepts the statements that nothing can come out of nothing and that what exists cannot perish; the sum of being is constant.

(Frr. 11 and 12) Fools—for they have no far-reaching thoughts, who suppose that what formerly was not can come into being or that anything can die and perish wholly. For there is no means whereby anything could come to be out of what in no way is, and it cannot be brought about or heard of[2] that what is should perish. Wherever one may thrust it, there it will always be.

We have also (fr. 17.32f.):

But what could increase this All? Whence could it come? And how also could it perish, since nothing is empty of these things?

The last words hint at the denial of void, which is more explicit in frr. 13

Nor is any part of the All empty nor yet overflowing,

and 14

Of the All, none is empty; whence then could anything enter it?

---

[1] Contrast Parm. 7.3ff. Other interpretations of these lines, claiming to see in them an antithesis between reason and the senses, are mentioned by Millerd, *Emped.* 25, n. 2. Karsten's punctuation with full stop after νοῆσαι (v. 12), thus separating ἄλλων from γυίων, is highly unnatural. As Millerd says: 'νόει here means simply "apprehend" and implies no distinction of knowing from perceiving with the senses. We are told to apprehend each thing by its appropriate means.'

[2] Reading ἄπυστον (Mangey) with DK. The fr. is quoted both in *MXG* (with ἀπρηκτον) and by Philo (with ἄπαυστον). For ἄπυστον cf. Parm. 8.21, and for an elaborate defence of ἄπαυστον see Bignone, *Emped.* 398f. It is also retained by Rostagni (*V. di P.* 264, n. 2), but his notion that the adjectives qualify ἐξαπολέσθαι is scarcely credible.

So far Parmenidean logic is inescapable. What is real cannot come to be or perish, and it is everywhere, since to admit emptiness is to concede the reality of what is not. But from this Parmenides had deduced two further conclusions—that reality was a unity and that it was immovable—which Empedocles did not find so compelling. By denying them, the more fundamental principles might be observed, without taking away all reality from the physical, perceptible world.

(Fr. 8) I shall tell thee another thing: there is no birth of any mortal things, nor any end in baneful death, but only mingling and separation of what is mingled; birth is the name given to these by men.[1]

Parmenides was right in denying that a plurality could ever be derived from an ultimate unity; but what if there was no ultimate unity, but a plurality of primary entities which had always existed? It is time to give up the tenet on which all cosmogony and cosmology had hitherto been openly or tacitly based, but which had been shown by Parmenides to lead logically to the abolition of cosmogony and the annihilation of phenomena: that is, the ultimate unity of all that exists. The new order is announced in fr. 6 (which is cited by Tzetzes as being from the first book 'On Nature'):

[1] φύσις more commonly meant 'constitution, permanent nature', but in this fr. has the sense which Aristotle explains as that of a verbal noun from φύω, 'as if the υ were long' (*Metaph.* 1014b16). He speaks again at *Phys.* 193b12 of φύσις ἡ λεγομένη ὡς γένεσις and in *Gen. et. corr.* (314b5) he interprets this very fragment in that way. Unfortunately he seems to have changed his mind, and in the 'philosophical dictionary' of *Metaph.* Δ, where he enumerates different senses of the word, he quotes the same fragment to illustrate φύσις as meaning ἡ τῶν φύσει ὄντων οὐσία (1014b35). This encouraged A. O. Lovejoy (*Philos. Rev.* 1909, 371 ff.) to argue that the point of the fragment must be that things other than the elements have no permanent nature but are always dying. He therefore took οὐδέ...θανάτοιο τελευτή to mean 'there is no end of death', i.e. death is always occurring, and maintained that to say there is no death of θνητά would be absurd. But in the light of phrases in the epic tradition, the genitive in θ. τελευτή can hardly be other than a defining one, and the phrase is a periphrasis for θάνατος. Cf. its use in Hes. *Scut.* 357, and θ. τέλος in *Il.* 3.309; also Mimnermus 2.6–7 Diehl.

Since Aristotle interprets the word both ways, his evidence must be discounted, but all other Greek testimony goes to confirm the interpretation that he gives in *Gen. et corr.* Plutarch writes (*Adv. Col.* 1112a): ὅτι γὰρ ἀντὶ τῆς γενέσεως εἴρηκε τὴν φύσιν, ἀντιθεὶς τὸν θάνατον αὐτῇ δεδήλωκεν ὁ Ἐ., thus showing that he regards both φύσις as equivalent to γένεσις and θ. τελευτή to θάνατος. So also Simpl. *De caelo* 306.3, *MXG*, 975b6. Empedocles can quite well have said that there is no (*real*) birth or death of (*so-called*) mortal things. This is what he believed, and the word θνητῶν is an implied rebuke. *Genesis* and death are only names for the process of mingling and separation of certain elements. Only Plutarch's interpretation makes good sense of the passage.

Burnet (see *EGP*, 205, n. 4) and Ross in his commentary on the *Metaphysics* followed Lovejoy. Heidel (*Proc. Am. Acad.* 1910, 98, n. 73), Heinimann (*Nomos und Physis*, 90), Kirk (*HCF*, 228f.) and Kahn (*Anaximander*, 23) take the view accepted here.

The Four Roots

Hear first the four roots of all things: bright Zeus, life-bringing Hera, Aidoneus, and Nestis who with her tears makes springs well up for mortals.[1]

The divine names here accorded to the elements are replaced elsewhere by plain language:

(Fr. 17.18) Fire and water and earth and the immeasurable height of air.

Indeed Empedocles has no fixed terminology, a fact of which the exigencies of metre probably offer no more than a partial explanation, the rest being the demand of the poetic imagination for concrete visual images. Fire appears also as flame and Sun (both Helios and Elektor the shining one, cf. *Il.* 6.513), water as rain and sea (both θάλασσα and πόντος), air as sky (Ouranos). (The Greek titles are listed in Gilbert, *Met. Theor.* 107, n. 3.)

Aristotle says (*Metaph.* 985 a 31) that Empedocles was the first to speak of four material elements, and his originality in this respect is usually granted without question. It is perhaps difficult to determine priority between him and the Pythagoreans, who certainly must have recognized the four elements before the end of the fifth century. (Cf. vol. I, 266 f.) Pythagorean influence on Empedocles was strong, as appears from the importance which he assigns to transmigration and abstention from flesh and beans; and it is noteworthy that he gives to his elements, as the source of all nature, the titles which the ancient Pythagorean oath applies to the tetractys. It 'contains the springs and root of everlasting nature',[2] and Empedocles calls the elements now the 'roots of everything' and now the 'spring of mortal things'. It also became clear in our examination of earlier thought (vol. I, 122 f., 313) that the conception of four primitive forms of matter was arrived at gradually rather than by a sudden inspiration. Its beginnings are in myth, and may be seen in the division of the universe in Homer (*Il.* 15.189 ff.) whereby the heavens fell to the lot of Zeus, the sea to Poseidon, and the misty darkness to Hades, while the earth was held by them all in common. From the earliest times it seemed to the Greeks that

[1] On the distribution of divine names between the elements see Additional Note (1) at end of section.
[2] πηγὴν ἀενάου φύσεως ῥίζωμά τ' ἔχουσαν. (See vol. I, 225.) Cf. Empedocles fr. 6.1 τέσσαρα τῶν πάντων ῥιζώματα and 23.10 θνητῶν...πηγήν. Rostagni (*V. di P.* 262, n. 2) concluded that the tectractys itself must have symbolized (among other things) the four elements. It is an attractive idea, for which, however, the positive evidence is slight.

the components of the world fell naturally into four main categories or states, whether one call them qualities or substances. The first philosophers had spoken of it as made up of the hot, the cold, the wet and the dry, or of substances in which these opposites manifest themselves: earth, water, air and fire. Heraclitus mentioned all four, in a passage which is only rejected by scholars on the ground of their own (*prima facie* improbable) belief that he did not recognize air (or rather *aer*, mist or vapour) as one of the main constituents of the world.[1]

If however one looks at Aristotle's mention of the four Empedoclean elements at a slightly earlier point in his account (984a8), it appears probable that the novelty with which he credits him is something slightly different and less disputable. With him for the first time the four take the rank of genuine *archai*: none is prior to any other, nor is there anything else more fundamental. Heraclitus may have mentioned them all, but he exalted the priority of fire; Thales and Anaximenes had promoted water and air respectively to be sole *arche* generating the rest; for Anaximander they came out of the *apeiron*, and for the Pythagoreans they were the final product of the One. All these rival claims had been made obsolete by the insistence of Parmenides that no unity can ever generate a plurality. Only by a plurality of equal and ultimate *archai* or elements can the phenomena be saved. Hence 'all these are equal and coeval, but each is master in a different province and each has its own character' (fr. 17.27f.). They are like Anaximander's opposites given an explicitly substantial character and with no *apeiron* behind them.[2]

[1] Cf. vol. 1, 453 with n. 2.

[2] Though standing mainly in the Italian tradition, Empedocles, it seems obvious, owed much to reflexion on the Milesian schemes. Suggesting that the four 'roots' are a development of the 'opposites' hot, cold, wet and dry, Reinhardt (*Parm.* 227) saw them as an extension of medical theory, especially that of Alcmaeon: the opposites that work in the human body (Alcmaeon fr. 4; see vol. 1, 346) have been extended to the whole of nature. This was also the opinion of Tannery, Gomperz and others. Millerd (*Emped.* 33) is critical of the idea that 'abstract qualities' like hot and cold could have furnished the origin of the theory. It would indeed be questionable if τὸ θερμόν, τὸ ψυχρόν, etc., had ever been regarded as 'abstract qualities', but this is surely not so. (Cf. vol. 1, 79.) In any case the origins of a major doctrine like this are complex. We may suppose that Milesian monism, Western medical theory, the compulsion to answer Parmenides, and the philosopher's own powers of observation all played their part.

Gomperz's note (*Gr. Th.* 1, 558f.) that the four elements occur in Hindu popular thought may incline one to suppose that they represent a universal human way of looking at the world. But to the Chinese it seemed equally natural to speak of five elements: fire, water, earth, wood and metal (Needham, *Science and Civilisation*, 11, 232ff.).

The Roots are True Elements

Although this doctrine of the four elements was dethroned immediately by Anaxagoras and the atomists, in a modified form it was restored as the basis of physical theory by Aristotle, whose tremendous authority supported it through and beyond the Middle Ages. In spite of the challenge of chemists like Boyle, it would commonly have been said even in the eighteenth century that the elements of bodies were earth, water, air and fire.[1] The change introduced by Aristotle was to suppose the elements capable of mutual transformation.[2] The theory of Plato's *Timaeus* also demanded this, but on a mathematical basis which in Aristotle's eyes was fanciful. Moreover for neither of these two were the 'elements' strictly elemental. Plato said that far from being letters, they were even more complex than syllables. They were only the most elementary form of perceptible substance. Behind them stood for Plato, with his Pythagorean ardour, the world of numbers and geometry, and for Aristotle 'prime matter' as a logically necessary postulate of change, though imperceptible and incapable of an existence unqualified by form.

The divine names given to the elements are not mere poetical ornaments. The way in which they are acted upon, as will appear later (pp. 156f.), shows them to be sentient. Indeed Empedocles carries the notion of the kinship of all nature so far as to say that nothing is without sense (frr. 103, 110.10). Being both sentient and everlasting, they are immortal, and so divine. 'The elements too are gods', reports Aristotle, and later the doxographers repeat that both the elements and their mixture (that is, the complete mixture in the Sphairos under the rule of Love) are gods.[3] Hylozoism may be modified, but its complete eradication is a gradual process, for its roots are old and deep, not only in previous philosophy but also in religion; and Empedocles, for all his intellectual gifts, was the reverse of irreligious.

[1] Thus J. F. Gmelin wrote, in his *Einleitung in die Chemie* of 1780, that we have 'very good reason to allow the name of elements to fire, water, air and earth, if we imagine them in their greatest purity'. (Quoted by F. A. Paneth in *Brit. Journ. for Philos. of Sci.* 1962–3, 146.)

[2] See *Gen. et corr.* bk. 2, ch. 6, where he points out the difficulties in which Empedocles involved himself by refusing to admit this transformation, and Additional Note (2), p. 146. On the consequences for alchemy see p. 148, n. 1.

[3] Arist. *Gen. et corr.* 333b20, Aët. 1.7.28 (DK, A32). This has been a subject of controversy in the past, but admits of no real doubt, as Bignone showed. For the older view see ZN, 961. Bignone quotes examples of the divinity of the elements from non-philosophical literature in *Emped.* 180, n. 4. They could be easily multiplied. It is difficult, for instance, to think of Gaia as anything but a goddess.

Empedocles

Additional Notes

(1) *The divine names of the elements* (p. 141)

The distribution of the divine names between the four elements has been in doubt since antiquity. (Fire is referred to less equivocally as Hephaestus in frr. 96 and 98.) Nestis alone is undisputed. She is obviously water, and the choice of such an obscure figure is explained when we learn from Photius that she was a Sicilian deity (Bignone, 542, n. 3). This Sicilian water-goddess cannot 'disappear from the scene' so easily as Kranz supposed (*Hermes*, 1912, 23, n. 1). According to him she is simply a personification of sobriety or temperance (*Nüchternheit*), and the word, as he says, occurs as early as Homer. There however it means 'fasting', as also in Aeschylus. Kranz seems to be thinking along the same lines as Hippolytus (A 33), who explains that water is the vehicle of nourishment without being itself nourishing; but the etymological connexion with νῆστις = fasting is not un-challenged. Bignone (542, n. 3) considered a more watery derivation (from ναίειν, cf. νῆσος), which had already been put forward by Simplicius (*De an.* 68.14), to be *evidente*. (See also ZN, 949, n. 1.) Moreover this 'Göttin Nüchternheit' is otherwise unheard-of, and it seems unlikely that Empedocles would put a new personification of his own alongside of popular gods like Zeus, Hera and Aidoneus.

Aidoneus, for Homer onwards an alternative form for Hades god of the underworld and the dead, would most naturally seem to represent the earth. So Aëtius (A 33) and most modern writers (e.g. Zeller, Diels, Bignone, Millerd). But Diogenes Laertius (8.76) identifies him with air, as do Stobaeus and Hippolytus. (See A 33.) The name means 'invisible', and Hippolytus argues that we see everything through air but cannot see air itself. Diels however (*Dox.* 89, and see Burnet, *EGP*, 229, n. 3) showed convincingly that whereas Aëtius represents the soberer tradition going back to Theophrastus, the others are based on a school of Homeric allegorists trying to reconcile Empedocles with Homer. Knatz in 1891 propounded the novel view that Aidoneus was fire, explaining the association of fire with the god of the underworld by reference to Sicilian volcanoes. This has no ancient authority, and in spite of the support of Thiele and Burnet (see *EGP*, 229, n. 3) is adequately refuted by Bignone (*Emped.* 543) and Millerd (31).

By Zeus all ancient authorities are agreed that Empedocles meant fire. Diogenes Laertius and Hippolytus call him πῦρ, and Aëtius (A 33) equates πῦρ with τὴν ζέσιν καὶ τὸν αἰθέρα. The latter phrase is repeated without πῦρ in Stobaeus, and could lead to confusion because whereas for these later writers αἰθήρ was equated with fire, in Empedocles himself it is an alternative name for air. (Cf. especially frr. 98, 100.5, 71.2, 109, also 115.9–11. For a possible reason for this see the quotation from Wightman on p. 225 below, and for the apparent exception in fr. 38.3–4 see p. 185, n. on *v.* 3.) Nevertheless, no scholars have tried to equate Zeus with air save those who, by allowing Aidoneus to usurp the place of fire, had put themselves under the necessity of finding another function for him. In the more philosophical poets like Euripides, who equated the gods with parts or aspects of the natural world, Zeus is spoken of as the fiery αἰθήρ of the upper heavens, beyond the dimmer spaces of ἀήρ. Empedocles doubtless had the same thought in mind.

The epithet φερέσβιος, life-bringing, applied to Hera immediately suggests the fruitful earth (γαῖα), which it describes in Hes. *Th.* 693 and *Hom. Hymn Apollo*, 341. Burnet remarked that it seemed only to be used of earth and corn. The epic associations led Diels to suppose that this identification too (made by Diogenes Laertius (8.76), Stobaeus and Hippolytus, A 33) was an error of the Homerists, but since Empedocles himself stood in the epic tradition the argument does not here seem so strong. It is also likely that Hera was, at least in origin, an earth-goddess (Guthrie, *Gks. and their Gods*, 68 ff.), though that may well have been forgotten by this time. The identification with earth is followed by Knatz, Thiele, Burnet and Kranz. On the other hand Aëtius (A 33) supposed that Hera is here the air, and this opinion has been held in modern times by e.g. Diels, Zeller, Bignone, Millerd. (See the arguments of Bignone, 543 f.) It is true enough that 'life-bringing' is a highly appropriate epithet for the air we breathe, though doubtful whether this would have weighed more with Empedocles than poetic precedent. Snell (*Philol.* 1943, 159 f.) argues from this epithet that Hera is the earth, and for Aidoneus as ἀήρ compares the epic Τάρταρον ἠερόεντα, etc.

Empedocles

If one must decide, it is perhaps safest to follow the Theophrastean tradition with Bignone and say that Zeus = fire, Hera = air, Nestis = water and Aidoneus = earth. Fortunately the question is of little importance for Empedocles's thought. It does however raise points of some interest for the history of Greek philosophical religion, and this note may serve as a starting-point for anyone who wishes to follow them up. Cf. also O. Gilbert's note, *Met. Theor.* 110, n. 2.

(2) *The immutable elements and fr. 26.2 (p. 143)*

The remains of Empedocles himself, as well as Aristotle's comments, leave no doubt that he conceived of the elements as immutable and indestructible. This was one of the cornerstones of his answer to Parmenides. But mention should be made of a difficulty which has been felt in connexion with the first two lines of fr. 26, which run:

ἐν δὲ μέρει κρατέουσι περιπλομένοιο κύκλοιο
καὶ φθίνει εἰς ἄλληλα καὶ αὔξεται ἐν μέρει αἴσης.

Simplicius quotes this fragment as coming 'a little after' fr. 21, and intends us to suppose that the subject is still the four elements. In any case much of the fragment is repetition of parts of fr. 17. Verse 1 = 17.29 (with the variant κύκλοιο for χρόνοιο) and *vv.* 5–6, 8–12 practically reproduce 17.7–13. And in fr. 17 it is quite clear that the elements are in question, or possibly in the latter part of the fragment the elements plus Love and Strife. These latter, however, can hardly be included here in view of *vv.* 5–6.

Simplicius (*Phys.* 160.14) thought that in *vv.* 1–2 Empedocles was asserting the mutual transformation of the elements, and in modern times too they have commonly been translated in some such way as: 'They perish into each other and grow out of (or originate from) each other.' Bignone (*Emped.* 533 ff.) avoids the difficulty by supposing that Empedocles is here making a concession to ordinary language as he admits to doing in fr. 9. Against this there is something in the argument of Verdenius (*Mnemos.* 1948, 12f.) that in fr. 9 he is speaking of the so-called birth and death of mortal creatures like animals and birds: he would not allow himself this language in speaking of the elements themselves. Still more to the point is Verdenius's reminder that the rendering involves a mistranslation of φθίνειν and αὐξάνεσθαι.

These words do not mean 'perish' or 'decline' and 'come into being': they mean 'grow smaller' and 'grow larger'. Plato and Aristotle were not inventing new technical uses when they distinguished αὔξησις and φθίσις both from γένεσις and φθορά and from ἀλλοίωσις. The sum total of each element is of course constant as are its qualities and functions (ἦθος and τιμή, fr. 17.28); but in any particular part of the cosmos they grow as particles of the same element come together, as described in fr. 37 αὔξει δὲ χθὼν μὲν σφέτερον δέμας αἰθέρα τ' αἰθήρ, and diminish as they are separated from their own kind and attached to another element—φθίνει εἰς ἄλληλα. (Cf. the use of πλήθει καὶ ὀλιγότητι in Arist. *Metaph.* 984a10.) Verdenius's suggestion that these words might mean 'in comparison with one another', as if εἰς were πρός, is surely untenable, and 'dwindle into one another' is not an impossibly condensed expression for what Empedocles was trying to say. On this view *v.* 1 does not necessarily refer to separate and successive world-periods; the elements 'prevail in turn' according to their varying proportions in individual things.

F. STRUCTURE OF MATTER: THE THEORY OF MIXTURE AND ITS RELATION TO ATOMISM

How by the mixture of water, earth, air and sun [fire] there came into being the shapes and colours of all mortal things that are now in being, put together by Aphrodite... (fr. 71).

The notion of elements has now for the first time acquired a definite meaning as forms of matter which are (*a*) ungenerated and indestructible, (*b*) qualitatively unalterable, (*c*) homogeneous throughout (fr. 17.35). In all this they are, as it were, the Parmenidean One multiplied by four, but in other respects they depart from that norm. Although Empedocles accepted the Eleatic denial of empty space, he did not admit as a necessary consequence that local motion was impossible. Given four substances instead of one, they could take one another's places, the last in a series of moving objects slipping into the place of the first, without needing empty space to move into.[1] With motion permitted, his

[1] See *MXG*, 976b22–9 (DK, 30 A 5). This is the motion later known as ἀντιπερίστασις, defined by Simpl. *Phys.* 1350. 32ff. (on Ar. *Phys.* 267a16), and exemplified by that of a fish through water (Strato fr. 63 Wehrli: Strato demonstrated it by the motion of a pebble in a sealed jar full

'beings' take on two characteristics denied by Parmenides to his single Being, which make the genesis of a cosmos possible: they are (*a*) in motion and (*b*) divisible. The latter is illustrated by fr. 22. 1–2: 'For all of these—sun, earth, sky and sea—are at one with their own parts which are scattered far from them in mortal things.' The divisibility and movement of the four 'roots' make it possible that 'there is no birth or death of mortal things, but only mingling and separation of what is mingled'. Apparent change is only rearrangement. 'There are just these elements', he writes, 'but by running through one another they alter their appearance: so far does mixture effect change' (21.13–14). Immediately after these lines Simplicius goes on to quote the picturesque simile of the painter's palette with which Empedocles illustrated the production of infinite variety out of the same few elements (fr. 23, Simpl. *Phys.* 160):

As when painters are decorating votive tablets, men well skilled and cunning in their craft, they take the various pigments in their hands, mixing in due adjustment more of these and less of those, and produce from them forms resembling all things, creating trees, men, women, beasts, birds and fishes that live in the water, yea and gods long-lived and highest in honours; so let not the falsehood subdue thy mind that there is any other source [i.e. than the elements] of all the countless mortal things that are plain to see.

The simile gains additional precision from the fact that Greek painters worked in terms of four basic colours (white, black, yellow, red), the same in number as the elements.[1]

of water). The importance of the idea that in a plenum circular or vortex-like motion is possible ('peas can move with the vortices of pea-soup') has been emphasized by K. R. Popper. Crediting it to Plato (though it must surely have been already in the mind of Empedocles) he writes (*Brit. Journ. for Philos. of Sci.* 1952, 147, n. 1): 'Plato's reconciliation and the theory of the plenum ("nature abhors a vacuum") became of the greatest importance for the history of physics down to our own day. For it influenced Descartes strongly, became the basis of the theory of ether and light, and thus ultimately, via Huyghens and Maxwell, of de Broglie's and Schrödinger's wave-mechanics.' (See also *idem, Conj. and Ref.* 81, n. 22. For the 'circular thrust' in Plato, see *Tim.* 80c τὸ δὲ κενὸν εἶναι μηδὲν περιωθεῖν δὲ αὐτὰ ταῦτα εἰς ἄλληλα, κτλ.)

[1] Democritus recognized these four colours as 'simple' (Theophr. *De sens.* 73, DK, 68 A135, p. 445 below), and ps.-Aristotle *De mundo*, 396b12 says it is by mixing these four that painters gain their effects. That Empedocles noted an actual correspondence between the colours and the elements is stated by Aëtius (1.15.3, A92), though Theophrastus criticizes him for allowing only for black and white in his explanation of the sense of sight. The eye is composed of fire (white) and water (black). How then, asks Theophrastus, if like is perceived by like, do we perceive mixed colours like grey? (*De sens.* 17, A86). He does not, as one might expect, raise the question in relation to the other two 'simple' colours, which leaves one in some doubt whether Aëtius was

It is not immediately obvious whether Empedocles was imagining matter as continuous and flowing or as made up of minute discrete particles; but without a particulate structure of matter it is difficult to picture the movements taking place as he describes them, and this was attributed to him in later antiquity from Aristotle onwards. Aristotle writes (*Gen. et corr.* 334a26):

What is the manner of change according to those who follow Empedocles? It must be like the putting together of a wall out of bricks and stones. Their 'mixture' must be of elements which persist, but are combined in small particles lying side by side.[1] In this way arise flesh and everything else.

So also, some centuries later, Galen (DK, A43, and cf. A34):

Empedocles too says that we and all other terrestrial bodies are made out of the same elements as Hippocrates names, not however fully blended with each other but lying beside and in contact with each other in small particles (μόρια).

Theophrastus (*De sens.* 11; DK, A86) had spoken of the nature of men in whom the elements are 'close-packed and broken up fine'.[2] The doxographers describe these particles in language suggestive of the atomists Leucippus and Democritus: 'Empedocles said that prior to the four elements were minimum particles (θραύσματα),

right to say that Empedocles recognized all four. (Cf. Diels, *Dox.* 222. Aët. 1.15.7 attributes four primary colours to Pythagorean theory also.) Certainly Theophrastus attributes them explicitly to no one before Democritus, but it is difficult to believe that the writer of fr. 23 did not have the four in mind.

The correspondence between elements and colours occurs also in Chinese thought. See Needham, *Science and Civilisation*, II, 238. It became an essential part of alchemy, both Western and Oriental. It should be noted, however, in case anyone should be tempted to see Empedocles as an ancestor of the alchemists, that if Aristotle had not overthrown his doctrine that the elements are indestructible and immutable, the basic theory of alchemy would have been impossible. On Empedocles's theory of colour see also Kranz in *Hermes*, 1912, 126–8.

[1] ἐκ σωζομένων...τῶν στοιχείων κατὰ μικρὰ δὲ παρ' ἄλληλα συγκειμένων. No other noun but 'particles' can well be supplied with the adjective: the μικρά correspond to the separate bricks and stones in the composite wall. The word μόρια itself is used by Aristotle at *De resp.* 473b3, where he speaks of πόροι in the body which are τῶν μὲν τοῦ σώματος μορίων ἐλάττους τῶν δὲ τοῦ ἀέρος μείζους. At *GC*, 325b5 he says that Empedocles was 'almost bound' to adopt the position of Leucippus that there are indivisible solid bodies.

[2] Cf. also Arist. *De sensu*, 441a4: water, according to Empedocles, contains in itself all flavours ἀναισθητὰ διὰ μικρότητα. Kranz (*Hermes*, 1912, 24f.) sees Empedocles's own terms for the smallest particles in the μέρη of fr. 96 (cf. μόρια in Galen) and the κέρματα which in fr. 101 are inhaled as scent by hunting dogs. μέρη is used again in fr. 22.1: the elements are ἄρθμια with their own μέρη (hence the attraction of like for like). Cf. ὕδωρ οἴνῳ μᾶλλον ἐνάρθμιον in fr. 91. Kranz's contention, though vigorously and dogmatically denied by Reinhardt (*CP*, 1950, 178), has much to be said for it. This is not of course to deny that when we get to Galen, his formulation of the two modes of mixture is made with reference to the Stoic κρᾶσις δι' ὅλου.

homoeomerous and as it were elements before the elements', and: 'He constructs the elements out of smaller bodies (ὄγκοι), which are the least of all and as it were elements of the elements.'[1] This may mean no more than that, for example, earth is an element but is composed of millions of minimum particles, each of which has all the properties of earth. If 'elements of the elements' means anything more, it is certainly wrong. Empedocles himself is emphatic that nothing must be thought of as prior to the 'four roots' with their inherent qualitative differences. Here he differs fundamentally from the atomists, who taught that the elements of everything are atomic bodies lacking all the sensible qualities (colours, sounds, flavours, smells) later to be known as 'secondary'. These resulted from the interaction of atoms from outside with those in our own bodies and were therefore subjective and arbitrary. Nevertheless the doxographers could scarcely have said what they did had there not been in Empedocles some evidence of 'least particles' such as Aristotle provides.[2]

The notion of the elements 'running through one another' was made more precise by the theory that they and their compounds contained microscopic (Arist. *Gen. et corr.* 324b30) passages or pores which might or might not admit the particles of other substances. It is most fully described in connexion with sensation (pp. 231 ff. below), but was also used to explain why some substances combined more easily

---

[1] Aët. 1. 13. 1 and 1. 17. 3 (DK, A 43). It would not be unlike the doxographers, with their unsubtle approach and zeal for conformity, to assimilate Empedocles's theory to the atomic, and if they did, it is possible to guess at the origin of this mistake. Asclepiades of Bithynia, a medical writer of the first century B.C., adopted a form of atomism based on that of Heraclides Ponticus. Both called their atoms ὄγκοι. Like the atoms of Democritus and Epicurus, they had no sensible qualities, yet Sextus (*Pyrrh. hyp.* 3.33) wrote of τοῖς περὶ Ἀσκληπιάδην...θραυστὰ εἶναι τὰ στοιχεῖα λέγουσι καὶ ποιά. (Cf. θραύσματα of Empedocles above.) The most reasonable explanation of this is given by Baeumker in *Problem d. Materie*, 326 n. By στοιχεῖα here Sextus means, not the ὄγκοι themselves, but the elements in the Empedoclean sense—earth, water, etc. For Asclepiades the ὄγκοι *are* στοιχεῖα πρὸ τῶν στοιχείων. Now Asclepiades in his theories also made great use of πόροι. We read for instance κατὰ τὸν Ἀσκληπιάδην στοιχεῖα ἀνθρώπου ὄγκοι θραυστοὶ καὶ πόροι. (Ps.-Galen 14.698 Kühn: whether he actually thought of the ὄγκοι as θραυστοί, and so not strictly atoms, is beside the present argument.) As Baeumker points out, the physical basis of Asclepiades's theories goes back not only to the atomists but also to Empedocles, and the confusion in the doxographic account probably owes something to this later combination of the two types of theory.

[2] Admittedly Aristotle's expression shows that he could find no explicit statement in Empedocles that the elements existed in the form of minimum particles. He was inferring from what he did find that Empedocles pictured them to himself in this way, and the balance of the evidence suggests that he was right. See also p. 152.

than others, for example water with wine but not with oil (fr. 91 and Theophr. *De sensu*, 12): it was a question of having 'pores' of the right gauge. 'Those substances can mingle whose pores are reciprocally symmetrical' (Arist. *Gen. et corr.* 324b34), or in Theophrastus's words, 'he accounts for mixture in general by symmetry of pores' (*De sensu*, 12).[1] Everything is continually giving off films or 'effluences'. A line of Empedocles on this subject has been preserved by Plutarch (*Qu. nat.* 916d, fr. 89):

Look at it in the light of Empedocles,

'Perceiving that there are effluences from all things that have come into being'.

Not only from animals and plants, or earth and sea, but also from stones, bronze and iron there is a continual and abundant outflow. Indeed it is this unbroken flux and movement which causes the destruction and perishing of everything.[2]

The doctrine is referred to by Plato (*Meno*, 76c), and Theophrastus confirms (*De sensu*, 20) that Empedocles invoked it as a cause of perishing or wasting away. 'If', he writes, 'wasting is caused by effluence, and scent also is a matter of effluence, things with the strongest scent ought to pass away the quickest.' His further criticism, that when Love is gaining there could be little or no sense-perception because objects would be drawing matter in, not sending it out, confirms what one would expect, that these effluences in our own world are due to the separating action of Strife. The actual entering of one body into another, through the pores, is according to Aristotle Empedocles's explanation of all action and passion in the physical world.

[1] Other examples: white particles fit the fire-*poroi* of the eye, black particles the water-*poroi* (Theophr. *De sensu* 7; DK, A86); films given off by iron press into the *poroi* of the lodestone (Alex., A89); nourishment from the earth fits the *poroi* of plants (Plut., see fr. 77).

Whether Empedocles himself used the word πόροι in this connexion is doubtful. In the surviving fragments we find various poetic equivalents, χόανοι or χοάναι in frr. 84.9 (as restored by Blass), 96.1, σύριγγες 100.2. But cf. 3.12 ὁπόσῃ πόρος ἐστι νοῆσαι. Since Empedocles attempted to explain thought, no less than sensation, on material lines, the word πόρος here can scarcely have the metaphorical sense which we naturally ascribe to it, and which it frequently has in other Greek writers. The brief statement of Philoponus (on *Gen. an.* 123.13; DK, A87) is not very informative. For Kranz's opinion see *Hermes*, 1912, 27, n. 2.

[2] Translating ὄλωλε as in DK. But Mr Sandbach points out to me that the MSS. of Plutarch have ὄδωδε, which may well be correct, not only as avoiding tautology but also in view of the reference to scent in Theophr. *Sens.* 20.

Aristotle was quick to point out the difficulty of reconciling this theory with the denial of void. His point that if the pores are full they are a superfluous hypothesis (*Gen. et corr.* 326b8) is, as a general criticism, captious, but in connexion with sensation they lead to serious difficulties which Empedocles does not seem to have faced. At present we may note simply that on this theory the elements must be constructed of parts which are never divided beyond a certain point, as otherwise everything could be fitted into everything else and there could be no question of an 'asymmetry' of pores. This too might be a consequence that he had not fully thought out, were it not for the positive evidence that he did regard matter as particulate in this way. That he was, seen through later eyes, a forerunner of the atomists without fully reaching their position is further borne out by Aristotle's remark (*De caelo*, 305a2) that he 'seems to mean' that the smallest body is 'divisible but will never be divided'. His particles remained physically intact although he had not advanced to the notion of theoretically indivisible magnitudes.[1] It is not surprising if the compilers of doxographies took him the whole way. He did in fact provide atomism with three of its fundamental tenets: the ideas of indestructible elements and smallest particles, and the reduction of all forms of change to mechanical mixture. They further took over and developed the theory that physical objects were constantly giving off films or 'effluences' (fr. 89) of microscopic particles, and used it as he did to explain sensation.[2]

G. LOVE AND STRIFE

We may now look at some passages of Empedocles at greater length and see the connexion of thought which they display. First comes one which Simplicius in one place describes as from 'the first book *On Nature*', and in another as coming 'right at the beginning'.

---

[1] Cf. the remarks of Luria, *Infinitesimaltheorie*, 136–8.

[2] The best account of the structure of matter in Empedocles is still that of Zeller, ZN, 954–60. See also Gilbert, *Met. Theor.* 107 n. 1, 120; Kranz in *Hermes*, 1912, 24f. and *Emped.* 46f., 83. Reinhardt's denial of a particle-theory (*CP*, 1950, 178) is arbitrary and ignores some of the evidence.

The foregoing discussion should have made it plain that the system of Empedocles must have preceded that of the atomists, and not *vice versa* as has occasionally been held in the past (e.g. by Diels; see Bignone, *Emped.* 248, n. 2).

(Fr. 17) I shall tell a twofold tale. At a certain time one alone grew (2) out of many, and at another it grew apart to be many out of one. (3) Double is the birth of mortal things and double their failing. (4) The one race is born and dies through the coming together of all things, (5) the other is nurtured and then vanishes as they scatter again. (6) They never cease thus to alternate continually, (7) now all coming together into one through Love, (8) and now again each one drawing apart by Strife's hatred. (9) Thus in that they have learned to grow one from many, (10) and as the one is divided turn into many again, (11) in this way they suffer becoming and have no steadfast life; (12) but in that they never cease from alternately coming together and separating, (13) they are for ever, unshaken on their circular path.

(14) But come, hear my discourse, for learning increases wisdom. (15) As I said before in disclosing the limits of my discourse, (16) I shall tell a twofold tale. At a certain time one alone grew (17) out of many, and at another it grew apart to be many out of one: (18) fire and water and earth and the immense height of air, (19) and cursed Strife apart from these and equal in every respect, (20) and Love among them, equal in length and breadth. (21) Her must thou see with the mind, nor sit with eyes bemused: (22) she it is who is acknowledged to be implanted in the limbs of mortals, (23) whereby they think kindly thoughts and do peaceful works, (24) calling her Joy by name and Aphrodite. (25, 26) No mortal man is aware of her as she circles round among these [i.e. the elements and Strife], but do thou listen to the unfolding of a discourse that is not deceitful. (27) All these are equal and coeval, (28) but each is master in a different province and each has its own character, (29) and they prevail in turn as time circles round. (30) And besides these nothing comes into being nor ceases to be. (31) If they were continually perishing, they would no longer be; (32) and what could increase this All? Whence would it come? (33) And how also could it perish, for nothing is empty of these things? (34) No, there are just these, but running through one another (35) they become now some things and now others and yet ever and always the same.

vv. 1–2. Alternative translation: 'It grew to be one alone out of many, and again grew apart...', the subject being unexpressed but understood to be the sum total of what exists. This would accord with the practice of Parmenides in speaking of his one Being.

vv. 4–5. The antecedent of τήν and ή must be, in sense, both γένεσις and ἀπόλειψις, and since it is these verbal nouns and not the θνητά themselves, the accusative must be regarded as 'internal' rather than expressing a direct object. Burnet's use of 'generation' ('The coming together of all things brings one generation into being and destroys it') is perhaps as satisfactory as can be expected in a translation.

v. 5. Panzerbieter's θρεφθεῖσα for the MSS. θρυφθεῖσα (retained by Wilamowitz) has been generally accepted as providing the parallel to τίκτει which seems to be needed.

vv. 7–13 = 26.5–6 and 8–12, save that *v.* 9 (= 26.8) is omitted in Simplicius's quotation of fr. 17. Its insertion is guaranteed by the corresponding passage.

v. 13. ἀκίνητοι. The gender is unexpected, following as it does on διαλλάσσοντα and other neuters. It is generally (Diels, Kranz, von Arnim, Bignone) attributed to the fact that the elements for Empedocles are gods. (Cf. fr. 6, p. 141 above.) Munding's unconvincing opinion (*Hermes*, 1954, 134) that the reference is to 'mortals' offers no solution.

For Aristotle's quotation and interpretation of these lines see p. 176, n. 4 below. The main contrast is the post-Parmenidean one between γίγνονται and ἔασιν, as I have tried to bring out in the translation.

v. 14. 'Learning increases wisdom.' Perhaps aimed at Heraclitus fr. 40 (vol. 1, 412).

v. 18. ἠέρος ἄπλετον ὕψος. ἄπλετον is the reading of Simplicius and Clement. Sextus, Pluturch and Athenagoras quote the line with ἤπιον, and Clement and Plutarch have αἰθέρος for ἠέρος. (Cf. p. 185, n. on *v*. 3 below.) The variants here may have no great importance, but may serve as a warning how far from certain we can be that in these quotations we have the exact words that Empedocles wrote. (In *v*. 14 the MSS. of Simplicius make Empedocles say: 'Drunkenness (μέθη) increases wisdom'!)

v. 19. ἀτάλαντον. The translation currently favoured is 'everywhere equally balanced' (KR), 'egualmente librata' (Bignone). But in Homer, where it is common (*Il*. 2.169, 5.576, 7.366, 12.463, 13.795), the word means 'equal' in any respect. Sometimes the respect is specified, e.g. in wisdom, in violence, in appearance. The only instance of the other meaning is in Aratus (*Phaen*. 22), so it is unlikely that it is intended here. Nor does the sense require it. Empedocles's point is that all six factors—the four elements and Love and Strife—are equal to each other. Of Love he says in the next line that it is 'equal in length and breadth', and of the elements in *v*. 27 that they are 'all equal'. Here he says the same of Strife. It is worth noting that in place of ἀπάντη Simplicius read ἕκαστον. If that is correct, Empedocles is saying in this and the preceding line that the four elements and Strife are all equal. Panzerbieter suggested ἑκάστῳ, which is an easier reading. (There is a similar variation between ἅπαντα and ἕκαστα in Simplicius's six citations of *v*. 7. See DK *ad loc*.)

Bignone was influenced by his assumption that Empedocles was describing the Sphairos, or universe under the supremacy of Love, but he is not here considering any single episode in the cosmic cycle: he is at the earlier stage of setting out the factors involved and describing what happens in general terms, as *vv*. 7–8, 16–17 and 29 make clear. I therefore attach no temporal significance to the fact that Strife is 'apart from these' and Love 'among them'. It will simply be the *ethos* (*v*. 28) of Strife to shun others, as it is of Love to embrace them. It must be remembered that, though they have extension, their action is not mechanical. Cf. e.g. *vv*. 8 and 22.9. The 'hatred' which Strife implants is part of its own nature.

v. 25. The reading μετὰ τοῖσιν is due to Brandis. The MSS. of Simplicius have μετ' ὅσσοισιν or ὅσσοισιν. The former makes good sense but is unmetrical, and Preller suggested γ' ὅσσοισιν. If something like that was what Empedocles wrote, it removes the contrast with δίχα τῶν which is part of the case for supposing that he has the Sphairos in mind. Zeller (ZN, 999, n. 2) approved Panzerbieter's μεθ' ὅλοισιν. Pfligersdorffer (*Poseidonios*, 110, n. 2) has an original notion of the meaning of this line: no man has seen Love circling round, because in fact she does not; a whirling motion would be most unsuitable for her! The point is that whereas everyone recognizes the power of Love in human affairs, her cosmic significance has been missed.

v. 30 emphasizes the Parmenidean truth that since the elements and Love and Strife are everlasting and are the only realities, nothing ever (in the strict sense) comes into being or perishes at all. It does not of course imply that they themselves come into being or perish. For this reason some translate the last half 'nor do *they* perish', but this is unnecessary and the change of subject is harsh.

vv. 31–5 show how much of Parmenides's logic Empedocles felt bound to retain. With αἰὲν ὁμοῖα cf. ὁμοῖον of the one Being in Parm. 8.22. The only change is to substitute pluralism for monism.

This passage affords an excellent illustration of Empedocles's method of interlocked argument and repetition, acknowledged as deliberate in *vv.* 15 f. Within the fragment *vv.* 16–17 repeat 1–2 and 12 repeats 6. Verse 29 = fr. 26.1. Verse 34 recurs in different contexts as 26.3 and 21.13, but the sentence is ended differently. Instead of 'become now some things and now others and yet ever and always the same' we have at 26.3 'become men and the other kinds of animal', and the lines which appear in this fragment as 7–8 are added immediately after as part of the same sentence, and followed by a further subordinate clause. At 21.13 the following line is 'become different; so much does mixture effect change'. It is an unusually clever and effective method of impressing upon a reader the unity and interdependence of all parts of the cosmic scheme.

The problem of motion was not solved by positing four elements instead of one. Parmenides had insisted that what exists could not move, and had made impossible the unreflecting hylozoism which had enabled earlier philosophers to avoid the question of a motive cause. Since the elements were to be as like the Parmenidean One as possible, Empedocles felt bound to introduce external motivators. Some have thought that this eliminates any idea of life, and brings us to the conception of inanimate bodies moved purely mechanically by external forces. Thus Cornford wrote:

Though the elements are called gods (because immortal) and given mythical names, they are not alive. As the conception of a bodily element grows clearer, the life is frozen out of it. The living force of motion is deposited by Empedocles in distinct substances.[1]

What these movers were we learn in this fragment. They too have 'mythical' names, Strife and Aphrodite or Love, the powers of repulsion and attraction. Since their effects are contrary, and both are active together, they represent something very like the simultaneous opposite tensions, the 'hidden harmony' of Heraclitus. As in Heraclitus also, it is only while the struggle between the contrary forces continues that a world of living creatures can exist:[2] the preponderance of either leads to the break-up of the cosmos and a state in which terrestrial life is impossible. Since both are active and opposed, the elements can never

[1] Unpublished lecture.
[2] Cf. Aristotle, *GC*, 315a16: ἄλλως τε καὶ μαχομένων ἀλλήλοις ἔτι τοῦ Νείκους καὶ τῆς Φιλίας.

be permanently in a state of mixture or separation, but alternate between the two, and at some point in either process a world of mortal creatures can be born. We notice already an advance in elasticity of language from the uncompromising 'It is or it is not' of Parmenides. Much later Aristotle was to say '"Being" is a word used in several senses', and patiently analyse and dissect it. That time is not yet, but the first step has been taken when Empedocles can write (*vv.* 9 ff.) 'In some way [i.e. in so far as different compounds are produced and resolved by the motions of the elements] things do come to be and perish, but in another [i.e. in so far as the moving elements are indestructible and unalterable in themselves] they *are* for ever.' He cannot avoid the language of becoming—he must say for instance that the elements '*become* now some things and now others'—but with remarkable awareness he has warned his readers of this (fr. 9): when the elements combine to form animals or plants, men say these are born, and when they scatter again men call it death, 'wrongly, but I comply with[1] custom myself'. Love and Strife are of course everlasting like the elements: 'Never will boundless time be emptied of these two' (fr. 16).

The contrary effects of Love and Strife may also be expressed by saying that Love represents attraction between dissimilars and Strife the attraction of like to like. The tendency of Strife to pull the elements apart from each other has as its natural corollary the gathering of each one together in a separate mass. Aristotle puts this clearly, though in his readiness to find fault with a predecessor he imputes to Empedocles an unreal inconsistency. 'At any rate', he writes (*Metaph.* 985 a 23), 'in many places his Love divides and Strife unites. When the whole is separated into the elements by Strife, fire and each of the others is collected into one; and when again under the action of Love they come together into one, it is necessary for the parts from each element to be separated once more.'

What fr. 17 says of the nature and working of the two forces, especially Love, is confirmed elsewhere, and casts serious doubts on the view that Empedocles has at last achieved the distinction between

---

[1] For ἐπίφημι I have borrowed the word used by Locke in speaking of secondary qualities, which have no right to be called qualities of the objects themselves, but 'which I, to comply with the common way of speaking, call qualities' (*Essay Concerning Human Understanding*, II, viii, 10).

inert matter and mechanical force. Love turns out to be no mythical name for an impersonal physical force attracting inanimate bodies to one another in the manner of magnetism or gravity. She is Aphrodite, the same power which men feel in their own hearts, filling them with thoughts of peace and lovingkindness, as Strife (or Anger as it is called in 21.7) induces hatred. In fr. 22 the elements are 'dear to one another' when Aphrodite unites them, and become hostile and grim by the *bidding* of Strife. In fr. 21 they come together in Love and 'are desired by one another'. Microcosm and macrocosm are governed by the same psychological principles. Empedocles has at last separated mover and moved, but we are not in the world of Descartes or Newton.[1] Indeed, for his forces to be mechanical, psychologically and morally neutral, would not have suited him, for he had also a religious message to preach, the message of the *Purifications*, and both were based on a single world-view. Some aspects of the physical world may incline one to forget this, but his own words confirm the dictum of Aristotle (*Metaph.* 985 a 4) that if one follows his meaning rather than his imperfect expression one will say that Love is the cause of good and Strife of evil. He presents a combination of physical and moral dualism unique in history, for at no other moment would it have been possible.

Another characteristic of these powers is equally disturbing to the mind of a later age. Aristotle, with his own clear-cut classification in mind, complained (*Metaph.* 1075 b 2) that in Love Empedocles confused the final, formal and material causes. It was 'the good', and at the same time 'both moving principle—for it combines things—and matter, for it is a part of the mixture'. Existence was still tied to extension in space, and so we read that Love was 'equal in length and breadth' to the elements. Her influence is not exerted without physical penetration. It is useless to argue whether the action of these powers is physical or psychological, for it is both. It could hardly be otherwise in an age when psychical faculties themselves were conceived materially as breath or blood.

[1] Even after Newton a scientist (Lorenz Oken) could still object to his theories that 'not by mechanical manipulation (*Stossen und Schlagen*) but by infusing life do you create the world. Were the planet dead, it could not be attracted by the sun.' (Quoted by Heisenberg, *Philos. Problems of Nuclear Science*, 36.)

(Fr. 22)   For all of these—the shining sun, earth, sky and sea—are one with their own parts which are scattered far from them in mortal things; and in the same way all that are fitted rather for mixture are assimilated by Aphrodite and hold one another dear.   But enemies are those that are farthest from each other in origin, composition and moulded form, in every way unaccustomed to unite and very grim by the bidding of Strife, because it has brought about their birth.

v. 2 Ἠλέκτωρ, 'the shining one', used in Homer as an epithet for Hyperion the sun (*Il.* 19.398, and cf. 6.513). Here the sun stands for fire, as sky for air.

v. 9 is corrupt. At the beginning Simplicius has νεικεογεννέστησιν and refers in his comment to τοῖς νεικεογενέσι, 'the things born of Strife'. Yet Panzerbieter's slight correction νείκεος ἐννεσίησιν, 'by the bidding of Strife', deserves its universal acceptance. The last word is also uncertain but the sense not much in doubt.

The first clause makes the point that the elements do not lose their separate identities when they mingle with each other to form a world. The rest of the passage refers to the fact that in the contest between the two opposing forces some bodies are formed which combine easily with others, and of these Love makes further compounds; whereas others are of a structure that forbids their mixture so that Strife has his way with them and they remain separate beings or substances. Examples are given in fr. 91 in the different behaviour of water in relation to wine and oil. This 'fitness for mixture' or otherwise is dependent on the size of the microscopic openings in each body.

The nature of the elements and their behaviour under the influence of Love and Strife is so important that Empedocles does not hesitate to repeat his points in different ways. Thus in fr. 21:

Come now, see this witness to my former words, should anything in them have been lacking in form: the sun white to see and hot all over, all the divine things which are bathed in heat (?) and the bright ray, and the rain in all things dark and cold; and from the earth spring things rooted and solid. In Anger all are diverse and sundered, but in Love they come together and are desired of each other. For out of these are born whatever was and is and will be—trees, men, women, beasts, birds and water-feeding fishes, yea and long-lived gods highest in honours. There are just these, but running through one another they alter their appearance: so far does mixture effect change.

v. 2. Some scholars (see Bignone and DK *ad loc.*) refer μορφῇ, possibly rightly, to the form or character of the elements, which is touched on in the next lines.

vv. 3–7 give poetic descriptions of the elements, as Aristotle saw (*GC,* 314b20). The sun is used for fire (as in 22.2, 71.2) and rain for water (as in fr. 98), and to vary the expression Empedocles says that earth is the element producing solid things rather than that it is solid itself. Verse 4 must therefore describe the air, but its exact text and meaning are uncertain. The 'divine things' were taken by Diels and Burnet to be the heavenly bodies, which are made of solidified air (A 60). (Bignone objected that these are not immortal, ἄμβροτα; but they were commonly thought to be divine, and Empedocles by his own confession makes use of popular expressions.) It is more likely that by the plural he intended only the particles of air, but the line remains obscure. It appears only in Simplicius whereas Aristotle and Plutarch quote *vv.* 3 and 5 consecutively. δσσ' εἴδει (= heat) τε is a conjecture of Diels for various unintelligible readings in the MSS. of Simplicius.

Since air for Empedocles is synonymous with sky (22.2), it is natural enough that he should speak of it as bathed in the heat and light of the sun.

v. 3. Fire was white for Empedocles as water was black (*v.* 5). Cf. Theophr. *De sensu*, 59 (A 69 a) and 7 (A 86). Aristotle glances at this passage in *GC* 315 a 10: καθάπερ λέγει τὸν μὲν ἥλιον λευκὸν καὶ θερμὸν τὴν δὲ γῆν βαρὺ καὶ σκληρόν.

v. 6. θελεμνά in DK is a correction of θελημνά or θελημά in Simpl. Hesychius has θέλεμνον· ὅλον ἐκ ῥιζῶν, but otherwise the word does not occur. θέλυμνα Sturz.

We have then six ultimate factors, four passive and two active. Although Love and Strife are invisible and unimaginably fine and tenuous (more so, obviously, than air or fire), and although their influence is in the first place a psychological one, their spiritual character is not yet completely divorced from physical form. Only by being in the world and mingling with the ever-living elements can they inspire them with the feelings which cause them either to come together in mutual embrace or to draw apart in cold exclusiveness each to itself. The secondary effects of these proceedings are physical and are the outcome of chance. How this happens will emerge in subsequent sections, which will show that those are fully justified who claim, in spite of the original psychological impulse (which they frequently ignore), that Empedocles deserves to go down to history as the first European to introduce into science the idea of a force operating on matter. At the same time the thoughts of a Sicilian Greek of the fifth century B.C. are not so simple as such critics sometimes think.

H. CAUSATION IN EMPEDOCLES: CHANCE, NECESSITY AND NATURE

It was held against Empedocles in antiquity, particularly by Aristotle, that having posited six and only six ultimate principles he then found them insufficient for the construction of a world and smuggled in two more, Chance (*Tyche*) and Necessity (*Ananke*). Some modern scholars, like Bignone (*Emped.* 306n.), have thought this a real weakness in his system. Aristotle writes (*GC*, 334a7): 'What is the prime mover and cause of motion? It cannot be Love and Strife, for they are the causes of a particular *kind* of motion.' What kind of motion, he has stated earlier (333b12): 'They are the causes of aggregation and segregation respectively.'[1]

In this chapter Aristotle sees things from his own viewpoint, namely the teleological. For him, as he says in the *Physics*, there are only two possible explanations of events, chance or purpose. Chance cannot be responsible for regularity (what happens 'always or for the most part'), therefore that must be the result of purposive causation. But in general nature does exhibit regularity (e.g. a grain of wheat always produces more wheat, never olives), therefore nature works teleologically. Chance events only occur occasionally, and argue failure of purpose rather than its absence.

With this outlook he could not fail to find Empedocles wrong-headed,[2] but it is not an outlook that all would share. For instance, Empedocles attributes the constitution of different organic substances to the proportion in which the elements are mixed in them. This proportion is a chance outcome of the interaction of Love and Strife. Now the word for proportion is *logos*, but *logos* had many other meanings in Greek, some of which have reference only to the behaviour of rational beings: it can mean thought or the result of thought. Aristotle commits what amounts to a play on words when he continues: 'What then is the cause of this *logos*? Not presumably fire or earth, but neither is it Love or Strife, for the one is the cause of aggregation, the other of segregation. The cause is the essential nature of each'—a shameless introduction of Aristotelian ideas which would have meant nothing to Empedocles—'and not solely "mingling

---

[1] Millerd agreed (*Emped.* 35): the evidence seems to prove 'that Love and Strife were not conceived by him as universal "motor causes", but as having the specialized function of effecting and dissolving certain combinations of the elements'.

[2] H. A. T. Reiche, in *Empedocles's Mixture*, argues that (as he says on p. 38) the role of mechanism in Empedocles is of purely secondary, subsidiary importance: 'Unlike Diogenes, he had no grounds for thinking of human reason and "technology" as anything other than a less perfect copy of, and approximation to, the unconscious purposefulness of Nature at its best.' This would make his position exactly the same as Aristotle's, and if it were true, Aristotle's repeated castigation of him as a mechanist would be incomprehensible.

and separation of what is mingled" as he puts it. But the right name for this is chance, not *logos*, for it is possible for things to be mingled fortuitously.'

There is no evidence that Empedocles used the word *logos* in this connexion,[1] and he certainly taught that organic substances and living creatures were produced by chance, though the fact that the elements could combine at all, and retain their union for a time, was due to the influence of Love. (One can hardly be surprised that Aristotle found this a little confusing, and asked impatiently in *De anima* (408a21): 'Is Love the cause of any chance mixture, or of mixture according to *logos*?'). Describing the formation of bone, he says after mentioning the proportions in which the elements were mixed: 'And they became white bones, joined by the wondrous cement of Love' (fr. 96), and again of blood, 'Anchored in the perfect havens of Cypris' (98.3). At the same time, indicating in the same fragment what the appropriate mixture is, he speaks of earth 'happening upon' equal quantities of the others, and in fr. 85 fire 'Chanced to meet' a little earth in the making of the eye: creatures with soft bodies over a hard skeleton 'chanced to get this flaccidity in the hands of Cypris' (75.2). Again he writes: 'By the whim of Chance all things think' (fr. 103), and 'in so far as the finest bodies met by chance in their fall' (fr. 104). In citing these examples, Simplicius adds (*Phys.* 331.10): 'One may find many such expressions in the *Physica* of Empedocles.' He is enlarging on the criticism of Aristotle (*Phys.* 196a11 ff.) that the earlier natural philosophers, including Empedocles from whom he quotes, though they give no explanation of chance, do make use of it. Most striking perhaps is Empedocles's use of chance as the sole explanation of favourable biological characteristics such as form the strongest weapon in the teleologist's armoury. It comes out best in his account of the evolution of animals by the survival of the fittest (pp. 203f. below), but may be illustrated by Aristotle's criticism in *De part. anim.* 640a19: 'Empedocles was wrong to say that many characteristics of animals are the result of accidental occurrences during their formation, for instance

---

[1] The word does not occur in the extant fragments, and he was perfectly capable of explaining without its use that organic substances were the product of elements combined in varying ratios, e.g. 4:2:2 for bone (fr. 96; possibly 4:2:1, see Simpl. *ad loc.*) and 1:1:1:1 for blood (fr. 98).

that the backbone is divided into vertebrae because·the contortion [of the foetus] has broken it.'¹

The fragments, then, confirm the fortuitous character of the formation of organic nature. In spite of his religious outlook and the choice of Aphrodite, spirit of harmony and goodness, as one of the motive powers, Empedocles, like the Ionians, is no teleologist in his description of the physical world. This in the eyes of Aristotle, as of Plato before him,² was a grave fault, but perhaps it is Empedocles and his predecessors who in this respect showed the more scientific outlook. There is little in the charge that he illegitimately smuggled in chance as an independent cause over and above those that he overtly recognized. Apart from the one poetic expression 'by the whim of *Tyche*', the noun does not occur in the fragments, the idea of chance or accidental occurrence being conveyed by verbs.³ Aristotle (*Phys.* 196a8) says that those who believe that there is no such thing as chance, but that every event has a definite cause, invoke the earlier philosophers for this view. These, they say, in their discussions of becoming and dissolution, ignore chance and act as if there were no such thing as a chance event. In his reply Aristotle only remarks that if they omitted to explain it, they ought not to have done so, since in fact they do avail themselves of the notion, as for instance Empedocles both in cosmogony and zoogony. Simplicius, who also had the poem, says the same (*Phys.* 331.15): 'Empedocles is less worth consideration [*sc.* than the atomists] since he appears to employ chance in minor matters but never explains what it is.' The natural conclusion is that Empedocles, like many in all ages, could speak of things 'just happening' or being 'accidental' without supposing chance to be a cause in its own right. His conception of it may become a little clearer after a brief discussion of *ananke*.

¹ Kranz (*Empedokles*, 58) took this to mean that the structure of the backbone was an accident in the distant past, the effect of which had persisted to the present day through heredity. As I read it, it is not a matter of phylogenetic evolution, but of an early stage in the development of the individual embryo. A. L. Peck in his Loeb translation also takes it in this way. If it is right, then the breaking, being something that happens regularly, does not satisfy Aristotle's criterion for a chance event (that it should not happen 'always or for the most part'), and he could have used that as an argument against its accidental character.

² Cf. *Laws* 889a–c, quoted in vol. I, 144. Bignone (*Emped.* 340, n. 3) conjectured that Plato was referring to the Sicilian medical school, especially Philistion. Rather perhaps to 'Sophists of his own day who advocated the Empedoclean physics' (Millerd, *Emped.* 40, n. 2), with the reservation that the physics here loosely described are not exclusively Empedoclean.

³ συγκυρῶ frr. 53, 59.2, 98.1, 104; τυγχάνω 85, 75.2.

Empedocles, like Parmenides, follows other poets and religious teachers in speaking of *ananke* as a personal power. In fr. 116 Love 'hates intolerable Ananke', and fr. 115 mentions a decree of Ananke. Its function in his system evidently puzzled the commentators, who are wildly inconsistent. Aëtius in one place calls it the One, of which the four elements are the matter and Love and Strife the form; in another, he describes it as a cause which makes use of the principles and elements. Plutarch simply identifies it with Love and Strife, whereas Simplicius lists it as a third creative cause. Elsewhere he attributes to Empedocles a more elaborate scheme in which the two contrarieties exhibited by the elements (hot–cold, dry–wet) are subsumed under the one pair Love and Strife, and that in turn under the monad *ananke*.[1]

We cannot say to what parts of the poem these writers are referring, but their phraseology shows that they were trying to remodel what they found there into Peripatetic or later forms. Empedocles's own lines are unlikely to have gone beyond the simple statement of Aristotle (*Phys.* 252a7): 'Empedocles appears to have meant that the alternate predominance as movers of Love and Strife is inherent in things of necessity.' In other words, in spite of the personification of *ananke*, he meant no more than that, the elements and Love and Strife being what they were, it could not have happened otherwise. One may compare the comment of Hippolytus on the 'decree of Ananke' in fr. 115 (*Ref.* 7.29; DK, I, 356f.): 'What he calls Ananke is the change from one to many caused by Strife, and from many to one by Love.'[2]

It must be remembered that for a Greek chance and necessity could be much the same thing. Orestes can be said to have died 'by necessary chance', which Tecmessa in the *Ajax* bewails as the worst of evils. Plato criticizes the cosmogony of non-teleological philosophers like Empedocles by saying that they make things happen 'necessarily by chance'. A little later he calls the same cause 'chance and nature

---

[1] Aët. 1.7.28, 26.1 (DK, A32 and 45); Plut. *De an. procr.* 1026 b (A45); Simpl. *Phys.* 465.12, 197.10.

[2] The *De providentia* of Philo has come down to us in a Latin version by devious ways, but its account of Empedocles coincides on the whole with corresponding Greek sources (Bignone, *Emped.* 341, n. 2). Of the earth it says (DK, A49): *terra vero in unum concurrens et* necessitate quadam *concreta in medio apparens consedit*. This illustrates the same point, for the concretion of the earth at the centre was the work of Strife. On the way that some ancient commentators exaggerated the role of *ananke* in Empedocles see also ZN, 968, n. 2.

Empedocles

(physis)'.[1] All this may sound strange, but represents a consistent view. *Physis* in the eyes of these men is a natural necessity inherent in each separate thing or substance, not a law of interaction between them. With each thing moving as its own *physis* dictates, the clashes between them will be fortuitous though caused by necessity. By 'chance' was meant 'a cause not manifest to human reason' as Aristotle was later to put it. We can be sure that rain will fall and flames rise, because it is in their *physis* to do so. But it is beyond our telling when and where a portion of fire will encounter a portion of water, and in what proportions they will mix. In effect, the formation of a cosmos is the undesigned and purposeless result of a clash between material substances each driven in certain ways by its own internal impulse. That is the essence of this type of cosmology, against which Plato and Aristotle directed their heaviest batteries in the interests of teleology.

This seems to uncover yet another active factor in the Empedoclean universe, the internal motive powers of the elements themselves. Certainly they are not dead matter which would remain completely inert unless acted on by external forces; but if we try to analyse Empedocles's notions of causes and forces and distinguish them in the Aristotelian manner, we shall be contorting his thoughts and forcing upon him a logic of which he was innocent. In these matters he was much nearer to the vagueness of popular thought. According to him, says Aristotle in *De anima* (415 b 28), plants grow downwards because earth tends downwards by nature, and upwards because fire tends upwards. Somewhat similarly in the chapter of *De gen. et corr.* already cited, in which he undertakes to show that Empedocles's views on motion and its causes are naive, he says: 'It is Strife that separates, yet *aither* is borne upwards not by Strife, but as he says in one place, naturally, and in another, by chance ("For thus it chanced to meet [the other elements] then in its course, but often otherwise"). Elsewhere he says that it is the nature of fire to move upwards, yet *aither*, he says, "sank into the earth with long roots".'[2]

---

[1] ἀναγκαία τύχη Soph. *El.* 48, *Aj.* 485 (cf. 803, Eur. *I.A.* 511; Plato, *Laws*, 806a); κατὰ τύχην ἐξ ἀνάγκης, φύσει καὶ τύχῃ, *Laws*, 889c. This is dealt with more fully on pp. 414ff.

[2] 334a1, Emped. frr. 53 and 54. Aristotle is here, rightly or wrongly (Gilbert, *Met. Theor.* 108, n. 1), identifying αἰθήρ with fire. According to Empedocles there was fire within the earth (fr. 52) as well as in the heavens.

Aristotle's head is full of his own ideas, of his distinction between 'natural' and 'enforced' motions and the theory that all natural motion must be directed towards a predetermined end. What he says amounts to no more than this, that in Empedocles's mind the movement of each of the elements was necessary and the concourse of elements fortuitous. Both were the result of 'nature', which was a necessary, not a teleological, cause. Thus he writes in the *Metaphysics* (1000b12): 'He offers no cause of the change itself, except that it is in the nature of things...as if it is *necessary* for them to change; but he suggests no cause for this necessity.' There is however another principle obviously at work in the elements, namely the attraction of like for like. Any portion of fire or earth has a natural tendency to seek out and join other parts of the same element. This too was a universal popular conception. Tannery, noting that for Empedocles it does not appear to be a transcendent force but an immanent property of matter, added rightly: 'Nous ne pouvons guère penser trouver autre chose à cette époque.' Ever since Homer, and no doubt long before, it had been believed that 'God always brings like to like' (*Od.* 17.218), and the principle appears in various guises in many rational thinkers including Democritus. Here again critics have claimed to detect Empedocles invoking another force besides those which have an acknowledged place in his system. It is admittedly more difficult to correlate with the external powers of Love and Strife, for as Aristotle remarked, in separating unlikes, Strife draws like substances together.[1] In the many passages where the principle is invoked, it is not always easy to decide whether Empedocles conceives himself to be speaking of an inherent property of matter or of the influence of Strife upon it, as for instance in fr. 90: 'So sweet seized upon sweet, bitter leaped upon bitter, acid came to acid, and hot rode upon hot.'[2] That it *was* an inherent property

[1] P. 156 above. Burnet (*EGP*, 233) writes that 'we must carefully distinguish between the Love of Empedocles and that "attraction of like for like" to which he also attributed an important part in the formation of the world'. I cannot see how anyone could be temped to identify this attraction with Love, which obviously has the opposite effect: the difficulty is to distinguish it from the influence of Strife.

[2] I have translated the aorists as past tenses (so DK), assuming them to refer to a stage in the evolution of the world. Burnet however, and Kranz in his *Empedokles*, render them as presents (gnomic aorists). Verse 2: possibly 'hot coupled with hot': θερμὸν δ' ἐποχεύετο θερμῷ Macrob., δαερὸν δ' ἐποχεῖτο δαηρῷ coni. Diels from Plutarch's δαλερόν. For the same principle cf. also fr. 110.9, 62.6.

of things, he would accept as axiomatic without much thought, and probably Burnet comes nearest the truth in the words (*EGP*, 233): 'It depends on the proper nature of each element, and is only able to take effect when Strife divides the Sphere.' (In more concrete terms, he thought that the attraction of like for like was explained by the doctrine of 'symmetry of pores'.) Empedocles's dominant aim was to rescue the real world from the unity and immobility into which Parmenides had frozen it. Consequently he would feel bound to start from a conception of it as apparently unitary and static, and show that the unity was not essential, and that motion and change could be introduced. This conception, in his system, was represented by the Sphere in which Love had so completely mingled the elements that their separate natures were indistinguishable. With this powerful force holding unlikes together, their natural tendency to seek their like would remain ineffective without the equally powerful intervention of Strife. Another reason for beginning with the state of 'all things together' would be that that was the way in which cosmogony always had started, from the age-old myths in which earth and heaven were one to the 'monist' systems of the Ionians. His Sphere of Love resembles especially the primal *apeiron* of Anaximander; it is 'hardly more than a clarification of the confusion of Anaximander's thought'.[1] His apparent unity becomes, as logically it had to be if the opposites were to be 'separated out' from it, a mixture. Empedocles had also, following Parmenides, made the original mass spherical, though at the same time it was unlimited— a combination of ideas which may also have been present to the mind of the earlier thinker (vol. 1, 85; cf. also for Empedocles p. 170 below).

In the physical theory of Empedocles we have a transitional stage in the history of ideas, to which modern thought-categories are not altogether relevant, and it is more rewarding to understand than to criticize. The separation of the notions of body and spirit was a very gradual process, which was not yet completed, even if it may be almost beyond our powers of expression to say just what stage it had reached. We have already met Heraclitus's conception of a 'rational fire'. In that there was as yet no hint of a separation, however plain it may seem that the difficulties of such a composite conception must lead to a break

[1] Cornford, *C.A.H.* IV, 564. Cf. my vol. I, 87.

very soon. Empedocles has made the break, depositing the motive force in two separate entities. Yet their action is psychological. It is love or liking and hatred or anger that strive for mastery among the elements, and of such impulses it is almost truer to say that they *animate* than that they move them. At least the bodies which submit to their action are not just dead stuff, and the bestowal of divine names on them is more than a poetic convention. Nevertheless the importance of Empedocles is not in the lingering traces of hylozoism but in the great step forward which he took by declaring that the elements were indestructible and immutable, that the cosmos was formed by a mixture of these unalterable roots in different proportions, and that the motion necessary to produce the mixture was caused not (in the loose Milesian way of thinking) by the elements themselves but by distinct forces working upon them.

I. THE COSMIC CYCLE

Further descriptive analysis of our present world, with details of the formation of organic substances and living creatures, will be best left until after consideration of the whole cosmic process. This will make clearer the respective roles of Love and Strife at the present stage of world-history. The process, described in fr. 17 (p. 153 above) and elsewhere, is curiously complex. There is a period when Love rules unopposed, having fused all the elements into a unity. Then Strife enters the Sphere and begins to separate them until finally he has taken full possession and each element is isolated from the rest. After this Love reasserts herself, pervades the whole once more and gradually brings the separated elements together until once more they are completely united. A universe of 'mortal things', such as that in which we live, is a temporary stage intermediate between the supremacy of Love and Strife, a product of the tension and conflict between them. To the old idea of cosmogony as a 'separating-out' from an original unity has been added a converse process of coming-together from a state of separation, which is cosmogonic no less than the other. 'Double is the birth of mortal things, and double their failing' (17.3). There is not one cosmogony, but an endless succession of worlds. 'Empedocles and Anaxagoras also produce other things by separation from mixture, but they differ in that Empedocles makes these things happen in a cycle but Anaxagoras once for all' (Arist. *Phys.* 187a23); or as Simplicius describes it more fully (*De caelo*, 293.18):

Others maintain that the same cosmos comes to be and perishes alternately, and again arises and perishes, and that this succession goes on for ever. Thus Empedocles says that Love and Strife gain the ascendancy in turn: Love brings all things together into one, destroys the cosmos created by Strife and makes of it the Sphere, whereas Strife separates the elements again and creates a world like this.

So much is clear, though when we come to consider the details of each stage of the cycle, the gaps in our knowledge of the poem raise problems which cannot all be solved with certainty.

First stage: the Sphere of Love

'They never cease thus to alternate continually, now all coming together into one through Love, and now again each one drawing apart by Strife's hatred' (fr. 17.6–8). Although the process is thus cyclic, the logical starting-point is (for reasons given in the preceding section) the state of unity, when Love has drawn all things together into one.[1] Of the resulting Sphere, Hippolytus has preserved a description (*Ref.* 7.29.13, fr. 29):

Of the shape of the cosmos, what it was like when ordered by Love, he speaks like this:

'No twin branches spring from its back, there are no feet nor nimble knees, no parts of generation, but it was a Sphere and in all directions equal to itself.'

The first surprise is perhaps to find Empedocles at pains to deny that the original mixture of the elements is anthropomorphic or theriomorphic. But for him it is a god, 'the most blessed god' according to Aristotle,[2] and its obvious prototype is the unitary cosmic divinity of

---

[1] Bignone (*Emped.* 220) adopts the contrary procedure, and Millerd (*Emped.* 53) thinks that Empedocles himself started from the separated elements. But her quotation from *GC*, 333b21 provides no argument, and in fact Aristotle's evidence is all against the supposition. Cf. rather *De caelo*, 301a14–18 (quoted on p. 173 below). More telling in favour of her thesis is a fact mentioned by Bignone that events belonging naturally to the period of Strife's advance are assigned to the second book of the *Physica* (fr. 62), and others suggesting the period of Love to the first (fr. 96). See his *Emped.* 567f. In 568, n. 2, however, his inference from the order of the recurrent cosmic cycle to the order of our own period of Strife is illogical.

[2] *Metaph.* 1000b3, and cf. *GC*, 333b21; Simpl. *Phys.* 1124.1.

Xenophanes. At the same time it illustrates the remarkable consistency which Empedocles was capable of maintaining between the different parts of his system. In our own imperfect world the highest manifestations of life, namely intelligence and knowledge, were achieved through the physical medium exhibiting the most nearly perfect blend of the elements.[1] It is in keeping that when an actually perfect blend is achieved, the product should be the highest form of all life, divinity. As in Xenophanes also it is unmoved. Further information comes from Simplicius (*Phys.* 1183.28):

> Eudemus understands the immobility [*sc.* of which Aristotle speaks at *Phys.* 252a9] to apply to the Sphere in the supremacy of Love, when all things are combined.
>
> 'Then neither is the swift body of the sun discerned', but as he [Empedocles] says,
>
> 'Thus everything is held fast in the close obscurity of Harmonia, a rounded Sphere[2] rejoicing in its circular stillness.'[3]

Another couple of lines (fr. 28), which after the Empedoclean manner repeat phrases from elsewhere in the poem but put one fresh point into

---

[1] Theophr. *De sensu*, 10 (A86). Cf. frr. 98, 105.3, and p. 215 below.

[2] σφαῖρος κυκλοτερής. The tautological expression no doubt owes something to εὐκύκλου σφαίρης in Parm. 8.43.

[3] See fr. 27. (I am afraid I find Minar's attribution of *vv.* 3 and 4 to the total supremacy of Strife, in *Phronesis*, 1963, 131f., quite unconvincing. For one thing, ἁρμονίη *does* mean Love in Empedocles.) The last words are μονίη περιηγέι γαίων. Whether the unusual word μονίη is from μόνος (solitude) or μένω (rest, motionlessness) is disputed. The majority of modern critics have translated it in the first way (DK, Burnet, Millerd, Bignone, Munding, Kranz, KR), but Jaeger, who like Zeller and LSJ renders it 'rest', has given a reasoned defence of this interpretation (*TEGP*, 141). One of Jaeger's parallels, the papyrus fragment of Tyrtaeus (1.15 in the second and 1.54 in the third edition of Diehl's *Anth. Lyr.*), must be admitted to be doubtful owing to the condition of the papyrus at this point. However, in the third edition, Diehl (or just possibly Beutler who published the fascicle after Diehl's death), though refusing to commit himself in the text as he had done before, not only repeats (from the original publication of the papyrus by Wilamowitz) but also adds to the references supporting the reading and the meaning 'steadfastness, staying where one is'. (Note especially καμμονίην in *Il.* 22.257.) Perhaps the most relevant comparison is the μίμνει of Xenophanes's spherical god (fr. 26, vol. 1, 374), since the influence of Xenophanes on Empedocles in this matter is pretty clear. The context in Simplicius makes it practically certain that at any rate he and Eudemus took the word to mean that the Sphere was motionless. More recently J. B. Bauer in *Hermes*, 1961, has again argued for the connexion of μονίη with μόνος, but would render it not 'solitude' (*Einsamkeit*) but 'oneness' or 'attainment of unity' (*Einssein*).

Περιηγής can also mean 'surrounding' rather than 'circular'. So Millerd (*Emped.* 60) translates 'the isolation that surrounds him', and DK (repeated by Munding, *Hermes*, 1954, 143) 'die ringsum herrschende Einsamkeit'. With Jaeger's translation of μονίη one could render it similarly 'the surrounding stillness'. In fact however, whatever be the exact reference of Aët. 1.5.2 (A47), Empedocles has no thought of any περιέχον. The limitless Sphere (fr. 28) contains all that is.

their context, state that the Sphere is 'altogether without limit'. Empedocles must have aimed this at the emphatic limitation of the spherical whole by Parmenides, but we do not possess (as we do with Melissus) his reasons for the change. It is clear however that he saw no incompatibility between limitlessness (in whatever sense; cf. vol. 1, 85) and spherical shape.

At this stage the Sphere is permeated through and through by Love, and Strife has been driven to its furthest limits: spatial relegation is the necessary concomitant of ineffectiveness. 'If Strife were not in among things [*sc.* as it is now], all would be one according to him', says Aristotle (*Metaph.* 1000b1), quoting the last half of fr. 36: 'As [the elements] came together, Strife retired to the outermost edge.' These spatial relationships are emphasized in fr. 35, which describes the gradual process whereby the full supremacy of Love is attained (pp. 178f. below).

The reign of Love, then, presents a Sphere containing the four elements so thoroughly blended by her co-presence with them as to be indistinguishable, with their normally antithetic characteristics in abeyance. (Cf. Philoponus in A41.) Consequently there is peace and rest, 'no division nor unseemly contention in the limbs'.[1] The whole is effectively, if temporarily, a unity, and is called a god, like the divine All of Xenophanes from which it derives and which enjoyed a similar tranquillity. Strife bides his time on the outer fringe of this Sphere. There is little point in asking in what precise sense it is a unity. Any explanation must be historical. Anaximander doubtless thought of his *apeiron* as a unity, but more critical ages, seeing that in some sense it must have contained the elements of a cosmos, described it as a mixture.[2] Empedocles, schooled by Parmenides, grasped that the unitary phase must contain the elements, since out of a strict unity no plurality could arise, and spoke of Love as uniting them 'into one' (εἰς ἕν). In

---

[1] Fr. 27a, quoted anonymously by Plutarch, but plausibly ascribed to Empedocles by Wilamowitz. That the Sphere is motionless is the general opinion of ancient critics (e.g. Simplicius and Eudemus quoted above, Arist. *Phys.* 252a7–10, where presumably κρατεῖν refers to the process of gaining the mastery), apart from the disputed question whether μονίη in Empedocles himself means 'rest'. Plato (as elsewhere in the *Timaeus*) is following Empedocles when he lays down the principle στάσιν μὲν ἐν ὁμαλότητι, κίνησιν δὲ εἰς ἀνωμαλότητα ἀεὶ τιθῶμεν· αἰτία δὲ ἀνισότης αὖ τῆς ἀνωμάλου φύσεως (*Tim.* 57e).

[2] Aristotle, *Metaph.* 1069b21; see also vol. 1, 86f.

writing of him Aristotle sometimes copies this phrase or calls the Sphere 'the One',[1] and at other times characterizes it as a mixture.[2] Empedocles had not advanced beyond the notion of mechanical mixture (as §F of this chapter should have made clear), but the important point is that under the unchallenged influence of Love the elements have become (*a*) so inextricably mingled, and (*b*) so 'dear' to one another that all their otherwise antagonistic characteristics have become subdued and indeed annihilated in an ineffable harmony.[3]

Second stage: the advance of Strife

'As Strife begins to gain once more, motion begins again in the Sphere: "For (fr. 31) one by one all the limbs of the god quiver."' So Simplicius (*Phys.* 1184.2) introduces fr. 31. A quotation which must have stood in close context with this is preserved by Aristotle (fr. 30):

But when great Strife waxed strong in the limbs and leaped to power as the time was fulfilled which is fixed for them in turn by a broad oath....

On this Aristotle comments (*Metaph.* 1000b12) that Empedocles offers no cause of the change itself: it seems to happen naturally. The words, he says, imply that the change is necessary, but the reason for this necessity is nowhere made clear. There is probably little more to be said about the way in which Empedocles tackled the problem—inescapable since Parmenides—of how to introduce motion into a motionless sphere. The Sphere was no longer a true unity, and motive powers existed. This seemed sufficient, and the question why one or other of the forces started to become effective at a particular time was

---

[1] *GC*, 315a6; *Metaph.* 984a10, 985a28, 1000a28 and b12.

[2] *Phys.* 187a23; *Metaph.* 1092b7 and 1069b22. In the last of these passages he couples Empedocles and Anaximander together. At one place (*Metaph.* 996a8) he even sees in Love an anticipation of his own notion of the undifferentiated substratum (ὑποκείμενον) of the physical world. We know that he was worried by Empedocles's apparent characterization of it as at once moving cause and part of the mixture, and here he is probably identifying Love with the Sphere in which it is everywhere supreme and the elements have lost their separate identities. Cf. for a more tentative statement 1001a14 (Burnet, *EGP*, 236, n. 1).

Aristotle also accuses Empedocles of contradicting himself by saying (*a*) that no element comes to be out of another element, and (*b*) that when everything save Strife is gathered together 'into one', each of them is born again from 'the one' (*GC*, 315a3).

[3] Ἁρμονίης πυκινῷ κρύφῳ, fr. 27. Cf. Plato, *Soph.* 242e ἓν εἶναι τὸ πᾶν καὶ φίλον ὑπ' Ἀφροδίτης.

answered on religious rather than on physical grounds. The 'broad oath' of these lines is repeated, and joined with the 'necessity' of which Aristotle speaks, in a quotation from the *Purifications* describing the fate of divine souls caught in the wheel of reincarnation (fr. 115.1–2):

There is an oracle of Necessity, an ancient decree of the gods, sealed with broad oaths.

The alternate waxing and waning of Love and Strife was ruled by the same eternal law as the cyclic wanderings of individual souls. One might guess at the physical means by which it happened. Possibly in the age-long struggle to win the victory and hold its gains, the victor temporarily exhausted his strength while his rival's powers were recouped. But ultimately it is a religious sanction governing macrocosm and microcosm alike, analogous to the cosmic justice which in Anaximander's world ensured that none of the opposites gained a final advantage over any other.

Strife, then, enters the Sphere and initiates a motion which disrupts it. As Love loosens her hold, the tendency of each element to seek its like asserts itself, and they begin to draw apart. In psychological or moral terms (equally important for Empedocles) the seeds of hate and exclusiveness are sown in the perfect harmony of the divine Sphere. In the course of their separation our world is formed, in which large masses of the elements have already been separated—the earth, the sea, the air, and (as he believed) fire at the circumference—but the process is not complete. 'Strife and Love are still fighting with one another' (Aristotle, *GC*, 315a16). For one thing each of the main masses still contains some portion of another element; we see rivers springing out of the earth, and fire erupting from beneath its surface. Secondly, there exists the variety of organic creatures which are formed of several elements mingled in different proportions.

A similar stage must of course be reached in the complementary period when Love is on the increase, but our own world is that of advancing Strife. On this point the explicit statements of Aristotle are in accord with what we know of Empedocles's own account. 'He says that the cosmos is similar now under the influence of Strife to what it was formerly under the influence of Love.'[1] In *De caelo* he gives an odd reason for this, but the passage is further evidence for the fact.

To make the world-process start from things in motion and separate is irrational. That is why Empedocles passes over the process of formation in the period when Love is prevailing; he could not have built up his universe by making it out of separate elements and combining them by Love. The elements of the cosmos *are* in a state of separation, so that its formation must have proceeded from unity and combination.[2]

Simplicius says the same thing several times, for instance *De caelo*, 590.19: 'He says that the elements were formerly combined by Love, and later as they became separated by Strife formed this world of ours.'[3] In Empedocles himself and the doxography the formation of the world is described as a separation of the elements from a primal mixture, first into their cosmic arrangement (A30) and then into living creatures. Thus in fr. 62 the first men and women originate from certain 'whole-natured', i.e. less differentiated forms of life, which in turn were constructed out of earth, water and fire as a result of fire struggling to rejoin its like.[4] Again, trees are both the earliest form of life and, cor-

---

[1] *GC*, 334a5. On the meaning of the phrases ἐπὶ τοῦ Νείκους νῦν...ἐπὶ τῆς Φιλίας cf. Simplicius, *Cael.* 587.24 ἐπὶ τῆς Φ. οὖν ὁ ᾽Ε. ἐκεῖνα εἶπεν οὐχ ὡς ἐπικρατούσης ἤδη τῆς Φ. ἀλλ᾽ ὡς μελλούσης ἐπικρατεῖν. A similar conclusion follows from Theophrastus, *De sensu*, 20: συμβαίνει δὲ καὶ ἐπὶ τῆς Φιλίας ὅλως μὴ εἶναι αἴσθησιν ἢ ἧττον διὰ τὸ συγκρίνεσθαι τότε καὶ μὴ ἀπορρεῖν, where ἐπὶ τῆς Φ. evidently refers to a different world-order from our own (τότε). (Millerd, *Emped.* 45.)

[2] *De caelo*, 301a14. I call Aristotle's reasoning odd because it would only be necessary to suppose cosmogony to occur at an early stage in Love's progress, just as it must occur at an advanced stage of Strife's. He is really arguing, not logically, but under the influence of the age-old idea that if there is to be cosmogony, it must proceed from mixture to separation. His statement here is confined to the genesis of the οὐρανός and perhaps of the inorganic world. He knew that Empedocles did describe the genesis of living things in the period of increasing Love, for he has just said so (300b29).

[3] Cf. also *ibid.* 293.18ff. (quoted above, p. 168), 528.11. Millerd objects (*op. cit.* 47) that Neoplatonic statements are here valueless because they only mean that this world is not the Sphere. Admittedly Simplicius had not a full appreciation of the cycle. For instance at 528.8ff. he misunderstands Arist. *De caelo*, 295a29 because he cannot conceive of the elements ever being wholly separated. Nevertheless I doubt if the criticism is relevant to the present passages, and on two of them Millerd notes that 'the order of treatment of Empedocles seems here to be observed'. Fortunately however we are by no means confined to Simplicius for evidence.

[4] It can hardly be argued that this account of the origin of the human race belongs to the other half of the cycle and not our own. When Empedocles does describe the origin of animal life by a reverse process of combination, later writers are careful to state explicitly that this takes place in the period of Love, but in all the many details of our own world they see, as one might expect, no reason to specify the period. (See Millerd, *Emped.* 49f.) It is in any case overwhelmingly

respondingly, contain the elements in a more thoroughly mingled state than others (A 70, pp. 208 f. below). Most significant of all, on the religious and moral side, our world exhibits a degeneration from an age of peace and harmony ruled over by Aphrodite to one of discord and slaughter (fr. 128).

The cosmogonic motion of the Sphere initiated by Strife is a revolving or whirling one (Greek *diné*). This is a simple inference from cosmology—the visible movements of the heavenly bodies—to cosmogony, followed also by Anaxagoras, who begins his cosmogony with a revolution initiated by *Nous*, and by the atomists. Its physical mechanism will be discussed later. Begun at a very early stage in the break-up of the Sphere, it brings about the separation of the rest of the elements 'by the impetus of the revolution'.[1]

Third stage: Strife triumphant

From passages like fr. 17.7–8 (= 26.5–6) and 21.7–8, it is evident that there comes a time when, in complete contrast to the union of the elements in Love, they are all completely separated by Strife.[2] But the surviving information is too scanty to answer all our questions about this state of things. There are only two lines of Empedocles,[3] which are, however, quoted by Plutarch in a descriptive context.

probable that he would follow all his predecessors, both mythical and philosophical, in the universal assumption that our world is the result of ἀπόκρισις from a πάντα ὁμοῦ and not the reverse, an assumption which continues in Anaxagoras and the atomists. The view of Zeller (ZN, 977) that our world is the world of increasing Love has been so often refuted that it can be disregarded. See e.g. Millerd, 50–2, Bignone, 561, and his appendix on the cosmic cycle in general.

[1] For discussion of the evidence see p. 186 below. The explanation of the origin of the δίνη given by the *Stromateis* (A 30) is plain enough, and there was no need for Zeller to say (ZN, 980, n. 1) that we have no record of it, or Munding (*Hermes*, 1954, 144) to say simply that the gradual growth of Strife, disrupting the Sphere, was itself pictured as a δίνη.

[2] Aristotle's paraphrases of these or other passages are in accord. So *Metaph.* 985 a 25: 'When the whole is divided into its elements by Strife, then fire is collected into one mass and so is each of the other elements'; and *De caelo*, 295 a 30: 'When the elements had been separated off by Strife....'

[3] Fr. 26a Bignone. See his *Emped.* App. 3 (599 ff.). It is difficult to understand how DK could combine these lines in their fr. 27 with those quoted by Simpl. *Phys.* 1183.30 ff., altering the end of the first one to do so. Plutarch states clearly that his quotation refers to the reign of Strife, and Simplicius that his describes that of Love; and it is entirely in keeping with Empedocles's manner that in describing two contrary states which yet have one important point in common (absence of the familiar features of our own world), he should draw attention to this fact by repetition of a half-line (pp. 136 f., 154 f. above).

In his dialogue *On the phenomenon of a face in the moon's circle*, he writes (926d):

Take care that you don't, by transposing each thing and relegating it to its natural place, bring about by your philosophy a dissolution of the cosmos and saddle things with the Strife of Empedocles—or rather rouse against nature the Titans and giants of old—and find that what you want to see, by separating all that is heavy from all that is light, is that mythical and fearful disorder and discord, when as Empedocles says:

> 'Neither is the bright form of the sun distinguished
> nor yet the shaggy earth[1] nor the sea.'

Earth had no portion of heat, nor water of air; nothing heavy was aloft, nothing light below; the principles [elements] of all things, unmixed, unloving and solitary, not admitting combination or association but avoiding and shunning one another and moving with their own stubborn motions, were in the state in which Plato [*Tim.* 53b] says everything is from which God is absent—that is, as bodies are when mind and soul have deserted them; until desirability came over nature providentially when Love, Aphrodite, or Eros was implanted in it, as Empedocles says and Parmenides and Hesiod.

The language of the sentence following the quotation leaves no doubt that Plutarch's speaker is still paraphrasing Empedocles. It suggests to him a comparison with the random motion of the Platonic chaos before the divine reason of the Creator got to work on it, and the comparison has this much point, that Empedocles too was describing a state of things furthest removed from the divinity of the Sphere. It does not follow that the motions themselves were similar, but the parallel would hardly have occurred to Plutarch if in fact the elements had been motionless under Strife as in the divine mixture brought about by Love. Their motion is confirmed by the passage in *De caelo* (301a14) where Aristotle says that Empedocles omitted to describe the cosmogony of the period when Love is taking over from Strife owing to the difficulty of describing a process of *genesis* from 'separate *and moving*' elements.

This evidence may be reinforced by more general considerations. When conflict and discord prevail, it is unlikely that the result would be peace and rest such as are the ultimate product of love and concord and

---

[1] Van Groningen (*Mnemos.* 1956, 221) has defended Plutarch's reading γένος against the μένος of Bergk and DK. He compares Hes. *Th.* 161.

(as Empedocles would agree with the Pythagoreans) are good and desirable states.[1] There was moreover, in Presocratic systems and especially since Parmenides, a general tendency to associate unity with rest, and plurality with motion.[2] There are however one or two ancient testimonies which might suggest a different state of things, and unfortunately in the absence of Empedocles's own words it is difficult to be certain. There is for instance an attractive simplicity about Zeller's explanation that

Both processes [*sc.* of separation and combination] continue until complete union on the one hand, or complete separation on the other, is achieved, and this is also the duration of the movement and life of nature, and the formation and destruction of individual things. As soon as the goal is reached, that movement ceases, the elements stop combining or separating—because they are completely mixed or separate—and will remain in this state until it is disturbed by a new impulse in the opposite direction.[3]

This interpretation goes back to Aristotle's statement in the *Physics* (250b26) that according to Empedocles 'things are alternately in motion and at rest, in motion when Love is making the one out of many or Strife many out of one, and at rest in the intervening periods'; and it depends on supposing that Aristotle is referring to two periods of rest. His precise meaning is by no means certain, and it has generally been thought that he was misled by misunderstanding *vv.* 9–13 of fr. 17 which he quotes. That is, that he has erroneously assumed ἀκίνητοι ('unchanged', of the everlasting elements) to mean 'unmoved'.[4] A

[1] Pfligersdorffer even says (perhaps a trifle too bluntly) 'Strife is movement, as Love is rest' (*Posidonios*, 110, n. 2).

[2] Thus when at the beginning of the *Physics* Aristotle enumerates the possible number and kinds of ἀρχαί, Simplicius (22.16) comments that he omits one theoretical possibility 'because the opinion has never been held that the ἀρχαί are many and motionless'. Cf. Aristotle himself at *Metaph.* 1004b29 στάσις τοῦ ἑνὸς κίνησις δὲ τοῦ πλήθους. For Parmenides of course, whom Empedocles respects to the limit compatible with the existence of a phenomenal world, the association of unity and rest was a matter of logical necessity.

[3] ZN, 971 translated. That the natural processes of this world have ceased, and that the elements can no longer continue the process of separation, is of course true, but for Zeller there was no more to be said. Evidently in his view this implied an absolute standstill.

[4] Aristotle's meaning was already disputed among his Greek commentators, see Simpl. *Phys.* 1125. Simplicius's own opinion was that Aristotle had taken ἀκίνητοι to mean literally unmoved, and this has been widely asserted since Zeller's time, e.g. by von Arnim, *Festschr. Gomperz*, 18; Millerd, *Emped.* 54; Bignone, *Emped.* 592, n. 1 and elsewhere; Cornford *ad loc.* in Loeb *Physics*; Ross, *Physics ad loc.*; Cherniss, *ACP*, 175; Munding, *Hermes*, 1954, 135; Solmsen, *HSCP*, 63, 277 and *Aristotle's System*, 223, n. 4; Kahn, *Anaximander*, 23. Whether or not Aristotle misunderstood ἀκίνητοι in this way (O'Brien (for whom see p. 183 below) argues that he did not), those who think he did still differ among themselves as to whether he was thinking of one period of rest in each complete cycle or two.

little later in the same book (252 a 7), Aristotle repeats his statement, but with 'period' in the singular: 'It happens to things of necessity that Love and Strife prevail and move them in turn, and they are at rest for the intervening period'; and his pupil Eudemus refers this period of rest only to the Sphere under the reign of Love (*ap.* Simpl. 1183.28).

Another of Aristotle's criticisms is puzzling. Empedocles believed, he says, that the earth is kept in its central position by the rapid revolution of the heavens, but this could not hold when the elements had been completely separated from one another by Strife: 'for he cannot adduce the vortex at this stage too' (*Cael.* 295 a 31). This has been taken as evidence that not only vortical motion, but all motion, will have ceased in the universe. But those who cite this and *Phys.* 250 b 26 ff. as un-equivocal evidence for Aristotle's opinion[1] should at least take into account the mention of 'separate and moving elements' at *Cael.* 301 a 14 as well.

In trying to describe the state of things when Strife is supreme our sources were in all probability making conjectures in the absence of anything on the subject in Empedocles's own poem.[2] It is natural to suppose that the separated elements were arranged in concentric circles with earth at the centre. This is perhaps implied by Aristotle's criticism about the vortex, and accords also with observation: at the advanced stage of Strife which the present cosmos has reached, the main masses of earth, water, air and fire have in fact adopted this arrangement. But it is nowhere explicitly stated.[3] Nor can we be certain how long Strife remained in undisputed sway. Most probably there

---

[1] So Millerd, *Emped.* 53 f.; Cherniss, *ACP*, 205. But cf. also Bignone, *Emped.* 562, n. 3. O'Brien offers an explanation based on the assumption that, since the state of complete separation is only momentary, the words refer to the time when Love is beginning to increase. Then, for the elements to become mingled, heavy things would have to move outwards, which is the contrary of the effect caused by a δίνη as Aristotle understood it.

[2] Thus Millerd concludes (p. 54): 'It is not impossible that Empedocles himself left the matter ambiguous.... Save in the brief initial summary there would be no need for an account of the transition from the end of the period of Strife to the beginning of the period of Love. Here he may have contented himself with some such statement as that "Strife had now won complete sway and separated the elements. Love re-entered and he withdrew to the depths of the world."' Zeller too (ZN, 971, n. 1) suggests that Empedocles may have given a detailed description of the Sphere but omitted, or only mentioned in passing, the opposite state of absolute separation.

[3] Bignone (pp. 223 and 562, n. 3) thinks it is shown by Arist. *Cael.* 295 a 30 in conjunction with Plut. *De facie* 926 f, where the elements are said to be disposed in order of weight or lightness. It is just possibly relevant to this point that Aristotle chides Empedocles, along with Anaxagoras, for having offered no explanation of lightness or weight (*Cael.* 309 a 19).

was only an instantaneous changeover from the completion of the separating process to the beginning of gradual reunion by Love. The cycle could then be divided into three equal[1] periods: Strife to Love, Sphairos, and Love to Strife. One would still have to describe the elemental relation as fourfold—completely united, separating, completely separated, uniting—but the third of these would be represented by a moment of transition only. This would explain the lack of any agreed explanation of what happens during the reign of Strife, and receives support from the difficulty of imagining any stability in a state of things where conflict and discord rage unchecked.

Fourth stage: the advance of Love

Our main source for this part of the cosmic cycle is some lines of Empedocles himself. Unfortunately their purport is not altogether clear, and they have lent themselves to a variety of interpretations.[2] As the situation will be understood here, they should be translated as follows (fr. 35, *vv.* 3ff.):

When Strife reached the lowest depth of the vortex, and whenever Love finds herself in the midst of the whirl, there all things come together to be one only—not suddenly, but combining from different directions at will.[3] And as they came together, Strife began to retire to the boundary.[4] Yet many remained unmixed alternating with those that were mingling, all those,

---

[1] At *Phys.* 252 a 31 Aristotle has the note: τὸ δὲ καὶ δι' ἴσων χρόνων δεῖται λόγου τινός. Like many of his notes, it is somewhat isolated and reads like an afterthought, but it seems to refer back to the statement ἐν μέρει τὸ πᾶν ἠρεμεῖν καὶ κινεῖσθαι πάλιν. This could refer to either a three-period or a four-period cycle (whether or not the reign of Strife in the latter were one of rest), for the brief jotting need mean only that each of the periods occupied the same time: it need not imply that the total of the periods of rest equalled the total of the periods of motion. I cannot believe in a reign of Strife that was also a period of rest, and would conclude that Empedocles had in mind either a three-period cycle or one in which the reign of Strife was much as Plutarch describes it.

O'Brien argues that complete separation is instantaneous but that the Sphairos lasts as long as the whole period of movement, from unity to separation and back again.

[2] See additional note, pp. 183–5 below.

[3] ἀλλὰ θελημὰ (or ἀλλ' ἐθελημὰ; there are no significant textual variants). Cf. Hes. *Erga*, 118: in the Golden Age the earth produced abundant crops of her own accord, and men ἐθελημοὶ ἥσυχοι ἔργ' ἐνέμοντο. Like the phrase ἀλλήλοισι ποθεῖται (21.8), this epithet reminds us that the elements are not inanimate. In response to Love they have the *desire* to combine. τὸ ἱμερτὸν ἧκεν ἐπὶ τὴν φύσιν as Plutarch says (*De facie*, 926f).

[4] Substituting fr. 36 for *v.* 7 of fr. 35 as given by Simplicius (a suggestion of DK adopted by KR). In Simplicius *v.* 7 is repeated as *v.* 16, and fr. 36 fits the context so well that in all probability Simplicius made an error in copying.

that is, that Strife still held back in suspense; for it had not all retired blame-lessly from them to the furthest ends of the circle, but parts of it remained within while other parts had passed out of the limbs. But as much as it continued to run forth, so there ever pursued it a gentle immortal stream of blameless Love. Then quickly those things grew mortal that before knew immortality, and those that were unmixed became mixed as they changed their ways.[1] And as they mingled a myriad tribes of mortal creatures were poured forth, endowed with all sorts of shapes, a wonder to behold.

As Love increases her power over the elements, which also means physically occupying an increasing area among them, Strife is gradually driven out to and beyond their confines. The view most commonly held today is that the same thing happens to Love as she is overcome by Strife. The two change places, each banishing the other outside the world and then invading it again from that position. On the transla-tion given above, the effect of Strife's re-entry is to drive Love towards the centre and force her to contract. As he continues his victorious progress he penetrates the whole sphere to its lowest (i.e. innermost) depth, and Love is penned into the very centre of the whirling mass— whirling, because the effect of Strife has been to make it rotate at ever-increasing speed (p. 186 below). The process resembles the systole and diastole of the heart, a physiological analogy which is quite in keeping with the tenour of Empedocles's thought. (See Burnet, *Thales to Plato*, 73.) The opening lines therefore describe the moment of Strife's supremacy. At this point, probably with no pause at all, Love once more begins to expand and, starting from the centre, the elements gradually unite with one another to form another world containing mortal creatures. Emphasis is laid on the gradual nature of this process and the reluctant and fighting retreat carried out by Strife. The meaning of immortal things becoming mortal is explained by what follows. They are the indestructible and changeless elements, which by mingling form mortal things like plants and animals. 'In that they have learned to grow one from many... they suffer becoming, but in that they never

---

[1] The reading of *vv.* 14 and 15 varied in antiquity and has been much discussed. The most recent treatment is that of Mr D. O'Brien, in *CR*, 1965, 1–4. I find his arguments convincing, and have followed them in preference to those of Miss Arundel (*CR*, 1962, 109–11) and Verdenius and Waszink (*Arist. on Coming-to-be*, 67).

cease...' (fr. 17.9ff., p. 153 above), though of course the language of becoming and perishing is not used strictly (fr. 9, p. 156). In this part of the cycle a natural world evolves by a process the reverse of that which occurred under the ascendancy of Strife. Instead of 'whole-natured' animate lumps in which separate limbs and organs gradually become distinct, we have the curious conception of isolated limbs combining at first haphazard into all sorts of strange creatures before they settled into the familiar species of a world like our own.[1] It is to this part of the cycle also that Bignone (*Emped.* 564f.) would refer a brief and puzzling sentence in Aëtius (1.5.2, A 47) that in Empedocles there is one cosmos only, 'but the cosmos is not the whole, but a small part of the whole: the rest is idle matter'. This idle or unformed matter would then be all that 'remained unmixed, alternating with the things that were mingling, all those, that is, that Strife still held back in suspense'; in other words, such portions of the four elements as had not yet been combined by Love to form the compound structures of the natural world. This is perhaps the best explanation, for it is certainly impossible to suppose that any unused matter existed, like the *apeiron* of Anaximander, outside and beyond the sphere of the four elements and Love and Strife; yet it is surprising that the doxographer should use the word *cosmos* without qualification to refer, not to the present world, but to that which forms the opposite phase of the cycle. (Cf. p. 173, n. 4 above.) The possibility of either a misunderstanding or a wrong attribution cannot be dismissed.[2]

Conclusion

In outline the world-process of Empedocles is plain enough. To divide it into four phases seems the clearest and most logical way of explaining it (even if one of them was instantaneous), though without any intention of

---

[1] Fr. 57 ('heads without necks, eyes lacking faces') is referred by Aristotle to the period ἐπὶ τῆς Φιλότητος (*De caelo*, 300b29), and both this state of things and the ox–men hybrids described in fr. 61 occurred κατὰ τὴν τῆς Φιλίας ἀρχήν according to Simplicius (*Phys.* 371.33). Their erroneous assignment by Philoponus (*Phys.* 314.6ff.) to an early stage in the dissolution of the Sphere seems to be due to his attempt to fit the texts to the Neoplatonic idea of a single world of generation only. (See Millerd, *Emped.* 48.) The zoogony of both worlds will be dealt with more fully later (pp. 200ff.).
[2] Zeller assumed misunderstanding (ZN, 981, n. 3).

claiming that they were so enumerated by Empedocles himself.[1] If they were, the misunderstandings of Neoplatonic and other commentators could hardly have arisen. But the evidence of Aristotle and Theophrastus (p. 173, n. 1 above), supported by the fragments, is decisive for the substantial correctness of the thesis that (*a*) the cycle contains two world periods, developed between the divine commingled Sphere of Love and the utter separation and estrangement of the elements under Strife, and (*b*) we are now living in the phase of Strife's increasing influence. In assessing the interpretations of the Neoplatonic writers, it is important to remember that they saw the early philosophers in the distorting mirror of their own belief in two everlasting realms of existence, the sensible and the intelligible. Simplicius as well as Philoponus attempted to find in Empedocles an early adumbration of this Platonic ontology, in which the divine Sphere represented the intelligible realm and the rest of the cycle was foreshortened into a picture of the sensible. The whole is, in their eyes, an analysis of the permanent constitution of reality and our relation to it, metaphorically expressed, for instructional purposes, in genetic terms.[2] It is all the more remarkable, and a tribute to his scholarly conscience, that Simplicius provides so much of the material from which we can reconstruct the unique Empedoclean scheme of two world-processes operating in contrary directions, and refuses to gloss over all the difficulties in his own simplified version.

The boldness of Empedocles's conception, and the thoroughness and consistency with which he applied its principles in a detailed explanation of the natural world, afford an extraordinary demonstration of the power of the human imagination disciplined, but not inhibited or rendered ineffective, by the intellect. He was, says Aristotle (*Metaph.* 985 a 29), the first to divide the motive principle into two contrary forces, and the question has often been asked, what the motive for such elaboration can have been. If he wished simply to restore reality to the physical world and its processes, and rescue them from the Parmenidean

---

[1] For some of the many conflicting theories of the cosmic cycle see ZN, 971, n. 1 and Bignone *Emped.* App. 2 (545–98, esp. 546, n. 1). The most influential of those denying a four-period cycle was von Arnim in *Festschr. Gomperz* (1902). This is summarized by Nestle (ZN, *loc. cit.*) and criticized by Bignone (591–8). The former calls it a two-period theory, the latter a three-period, but in any case it is not the three-period theory suggested on p. 178 above.

[2] Simpl. *De caelo*, 305.21, 530.24, *Phys.* 34.8; Philop. *Phys.* 24.9.

denial of motion and plurality, then a single cause and a single process would have sufficed, once plurality had been restored within the ultimate constitution of matter. This was how the case appeared to Anaxagoras: given a plurality of qualitatively different elemental 'seeds', only *Nous* was required to set the mass in motion. The only convincing answer is that for Empedocles the moral and religious order was as important as the physical, and in equal need of explanation. For this he turned to the primeval force of Love,[1] which since Hesiod and the Orphic writers, if not earlier, and even in the 'Way of Seeming' of Parmenides himself, had been recognized as a cosmogonic as well as a moral power. But Love could not explain everything. 'Since nature plainly contained things contrary to the good—not only order and beauty but disorder and ugliness—and the bad outnumbered the good and the worthless the fine, [Empedocles] introduced Love and Strife, each of them the cause of one of these qualities' (Arist. *Metaph.* 984b32). Empedocles was haunted also by another ancient dogma which told of increasing disharmony between man and nature and his degeneration from a physically and morally superior type. Linked in his mind with this tradition of a past Golden Age was the belief current in his own Western lands that the bodily existence of men is a punishment imposed on essentially divine spirits. Why had they fallen? What was the source of pain and evil? If Love was active as a unifying force both in the world at large and in the hearts of men (fr. 17.22 f.), must there not be another and even stronger power now urging both in the direction of disintegration and evil? And what could this be but Love's opposite, cursed hatred, strife (*Eris*), Ares?[2] Given two opposing forces, they might have remained eternally locked in an indecisive struggle like the 'everlasting fire' of the Heraclitean cosmos; but this would have left unexplained the degeneration from a Golden Age of bounteous, beneficent nature and sinless man; and if that demand was to be satisfied, then the Greek, with his instinct for symmetry and reciprocity (one thinks, for example, of the 'justice' of Anaximander),

---

[1] Though he calls this force Aphrodite, Cypris and Φιλότης, the name Eros does not actually occur in the extant fragments. This however may well be accidental as Kranz supposed (*Emped.* 43).

[2] The contrasting pair Φιλότης and Ἔρις (cf. Emped. fr. 20.4) occur already in Hesiod (*Th.* 224f.) among the progeny of Night.

and his conception of time as a circular rather than a linear process, demanded that there should be a compensating age of increasing Love. That this era lay beyond the bounds of our experience was no barrier to his ever-fertile mind.[1]

Additional note: the interpretation of fr. 35

The interpretation of these difficult lines given on pp. 178 ff. was only reached after much heart-searching and represents a reversal of my previous opinion undergone in the course of writing. Ever since I listened to Cornford's lectures and first read Burnet's *Early Greek Philosophy* I had taken it for granted that *vv.* 3 and 4 described the Sphairos of the reign of Love. Strife was outside (ἐνέρτατον ἵκετο βένθος), and Love 'in the middle of the whirl', which must be supposed to mean 'occupying the whole of it'. Under her influence the elements now join together, though not all at once (*vv.* 5 and 6), so as to allow of the formation of a world of creatures out of the partly-mixed elements (though one would have thought that once Love was everywhere in the sphere she would already have brought about complete union).

The other interpretation, that *vv.* 3 and 4 describe the victory of Strife, who has penetrated from circumference to centre and penned Love in the very middle, was given by Burnet in *From Thales to Plato* (1914), p. 73, though without discussion, and curiously enough in all three editions of *EGP* (1892, 1908 and 1920) he writes that as Strife enters the sphere Love is driven outside it. The case for the supposition that Love is driven to the centre by Strife's predominance has tended to go by default, since of the few scholars who have adopted it none has done more than state it without argument. (Besides Burnet, see e.g. Robin, *Greek Thought*, Eng. tr. 104.) However, Mr D. O'Brien,

---

[1] Ch. Mugler (*Devenir Cyclique*, 46 f.) points out that there can also have been a purely scientific or physical justification for the introduction of the two opposing forces. In Anaximander, differentiation (ἀπόκρισις) creates a world which is destroyed by reabsorption. Empedocles saw that differentiation itself, if continued unchecked, would be equally destructive to organic structures. It was, Mugler suggests, this discovery that gave him the idea of substituting for the unique force of Anaximander the antagonism of two contrary forces counteracting each other. I may have done less than justice to this interesting suggestion, but I am sure it is equally mistaken to leave out the religious and moral motives which I believe to have had even more influence in bringing Empedocles to his conception. Mugler goes on to detect in him a first sketch of the oscillation between actual and potential energy, familiar in modern physics, as well as the law of the conservation of energy and the second law of thermodynamics.

who has recently subjected the fragment to a detailed examination for a forthcoming study of Empedocles, has concluded that it is correct. The experience of defending the opposite view in discussion led me to make the effort to re-read the lines with a completely open mind, as if for the first time, and this has finally brought me to see the interpretation now given here as much the most natural. No doubt obscurities remain, and the idea of Love as *compressible* is not an easy one to absorb; but probability lies in that direction.

The full case must await the publication of Mr O'Brien's work, but the points which have chiefly struck me on an unbiased re-reading of the fragment are these.

(1) The difficulty of believing that ἐνέρτατον βένθος δίνης in *v*. 3 means the same as ἔσχατα τέρματα κύκλου in *v*. 10 rather than its antithesis. (This had always troubled my conscience to some extent.)

(2) The translation of the verbs in *v*. 10 as if Strife and Love were passing each other like trains on the up and down lines. ἐπῄει in the context of ὑπεκπροθέοι is much more likely to mean 'pursued'. (For ὑπεκπροθέω of one pursued cf. *Il.* 21.604; *Od.* 8.125.)

(3) The difficulty of tenses and sequence of events in *vv*. 3–5. When Strife *had arrived* (ἵκετο) at the ἐνέρτατον βένθος, and Love *was*[1] in the middle of the whirl, only then do all things *come together gradually* (συνέρχεται οὐκ ἄφαρ). If this describes the triumph of Love, surely the *process* of combination, bringing about and then destroying a world of living creatures, should be complete. It seems better to assume that we are at the opposite point of the cycle, and that the complete separation of the elements was momentary, as suggested already on p. 178. Once Strife has reached its furthest extent and confined Love to the very centre, then *there* (ἐν τῇ δή, *v*. 5), i.e. where the unifying power of Love was, they begin gradually to combine again. I should prefer not to consider here any further details of Love's position, for which the evidence does not exist, but in placing her initially (that is, at the beginning of her activity) at the centre of the whole mass, from which

---

[1] Subjunctive γένηται with perfect sense followed by a present indicative. O'Brien draws attention to Goodwin, *Moods and Tenses*, §90. The change of mood he has defended by comparison with the Homeric similes illustrated in Goodwin, 547–9, as indicating a change in Empedocles's mind from thinking of one cycle only (ἵκετο) to a general contemplation of the endless succession of cycles.

she sets about her cosmogonic work, Empedocles must surely have had the goddess of Parmenides in mind. She too was the goddess of sexual union and mother of Eros, and in her turn seems to have owed something to Pythagorean teaching (pp. 62ff. above).

J. COSMOGONY AND COSMOLOGY

(1) *Cosmogony*

That Empedocles omitted any account of cosmogony by combination in the period of increasing Love is stated by Aristotle (p. 173 above) and borne out by the silence of the fragments and secondary authorities. Of the genesis of our own world, which as in earlier systems was a process of 'separating-out', we have some description, though the doxographers have unfortunately not thought fit to quote much from Empedocles himself. This is the more tantalizing in that Clement has preserved the four lines in which he promises to tell of it (fr. 38):

But come now, I shall tell thee the beginning, from which everything that we now see became manifest: earth and billowy sea, the damp atmosphere and *aither* the Titan fastening his circle tight round everything.[1]

The most informative passage is from the *Stromateis*, and runs as follows (A30):

Empedocles of Acragas posits four elements, fire, water, air (*aither*) and earth, and Love and Strife as their cause. He says that air [*aer*: the late

---

[1] Notes on the translation:—

v. 1. This line as the received text of Clement has it (λέξω πρῶθ' ἥλιον ἀρχήν) is nonsense, but whether or not Empedocles mentioned the sun, he is at least promising to reveal the ἀρχή of our familiar world, as the next line makes clear.

v. 2. ἐξ ὧν δῆλ' ἐγένοντο Weil (who compares fr. 23.10), adopted by DK. The text of Clement has δὴ ἐγένοντο, 'from which there came into being'.

v. 3. ὑγρὸς ἀήρ. ὑγρός need not of course have its literal sense of 'damp'; it may mean pliant, mobile, 'buxom'. The translation is based on the fact (for which cf. Kahn, *Anaximander*, 124 f.) that the lines refer, not to the four 'roots' in their purity, but to the main masses as they now appear to us (τὰ νῦν ἐσορῶμεν). ὑγρὸς ἀήρ is thus the contaminated atmosphere of the sublunary world, and Τίταν αἰθήρ (appropriately translated 'Sky' by Kahn) the clear bright substance of outer space. (On Τίταν see further pp. 193 f. below.) Common Greek speech was content with the term αἰθήρ, but once the four-element cosmology had been put forward, philosophers differed over the question whether it should be identified with air (pure) or fire. Finally it was established as a fifth element (vol. 1, 270ff.). In Empedocles it is regularly the word for air, which in its elemental state was the first to be separated out of the mixture and formed the outer shell of the cosmic sphere. (Cf. additional note 1, p. 145.) In the passage from the *Stromateis* to be discussed immediately, it is clearly distinguished from fire. See further in text.

author reverts to his own terminology] was separated off from the primal mixture[1] and spread around it in a circle. After air, fire burst out, and having nowhere else to go ran out under the solid mass of air.[2] There are two hemispheres revolving round the earth, one entirely of fire and the other a mixture of air [or mist, *aer* again] and a little fire. This he supposes is the night. The start of the revolution is due to the accident that the fire weighed down and overbalanced the mass.[3]

The essential motion initiated by Strife is that of the separation of the elements from each other and the attraction of like to like in ever-increasing masses. In Empedocles's own words (fr. 37): 'Earth augments its own body, and air augments air.' (Cf. also fr. 90.) This however immediately creates a lack of balance in the former perfectly blended Sphere, and since the mass is still approximately spherical in shape, the differing weights of the two first elements to be separated out produced in it the rotation which still persists.[4] This rotation has been gradually accelerating, as is to be expected when one remembers that it began from the absolute immobility of the Sphere of Love. Therefore, since the sun is carried round by the motion of the whole sphere, the days have been gradually growing shorter.

When the human race was first generated from out of the earth, the day was of the length that ten months are now, owing to the slowness of the sun's advance. As time went on, it became the length of seven months (Aët. 5.18.1, A75).

The consistency with which Empedocles applies the first principles of his cosmogony is remarkable. If at all possible he connects their

---

[1] ἐκ τῆς πρώτης κράσεως. Though meaning no more than that air was the first element to be separated out of the mixture, the phraseology may afford some slight additional support to the view, on other grounds reasonable, that Empedocles began his account of the cosmic cycle from the Sphere of Love.

[2] This translation of τοῦ περὶ τὸν ἀέρα πάγου follows Bignone, *Emped.* 327, n. 2.

[3] Text corrupt. See Bignone, 328, n. 1. But the meaning cannot be other than that fire was concentrated in the upper hemisphere to begin with, and being heavier than the pure air, caused the whole sphere to start revolving.

[4] I cannot see how this account of the mechanism whereby Strife brings about the δίνη is inconsistent with the mention of the δίνη in fr. 35, nor, therefore, the necessity to have recourse, as Bignone does, to the improbable hypothesis that the δίνη belongs to a different cosmic period. Pfligersdorffer (*Posidonios*, 110) points out correctly enough that the δίνη is not the original motion, but occurs only after the separation of air and fire. The motion originated by Strife, in keeping with his character, is one of separation pure and simple. Its further results are accidental consequences of the separation (ἀπὸ τοῦ τετυχηκέναι..., A30).

application with some phenomenon in the present world, in this case by a fanciful parallel with the birth of children after seven or ten months' gestation.[1]

The implication that fire is heavier than 'air' has been thought strange, but only because of our habit of equating the four elements of Empedocles with the four sublunary elements of Aristotle's five-element doctrine. In fact, although we use the Aristotelian nomenclature, this 'air' is for Empedocles, both in name and nature, *aither*. The Greeks, owing to their enviable climate, had always made a distinction between *aither*, the brilliant upper sky, divine itself and the abode of divinity, and the dimmer *aer* at cloud-level and below.[2] To the natural philosophers, until the explicit adoption of the five-element theory, *aer* was simply *aither* contaminated with grosser matter such as moisture. This had to be so for Empedocles, in whose system there were only four pure elemental substances, and hence when he speaks of *aither* he means this bright divine essence which in its purity occupies (as the account here quoted says) the outermost regions with fire beneath it. In the terrestrial regions we experience it as atmospheric air or in even more adulterated forms, but as one of the four 'roots' it might be less misleading to call it 'ether'. The familiarity of the quartet fire, water, earth and air makes this impracticable (hence, like Empedocles, 'I conform to custom myself'), but it is essential to be aware that this is not the sublunary air of Aristotle. It is an element whose main mass is more distant from the earth, and nearer the outer confines of the round universe, than is the main mass of fire. Aëtius's version of the separation of the elements, which also includes the further stages, brings out the distinction well (2.6.3, A49):

Empedocles says that the *aither* [pure elemental air] was first separated off, fire second, and after that earth. From earth, as it was excessively constricted by the force of the revolution, water gushed out, and from water the *aer* [sublunary atmosphere] was evaporated. The heaven was formed out of *aither* and the sun of fire, and from the rest was condensed the terrestrial realm.

---

[1] It was commonly believed that babies born after seven months could survive, and those born after forty weeks, or ten lunar months, had a particularly good chance of survival; but that those born after eight months invariably died. See e.g. Hipp. *De septimestri*, 4 and 7 (VII, 442 and 446 Littré).

[2] Vol. I, 466, 470f.

The idea of the crystalline heaven, so familiar in the middle ages and already hinted at in Parmenides (A 37) and possibly in Anaximenes,[1] here becomes explicit. The *Stromateis* spoke of the 'solid mass' (πάγος) of air, and this is further developed in Aëtius. Air, it appears, was 'frozen' into solidity by the action of fire.

Empedocles says that the sky is solid, made of air congealed by fire in the manner of ice. It encloses fiery and airy substance in each hemisphere respectively.[2]

The apparently bizarre speculations of the early thinkers are rarely entirely divorced from observation, but sometimes depend on rather extravagant extrapolation from it. Thus the hardening action of fire appears in a more credible form when Empedocles speaks of the drying out of the earth at the time when it produced the first living creatures:

So then Cypris, after she had moistened the earth with water, as she fashioned the forms of living things gave them to swift fire to harden.[3]

Here the goddess plays Prometheus, and is compared to a potter baking clay figures in the kiln. In fr. 34 the image is that of a baker mixing flour and water, which again will be hardened into a crust by fire. The process is similar to that in the cosmogony described by Diodorus (1.7.2 f.). The earth 'was muddy and altogether soft, then first of all it underwent hardening[4] as the fire of the sun shone down upon it, next the heat caused its surface to boil up', and in this state it produced the fertile bubbles in which life made its first appearance. Somewhat similarly Archelaus in the late fifth century taught that water under the

---

[1] See vol. I, 135 ff.

[2] Aët. 2.11.2 (A51). The ice-like or glassy nature of the sky is reiterated by D.L. (8.77) and other writers cited in A51. Aët. 2.13.11 (A54) says that the stars συνδεδέσθαι τῷ κρυστάλλῳ.

[3] Fr. 73. These lines, says Simplicius, came 'a little after' fr. 71 in which the birth of mortal things is mentioned. They sound as if they referred to the zoogony of the period of increasing Love. Earth and water, hitherto separated, are being mixed. Under Strife the same effect would be produced as the water, effectively homogeneous with earth in the Sphere, is forced out on to its surface. For the reading and translation of εἴδεα ποιπνύουσα see Bignone, 455 f., 206, n. 4. It is supported, as DK note, by frr. 22.7 and 71.3.

[4] πῆξις. πήγνυμι (meaning both to solidify and to freeze) was used frequently by Empedocles himself, showing how often he thought of the process of creation as a hardening or solidifying. In fr. 56, 'Salt is solidified when struck by the onset of the sun's rays', it can be translated literally; but in the following cases one can only render it by 'make': fr. 15.4 πρὶν δὲ πάγεν τε βροτοί, 86 ἐξ ὧν ὄμματ' ἔπηξεν...'Αφροδίτη, 107.1 ἐκ τούτων πάντα πεπήγασιν ἁρμοσθέντα, 75.1 τὰ δ' ἔκτοθι μανὰ πέπηγε. The doxographers speak of the πάγος of the air (A30), and of ἀέρος συμπαγέντος (A51); the moon is a πάγος ἀέρος, πεπηγὼς ὑπὸ πυρός (A60). The fragments justify us in supposing that they are reproducing the philosopher's own terms.

action of heat formed not only mist but also earth (DK, 60 A 1 and 4, p. 342 below). The strange notion that heat should solidify water as well as vaporizing it may perhaps receive some illumination from the Aristotelian *Problemata*. These base a question on the observed fact that a deposit crystallizes from the water of hot springs on the rocks over which it flows. 'Why are stones formed by hot water rather than by cold?... The cause of the petrifaction is the heat, just as Empedocles says that rocks and stones and hot waters are formed.'[1] The *naïveté* of Empedocles on this point is somewhat redeemed by the statement which Plutarch attributes to him (see A 69) that rocks have their origin in 'the fire that burns in the depth of the earth'. This wins praise from Bignone (p. 72) as a recognition of the important theory of the plutonic origin of rocks. Nevertheless to Empedocles their origin from hot water was an equally logical inference from observation: the essential is the presence of heat.

To Empedocles the creation of the various contents of the physical world appeared in general as a process of hardening, solidifying, or 'setting'. (Cf. n. on previous page) The agent of this 'setting' was fire, which no doubt is the reason why Aristotle saw fire as occupying a special position in his system, over against the other three elements:

(*GC*, 330 b 19)   Some, like Empedocles, posit four elements as primary. Yet he too reduces them to two, for he opposes all the others to fire.

(*Metaph.* 985 a 31)   He was the first to say that the material elements are four, yet he does not employ them as four but as two only, putting fire by itself and treating the others—earth, air and water—as a single substance. So one would suppose from a study of his verses.

We find a hint of this special position of fire as agent in the zoogony of fr. 62 (p. 206 below). Otherwise it is not obvious in the extant fragments, and Aristotle like the doxographers must have had other passages in mind. He may also have been inclined to exaggerate its significance, since he and Theophrastus themselves attached great importance to the activity of fire and heat in contrast to the passivity of

---

[1] *Probl.* 937 a 11 (A 69). Cf. Hippocr. *De aëre*, etc. 7 (II, 29 f. Littré): among waters injurious to health are those springing from earth where hot waters are found, or iron, copper, silver, gold, sulphur, alum, bitumen or soda: ταῦτα γὰρ πάντα ὑπὸ βίης γίγνονται τοῦ θερμοῦ.
The action of heat in both solidifying and liquefying is discussed by Aristotle, who also classifies substances according to whether they are solidified by heat or cold. See *PA*, 649 a 29 ff., *Meteor.* 388 b 10 ff., 382 b 31 ff.

Empedocles

the other forms of matter.[1] For Empedocles all the elements remained 'equal, coeval, each master in a different province and with its own character' (fr. 17.27); but the province of fire was certainly to be active and creative. In this he had many predecessors.[2] He was moreover a native of Sicily, that violent land where the soil is baked hard and dry by the fierce radiance of a sun more African than European, where by evaporation salt is extracted from the sea commercially in large quantities,[3] and the earth sends up fiery lava from Etna and in several places springs of hot water.

(2) Shape of the cosmos

Although the doxographers refer to the cosmos as a sphere, and its halves as hemispheres, Aëtius in one place says that strictly speaking it was egg-shaped, with its height (distance from earth to sky) less than its breadth.[4] The comparison was probably suggested to Empedocles, not by any observed facts, but by the poems of the Orphics, in whose cosmogony a world-egg gave birth to the generative power of Love (Eros–Phanes) before the existence of heaven and earth, which were subsequently formed from the two halves of the egg. His religious views are very close to those of the Orphics. The parallel may have extended to more than the shape. In his introduction to the *Phaenomena* of Aratus, Achilles writes:

The arrangement which we have assigned to the sphere the Orphics compare to that in eggs. The sky is analogous to the shell, and as the *aither* is suspended in a circle from the heaven, so is the skin (ὑμήν) from the shell.[5]

---

[1] Cf. e.g. *Meteor.* 379a15 καὶ γὰρ γῆ καὶ ὕδωρ καὶ ἀὴρ σήπεται· πάντα γὰρ ὕλη τῷ πυρί ἐστι ταῦτα, and the role of fire as agent of growth in Theophrastus's *Hist. plant.* and *De causis plant.*

[2] Most recently Parmenides. See pp. 58ff. above.

[3] In ancient times at Acragas itself, though nowadays the salt-pans can be best observed at Marsala. (Cf. fr. 56.)

[4] Aët. 2.31.4 (A50). A translation is: 'Empedocles says that the height from the earth to the sky, that is the elevation from ourselves, is less than the dimension in breadth. The heaven extends further in the latter direction, because the cosmos lies like an egg.' Zeller (ZN, 980, n. 2) was inclined to take the words ᾠῷ παραπλησίως κεῖσθαι as referring strictly to position only, claiming that the rest of the description applied better to a flattened spheroid. Nestle however added to the note that in all probability Empedocles had borrowed the ancient conception of the world as an egg, and the introduction of the word (assuming that it is his) certainly suggests this. That it should have precisely the shape of a bird's egg may not have seemed necessary.

[5] Kern, *Orph. Fr.* 70, p. 150; DK, vol. 1, p. 11. For the egg see especially the cosmogony of Aristophanes's *Birds*, 693ff. Achilles is a writer of perhaps the third century A.D., but for the

This arrangement has a certain resemblance to that of Empedocles's cosmos, with sky corresponding to his *aither* which formed the outermost sphere, and *aither* to his fire which 'ran out under the solid mass' at the circumference. Empedocles was much impressed by the analogy between the members or parts of the animal and vegetable world (fr. 82, p. 209 below), and for him and his contemporaries the world itself was the supreme and universal animal. It is possible that the word 'crystalline' was used in connexion with eggs (vol. 1, 137), and Leucippus compared the surface of the round universe to a skin or membrane (ὑμήν, D.L. 9.32). It is an interesting if somewhat speculative idea that the long-lived and influential notion of the crystalline sphere (later spheres) may have owed its origin to the macrocosm–microcosm analogy and the idea that the universe was essentially an enormous egg. Whether its outer envelope should be compared to skin or shell seems to have been something on which the natural philosophers differed.

Nothing is recorded of what Empedocles thought about the absolute size of the cosmos, but he said that the sun is the same size as the earth and twice as far above the moon as the moon is above the earth. Since the orbit of the sun is at the periphery of the cosmos, the vertical radius of the cosmos is three times the distance of the moon from the earth.[1] He followed the Pythagoreans in assigning right and left sides to the cosmos, an idea which is bound up with that of the animate nature of the universe.[2]

(3) *The sun and the two hemispheres*

He believed, as did Anaxagoras, that the celestial North Pole was originally at the zenith, and that the axis of the universe was later tilted. For this, according to Aëtius (2.8.2, A58), he gave a mechanical explanation:

---

credentials of the world-egg as an Orphic conception see Guthrie, *Orph. and Gk. Rel.* 92 ff. The idea occurs in the most widely separated places. In China in Han times an astronomical theory was current according to which heaven and earth are shaped like an egg, earth being enclosed by the sphere of heaven just as the yolk of an egg is enclosed by its shell (Kramer, *Mythologies of the Anc. World*, 384, and for an identical conception in Iranian mythology, *ibid.* 339).

[1] Aët. 2.21.2, 31.1 (A56 and 61). Consistently with this, he said that the sun was larger than the moon (D.L. 8.77).

[2] Aët. 2.10.2 (A50). For the Pythagoreans see Arist. *De caelo*, 284 b 6, where also the connexion of right and left with sensation and the power of locomotion is brought out.

He says that as the *aer* gave way before the onrush of the sun [i.e. the dark hemisphere before that of the light; see below], the poles[1] were tilted, so that the northern parts were heightened and the southern lowered, and the whole universe affected similarly.

Still relying on the secondary sources, we learn that the stars are 'fiery, made from the fiery element which the air contained within itself and squeezed out at the first separation'. They are not, therefore, as they were for Xenophanes, the result of exhalations from earth-level, a difference which seems to reflect the different religious outlook of the two men. The fixed stars are imbedded 'in the crystal', but the planets move freely.[2]

The sun is also commonly described as being of fire. Diogenes (8.77) calls it 'a great concentration of fire', and Aëtius (2.6.3, A49) says that as the elements separated the sky was formed of *aither* and the sun of fire. Only the *Stromateis* (A30) say that 'the substance of the sun is not fire, but a reflexion of fire like that from water'. Each of these sources is perhaps over-simplifying the case. Aëtius in another passage (2.20.13, A56) credits Empedocles with a complex theory about the sun which is not altogether easy to understand.[3]

Empedocles assumes two suns: (1) the archetype, which is fire in one hemisphere of the cosmos. It fills the hemisphere, and is always stationed opposite its own reflexion; (2) the visible sun. This is a reflexion in the other hemisphere, namely the hemisphere which is filled with air [or darkness, *aer*] mixed with heat. It arises by reflexion from the earth—which is circular[4]—on to the crystal-like sun, and is carried round with it by the motion of the fire. In brief, the sun is a reflexion of the fire surrounding the earth.

This may be supplemented by a further sentence of Aëtius (2.21.2, A56) that 'the sun-by-reflexion is equal to the earth', and a line of

---

[1] τὰς ἄρκτους, the north and south poles. Cf. Arist., *Meteor.* 362 a 32, ἡ ἑτέρα ἄρκτος of the south pole. For the rest see Heath, *Aristarchus*, 91 f.

[2] Aët. 2.13.2 and 11 (A 53 and 54). The fixing of the stars ἐν τῷ κρυστάλλῳ suggests that he may have been copying a theory of Anaximenes, but there are obscurities and difficulties about the attribution, and it is by no means clear that Anaximenes distinguished between fixed stars and planets, though some have thought he did. See vol. I, 135 ff.

[3] Some earlier views are mentioned by Millerd, *Emped.* 66. Gilbert, *Met. Theor.* 683 f.; Dreyer, *Plan. Systems*, 24 f.; and Bignone, *Emped.* 240, 346, n. 2, may also be consulted. Bignone is brief, on the ground that no certain conclusion is possible from the evidence, a view which is shared by Millerd, DK, and others. See also Kranz in *Rh. Mus.* 1957, 123 f.

[4] The word is κυκλοτερής, not the ambiguous στρογγύλος.

Empedocles himself which is quoted in passing in Plutarch's *De Pyth. or.* (400b, see Empedocles fr. 44): 'You laugh at Empedocles for saying that the sun, originating about the earth by reflexion of light from the sky, "flashes back to Olympus with fearless countenance".'

In the absence of the original it is unlikely that we can reproduce his theory with certainty from these partial and distorted data. Most probably the sun (in the ordinary accepted use of the word) is a reflexion of the whole fiery hemisphere thrown back on to it in some way from the earth. When the *Stromateis*, to emphasize that it is only a reflexion, say that it is not itself fire, they falsify Empedocles, since for him a reflexion consisted of effluences of particles from an object, collected and packed together on the reflecting surface; that is, they are of the same material as the object itself.[1] The term *anaklasis* (bending back, re-flexion) was used not only of reflected light or images, but also in connexion with the use of convex mirrors as burning-glasses,[2] and this is obviously what was in Empedocles's mind here. The whole bright fiery hemisphere shines on to the earth, where its light and fire are collected into a focus and then thrown back as a 'great concentration[3] of fire', as Diogenes has it, to form the sun. The daily revolution of the sphere carries the sun round with it. It is natural that Empedocles should have been neither accurate nor very clear about the laws governing the direction of reflexions. This fits most of the testimony, including any hints that we have in the fragments of the poem itself. Thus in fr. 41 it is said of the sun that 'when gathered [or massed, ἁλισθείς] together he circles round the great heaven'. Kranz with some plausibility takes fr. 44, that the sun 'flashes back to Olympus with fearless countenance', introduced by Plutarch with the remark that it originates by reflexion of light from the sky, together with fr. 38.4 (quoted above, p. 185), as being the lines which together gave rise to the 'two-sun' description of Aëtius. 'Titan' suggests a reference to the

[1] Aët. 4.14.1 (A88). The point is made by Millerd, *Emped.* 68.
[2] See e.g. Theophrastus, *De igne*, 73 (III, 72 Wimmer): ἀπὸ μὲν τοῦ ἡλίου φῶς ἅπτουσι τῇ ἀνακλάσει ἀπὸ τῶν λείων. The reports about Empedocles are evidence that this technique was understood in his time.
[3] ἄθροισμα. Cf. the use of ἀθροισμός by Theophrastus, *De igne*, 73, in connexion with burning-mirrors.

sun,[1] and at the same time it is the *aither* which circumscribes all things. This is the fire-filled half of the crystalline hemisphere considered as 'archetypal' sun, whereas what 'flashes back to Olympus' (that is to the sky, identical with '*aither* the Titan') is what *we* call the sun, the dazzling and burning concentration thrown back from the earth.

It is incredible that this theory should not be in some way connected with the Pythagorean ideas about the sun attributed to Philolaus.[2] Philolaus was the younger man, but one cannot be certain about the chronological relationship of the two theories. Both were of course known to Theophrastus, on whom Aëtius, our immediate source for both, will have been relying, and from what is said of the Philolaic view in particular one may judge that he thought them rather absurd. His suggestion that it might even imply a third sun is only a captious criticism, and it is possible that the talk of 'two suns' is also a matter of interpretation and that he had rather lightly thrown the two theories together. They could not have been identical, since Empedocles's scheme lacked the central fire of the Philolaic, and it may be a confusion here that led Aëtius to speak of the sun as reflected in the other, dark hemisphere. This is the hemisphere of night, nor is it easy to see how in that case, if it originated from the fiery hemisphere, it could be reflected off the earth. Millerd tried to meet the objection that if the sun were in this hemisphere it would be bright day, by saying that 'fire is not perceived unless it approaches the eye. It may be spread out in the heavens through the whole hemisphere that encircles us without our perceiving it. It may travel from one hemisphere to the other in large quantities without coming to us.'[3] Even if this were correct, the idea

---

[1] Kranz makes this point in *Philologus*, 1961, 290–5. Titan itself as a name for the sun does not elsewhere occur until the Christian era, when it is frequent in poetry, but he nevertheless is a Titan, namely Hyperion, as early as Homer (*Il.* 19.398; *Od.* 1.24) as well as in later classical writers. Alternatively he is the son of Titans (Theia and Hyperion in Hes. *Th.* 371–4; Hyperion, *ibid.* 1011, *Od.* 12.176; *Hom. Hymn Dem.* 26).

[2] See vol. 1, 284f. To make a small additional point, both used the name Olympus for the highest heaven. Cf. Empedocles, fr. 44 (quoted in text) and Philolaus A 16. Diels (*SBB*, 1884, 353) thought that the origin of the reflexion-theory of the sun was incomprehensible without presupposing the reflexion from Philolaus's central fire.

[3] *Emped.* 68. This, she says, is the target of Aristotle's criticism in *De an.* 418 b 20, and not the statement that light is a moving body and takes time to travel. In its context it 'refers rather to the possibility of light being present in a medium without "actualizing" it, that is, without being perceptible through that medium'. I cannot detect this reference, unless ἡμᾶς δὲ λανθάνοντος be taken to mean that we do not see the light, whereas it obviously means that we do not see the

that the hemisphere of fire could be the nocturnal one, because the fire in it escapes our eyes, is disproved by the *Stromateis* (A30), which state that not the fiery hemisphere but the hemisphere of *aer* 'mixed with a little fire' (presumably the stars) 'is the night'. It is also incompatible with frr. 48 and 49 of Empedocles himself, in the setting in which they are presented.

Fr. 48 (Plut. *Qu. Plat.* 1006f): The pointers of sundials by staying still and not changing their place with the shadows become instruments and measures of time, like the earth which intercepts the sun when the sun passes below it, as Empedocles says:

'The earth makes night by blocking the lights.'

Fr. 49 (*Plut. Qu. conv.* 720e): The *aer* being dark (as Empedocles says,

'belonging to lonely, blind-eyed[1] night')

gives back through the ears what it takes away from sight of the power of perceiving ahead.

Fr. 49 substantiates the statement of the *Stromateis* that the hemisphere of *aer* is that of night, and fr. 48 shows that Empedocles believed the dark effect of the nocturnal hemisphere to be ensured by the screening off of the sun's light by the earth. It has been claimed as an advance on his part that by attributing night to the shadow of the earth he had outgrown the earlier idea that darkness was a substance in itself, a kind of mist or exhalation.[2] In fact however night was still a sky-ful of *aer*, and the part played by the earth's interposition was simply to ensure that the darkness of this substance was not counteracted by

movement of the light. That light takes time to travel is an anticipation of modern knowledge, but for Empedocles it followed naturally from his view that light is a material substance 'flowing from the light-giving body' (Philop. *De an.* 334.34, A57). It is stated by Aristotle, *loc. cit.*: 'Empedocles, and any other who says the same, are wrong in speaking of light as travelling and being at a given moment between the earth and the surrounding sphere'; and again *De sensu*, 446a26.

On the other hand Millerd does draw attention to something generally overlooked: not only does Aëtius say that the sun is a reflexion in the darker hemisphere, but Plutarch (*De facie*, 922c, A60) speaks conversely of people who grumble at Empedocles for making the moon a solidification of air *surrounded by the sphere of fire*. I cannot claim to understand from this what Empedocles himself said, but it certainly does not explain how the sun could be a reflexion from the dark sphere, on Millerd's view or any other.

[1] The received text of Plutarch has ἀγλαώπιδος, but this word is otherwise unknown, and ἀλαώπιδος has been universally accepted since it was first suggested by Xylander (1532–76). Hesychius defines it by σκοτεινή, οὐ βλέπουσα, and a masc. ἀλαωπός is used of fog (ὁμίχλη) by Nonnus, *Dionys.* 25.282.

[2] So Burnet, *EGP*, 239. What is said above modifies a statement at vol. I, 126.

illumination from the light hemisphere. The only reasonable conclusion (in which we have many predecessors, for example Tannery, Gilbert, Heath, Burnet) is that the report of Aëtius is mistaken, either because he paraphrased Theophrastus unintelligently or, more probably, because Theophrastus himself gave an ironically confused account of what were to him archaic and unscientific theories.[1]

A further report about the sun is : 'The sun turns because it is prevented by the sphere surrounding it, and by the tropic circles, from continuing for ever on a straight course' (Aët. 2.23.3, A58). As often, the doxographer seems to have indiscriminately combined two statements. That the sun's course is regulated by the inner surface of the sphere seems aimed at the bizarre theory of Xenophanes (A41a) that a series of suns succeed one another, travelling on indefinitely in a straight line. How Empedocles conceived of the tropic circles, and in what way they could prevent the sun's further passage North or South, is not said. It is presumably connected with his explanation of the seasons, which is said to have been that 'it is winter when the *aer* through condensation predominates and is forced into the upper part, and summer as fire predominates whenever it is forced into the lower.'[2] That is, in winter the darkness which fills one half of the cosmic sphere overflows into the fiery half, and in summer the fiery half encroaches on the dark. 'The idea seems to be that the greater half of the sphere takes longer to revolve about a particular point on the earth's surface than the smaller half, and that this explains why the days are longer in the summer than in the winter' (Heath, *Aristarchus*, 88). But no reason is given for the successive encroachments. They could have been a kind of tidal effect caused by the cosmic whirl, which was in its origin due to a certain lack of equilibrium between the dark and the bright spheres.

Amid so much that seems pure imagination, it is refreshing to recall that Empedocles was aware of the true cause of eclipses. The sun is

---

[1] Cf. Burnet, *EGP*, 238, n. 4, 298, n. 1.

[2] Aët. 3.8.1 (A65). Diels construed βιαζομένου as deponent, understanding τὸν ἥλιον as object. Bignone, defending this, says that 'in the doxographic text from which the note is taken, the sun is mentioned a little earlier'. (*Emped.* 350, n. 2.) The mention of the sun in ps.-Plut. is at the end of the previous section, before the heading περὶ χειμῶνος καὶ θέρους, so that the carry-over would be extremely harsh. In Stobaeus it does not occur at all.

eclipsed 'when the moon passes beneath it', says Aëtius. He may have learned this from the Pythagoreans, for Aëtius attributes the same explanation to both; but these later attributions of astronomical discoveries are very uncertain, and for Empedocles we have his own words. 'The moon', says Plutarch, 'often conceals and obliterates the sun. As Empedocles says: "She cuts off his rays as he passes above her, and darkens as much of the earth as is the breadth of the pale-eyed moon."'[1] Altogether, in spite of their fanciful aspects, his theories about the sun are considerably more advanced and subtle than those of Heraclitus and Xenophanes, with their suns lost and replaced every day and their extraordinary ideas about eclipses. Unlike them, he gives the impression of a man who wants to come to grips with the problems of nature for their own sake.

(4) *The moon*

His views about the moon are thus stated in the account of the *Stromateis* (A30):

He says that the moon was formed separately of the *aer* cut off by the fire, which solidified like hail. It has its light from the sun.

Aëtius says that it is 'compacted air, resembling cloud, solidified by fire, so that it is a compound', and Plutarch describes it as 'a solidification of air resembling hail'. Its shape was that of a disc or lentil, that is, round with convex sides, not spherical.[2] The evidence that Empedocles knew it to be lit from the sun is stronger than that for Parmenides. He imitated the punning line of Parmenides that called it a 'foreign light',[3] and Plutarch quotes another original verse in the following context:

There remains then the theory of Empedocles that the moonlight which we see comes from the moon's reflexion of the sun. That is why there is neither

---

[1] Aët. 2.24.7 (A 59); Plut. *De facie*, 929 c (fr. 42). Verse 1 of the fr. should possibly run: 'She cuts off his rays to the earth from above', for the text is uncertain. ἀπεσκεύασε...ἐς τ' αἶαν καθύπερθεν MSS., ἀπεσκέδασεν...ἐς γαῖαν Xylander, ἀπεστέγασεν...ἐς τ' ἂν ἴῃ DK. Hippolytus ascribes the statement of the cause of eclipses to Empedocles's contemporary Anaxagoras. (P. 306 below.) It is very possible that in this he was the discoverer and Empedocles the follower.

[2] Aët. 2.27.3; Plut. *Qu. Rom.* 288b, *De facie*, 922c (all in A60); D.L. 8.77.

[3] Fr. 45. See p. 66 above. In quoting this fragment, Achilles connects it with the 'opinion of the majority' that the moon is an ἀπόσπασμα τοῦ ἡλίου. There is no reason to think that Empedocles believed this, and Heidel proposed a correction to ἀπόφασμα (reflexion). See Bignone, *Emped.* 346, n. 1. Zeller thought the phrase could mean no more than that it gets its light from the sun.

warmth nor brilliance in it.... To the contrary, just as voices when they are reflected produce an echo which is fainter than the original sound and the impact of missiles after a ricochet is weaker,

'Thus having struck the moon's broad disk, the ray'

comes to us in a refluence weak and faint.[1]

Even if the discovery must be credited to Anaxagoras (p. 306 below), Empedocles could have known of it also. Nothing is recorded of his explanation of the phases or eclipses of the moon, though Heath (*Aristarchus*, 91) suggested that its 'mixed' composition might be intended to account for the former. The description makes its formation identical with that of the outermost sphere as also given by Aëtius (A51), which may be why the *Stromateis* takes the trouble to add the word 'separately' (καθ' ἑαυτήν).

(5) *The earth*

Nothing has survived about the shape of the earth,[2] and it is uncertain whether he believed it to be spherical. Neither Anaxagoras nor Democritus did so, and the implication of Aëtius that the axis of the cosmos was originally perpendicular to the earth's surface suggests that this was flat: the two ideas are combined in Anaxagoras.[3] It remains in the centre of the universe not because it is supported by air or anything else, nor yet because, as Anaximander so ingeniously supposed, it has no reason to move in one direction rather than another, but by the action of the cosmic whirl.

Some, like Empedocles [says Aristotle], say that the motion of the sky as it rotates in a circle at a higher speed [*sc.* than would be the earth's in falling] prevents the earth from moving. It is like the water in cups, which when the cup is swung round in a circle does not fall though it is often underneath the bronze and it is natural for it to move downwards. The reason is the same.[4]

---

[1] Fr. 43 in Plutarch, *De facie*, 929e, trans. Cherniss.

[2] Unless one includes the negative evidence of his scorn of Xenophanes for saying that its depths are ἄπειρονα (fr. 39; cf. vol. I, 394).

[3] For Anaxagoras see pp. 305, 310 below; cf. also vol. I, 294, and for Parmenides p. 64 above. The flatness of the earth in Empedocles is however by no means certain, and there is some force in the arguments of Millerd, *Emped.* 63, n. 6. Contrast Heath, *Aristarchus*, 91 f.

[4] *De caelo*, 295a17. At 300b3 there is another reference to Empedocles as saying that the earth 'remains at rest owing to the vortex', and cf. the criticism at 295a31 (p. 177 above). The demonstration of centrifugal force by means of the rapidly whirled cup of water is not in fact relevant to the case of the earth. A good appreciation of Empedocles's merits and limitations

This is one example out of several which indicate a genuine desire on the part of Empedocles to base his conclusions about the natural world on observation, even if at that early stage of science the inference was inaccurate. Like the illustrations of the lantern (fr. 84) and the clepsydra (fr. 100), it is simply a matter of drawing analogies from well-known phenomena, not of controlled experiment. The trick with the rotating cups will have been part of the stock-in-trade of jugglers at fairs, as Gomperz tells us it still is (or was in his lifetime).

(6) *The sea*

The sea is water originally contained within the earth, which burst out as the earth was squeezed like a sponge by the force of the cosmic whirl. In some way the heat of the sun was combined with this as a causal factor, thus enabling Empedocles to invoke the microcosm—macrocosm analogy, which for him was very real. The sea was 'the sweat of the earth' (fr. 55), exuded under heat, and, like other sweat, salt. Aristotle (*Meteor.* 357a24) dismissed this as a ridiculous and meaningless metaphor, but for Empedocles it was more than that. The sea was not entirely salt however, but contained an imperceptible quantity of fresh water, which produced nourishment for fish.[1]

Certain features of this cosmology of Empedocles make it fairly clear that he had studied Parmenides's world of seeming no less than his way of truth. The two hemispheres, one of fire and the other of *aer* mixed with a little fire, suggest a derivation from the circular bands,

here is given by Gomperz, *Gr. Th.* I, 242. Mugler (*Dev. Cycl.* 37) thinks that Aristotle may have been misled by the poetic diction of Empedocles, who intended to describe something different, namely the behaviour of a solid body floating in a liquid contained in a cylindrical or spherical vessel. Cherniss on the other hand (*ACP*, 204, n. 234) says that the simile must have been intended to explain, not why the earth does not fall, but why the outer water, air and fire do not fall upon the earth. He refers to Heidel, *Heroic Age of Science*, 188. This would form a parallel to the theory of Anaxagoras (p. 302 below); the only doubt is whether such a gross misunderstanding of Empedocles was possible.

[1] The doxographic notices are: (*a*) Aët. 2.6.3 (A49) 'From earth as it was excessively constricted by the force of the revolution, the water gushed out'; (*b*) *idem* 3.16.3 (A66) 'Empedocles calls the sea the sweat of the earth, as it was scorched by the sun owing to the increasing compression'. Tzetzes (see A66) has a picturesque description of the chaotic state of things when the world was young: 'According to Empedocles the natural philosopher, the elements were still in disorderly motion even after the appearance of earth and sea: at one time fire would get the upper hand and burn things up, and at another the surge of water would overflow and submerge them.' On the fresh water in the sea, Aelian, *Nat. an.* 9.64 (A66), p. 241 below, and for the same belief in Democritus see p. 424.

one made of rare matter, another of dense, 'and others between these mixed of light and darkness'. The moon, too, for Parmenides, was a compound of both *aer* and fire. (See A 37, pp. 61 f. above.)

K. THE FORMATION OF LIVING CREATURES

We have already seen how in general, 'chemical' terms the various forms of life arise. What is truly existent cannot be born or perish or change, but strictly speaking only the four elementary substances exist: life results from mixtures of these substances in certain proportions. According to the stage in the cosmic cycle at which it occurs, a thing may both be born and perish by either the coming together or the dissolution of the elements (fr. 17. 3–5). Into this new framework are fitted the current ideas (going back to Anaximander, and in mytho-logical form further still) of life as originating in moistened earth under the action of heat. So in fr. 73 Love, the agent of mixture, mingles earth with water, fashions the living creatures in it, and hardens them by fire.[1] Fr. 62 describes a similar process.

The evolution of animal life was related to the cosmic cycle in a way that can be seen from a passage of Aëtius supplemented by quotations from Empedocles and other testimony. The doxographer does not make it clear, as he was probably not clear himself, that he was describ-ing, not a continuous evolution, but two contrary processes. Never-theless the passage can be read as a concise summary of the Empedoclean doctrine. It distinguishes four stages as follows.[2]

---

[1] Bignone (*Emped.* 427) has shown it to be probable that frr. 34 and 73 should be joined as the two halves of a simile. ['As a baker puts cakes in the oven], having cemented the meal with water, so Cypris after she had moistened the earth with water, as she fashioned the forms of living things gave them to swift fire to harden.' The custom of making cakes in the form of animals and men would add point to the simile. Another simile describing the work of Love in forming compounds is fr. 33: 'As when fig-juice fixes and binds white milk.' Fig-juice was used as rennet, and the line is adapted from Homer, *Il.* 5.902. Here it may have a more par-ticular physiological reference; cf. Plut. *Qu. nat.* 917 a (A 78): 'Some say that tears are extruded like whey from milk when the blood is stirred up; so Empedocles.'

[2] Aët. 5.19.5 (A 72). The passage has been the subject of considerable discussion, but since it seems to admit of a straightforward interpretation references to other views would be more likely to cloud the issue than to clarify it. To mention only one of the most recent, Minar in *Phronesis*, 1963, 141 ff., supposes all four stages in Aëtius to be contained within the period of increasing Love. But his assumption that to do otherwise involves confining sexual generation entirely to the epoch of Strife places an entirely undeserved reliance on the completeness of the doxographer's summary. At the same time he has to explain the absence of information about the period of increasing Strife as due at least in part to 'the fragmentary nature of our tradition' (p. 143).

Empedocles says (i) the first generations of plants[1] and animals were not entire, but divided, with parts not grown together; (ii) the second, in which the parts grew together, were like creatures of fantasy; (iii) the third was the generation of the whole-natured; (iv) the fourth was no longer engendered from the elements[2] like earth and water but from each other, when for some their nourishment became thick and for others the beauty of women excited the seminal motion.[3] The kinds of all living creatures were distributed according to the character of their mixture: some had a more natural inclination to water, as many as had a preponderance of fire flew up into the air,[4] the heavier made for the earth, and those in whose composition the elements were equally balanced....[5]

(i) This is the earliest stage of organic life in the period when Love is gaining and the process of evolution is from separation to combination. Empedocles describes it in the lines of fr. 57, which is expressly ascribed by Aristotle to this period and by Simplicius to the first stage of it:[6]

On the earth[7] many heads sprang up without necks, arms wandered bare, bereft of shoulders, and eyes strayed alone in need of foreheads.

---

[1] See n. 1 on next page.

[2] ἐκ τῶν ὁμοίων. That the elements are referred to is clear from what follows. Suggested emendations are discussed in Bignone, *Emped.* 356, n. 6, but seem unnecessary. The elements are ὁμοῖα (ἠνεκὲς αἰὲν ὁμοῖα fr. 17.35; cf. 62.6: the same characteristic is alluded to in 22.1 ἄρθμια μὲν γὰρ ταῦτα ἑαυτῶν πάντα μέρεσσιν) because each is modelled, as closely as appearances allow, on the Parmenidean One, which was πᾶν ὁμοῖον (fr. 8.22). The meaning of ὁμοῖον here is 'internally consistent', 'homogeneous'. This is what the elements are as such, until by the action of Love they are made ὁμοῖα with each other (fr. 22.5) and persuaded to mingle in the formation of the organic world. When the mingling is complete, in the perfect Sphere, everything is ὁμοῖον in both senses. (It is ἶσος ἑαυτῷ, fr. 29.3.)

[3] The distinction is between the lower animals, for whom the sexual impulse is purely physiological, and man, who has an aesthetic sense as well.

[4] τὰ δὲ εἰς ἀέρα ἀναπτῆναι ὅσ' ἄν is the emendation of Diels for the MSS. ἀναπνεῖν ἕως ἄν (or ὡς ἄν). Although this could be translated, the correction should probably be accepted. Cf. the parallel account of Diodorus (1.7.5) τὰ μὲν πλείστης θερμασίας κεκοινωνηκότα πρὸς τοὺς μετεώρους τόπους ἀπελθεῖν γενόμενα πτηνά, and p. 206 below.

[5] After this, *incerta omnia* (Diels), for the scribe's attention wandered and he made nonsense of the last few words. They must have said that those of balanced composition were at home in more than one element. These will be plants, of which Theophrastus says (*De caus. plant.* 1.12.5, p. 21 Wimmer; see A70) that Empedocles divided their substance, assigning earth to the downward thrusting roots and air to the upward growing shoots. Cf. Arist. *De an.* 415b28.

[6] καθάπερ 'Ε. φησι γίνεσθαι ἐπὶ τῆς φιλότητος, Arist. *De caelo*, 300b29. Cf. Simpl. *Phys.* 371.33.

[7] τῇ μέν. The translation is confirmed by Arist. *GA*, 722b25–6.

This provides concrete illustrations of the fantastic situation outlined in fr. 20, taken from Simplicius (*Phys.* 1124.9):

Here too [*sc.* in the sublunary world] Empedocles says that Strife and Love prevail in turn among men and fish and beasts and birds, when he writes:
  'This is manifest throughout the mass of mortal bodies. At one time all the limbs which belong to the body, in the prime of blooming life, come together into one through Love. At another, severed by evil spirits of discord, they wander, each separately, on the shores of life; and it is the same for bushes, and fishes housed in water, and beasts with their mountain lairs and birds of winged flight.'[1]

Aristotle's criticism amplifies the picture slightly (*GA* 722b17):

It is impossible for large members to survive and be alive in separation, which is Empedocles's account of generation under Love. 'Many heads', he says, 'grew up without necks', and later they were joined together.[2]

Simplicius, in describing with the aid of fr. 35.9–13 the state of things when Love was gaining but Strife still active and vigorous, adds:

In this state of things the members were still 'single-limbed' [formed of one limb only][3] from the separation wrought by Strife, and wandered about longing to combine with each other.

---

[1] This fr. is given a different application by Bignone, *Emped.* 410, but the interpretation of Diels, which he stigmatizes as erroneous, is more likely to be right (at least in its general reference to the evolutionary cycle, if not in detail). Bignone's objection to it (571, n. 1) is that it includes plants among the organisms whose parts once sprang up separately and were joined at random, whereas Aristotle in a bantering mood says that Empedocles should have mentioned 'olive-headed vines' as well as 'man-headed oxen' (*Phys.* 199b10), and Simplicius *ad loc.* (382.30) confirms that he left them out. It is however scarcely possible, considering his elaborate striving after consistency, that Empedocles failed to assume the same process for plants as for animals. If he confined himself to a general reference like the above, Aristotle was still entitled to have his joke about the man who specified the animal monsters (which were already well known in Greek mythological tradition) but did not dare to enumerate the surprising products of his scheme in the plant world. The inclusion of plants by Aëtius is some confirmation that this was so. It is difficult to believe, as Bignone would have us do, that the words of fr. 20 describe the individual in health and sickness. Still more improbable is the proposition of Kranz, advanced without argument (*Emped.* 361), that the subject of these lines is sexual intercourse.

[2] Bignone (*Emped.* 569) sees here an affinity between Empedocles and the Orphic doctrine cited by Aristotle, *GA*, 734a16, that the parts of animals come into being not simultaneously but one after the other, 'like the weaving of a net'. There however Aristotle is referring to the formation of the foetus in the womb, not to Empedocles's fantastic theory of the origin of life in another part of the cosmic cycle.

[3] See fr. 58. The compound adjective μουνομελῆ is clearly Empedocles's.

'But when *daimon* engaged more and more with *daimon*',[1]
as Love continued to gain over Strife,

'it came to pass both that these things[2] came together as each happened to meet, and also many others besides them sprang up in continuous succession' (fr. 59).

This fragment must have been written in close proximity to 35.16f.

And as they [the elements] mingled, a myriad kinds of mortal creatures were brought forth, endowed with all sorts of shapes, a wonder to behold.

The chance coming together of the separate limbs and organs marks the transition to the second stage. Similarly, Simplicius says elsewhere (*Phys.* 371.33) that under the rule of Love, *first* the parts of animals such as heads, hands and feet appeared here and there at random, *then* they came together and gave rise to the monsters about to be described.

(ii) For the second stage of Love's advance we have four surviving lines of Empedocles (fr. 61):

Many were born with faces and breasts both front and back, oxen with the heads of men, and conversely there sprang up creatures in human form with the heads of oxen, and mixtures partly of men and partly of women's nature, fitted with shadowed[3] [private] parts.

Plutarch preserves, along with the man-headed oxen, another phrase (fr. 60): 'shambling [cattle] with countless hands'.[4]

It is at this stage that we have the theory of the survival of the fittest which some modern commentators have likened to Darwin's. No words of Empedocles on the subject have survived. Aristotle refers to it briefly in a passage where he is setting forth, in order to refute it,

---

[1] That is, as the struggle between Love and Strife continued and intensified. The comments interpolated by Simplicius show that he at least thought that they (not, as Zeller supposed, the elements) are the δαίμονες in question. For μίσγεσθαι of engaging in combat cf. e.g. Hom. *Il.* 4.456.

[2] 'Dieses' in the translation of DK should be 'Diese'.

[3] Or 'sterile'. Diels suggested στείροις, a probable conjecture.

[4] εἰλίποδα. The epithet is a standing one for cattle, and cattle only, in Homer. In the same meaning it occurs later without the noun in Theocritus 25.131. M. Timpanaro Cardini (*Physis*, 1960, 8) thinks that by ἀκριτόχειρα Empedocles did not mean 'with innumerable hands' but 'with hands not articulated into separate fingers', suitable appendages for mixed animal and human creatures. This is probable. The word is presumably modelled on the Homeric ἀκριτόφυλλος and ἀκριτόφωνος. The former (*Il.* 2.868) undoubtedly means that the leaves were plentiful, but does so by calling them 'indistinguishable'. (Lieselotte Solmsen in *Lex. d. frühgr. Epos*, s.v.: 'mit nicht zu unterscheidenden, dichten Blättern.') ἀκριτόφωνος is applied to the speech of Thersites in *Il.* 2.246, where confusion rather than profusion seems to be in point.

the anti-teleological view according to which any apparent signs of purpose in nature (e.g. that front teeth should be sharp for biting, and the molars flat to reduce the food to a digestible smoothness) are in fact only fortuitous.

Similarly [he continues (*Phys.* 198 b 27)] with other organs in which we seem to see a purpose. Where everything turned out in a way which simulated purpose, those creatures survived because *by chance* they were constituted in a suitable way; whereas all that were not so constituted perished, and continue to perish, as Empedocles says the 'man-headed oxen' did.

Commenting on this passage, Simplicius is rather more informative. After quoting fr. 62, *vv.* 2–3, he continues (*Phys.* 371.33):

Empedocles says that during the rule of Love first of all there came into being at random parts of animals such as heads, hands and feet, and then there came together those 'oxen with the heads of men', 'and conversely there sprang up', naturally, 'men with the heads of oxen', that is, compounded of ox and man. As many of these parts as were fitted together in such a way as to ensure their preservation became animals and survived, because they fulfilled mutual needs—the teeth tearing and softening food, the stomach digesting it, and the liver converting it into blood. The human head, when it meets a human body, ensures the preservation of the whole, but being inappropriate to the ox-body it leads to its disappearance. All that did not come together according to the proper formula [*logos*] perished.

Whatever the superficial resemblances of this conception to nineteenth-century theories of evolution,[1] it was obviously reached

---

[1] They were probably rated most highly by Gomperz, *Gr. Thinkers*, I, 244. We must at least agree that they represent an attempt to explain the apparent evidence of design in nature by purely natural, or, as the Greeks would say, 'necessary' causes. This reliance on blind automatism and neglect of the final cause in Empedocles is repeatedly castigated by Aristotle. That is the intention of his criticism at *Phys.* 199b9. Cf. also 196a20–5, *GC*, 333b15, *Metaph.* 1000b12, *De caelo*, 300b25–30, *PA*, 640a19, *De resp.* 473a15.

For a sceptical view see Millerd, *Emped.* 58. She thought that Simplicius was mistakenly attributing to Empedocles a view which Aristotle assigned to others, with only a purely incidental mention of Empedocles. This is perhaps a *possible* way of reading *Phys.* 198b27, but I do not think it a likely one, especially in view of his criticism of Empedocles on the same ground elsewhere. Nor do I see the force of Zeller's remark (ZN, 989, n. 3), approved by Millerd, that an evolutionary theory based on chance could not appear until the teleological explanation had been developed which it was intended to replace. Rather was the philosophic (as opposed to naïve mythological) expression of teleology developed by Socrates, Plato and Aristotle as a deliberate attack on the automatism of earlier science. Luria, *Anf. d. gr. Denkens*, 1963, 153, n. 208, also takes an extreme sceptical view, but for a different assessment see M. Timpanaro Cardini in *Physis*, 1960.

from very different premises and formed an integral part of a cosmological system which by nineteenth-century standards was fanciful in the extreme. It does not refer to development in the present world, but to an era in which evolution proceeded in the opposite direction. The monsters described are reminiscent of various figures in Greek mythology, and it is fair to assume that Empedocles had these in mind, for he was always glad to show that his carefully constructed system accounted for phenomena known or believed in by his countrymen. The Minotaur provided a bull-headed man, and other mixed forms included centaurs and the Chimaera (lion's head, goat's body, and serpent's tail). Bisexual beings were by no means confined to Hermaphroditos, whose cult seems to have been introduced at Athens during the fifth century. Considering the affinities of Empedocles's doctrines, some have been tempted to think also of Phanes, in Orphic literature the creator and first ruler of the gods and the world. Orphic verses described him as bisexual and as having the heads of a ram, a bull, a lion and a snake.[1] But although Phanes himself might be said to belong to the past, in so far as a god can (he was swallowed by Zeus), it is hardly likely that Empedocles would have wished to include this great cosmic figure among the transient non-viable creatures which his lines describe. More obviously in the same tradition (whatever its origin) are the early human beings comically described by Aristophanes in Plato's *Symposium* (189d ff.). These were spherical in shape and in every way double, with four hands, legs and ears, two faces, and the sexual parts of both male and female.[2]

[1] See Guthrie, *Orph. and Gk. Rel.* 101 f. and 145, nn. 24 and 25, for evidence for this paragraph.

[2] Some have thought that they resemble rather the οὐλοφυεῖς of the early stages of Strife's progress. The 'wholeness' of their androgynous nature, and their spherical shape, can be thought to point in this direction, and their modification into ordinary men and women was the result of a drastic act of separation. Also it can be argued that the οὐλοφυεῖς, assuming that they were biologically sufficiently advanced in the first place, would lead happier and better lives than ourselves, since Love was more powerful then than now; and the Aristophanic hermaphrodites were happier than their monosexual successors.

On the other hand, (1) Aristophanes's creatures have even more limbs and sexual parts than we do, whereas the οὐλοφυεῖς have none; (2) bisexual beings occur among the monsters of fr. 61; (3) in Empedocles the human beings of an age when Love was more powerful were not only happy but morally perfect and pious worshippers, whereas Aristophanes's creatures were so impious that they tried to storm heaven and attack the gods. Plato's mind was well stocked with traditional motifs, but it is unwise to look too closely at the tale which an imaginative genius puts into the mouth of one of the greatest of comic poets. I cannot myself believe that the οὐλοφυεῖς τύποι had any kind of human form. Cf. p. 211 below.

From fr. 61 and the comments of Aristotle and Simplicius it follows that there was a third stage in the period of increasing Love, not mentioned by Aëtius: when the monstrosities had been weeded out by natural causes, there remained men, women and animals who were the counterpart of those in our own era.[1] Since Love unites heterogeneous elements, it is presumably to this stage that Aristotle refers when he says that 'the hottest animals, those containing most fire, are aquatic, to escape the excess of heat in their own nature'.[2] This is the contrary of what is said at the end of the Aëtius passage (p. 201 above), that animals seek the element most akin to the one which preponderates in themselves. That applies to the present era of increasing Strife, in which each element is attracted to its like.

(iii) The third stage mentioned by Aëtius is an early stage in the advance of Strife. 'Whole-natured' (or growing as a whole, οὐλοφυής) is the word used by Empedocles himself in the following description (fr. 62):

Come now and hear this, how fire as it was separated raised up the nocturnal[3] scions of men and pitiable women: it is no erring or ignorant tale. Whole-natured forms first sprang up from the earth, having a portion of both water and heat. These the fire sent up, wishing to come to its like. Not yet did they display the comely shape of limbs, nor voice nor the part proper to men.

Here we see the work of Strife in that fire, still mingled with the other elements, is being separated and impelled to reach its like, the

---

[1] It may be useful to compare what is said about the corresponding stage of the cosmic cycle (pp. 178 ff. above).

[2] *De resp.* 477a32 (cf. *PA*, 648a25, p. 78 above). So also Theophrastus, *CP*, 1.21.5 (DK, A73). It is true that Aristotle gives no hint that he is not speaking of the present world, but this is provided by Theophrastus in the next chapter of *De causis plant.* (1.22.2–3, II, 43 Wimmer): ἐπεὶ καὶ Ἐμπεδοκλεῖ πρὸς τοῖς ἄλλοις καὶ τοῦτ' ἄτοπον...τὸ γεννήσασαν ἐν τῷ ξηρῷ τὴν φύσιν μεταίρειν εἰς τὸ ὑγρόν· πῶς γὰρ ἂν διέμενεν ἢ πῶς οἷόν τε καὶ διαμένειν ὁντιναοῦν χρόνον εἴπερ ἦν ὅμοια τοῖς νῦν; ἔτι δ' αὐτὸ τὸ συμβαῖνον κατὰ τὴν νῦν γέννησιν ἀποσημαίνει. Here he adds two points: (*a*) that on Empedocles's theory living creatures changed their habitat after birth, those born on dry land taking to the water, (*b*) that this referred to another epoch, not the present one. Empedocles fr. 74 φῦλον ἄμουσον ἄγουσα πολυσπερέων καμασήνων may possibly be part of a description of (*a*). The subject must be Love, who 'leads' or 'conducts' the fish to the water. A reverse process occurred in Anaximander (A30, vol. I, 102).

[3] ἐννυχίους, literally 'in the night'; used of the dwellers in the darkness of Hades by Sophocles, *O.C.* 1558; in Homer and Hesiod of doing anything by night. These early forms of life arose on the earth even before there was a sun, as is explicitly said of another early form of life, namely trees and plants (A70, p. 208 below).

fire in the earth reaching outwards towards the large mass of fire at the circumference of the cosmos. In this process curious living forms arise compounded of earth mixed with water and fire, without limbs, organs, or distinction of sex. The unifying force of Love is still strong.[1] The fourth element of air is not mentioned (so Bignone suggested) because air is a component of blood and fleshy tissue (fr. 98) which these living masses do not yet possess.[2] It could be absorbed later from the surrounding atmosphere. It is likely enough that Empedocles took these pains to impose consistency on his scheme, but in the choice of the three elements he would also be influenced by ancient traditions of the origins of life. In Hesiod (*Erga*, 59 ff.) Zeus ordered the god of fire to mix earth and water to make the first woman. For Anaximander life arose from water and earth when they were heated. In Empedocles fire retains the active role, as its heat penetrates the mixture.

The general notion of earth as literally the mother, from within whom not only plants but also the first animals and men originated, is of course so old and universal as hardly to need illustration. Among the Greeks it is reflected in myths like that of Cadmus and the 'sown men' of Thebes, of Jason sowing the dragon's teeth, of many autochthonous heroes and *gegeneis* (earthborn), of Deucalion and the renewal of the human race after the flood from 'the bones of our mother' (i.e. stones). Tales of the marriage of earth and sky symbolize the need of water to make earth fertile. Serious beliefs in the spontaneous generation of small animals like mice from the earth were buttressed by the conviction that the earth had in the past possessed even greater generative powers.[3]

(iv) The fourth stage, a later one in the advance of Strife, is that in which we now live. Advancing discrimination and articulation have brought into being the familiar world of self-reproducing male and female creatures, divided into fishes, birds and land-animals. Love of

---

[1] A weak point of Minar's account in *Phronesis*, 1963, is the failure to see that sexual differentiation, like any differentiation, is not a good but the work of Strife. Note the sexlessness of the deity of frr. 29 and 134. That the sexes are *attracted* to one another may be Love's doing, though Hippolytus says that their intercourse is the work of Strife (see *Ref.* 7.29.22, 30.4, pp. 214, 216 Wendland), but that is a very different thing.

[2] See Bignone, *Emped.* 581, and cf. the elaborate reconstruction of Reiche, *Empedocles' mixture*, etc. 62 f. with its comparison between phylogeny and ontogeny.

[3] For some details see Guthrie, *In the Beginning*, chh. 1 and 2, and cf. vol. I, 291 f., 385 ff.

Empedocles

course is still at work, but her power is weakening, and with the effect of this in the human sphere we pass from the poem on nature to the *Purifications*, which tells of the moral degeneration brought about by increasing Strife. The remark in Aëtius about women's beauty may be compared with a line of Empedocles which as printed in DK speaks of the desire that comes upon a man through sight (fr. 64, quoted by Plutarch in connexion with sexual love).[1]

What Empedocles said about trees may fittingly find a place here, for besides having a considerable general interest, it shows them as a kind of living fossil, a primitive form of life which has persisted to the present day. Aëtius paraphrases it thus (5.26.4, A 70):

Empedocles says that trees were the first living things[2] to grow out of the earth, before the sun was spread around[3] and day and night were distinguished. Owing to the matching of the elements in their mixture, they combined the formula for male and female. They grow by being pushed up by the heat in the earth, so that they are parts of the earth just as embryos in the belly are parts of the womb. Fruits consist of the excess of water and fire in the plants. Those that have insufficient moisture lose their leaves in summer as it evaporates, but those that have more, like the laurel, olive and palm, retain them.[4] Differences in flavour are due to the composition of the soil, and the different ways in which the plants draw the homoeomerous substances from that which nourishes them.[5] So with vines, it is not the differences in the vine that make a drinkable wine,[6] but differences in the soil that sustains them.

[1] See Plut. *Qu. Phys.* 917c. The reference to sight is due to a conjecture by Wyttenbach. Cataudella (*Riv. di filol.* 1960, 128f.) suggests a reading closer to the MSS., but I find the allusion to the aphrodisiac effects of the digestive process more in keeping with Catullan impudence (he quotes Catullus 32.9 as a parallel) than with the present context. In any case Plutarch quotes the line to illustrate the effects of proximity, not satiety, which he has mentioned earlier as a distinct alternative.

[2] I take ζῷα to mean living creatures *as we know them*: Empedocles is not saying that trees preceded the 'whole-natured'.

[3] περιαπλωθῆναι, which Diels thought 'omnino ineptum' (*Dox.* 439), is now usually justified by reference to Empedocles's curious theory of the sun (pp. 192ff. above).

[4] Plutarch (*Qu. conv.* 649c, on frr. 77–8) says that Empedocles attributed evergreenness to ὁμαλότης κράσεως and συμμετρία πόρων. These enable the nourishment to flow smoothly and regularly and so in sufficient quantity. Since the food is drawn from the earth in the form of moisture, the two explanations are complementary. Plutarch's describes the mechanism whereby the evergreens obtain their larger supply of moisture.

[5] This idea is elaborated in Hippocr. *De morbis*, 4.34 (VII, 546 Littré).

[6] I see no necessity to alter the MSS. χρηστικόν το χρηστὸν τόν with Diels. For a further remark on the nature of plants see p. 201, n. 5 above. A quotation from Empedocles himself (fr. 81) says that wine is water from the bark, putrefied or fermented in the wood.

The Nature of Trees

Trees, then, are the nearest in the present world to the original 'whole-natured' forms of life. Like them they are still rooted in the earth, from which they are pushed up by the heat within it, and still combine the characteristics of both sexes, because the persistent influence of Love combines their elements in a manner nearer to the perfect mixture of the Sphere than that of more recent formations.

A further point of interest in the account is the analogy between vegetable and animal life. The doxographer applies to trees the word (3ῷα) usually confined to animals, probably because it appeared in Empedocles. For him, with his belief in the kinship of all life, there was no firm distinction. One may compare his own expression 'tall olive-trees bear eggs' (fr. 79), the assertion in fr. 82 that hair, leaves, scales and the wings of birds are 'the same', and the description of the ear as a 'shoot (or sprout, ὄzος) of flesh' (Theophr. *De sensu* 9, A 86). According to the *De plantis* both he and Anaxagoras attributed desire, pleasure and pain to plants, and the latter, as well as Democritus and Plato, called them 'earth-rooted animals'.[1] The parallel between young plants and embryos is echoed in the Hippocratic treatise *On the Nature of the Child* (27, VII. 528 Littré):

All things that grow in the earth live off the moisture in the earth, and the moisture in them depends on the moisture in it.[2] So also the child lives off its mother in the womb, and its health depends on hers. If anyone considers what has been said on this subject from beginning to end, he will find a similarity between the whole nature of the products of the earth and those of human generation.

These remarks may owe something to Empedocles, but are more reasonably taken as arising out of the old and very general belief in the earth as the original mother of all living things alike. The same analogy is turned into nonsense by Aristophanes in the *Clouds* (232), where the word 'moisture' (ἰκμάς) plays a part as in the Hippocratic

---

[1] [Arist.] *De plantis* 815 a 15, Plut. *Qu.nat.* 911 d (DK, 31 A 70, 59 A 116). Cf. Plato, *Tim.* 77 a–b.

[2] Moisture, ἰκμάς. The parallel with human life is developed a little further on (p. 544 Littré): ἐπὴν δὲ φάγῃ ἢ πίῃ ὁ ἄνθρωπος, ἕλκει τὸ σῶμα ἐς ἑωυτὸ ἐκ τῆς κοιλίης τῆς ἰκμάδος τῆς εἰρημένης ...ὥσπερ ἐπὶ τῶν φυτῶν ἕλκει ἀπὸ τῆς γῆς ἡ ὁμοίη ἰκμὰς τὴν ὁμοίην.

On the embryo see also p. 498 καὶ δὴ καὶ διοзοῦται ὡς δένδρον, which may be compared with the use of ὄzος of the ear by Empedocles.

writer: 'The earth draws to itself perforce the moisture of the mind—the same phenomenon may be observed in cress.'

The full significance of the analogy between animal and plant life comes out in the religious poem, where we learn that the same soul may migrate from one to the other (frr. 117 and 127; p. 250 below).

This evolution of life in the world of Strife, as it emerges when stages (iii) and (iv) of Aëtius are combined with the fragments of Empedocles himself, has many points of resemblance to other accounts, notably the anonymous one retailed by Diodorus in the first century B.C.[1] According to this, the earth at its first formation was soft and muddy. The sun's warmth caused its surface to 'ferment', and some of the wet parts swelled up and produced a kind of bubbles with a thin skin. These grew and developed, absorbing nourishment at night from the marsh-mists and hardening by day under the heat of the sun. When fully developed, the membranes were burst by the heat and 'all kinds of animals were born'. Subsequently, as in Aëtius's report of Empedocles, those containing most heat grew wings and took to the air, the earthy became reptiles and other animals, and the moist took to the water. Later still, the earth became too hard to generate in this way and animals were reproduced by copulation with each other. A similar report is given by Lucretius (5.805 ff.).

These late and derivative accounts no doubt owed much to Empedocles himself, though Anaximander had already described the earliest animals as born in warmed moisture and enclosed in a kind of 'bark', which split as they came to dryer surroundings (A 30; vol. 1, 102). Possibly one may restore some of the missing parts of Empedocles from these other accounts in the same tradition. What he said about the transition from the 'whole-natured forms' to men, women and animals has not survived. Simplicius however, following up Aristotle's anachronistic claim that they must in fact have consisted of

---

[1] Diod. 1.7. The origins of the cosmogony and zoogony of Diodorus are a matter of lively controversy. W. Spoerri has devoted a book to the subject, *Späthellenistische Berichte über Welt, Kultur und Götter* (1959), in which references will be found. He believes that Diodorus has worked his material into a systematic whole which shows unmistakable signs of the thought of his own period. This however is not undisputed, and the chapter certainly contains passages of purely Presocratic matter some of which must be traceable to Empedocles. For a summary of recent discussion see my *In the Beginning*, 122, n. 10 and review of Spoerri in *Gött. Gel. Anz.* 1963.

sperma, says that 'whole-natured' is a very good description of *sperma*, since it, like them, contains the form of man in potentiality and *is* every part of the body in an undiscriminated state; 'whereas', he continues, 'no part of the body is the other parts once separation has taken place among them *and the whole-natured has been torn apart*' (*Phys.* 382).[1] It is a probable inference that the 'whole-natured forms' which grew out of the earth were these 'wombs' as the Epicureans later called them, in which, as the work of 'separating-out' proceeded (the action of Strife reminds us once again of the *ekkrisis* of Anaximander), the various forms of animal life could develop.[2]

L. THE STRUCTURE OF ANIMATE NATURE: PHYSIOLOGY

(1) *The ratio of the mixture*

To explain organic tissues Empedocles makes use of the characteristically Pythagorean notion of proportionate mixture. Living things at least are compounded of the elements in certain definable mathematical ratios. This proportion Aristotle calls the *logos* of the mixture, which, whether the word was used by Empedocles or not,[3] enables him to take advantage of its ambiguity to relate the theory to his own system of causation.

In the first chapter of *De partibus animalium* Aristotle is defending his favourite thesis that the 'nature' of anything, defined here as its completed structure,[4] is a principle or cause prior to the matter. At 642 a 17 he says:

It is the nature of a thing, rather than its matter, which is a principle (*arche*). Empedocles too sometimes hits upon this principle, guided by the truth itself, and is compelled to assert that the essence or nature is the *logos*, for instance when he explains what bone is; for he defines it not as one of the elements, or two or three or all of them, but as the *logos* of their mixture.

---

[1] διασπασθέντος τοῦ οὐλοφυοῦς. In Anaximander, A 30 (Aëtius) we have περιρρηγνυμένου τοῦ φλοιοῦ, and in a Latin version 'ruptis illis'.

[2] The inference is drawn by Bignone, *Emped.* 580–4. The 'wombs rooted in the earth' occur in Lucr. (5.808) and Censorinus, *De die nat.* (4.9). R. Philippson in *Phil. Woch.* 1929, 672f., produced some evidence to suggest that they originated with Democritus. It is relevant to compare the embryological analogy applied to trees in Aëtius's version of Empedocles.

[3] P. 161 above.

[4] τέλος τι πρὸς ὃ ἡ κίνησις περαίνει (641 b 24).

This ratio, then, is what constitutes bone. It is what Aristotle calls the form or essence of bone, its *logos* in the sense of definition, as opposed to its matter, that is, the elements which are combined in the specific ratio.

Repeating this information in *De anima* (410a1), Aristotle quotes the actual formula of Empedocles for bone:

Each of these [compound bodies] consists of the elements not in any haphazard state, but in a certain proportion and mode of composition, as Empedocles says of bone:

'The kindly earth received in its broad melting-pots[1] two parts of the glitter of Nestis out of eight, and four of Hephaestus; and they became white bones, wondrously joined by the cement of Harmonia' (fr. 96).[2]

Thus bone consists of four parts of fire, two of water, and two of earth to make up the total of eight. The preponderance of fire may have been suggested, as Simplicius thought, by the whiteness and dry hardness of bone.[3] Aëtius (5.22.1, A78) gives the formula for certain other animal tissues as well:

Empedocles says that flesh originates from the four elements mixed in equal quantities, sinews from fire and earth mixed with double the quantity of water, the claws or nails of animals from the sinews in so far as these are chilled by contact with the air, bones from two parts of water and earth to four of fire, these parts being mixed within the earth.[4]

---

[1] χόανος 'melting-pot' rather than 'funnel' as it has most often been translated in English. Cf. Hom. *Il.* 18.470, Hes. *Th.* 863. The metaphor is from metal-working. (See also Solmsen in *JHI*, 1963, 477.) The translation 'funnels' has probably been influenced by the belief that (as is no doubt true) the reality behind the metaphor is the πόροι or tiny channels which make mixture possible (pp. 150 f. above).

[2] The last line is added by Simplicius, *Phys.* 300.24.

[3] Simplicius (*De an.* 68, see Emped. fr. 96) also says that the formula is in fact 4 of fire, 2 of earth and 1 each of air and water. He supposes that Nestis is here used to cover both of the last two. This is scarcely possible, though it would explain a troublesome little point, namely why Empedocles should speak of a proportion of 4:2:2 rather than 2:1:1. Theophrastus also (*De sensu*, 23) speaks of both bone and hair as comprising 'all the elements'. See however Aëtius above. (This modifies a statement in vol. 1, p. 275, n. 2.)

[4] Further light is thrown on the last few words by the summary of cosmogony in the Hippocratic *De carnibus*, ch. 3 (VIII, 586 Littré), which seems to owe something to Empedocles: 'With a long period of heat, what was formed from the putrefaction of the earth and was fatty and retained the smallest quantity of moisture was most quickly burned up and became bones.' The theory of the origin of life from a primitive 'putrefaction' of the earth appears in a variety of authorities. For its currency in Presocratic thought cf. Plato, *Phaedo*, 96b.

Of these examples we have the first in Empedocles's own words (fr. 98):

Earth chanced in about equal quantity upon these, Hephaestus, water, and shining *aither*, anchored in the perfect harbours of Cypris, either a little more or a little less among more of them.[1] From these arose blood and the various forms of flesh.[2]

Cornford[3] was strongly of the opinion that the principle of specific ratios was confined to organic compounds: it is the presence of definite numerical proportion that distinguishes living creatures and their parts from inorganic masses. He thought it probable that the tissues of plants were included, since these also have life and soul, but nothing else. Millerd too (*Emped.* 40f.) saw no evidence that the principle was generalized, and used this as an argument against those who, like Gomperz, have claimed for Empedocles that he anticipated the modern chemical principle of proportional combination. She herself would confine it to the actual examples mentioned (bone, blood, flesh, sinew), and held that the phrase used by Aristotle—'*logos* of the mixture'— has given to modern interpreters a false impression of universality. Bignone on the other hand maintained that frr. 23[4] and 71 (which he said are to be connected) at once extend the principle to the whole animal and vegetable world, and in fact the 'harmonious mixture' of fr. 23 implicitly affirms its universality.

Much depends on the meaning of the word *harmonia*. When used as a proper name it is the divine power also called Philia, Aphrodite and

---

[1] εἴτε πλεόνεσσι Panzerbieter for the εἴτε πλέον ἐστι of Simplicius.

[2] ἐξ ὧν αἷμά τε γέντο καὶ ἄλλης εἴδεα σαρκός. (Literally 'the forms of different flesh', but cf. 26. 4, ἄλλων ἔθνεα θηρῶν. I doubt if DK's 'sonst die Arten von Fleisch' quite hits the mark.) This reads as if blood itself were a form of flesh, as indeed it must have been since the same formula applies to both. The Greek word σάρξ, which from Homer onwards was used regularly in the plural, covered a wider field than our 'flesh'. (Cf. the content of the Hippocratic *De carnibus*.) Presumably however blood contained a larger proportion of water than did flesh. Perhaps Empedocles intended to allow for this with his 'about equal' and 'a little more or a little less'. These phrases at least confess that the doctrine of strict proportion as constituting the essential distinction between specific organic substances was relaxed to take account of observed differences within what was regarded as a single kind. The same may have been done for bone: cf. the distinction drawn in *De carn.* between the composition of solid and porous bones (VIII, 588 L.). (Bignone, *Emped.* 469 n., suggested that the language of approximation was used to allow for the presence of Love as well as the elements. Although Love was certainly present, I do not think this a likely way of alluding to the fact.)

[3] In lectures.　　　　　　　　　　　　　[4] Translated on p. 148 above.

Cypris, which is the cause of *all* mixture. She it is who *joins things together* (συναρμόζει, of Aphrodite in fr. 71.4), and in this case it would seem that neither the noun nor the verb can be confined to the special sense of 'combine in fixed proportion'. As a common noun, on the other hand, at least for the Pythagoreans with whom Empedocles had strong affinities, it connotes combination in mathematical ratio (vol. I, 220, 223), and that is how Bignone regarded it in the simile of the mixing of paints in fr. 23.4: 'mixing them in *harmonia*, more of these and less of those'. Indeed his whole belief in the universality of the principle depends on this. Yet what painter ever obtained his desired shade by conforming to a recipe which laid down a numerical proportion between the pigments, like a dispenser making up a medical prescription? The thought is rather of the harmonious, that is pleasing, effect produced than of the means of its production.

Aristotle, it is said, provides evidence that Empedocles did not apply proportion universally, for he censures him on this account as inconsistent. In the *Metaphysics* he sums up his review of the early thinkers by saying that they were all groping after the four aspects of causation in which he himself believed, but could not state them clearly at a time when philosophy was still in its lisping infancy.

So Empedocles [he continues (993 a 17)] says bone exists by the *logos*; that is, the essence and substance of the thing. But it was equally necessary that flesh and everything else should be the *logos*, or else none of them. That will be the cause of flesh and bone and everything else—not the matter that he alleges, fire and earth and water and air. If anyone else had said so, he would have had to agree, but he has not put it clearly.

This is a criticism on grounds of inadequate and obscure expression. Empedocles, it would seem, stated the ratio of mixture of the elements of a few organic substances like bone, and emphasized that it was this ratio that imparted their specific character to them; but in the case of most other substances he was content to name their elements alone, although if the point had been put to him, he would have had to agree that their specific character depended also on the proportions in which these elements occurred. This is obvious, since otherwise it would have been impossible to produce the manifold variety of nature from four elements only.

Elsewhere Aristotle seems to say that Empedocles's theory demands a rationally proportionate mixture in every compound substance (*De an.* 409b32):

It is the same with any other compound at all. Each of them consists of the elements not in any haphazard state, but in a certain *logos* and mode of composition, as for instance Empedocles says of bone. . . .

So also Simplicius introdùces fr. 96 by saying (*Phys.* 300.19): 'He makes flesh and bone *and all the rest* by a certain *logos*.'[1]

In the absence of the philosopher's own words, any interpretation of this evidence must be hazardous. It seems most likely however that Empedocles believed all natural substances, metals and minerals as well as organic tissues, to be differentiated from one another by a different proportion of the four common elements in their mixture. He gave only a few examples of this,[2] all from the highest and most important stratum of existence, namely animal life, and was upbraided by Aristotle for neglecting to extend these explanations further; but his Pythagorean faith in the kinship of all nature makes it improbable that he regarded inanimate objects as composed on an entirely different basis from animate. The difference would be one of degree, and would amount to this, that the lower anything was in the *scala naturae* the more unequal would be the balance of the elements within it. This is suggested by the fact that the highest manifestation of physical life, namely rational thought, has for its organ the blood,[3] in which the elements display the nearest possible proportions to those in the divine Sphere, namely one to one.[4] Love is the power which unites different elements with each other. It has been shown earlier (p. 161) that the products of these

---

[1] Aristotle's argument concerns those who say that perception is of like by like (as e.g. Empedocles in fr. 109). This leads to the absurd conclusion that the perceiving soul must contain the substance of all the infinite number of things which it perceives. It is no use saying simply that it contains the four elements out of which they are all composed, for how then could it be aware of the objects as separate wholes? Their specific character depends not on the common elements but on the *logos* in which in each separate case they are combined.

The words καὶ τῶν ἄλλων ἕκαστον in Simplicius might mean only 'each of the other organic tissues', but in the light of Aristotle's reference to ἄλλο ὁτιοῦν τῶν συνθέτων should probably be interpreted more widely.

[2] Though not without its dangers, it is perhaps permissible here to quote Bignone's dictum that Empedocles was after all writing a poem, not a treatise (*Emped.* 363, n. 1).

[3] Fr. 105, p. 229 below. (For Michael Servet in the sixteenth century the soul had its seat in the blood. See Toulmin, *Arch. of Matter*, 308.)

[4] Fr. 98 (p. 213 above) and Theophr. *Sens.* 10.

unions, in a world where Love is opposed by Strife, are chance effects, and there is nothing in the evidence here considered to alter that conclusion. The precise description of the proportions constituting certain selected organic tissues might give the impression that Love was working alone to produce those particular blends, but there is no reason to distinguish the principle underlying their structure from that which brought about any other compound substances. To demonstrate that Empedocles 'says that the parts of animals also came into being by chance', Simplicius (*Phys.* 331.5) quotes among other examples the first line of fr. 98 describing the composition of blood itself. Yet at the same time he can say (300.25) apropos the composition of bone in fr. 96: 'That is, it happens by divine causation, mostly by Love or Harmonia, for it is by her cement that they are joined.' Aristotle saw no answer to his question: 'Is Love the cause of any chance mixture, or of mixture according to *logos*?' The answer is that it is only from his own teleological viewpoint that there is any essential difference between chance and *logos*. The latter word, with its double significance of 'proportion' and 'formal–final cause', is his own importation.

(2) *Medicine and physiology: reproduction*

The Sicilian school of medicine took its place alongside those of Cos, Cnidus and Rhodes, and Empedocles was generally looked on as its founder. Galen wrote:

In former days there was great rivalry between Cos and Cnidus as they endeavoured to outdo each other in the number of their discoveries. These were the two surviving branches of Asclepiads after the decline of Rhodes, and they were joined in that 'noble wrangling', which Hesiod eulogized, by the physicians of Italy, Philistion, Empedocles, Pausanias and their colleagues. There were then these three impressive groups of physicians competing with each other. The Coan school was fortunate in having the most and the best practitioners, but the Cnidian ran it close, and the Italian too was of no small merit.

Philistion, an influential physician and writer on medicine in the fourth century, was a native of Locri, but was also referred to as 'the Sicilian' from his connexion with the school. It was, says Pliny, known from its reliance on observation as the empirical school, and began with Acron of Acragas who owed his reputation to the fact that (like Pausanias) he was a pupil of Empedocles.[1]

In the surviving remains of Empedocles there is little information about disease or its therapy; but we have not only his claim to impart such information in frr. 111 and 112 (p. 132 above), but also evidence of a consuming interest in the body and its functions. The influence of his physiological theory is obvious in what we know of the theories of later physicians like Philistion and Diocles, and of Plato himself. In this respect the *Timaeus* owes an obvious debt to Empedocles, partly at least through the medium of Philistion with whom in all probability Plato was personally acquainted.[2]

The arrangement of the elements in organic bodies, which is the work of Love, is illustrated by examples of flesh-covered creatures and those which have hard parts on the outside. In the latter it differs, he points out, from the order of the main masses in the world, which are already largely the work of Strife and forecast the order that they will assume when entirely separated.

(Fr. 75)   Those of them that are solid within and rare without, having got this flaccidity in the hands of Cypris.

(Fr. 76)   This you find in the heavy-backed shells of the sea-dwellers, tritons and turtles of stony hide. There you will see earth [the heaviest element] lying on the surface of the skin.

Empedocles shows especial interest in animal reproduction. He believed that the female as well as the male provides semen, different parts of the offspring being formed from the semen of each (fr. 63, Arist. *GA*, 722b10). The necessity for a correct mixture of the two suggested to him an explanation of the sterility of mules, though we have only Aristotle's account of this,[3] and he confesses to having found it obscure. The reason as he gives it (*GA*, 747a34) is that though the semen of both horse and ass is soft, their mixture solidifies as the

---

[1] Galen 10.5 (Wellmann, *Frr. gr. Ärzte*, 109f., part in DK, 31 A3); for Philistion 'the Sicilian', D.L. 8.86 on the authority of Callimachus (he probably worked in Syracuse, Wellmann, 68); Pliny, *N.H.* 29.1.5 (DK, 31 A3).

[2] Cornford, *Plato's Cosmology*, 334; Jaeger, *Diokles*, 9f.

[3] Aët. 5.14.2 (DK, A82) must be rejected. It is inconsistent with Aristotle and seems to be due to confusion with another philosopher (Bignone, *Emped.* 366, n. 2; Lesky, *Zeugungslehren*, 31, n. 1). On symmetry of pores and sterility of mules cf. ZN, 991, n. 1.

Empedocles

'hollows' of each fit into the dense parts of the other. This type of mixture, Empedocles says, makes soft bodies hard, as happens when copper is alloyed with tin. (Even this explanation of the hardness of bronze is wrong, remarks Aristotle.) The passage affords yet another instance of how he applied his general principles (in this case the doctrine of 'symmetry of pores', pp. 150f. above) to a particular case.

Sex is determined by temperature, males being hotter than females.[1] So Aristotle (*GA*, 764 a 1):

Others claim that the differentiation of sex takes place within the womb.[2] Thus Empedocles says that what enters a hot womb becomes male, what enters a cold womb female. The heat or coldness is determined by the flow of the menses, which may be either colder or hotter, older or more recent.[3]

Again at 765 a 8: 'We must also face the argument of Empedocles, who differentiates male from female by the heat of the womb.' This applies to the original formation of animals within the earth as well as to the embryo in the womb. Of Empedocles himself we have the following lines: (fr. 65) 'And it was poured out in the purified parts;[4] some become women, when they have met with cold...' and (fr. 67.1) 'For in the warmer part of the earth appeared that which engendered the male'.[5]

Multiple births were due to superabundance and division of the semen. Family resemblances 'follow the preponderance of the seed';

[1] Arist. *PA*, 648 a 29–31, quoted on p. 78 above. See Lesky, *op. cit.* 31 ff., *Die Wärmetheorie des Empedokles*.

[2] As opposed to those who say that it is already present in the semen.

[3] Empedocles himself may have been more lucid than this summary of him. Presumably the meaning is, as Platt says (*ad loc.* in Oxford trans.), that if conception takes place directly after menstruation the offspring is male, if later female. But according to Galen (*ad fr. 67*) it was a question of the right-hand side of the womb being warmer than the left, whereas the words of Censorinus (5.4, DK, A81) would seem to imply that sex depended on the semen coming from the right (male) or left (female) testicle. At least 'ex dextris partibus profuso semine' does not appear to refer to the receiving womb. (See also G. E. R. Lloyd in *JHS*, 1962, 60, n. 19. He thinks Censorinus's interpretation should probably be ruled out.) Empedocles's own statement has not survived.

[4] ἐν καθαροῖσι. καθαίρεσθαι, κάθαρσις are words used of menstruation.

[5] The edd. of Galen have ἐν γὰρ θερμοτέρῳ τὰ κατ' ἄρρενα ἔπλετο γαίης (with hiatus), which Diels emended to τοκὰς ἄρρενος ἔπλετο γαστήρ. Seeing however that Empedocles shared the widespread view that the earth was the original mother of animals and men, and believed that the first males arose in the eastern and southern parts of the earth because these were warmer (Aët. 5.7.1, A81), it hardly seems necessary to alter the last word. Cf. Guthrie, *In the Beginning*, ch. 2 with n. 8.

a lack of resemblance to either parent results 'when the heat of the semen has evaporated'.[1]

In human beings the differentiation of the parts in the embryo begins from the thirty-sixth day and is complete from the forty-ninth. Male embryos take shape more quickly than female, and the right-hand parts than the left. The heart is the first organ to be formed, because it above all contains the life of a man. The navel brings together four vessels, two venous and two arterial, through which sanguineous and breathy material is conveyed to nourish the embryos. These substances according to Empedocles originate in the liver.[2]

He believed that menstruation occurs in women when the moon is waning, a superstitious idea with which Aristotle is rather surprisingly inclined to agree, though more tentatively. Aristotle also gives a reason, which since it is connected with change of temperature is likely to have weighed with Empedocles before him.[3]

Of the drawing of the infant's first breath Aëtius reports (4.22.1, A74):

Empedocles says that the first breathing of the [first?] living creature is [was?] caused[4] by the retreat of the moisture in the infants and the entering

---

[1] Aët. 5.10.1 and 11.1 (A81). The meaning of the clause about resemblances may be inferred from the fuller statement of the Hippocratic *De genitura* 8 (VII, 480 L.): semen is provided by the bodies of both parents, and those parts of the offspring which contain more of the seed of one parent will resemble the corresponding parts of that parent. But according to Empedocles temperature was effective here too, as well as in determining sex, if we may trust Censorinus. (A81, but see Lesky, *op. cit.* 36f. on these passages.)

[2] All these statements depend on secondary sources, Aëtius, Censorinus and Soranus. See A83, 84, 79. On the question which organ was formed first, opinion in the fifth century differed according to the view taken of what was the central and most vital organ. Thus Alcmaeon (A13) and Anaxagoras (A108) said it was the brain. For Democritus see p. 467 below.

[3] Soranus (early second century A.D.) quoted in A80, Arist. *GA*, 738a16ff., repeated at 767a2 and *HA*, 582a34. Other physicians, says Soranus, thought menstruation more likely to occur at full moon (Wellmann, *FGÄ*, 1.197), whereas he himself took the sensible view that the time of onset differed for different women.

[4] The MSS. have τὴν ἀναπνοὴν τοῦ πρώτου ζῴου γενέσθαι. Diels (*Dox.* 411) excised πρώτου and altered to γίνεσθαι, comparing 5.15.3. DK and Bignone (*Emped.* 359) have restored the original text, but the corrections are strongly defended by Reiche, *Emp.'s Mixture*, 67. I do not think that by τὸ πρῶτον ζῷον Empedocles would necessarily have meant the 'whole-natured' as Reiche insists (he is inclined in general to press on Empedocles a scientific precision which may be excessive), and the MS. reading is favoured by the opening words of the next sentence, τὴν δὲ νῦν κατέχουσαν, which Bignone translates 'Nella condizione presente'. (The unexpressed noun is ἀναπνοήν.) The passage may be compared with the brief account of the same phenomenon by Philolaus (vol. 1, 278f.). Philistion like Philolaus believed the purpose of breathing was to cool the ἔμφυτος θερμασία (Wellmann, *FGÄ*, 71), and refrigeration was also its primary function in Aristotle.

of air from outside into the vessels by way of the void thus created. Immediately afterwards exhalation was caused by the innate warmth in its surge towards the surface driving out the air, and inhalation as it retreated inwards and allowed the air to return.

(3) *Respiration*

On respiration in general we have one of Empedocles's most picturesque passages (fr. 100). Modern interpretations of it differ, and the differences affect the translation itself. The following translation is based on that of N. B. Booth, and goes against the view generally accepted until recently, though this had already been challenged by D. J. Furley.[1] Whatever interpretation is adopted, one must admit that Empedocles does not seem to have thought of all the problems raised by his theory and that his poetical language is at some points irretrievably vague.

This is the way that all creatures breathe in and out. All animals have tubes of flesh, containing little blood, stretched out deep inside the body.[2] At their mouths the furthest ends of the nostrils[3] are pierced through with close-set holes, so that the blood is kept out but a free pathway for air is opened through the passages. Then whenever the delicate blood runs away from here, the blustering air rushes in with furious surge, but when it leaps back, the animal breathes out. It is as when a girl plays with a water-lifter (*clepsydra*) of shining bronze. When she puts the opening of the neck against her fair hand, and dips the vessel into the yielding mass of bright water, no liquid enters, but the bulk of air falling from within on the close-set holes prevents it until she uncovers the compressed stream of air. Then as the air gives way, the water duly enters. Similarly when water occupies the interior of the bronze vessel and the opening or passage is stopped by human flesh, the air

---

[1] In *JHS*, 1957 (1), 31–4. See p. 224, n. 2 below. Mr Booth's article is in *JHS*, 1960, 10ff. Signora M. Timpanaro Cardini in *Parola del Passato*, 1957, had independently come to much the same conclusions as Booth.

[2] Here the vagueness of terminology begins to make itself felt. πύματον simply means last, hindmost or furthest. DK and others have taken πύματον σῶμα to mean the surface of the body, that which comes last as seen from the inside. On Booth's interpretation we are looking in from the outside. Signora Cardini's is slightly different (*loc. cit.* 259).

[3] ῥινῶν ἔσχατα τέρθρα. According to Burnet, DK and many others (following Karsten and Lommatzsch), ῥινῶν is pl. of ῥινός, skin. Timpanaro and Booth derive it from ῥίνες, nostrils. It was so understood by Aristotle, whom Diels thought guilty of a 'ridiculous misunderstanding'. Professor Verdenius tells me (by letter) that he cannot accept Booth's translation of πύματον, and believes ῥινῶν to mean skin, the pl. being due to metrical compulsion and perhaps also to a desire to play on the double meaning: the skin on Empedocles's theory is a collection of nostrils.

outside trying to get in keeps back the liquid, commanding the surface[1] about the gates of the gurgling strainer, until she releases her hand. Then, the opposite of what happened before, the air rushes in and the water duly rushes out. So with breathing, when the blood coursing through the body leaps back to the inner recesses, straightway a stream of air comes surging in, but when it returns, an equal quantity goes back and is breathed out.

The essential and agreed point of this account is that the rhythm of breathing depends on an oscillatory movement of the blood. On the translation given here, there are tubes containing a little blood[2] coming from within the body and ending at the back of the nostrils. Here the inner surface of the nostrils is pierced with holes so tiny that they are impenetrable to blood but not to air. As blood pulses forward and fills the tubes, the air is driven (breathed) out through these holes, while the blood itself can go no further than the tiny perforations. When the blood retires, air is drawn in again through the same perforations.

The clepsydra described here was a device for lifting liquid from one vessel (say a large jar of wine) and releasing it into another (say one of the broad flat drinking-cups in use in Greece).[3] It would be especially useful when the liquid was low in its receptacle. Its nature and working are thus described by Simplicius (*De caelo*, 524; cf. *Phys.* 647.26). It is 'a narrow-necked vessel having a broader base pierced with small holes, now called *hydrarpax* ("water-snatcher")'. In language which might be a prose paraphrase of Empedocles, he goes on to explain that when it is let down into water with the upper orifice closed, the water does not enter through the holes because the air collected within exerts pressure against it and prevents it from coming up, having itself nowhere else to go. When the obstruction is removed from the opening at the top, the water enters and the air gives place to it. If the upper opening is again covered when the clepsydra is full of water, the water

---

[1] The language, as Millerd remarks (*Emped.* 73), suggests a metaphor from a siege; but the double meaning of ἄκρα κρατύνων ('commanding the heights') can hardly be kept without detriment to the sense.

[2] λίφαιμοι, 'partly filled with blood' (Booth) rather than 'bloodless' as previous translators. Cf. Arist. *De resp.* 473 b 2 φλέβας . . . ἐν αἷς ἔνεστι μὲν αἷμα, οὐ μέντοι πλήρεις εἰσὶν αἵματος.

[3] Its use in serving wine is described by Hero of Alexandria (*Pneum.* 1.7, vol. 1, p. 56 Schmidt).

cannot run out through the holes at the bottom because that would cause a vacuum in the vessel, since air cannot enter to replace it either through the closed mouth or through the bottom where the water stops up the holes.[1]

Two operations are described in the simile. Each deals with the effect of unstopping the previously stopped opening in the top of the clepsydra, and inspiration and expiration respectively are compared with these effects. In the first, the stopped clepsydra contains no water, but uncovering the upper hole allows water to enter through the strainer at the bottom as the air escapes through the top. In respiration, the inspired air corresponds to the water, and the blood to the air that retreats and makes way for it. Secondly, the girl starts by holding up the clepsydra with water in it and her finger over the top, so that there is no downward pressure of air on the water and it stays where it is because of the upward pressure on the small holes in the bottom. She takes her finger off and the water runs out. This illustrates expiration; the air entering and forcing the water out corresponds to the blood rushing up the tube, and the water to the air which is expelled through the nostrils. In the body the blood is of course halted at the mouth of the tube by the fineness of the perforation, whereas in the clepsydra the air will follow the water through the holes, but the simile is quite close enough to illustrate the process as Empedocles imagined it. We may agree with Booth that there is no great improbability in his having made air in the simile correspond to the blood, and the air that is breathed out correspond to the water in the simile.

According to earlier interpretations the theory expounded is that we breathe through the skin all over our bodies.[2] It is unfortunate that the relevant noun *could* mean either 'nostrils' or 'skin', though the

[1] The interpretations of Burnet and Millerd are vitiated by their assumption that the clepsydra in question is the water-clock which has a superficial resemblance to it and borrowed its name. See H. Last in *CQ*, 1924, 169–73, and Guthrie, *Aristotle on the Heavens* (Loeb ed.), 226, n. (a). A full description of its working occurs in [Arist.] *Probl.* 914b9ff., where it is said that Anaxagoras also offered an explanation of the phenomena involved. There is no evidence to show whether he was interested in the problem for its own sake or, like Empedocles, was using the clepsydra as an analogy.

[2] E.g. Ross, *Parva Nat.* 314: 'Whether we like it or not, Empedocles definitely refers to tubes extended all over the surface of the body.' Ross agrees that this is 'a very paradoxical account of breathing'.

latter would imply an unusual and poetic use of the plural.[1] Introducing the quotation Aristotle says (*De resp.* 473 b 1):

He says that inspiration and expiration take place because there are veins[2] containing some blood, but not filled with it, and these veins have passages leading to the outer air, smaller than bodily particles, but larger than those of air. Now it is in the nature of blood to move up and down, and so when it sinks down the air flows in—which is inspiration—and as it rises up the air is forced out in expiration. [There follows the quotation.]

In criticism of this Aristotle says (473 a 17):

He speaks of breathing through the nostrils (μυκτήρων) and thinks he is referring to the essential process of breathing, whereas there is also breathing from the chest through the windpipe, and without it there is no breathing through the nostrils. Moreover animals can be deprived of breathing through the nostrils without coming to harm, but if they cannot breathe through the windpipe they die.

Evidently Aristotle saw nothing in Empedocles about breathing all over the skin. In view of this passage, the words 'to the outer air' in the previous one cannot mean the external surface of the skin all over the body, but must indicate the inner surface of the nostrils, which is equally in contact with the air. Similarly, Aëtius (4.22.1, DK, A 74) speaks of the blood as travelling to the surface (εἰς τὴν ἐπιφάνειαν) and driving out the air through the nostrils.[3]

A strong point in favour of the established interpretation is that a theory of breathing through pores in the skin is expounded by Plato in the *Timaeus* (79 c), who probably took it from Philistion the physician of the Sicilian school.[4] In general the influence of Empedocles on the *Timaeus* is marked, and moreover the principle behind Plato's theory of the 'circular thrust' is the Empedoclean one that there is no such thing as empty space. On the interpretation followed here, it must be admitted that Empedocles does not seem to have allowed for this

---

[1] See Timpanaro Cardini, *P. del Pass.* 1957, 261, n. 3, and p. 220, n. 3 above.

[2] On φλέβας see Cardini, *loc. cit.* 258 f.

[3] ῥινῶν as in Empedocles. As Booth says, Aëtius does not usually keep Empedocles's poetical language in his dry prose summaries, and would be most unlikely to retain ῥῖνες in the unfamiliar sense of 'skin' or 'skins'. To Reiche (*E.'s Mixture*, etc. 74) and others Aëtius is merely copying Aristotle's mistaken identification of the word with 'nostrils'.

[4] To whom is attributed in *Anon. Lond.* 20.45 a theory that we breathe 'not only through the mouth and nostrils but also all over the body'.

explicitly.[1] It would not be astonishing, however, if this difficulty had not occurred to him and Philistion or Plato had rectified the omission by a more sophisticated theory. No doubt the last word has not been said, but to quote Booth again:

If both Plato and Philistion believed that breathing occurred through pores in the skin, this is admittedly an argument in favour of Diels's interpretation of ῥινῶν as skin. But it is not nearly so strong as the arguments against: Aristotle's evidence, the improbability of ῥινῶν meaning anything other than 'nostrils' in an account of breathing, the still greater improbability of Empedocles having made no mention of the nose in an account of breathing.[2]

Two claims are often made for this fragment which are incidental to its physiological subject. First it is said that in it Empedocles proves the corporeal nature of air, as distinct from empty space or rarefied mist (*aer*). So for instance Burnet (*EGP*, 229):

Aristotle laughs at those who try to show there is no empty space by shutting up air in water-clocks and torturing wineskins. They only prove, he says, that air is a thing. That, however, is exactly what Empedocles intended to prove, and it was one of the most important discoveries in the history of science.

This of course was not his main purpose here, nor could he well have written as he did if he believed that preparatory to his explanation of breathing he must prove as a startling new fact that air was a thing. The clepsydra was in common use, and everyone must have known that the invisible air could resist pressure and keep away another body. Nor does Burnet do justice to the point which Aristotle is making in the passage he refers to (*Phys.* 213a25). Those who play with inflated

---

[1] 'If Empedocles did not believe in a void...then he must have supposed that something was displaced by the blood deep inside the body; this would presumably be air, which would then have to go somewhere' (Booth, *JHS*, 1960, 14). On the theory of Philistion see also Cardini, *loc. cit.* 261–4.

[2] Booth is arguing against the view of D. J. Furley, which deserves mention in conclusion. Even though Empedocles believed, says Mr Furley, that we breathe all over our bodies, he must have known that we also breathe through the nose and mouth; and he suggests that difficulties of interpretation are avoided if we assume that the top vent of the clepsydra corresponds to nose (or nose and mouth) and the strainer at the bottom to the pores in the skin. We breathe in through the nose as we breathe out through the pores, and *vice versa*, a process made possible by the oscillation of the blood. The attraction of this explanation lies in the neat way that it allots a function to both of the characteristic features of the clepsydra, but as Booth has shown, it is not without difficulties, and since the whole principle of the clepsydra depends on the upper opening as well as the perforated bottom, the former is by no means otiose on the other explanations.

wineskins and clepsydras think, says Aristotle, that they have sufficiently refuted the philosophers who hold that true void exists. All they do is to prove that air is a thing (one is tempted to supply 'and everybody knows that'), whereas, he goes on, 'what is needed is not a proof that air is a thing, but that there is not an interval distinct from bodies... which breaks the continuity of the whole body, or even outside the whole body, which remains continuous. That is what Democritus and Leucippus and many other scientists maintain.' To demonstrate that air is a thing is obviously inadequate as a refutation of this position.[1] The denial of void was something that Empedocles accepted from Parmenides on the Parmenidean grounds that empty space is 'what is not'.[2] Anaximenes a century earlier already regarded invisible air[3] as a corporeal substance. The novel contribution of Empedocles is that as the first philosopher with a pluralistic doctrine he was the first to regard air as a pure element incapable of transmutation into any other; but this he has said in different connexions and it has nothing to do with the observations on the clepsydra.

The second claim made for this passage is that it is a striking instance of experimental method in the early days of Greek science. Some have even given it on this account a scientific importance above anything else that Empedocles said or did. Both claims are combined, for example, by Benjamin Farrington in the statement that 'his great contribution to knowledge was his experimental demonstration of the corporeality of the viewless air.... Empedocles undertook an experimental investigation of the air we breathe', and by W. P. D. Wightman who writes: 'By actual experiments with closed vessels under water he had shown the existence of a distinct, corporeal substance (αἰθήρ) different from the misty, ill-defined ἀήρ of Anaximenes.'[4] Others have denied the status of experiment to what Empedocles describes.[5] It is certainly not what is understood as experiment by a modern scientist. The quotation does not even suggest that Empedocles had performed the operation

---

[1] Cf. Simpl. *Phys.* 647.30. In the *Pneumatica* of Hero of Alexandria (*prooem*, vol. 1, 4–6 Schmidt) the corporeality of air is demonstrated, in the same way as by Empedocles, in the course of an argument designed to prove that vacua do exist, dispersed between the particles of bodies like air, fire and water!

[2] See pp. 139 f. above.   [3] ὄψει ἄδηλον, Hippol. *Ref.* 1.7.1, A 7.

[4] Farrington, *Greek Science*, 1, 55; Wightman, *Growth*, 15, n. 1.

[5] E.g. Cornford, Vlastos, Furley. See Furley, *JHS*, 1957 (1), 31 and 34.

himself. The clepsydra was not only a familiar utensil; its properties made it a plaything for children, whom he had seen amusing themselves with it. What he gives is a simile, an acute inference from observation of an everyday occurrence; and as Cornford remarked, 'to draw a clear-sighted inference from familiar experience is not the same thing as to practise the experimental method as it is understood today'. Such explanation of natural phenomena by means of illuminating comparisons with the practical arts was a favourite device of Empedocles. We have seen how the elements are mingled like the colours on an artist's palette, the action of heat on wet substance to make living creatures suggests the skill of baker or potter, and the hardening of male and female semen is like the mixture of two soft metals in an alloy. The water which issues in hot springs, he thinks, must be heated within the earth by a system of coiled channels like the coiled pipes of a water-heater which ensure that the water passes through the same fire often enough to heat it, and so, after going in cold, flows out hot (Seneca, *Nat. qu.* 3.24.1, A68). The clepsydra 'experiment' is in line with these analogies.

(4) *Sleep and death*

Aëtius (5.24.2, A85) records that in Empedocles's view sleep resulted from a cooling of the blood to the appropriate extent; death ensued when the heat left it completely. In another statement, partly obscured by corruption,[1] he says that according to this view death is common to body and soul (*psyche*). This is consistent with the function of the blood as centre of the cognitive faculties (fr. 105), and is perfectly credible if we remember (*a*) that *psyche* is the doxographer's word and unlikely to have been used by Empedocles, (*b*) that it refers to the capacity for physical life, and for the cognition, through the senses and reasoning powers, of the world around us. This is something different

---

[1] 5.25.4. There is obviously a lacuna in the words Ἐ. τὸν θάνατον γίγνεσθαι διαχωρισμὸν τοῦ πυρώδους ἐξ ὧν ἡ σύγκρισις τῷ ἀνθρώπῳ συνεστάθη, since they provide no plural antecedent for ὧν. Reiske adds ⟨καὶ γεώδους⟩ and DK (A85) add the other two elements besides, making the sentence mean simply that death is a disintegration of all the elements of which the human body is formed. But the important thing was the departure of *heat*, as is shown not only by 24.2 but by the special part played by fire in Empedocles's system (p. 190 above), especially in connexion with life (pp. 206 f.: growth is due to the presence of heat, Aët. 5.27.1, A77). Possibly the restoration needed is διαχωρισμὸν τοῦ πυρώδους ⟨ἀπὸ τῶν στοιχείων⟩ ἐξ ὧν κτλ. (This was written before seeing the rather similar suggestion of Cataudella, *Riv. di Filol.* 1960, 127.)

from the migrating *daimon* of the *Purifications*.[1] In making heat the vehicle of life Empedocles was no doubt following Parmenides,[2] but the notion was pretty well universal in Greek thought then and later, down to the 'vital heat' of Aristotle.

(5) Madness

Presumably Empedocles must have written of illness and its cure, and we remember the service he rendered to the fever-stricken Selinuntines; but the only extant reference (appropriately enough, considering the spread of his interests between the *Physica* and the *Purifications*) is to mental illness, or affections of the soul. A late medical writer, Caelius Aurelianus (*Morb. chron.* 1.5, A98), attributes to him the origin of the belief that madness (*furor*, Greek *mania*) is of two sorts. One is a consequence of 'purification of the soul' (*ex animi purgamento*),[3] the other of 'mental alienation due to physical causes, namely imbalance of mixture'. *Mania* to the Greeks was by no means necessarily an evil: it might be a sign of divine possession, as in the Dionysiac *mania* of the maenads or the behaviour of the Pythia when prophesying. Plato in the *Phaedrus* (244a) speaks of 'the greatest of blessings coming to men by *mania*', and of this good *mania* he distinguishes three recognized kinds: that of prophets, healers and poets. All three were exemplified in Empedocles himself, a condition which he attributed to the high degree of purification that his soul had attained. (Cf. fr. 146, pp. 250 f. below.) All men have inherited a load of impurity—they are 'distraught with grievous wickedness' (fr. 145)—but by following the precepts of the *Purifications* they can shake it off and reach the exalted state which culminates in apotheosis.

Pathological madness, on the other hand, is caused by an 'unbalanced mixture', which must be that of the elements in the blood. Blood is

---

[1] Reiche (*E.'s Mixture*, 19) thinks differently. The whole question of Empedocles's beliefs about the soul and its immortality will be discussed more fully in connexion with the *Purifications*.

[2] Cf. the ἔκλειψις τοῦ πυρός in a corpse, Theophr. *De sensu*, 3 (p. 67 above).

[3] Bignone (*Emped.* 385, n. 1), though referring this rightly to the doctrine of the *Katharmoi*, surely goes astray in his translation of *purgamentum*. It renders the Greek κάθαρσις or καθαρμός. The correct explanation is given by A. Delatte, *Conceptions de l'enthousiasme*, 21–5, assuming, that is, that Caelius Aurelianus is a trustworthy source. Some may prefer the cautious scepticism of Hackforth, who very properly reminds us that we are dealing with a writer of the fifth century A.D. (*Plato's 'Phaedrus'*, 58).

the organ of thought (fr. 105), and this is expanded by Theophrastus thus (*De sensu*, 10–11, A86):

Men think mainly with the blood, for there the elements of the body are most thoroughly[1] mingled. Those then in whom the mixture is equal or nearly so, with the elements neither too far apart nor too small nor too large, are wisest and keenest of perception, and so, in proportion, are those who come nearest to them; whereas those in the opposite state are most witless.

There is a faint foreshadowing here of the remarkable assurance with which Plato in the *Timaeus* (86b ff.) assigns somatic causes to psychological disturbances, including those which lead to intemperate and criminal behaviour.

M. COGNITION, THOUGHT, SENSATION

On this topic more information is available about Empedocles than about most other Presocratics, mainly because Theophrastus in his critical-historical treatise on the senses gives more space to him than to any other except Democritus.[2] He says moreover (§2) that Empedocles himself, in defending his view of sensation as due to the action of similars, went into more detail than others about the working of each separate sense.

(1) *All cognition is of like by like*

Men think with the blood, and sensation also is a purely physical process. That is why Aristotle says that for Empedocles and other early thinkers 'sensation and thought were the same'. He means that 'they all assume thought to be corporeal like sensation, and that like is both perceived and thought of by like'. This point he illustrates by two lines of Empedocles: 'Man's wit is increased with reference to what is present', and (in a fuller and more accurate version in the *Meta-*

---

[1] Or 'most equably'. For A. Frenkian's correction of the MS. ἐστι (expunged by DK following Mullach) into ἴσα, see *Philologus*, 1963, 313.

[2] Theophrastus's work on the senses is generally reproduced (as in the present work) only in scattered sentences in the writings of historians of Greek philosophy or psychology. For the work as a whole readers may be referred to G. M. Stratton, *Theophrastus and the Greek Physiological Psychology before Aristotle*, which provides a complete text, translation and notes.

With the present section compare in general the relevant parts of Beare, *Gk. Th. of Elem. Cogn.*

physics) 'As much as men change their nature, so much it also befalls them to think different thoughts'.[1] In fr. 105 Empedocles says of the heart that it is 'nurtured in the sea of pulsing blood, where especially is what men call thought: for the blood around the heart is thought'.[2] Theophrastus gives another relevant quotation (fr. 107), putting it in its context as follows (*De sensu*, 10). After describing the working of the senses he continues: 'Pleasure is induced by what is similar in respect to its parts and their mixture, and pain by the opposite. He speaks in the same way of knowledge and ignorance: knowledge is by similars, ignorance by dissimilars, thought being the same as sensation or very like it.'

Both sensation and thought, then, are special instances of the universal principle that like acts on like. This is unequivocally stated of sensation in frr. 109 and 107:[3]

With earth we see earth, with water water, with air the divine air, but with fire destructive fire, with Love Love and with Strife we see dismal Strife; for out of these are all things formed and fitted together, and with these they think and feel pleasure and pain.

The crudity of this general theory offended Aristotle. We may admit, he says (*De an.* 409b23), that the soul is composed of the elements and therefore can recognize and perceive them; but how is it to distinguish between their myriad compounds and know what is god or man or flesh or bone, things whose distinctive essence consists in the different proportions in which the elements are mixed? If like is known by like, must we say that the soul contains not only the elements but stones or men?

Apart from the fact that at this stage in the history of science a satisfactory account of the physiological basis of sensation is hardly to be expected, the faults of Empedocles's theory are largely due to his heroic attempt to explain all details in the natural world by reference to his

---

[1] Arist. *De an.* 427a22, *Metaph.* 1009b18; Empedocles frr. 106, 108. In the *Metaph.* Aristotle paraphrases fr. 106 as 'when we change our condition we also change our thinking'.

[2] In *v.* 1 τεθραμμένη is Grotius's emendation for MS. τετραμμένα. 'Thought', i.e. νόημα. For the meaning of νοεῖν and its correlatives see pp. 17 ff. above. In fr. 107 the verb φρονεῖν is used apparently synonymously. The author of the Hippocratic *De corde* says that the mind (γνώμη) resides in the left ventricle, which rules the rest of the soul (IX, 88 Littré).

[3] In the light of Theophrastus's words just quoted (*De sensu*, 10) I do not think it can be doubted that frr. 109 and 107 form a single quotation.

basic cosmological principles. This economy of explanation is strikingly illustrated by what he says in fr. 110:

If thou shouldst plant these things in thy firm understanding and contemplate them with good will and unclouded attention,[1] they will stand by thee for ever every one, and thou shalt gain many other things from them; for these same things grow into every personality, according to the nature of each man. But if thou shouldst hanker after things of a different sort, such as in human life come in their thousands, sorry matters that blunt men's thoughts, quickly will these things desert thee as time goes on, desiring to come to their own kind; for know that all things have wisdom and a portion of thought.

The combination of physical and mental in these lines is difficult to transfer to an alien language and age. Empedocles seems simply to be telling his disciple to attend well to his teaching, but a more peculiarly Empedoclean meaning is suggested first of all by the words 'according to the nature (*physis*) of each man'. They recall fr. 108: 'As much as men change their nature, so they think different thoughts', which Aristotle, presumably with knowledge of its context, quoted to illustrate the point that thought is corporeal and affected by bodily alterations. The physical implications are confirmed when we read that 'these things', if neglected for less worthy objects, will run away because the desire to return to their own kind (like to like) will become irresistible. If Pausanias holds fast to his master's teaching, it goes without saying that he will be acting in accordance with the good power of Love; if he neglects it he is giving Strife, the evil power, its opportunity; and Love and Strife are at the same time the forces that unite unlikes and likes respectively. As Strife grows stronger in the cosmos, the elements dissolve their associations and each returns to its own. Thought is blunted when the mixture of elements in the blood is disturbed, and this is what will happen to the man who is seduced by 'many sorry matters' from cultivating the power of Love in himself. No wonder editors have been in doubt whether 'these things' refers

---

[1] This gives the bare sense, but the echoes of terms used in the mysteries (καθαρός, ἐποπτεύω, μελέτη) have been remarked by several scholars. See DK *ad loc.*, Souilhé in *Arch. de Philos.* 1932, 441, n. 2; Bignone, *Emped.* 480ff.

The text in Hippolytus has a number of corruptions, for which see DK, but the sense is scarcely in doubt. The last line is correctly quoted by Sextus. The address in the 2nd person singular indicates that the passage comes from the *Physica*.

to Empedocles's teaching or to the elements. In his system of thought the two cannot be cleanly separated. Even the elements are conscious. 'Desiring to come to its own kind' reminds us of the converse situation in fr. 21.8, where under the influence of Love the elements 'are desired by one another' (p. 157 above).

(2) *Pores and effluences*

In more detail the action of like on like in sensation was explained by applying the theory of the porosity of matter on which something has already been said (pp. 150 f. above). This is stated by Aristotle as follows (*GC*, 324b25):

Some[1] believe that everything is acted on by the agent (that is the proximate agent which is most properly so called) entering it through certain pores, and this they claim is the explanation of sight and hearing and all our other senses; further that things are seen through transparent bodies like air and water because such bodies have pores too small to be seen but arranged in close-packed rows, and the more transparent a body is, the closer are the pores. Some, of whom Empedocles was one, advanced this theory in respect of certain bodies—not only those which act and are acted on, but they also say that mixture takes place between bodies whose pores match each other in size.

So also Theophrastus (*De sensu*, 7):

Empedocles explains all the senses on the same lines, saying that sensation takes place by a process of fitting into the pores of each organ. This is why they cannot distinguish each other's objects: some have pores too wide, others too narrow for the sense-object, so that some pass through without making contact while others cannot enter at all.

What actually fit into the pores are films or effluences (ἀπορροαί) which physical objects are constantly giving off. They are mentioned in one extant line of Empedocles (fr. 89: 'Knowing that there are effluences from all things that have come into being') which Plutarch expands by saying that there is a continual outflow from everything—

---

[1] Cf. Aët. 4.9.6 (DK, 28 A 47): 'Parmenides, Empedocles, Anaxagoras, Democritus, Epicurus and Heraclides say that particular sensations take place according to symmetry of pores; the proper object of each sense fits into the sense-organ.' The tendency to group philosophers together is characteristic of the doxographers, and if Parmenides held this theory there is no other evidence for it.

organisms, minerals, land and sea—and that this is what finally causes their decay (p. 151 above). Plato (*Meno*, 76c) brings in this general theory with reference to vision, in which connexion it is most frequently cited:

You agree with Empedocles that there are certain effluences from existing things?

Certainly.

And pores to which and through which the effluences make their way?

Yes.

Some of the effluences fit into some of the pores, whereas others are too fine or too coarse?

That is so.

...Colour then is an effluence from shapes commensurate with sight and perceptible by it.

An example of how the theory works outside the field of sensation is provided by the curious explanation of magnetism, of which we have the following account:[1]

On the reason why the lodestone attracts iron. Empedocles says that the iron is attracted to the stone by the effluences which issue from both, and because the pores of the stone are commensurate with the effluences from the iron. The effluences from the stone stir and disperse the air lying upon and obstructing the pores of the iron and when this is removed the iron is drawn on by a concerted outflow. As the effluences from the iron travel towards the pores of the stone, because they are commensurate with them and fit into them the iron itself follows and moves together with them.

The Greek commentator sees a number of objections to this, based on the universality of the doctrine of pores and effluences. Why should not the magnet follow its own effluences and be drawn towards the iron instead of *vice versa*? Why do not other bodies have the same effect on iron? Why indeed are not quite different pairs of bodies similarly affected, seeing that Empedocles mentions many others as having com-

---

[1] A89, from the *Quaestiones* of Alexander of Aphrodisias, probably dependent on Theophrastus. With this explanation of magnetism should be compared pp. 372, 426 below. The attractive power of the lodestone was known to the Greeks from the time of Thales if not before, and in Roman times at least its repelling power also, though they had no understanding of the principle of polarity. They made no practical use of it (e.g. they did not, like the Chinese, invent the compass), nor did they make artificial magnets. For a brief statement of their knowledge of magnetism, see Cohen and Drabkin, *Source Book*, 310, and for a fuller account Rommel in *RE*, XIV, 1, 474–86.

mensurate pores and effluences? Here he quotes fr. 91 (p. 151 above). The universal application of the doctrine is also seen by Theophrastus as a difficulty in applying it to sensation.

How [he asks (*De sensu*, 12)] will living creatures differ as regards sensation from everything else? Sensible objects fit into the pores of inanimate things as well, for he explains all mixture by symmetry of pores. That is why oil and water do not mix (fr. 91), in contrast to other liquids and all the substances whose particular capacities to mingle he enumerates. Thus everything will be capable of sensation, and mixture, sensation and growth will be the same thing; for he explains everything by symmetry of pores, unless he posits some distinctive cause in addition.

The same applies to thought (§23): everything will share in it, for its causes are the same as those of sensation.

In this case, however, the attack misfires, for it was in fact fundamental to Empedocles's whole system that there is no distinction between animate and inanimate and everything has some degree of awareness and power of discrimination. Fr. 103, 'Thus then by the will of Fortune all things think', is not conclusive proof of this, any more than fr. 102, 'Thus then everything has breath and smell', means that everything in the world breathes and smells. It is however unambiguously stated at the end of fr. 110 (p. 230), and demonstrates once again how the general forces governing the universe are never forgotten by Empedocles when he comes to work out its details. Nothing that was without feeling could be subject to the action of Love and Hatred, and these are the sole activating forces, acting alike on the elements, inorganic compounds, plants, animals and men. This is not to say that there is no distinction between the workings of the human mind and the cognitive powers of an oyster. Aristotle's bald statement that for Empedocles 'sensation and thought are the same' is only intended to bring home the truth that both result from equally corporeal causes. There is a clearly defined hierarchy in nature, but it is a matter of degree only: no radically new process is involved at any stage. In all this Empedocles was partly moved by the religious considerations which find expression in the *Purifications*, namely the possibility of transmigration from one form of existence to another, and the struggle to graduate from lower to higher forms. To Theophrastus the idea that fire or stone should have some measure of cognition was ridiculous, as it was to Aristotle, who noted that parts even of an animal's body, such as bones, sinews and hair, seem wholly insensitive.[1] They did not therefore think it incumbent on them to waste time on the train of thought which had led Empedocles to his curious conclusion. More pertinent perhaps are the questions which they raised concerning the physical apparatus of pores and effluences. This is criticized by Aristotle, and more briefly and trenchantly by Theophrastus,[2] who simply asks: are the pores full or empty? If empty, Empedocles is contradicting himself, since he does not believe in the existence of empty space; but if they are never empty, but the pores, say, of an animal are always full of extraneous matter so constituted as to fit into them, the animal will have sensations all the time.

These are questions which Empedocles would hardly have been prepared to answer, and there is little point in inventing answers for him.[3] He would not contravene his Parmenidean principle of the impossibility of void: there was a continuous flow of some sort of matter through the pores, even if only of air as in his account of breathing;[4] but this might not be sufficient to produce any strong sensation.

(3) *Vision*

Early Greek theories of vision fall into three groups. According to one the eye was the agent, sending out rays from its own 'fire' to the object; according to another it received more or less passively 'effluences' or 'images' directed to it from the object; in the third, both eye and object are active, the eye sending out rays which mingle with the effluences from the object. The Pythagoreans and their associates seem to have emphasized the first aspect, the atomists the second, while the

---

[1] *De an.* 410a30, taken up by Theophrastus in *De sensu*, 23.

[2] Arist. *GC*, 326b8ff.; Theophr. *De sensu*, 13.

[3] Luria makes an interesting suggestion in his *Anf. gr. Denkens* (p. 87), that when Empedocles said that there were *poroi* everywhere he was describing a property or capacity (*Fähigkeit*) of bodies, the capability of yielding and leaving a narrow passage for an entering body. When a body pushes in, it fills the *poros*; where no body has yet penetrated, the *poros* exists only as a possibility. This perhaps smacks rather of Aristotelian potentiality, but it might be supported by the reflexion that from earliest times (e.g. Hom. *Il.* 2.592, 14.433) πόρος meant a ford, and there is no gap in the water of the river until a body makes its way through.

[4] Cf. Philop. *GC*, 178.2 (A87): ἴσμεν δὲ ὅτι οἱ τοὺς πόρους ὑποτιθέμενοι οὐ κενοὺς ὑπετίθεντο τούτους, ἀλλὰ πεπληρωμένους λεπτομερεστέρου τινὸς σώματος οἷον ἀέρος.

combination is represented by Empedocles and Plato.[1] The exact nature of Empedocles's theory is difficult to recover, and obscurities must probably remain; but if we take his own fr. 84 in conjunction with Theophrastus, and add the criticism of Aristotle, we must conclude that he adopted some form of the third way. The evidence consists chiefly of a long quotation from his own poem and the full, though not always lucid, description of Theophrastus. As with breathing, Empedocles uses a simile from human invention to explain how the eye sees (fr. 84):

As when a man, thinking to go out through the wintry night, makes ready a light, a flame of blazing fire, putting round it a lantern to keep away all manner of winds; it divides the blasts of the rushing winds, but the light, the finer substance, passes through and shines on the threshold[2] with unyielding beams; so at that time[3] primeval fire, enclosed in membranes, gave birth[4] to the round pupil in its delicate garments[5] which are pierced through with wondrous channels. These keep out the water which surrounds the pupil, but let through the fire, the finer part.

Simplicius tantalizingly quotes four separate lines which evidently have to do with the eye or vision, but only in passing, to illustrate other topics, so that they tell us little or nothing of Empedocles's mind on the subject. In his discussion of the role of chance in the generation of parts of animals (*Phys.* 331.3), he gives fr. 85: 'The gentle flame [of the eye] met with a very little earth.' At *Cael.* 529.21, speaking in general of the works of mixture caused by Love, he says:

Again when he is speaking of the making of our bodily eyes he introduces this line (fr. 86):

   'Out of which divine Aphrodite formed eyes',

---

[1] Cf. A. E. Haas in *Arch. f. Gesch. d. Phil.* 1907. Haas is rather more definite in his division and assignment of the theories than the evidence warrants.

[2] The usual meaning of βηλός, so translated by Burnet, G. R. T. and W. D. Ross, Millerd, Beare. Alex. *ad loc.* says that here it means οὐρανός, and so Diels. But this seems to be a late sense, found only in Quintus Smyrnaeus and then with the qualification ἀστερόεις, and the vividness of Empedocles's picture is better served by the classical meaning. Bignone's 'horizon' suggests the power of a modern searchlight rather than a horn lantern.

[3] I.e. the time when 'Aphrodite created eyes' (fr. 86, cf. 95). Burnet and Beare understand Love herself as the subject here, and make fire the object, but this seems unlikely.

[4] The MSS. vary between λοχάζετο and ἐχεύστο: λοχεύσατο Förster, followed by Ross. If λοχάζετο is correct the meaning seems to be 'lay hidden in the pupil'.

[5] κούρη means both the pupil of the eye and a girl. Hence Empedocles's use of ὀθόναι, 'fine linen' (? swaddling clothes), for the membranes round the pupil.

and a little later (fr. 87):

'Aphrodite having wrought them with rivets of love';

and when he is giving the reason why some see better by day and others at night he says (fr. 95):

'When first they grew together under the hands of Cypris.'

Simplicius could so easily have given us the lines about some animals seeing better by day and others by night (to which Empedocles seems to have attached surprising importance),[1] but as he has not, we must take this and the rest of the theory from Theophrastus, whose account (*De sensu*, 7) is partly based on the lantern simile of fr. 84:

He says that the interior of the eye is fire, and around it are earth and air through which, being fine in texture, it penetrates like the light in lanterns. The pores of fire and of water are arranged alternately. By those of fire we perceive white objects and by those of water black,[2] for each class of objects fits into each kind of pore. Colours are brought to the eye by effluence. Eyes are not all composed alike from the contrary elements,[3] and some have the fire in the centre, others on the outside. This is the reason why some animals have keener sight by day and others by night: those that contain less fire, by day, for the light within them is compensated[4] by that without; and those that contain less of the opposite element [i.e. water], by night, for then they in turn have their deficiency made up. In the reverse conditions the contrary is true. Even[5] those with a greater quantity of fire are dim-sighted by day, for then it is increased still further and stops up and occupies the pores of water. The same thing happens by night to those in which water preponderates. The disability persists until for the latter group the water is intercepted by fire from outside,[6] and for the former the fire is intercepted

---

[1] The ability to see at night was ascribed by the ancients not only to certain animals but also to some men, e.g. Tiberius (Haas, *Archiv*, 1907, 359).

[2] For this apparent limitation cf. p. 148, n. 1 above.

[3] The text as it stands is corrupt or incomplete. This rendering (which differs from DK) is closer to that of Stratton, *Gk. Physiol. Psychol.* p. 164, n. 28.

[4] For a similar use of ἐπανισόω see Plato, *Prot.* 321 a.

[5] '*Even* those', because one would expect them to see better then, since in general like is perceived by like. But the sunlight 'gets into the eye and chokes up the pores so that the water in the eye by which the dark colours are seen is unable to do its work and the animal is just blinded and dazzled by light, and the more easily the greater amount of fire, as compared with water, it already had in its eye' (A. E. Taylor; see Stratton, *op. cit.* p. 166, n. 32). Aristotle also noted the fact that too strong a stimulus from its proper object could damage, instead of intensifying, a sense-organ's power of reception, and accounted for it after his own fashion (*De an.* 424a28).

[6] I.e. until its passages are stopped by the fire. 'It does not cease to be there but is rendered inactive by the stopping up of the πόροι through which it would otherwise issue forth and be operative' (Taylor; see Stratton, *loc. cit.* n. 33).

by vapour. Each condition is cured by the contrary. The best and best blended eye is one which is composed of equal amounts of fire and water. This is roughly what he says about vision.

Aristotle adds the information that the preponderance of fire or water may be learned from the colour of the eye (*GA*, 779b15):

It is wrong to suppose, as Empedocles does, that blue eyes are fiery whereas black eyes have more water than fire, and that for this reason the blue do not see well by day owing to lack of water, and the others by night owing to lack of fire.

As has often been noted, the prominence of fire and water in the operation of the eye suggests the influence of the Italian Alcmaeon, who taught that the eyes contain fire and 'see through the water surrounding them'. Nevertheless for Empedocles they are made up of all four elements, as appears from fr. 85 which mentions earth, from Theophrastus, and from fr. 109 (p. 229 above). It must also be remembered that Alcmaeon belonged to the opposite school of thought from Empedocles, which explained sensation as the interaction of dissimilars (vol. 1, 347f.).

According to Theophrastus, colours are carried to the sight through effluence from their objects, as in Plato's Empedoclean definition. Aristotle (*De sensu*, 437b23) accuses Empedocles of inconsistency in that he sometimes explains vision by light issuing from the eye (as in fr. 84, which he quotes) and sometimes by emanation travelling to the eye from the object. It is very probable that Empedocles thought of both factors as effective without working them into a coherent theory as was done later by Plato (*Tim.* 45b–c, 67c–d).[1]

Empedocles also tried to explain mirror-images, a phenomenon which (as Taylor remarked[2] in connexion with the disproportionate attention given to it by Plato in the *Timaeus*) must have seemed

---

[1] This is what Professor W. J. Verdenius would call 'a confession of impotence'. For his own solution of the contradiction between light issuing from the eye, and effluences from the object entering the pores, see his article in *Studia...Vollgraff...oblata*, 155–64. Ch. Mugler (*Devenir Cyclique*, 52ff.) argues from the words ότὲ μὲν...ότὲ δέ in Aristotle that there were two theories, one valid for our present world of increasing Strife, the other for its counterpart under increasing Love. Aristotle's 'remarque trop concise' has misled commentators. But Aristotle nowhere shows awareness of such a distinction, and says without qualification, like Theophrastus, that Empedocles explained sensation as of like by like (e.g. *De an.* 410a28, 427a23–28). Cf. also Bignone, *Emped.* 249, n. 2, 381, n. 1, who notes that Theophrastus mentions only the effluences as playing any active part in the act of vision. In this his account agreed with Plato's theory. See also Kranz, *Hermes*, 1912, 42.   [2] Comm. on *Tim.* 285.

Empedocles

especially perplexing to scientific students unacquainted with the simplest laws of optics. On this we have only an inadequate summary in the *Placita* of Aëtius (A 88):

Concerning images in mirrors, Empedocles says that they are produced through the effluences which collect on the surface of the mirror and are condensed[1] by the fire which is expelled from the mirror and carries with it the air in front into which the streams are carried.

In his general theory of vision, Plato followed Empedocles fairly closely, though if Aëtius is to be trusted he departed from him in his explanation of mirror-images by making no use of 'air'.[2] Nevertheless the part played by the two 'fires', internal and external, in his theory, may throw some light on the account of Empedocles's view. Plato says:

As a result of the combination of the two fires, inside and outside,[3] and again as a consequence of the formation, on each occasion, at the smooth surface, of a single fire which is in various ways changed in form,[4] all such reflexions necessarily occur, the fire belonging to the face [i.e. the face seen in the mirror] coalescing, on the smooth and bright surface, with the fire belonging to the visual ray.

(4) *Hearing*

No statement of Empedocles himself on hearing has been preserved, and we have only brief notices by Theophrastus and Aëtius.

Theophr. *De sensu*, 9 (DK, A 86): Hearing is caused by sounds from outside.[5] When the ear is stirred by the noise it resounds within,[6] for it is like

[1] πιλουμένας in the version of Stobaeus; ps.-Plut. has τελειουμένας.

[2] Air figures largely in the account of Lucretius (4.279ff.), which led Taylor to suspect the possibility of Epicurean contamination in what the *Placita* say of Empedocles. More probably Lucretius was following Empedocles, and his explanation may usefully be read in conjunction with Empedocles A88.

[3] I.e. inside and outside the eye. In Plato's theory a 'stream of fire' (ray of light) issues from the eye and coalesces with the 'fire' (daylight) around it to form a single elongated body of light. This body of light, falling upon the light reflected from an external object, i.e. its colour (which is conceived as a motion: here Plato's extremely condensed account must be supplemented from what he had already written in the *Theaetetus*, 153e, 156a–e), transmits the motions back to the eye.

[4] 'This probably refers forward to the transposition of right and left mentioned in the next sentence, and also to the distortions due to the mirror having a curved surface' (Cornford, *P.'s C.* 155).

[5] ἔξωθεν MSS., Diels *Dox.*, Burnet. Karsten altered to ἔσωθεν and is followed by DK, but Beare (*Gk. Th. of Elem. Cogn.* 97) gave reasons for rejecting this.

[6] Diels's insertion of ἀήρ as subject has been generally followed, but hardly seems necessary, though Aristotle, *De an.* 419b34–5 is cited in its favour. It is easy to understand that the ear is meant, since ἀκοή is used indifferently for the sense of hearing and its organ the ear (so the next sentence), as ὄψις for the eye in §7. The translation follows the κινηθῇ ἠχεῖν of *Dox.* and DK for the ungrammatical readings of the MSS.

a bell reproducing sounds in the same volume:[1] he calls it 'a shoot of flesh'. The air when it is stirred strikes against the solid parts and produces a sound.

Aët. 4.16.1 (A93): Hearing occurs in the impact of air on the cartilaginous part, which he says is like a bell that hangs swinging within the ear and is struck.

It is difficult to construct a detailed physiological picture from these meagre descriptions. Beare thought that by cartilage Empedocles meant some structure which he had found by dissection, but more probably he was relying less on observation than on a preconceived notion of how the ear must work if hearing was to conform to his general principle of sensation by physical contact.[2] In this case the effluences are waves of air set in motion by whatever caused the sound outside. (That *every* sensation is a matter of effluences fitting into pores is stated by Theophrastus, *De sensu*, 7, 20.) They enter the ear and reproduce the sound by striking a resonant cartilaginous member. In the naively materialistic view of Presocratic thought this sufficed for explanation. Aristotle advanced to the distinction between the physical organ, which was a *sine qua non* of sensation, and the act of sensation itself which was a psychical event supervening on the physical affection of the organ. Armed with this distinction his pupil Theophrastus proceeds to criticism of Empedocles (*De sensu*, 21):

He explains hearing by sounds within the ear, but it is absurd to think that he has made it clear how creatures hear by positing a noise inside, as of a bell. We hear external sounds by this, but what makes us hear the bell itself? This is just what still remains to be asked.

The theory of Empedocles resembles that of Alcmaeon in so far as air in the ear produces an echo of sounds outside, though the two philosophers differed on the basic principles of sensation and thought (vol. I, 347 f.).

---

[1] If the MSS. are correct, the literal meaning is 'a bell of the equal sounds'. 'Echoes that resemble the sounds outside', Millerd. Others have suspected the text. See A. E. Taylor in Stratton, *Gk. Physiol. Psychology*, 167.

[2] If this sounds defeatist, readers may consult the attempts at physiological explanations by Beare (*Gk. Th. of Elem. Cogn.* 95–9) and Millerd (*Emped.* 86 f.).

(5) *Smell*

By putting together two single-line quotations, a dubious couplet of Empedocles on this topic has been recovered. It refers to a hunting-dog, and most probably ran (fr. 101):

Tracking down with his nostrils the particles from the bodies of wild beasts, (the scent?) of their feet which they leave in the tender grass.[1]

These particles, or fragments, constitute the 'effluences' which Empedocles's theory of sensation requires, as may be gathered from the context in Plutarch's *De curiositate*.

The only other extant fragment on the subject is quoted by Theophrastus (*De sensu*, 22) to emphasize that Empedocles insists on breathing as the essential cause of smell, 'even adding at the end as if to set a seal on it (fr. 102): "In this way then all things have received a share of breath and odours."'

Theophrastus's own report (*ibid.* 9) is:

Smelling is due to the act of breathing, for which reason those have the keenest sense of smell in whom the movement of the breath is most vigorous, and the strongest scent flows off from fine-textured and light bodies.

There remains only Aët. 4.17.2 (A94):

Empedocles says that scent enters together with the breathing that is effected by the lungs. At any rate when the breathing becomes laboured, its roughness prevents our smelling as well, as in people suffering from catarrh.

Presumably the last sentence corresponds to something that Empedocles said, but if so, it deserved at least a mention when among his many severe criticisms of the theory Theophrastus writes that hard breathing is of no assistance to smelling 'if the sense-organ is unhealthy or in some way obstructed'.

---

[1] Verse 1 is quoted by Plutarch (*De curios.* 520e), quite by the way, in a passage on the evils of inquisitiveness, and again more relevantly (*Qu. nat.* 917e) in trying to answer the question why spring is a bad season for scent in the hunting field. (κέρματα, 'fragments', is taken from Anon. *in Plat. Theaet.*, in place of various unsatisfactory readings in the MSS. of Plutarch. See crit. n. in DK.) Verse 2 is from ps.-Alexander's *Problemata* (22.7 Usener), which however omits the beginning. This has been variously restored as πνεύματά θ', ὀσμᾶθ' and ζώονθ' ὅσσ' (the last from a statement in ps.-Alex. and Anon. *in Plat. Theaet.* that dead animals provide no scent).

(6) *Taste and Touch*

Theophrastus (*De sensu*, 9) says that Empedocles gives no specific account of the processes of either taste or touch, nothing in fact but the general statement, applicable to all sensation, that it is a matter of effluences fitting into pores. This may be true of the processes, but he seems to have had an interest in the composition of flavoured substances. According to Aristotle (*De sensu*, 441 a 4) he believed water to contain every sort of flavoured particle in sizes and quantities too small for any particular flavour to be perceived. This must be connected with a remark of Aelian: 'Empedocles of Acragas says that there is some sweet water in the sea, not perceptible to all, but serving to nourish the fish; and that the cause of this sweetness in the brine is a natural one.'[1] This sounds like a deliberate contradiction of Heraclitus (fr. 61, vol. I, 445), who adduced the fact that sea-water was life-giving to fish but fatal to man as proof of the identity of opposites. There is also the passage on the flavours of wine and other vegetable products quoted on p. 208 above.

The statement that water could be without perceptible flavour while containing within itself all flavours in quantities too small to be discerned shows how Empedocles prepared the way for Anaxagoras and the atomists. For Anaxagoras, in the initial state of the world when 'all things were together', 'none could be distinguished for their smallness';[2] and the whole atomic theory depended on the existence of particles below the level of sensation.

As to touch, Theophrastus is especially critical of the omission of an explanation, because of the difficulty of reconciling it with the general theory of effluences. In a way, of course, Empedocles has reduced all sensation to touch, that is, to a matter of physical contact (ἅπτεσθαι) though not of the specific sense of touch (ἁφή). This was an inevitable consequence of the materialism of early theories of sensation, and was made more explicit by Democritus.[3]

---

[1] *Nat. an.* 9.64, A66. See Beare, *Gk. Th. of Elem. Cogn.* 162.

[2] Anaxagoras fr. 1. It is admittedly not certain that Empedocles's work preceded that of Anaxagoras and would be known to him (p. 128, n. 4 above).

[3] Cf. Arist. *De sensu*, 442 a 29: Δημόκριτος δὲ καὶ οἱ πλεῖστοι τῶν φυσιολόγων, ὅσοι λέγουσι περὶ αἰσθήσεως, ἀτοπώτατόν τι ποιοῦσιν. πάντα γὰρ τὰ αἰσθητὰ ἁπτὰ ποιοῦσιν.

(7) *Pleasure and pain*

The sensations of pleasure and pain are mentioned in fr. 107 (p. 229 above), and Theophrastus reports (*De sensu*, 9) that pleasure is excited when the sense-organs encounter objects similar to them in their parts and in the mixture of the elements in their composition, and pain when the objects are dissimilar. More succintly in §16 he says that Empedocles explains pleasure by similars, pain by dissimilars, and quotes in this connexion *vv.* 6 and 7 of fr. 22 (p. 158 above): 'But enemies are those that are furthest from each other in origin, composition and moulded form.'

There are also two relevant statements in Aëtius:

4.9.15 (A95): Empedocles says that pleasure occurs by the action of likes on likes, and in the making up of what is lacking, so that desire is the reaching after kindred substance in what lacks it. Pain is caused by contraries, for all things that differ in their composition and in the blend of the elements are hostile.

So also 5.28 (A95):

Desire in animals corresponds to their lack of the elements which constitute each one.[1]

Thus pleasure and pain are spoken of, as Theophrastus says (§16), purely in terms of physical sensation. In his account Empedocles differs from Anaxagoras, who, we are told, held the curious theory that all sensation is accompanied by pain (Theophr. §§ 17, 29, p. 318 below).

(8) *Conclusion*

For the explanation of the individual senses, Empedocles's own words are in most cases lost. Where we have them, in the case of sight, the account is in highly poetical terms and takes the form of a simile, so that translation and interpretation are controversial. It must be remembered therefore that the sources on whom we rely for the other senses were probably faced by similar difficulties. The figurative language of fr. 84 is reduced by Theophrastus to the simple statement that

[1] I omit the rest in the text as being corrupt. See note in *Dox.* 440. The restoration in DK may be translated: 'pleasure arises from what is proper to the mixture of kindred and similar substances, and distress and ⟨pains from the contrary⟩'.

fire passes out through the other elements in the eye 'like the light in lanterns'. It is at least possible that when he speaks of a part of the ear as being 'like a bell', he is similarly condensing a number of lines over which the moderns would differ no less if they had the text before them. It is unwise therefore to place too much reliance on the details of the doxographic reports or build elaborate physiological theories on such foundations.

The essential point is that for Empedocles all cognition, thought as well as sensation, is in some way reducible to the interaction of physical bodies. We obtain knowledge of the world in which we live because it and we are composed of the same elements, and where those elements are blended in similar proportions, consciousness and awareness are the result. Thus knowledge depends on physical condition, which affects our relations with the external world (frr. 106, 108). This seems to be a rationalization of an idea already expressed more obscurely in early poetry.[1] Moreover, everything in the natural world, including animals and men, is only a temporary combination of the elements brought about in the course of a struggle between two forces, one seeking to unite and the other to separate them. Here lies the chief difficulty in reconciling the physical poem with the *Purifications*, which introduces us to an immortal part of living creatures capable of surviving the dissolution of a series of bodies and finally emerging as divine.

Another fundamental consequence of the physical explanation of cognition is the disappearance of any sharp line of cleavage between animate and inanimate. All things have a share (though not an equal share) of consciousness. In this way a physical account is given of the belief in the kinship of all existence which runs through Empedocles's religious as well as his scientific thinking.

Of the limited powers of sensation and thought as means of apprehending reality something has already been said (pp. 138 f. above).

[1] Cf. Homer, *Od.* 18.136f., Archilochus fr. 68 Diehl.

Empedocles

N. THE 'PURIFICATIONS'

(1) Introduction

The title of this work, in Greek *Katharmoi*, signifies means of purification, either by lustration, libation, sacrifice and other forms of ritual, or by obedience to certain precepts of restraint. Such purification was necessary when, whether wittingly or unwittingly, a man had made himself unclean by offending against some divine ordinance. The causes of this *miasma* or *mysos* might range from homicide to accidental trespass in a sacred grove. When Creon announces that the plague at Thebes is caused by a *miasma* which Apollo has bid them get rid of, Oedipus asks: 'By what *katharmos*?' (*O.T.* 99). When as an old, blind man Oedipus has wandered into the grove of the Eumenides at Colonus, the Athenian elders tell him he must make a *katharmos*. The required procedure varied, but naturally, being essentially a cleansing, it often involved water, as in this instance, where the first thing Oedipus has to do is to draw water from an ever-flowing spring. In the *Seven against Thebes* (738) it is asked, When once the ground has drunk the dark blood of slaughter, who can provide a *katharmos*, who can *wash* it away? In Sophocles again (*O.T.* 1227f.) the messenger says that neither of the two great rivers Istros and Phasis can 'wash with *katharmos*' the stain from the house. An example of this type of *katharmos* is found in the poem of Empedocles himself. Theo Smyrnaeus, comparing progress in Plato's philosophy to the stages of initiation in the mysteries, says that the first stage is *katharmos*, which corresponds to education from childhood upwards in the right subjects: and just as Empedocles says one must cleanse oneself 'by drawing water from five springs in unyielding bronze',[1] so for Plato this education consists of five subjects.

Empedocles was not the only one to apply the term to a written work. In the *Republic* (364e) Plato speaks contemptuously of begging priests and prophets who claim to have the power to absolve from guilt through sacrifices and incantations. Quoting the authority of books attributed to Musaeus and Orpheus, they persuade individuals

---

[1] Fr. 143. The readings in DK should be compared with those of Hiller's text of Theo Smyrnaeus (15.7–11).

and cities that there are means of release and *katharmoi* to be accomplished through sacrifices and 'childish amusements'. In the form of *teletai*, these rites can secure immunity from punishment after death. Empedocles also is in the Orphic ambience, and it is possible that some of the books mentioned were entitled *Katharmoi*. In the *Frogs* of Aristophanes (*v.* 1033) we read that Orpheus taught *teletai* and abstention from killing, Musaeus healing and oracles, and Hesiod the lore of farming. The mention of Hesiod puts them in a literary context, and a scholiast on the passage says that Musaeus '*composed katharmoi*'. Similarly the Suda says of Epimenides that he '*wrote* certain mysteries and *katharmoi*'.

Practical precepts in the extant fragments of the *Katharmoi* of Empedocles include, besides the rite of purification by water, abstention from meat and beans and from laying hands on the bay: according to Hippolytus they also included sexual continence.[1] The rest of the poem puts these precepts in their cosmic setting and explains their necessity, by telling of the fate of the souls of all living creatures. They are immortal *daimones* whose home is with the blessed, but who have been seduced by Strife into sin and are now exiled by an inexorable decree and condemned to be tossed in torment from one element to another of the sublunary world. Only by strict adherence to the rules of purity, and by gaining an understanding of the divine nature, will they escape from the round of incarnation in separate animal bodies and regain the company of the gods. This is the tale which we have now to reconstruct in as much detail as the surviving information will allow. Love and Strife continue to play their part in it as they did in the description of the world of nature and its processes, but here of course the emphasis is on the moral rather than the physical effects of unification and division. Strife brought about our falling away from a former state of divine unity, and to restore it is to co-operate with Cypris, who reigned in the age before murder, perjury and other causes of division were known.

---

[1] Frr. 128, 136, 139, 141, 140; Hippol. *Ref.* 7.29 (*ad* fr. 115).

Empedocles

(2) The opening of the poem

The first lines of the *Purifications* run like this (fr. 112):[1]

Friends, who inhabit the great town that looks down on yellow Acragas,[2] up on the heights of the citadel, intent on fine works, harbouring with honour the stranger, unacquainted with want,[3] I bid you hail. I an immortal god, no longer a mortal, go about among you all, honoured as is meet,[4] crowned with fillets and blooming garlands. When with these[5] I come to flourishing cities, I am an object of reverence to men and women. They follow me in their thousands, asking whither leads the way to profit, some desiring oracles, whereas others seek to hear the word of healing for every kind of disease, long time transfixed by sore anguish.

This is a good example of the lofty arrogance which formed one facet of the many-sided character of its author. Though paradoxical, it is not at all unnatural that such a passionately religious soul should at one moment reflect on his immense superiority to the common man, and thinking of his imminent release and apotheosis speak as if they were already achieved, and at another bemoan the sin and the cruel fate which has dragged him down to this earth 'a fugitive and a wanderer from the gods' (fr. 115.13). His language here recalls (not accidentally, we may be sure) the words in which the guardians of the other world address a nameless initiate after his death: 'Happy and blessed one, thou shalt be god instead of mortal.'[6] The same arrogance and claims to

---

[1] ἐναρχόμενος τῶν Καθαρμῶν D.L. 8.62.

[2] Presumably the river of that name rather than the rock as Burnet and some others have thought.

[3] Verse 3 is missing in D.L. and supplied from Diod. 13.83 (quoting Timaeus). It was rejected as spurious by H. Fränkel but defended by Wilamowitz, *SBB*, 1929, 628. κακότητος is usually translated 'evil' in a moral sense, and I had so understood it until Mr Sandbach pointed out to me that poverty or ill-fortune was a more likely meaning as applied to the wealthy, pleasure-loving (and meat-eating) Acragantines. If the author of the Orphic *Lithica* had this line in mind—and it looks as if he did—he at least took it in that sense (*vv.* 15 f. ὄλβῳ ʒώειν τερπομένοισιν, ἀπειρήτοις κακότητος).

[4] Kranz's opinion (*Emped.* 27, 129) that Empedocles is not here claiming divinity for himself, but only saying that in the eyes of the Acragantines he *appears* a god, seems to strain the Greek. ὥσπερ ἔοικα, 'as is proper for me'; cf. Reinhardt, *CP*, 1950, 171.

[5] Bignone takes τοῖσιν to refer to the ταινίαι and στέφη, which follows the most natural word-order. Possibly, however, Diels may have been right in saying that it referred back to πᾶσι in *v.* 5 and was explained by the following ἀνδράσιν ἠδὲ γυναιξί.

[6] ὄλβιε καὶ μακάριστε, θεὸς δ' ἔσῃ ἀντὶ βροτοῖο, Kern, *Orph. fr.* 32c, p. 107.

246

supernatural powers appear in his promises to Pausanias in the poem on nature (fr. 111):

Thou shalt learn all drugs that exist to ward off ills and old age, since for thee alone will I accomplish all this. And thou shalt stay the power of the un-wearied winds which sweep upon the earth and lay waste the fields with their blasts, and, if thou wish, bring back their breath again. After dark rain thou shalt cause a seasonable drought for men, and after summer's drought bring on the streams that nourish the trees as they pour [? word dubious] from the sky. Thou shalt bring back from Hades the strength of a man who has died.

Most prominent among the gifts that Empedocles has to offer are healing and prophecy, and from fr. 146 we learn that prophets and physicians are among those who have won through to their last incarnation and are ready to join the gods.

His conscious superiority puts him above the human struggle, and he continues (fr. 113): 'But why am I hot against these men, as if it were some great thing for me to surpass mortals doomed to destruction?'[1]

This reminds us of the statement of Aristotle that he was indifferent to office, and of Timaeus that his political life was in contrast to the egotism of his writings.[2]

In speaking of divine matters his tone is different from that appropriate to an investigator of nature relying on the partial powers of human sensation and reason (fr. 2, pp. 138 f. above). Then he asked the Muse to vouchsafe only 'what is lawful for creatures of a day to hear' (fr. 3). Now his prayer is this (fr. 131): 'If, immortal Muse, for the sake of a creature of a day it pleased thee to consider my endeavour, attend once more to my prayer, Calliope, as I make plain a good discourse about the blessed gods.'[3] He knows that what he now says is the truth:[4] 'Friends, I know that the truth is in the words which I shall

[1] Quoted by Sextus after *v.* 5 of fr. 112, with the words καὶ πάλιν. τοῖσδ' ἐπίκειμαι, 'attack these men'. So Wilamowitz, and a glance at the lexicon bears him out.

[2] Arist. *ap.* D.L. 8.63, Timaeus, *ibid.* 66. Cf. p. 132 above. The exact reference of the words cannot be recovered in the absence of context, but Empedocles was πάσης ἀλλότριος ἀρχῆς, scorning the struggle for power, and the sentiment seems to be that of 'I strove with none, for none was worth my strife'.

[3] I follow Wilamowitz and Reinhardt (*CP*, 1950, 174) in taking the 'creature of a day' to be Empedocles himself (cf. fr. 3.4, of which this may be a deliberate echo), and the reference to be to the π. φύσεως. ἐφημερίων has been variously interpreted: as a neuter by Diels and Burnet, as a reference to Pythagoras (fr. 129) by Kranz. I am not inclined to attribute this fr. to the π. φύσεως with Bignone (*Emped.* 637f.).

[4] Fr. 114. The opening ὦ φίλοι guarantees its provenance from the *Katharmoi*.

speak, but hard and painful is the entry of belief into the minds of men.'
Here again, in the sphere of knowledge and its attainment, we meet
the combination of pride and humility which was noteworthy also in
Heraclitus (vol. I, 414). Pride in possession of certain truth is the mark
of the seer who believes himself divinely inspired; consciousness of the
fallibility and inadequacy of the human faculties belongs rather to the
scientific mind. What we are witnessing in these men (in Empedocles
far more fully than in Heraclitus) is the gradual transformation of the
seer into the philosopher. That is what makes the essential unity of
their thought so difficult to comprehend, while at the same time it lends
them an absorbing interest. Part of Empedocles's knowledge, he
knows, is derived from ordinary everyday experience, but part of it
from his privileged access to a world of gods or spirits.[1]

(3) *The Golden Age of Love*

The idea of a bygone age in which men and women of perfect moral
character lived, as in the Garden of Eden, under perfect natural conditions was much older than Empedocles and may have come to the
Greeks from Oriental sources.[2] In Greek literature it first appears in
Hesiod: the epithet 'golden' (not used by Empedocles so far as we
know) applied to the goodness of the men, and except for their
mortality they lived like gods; pain was unknown, death came like
sleep, and earth bore her fruits without human toil.

This ancient and widespread belief Empedocles wove into his
cosmogony as the age of Love. It was not of course the cosmic reign
of Love, when the elements were fused in the one divine Sphere and
no human beings existed; but since throughout our present era Love
has been losing and Strife gaining in power, it is obvious that when
men were first formed Love was a stronger force. This may be called
the reign of Love in the human sphere, and it is thus described (fr. 128):

Among them was no war-god Ares worshipped, nor the battle-cry, nor was
Zeus their king nor Kronos nor Poseidon, but Cypris was queen. Her they
propitiated with pious offerings, painted figures and variously scented
unguents, sacrifices of unmixed myrrh and fragrant incense, and they poured

---

[1] For further development of what is said here, see Cornford, *Princ. Sap.* ch. 7, The Philosopher as Successor of the Seer-poet.
[2] See references in Guthrie, *In the Beginning*, 135, n. 9.

on the ground libations of yellow honey. But no altar was wet with the shameful[1] slaughter of bulls; nay it was held the foulest defilement to tear out the life (θυμός) and devour the goodly limbs.

The age of simplicity and happiness was traditionally the age of Kronos, 'Saturnia regna'. Servius says that according to some theogonies, including the Orphic, an age of Poseidon followed that of Zeus.[2] For Empedocles the ruler of the age of blessedness is none of these, but Aphrodite. Nature as well as man was under her dominant influence, and so, as in other golden ages (fr. 130), 'all things were tame and kindly to man, and lovingkindness was kindled abroad'. Trees bore leaves and fruit in abundance all the year round, in a climate that was like a perpetual spring, as in the mythical gardens of Alcinous.[3]

(4) *The sin of bloodshed: reincarnation*

The description of the state of innocence prepares us for the discovery that the sin which put an end to it was the killing and eating of animals. The solemn terms in which Empedocles pronounced the law against this have been preserved by Aristotle (*Rhet.* 1373b6), quoting fr. 135:

...as Empedocles says about not taking life. It is not, he says, right for some and wrong for others,
'But this, the law for all, extends unendingly through the wide-ruling air and through the immense light of heaven.'

As a transgressor himself, he feels passionately his own disgrace (fr. 139): 'Alas, that the pitiless day did not destroy me before I thought to

---

[1] The epithet is doubtful: see DK *ad loc.* ἀρρητοῖσι is perhaps the most likely. For Scaliger's ἀκρήτοισι (in the sense of 'violent') may be quoted Aesch. *P.V.* 678 ἄκρατος ὀργὴν Ἄργος, and perhaps *Anth. Pal.* 9.71, v. 2, ἄκρατον καῦμα.

[2] Serv. *ad Virg. Ecl.* 4.10: quidam deos et eorum genera temporibus et aetatibus dispescunt, inter quos et Orpheus, primum regnum Saturni, deinde Iovis, tum Neptuni, inde Plutonis.

[3] Frr. 77-8, cf. Hom. *Od.* 7.114-19. The sense is clear from Theophr. *CP*, 1.13.2, whatever the exact restoration of the first line. Editors have differed over the assignment of the lines to the *Katharmoi* or the Π. φύσεως. If they belong to the latter, this is only because 'auch in der Bildung der Welt gab es ein goldenes Zeitalter' (Diels, and cf. Bignone, *Emped.* 458). Certainly Empedocles explained evergreenness on his own physical principles, for Plutarch (*Qu. Conv.* 649c, see p. 208, n. 4 above) says that it is due to 'symmetry of pores' allowing the nourishment to flow evenly and regularly into the plants, and this has generally been taken to refer to the age of Love. Yet Plutarch only quotes the word ἐμπεδόφυλλον, and in the context seems to be explaining the evergreen trees of the present world, not referring to a different state of things in the past. Possibly then, as Wilamowitz was inclined to believe, the two lines as put together by Karsten and given by DK represent a conflation of two statements, one from each poem. Such doubts illuminate the strong logical bonds between the two.

bring the impious food to my lips!' Here we are on Pythagorean ground, and, as we should expect, the basis of the law is the doctrine of transmigration. So fr. 136: 'Will ye not cease from ill-sounding slaughter? See ye not that ye are devouring one another in the heedlessness of your mind?' and with greater vividness fr. 137:

The father lifts up his own son changed in form, and slaughters him with a prayer in his great folly. Others look on beseeching as he sacrifices;[1] but he, deaf to their protestations, slays him and makes ready in his halls an evil feast. Even so son seizes father and children mother, and tearing out the life they feed on kindred flesh.

The sacrificial animal may be one's own dead relation, 'changed in form'. Empedocles also included in his poem the Pythagorean injunction to abstain from beans, in a line (fr. 141) which was also attributed to the Orphic writings. This itself was due to a curious belief in an affinity between beans and human life. (See vol. 1, 184f.).

The notion of transmigration is pursued in other quotations, in which it is made plain that the soul may live in plants no less than animals. Of himself Empedocles says (fr. 117): 'Before this have I been a boy and a girl, a bush and a bird and a dumb fish of the sea.'

There is a hierarchy of lives, men being a higher form than animals, animals than plants. Within these main kinds the gradations persist. 'Empedocles too says', writes Aelian, 'that the best move is into a man, but if his lot transfer him to a beast, then a lion, or if to a plant, a bay.' Empedocles's words are these (fr. 127): 'Among beasts they become lions with their lairs on the mountains, their beds on the ground, and bays among the leafy trees.'

Within mankind the distinction persists, and those souls that have won their way to the threshold of apotheosis are incarnated in the highest forms of humanity (frr. 146–7):

At the end they become prophets, bards, physicians, and princes among men on earth. Thence they arise as gods highest in honour, sharing hearth and table with the other immortals, free from human sorrows, unwearied.[2]

---

[1] Text corrupt. I have followed Bergk and Bignone (*Emped.* 503). DK print οἱ δ' ἀπορεῦνται λισσόμενον θύοντες, which KR render: 'and the people are distracted as they sacrifice the imploring victim'. But the sacrifice is performed by the head of the household.

[2] The language deliberately recalls the Π. φύσεως. Cf. fr. 21.12 θεοί...τιμῆσι φέριστοι, and v. 10 ἐβλάστησε. (See also n. 4 on next page).

We remember that Empedocles himself was prophet, bard and physician, and was offered the highest place in the state. His apotheosis is immediate and assured. That is the justification for his triumphant cry to his fellow-citizens: 'I an immortal god, no longer a mortal.'[1]

Another fragment on transmigration has a special interest in that it refers to a particular man, who is, beyond all reasonable doubt, Pythagoras.[2]

(Fr. 129) There was among them[3] a man of surpassing knowledge, who possessed vast wealth of understanding, master of all manner of skills. When he reached out with all his mind, he saw easily every single thing that is, in ten, yea and twenty lives of men.

(5) *The fallen spirits*

The impressive fr. 115 introduces the doctrines that have appeared in other quotations—bloodshed as the cardinal sin, the cycle of reincarnation—but develops the idea that the souls which go the round of mortal bodies are in themselves divine spirits: the divinity to which they ultimately attain is a return to their original and proper state. Their fall is related thus:

There is an oracle of Necessity, an ancient decree of the gods, eternal, sealed with broad oaths:[4] when any errs and pollutes his own limbs with the blood of slaughter, or following Strife (?) swears a false oath[5]—the spirits whose portion is length of life—they must wander for thrice ten thousand seasons[6]

---

[1] Fr. 112.4 (p. 246 above), already dubbed ἀλαζονεία in antiquity (Timaeus *ap.* D.L. 8.66), but defended by an explanation of its religious significance in Sextus, *Math.* 1. 303 (perhaps quoting Posidonius, Reinhardt, *Pos.* 417).

[2] See vol. I, 160f., 161 n. 1.

[3] ἐν κείνοισιν. Porphyry, who quotes the fragment, gives no clue as to who these are. They are commonly held to be the men of the Golden Age of Love, and some have seen this as a difficulty for the identification of the subject with Pythagoras. (Cf. Minar, *Phronesis*, 1963, 140, n. 2.) Rostagni (*V. di P.* 229f.) takes it as meaning 'among early prophets'. Even if it refers to the time when Cypris was queen, is it not possible that the numerous incarnations of Pythagoras might reach back into the age of Love? For some of his previous incarnations see vol. I, 164. For recent support of the identification with Pythagoras see Burkert, *Weish. u. Wiss.* 113 f.

[4] The language of *v.* 2 recalls the Π. φύσεως (fr. 30.3), where the alternate rule of Love and Strife is said to be appointed 'by a broad oath'. Similarly *v.* 8 echoes 35.15.

[5] Verse 4 is incomplete in Hippolytus and omitted by Plutarch. On its genuineness see Wilamowitz, *SBB*, 1929, 634 (against) and Rathmann, *Quaestt. Pyth. Orph. Emped.* 98f. (for).

[6] I.e. probably 10,000 years, the time in which a soul completes its cycle of incarnations according to Plato, *Phaedrus*, 248e. So Dieterich, *Nekyia*, 119, though Rohde (*Psyche*, 404, n. 78) disagreed. Herodotus (2.123), speaking of belief in reincarnation in general terms, mentions

away from the blessed ones, being born through time in all manner of forms of mortal creatures which tread in turn the troublous paths of life. The mighty heavens pursue them to the sea, the sea spews them out on to the floor of the earth, earth to the rays of the shining sun, and he casts them into the circling heavens.[1] One receives them from another and all abhor them. Of these I too am now one, an exile from the gods and a wanderer, having put my trust in raving Strife.

The notion of gods undergoing a fixed period of exile from heaven for wrongdoing, and specifically for perjury, is taken by Empedocles from Hesiod's *Theogony*, lines 793–804. The most binding oath that the gods can swear is by the waters of Styx, says Hesiod, and continues:

Whoever of the gods who dwell on the summits of snowy Olympus pours out this water in swearing falsely, he lies a full year without breath. Nor does he touch the nourishment of ambrosia and nectar, but he lies breathless and voiceless on a strewn couch, enveloped in cruel torpor. When this sickness is over, at the end of a great year, one trial after another, each more difficult, awaits him. Nine years is he kept from the ever-living gods, for nine whole years having no share in their councils or their banquets; but in the tenth he rejoins the assembly of the immortals who dwell in Olympus.

These are the popular gods of Homeric belief. To this traditional material Empedocles has added the Pythagorean doctrine of transmigration of souls and the cycle of births.[2] In this connexion an illuminating comparison is with a passage of Pindar, a contemporary of Empedocles who visited Sicily. Plato quotes it in the *Meno* to illustrate the doctrine that the human soul is immortal and undergoes many births.

Those from whom Persephone receives requital for ancient doom, in the ninth year she restores again their souls to the sun above. From them arise noble kings, and the swift in strength, and greatest in wisdom; and for the rest of time they are called heroes and sanctified by men.[3]

3000 years. In any case the parallel with Hesiod, *Th.* 799, suggests that Empedocles had a 'Great Year' in mind (see vol. 1, 282), as also does Plato, *Politicus* 272d–e, where the time taken for souls to complete their allotted number of births coincides with a world-cycle. On the other hand those may be right who think that τρισμύριαι here, as often elsewhere, stands only for an indefinitely large number. (So Zeller, Rohde, and Millerd, *Emped.* 55, n. 3.)

[1] ἔμβαλε δίναις, a somewhat incongruous reminder of Nausicaa playing with her maidens, *Od.* 6.116.

[2] Pythagorean: see vol. 1, 186, 318f.

[3] Pindar fr. 127 Bowra; Plato, *Meno*, 81b.

Here again the soul (*psyche* in Pindar) is being punished for an ancient wrong,[1] and when men have purged it they become 'sanctified heroes' after a final incarnation in the highest forms of humanity, as kings or men of outstanding physical or mental gifts. In Plato's *Phaedrus* the cycle from each birth to the next takes 1000 years, and normally[2] ten of these must be completed before a fallen soul can regain the society of the gods which it enjoyed before its fall (though not itself a god; in Plato's version the gods are flawless and do not fall).

It looks as if these accounts have a common basis, so that the 'ninth year' of Pindar corresponds to the 9000th of Plato, and also of Empedocles if we may assume that his 'seasons' represent a third of a year. There existed a systematic body of religious doctrine, commonly and with good reason known as Orphic,[3] which was current especially in Western Greece, and by individual writers of genius could be modified to suit their own purposes. The word *daimon* in *v.* 5, translated 'spirit' because that makes it easier to comprehend as something incarnated in mortal bodies, could without confusion be rendered 'god'.[4] Of these Empedocles says that he himself is one, an 'exile from the gods'.[5] In frr. 146–7 he describes the purified souls in their last incarnation as the highest forms of humanity, 'whence they arise as gods, highest in honour, sharing hearth and table with the other immortals'. Just so the exiled gods in Hesiod return to the banquets of the immortal gods. Empedocles has been called, usually with some disparagement, an eclectic. It is obvious that he has made use of a variety of existing beliefs, but the achievement of constructing his own grand system is scarcely lessened thereby. Every religious and philosophic writer, however individual a genius, is eclectic if the word is

---

[1] Literally 'grief' (πένθος). Behind this is probably the Orphic story of the composite origin of men from the earth-born Titans and the god Dionysus whom they killed and ate. For men this horrid crime was a misfortune rather than a sin. See H. J. Rose in *Greek Poetry and Life*, 79 ff., and *Harv. Theol. Rev.* 1943.

[2] Specially worthy souls may be released after three incarnations (Plato, *Phaedrus*, 249a; Pindar, *Ol.* 2.68).

[3] See Guthrie, *Gks. and their Gods*, ch. 11, and index to vol. 1, *s.v.* Orphics. Kranz (*Emped.* 32) draws attention to some differences between the Pindar fragment and Empedocles. For Pindar's belief in transmigration *Ol.* 2.56–77 is also to be compared.

[4] On the meanings of *daimon*, see vol. 1, 318. Love and Strife are also called *daimones* (fr. 59).

[5] φυγὰς θεόθεν. A similar phrase is used by Aeschylus of Apollo (*Suppl.* 214): φυγάδ' ἀπ' οὐρανοῦ θεόν.

taken in its strictest sense. The adaptation of traditional material to his own cosmology is seen here in the dramatic description of the guilty spirit's stormy journey through the four elements, and their indignant rejection of it (it must be remembered that 'the elements too are gods', p. 143 above), and in the mention of Strife as the evil influence.

Empedocles dwells in moving terms on the horrors of this world and the woes of the soul when it has been 'clothed in an alien garment[1] of flesh' by Necessity[2] (fr. 126). He speaks out of the anguish of personal experience. 'I wept and wailed when I saw the unaccustomed place' (fr. 118). And again (fr. 124):

'O alack, O wretched race of mortals, O sore unblest; out of such contentions and groanings were ye born.' And in an isolated fragment of a sentence (fr. 119): 'From what high rank and what a height of bliss....' This world to which we have come is a 'roofed-in cave', a 'joyless place' where 'Murder and Anger and tribes of other spirits of death, and parching diseases and wastings and the works of flux wander in darkness over the meadow of Doom'.[3]

---

[1] The exact force of ἀλλογνώς, which does not occur elsewhere, is difficult to determine. Perhaps the most helpful parallel is ἀλλογνώσας Κροῖσον in Hdt. 1.85 ('failing to recognize'). The *daimon* is unrecognizable in its sorry guise. The χιτών is probably less metaphorical than it might appear, since the word is frequently used of skin or membrane in the Hippocratic writings and Aristotle. (See LSJ and p. 408, n. 1 below.) Possibly Empedocles even has in mind his own description of the origin of men and women from the 'whole-natured forms' that arose out of the earth. We have noted resemblances between these and the bubbles of life which others described as growing out of a sort of fermentation on the earth's surface (p. 210 above). An account of this type in the Hippocratic corpus (*De carn.* 3, 8.586 Littré) describes these fermentations as οἷόν περ χιτῶνας. The word also occurs in a religious context similar to the present one. The papyrus fragment of a poem, Orphic in character, about the next world speaks of being free from the flesh (ἄμμορος σαρκῶν) and of the 'shadowy garment of a mortal body' θνητῶν μελέων σκιόεντα χιτῶνα), words which recall both this fragment and the σκιερὰ γυῖα of fr. 61.4. There is also mention of the agency of Ananke. See the publication by R. Merkelbach in *Mus. Helv.* 1951, 10. (The poem is of late date, so that imitation of Empedocles cannot be altogether excluded.)

[2] Porphyry, who quotes the fr., describes the subject of περιστέλλουσα as εἱμαρμένη καὶ φύσις, whom Empedocles calls δαίμων. This must be the Ἀνάγκη of fr. 115.

[3] Frr. 120 and 121. Hierocles in quoting fr. 121 refers it to the earthly regions. Porphyry says that fr. 120 is spoken to the souls by their ψυχοπομποὶ δυνάμεις. The epithet (cf. Hermes *psychopompos*) suggests souls being conducted to the underworld, and Wilamowitz (*SBB*, 1929, 638) thought that both these frr., as well as fr. 118, referred to life in Hades, not on earth. He cited the darkness and the meadow, which he compared to the asphodel meadow of the Homeric Nekyia, and especially the meadow in the myth of Er (Plato, *Rep.* 614e). According to him, what happens here corresponds to that myth. The *daimon* (Empedocles himself) is distressed because the Keres and their train are telling him in the other world that he must be incarnated on earth. Maass (*Orpheus*, 113, n. 150) and Rathmann (*Quaestt. Emp. Pyth. Orph.* 100) took the same view, but Jaeger has argued for the other in *TEGP*, 149: 'There is undoubtedly a reference to the

It is, as he has taught in the poem on nature, a world of mortal things that are born, decay and perish. For Empedocles, as for the earlier natural philosophers, this is inseparable from its character as a world of 'opposites', and in the language of the *Purifications* some of these pairs are presented in personified, or demonic form (frr. 122 and 123):

There were the Earth-maiden and far-seeing Sun-maiden, bloody Discord and grave Harmonia, Beauty and Ugliness, Haste and Tarrying, lovely Truth and black-haired Obscurity, Growth and Decay, Repose and Waking, Motion and Stability, Greatness with many crowns and Sordidness, Silence and Voice.[1]

With these allegorical pairs of figures Empedocles expresses, in almost Heraclitean fashion, the co-existence of opposites physical, moral and aesthetic, without which the natural world could not exist. This world, as in the poem on nature, is clearly to a large extent under the sway of Strife, and to this unsatisfactory realm the souls of men are bound for ever if they will not listen to the prophetic voice of Empedocles and abjure Strife and all his works: 'Wherefore, distraught by grievous wickedness, never will ye relieve your heart of wretchedness and sorrow' (fr. 145). It is possible that in the lost portions of his poems Empedocles recounted a full theogony like Hesiod, 'Orpheus' and other *theologoi*. In the poem on nature he mentioned 'long-lived gods, highest in honour', along with trees, human beings, animals, birds and fish, among the products of the four elements and Love and Strife (fr. 21. 12), and in introducing fr. 128 Porphyry says that it occurs 'when he is writing on the generation of the gods (θεογονία) and on sacrifices'.

terrestial world in the words "We arrived in this roofed-in cave".... We have strong evidence elsewhere that the conception of the world as a cave is Orphic.' Jaeger is supporting Rohde (*Psyche*, Eng. tr. 403, n. 75), with whom Bignone (*Emp.* 493 f.), Kranz (*Hermes*, 1935, 114, n. 1), Millerd (*Emped.* 93, n. 5) and Dodds (*Gks. and Irrational*, 174, n. 114) also agree. The Orphic image of the cave, as everyone knows, was also applied to this life on earth by Plato. (See Bignone, 493, for passages indicative of Orphic origin.) That the description should recall the underworld is only natural, for true to the Orphic tradition Empedocles regards the life of the soul as belonging to a higher region, and banishment to earth as the equivalent of death. To the Orphics 'the body is a tomb' (Guthrie, *Gks. and their Gods*, 311, n. 3).

[1] All the nouns are of feminine form, and some have epithets indicating their personification, which nevertheless is extremely difficult to make plausible in translation, save by the device, adopted by some, of writing Lady this and Lady that. In composing the catalogue Empedocles evidently had in mind the catalogue of Nereids in the *Iliad* (18. 39 ff.), which besides names suitable for sea-nymphs has also some more abstract, including Νημερτής. In general however the lists are quite different, and the contrasting pairs are Empedocles's own.

It is not certain that the two fragments belong together, nor is either vouched for as coming from the *Katharmoi* to which they seem most naturally to belong.

(6) *The way to salvation*

In general the soul must learn 'to fast from evil' (fr. 144), an isolated and striking phrase quoted by Plutarch. It must lead a pure life, practising the *katharmoi* recommended and above all abstaining from flesh. There is also something else, the knowledge of the divine which the pure soul may hope to attain (fr. 132): 'Blessed is he who has obtained the riches of divine wisdom, and wretched he who has a dim opinion in his thought concerning the gods.'

Since like is known by like, to know the divine is to be assimilated to it as in Pythagorean belief (vol. I, 211). 'With earth we see earth, with water water.' If then we become clearly aware of the nature of divinity, there must be a divine element in ourselves. It is not to be grasped by the bodily organs (fr. 133, quoted by Clement of Alexandria):

For the divine, says the poet of Acragas,
'Is not to be reached and made accessible by the eyes, nor grasped with the hands, though by this way the broadest path of persuasion enters the heart of men.'

This is because (fr. 134):

Neither is the god furnished with a human head on a body, nor do two branches spring from its back, it has no feet, no swiftly-moving knees, no hairy genitals; but it is only a mind, holy and beyond description, darting through the whole cosmos with swift thoughts.[1]

The criticism of anthropomorphism recalls that of Xenophanes, whose god was 'in no way like mortals either in body or mind', but 'sees, perceives and hears as a whole' and 'remains in the same place, not moving at all, but without toil makes all things shiver by the

---

[1] The fr. is thus introduced by Ammonius (see DK): 'Wherefore the sage of Acragas also, having censured the myths of the poets which represent the gods as having human shape, expressed himself thus, principally about Apollo, of whom he had just been speaking, but similarly in his general explanation of divinity as a whole: "Neither is it furnished", etc.'

D.L. (8.57) said that Empedocles composed a proemium to Apollo which was burned. Apart from that and a doubtful reference in Genethlius (A23, cf. Wilamowitz, *SBB*, 1929, 644), this is the only mention of the name in connexion with Empedocles. It does not occur in any fragment. It is therefore impossible to be certain how he used it, but since Apollo was the patron deity of the Pythagoreans it is not unlikely that he applied it to his own non-anthropomorphic highest divinity. Bignone (*Emped.* 642) supposed it to have been an alternative name for the sun.

It is very possible that frr. 133 and 134 form a single quotation, as DK suggest.

impulse of his mind'.[1] More important, it is obviously meant to recall the description of the divine Sphere of the elements united under Love (fr. 29). Two whole lines are identical in both, or practically so; then for the last line, 'but it was a Sphere, and in all directions equal to itself', is substituted 'but it is only a holy mind', etc. This raises the whole question of Empedocles's theology, on which something must be said before we can consider the ultimate destiny of the fallen gods in mortal bodies.

(7) The gods

The evidence for Empedocles's theological beliefs is not of course confined to the *Purifications*, but may be conveniently considered together in a chapter dealing with the religious aspect of his thought. The mind of a mystic on this subject does not lend itself to logical analysis,[2] and we are further hampered by the fragmentary state of the poems. Certainty on all points is therefore unattainable, but it is well to remember at the outset that 'god' is by no means an exact equivalent of the Greek *theos*. G. M. A. Grube, repeating the acute remark of Wilamowitz that *theos* is primarily a predicative notion (not 'God is love' but 'Love is a *theos*'), remarks that 'any power, any force that we see in the world, which is not born with us and will continue after we are gone, could thus be called a god, and most of them were'.[3]

Our reading of the poems has shown that Empedocles recognized at least the following categories of gods:

(1) The four elements.

(2) Love (Aphrodite, Cypris) and Strife.

(3) Certain products of the elements. In fr. 21 it is said that from them grow trees, men, women, beasts, birds, fish, 'and long-lived gods highest in honour', and the same list is repeated in the simile of paints

---

[1] Xenoph. frr. 23–6, vol. 1, 374.

[2] In strict logic one might for instance ask: if incarnation is for the *daimones* a punishment for perjury and bloodshed, and if the souls of men are incarnate *daimones*, how is it that there was a period of human life when men were sinless and had not yet killed? I do not think this question would occur to Empedocles, nor is the origin of moral evil ever capable of rational explanation by one who holds that man is made in the image of God, be he Empedocles, Plato or the author of the Book of Genesis. There are truths of religion for which myth is the only possible form of expression.

[3] Grube, *Plato's Thought*, 150, quoting Wilamowitz, *Platon*, 1, 348. This should make us chary of speaking, as some scholars have done, of 'the God of Empedocles', and then trying to identify this one god.

on a palette, fr. 23.8. This allows for the gods of popular belief, and since Greek mythology contained stories of gods being born (e.g. Apollo and Artemis, Hermes, Dionysus and Zeus himself) and dying (like Dionysus and the Cretan Zeus) it is not surprising to find that, though long-lived, they are subject to ultimate dissolution.[1]

(4) The Sphere in which the four elements are perfectly blended with Love (p. 168 above).

(5) The holy Mind of fr. 134.

(6) The *daimones* or spirits who for their sins are caught in mortal bodies, but if they learn to live in purity will finally arise again as 'gods highest in honour' (the same phrase as that used of the long-lived gods formed from the elements in frr. 21 and 23).

Empedocles also speaks, like any other Greek poet, of gods in the plural without further specification. In fr. 131 he prays to the Muse as he 'sets forth a good discourse (or tale) about the gods', and in 132 he speaks of those who have only a dim opinion about the gods. This is a Greek way of speaking which does not exclude the possibility that he had a peculiar theology of his own. Xenophanes, that staunch upholder of the unity of God, could also speak of 'being unmindful of the gods' when the context was appropriate (fr. 1.24). That the world was peopled with divine spirits was a universal belief which Empedocles no doubt took for granted. A Greek could multiply such spirits with the greatest of ease, as he does himself in frr. 121–3, and it by no means follows that all had to be given a fundamental position in his physical and theological system. Kranz may even have been right in comparing the traditional gods in Empedocles, the products of the four divine 'roots', to those of Epicurus: he did not deny their existence, but assigned no influence to them.

What must be taken seriously, for their cosmic or human significance, are the Sphere of Love, the holy Mind, and the *daimones*, and their relations with each other. The identical wording of the lines describing in negative terms the non-anthropomorphic character of Sphere and Mind had naturally led some to identify the two. This was done by Diès, Souilhé and Jaeger. An obvious difficulty is that the Sphere exists only at a certain stage of the cycle, and that during its perfection

---

[1] Xenophanes was less accommodating to popular belief. See his fr. 14 and vol. 1, 371 f.

there is no cosmos in the ordinary sense. 'Darting through the whole cosmos' would be a strange description of it. To this Diès replied that the globe retains its divinity and power of thought in its disintegrated state. Each particle is, 'more or less confusedly', divine and thinking (fr. 110. 10), retaining as it were a memory of the original felicity of the Sphere. Something similar must have been in Jaeger's mind when he identified the Sphere with the holy and unutterable Mind, and on another page wrote that 'this highest God is essentially akin to the single world-controlling intellectual God of Xenophanes, except in the fact that it never remains fully realized in this world'.[1]

Although these views are comprehensible, it is a little confusing to identify with the perfect Sphere of Love the divine element in a state of things when the perfect Sphere no longer exists as such. Bignone thought it best to identify the holy Mind of fr. 134 with Love or Aphrodite. He drew attention (*Emped.* 643) to the phrasing of fr. 17: it is by Love that men *think* kindly *thoughts*, and she is circling or whirling (ἐλισσομένην) among the elements, as the Mind darts through the cosmos. Reiche combines the two views when he says (*Mixture*, etc. 36) that the words 'holy and unutterable mind' refer 'not only to the force of Love, but to the Sphairos in particular', and he concludes (p. 38):

While Anaxagoras's Nous is *wholly* outside the corporeal plenum-mechanism, Empedocles's 'holy and unutterable mind', being itself Sphairomorphic mixture, is only in part (i.e. qua Love) outside that mechanism. In addition, it permeates it in the form of the demons within plants, beasts, and men, and so keeps the 'mechanism' in motion from within.[2]

The tendency to impose a kind of monotheism on Empedocles, to seek as Diès did for 'Le Dieu d'Empédocle', goes back to Hippolytus, whom Diès in fact quotes in this connexion, interpreting in this way the Christian bishop's comment on the line (fr. 115.13) in which Empedocles calls himself an exile from the divine: 'That is, he gives

---

[1] Diès, *Cycle Mystique*, 91 and 93; Jaeger, *TEGP*, 153 and 162. The Sphere is called εὐδαι-μονέστατον θεόν by Aristotle (*Metaph.* 1000b3), clearly with reference only to its perfect state, for he complains that, having no Strife in it, it can have no knowledge of Strife, and hence is less wise than other, presumably inferior, beings.

[2] It should be mentioned that both Bignone and Reiche assign fr. 134 to the Περὶ φύσεως. See p. 135, n. 3 above. It does not seem right to say that in the present state of things Love itself is altogether outside the 'corporeal plenum-mechanism'.

the name of God to the One and its unity, in which he had his being before being torn away by Strife and born among these many creatures of the world which Strife ordered' (*Ref.* 7.29, quoted by DK *ad loc.*). To interpret the *adytum cordis* of a man like this is impossible, at least on our insufficient evidence, and it must be admitted that the fragments tell nothing of the relationship of the divine Mind to Love or to the Sphere. The resemblances between fr. 134 and fr. 29 suggest at least that the Mind is a strong force for unity, and one would suppose that Love represents its working in so far as it enters the cosmos, where it is opposed by the evil and disruptive force of Strife. That the Mind is the highest form of divinity we need not doubt, especially considering its affinity with the one god of Xenophanes. We may also say that although there is as yet no formal distinction between material and spiritual, Empedocles has brought it a step nearer by the language of fr. 133. The divine is at least invisible and intangible.

Anything further is conjectural. It may be that some help is to be found in another comment of Hippolytus, overlaid though it is with later terminology and ideas. He writes:

Empedocles says that there is the cosmos ordered by Strife, the evil one, and another, intelligible cosmos ordered by Love. These are the two contrasting principles of good and evil. Between the contrasting principles is the just *Logos*, in accordance with which the things which were sundered by Strife are joined together and brought into harmony with the One by way of Love. This same just Logos which works on the side of Love he addresses as the Muse, and calls to be his helper.[1]

The idea of an 'intelligible world' is a Platonic importation, although once the Platonic distinction between sensible and intelligible worlds was established, the assimilation of Empedocles's system to it was pardonable, considering that he too spoke of divinity as something that cannot be seen or touched. The expression 'just *Logos*' comes from Stoicism, like 'right *Logos*' in Sextus, when he says in connexion with fr. 2 that according to some interpreters the criterion of truth in

---

[1] *Ref.* 7.31.3, p. 216 Wendland (not in DK: see Bignone, *Emped.* 636f.): κόσμον γάρ φησιν εἶναι ὁ Ἐμπεδοκλῆς τὸν ὑπὸ τοῦ Νείκους διοικούμενον τοῦ πονηροῦ, καὶ ἕτερον νοητὸν τὸν ὑπὸ τῆς Φιλίας, καὶ εἶναι ταύτας τὰς διαφερούσας ἀρχὰς δύο ἀγαθοῦ καὶ κακοῦ, μέσον δὲ εἶναι τῶν διαφόρων ἀρχῶν δίκαιον λόγον καθ' ὃν συγκρίνεται τὰ διῃρημένα ὑπὸ τοῦ Νείκους καὶ προσαρμόζεται κατὰ τὴν Φιλίαν τῷ ἑνί. τοῦτον δὲ αὐτὸν τὸν δίκαιον λόγον τὸν τῇ Φιλίᾳ συναγωνιζόμενον Μοῦσαν ὁ Ἐμπεδοκλῆς προσαγορεύων καὶ αὐτὸς αὐτῷ συναγωνίζεσθαι παρακαλεῖ.

Empedocles is not the senses but the 'right *Logos*'. But here also, as Bignone says, it is reasonable to suppose that the context of these fragments contained some doctrine which made possible an interpretation in that sense.[1] If one may venture to penetrate through the veil of later thought to what that doctrine may have been, the *dikaios logos*, the Hellenic spirit of just proportion, which we know from the fragments to have played an essential part in the *harmonia* of Empedocles's world, seems to stand outside this cosmos in which Love acts as its agent—or rather, *is* the *Logos* in so far as it penetrates the physical cosmos. What later writers call the *Logos* in Empedocles may therefore be what he named the holy Mind, the divine element as was the '*Logos* existing for ever' of Heraclitus. Its relation to the world may be best understood if we suppose Empedocles to have had always at the back of his mind the contemporary religio-philosophic world-picture, which I have suggested[2] would be instinctively retained by even an original thinker of the fifth century, just as even an original pre-Copernican in the Middle Ages would assume that the sun went round the earth. According to this picture, the cosmic sphere, with its conflicting elements and perishable compounds of them, is surrounded by 'the divine', which also penetrates the cosmos and inevitably suffers some degree of contamination or

---

[1] Bignone (*Emped.* 637f.), and, for the Stoic source of Hippolytus and Sextus (*Math.* 7.122), see *ibid.* 647f. In connexion with Hippolytus's identification of the δίκαιος λόγος with the Muse, it is interesting that Sextus, a little later in the same discussion of the κριτήριον (ch. 124), introduces fr. 3, which like fr. 131 contains an invocation to the Muse, by saying that the evidence of the senses is trustworthy τοῦ λόγου τούτων ἐπιστατοῦντος. Rostagni (*Verbo di P.* 217, n. 3) draws attention to the special significance of the Muses to the Pythagoreans as bringers of ἁρμονία. I have pointed out above (p. 161, n. 1) that the word λόγος does not occur in the extant fragments, but Vlastos has noted with equal justice that there is no reason why Empedocles should not have used it himself (*Philos. Rev.* 1950, 45, n. 59).

[2] See vol. 1, 271f., 469–71. Empedocles may have said explicitly that the region of evils reached as far as the moon, but that the heavens above the moon, being of purer substance, were free from them—a view commonly expressed in Hellenistic writers. This is stated by Hippolytus, but only in the scanty and wildly inaccurate summary of his first book, in which he claims that the teaching of Heraclitus and Empedocles is identical, attributing *ecpyrosis* to the latter, and Love and Strife as ἀρχαί to the former! The only other hint of it is in Simplicius (*Phys.* 1124.4), where after interpreting the Sphere of Love in Neoplatonic terms as the intelligible world, and that dominated by Strife as the sensible, he adds that one may see both unity and division in this world too: 'the first in the sky, which might plausibly be called a sphere and god, and the second in the region below the moon'. If we could suppose (as many do) that in the present world of Strife's dominance Love's influence is strongest in the outer spaces and she is abandoning the centre to her opponent, this would provide a neat correspondence between physical and religious doctrine. But at present, as I have said (pp. 183 ff. above), I think a correct reading of fr. 35 forbids it. (DK omit these passages of Hippolytus and Simplicius, perhaps wisely.)

Empedocles

dilution in the process. For the mystic, small portions of it are imprisoned in the bodies of men and animals, and even of plants. According to a widespread belief it was the 'divine *aither*' (Aesch. *P.V.* 88), into which the immortal mind of a man plunged at death (Eur. *Hel.* 1014).

Another quotation from Euripides reflects his reading of the philosophers and comes closer to Empedocles's own ideas:[1] 'All things return, the products of earth to earth, but those that have sprung from aetherial seed go back to the vault of heaven. Nothing dies that is born, but separated one from another they reveal a different form.' In this striking passage Euripides echoes the words of Empedocles fr. 8, that there is no such thing as death, but only separation of what has been unified, and shows how easily such an apparently physical doctrine could be combined with a religious belief in fallen spirits and their ultimate reunion with the divine nature. The doctrine of 'like to like' and the combination of earthly and heavenly in mortal creatures could take their place together in a rational scheme of the natural world, yet recur in the Orphic myth of the origin of the human race from the earth-born Titans who had devoured Dionysus and were reduced to ashes by the thunderbolt of Zeus; and another parallel to the lines of Euripides is found in the mystic's boast inscribed on a gold tablet from a South Italian tomb: 'I am a son of Earth and starry Heaven, yet is my lineage of Heaven.'[2]

Empedocles did not give the popular name *aither* to divinity in its uncontaminated state. This word, which in earlier and contemporary literature had been somewhat loosely and ambiguously used,[3] he appropriated for one of his four 'roots', air in its elemental purity. This divinity was something different from the four elements, non-sensible,

---

[1] Eur. fr. 839N. The origin of the thought in this passage is commonly sought in Anaxagoras, fr. 17, but that fragment contains nothing original, and the phraseology of Euripides recalls rather Empedocles. With ν. 14 μορφὴν ἑτέραν ἀπέδειξεν cf. Empedocles fr. 137.1 μορφὴν ἀλλάξαντα and 21.14 γίγνεται ἀλλοιωπά. See also fr. 8 (p. 140 above). Similarly, Eur. fr. 52.3–5

τὸ γὰρ πάλαι καὶ πρῶτον ὅτ' ἐγενόμεθα,
διὰ δ' ἔκρινεν ἁ τεκοῦσα γᾶ βροτούς,
ὁμοίαν χθὼν ἅπασιν ἐξεπαίδευσεν ὄψιν

suggests a poet's recollection of the undifferentiated forms which χθονὸς ἐξανέτελλον in Empedocles fr. 62.

[2] Kern, *Orph. Fr.* 32a, from Petelia, a city some twelve miles from Croton. Dated to the fourth or third century B.C.

[3] Essentially it was the bright upper atmosphere of a clear Mediterranean sky, as distinct from the lower atmosphere or ἀήρ including cloud and mist. Consequently it was sometimes regarded as a form of air, and at other times as fire. (See vol. I, 466 and p. 185, n. on ν. 3 above.)

to be apprehended only by the responsive element of divinity in ourselves. It was probably (though to affirm this goes slightly beyond the evidence) the element of intra-cosmic Love or goodness, 'whereby men think kindly thoughts and do peaceful works'. By separating divinity from the four elements Empedocles may have assisted the emergence of the 'fifth element', which when we meet it fully developed in Aristotle is divine, the substance of the stars which are gods. Possibly, however, although he did not advance to the idea of purely incorporeal being, he was nearer to it than some of his successors when he refused to identify it with any of the 'roots' but called it 'only a holy and inexpressible mind'.

It may seem strange, perhaps indefensible, to believe in a divine Mind and in our own true selves as incarnated, individualized fragments of it, and at the same time to explain the physical universe by causes which interact in a purely fortuitous way. Yet it was of the essence of early Greek mysticism to hold, not that the divine was responsible for the ordering of matter as it is, but that the whole cosmic order was the enemy of divinity. We think in terms of Platonism and Christianity, but it was a conscious protest against the prevailing view when Socrates and Plato argued that if there is a divine Mind, then it must have ordered the world for the best.

(8) *The nature and destiny of the 'soul'* [1]

The Greek word *psyche*, which is usually translated 'soul', occurs only once in the fragments of Empedocles, in the sense of 'life'. To take life is to draw off the *psyche* (fr. 138). It is improbable that he used it either for the combined faculties of sensation and thought, which depend on the blood and other bodily organs, or for the divine spark in us which is alien to the body and which he called *daimon*. By using the word 'soul' to cover both of these, earlier interpreters puzzled themselves or accused Empedocles of blatant inconsistency in saying in the poem on nature that the soul died with the body, and in the *Purifications* that it was an immortal spirit. That particular difficulty should no longer trouble us. The faculties whereby we live in the body and have cognizance

---

[1] With this account should be compared that of Kahn, 'Religion and Natural Philosophy in Empedocles' Doctrine of the Soul', *Arch. f. Gesch. d. Phil.* 1960.

of the physical objects around us consist of various blends of the same elements as these physical objects—necessarily so, for like is perceived by like. That in us by which we are capable of having knowledge and understanding (as opposed to 'dark opinions') of the divine is quite different, since by the same rule it must itself be divine. The Hesiodic lore of the spirits of heroes becoming 'good *daimones*' after their death had already been developed and altered by Orphic and Pythagorean doctrine, but Empedocles probably still had it in mind, and he (or his Orphic sources) had combined it with the story of gods exiled from heaven for their sins. In Hesiod the men of the Golden Race after their death became 'good *daimones* through the will of great Zeus, dwelling on earth, guardians of mortal men, who watch over righteous and evil deeds, going up and down over the land clad in darkness' (*Erga*, 121–5). Empedocles may have thought also of the spirits of men, between incarnations and before final apotheosis, as performing a similar function, for Hippolytus says: 'Empedocles spoke much about the nature of *daimones*, saying that there are a great many of them and they go up and down directing earthly affairs.'[1] It should not be necessary to enlarge further on the fact that the word 'soul' has been commonly used to cover what in ancient belief were two distinct entities, for this has been done earlier in connexion with the Pythagoreans. (See vol. I, 317–19.) The duality was surprisingly persistent, for it appears even in Aristotle. His general theory of *psyche* as the actuality of an organic body left no room for belief in immortality, in which in his maturity he had little interest. He was no mystic, scoffed at the idea of transmigration, and had nothing to say about rewards or punishments in a future life. Yet it still seemed to him that there must be one human faculty, namely *nous* or the power of intuitive apprehension, which falls outside the general nature of the *psyche*. It 'appears to be a generically different manifestation of soul, which alone is capable of separation, as the eternal from the perishable'. *Nous* alone 'enters from outside and alone is divine'.[2]

---

[1] *Ref.* 1.3, p. 9 Wendland. The authority of this first book of Hippolytus must be admitted to be dubious. Cf. p. 261, n. 2 above.

[2] *De an.* 413 b 24; *GA* 736 b 27: cf. also *Metaph.* 1070 a 25. The doctrine of the 'active reason' in *De an.* 3.5 may point in the same direction, but since it is the most disputed passage in all ancient philosophical literature, it is best left out of the present exposition.

The Fate of the Daimon

In Empedocles, what enters from outside, alien to the body in which it finds itself, is the *daimon*. It is there as a punishment for following the ways of Strife, and to earn its release it must turn, like the blessed ones of an earlier age, to the worship and service of Aphrodite or Love. Its final reward is to be for ever rid of the body and restored to divine status. More than that the fragments do not say, but the nature both of his system and of similar religious statements of the time encourages a guess: it achieves a mode of union with the source of all unity, harmony and goodness, and with the divine Mind to which it proved its affinity even on earth, by turning away from the elemental compounds and seeking, like to like, the knowledge of what is not to be seen with the eyes or grasped with the hands. As the Orphic devotee suppressed the Titanic and cherished the Dionysiac within him, so the follower of Empedocles must abjure the works of Strife and cultivate the spirit of Cypris. Of all this—Love, divine Mind, *daimones*—we have learned something in the preceding pages. Time, the loss of the greater part of his poems, and the unique character of Empedocles himself forbid us to hope for certainty on all the ultimate beliefs which he drew *ex adyto tamquam cordis*. But not the least part of his fascination lies in the way that, as we saw at the beginning and now know better, he typifies the complexity of the Greek mind of his time. Some love the Greeks for their rational achievement, their classical sense of form, proportion, symmetry and order. Others exalt the romantic, Dionysiac strain of *enthusiasmos* in which reason abdicates and man feels the ecstatic joy of possession by the god. We may be capable of responding to one side only of this contrast, but if we would do justice to the Hellenic spirit we must recognize that it included both; and we are helped to understand this by the knowledge that they were combined not only in one people but in one man, Empedocles of Acragas.

IV

ANAXAGORAS

With Anaxagoras we return from Western Greece to Ionia, both geographically and in spirit. Coming from Clazomenae near Smyrna, he is described as a philosophical heir of Anaximenes,[1] and certainly the spirit of the old Milesian school is revived in him. Uncomplicated by the passionate religious feelings that moved Empedocles, his thought returns to the Ionian tradition of free inquiry, motivated by curiosity alone and governed by a purely scientific temperament. The change is also marked, as we might expect, by a return to prose as the medium of expression. He deserves special notice as the man who brought Ionian physical speculation to Athens at the height of her political and intellectual development, for he spent thirty years of his life there and was a close friend of Pericles.

(1) Date and life

Anaxagoras son of Hegesibulus of Clazomenae was older, but only a little older, than Empedocles. Which of the two produced his work first is a matter of controversy, but the opinion may be hazarded that Empedocles links up more directly with Parmenides, and that Anaxagoras wrote slightly later and possibly with knowledge of the poems of Empedocles.[2] He was born, it would seem, about 500 B.C., and the thirty years which he spent in Athens ended in his exile to Lampsacus, where he died about 428 (the year of Plato's birth, as Hippolytus remarked) aged seventy-two. His book was finished later than 467, the year of the fall of the meteorite at Aegospotami (p. 302 below). So much may be said with confidence, though the more detailed chronology of his life is a matter of some dispute.[3] Coming from a wealthy family,

---

[1] Late writers call him, impossibly, a pupil of Anaximenes (DK, A7). Their source will be the description of him by Theophrastus (ap. Simpl. Phys. 27.2, A41) as κοινωνήσας τῆς Ἀναξιμένους φιλοσοφίας, which may be contrasted with the κοινωνήσας τῷ Παρμενίδῃ τῆς φιλοσοφίας said of Leucippus (ibid. 28.5). See p. 384 below.

[2] See p. 128, n. 4 above.   [3] See additional note 1, pp. 322ff. below.

he showed no interest in money but gave up his inheritance and the political influence that it might have brought, to devote himself single-mindedly to science and philosophy. This is mentioned by Plato, and Aristotle comments more than once on his lack of interest in practical matters. There was also a story current in Aristotle's time that when asked why to be born was better than not to be born (a form in which pessimism about human life was often expressed by Greek poets), he replied that a man would choose to be born 'in order to study the heavens and the whole universe'. Clearly there was factual foundation for the character of typical unworldly philosopher which he assumes in later writers. It was said that when he received at the same time the news of his own condemnation and the death of his son (or sons), he commented on the former, 'Both my judges and I were sentenced long ago by nature', and on the latter, 'I knew that I had begotten them mortal'.[1] Again, when he was reproached for his lack of interest in public affairs, as implying neglect of his fatherland, he is said to have replied that he did indeed care for his fatherland—pointing to the heavens. The implication, that he belonged to the whole cosmos, was not intended to indicate any sympathy with the religion of his time, to which, at least in its more superstitious forms, he is consistently represented as in opposition. Plutarch tells that a countryman brought to Pericles the head of a ram which had a single horn growing from the middle of its forehead. The soothsayer Lampon interpreted this as meaning that of the two rivals for supreme power, Pericles and Thucydides, that one would prevail to whom the head had been brought. Anaxagoras however had the skull split open and in a brief anatomical lecture explained the natural reasons for the anomaly. The people, says Plutarch, were full of admiration for his knowledge, but transferred their admiration to Lampon when a short time afterwards Thucydides fell and Pericles took over sole control of Athens.[2]

In Plato's *Phaedrus* (270a), Socrates is maintaining that all great arts, including rhetoric, demand a study of nature, and says: 'This is

---

[1] Plato, *Hipp. Maj.* 283a, Ar. *EN*, 1141b3, 1179a13, *EE*, 1216a11. Cf. D.L. 2.6, 10, 13, and Galen, *De plac. Hipp. et Plat.* 392f. Müller (DK, A1, 13, 30, 33).
[2] D.L. 2.7, Plut. *Per.* 6.

what Pericles acquired to supplement his natural gifts. In Anaxagoras he found, I think, that kind of man, stored his mind with astronomical lore and learned the nature of mind and thought [or 'of wisdom and folly']—matters on which Anaxagoras was continually discoursing—and drew from it what was useful for the art of speaking.' The famous association of the two men is also mentioned in the *First Alcibiades*, which if not by Plato himself is at any rate a fourth-century work, and by Plato's contemporary Isocrates, as well as by later authorities.[1] Plutarch and Diodorus agree that the prosecution of Anaxagoras for impiety was at least partly due to the desire of Pericles's political opponents to attack him through his friendship with the atheistic scientist. The same charge was brought against Aspasia. Plutarch tells us that a special bill was introduced by Diopeithes, a well-known religious fanatic, framed in general terms against 'those who do not acknowledge divine things or who give instruction about celestial phenomena', with this particular aim of discrediting Pericles through Anaxagoras.[2] A specific charge against him was that, in the Ionian tradition, he denied the divinity of the heavenly bodies. 'He called the sun a fiery stone' is the wording given in our later authorities, and in the *Apology*, when Meletus asserts that Socrates 'says the sun is a stone and the moon earth', Socrates asks him if he thinks it is Anaxagoras that he is accusing, 'whose books are full of that sort of thing'.[3]

Anaxagoras was exiled, and ended his days at Lampsacus on the southern shore of the Hellespont, where he was honoured in life and remembered after death. There is a pleasant story that when the authorities of the city encouraged him to name a wish, he asked that the children might be given a holiday in the month of his death. The Lampsacenes gave him public burial and, says a writer of the fourth century B.C., 'honour him to this day'.[4] Before his death he may have had time to teach and found a school there. Eusebius says that his pupil Archelaus of Athens (the teacher of Socrates) 'succeeded to the school of Anaxagoras in Lampsacus',

---

[1] *Phaedrus*, 270a, *Alc. I*, 118c, Isocr. π. ἀντιδ. 235, and see in general DK, A13, 15, 17.
[2] Plut. *Per*. 32, Diod. 12.39 (A17).   [3] See p. 307, n. 3 below.
[4] Alcidamas the pupil of Gorgias, quoted by Aristotle, *Rhet*. 1398b15.

and A. E. Taylor argued strongly for the existence of a school of philosophers in the city which it is most reasonable to account for in this way.[1]

Another who is said to have been, like Pericles, his pupil is Euripides. For this however we have nothing like the authority of Plato. All the testimonies are much later, and could have arisen out of references in the plays, which certainly show that Euripides was a keen follower of current theories of nature, and familiar with Anaxagoras's works; and, as Socrates says in the *Apology* (26d), these could easily be bought in the city for a drachma at the most. The most obvious allusion is the description of the sun as a 'rock' and a 'golden clod' in a chorus of the *Orestes* and a fragment of the *Phaethon*.[2]

(2) Writings

Diogenes Laertius (1.16) lists Anaxagoras among those who wrote only one single treatise (ἓν σύγγραμμα). It was, he says (2.6), 'written in an attractive and dignified style'. This is of course the *Physica*, in which he set forth his views on the first principles, matter and the moving cause, and described the origin and present constitution of the cosmos. A copy was still available to Simplicius in the sixth century A.D., and, in commenting on passages of Aristotle which deal with Anaxagoras, he gives a number of quotations of varying length, which constitute practically all the fragments that we still possess. They include the opening words of the treatise, and seem to be all from the first book, with the result that, so far as first-hand acquaintance goes,

---

[1] Eus. *Praep. Ev.* 10.14.13 (DK, A7); Taylor, *CQ*, 1917, 85–7. It is difficult to see why Taylor should make so much of the mention, at the beginning of Plato's *Parmenides*, of a group of keen philosophers at *Clazomenae* as evidence for the foundation by Anaxagoras of a school at *Lampsacus*. Taylor also says that in Roman imperial times Lampsacus placed his figure on its coins. I cannot trace this (he gives no reference), and suspect that Taylor has confused Lampsacus with Clazomenae. The philosopher's birthplace did put him on coins of both Hellenistic and Roman times. He holds a globe, possibly in allusion to the story that he took the whole cosmos for his fatherland. Examples are: (1) *B.M. Cat. Ionia*, p. 28 and pl. VII. 4. After 300 B.C. Anaxagoras seated on a globe (though DK, A27 call it a column-drum) and holding a smaller globe (?) in raised right hand. (2) *Ibid.* p. 32 and pl. VII. 9. Time of Commodus. Anaxagoras standing, holding a globe in extended right hand. (3) *Hunterian Cat.* II, p. 323 and pl. L. 9. Bust of Anaxagoras holding globe (?) in raised right hand, with the first five letters of his name. No. 2 has been used for the cover-design of this book.

[2] See additional note 2, pp. 323 ff. below.

we are better acquainted with the general principles than with the details of Anaxagoras's system.[1]

Some have assumed from a sentence in Plutarch that when in prison he wrote a work on the problem of squaring the circle, but as Burnet pointed out, the words probably mean no more than that he beguiled the time by attempting to work out the problem with figures on the floor.[2] More plausible perhaps is the report that he wrote a treatise on scene-painting and perspective. The authority is Vitruvius, who says that after Agatharchus, who painted scenes for Aeschylus, Democritus and Anaxagoras both wrote on the art of how to produce 'definite representations of buildings in scenic pictures and to bring it about that of objects on a vertical plane surface some appear to retreat and others to stand out'. This started an interesting speculation in the mind of Erich Frank, who connected it with the statements of Plutarch that he 'produced the first and clearest explanation in writing of the illumination and shadow of the moon', and of Hippolytus that he 'first cleared up the question of its eclipses and shinings'. Anaxagoras, said Frank, applied the discovery of perspective, made in his time and treated by himself and Democritus, to the whole world. As a result he was the first to construct the cone of the earth's shadow and prove geometrically the necessity of eclipses when the moon or sun entered it. Frank even went so far as to say, relying on Hippolytus, that he used the laws of perspective to estimate the sizes and distances of the sun and moon, and recognized the marks on the moon as shadows caused by mountains. With Anaxagoras the world practically gains a new dimension in the Greek consciousness.[3]

---

[1] That Simplicius possessed the whole work seems indubitable from the manner of his handling it throughout his commentary, though a slight doubt might be raised by the expression ὅσον ἐμὲ εἰδέναι at *Phys.* 176.17.

[2] Plut. *De exil.* 607f ἀλλ' 'Α. μὲν ἐν τῷ δεσμωτηρίῳ τὸν τοῦ κύκλου τετραγωνισμὸν ἔγραφε, Burnet, *EGP*, 257, n. 5. In any case the historical value of the anecdote, which occurs among others designed to show that a man may be happy and virtuous whatever his surroundings, must not be exaggerated. Proclus indeed (*Eucl.* 65.21, A9) says that he 'applied himself to many geometrical problems', but if so, nothing is known of his work in this field. Consequently the interesting suggestion of Frank (*Plato u. d. sog. Pyth.* 48 and 348), that he used his revolutionary assertion of the infinitesimal (p. 289 below) to solve this problem by the method of exhaustion, is highly speculative.

[3] Vitruvius, 7, *prooem.* 11 (A39), Plut. *Nicias*, 23 (A18), Hippol. *Ref.* 1.8.10(A42). See Frank, *Plato u. d. sog. Pyth.* 22f., 234f. It is of course true that Anaxagoras held the moon to be an earthy body with mountains, plains and ravines on its surface. (See p. 308 below.)

No Becoming but only Mingling and Separation

This extension to the cosmos of ideas derived from the laws of perspective as applied to scene-painting is not impossible, and as a possibility is too interesting to pass over. But it is a precarious structure, and its foundation in the statement of an Augustan writer on architecture cannot be claimed as unshakably firm.[1]

(3) The problem of becoming

Like Empedocles, Anaxagoras accepted the Parmenidean canons that there is no empty space[2] and that coming-into-being and perishing into not-being are strictly impossible, and in general terms he accepted the same alternative. 'There is no birth nor death,' Empedocles had said, 'but only mixture and separation of what has been mixed' (fr. 8). Anaxagoras put it thus (fr. 17): 'The Greeks have a wrong conception of becoming and perishing. Nothing comes to be or perishes, but there is mixture and separation of things that exist. Thus they ought properly to call generation mixture and extinction separation.' We notice at once a difference between the two men. Empedocles had insisted on a *double* process: both mixture and separation could in their turn be the cause of both generation and destruction, two moving forces were

---

[1] We need not agree with Burnet (*EGP*, 257) in regarding it as a 'most improbable story' that Anaxagoras wrote a treatise on perspective. The passage in Vitruvius is expertly criticized by E. Pfuhl in vol. 2 of his *Malerei u. Zeichnung der Griechen*, pp. 615, 666, 674–7. His main caveat is against exaggerating the achievements of Agatharchus. The creator of illusionistic painting (involving both perspective drawing and the use of light and shade to simulate solidity) was Apollodorus, whose inventions must be dated about (and not later than) 430. Agatharchus, Pfuhl thinks, with his very modest *Kulissenmalerei*, posed rather than solved the problem, Anaxagoras took the first steps towards a theoretical understanding of it, and the first full masters of perspective in practice and theory were Apollodorus and his philosophical contemporary Democritus (p. 676).

[2] This however, as Gigon has suggested (*Philologus*, 1936–7, 20–2), may not have played an important part in his system. It is not mentioned in the extant fragments, nor in the doxography when it is concerned with the ἀρχαί. Aristotle coupled Anaxagoras with Empedocles at *De caelo*, 309a19, and at *Phys.* 213a22 he writes: 'Those who try to demonstrate that there is no void do not disprove what people mean by void but are in error. Such are Anaxagoras and those who use his manner of disproof. What they prove is that air is something, when they torture wineskins to show that it is powerful, and enclose it in clepsydras.' (Cf. pp. 224f. above.) As Gigon says, we cannot believe that Anaxagoras's contemporaries took the air in an inflated skin to be nothing, and he suggests that the point may have lain rather in the ἰσχυρός, since Anaxagoras wishes his readers to believe that the air is strong enough to support the whole earth (ἰσχυρότατον ὄντα, Hippol. *Ref.* 1.8.3, A42). It is also capable of pushing back the sun and moon at the limits of their courses (*ibid.* §9). The absence of void is mentioned once more in Aristotle in connexion with the breathing of fish (*De resp.* 471a2 οὐ γὰρ εἶναι κενόν), and later by Lucretius (1.843f. *nec tamen esse ulla idem parte in rebus inane concedit*).

271

posited and the cosmic process was cyclic. With the religious motive removed, a single force suffices and the cosmogonic process is in one direction only.

The solution of Empedocles had been to suppose that there was only a strictly limited number of elemental substances which deserved to be called existent. The rest, the world of 'mortal' things which we suppose to be real, consisted simply of mixtures of the four 'roots' in different proportions, which could be dissolved without infringing the rule of 'no becoming'. The condition laid down by Anaxagoras was stricter. On the Empedoclean theory, if it were possible to divide a piece of (say) flesh into small enough fragments, the elements would come to light and it would be flesh no longer. But Anaxagoras held that if this were even theoretically possible, then a definite substance, flesh, could perish. There was no reason for singling out certain forms of matter like earth or water as primary. Why should they be said to 'exist' more than others? 'How can hair come out of not-hair, and flesh out of not-flesh?' (fr. 10). All the infinite number of natural substances, flesh, bone, hair, sinew, wood, iron, stone, etc. must be equally real. The problem is most clearly seen in nutrition, and some passages suggest that it was in fact the phenomenon of nutrition which led Anaxagoras to consider it in this way. Besides fr. 10 just quoted, one may cite Aët. 1.3.5 (A46):

It seemed to him a baffling problem how anything can come into being out of what is not, or perish into what is not. Yet we take in nourishment which is simple and uniform, bread and water, and from this nourishment grow hair, veins, arteries, flesh, sinews, bones and the other parts of the body. (So also Simpl. *Phys.* 460.15, A45.)

Clearly therefore, if the rule of 'no becoming, but only mingling and separation' is to be kept, Anaxagoras had set himself a much harder task than Empedocles's, and the answer will have to be correspondingly more complex.

(4) *Mind*

'All things were together, then Mind (*Nous*) came and set them in order.' This, says Diogenes (2.6), was the opening of Anaxagoras's book; and though we can see from Simplicius that it is rather a distillation of his meaning than a verbatim quotation, it does indeed put his whole theory of cosmogony in a nutshell. An account of his system has therefore to face two main questions: (*a*) What is the nature and function of Mind? (*b*) What theory of the nature of physical reality lies behind the statement that all things were together?

The following are the actual surviving quotations from Anaxagoras's book which deal with Mind:

(Fr. 12) The rest have a portion of everything, but Mind is something infinite[1] and independent, and is mixed with no thing, but alone and by itself. If it were not by itself, but were mixed with any other thing, it would have had a share of all things if it were mixed with any, for there is a portion of everything in everything, as I have said before. [Cf. fr. 11 below.] And the things mixed in it would have prevented it from controlling anything as it can when alone and by itself. It is the finest and purest of all things, and has all judgment of everything and greatest power; and everything that has life, both greater and smaller, all these Mind controls; and it controlled the whole revolution, to make it revolve in the beginning. At first it began to revolve in a small part, but now it revolves over a larger field and will include a larger one still. And the things that are being mingled and those that are being separated off and divided, Mind determined[2] them all. Mind set everything in order, what was to be, what was[3] but is not now, and all that now is and shall be, and this revolution in which revolve the stars, sun, moon, air and fire[4] that are being separated off. This revolution[5] caused the separating off. The dense is separated from the rare, the hot from the cold, the bright from the dark, the dry from the wet. There are many portions of many things, and no one thing is completely separated or divided from another

---

[1] For the meaning of *apeiron* here, see p. 276 below.

[2] Or 'knows'. With some hesitation I have adopted this translation of ἔγνω (past tense as in Hdt. 1.74.4, etc.), for which see Lämmli, *Chaos zum Kosmos*, 1, 53 and n. 420. The close connexion between knowledge and power is well brought out in Arist. *De an.* 429a19. It should however be noted that Simplicius took the word to mean that Mind *knows* all things (*Cael.* 608.27–31). His comment, ἡ γὰρ γνῶσις ὁρίζει καὶ περατοῖ τὸ γνωσθέν, implies, in its context, not so much that knowledge has the power to determine, as that what cannot be determined or limited cannot be the object of knowledge.

[3] At *Cael.* 608.29, Simplicius quotes as a single sentence καὶ τὰ συμμισγόμενά τε καὶ ἀποκρινόμενα πάντα ἔγνω νοῦς, καὶ ὁποῖα ἔμελλεν ἔσεσθαι καὶ ὁποῖα ἦν. Since ancient books had no punctuation, inconsistencies like this are almost inevitable. To carry on the sentence as in the *De caelo* quotation would make the next one begin without a connecting particle.

[4] αἰθήρ in the Greek. Aristotle says in three separate places that Anaxagoras used the word αἰθήρ for fire, deriving it literally, as Simplicius notes, from αἴθειν. See Arist. *De caelo*, 270b24, 302b4, *Meteor.* 369b14, Simpl. *Cael.* 119.2.

[5] αὕτη MSS., Burnet, KR. DK print Schorn's conjecture αὐτή, 'the revolution itself'.

save Mind. Mind is all alike, both the greater and the smaller. Nothing else is like anything else,[1] but those things are and were most plainly each thing, of which there are most in it.

Parts of this quotation refer to aspects of the constitution of matter which must be left till later, but it has been quoted entire to put the description of Mind in its full functional context.

(Fr. 11) In everything there is a portion of everything except Mind, and in some things is Mind too.

(Fr. 13) After Mind initiated motion, it began to withdraw[2] from all that was moved, and all that Mind moved was divided. And as this motion and division went on the revolution caused it to be divided much more.

(Fr. 14) Mind, which is for ever, is assuredly even now where all other things are also,[3] in the great quantity surrounding and in the things which have been brought together and those which have been separated.

The general opinion of ancient critics was that Anaxagoras had taken a tremendous step forward by clearly separating, for the first time, the moving cause from the matter moved, and by characterizing this separate cause as Mind or Intellection. On the other hand he had shown a tendency to confine the action of Mind to the first step of initiating motion in what had been a motionless mass. The rest of the process he explained by the operation of non-intelligent causes: the motion set going by mind being a rotatory one, everything else followed through the mechanical action of a vortex on the bodies caught up in it. Plato makes Socrates say (*Phaedo*,

---

[1] A. Wasserstein (*CR*, 1960, 4f.) suggests deleting οὐδενί. Mind is 'all alike' internally, i.e. is homogeneous, and the logical contrast is to say that every other thing is *not* alike, in the same sense, namely because each contains a portion of everything else, rather than that the other things do not resemble each other. This makes Anaxagorean sense, but hardly seems necessary. Cf. M. E. Reesor, *CP*, 1963, 30f. and n. 4, and p. 291 below; also Simpl. *Phys.* 156.8 οὐδὲ γὰρ τῶν ἄλλων οὐδὲν ἔοικε τὸ ἕτερον τῷ ἑτέρῳ.

[2] καὶ ἐπεὶ ἤρξατο ὁ νοῦς κινεῖν, ἀπὸ τοῦ κινουμένου παντὸς ἀπεκρίνετο. The obvious subject of ἀπεκρίνετο is νοῦς. So Heidel, *Proc. Am. Ac.* 1913, 731 ('it began to withdraw') and DK ('sonderte er sich ab'). Others however translate it impersonally, as Burnet, *EGP*, 260 ('separating off took place'), Raven, KR, 373 ('separation began'), Lämmli, *Chaos zum Kosmos*, I, 108 ('da wurde von allem, was da bewegt wurde, abgeschieden'); but this is a less natural translation of the Greek. See also ZN, 1235, n. 2. On Heidel's translation, 'νοῦς gives the first impulse only, then withdraws to its condition of isolation; the revolution, once started, of itself accelerates and its effects in the segregation of like to like in the πάντα ὁμοῦ increase. Cf. ἡ περιχώρησις αὐτή fr. 12.' This passage, which as Heidel says is confirmed by fr. 12, affords the justification for the complaint of Plato and Aristotle.

[3] The MSS. of Simplicius have ὁ δὲ νοῦς ὅσα ἐστί τε κάρτα..., from which in its context no sense can be extracted. Translated here is Diels's conjecture ὃς ἀεί ἐστι τὸ κάρτα....

97 b ff.) that when he heard someone reading from a book of Anaxagoras that Mind was the prime cause and had set everything in order he was delighted, but that reading further brought bitter disappointment, for he found the author making no use of Mind in the actual ordering of things but putting it all down to 'airs, ethers, waters and many other strange things'. The reason for Socrates's disappointment was that he was looking for a teleological explanation of the world and thought it the only explanation possible on the assumption that it was controlled by Mind. Mind must have ordered things for the best, so that in Mind's world, if one wanted to know the reason why anything was generated or destroyed, it should only be necessary to ask in what way it was best for it to exist or to be affected. But this was not the method of Anaxagoras.

Aristotle echoed Plato's verdict. Anaxagoras, by affirming that just as living creatures have *nous*, so in nature as a whole *nous* is the cause of the cosmos and of motion everywhere, 'stood out like a single sober man by comparison with the wild assertions of his predecessors' (*Metaph.* 984b15). On the other hand (985a18), he 'uses Mind as a mechanical device for world-making. When he is at a loss for the reason why something necessarily is, then he drags it in, but elsewhere he explains events by everything rather than Mind.'[1]

In later antiquity Proclus (*in Tim.* vol. I, p. 2 Diehl) varies the metaphor by saying that Anaxagoras appears to have seen that Mind was the cause of becoming 'while the others were asleep', but for the rest he is content to quote the *Phaedo*. Simplicius however comments with more independence on Socrates's criticisms:

'That for which Socrates in the *Phaedo* blames Anaxagoras,' he writes (*Phys.* 177.9), 'namely that for the causes of particular events he makes no use of Mind, but only of materialistic explanations, is in fact the method proper to a study of nature. For that very reason even Plato himself in the *Timaeus*,

---

[1] It would appear, then, that Aristotle's praise of Anaxagoras is due not so much to the nature of his motive cause as to the fact that he provided a separate motive cause at all. Some have thought this an indication that Aristotle looks on him as prior in time to Empedocles. More probably he does not regard the concepts of Love and Strife as being strictly separate from the elements. Love for instance seemed to him to combine in an unsatisfactory way the characteristics of material and of efficient cause (ἀρχὴ γὰρ καὶ ὡς κινοῦσα...καὶ ὡς ὕλη· μόριον γὰρ τοῦ μίγματος, *Metaph.* 1075b3). His criticism of Anaxagoras was echoed by his pupil Eudemus (see A 47 *ad fin.*).

after he has stated in general terms the cause responsible for all things, when he comes to details cites as causes differences of size and shape, hot and cold and so on. Socrates however, because he wants to demonstrate the teleological explanation, mentions Anaxagoras as making use of the material but not the final cause.'

This is an acute assessment, and shows how much Plato's interest in secondary causes had grown by the time that he attempted, in the *Timaeus*, to emulate his predecessors by putting together for himself a complete cosmogony, cosmology and descriptive account of animate and inanimate nature. It will be of interest to keep these Greek verdicts in mind when we are examining the fragments ourselves.

'Mind is something *apeiron* and self-ruling, and is mixed with no thing.' It is *apeiron* in all the main senses of that word: infinite or indefinite in extent, for it is wherever matter is (fr. 14), and that is composed of particles infinite in number (frr. 1 and 2); infinite in time, for it exists for ever (fr. 14); and internally without boundaries, for it is homogeneous, 'all alike' (fr. 12 *ad fin.*). It is unmixed, 'for if it were mixed with any other thing it would have a share of all things, for there is a portion of everything in everything'. If Mind were a part of the mixture, it would have something of *every* kind of matter in it, for that is a condition of existence of matter. Everything contains portions of every other thing. This is basic to Anaxagoras's theory of matter, to which we shall come later. 'And the things mixed in it would have prevented it from controlling anything as it can when alone and by itself.' Here we have, clearly stated by Anaxagoras himself, what in the eyes of Aristotle and others was his greatest achievement, namely the realization that the moving and controlling force must be entirely separate from the matter which it moves.

'It is the finest and purest of all things, and has all knowledge of everything and greatest power.' The epithets used are *lepton* and *katharon*. *Lepton* is a word commonly used with a material denotation, applied to finely woven materials, spiders' webs, finely ground powder and so forth, and its use here has sometimes been taken as evidence that Mind is still being thought of as corporeal.[1] Since however it is already

---

[1] 'It is the "thinnest" of all things, so that it can penetrate everywhere, and it would be meaningless to say that the immaterial is "thinner" than the material' (Burnet, *EGP*, 268).

used of counsel or wisdom (μῆτις) in the *Iliad*, it is hardly worth repeating the many occasions on which it is used with similar non-material subjects in classical Greek.[1] If Anaxagoras had at last grasped the idea of non-material existence, he obviously had not the vocabulary in which to express it. Even now it is notoriously difficult to speak of mind or spirit without borrowing the terminology of the material world. ('Spirit' itself is an example.) Knowing no positive epithets to apply to the non-material as such, Anaxagoras could only describe it negatively as not being matter. This he seems to do emphatically in his repeated insistence that it is entirely separate from the mixture of everything which we should call matter. Mind is *that aspect* of Anaximander's *apeiron* which 'steers all things', *that aspect* of Heraclitus's fire which deserved the name of *logos* and was wise; but the divine and ruling faculty of Anaximander's *arche* has been recognized as incompatible with its identification with a corporeal mass, the *logos* of Heraclitus has been released from its uncomfortable association with fire.

This judgment is in no way affected by the use of the epithet *lepton*. If it needs to be qualified at all, it must be by the hint later in fr. 12 that there can be 'greater and lesser' quantities of Mind, and the statement in fr. 14 that it is 'where all other things are'. It may be that Anaxagoras thought of Mind as being, though invisible and intangible, extended in space. *Apeiron* probably does imply that in order to control the mass, it had in some way to permeate it, although at the same time keeping itself separate from the bodies within it. Yet the phrase 'the greater and the lesser' is introduced for the purpose of once again contrasting Mind

---

[1] *Il.* 10.226, 23.590. For other examples see LSJ. It is applied to νοῦς itself in Eur. *Med.* 529, and in fifth-century literature also to λῆροι, φρένες, ἐλπίς, μῦθοι. It would be perverse to argue that since philosophers themselves are at this time only on the threshold of an explicit distinction between mind and matter, others can have been conscious of no such distinction and may have thought of the entities just listed as being of the same order as blood or wood. (The φρένες were of course originally a part of the body.) The point is that they were fully capable of using a word metaphorically, and were obviously doing so in the cases cited. Homer also speaks of ὑφαίνειν μῆτιν (*Il.* 7.324, etc.), but we do not suppose on that account that he thought of a μῆτις as something made of wool or string. P. Leon has some sensible remarks on this point in *CQ*, 1927, p. 139.

As for mind being a χρῆμα, one must reflect that Plato in the *Protagoras* (361b) could call justice, temperance and courage χρήματα. Lämmli in *Chaos zum Kosmos*, n. 472 also cites Eur. *Bacchae*, 1152, but the reading there is not certain, though Dodds (*Bacchae*, 1944, 206) thinks there is 'something to be said for P's χρῆμα.' If so, we have it applied in the fifth century to τὸ σωφρονεῖν τε καὶ σέβειν τὰ τῶν θεῶν.

in every way possible with the corporeal constituents of the mixture. Smaller and greater parts of this do differ, for it is not homogeneous but made up of portions characterized by different physical factors which in the aggregate are manifest to sense, whereas 'Mind is all alike, in any quantity'. If any shred of materialism remains, it is very slight indeed.[1] A Christian who believes that God 'dwelleth not in temples made with hands' will still say that he is 'everywhere'.

Next we are told that Mind has a special relation to the organic world. 'Everything that has life', fr. 12 continues, 'both greater and smaller, all these Mind *controls*; and it *controlled* the whole revolution, to make it revolve in the beginning.' Here is another handle for the criticism of Plato and Aristotle. We note the different tenses. Mind was necessary to start the revolution in the beginning, for another epoch-making innovation of Anaxagoras was to say explicitly that everything started from a state of rest into which motion had to be introduced for the first time. The cosmos is not just a stage in an endless cyclical process as with Empedocles. Aristotle reports (*Phys.* 250b 24): 'He says that all things were together and at rest for an infinite time, then Mind set them in motion and divided them.' Once the initial push had been administered, the revolution continued of its own momentum at an ever-increasing speed. The control of Mind over living creatures, on the other hand, continues still. That life should stand in a specially close relation to the intelligent cosmic force is a natural assumption and in line with earlier thought. Living things in fact contain it. This

---

[1] The difficulty of conceiving anything as existing, in any sense, which was not extended in space, may be illustrated by a comparison with a later age. Basil Willey writes in *The Seventeenth Century Background* (p. 165): 'Such authority had the notion of "Extension" in the seventeenth century, as the essential attribute of the admittedly "real" (matter), that unless one could attribute "extension" to a substance, that substance was in danger of evaporating into nothingness. This was Henry More's fear for "spirit"; Descartes by affirming spirit as a mere abstraction was really, in spite of all appearances to the contrary, beginning upon the slippery slope towards materialism and atheism. It was safer, in More's opinion, to admit frankly that extension is a necessary attribute of all that exists, and to demonstrate, further, that spirit, as a real being, must be extended also. He was anxious to claim extension for spirit, "that it may be conceived to be some real Being and true Substance, and not a vain Figment, such as is everything that has no Amplitude and is in no sort extended". (*True Notion of a Spirit*, p. 41.)' So that matter may still be differentiated from spirit, More denies that extension is the formal principle of matter, for which he substitutes impenetrability. Spirit is penetrable. Secondly, extended matter is divisible, extended spirit 'indiscerptible'. Its extension is different from material extension. He describes it as 'metaphysical extension', 'a fourth dimension', or 'essential spissitude'.

Capelle writes very sensibly about νοῦς in *Neue Jahrbb.* 1919, 177 ff.

must be the reference when in fr. 11 Anaxagoras makes an apparent exception to his rule that material things contain a portion of all other things except Mind. 'In some things there is Mind too.' Aristotle concluded that Anaxagoras did not distinguish between Mind and life (*nous* and *psyche*):[1]

In many places he says that the cause of what is good and right is Mind,[2] but elsewhere that it is *psyche*; for he says that Mind is in all that lives, both great and small, high and humble, whereas Mind in the sense of wisdom does not appear to be in all animals, or even in all men.

There is then a portion of Mind in living things, 'controlling', i.e. animating them. It still remains distinct from body-substance, and no inconsistency other than a purely verbal one is involved.

That is practically all our information about Mind. To sum up:

(1) As its name implies, it is conscious and intelligent, and its knowledge and judgment know no limitations. It is nowhere in the extant fragments called God, but this may be accidental and it is impossible that Anaxagoras should not have thought of it as divine (θεῖον).

(2) It is completely separate from 'things' (χρήματα), and entirely homogeneous and self-consistent (ὅμοιος), whereas the 'things' display an infinite variety. This means that if not imagined as completely incorporeal, it is very nearly so, and Anaxagoras has adopted every means at his command to contrast it with the material.

(3) It governs itself and is ultimately responsible for all movement of matter. In particular it introduced rational order and arrangement (διεκόσμησε), which are the outcome of circular motion (περιχώρησις).

(4) It retains a special form of control over the organic world, and seems to be identical with the *psyche* or animating principle in living things.

(5) *Theory of Matter*

There is much dispute over what Anaxagoras meant to say in his account of the nature of matter. The most recent tendency is to claim that earlier interpreters have been over-subtle and introduced complica-

---

[1] *De an.* 404b1. Cf. 405a13 and p. 316 below.

[2] This is interesting. It does not emerge from the extant fragments, and if true, forms an important qualification to the criticism that Mind is used as a mere mechanical cosmogonic device.

tions into what was an essentially simple scheme. I fear that any reader who starts with this impression will be doomed to disillusionment. The idea that Anaxagoras's scheme is anything but remarkably subtle and complex could hardly survive a reading of, for example, fr. 3, where he tells us among other things that 'there is always a larger than the large, and it is numerically equal to the small'. As with the bigger problem of Heraclitus, I shall attempt a continuous exposition without too many confusing digressions to take account of opposing views. In this case it is particularly difficult to do justice to the opinions of other scholars by bringing them in piecemeal in the course of a different version, and anyone who wishes to make up his own mind after an impartial survey of modern interpretations as well as the ancient evidence must be advised to read the others in their entirety.[1] My debt to them will then become plain.

Of the ancient evidence the words of Anaxagoras himself must of course be given priority, but since the extant quotations amount in all to little over three average-sized pages of print, they must be supplemented at times by a prudent use of his critics and commentators from Aristotle onwards. In particular, to judge the meaning of the fragments properly, it is worth while looking at them in the order in which Simplicius presents them, and in the context of his own explanations. This is something to which perhaps sufficient attention has not been paid in the past, and, at the risk of some repetition, I have set out the most important passages of Simplicius, with a few others, in translation.[2]

---

[1] Among recent accounts the following should be noted: Bailey, *Greek Atomists and Epicurus* (1928), Appendix 1, pp. 537–56 ('On the Theory of Anaxagoras'). Cornford, 'Anaxagoras' Theory of Matter', *CQ*, 24 (1930), 14–30 and 83–95. Peck, 'Anaxagoras: Predication as a Problem in Physics', *CQ*, 25 (1931), 27–37 and 112–20. O. Gigon, 'Zu Anaxagoras', *Philologus*, 91 (1936–7), 1–41. Vlastos, 'The Physical Theory of Anaxagoras', *Philos. Rev.* 59 (1950), 31–57. Raven, 'The Basis of Anaxagoras's Cosmogony', *CQ*, 48 (1954), 123–37. R. Mathewson, 'Aristotle and Anaxagoras: An Examination of F. M. Cornford's Interpretation', *CQ*, 52 (1958), 67–81. M. E. Reesor, 'The Meaning of Anaxagoras', *CP*, 55 (1960), 1–7, and *The Problem of Anaxagoras*, *CP*, 1963, 30–3. C. Strang, *The Physical Theory of Anaxagoras*, Arch. f. Gesch. d. Phil. 1963, 101–8. The interpretation of Tannery in the second edition of *Pour l'Hist. de la Sc. Hellène* (1930), with which some later accounts (notably those of Burnet and Cornford) have much in common, will be found adequately referred to in some of the above. So far as I know, the first radical challenge to the Tannery–Burnet explanation came from Capelle in *Neue Jahrbb.* 1919, 172 ff.

[2] See Appendix, pp. 327 ff. below.

Theory of Matter

We have seen (p. 271 above) that the theory is another attempt to retain the reality of the physical world in face of the apparently inescapable Eleatic denial that anything comes into being or perishes. As Aristotle phrased it (*Phys.* 191 a 30): 'Neither does what is come into being (for it *is* already) nor could anything come into being out of what is not.' More than this, it is an attempt to restore as far as possible the *Milesian* world. In reading Anaxagoras's views on the composition of matter we are constantly reminded of Anaximander or Anaximenes.[1] At the same time Anaxagoras seems to have been impressed not only by Parmenides himself but also by the more paradoxical arguments of his follower Zeno, for example, that if there were many things they would be at the same time both small to vanishing point and infinitely large.[2]

When one takes into account also the condition already mentioned, that *every* natural substance must be assumed to have existence in the full Parmenidean sense, it is obvious that a solution of the problem of *genesis* is going to call for remarkable ingenuity on the part of Anaxagoras, and that it will be no simple task to interpret it from his fragmentary remains. There is however one difficulty which haunted the subject until recently but which I am sure is imaginary, and has been clearly shown to be so by A. L. Peck (*CQ*, 1931, 27 ff.). We may get this out of the way first. It is a difficulty which particularly affected Cornford's account, and can be best stated in his own words (*CQ*, 1930, 14):

The theory rests on two propositions which seem flatly to contradict one another. One is the principle of Homoeomereity: A natural substance such as a piece of gold consists solely of parts which are like the whole and like one another—every one of them gold and nothing else. The other is: 'There is a portion of everything in everything', understood to mean that a piece of gold (or any other substance), so far from containing nothing but gold, contains portions of every other substance in the world. Unless Anaxagoras was extremely muddleheaded, he cannot have propounded a theory which simply *consists* of this contradiction.

[1] This is well brought out in Gigon's article in *Philologus*, 1936–7.

[2] Zeno, frr. 1 and 2; see p. 89 above. The reaction of Anaxagoras to Zeno has been emphasized in particular by Gigon, *loc. cit.*, Raven, *CQ*, 1954 and KR, 370–2. So far as chronology goes, the relationship might have been reversed, for the two were contemporaries, and some have supposed that Zeno was attacking Anaxagoras. See the discussion in Luria, *Qu. und Stud.* 1932, 107 ff.

Now Anaxagoras certainly said 'There is a portion of everything in everything'. We have it in his own words (ἐν παντὶ παντὸς μοῖρα ἔνεστιν) repeated more than once (frr. 11, 12) and restated in different terms elsewhere. This then is a principle which any explanation of his theory must take into account. On the other hand there is no good reason at all to suppose that he held any 'principle of homoeomereity', in the sense that a natural substance 'consists solely of parts which are like the whole and like one another'. No fragment says this, it is inconsistent with what the fragments do say, and moreover it is not difficult to see how the mistake arose.

It arose because Aristotle says that Anaxagoras 'makes the *homoiomerē* [homoeomers, "things of like parts"] elements'.[1] He goes on immediately, however, to exemplify what he means by the word: 'Anaxagoras makes the homoeomers elements, such as bone, flesh, marrow, and whatever else has parts synonymous with the whole', and a few lines later, contrasting him with Empedocles, 'Anaxagoras on the other hand says that it is the homoeomers that are simple and elemental, and earth, fire, water and air are compounds, being in fact a collection of seeds of the others'.[2] Again at *De caelo*, 302a28:

Anaxagoras is opposed to Empedocles on the subject of the elements. Empedocles's view is that fire and earth and the other substances of the same order are the elements of bodies, and everything is composed of them. According to Anaxagoras, on the other hand, the homoeomers are elements (flesh, bone and other substances of that order), whereas air and fire are a mixture of these and all the other seeds, for each consists of an agglomeration of all the homoeomers in invisible quantities.

Now it is unlikely that Anaxagoras used the word *homoiomerē*,[3] and there is no reason to think that Aristotle intends in these passages to saddle him with any doctrine that however far one divides any of his

---

[1] τὰ ὁμοιομερῆ στοιχεῖα τίθησιν, *GC*, 314a18.

[2] Cherniss (*ACP*, 108, n. 444) claims that this is to translate the sentence as if τούτων were ἐκείνων. τούτων, he says, must refer to the σύνθετα, earth, air, fire and water. He does not supply a translation, but if he did it would presumably be (retaining πανσπερμία for which no English word exists) 'for there is a panspermia of them'. The argument is, he says, that 'the nature of the four bodies is that of a πανσπερμία'. The point had not occurred to me until I read his note, but I still think the generally accepted rendering is the right one in this particular sentence, in which τούτων replaces ἐκείνων for the sake of its repetition of ταῦτα. This repetition removes ambiguity.

[3] See additional note 3, pp. 325f. below.

elements the parts will always be like the whole. We may in the end find that there is a sense in which that is true, but we are under no obligation to look on it from the beginning as a condition that must be satisfied. All that Aristotle is doing is to indicate what sort of substances Anaxagoras regarded as elemental, and this he can do most simply by saying that they are the substances which *he himself* calls homoeomerous; and to remove any shadow of doubt he adds examples— flesh, bone, marrow, etc.

In Aristotle's scheme, matter exists at four main levels of complexity. At the most fully developed level are complete living creatures, plants, animals and men. These are made up of features and organs—eyes, noses, hands, hearts, livers, fruits—which Aristotle calls non-homoeomerous because they cannot be broken up into things of the same name: a heart does not divide into small hearts, and so on. These in their turn are composed of homoeomerous substances, defined as those 'of which the part is identical in name and nature with the whole'.[1] They include animal bone and tissues, wood, bark, sap and other plant tissues, ores, metals and stones, and in their turn are compounds of the four elements or simple bodies, earth, water, air and fire.[2] With them we reach the simplest corporeal entities, though even these are conceptually divisible further into matter and form.[3]

It follows that for Aristotle what he calls homoeomers—flesh, bone, hair, etc.—are not elemental, and to bring out the peculiarity of Anaxagoras's doctrine he says that for him these are elements. He is 'using the term as a convenient one of his own (and therefore readily intelligible to his listeners) to denote the substances it regularly denotes in his own philosophy. Nothing further need be assumed.' (Peck, *loc. cit.* 28 f.)[4]

---

[1] ὧν ἑκάστῳ συνώνυμον τὸ μέρος ἐστιν, *GC*, 314a20. συνώνυμον, as distinct from ὁμώνυμον, implies that the community of name is based on genuine community of substance.

[2] The most complete list of ὁμοιομερῆ is at *Meteor.* 388a13ff., where also are mentioned the ἀνομοιομερῆ that are made up out of them. Occasionally the elements themselves are described as homoeomerous (*Metaph.* 992a7, *Top.* 135a24–b6), but not when Aristotle is attending strictly to classification. At *Meteor.* 384b30, for instance, he says: ἐξ ὕδατος καὶ γῆς τὰ ὁμοιομερῆ σώματα συνίσταται. It is to animal and vegetable tissues that the word is more especially applied.

[3] The formal aspect of the simple bodies is provided for Aristotle by the contrary qualities hot, cold, wet and dry. Each element is characterized by a pair of these. (*G.C.* bk. 2, ch. 1, 329a24ff., and ch. 3.)

[4] This comes out especially clearly at *Cael.* 302b11ff., where he argues that Anaxagoras was wrong to say that all ὁμοιομερῆ are elements, for an element must be simple, and not all ὁμοιομερῆ are simple.

In order to conform to both his principles, that (*a*) there is a portion of everything in everything but (*b*) everything is infinitely divisible into parts homogeneous with itself, Cornford adopted in essence the explanation of Tannery which Burnet had also approved. In certain passages of Anaxagoras there is mention of what we, following Aristotle, call the opposites: the hot and the cold, the wet and the dry, the dense and the rare and so on. 'Opposites' is a neutral word which does not prejudge the question of whether they are qualities or material substances possessing the qualities. Tannery was undoubtedly anachronistic in assuming that 'the hot' and 'the cold' were qualities for Anaxagoras in precisely the sense in which heat and coldness were understood in his own time. Alive to this danger, Cornford called them 'quality-things' (*loc. cit.* 87), on the supposition that, since the notions of substance and quality were not yet clearly distinguished, they partook of the nature of both.[1] The solution proposed was that in the sentence 'there is a portion of everything in everything', the 'things' or 'factors'[2] referred to in the neuter expression παντός ('of everything') are these opposites. The statement would then mean, not that in all gold there is a portion of everything else—flesh, hair, wood, etc.—but (to use more modern terminology) that everything must have a certain temperature, some degree of moisture or dryness, some resistance and some colour.

As to this, one can only agree with Raven[3] that it is impossible that

[1] Cyril Bailey had some excuse for saying in a private letter to Cornford: 'I still don't understand what you mean by a "quality-thing".' His comments are of some interest: 'You say p. 93...that "these quality-things exist only in the seeds". But what does this really mean? If it means "qualities" I could agree, but you show admirably, what I have always thought, that that is not a possible conception for Anaxagoras. What then is your hot quality-thing? You say on p. 84 a "thing whose nature consists entirely in the single property of hotness". Is it concrete? Then it must be a hot piece of matter. And if so, (*a*) you must come down to it by infinite division, you must some time be able "to separate hot and cold with a hatchet" [fr. 8: I hope to show that this would not necessarily be so for Anaxagoras], or (*b*) it must have other attributes as well. If it's not concrete, then it's a quality.'

[2] Nowhere so much as in an exposition of Anaxagoras does one envy the Greek its neat and easy use of the neuter plural adjective without noun. As it is, readers will have to put up with frequent repetition of the clumsy and characterless English word 'things', for which the Hellenists among them will, I hope, make allowances.

[3] And with Bailey, who before Raven had written in the letter previously quoted: 'I do find it awfully difficult to believe that this really means "in every simple natural substance there is a portion of all the pairs of opposites". At least it is a very odd way of saying it. I find it equally difficult to get over the strong tradition (in Lucretius and elsewhere) that it was by means of this saying that Anaxagoras undertook to explain the phenomenon of change. I can't think they can have been so wrong as to the context in which it occurred.'

anyone should have written the simple sentence ἐν παντὶ παντὸς μοῖρα ἔνεστιν ('there is a portion of everything in everything') and meant by παντός something quite different from παντί. Moreover the idea that the first 'everything' meant every natural substance and the second one meant every 'opposite' was only introduced to save the principle of homoeomereity by allowing every substance to be infinitely divisible into parts of that substance only, and I hope it has been made clear that such a principle in Anaxagoras is no more than a ghost which may now be considered laid.

I suggest (or rather I am convinced) that for Anaxagoras there was no difference in the mode of their being between the opposites (so-called, but not by him as far as we know) and other substances like flesh and gold. Taking a first glance at fr. 4, we find him speaking of 'the mixture of all things (χρήματα), the wet, the dry, the hot, the cold, the bright, the dark, since there was much earth in it and an infinite number of seeds'. Evidently all these alike are for him *things*, components of the mixture. In fr. 3 he says that of the small there is no smallest and that there is always a larger than the large. No difficulty has ever been felt about the meaning of 'the small' and 'the large' here: everyone assumes without question that they mean small and large things, or particles of matter, for it is in fact obvious that in the context they could not mean anything else. Why then should we suppose that when Anaxagoras speaks of 'the hot' and 'the cold' he means something of a different order of being, not hot or cold substances but 'quality-things'? Aristotle bears out our contention when in contrasting Empedocles and Anaxagoras he says (*Phys.* 187a 20) that they both make a world by separation from a mixture, but whereas for Empedocles it contains the four elements only, for Anaxagoras it includes 'the homoeomers and the opposites'. A little later (187b 4), explaining that the process of separation is never complete, he says: 'Nothing is purely and wholly white or black or sweet or flesh or bone', as if it were quite natural, in speaking of Anaxagoras, to put white and black, flesh and bone in the same category.

This combination of Aristotle's phraseology with the actual fragments seems conclusive, and I shall assume that for Anaxagoras the hot, the cold, the wet, the bright, the black, etc., were substances having these characteristics, substances on the same footing as flesh and bone, just as the small and the large obviously are in fr. 3.[1]

Anaxagoras's general line of thought was this: nothing can come out of nothing, yet everything appears to be generated out of everything else; therefore everything must contain everything else. 'How', he asks (fr. 10), 'could hair come from what is not hair, or flesh from what is not flesh?'

Aristotle puts his argument thus (*Phys.* 187 a 32):

If everything which comes to be is generated either from existing things or from the non-existent, and the latter is impossible,... they [i.e. Anaxagoras and those who think like him] supposed the other alternative to be necessary, namely that things come into being from things that exist and are already present, but owing to their minute size are imperceptible to us. For that reason they say that everything is mixed in everything, i.e. because they saw everything coming into being out of everything; but things look different, and are called by different names, according to that which predominates numerically in the mixture of an infinite number of constituents. Nothing is purely and wholly white or black or sweet or flesh or bone, but the nature of each thing appears to be that of which it contains most. [The last words are a faithful paraphrase of the end of fr. 12.][2]

---

[1] And fr. 6. One may also note Melissus fr. 8 σίδηρος καὶ χρυσὸς...καὶ μέλαν καὶ λευκόν, a passage which Burnet (*EGP*, 328) and Diller (*Hermes*, 1941, 363) suppose with good reason to be directed against Anaxagoras. F. M. Cleve, *The Philosophy of Anaxagoras*, 7, notes that when Anaxagoras wants an abstract word to describe a quality he has it to hand: cf. ταχυτῆς in fr. 9. Additional evidence that Anaxagoras put all these in the same category is provided by the scholiast on Gregory Nazianzen who quotes fr. 10. Since he describes Anaxagoras airily as 'talking nonsense', he is not perhaps the most reliable of witnesses, but it looks as if at this point he is doing his best to paraphrase something that Anaxagoras actually said. He gives fr. 10 in the following context: 'He talked nonsense about all things being mixed with each other, and becoming separated as they grow. In the same germ (γονῇ) there are hair, nails, veins, arteries, sinews, bones, which happen to be invisible because they are in such small parts but are divided as they grow. "For how", he says, "could hair come from what is not hair and flesh from what is not flesh?" This he asserts not only of bodies but also of colours: the black is in the white and the white in the black; and he made the same assumption about weights, supposing the light to be mixed with the heavy and *vice versa*.'

Vlastos approves Cornford's 'quality-things', but says that 'powers' is a better word still for hot, cold, etc. 'The current term for "quality" was *dynamis*, power' (*Philos. Rev.* 1950, 41 f.). But in the passage of *VM* to which he refers, they are referred to not as *being*, but as *having* powers (παντοίας δυνάμιας ἔχοντα).

[2] Cf. the scholiast on Gregory Nazianzen quoted in previous note. It is presumably the same point that Anaxagoras put in the form of a paradox when he said that snow is black because it is frozen water and water is black. (Sext. *Pyrrh. Hyp.* 1.33, A97.) Though it appears white to the eye, some portions of the black must have remained in it.

A Portion of Everything in Everything

This idea of Anaxagoras is most clearly exemplified in our own growth and nutrition and that of plants.[1] We may eat nothing but bread and vegetables, and these apparently turn into flesh and bone and all the other constituents of our bodies. Since then on Parmenidean principles no new thing can come into existence, these constituents must have pre-existed in the corn or leaves, only in quantities too minute to be discerned. 'Anaxagoras plausibly says that flesh from the food is added to our flesh' (Arist. *GA*, 723 a 10). Cornford objected that in fact everything does *not* turn into everything else; if it did, we could be nourished by copper or cork. This was one of his reasons for supposing that 'a portion of everything in everything' does not mean what it plainly says. To explain the changes that can actually be observed to occur, it is only necessary to suppose that *some* things are in *some* things.[2] Nevertheless, Anaxagoras did say 'there is a portion of everything in everything', and if this is to be given its natural meaning, some explanation must be sought. It can be found in a statement attributed to Anaxagoras (though not in an actual extant fragment) that the change may be mediate and not direct. Simplicius's statement of the theory (in his comment on the passage of Aristotle's *Physics* just quoted, 460.8) is this:

Aristotle shows that Anaxagoras had not only to call the whole mixture infinite in size, but also to speak of each homoeomer as having everything in it just like the whole. They are not only infinite but infinite times infinite. [This is confirmed by fr. 6.] To this view Anaxagoras was brought by his belief that (*a*) nothing comes to be out of the non-existent, and (*b*) everything is nourished by its like. He saw (*a*) that everything comes to be out of everything, *if not directly then serially*[3] (as air from fire, water from air, earth from water, stone from earth, and fire again from stone), and (*b*) that by taking in the same food, e.g. bread, a great variety of things is brought into being—flesh, bones, veins, sinews, hair, nails, feathers also and horns in certain cases—and like is nourished by like; wherefore he supposed that

---

[1] Cf. fr. 10 and Aët. 1.3.5 (p. 272 above), as well as Simplicius's statement on this page. Plato, *Phaedo*, 96d is also a clear reference to Anaxagoras.

[2] Cornford, *loc. cit.* 19–21. As an explanation of nutrition, the theory of 'everything in everything' seemed to him uneconomic. It is an axiom of science that the more economic hypothesis must be preferred, but is this one, scientifically speaking, less economical of assumptions than 'some things in some other things'? If by economical we mean simple, ἐν παντὶ παντὸς μοῖρα is surely the best choice, for the task of drawing up a list of exactly what things must be contained in what other things, to account for the observed changes and no more, would be a formidable one.

[3] εἰ καὶ μὴ ἀμέσως ἀλλὰ κατὰ τάξιν.

these things are in the food. Similarly, assuming water to be the nourishment of trees, water contains wood, bark, leaves and fruit. Hence he said that everything is mixed in everything and coming-to-be takes place by separation.

Elsewhere (162.31), after repeating the premise that nothing can come from nothing, he goes on:

Therefore in the homoeomerous mass[1] there are flesh, bone, blood, gold, lead, sweet and white, but in quantities too small to be perceived by us, all being in all. For how could everything be seen to be generated from everything (*even if through other intermediaries*)[2] if everything was not in everything?

To say that earth is generated from fire sounds as absurd as to say that flesh comes from gold. But it is perfectly possible to believe that fire turns to vapour, vapour condenses into water, and water (as Anaximenes held) into earth and stones. Similarly, Anaxagoras can have thought, gold cannot turn directly into flesh, but it may be subject to a series of transformations, at the other end of which is an edible plant which does contain enough portions of flesh, etc., to nourish the body.

What then in detail was Anaxagoras's view? Let us take first the state of things as they now are, and afterwards the process by which they reached it, that is, the cosmogony.

In fr. 4, which Simplicius informs us came soon after the beginning of the first book *On Nature*, he writes:

This being so, we must suppose that there are many things of all kinds in all the things that are being mingled, and seeds of all things with every sort of shapes and colours and flavours.

And in fr. 6:

And since both the large and the small have portions equal in number, in this way too everything must be in everything. Separate existence is impossible

---

[1] ἐν τῇ ὁμοιομερείᾳ. I take this to be a collective singular: cf. additional note (3), pp. 325 f. below. Note how here again sweet and white are listed on a par with flesh, gold, etc., as constituents of the mixture.

[2] εἰ καὶ διὰ μέσων ἄλλων. Cf. on this point R. Mathewson, *CQ*, 1958, 74 f. It must also be remembered that more transformations were thought possible in the ancient world than would be accepted now, e.g. Simplicius mentions, alongside the production of vapour from water, that of wasps from horses (*Phys.* 162.31).

but everything has a portion of everything. When it is impossible for there to be a smallest, nothing can become separated or by itself, but just as in the beginning so now all things are together. Everything contains many things, the larger and the smaller containing an equal number of the things that are being separated off.

The phrase τοὐλάχιστον μὴ ἔστιν εἶναι ('It is impossible for there to be <anything which can be called> the smallest') implies that a piece of matter is, in theory if not in practice, infinitely divisible into ever smaller pieces, and this principle of infinite divisibility[1] is stated more fully in fr. 3:

Of the small there is no smallest, but always a smaller (for what is cannot not-be);[2] but similarly there is always a larger than the large, and it is numerically equal to the small, whereas in relation to itself each thing is both large and small.

The last clause means that each thing in and by itself (πρὸς ἑαυτό, in comparison with itself rather than with anything else) may be regarded as both great (because composed of an infinite number of parts or ingredients) and small (because its parts are themselves infinitesimally small).[3]

It is here that Anaxagoras seems to take up the challenge of Zeno, who thought he could reduce the notion of plurality to absurdity by saying that if things were many they would have to be at the same time infinitely great and so small as to have no magnitude at all. Anaxagoras's reply shows an understanding of the meaning of infinity which no Greek before him had attained: things are indeed infinite in quantity and at the same time infinitely small (ἄπειρα καὶ πλῆθος καὶ σμικρότητα, fr. 1), but they can go on becoming smaller to infinity without thereby becoming mere points without magnitude. Another argument against plurality was that its separate components must be both infinite in number (because between any two of them there must always be some-

---

[1] This phrase must be read in the light of the caution on p. 298, n. 2 below.

[2] If the division of something into smaller and smaller pieces could ever come to an end, this would mean that there was nothing further to divide; i.e. by cutting up an existing thing one would have reduced it to non-existence. This would contravene the Parmenidean canon ὅπως ἔστιν τε καὶ ὡς οὐκ ἔστι μὴ εἶναι (frr. 2–3), which Anaxagoras here repeats in all its purity and starkness. Zeller's τομῇ for τὸ μή expresses Anaxagoras's meaning exactly, but it is doubtful whether he would have considered οὐκ ἔστι οὐκ εἶναι to be tolerable Greek.

[3] Raven, *CQ*, 1954, 127f.

thing else, if they *are* two and therefore separate), and finite because 'they must be neither more nor less than they are'. This contention Anaxagoras simply denies (fr. 5): 'Now that these things have been separated, it must be recognized that all things are neither less nor more (for there cannot be more than all), but all are equal.' Even an infinite number is no more and no less than it is. The polemical echoes of Zeno are unmistakable.[1]

We can have no doubt by now of the subtlety and originality of Anaxagoras's thought. He has not only grasped the notion of strict infinity (and in particular of the infinitely small),[2] but, having realized what it implies, accepts the consequences as few Greeks were willing to do. For instance if a body contains an infinite number of ingredients, then however far it may be divided up, each successively smaller portion will still contain an infinite number of ingredients; and so, as Simplicius said, things are 'not only infinite but infinite times infinite'.[3] Thus the statement that there is no smallest and no largest is logically connected with the statement that there is an equal number of portions in the large and the small.

Here however we must take into account something which may not seem easy to reconcile with the points already made,[4] but which we must accept as credible to Anaxagoras and indeed the essential condition for the genesis of a cosmos. Everything contains a portion of

---

[1] Zeno, frr. 1–3, pp. 89 ff. above. The comparison is made by Gigon, *Philologus*, 1936–7, 4, and Raven, *CQ*, 1954, 125 ff. Anaxagoras 'applies to physical matter the arguments that had earlier been employed by Zeno in connexion with mathematical magnitude'.

[2] This is lucidly expressed by Vlastos, *Philos. Rev.* 1950, 41. (The criticism of him by C. Strang in *Archiv*, 1963, does not seem to me to be cogent.) That Anaxagoras did grasp the implications of the infinitely small emerges also from the criticism of Aristotle, to whom the idea of infinity, except as a purely logical concept, was anathema. At *Phys.* 187 b 30 he thinks to face Anaxagoras with a dilemma: 'If the process of separation ever comes to an end, everything will not be in everything, for [*sc.* from an original mixture containing water and flesh] in the remaining water there will be no flesh; if on the other hand it does not, but it is always possible to take away something further, there must be in a finite magnitude an infinite number of equal finite parts. This is impossible.' Except for the word 'equal', which is an unwarranted addition of Aristotle, the second alternative represents Anaxagoras's view and was not to his mind impossible at all.

[3] *Phys.* 460. 10, οὐ μόνον ἄπειρα ἀλλ' ἀπειράκις ἄπειρα. 'The main characteristic of the infinite set [is] the fact that it contains subsets which are equivalent to the whole' (Wasserstein, *JHS*, 1963, 189). Luria illustrates the idea of an equal number of portions in the large and the small by the figure of a number of concentric circles with a number of radii in them. The smallest is divided into the same number of parts as the largest. (*Anf. gr. Denkens*, 103.)

[4] The difficulty is however alleviated by a consideration of Luria's illustration mentioned in the previous note.

everything else, and a large piece of something contains as many portions as a small piece of it, though they differ in size; but every substance does *not* contain all the infinite number of substances *in equal proportions*. So he says at the end of fr. 12: 'Mind is all alike, both the greater and the smaller. But apart from Mind, nothing is like anything else, but those things are and were most plainly each thing, of which there are most in it.'

This passage could be the source of Aristotle's true remark that 'things come into being from things that exist and are present, but owing to their minute size are imperceptible to us' (*Phys.* 187a36). We must suppose that what we call a piece of bone contains portions of all the infinite variety of substances, but that the portions of bone predominate and most of the rest are present only in imperceptible quantities. I say most of the rest, because we also call it hard, white and brittle, and in Anaxagoras's language I believe this would mean that it also contains predominating quantities of the hard, the white and the brittle.[1]

This would be more difficult to understand and accept if we supposed that there is even a theoretical possibility of the portions of any one substance ever existing separately from the rest. But the infinite divisibility of matter makes this impossible. As he says himself in fr. 6: 'When it is impossible for there to be a smallest, nothing can become separated or by itself, but just as in the beginning, so now all things are together.' Again in fr. 8, where he gives the opposites as examples: 'The things in the one world-order are not separated from one another nor cut off with an axe, neither the hot from the cold nor the cold from the hot.' Here is another rather difficult but not impossible idea which

---

[1] Vlastos objects (*Philos. Rev.* 1950, 52f.) that this would make the bone-portions redundant. Taking flesh as his example, he writes: 'Flesh has any number of qualities: it is red, soft, heavy, etc. Given these powers in the required ratio, the result would *be* flesh. Why then need we mix flesh-seeds (or any other seeds) *to* [*sic*: the italics are Vlastos's] these powers to produce flesh?' (I am not concerned at the moment with the rightness of using the word 'seeds' in this connexion.) The temptation is irresistible to put beside this the words of William Whewell in the nineteenth century: 'An apple which is red, and round, and hard, is not merely redness and roundness and hardness; these circumstances may all alter while the apple remains the same apple.' (*Philos. of the Inductive Sciences*, 2nd ed., vol. 1, 405.) Whewell was of course arguing in favour of the distinction between quality and substance, but even before Aristotle had made that distinction explicit, it might seem to a philosopher on somewhat similar grounds that bone or flesh must contain 'boneness' or 'fleshness' as well as hardness or softness, redness or whiteness: that is, in Anaxagoras's more concrete terms, bone or flesh as well as the hard and the white, the red and the soft, etc. This may not appear a tenable point of view to ourselves, but that is a different matter.

Anaxagoras asks us to assimilate: the manifold world has evolved by a process of separation or division (ἀπόκρισις, διάκρισις) from an original mixture of all things, yet in spite of the separation that has taken place, everything still contains some of everything else: 'as in the beginning, so now all things are together.'[1]

Here an account of Anaxagoras's views on the constitution of matter may well stop. Ever since Aristotle expositors have taken it further by asking themselves the question: 'What for Anaxagoras are the elements or first principles (ἀρχαί or στοιχεῖα)'? In so far as this question admits of an answer, it must be that which Aristotle gives, namely the 'homoeomers' flesh, bone, hair, sinew, wood, bark, gold, iron, etc.[2] But there is no evidence in the remains of Anaxagoras's own writings of any word for elements or principles, and it is possible that by introducing them we should be distorting his thought and putting questions that he did not ask. In what sense can one speak of elements in a ὁμοῦ πάντα, an 'all things together', which exists now as in the beginning? Aristotle at least was led into confusion by thinking in this way. One thing that has emerged with certainty from our examination is that for Anaxagoras there is no such thing as a simple body, and for Aristotle

---

[1] Vlastos (*Philos. Rev.* 1950, 125 f.) quotes with approval the following from Cleve's book on Anaxagoras (87 f.): 'From his presuppositions Anaxagoras must have concluded that in bread and the other victuals seemingly dissimilar the same had to be contained as was contained in flesh, in blood, in bone, etc. This, however, did not mean that the ones consisted of the others, but that both consisted of the same *thirds*—namely, of *those ultimate elements*: rare- and dense-moiras, bright- and dark-moiras, warm- and cold-moiras, moist- and dry-moiras, etc.' (I have italicized the words that seem to me open to criticism.) Vlastos adds: 'In other words, flesh, constituted of the various qualitative ingredients in a given ratio, contains bone, hair, etc., not (as Lucretius and other commentators, ancient and modern, have imagined) in the form of discrete particles, but simply through the fact that its own ingredients, being the same as those of bone, hair, or any other substance, need only be taken in the ratio appropriate to bone or hair to "generate" bone or hair.'

It is a little rash to dismiss not only Lucretius but 'other commentators, ancient and modern'; and in fact it is not 'rare- and dense-moiras, etc.', as distinct from bone, hair, etc., that are the ultimate elements. Aristotle and Simplicius put it beyond doubt that the Aristotelian homoeomers (bone, hair, etc.) are themselves ultimate. Aristotle several times says that these are στοιχεῖα in the sense in which Empedocles's ῥιζώματα were, and Simplicius (who made his own study of the text) says for example at *Phys.* 167.9, ἐκ τῶν τοιούτων δὲ ὁμοιομερῶν σύγκειται τὰ ζῷα καὶ εἰς ταῦτα διαιρεῖται κατὰ Ἀναξαγόραν. οὐδὲν γὰρ τούτων ἀνωτέρω κατ' αὐτόν.

It could also be misleading to say that ancient commentators 'imagine' the homoeomers to be in the form of *discrete* particles. Aristotle and Simplicius clearly understood the capital and essential point made by Anaxagoras in fr. 12, that 'no one thing is completely separated off or divided from another save Mind'.

[2] Peck would exclude inorganic substances, *CQ*, 1931, 29–31.

it is axiomatic that an element must be simple. ἁπλᾶ σώματα and στοιχεῖα are synonymous. In one place this betrays him into calling Anaxagoras's 'elements' simple, an easy slip when he is contrasting him with Empedocles. In the view of Empedocles, he says (*GC*, 314a 26), fire, water, air and earth are elemental and simple rather than 'flesh, bone and such homoeomers; but Anaxagoras and his followers call the latter simple and elemental (ἁπλᾶ καὶ στοιχεῖα) and earth, fire, water and air compounds of them'. When however in *De caelo* (302a 28) he repeats the contrast with Empedocles in slightly different words, he omits 'simple' and calls them elements only; and a little later (302b 14) he is accusing Anaxagoras of inconsistency in that he calls all homoeomers elements, whereas not all homoeomers are simple. Elsewhere too he shows his awareness that the 'homoeomers' are not simple for Anaxagoras, for example at *Phys*. 187b 4 (p. 285 above), where he paraphrases the end of fr. 12. So also Simplicius, quoting or paraphrasing Theophrastus, wrote:[1]

Of those who posited principles infinite in number, some called them simple and homogeneous, others compound and heterogeneous and contrasted, but designated by that which prevails; for Anaxagoras...claimed that all the homoeomers, such as water or fire or gold,[2] are ungenerated and indestructible, and that it is combination and division alone which give them the appearance of generation and perishing, for everything is in everything, but each is designated by that which prevails in it.

My final suggestion is therefore that Anaxagoras did not put the question of the nature of matter in its Aristotelian form: 'What are the elements of physical bodies?' He asked rather: On what hypothesis of the nature of matter can one explain the apparent change of one sub-

---

[1] *Phys*. 26.31, assumed by Diels (*Dox*. 478) and DK (A41) to be from Theophrastus's *Phys. Opin*. On this see also Vlastos, *Philos. Rev*. 1950, 57, n. 84.

[2] The inclusion of two of the Empedoclean and Aristotelian elements, water and fire, among the homoeomers is probably due to a misunderstanding of Arist. *Metaph*. 984a 13, from which Theophrastus or Simplicius will have taken the statement that the homoeomers are everlasting. Aristotle says there: σχεδὸν γὰρ ἅπαντα τὰ ὁμοιομερῆ καθάπερ ὕδωρ ἢ πῦρ οὕτω γίγνεσθαι καὶ ἀπόλλυσθαί φησι, συγκρίσει καὶ διακρίσει μόνον, ἄλλως δ' οὔτε γίγνεσθαι οὔτ' ἀπόλλυσθαι ἀλλὰ διαμένειν ἀίδια. I take this to mean, *not* 'all the homoeomers such as water or fire...' but 'all the homoeomers come into being and perish in the same way as (οὕτω...καθάπερ) water or fire'. That Aristotle, rightly or wrongly, did not suppose water or fire to be on the same level of complexity for Anaxagoras as flesh or bone is clear from the passages already quoted in which he contrasts him with Empedocles.

stance into another (as exemplified *par excellence* in the phenomenon of nutrition) without assuming the creation of new substance which is forbidden by the law of Parmenides? And he answered in effect that none of the popularly recognized forms of physical substance was prior to any other, because in a portion of any one of them, of whatever size, there already existed portions of all the others, though in quantities beneath the level of our perception. This answer was made possible by the conception of the infinitely small, a conception which had been put into his head by a reading of Zeno, though Zeno had only mentioned it in order to dismiss it as absurd.

(6) *The initial state: cosmogony*

How then, and from what, did the cosmos originate? Anaxagoras opened his treatise with a description of the original state of matter, and the quotations from this early part of his work are best seen in the setting in which Simplicius has handed them down (*Phys.* 155.23):

Anaxagoras's view that homoeomers infinite in number become separated off from a single mixture—all things being in everything but each one characterized by that which predominates—he makes clear by what he says at the beginning of the first book of his *Physics* (fr. 1): 'All things were together, infinite both in number and in smallness; for indeed the small was infinite. And when all things were together, none was discernible because of their smallness, for *aer* and *aither* embraced all things,[1] both of them being infinite; for these are the greatest in the collection of all things, both in number and in size.' A little later he says (fr. 2): '*Aer* and *aither* become separated off from the mass surrounding, and the surrounding is infinite in number.' And a little later (fr. 4): 'This being so, we must suppose that there are many things of all kinds in all the things that are being mingled, and seeds of all things with every sort of shapes and colours and flavours. Before they were separated,' he says,[2] 'since all things were together not even any colour

---

[1] κατεῖχε πάντα. κατεῖχε is difficult to translate. 'Prevailed over' Burnet, 'occupied (?)' Cornford, 'covered' Raven, 'hielt nieder' DK, 'enthalten' Gigon (who says of DK's rendering that it is 'sachlich kaum zu verstehen'; but on this see also Lämmli, *Chaos zum Kosmos*, II, 102, n. 379). Things, says Gigon, are contained in *aer* and *aither* as in their original form ('als in ihrer Urgestalt'); the notion to be conveyed seems to waver between that of a spatial container and that of a primal form or state. Probably 'contained' comes as near to the meaning as any English word.

[2] At this point Simplicius has omitted a passage mentioning the beginning of living things and the existence somewhere else of men other than ourselves (p. 314 below), which he quotes after the preceding sentence at *Phys.* 35.3. But see p. 314, n. 1.

could be discerned. That was prevented by the mixture of all things—the wet and the dry, the hot and the cold, the bright and the dark, since there was much earth[1] in it and an infinite number of seeds[2] in no way resembling each other; for not even any of the other things resemble each other.'

The sentence '*aer* and *aither* embraced (or contained, or concealed) all things'[3] does not mean that *aer* and *aither* were already separated in the original mixture of all things together, though they were, as fr. 2 tells us, the first to become distinct once the process of separation had begun. As we have seen, one of the most striking things about Anaxagoras in Aristotle's view was his diametrical opposition to Empedocles on the subject of elements. Empedocles said earth, water, air and fire were primary and all other bodies such as flesh and bone the result of their mixture, whereas in Anaxagoras's scheme they themselves were a mixture of the homoeomers in invisible quantities (*De caelo*, 302b1). Now *aer* and *aither* or fire were in the beginning the two extreme states of matter, *aer* containing what is predominantly dense, cold, wet and dark, and *aither* what is predominantly rare, hot, dry and bright.[4] In the beginning all these and other contraries were together, and the best way that Anaxagoras can think of to describe this condition in which none of them was distinct is to say that *aer*-and-*aither* together held the field.[5] When the cosmogonic revolution starts, they are the first to be separated off (fr. 2). This is described also in terms of their contrasting qualities in fr. 15: 'The dense, wet, cold and dark collected here where they are now,[6] and the rare, hot and dry receded to the further region of the *aither*.'

[1] Peck (*CQ*, 1931, 115) adopts the alternative of taking the genitive γῆς as exactly parallel to χρημάτων, i.e. objective after σύμμιξις. But Cherniss's opinion that it is 'a genitive absolute giving the cause of the preceding statement' seems more probable. (See Vlastos, *Philos. Rev.* 1950, 33, n. 17.)

[2] On reading and translation here see Cornford, *CQ*, 1930, 28, n. 2.

[3] It is best to keep the Greek words here. *Aer* is not air, but dark, cold, damp mist; and *aither*, as has been explained (p. 273, n. 4 above), is fire, which, as in Empedocles and others, is believed to exist in greatest quantity in the outer regions of the spherical cosmos.

[4] Theophr. *De sens.* 59 (A70): τὸ μὲν μανὸν καὶ λεπτὸν θερμόν, τὸ δὲ πυκνὸν καὶ παχὺ ψυχρόν, ὥσπερ 'Α. διαιρεῖ τὸν ἀέρα καὶ τὸν αἰθέρα. Cf. also Hippol. *Ref.* 1.8.2 (A42).

[5] κατεῖχε πάντα. Note that the singular verb is used, though the subjects are not neuter: *aer–aither* is an amalgam.

[6] Some adopt the reading of the Aldine ed., 'where now is earth'. This is based on Hippol. *Ref.* 1.8.2: 'The dense, wet, dark and cold and all heavy things came together in the centre, and from them the earth was compacted', and doubtless represents Anaxagoras's doctrine, but it is unnecessary to alter the text here.

The original undifferentiated mass was motionless. 'He starts his cosmogony from immobility.'[1] The motion introduced by Mind was the rotation (περιχώρησις) which still continues, as the wheeling of the heavenly bodies shows. We have Anaxagoras's own words (fr. 12):

Mind controlled the whole rotation so that it started to rotate in the beginning. It first began to rotate in a small part, but now it rotates over a larger field and will include a larger one still.... And all things that were to be, all that were but are not now, all that are now or shall be, Mind arranged them all, including this rotation in which now move the stars, sun and moon, air and fire that are being separated off. Dense is separated from rare, hot from cold, bright from dark, dry from wet. But there are many portions of many things, and no one thing is completely separated or divided from another except Mind.

The last sentence should need no comment after our examination of the structure of matter. The notion that the rotating cosmos was at first small, and is continually growing by drawing in more of the infinite surrounding it, is interesting, particularly in the light of some recent cosmogonical theory. The only clear ancient parallel is the way that the Pythagorean cosmos grew from a seed by drawing in the infinite in its various forms of breath, time and void.[2] Even in this, so far as our evidence goes, there is no suggestion that the cosmos is still growing. The notion of the universe as an organic growth was shared by Anaximander,[3] but again there is no suggestion from his remains that it is gradually growing in size. However, our information about Anaximander is regrettably scanty, and, in view of the other parallels between his cosmogony and that of Anaxagoras, it seems possible that he entertained a similar idea.

Fr. 13 (p. 274 above) also speaks of Mind initiating the movement,

---

[1] Arist. *De caelo*, 301a12. Cf. *Phys.* 250b25: ὁμοῦ πάντων ὄντων καὶ ἠρεμούντων τὸν ἄπειρον χρόνον, κίνησιν ἐμποιῆσαι τὸν νοῦν καὶ διακρῖναι. From Arist. *Phys.* 205b1 we learn of an argument of Anaxagoras's on this topic: the *apeiron* (i.e. the whole mass, cf. fr. 2) is stationary because it στηρίζει itself (fixes, holds fast). This is because it is contained in itself, for there is nothing else around it, and wherever a thing is, there it is its nature to be. (Therefore, presumably, it is the nature of *apeiron* to be in itself; therefore it supports itself in its existing position. So Ross *ad loc.*) Gigon (*Philol.* 1936–7, 30f.) notes that here again we see Anaxagoras adapting an Eleatic argument, which goes back in the last resort to Parm. fr. 8.29: ταὐτόν τ' ἐν ταὐτῷ τε μένει καθ' ἑαυτό τε κεῖται.

[2] Vol. I, 276ff., 281.   [3] Vol. I, 90f.

and says that everything which Mind moved tended to separate, and that the rotation hastened the process of separation; and fr. 9 remarks on the tremendous speed of the rotation, many times greater than the speed of anything on earth.

We have seen that a portion of any substance, of whatever size, contains portions of any other substance, though not in equal proportions. In bone, the proportion of bone exceeds that of other substances and so gives it its perceptible character as bone. This proportion would be maintained however small a speck of bone we imagine, even far below the level of perception, for 'the large and the small have portions equal in number' (fr. 6 *init.*).

Now in the original, static mixture it would seem most natural (at least, for I must be personal here, it would seem so to me) to suppose that the fusion of everything was thorough and complete, so that no one thing prevailed over any other in any part of it. Since in origin the process is not merely mechanical but an *ordering* controlled by Mind, the first step could be for portions of each substance to coagulate and form microscopic specks in which they predominated over the others, and out of which pieces of bone, flesh, etc., could be amassed in perceptible quantities as like continued to seek its like in the cosmic whirl. This however is not what the texts say. Not only does Anaxagoras insist that 'just as in the beginning, so now all things are together' (fr. 6), but he also says unequivocally in fr. 4 that in the original 'all-things-together', before separation began, when not even any colour was discernible, there were not only the opposites and a lot of earth, but also 'an infinite number of seeds *in no way resembling each other*'. This is exactly the state of things now, when, as he says at the beginning of the same fragment, all compounds contain 'seeds of all things with every kind of shapes, colours and flavours'.

The original state of matter, then, was a mixture complete to this extent, that to an imaginary observer it would have appeared uniform, just as would the *apeiron* of Anaximander before the opposites were separated out from it. But Anaxagoras is writing under the stern eye of Parmenides. He knows that because plurality can never be produced out of strict unity, this apparently uniform matter must in fact be a mixture of everything that is subsequently to be produced. Its unity

297

must be only in the eye of the beholder—and, like Empedocles, he emphasized the inadequacy of the senses, saying that 'through their weakness we cannot judge the truth';[1] therefore (one may suppose him to have argued) the distinctions which we now perceive between substances must have been there from the beginning, only in measures too fine for our coarser faculties to pick up. And this led him to the original and, it may well be thought, remarkably mature conception of different kinds of matter as retaining, in however small a quantity, the same infinite number of ingredients in unchanging proportions.[2]

The mentions of 'seeds' by Anaxagoras in fr. 4 have attracted much attention and led to much dispute.[3] He says there, first, that in the present world everything contains 'seeds of all things with every sort of shapes and colours and flavours', and secondly, that before the cosmic separation began, the original mixture contained the opposites, much earth, and 'seeds infinite in number'. In addition, Aristotle says (*De caelo*, 302b1) that according to Anaxagoras air and fire are a mixture

---

[1] Fr. 21. See further p. 319 below.

[2] I have avoided here the later and convenient phrase 'infinite divisibility' (cf. Lucretius's *neque corporibus finem esse secandis*, 1.844) because the notion of infinite divisibility has troubled some critics as involving a vicious regress. As it presented itself to Anaxagoras, it would certainly not have troubled him. The infinity of ingredients in the same unequal proportions in any portion of matter, however small, is the cornerstone of his cosmogony, for it ensures that even in the original fusion, however large or small a portion be taken, there is the lack of homogeneity which makes possible the later emergence of distinctions in perceptible bulk. The acceptability of the infinite regress (if one likes to call it that) is the great discovery which enables him to parry, and even destroy, the weapons of Zeno. Raven also (KR, 378) defends Anaxagoras on this point, but it could be misleading to say as he does that the infinite regress 'must be at least momentarily halted' if a sensible world is to be built up. Anaxagoras describes a state, not a process. Gigon's observation is helpful (*Philologus*, 1936–7, 17), that to speak of infinite divisibility (a specifically mathematical problem) is to look back at Anaxagoras from Aristotle, whereas he himself was starting from Parmenides and Zeno.

[3] The fullest treatment is that of Vlastos, 'Phys. Theory of Anaxagoras, I. The Seeds', *Philos. Rev.* 1950, 32–41. My quotations from him must not be taken to indicate agreement with everything in this section. His statements that in Empedocles the elements are exempt from intermutation *and mixture*, and again that in Empedocles as well as Parmenides being and *mixture* are incompatible, are at first sight puzzling. It is of course solely because the elements (the only ὄντα) undergo mixture that according to Empedocles the sensible world can be accounted for. Vlastos's meaning is (as he has explained to me) that there is no radical, 'chemical' fusion of one element with another but only juxtaposition of minute parts of each (the view taken in ch. III, § F of the present work). The somewhat difficult sentence (p. 37, n. 29): 'mortality and mixture is predicated not of their [sc. the elements'] being but of their temporary conjunction' means, I understand, that although the elements do mix to form perishable compounds, the terms 'mixture' and 'mortal' cannot apply to an element *per se*.

of homoeomers like flesh and bone 'and all the other seeds', and to express the same idea elsewhere calls them a *panspermia*, or aggregation of seeds, of the homoeomers.

Vlastos has rightly emphasized that in thus enlarging the scope of the word 'seed' beyond the organic sphere Anaxagoras must have had the biological analogy in mind. It may well have been more than an analogy, for the notion that the whole world and everything in it was organic long outlived the transition from mythological to rational thought and is discernible in Anaximander,[1] a predecessor for whom Anaxagoras had especial regard. The contemporary scientific view of a seed,[2] as seen in philosophers and medical writers, Vlastos describes as follows (*loc. cit.* 34):

A seed is a compound of all the essential constituents of the parent body from which it comes [the 'pangenesis' theory][3] and of the new organism into which it will grow [the 'pre-formation' theory]. In its ovular or uterine environment (or, in the case of vegetable seeds, in the earth) the compound grows on the principle of 'like to like', each ingredient of the seed being 'nourished' by bits of the same stuff supplied by its environment. That this is Anaxagoras's own notion of a 'seed' is what we should expect, and the expectation is confirmed explicitly in B 10.[4]

Anaxagoras's theory of nutrition is complementary to that of the seed, depending as we have seen on the same principle that 'hair cannot come from not-hair'. Vlastos regards the extension of the word 'seed' to inorganic matter as a terminological innovation so radical that, while not agreeing with them, he feels sympathy with those who, like Peck, refuse to believe in it and try to limit the word in the fragments to the seed of plants or animals. But the explanation of inorganic nature in terms appropriate to organic is rather, as I hope I have shown, a sign of conservatism, as well as providing, in the current conception of a seed, the key that he needed to explain how everything comes to be

---

[1] Vol. I, 90–2.

[2] Greek *sperma*, which includes both the seeds of plants and the sperm of animals and men. The use of the same word was facilitated by the Greek belief that, as the Hippocratic *De nat. pueri* has it (27, VII. 528 Littré), 'the nature of what grows out of the ground and that of men is entirely similar'.

[3] So named by Vlastos on the next page. But if understood as the theory that semen is derived from all parts of the body, this is unlikely to be earlier than Democritus (p. 467, n. 1 below).

[4] For fr. 10 see p. 286, n. 1 above.

out of everything else.[1] It is obvious that he took the phenomenon of nutrition (flesh apparently coming from not-flesh) as the pattern of every kind of change and assimilation.[2]

We may conclude that by a 'seed' in fr. 4 Anaxagoras meant an imperceptibly small bit of any kind of substance, that is, one containing that particular substance in greater proportion than all the others which of course are also in it. This is the seed or germ from which that substance is built up in larger, perceptible quantities. (As Simplicius puts it: 'That appears as gold in which there is much gold, although it contains all things.')[3] There is of course no fixed size for such a seed: the theory of Anaxagoras precludes anything of the nature of atoms. But since even in the beginning matter had these internal distinctions of proportion, this probably did not seem to Anaxagoras to be an objection. Given internal distinctions in the original formation, it was possible, once the revolution was started by Mind, for the substances to come together and build themselves up into perceptible quantities.

We have seen how the revolution first caused dense, wet, cold and dark matter to settle in the centre, and the rare, hot and dry to recede to the farther reaches of the sky. This is in accordance with general ancient belief about the action of a vortex. So Aristotle says in *De caelo* (295 a 10) that in earlier cosmogonies earth came together at the centre 'being brought there through the action of the vortex [or whirl].

---

[1] Vlastos attaches great importance to what he calls the 'precise and technical' use of σπέρμα in Anaxagoras fr. 4. The sharp contrast which he sees between this and the 'vague and general fashion' in which it had hitherto been used causes him to dismiss as irrelevant such expressions as σπέρμα πυρός (*Od.* 5.490), πῦρ ἐξ ἑνὸς σπέρματος ἐνθορόν (Pind. *Pyth.* 3.37), and the identification with σπέρμα of the unit from which the world is derived when Aristotle is discussing Pythagorean theories (*Metaph.* 1091 a 16, 1092 a 32; vol. I, 276–8). I cannot believe that these expressions were wholly metaphorical, and they provided a precedent for the idea of σπέρματα of inorganic substances which would make Anaxagoras's more precise conception a natural and easy one to accept.

[2] The community of ideas between the making of a cosmos in Anaxagoras and the growth of the human body in contemporary physiology becomes plain when one compares Anaxagoras frr. 15 and 16 with a passage like this from the Hippocratic *De genit.* 17 (VII, 496 Littré) on the formation of the embryo: ἡ δὲ σὰρξ αὐξομένη ὑπὸ τοῦ πνεύματος ἀρθροῦται, καὶ ἔρχεται ἐν αὐτῇ ἕκαστον τὸ ὅμοιον ὡς τὸ ὅμοιον, τὸ πυκνὸν ὡς τὸ πυκνόν, τὸ ἀραιὸν ὡς τὸ ἀραιόν, τὸ ὑγρὸν ὡς τὸ ὑγρόν· καὶ ἕκαστον ἔρχεται ἐς χώρην ἰδίην κατὰ τὸ ξυγγενὲς ἀφ' οὗ καὶ ἐγένετο· καὶ ὅσ' ἀπὸ πυκνῶν ἐγένετο πυκνά ἐστι, καὶ ὅσα ἀπὸ ὑγρῶν ὑγρά...καὶ τὰ ὀστέα σκληρύνεται ὑπὸ τῆς θέρμης πηγνύμενα. (πήγνυμι could mean both to solidify by fire and to freeze.) This operation of the principle of like to like in the physiological world is then illustrated by a purely physical experiment involving earth, sand and metal filings in a bladder filled with water.

[3] *Phys.* 27.8, from Theophrastus.

They all name this as the cause, reasoning from what happens in liquids and in the air, where larger and heavier bodies always move towards the middle of a vortex.' So the process continues (fr. 16): 'From these things as they are separated off, earth is compacted; for water is separated off from the clouds, and earth from water, and from the earth stones are compacted by the cold, and they move outwards more than water.'[1]

The first stages of the cosmogony follow the order of Anaximander, who said that at the birth of the cosmos something capable of generating hot and cold was separated off[2] from the *apeiron*, and from this there grew first a sphere of fire enclosing the *aer* round the earth. As it proceeds, Anaxagoras seems to have made use also of the condensation theory of Anaximenes. The two processes, of the separation of dissimilars and of condensation, are combined through the common assumption that like is attracted to like. Thus the Milesian ideas are retained with the modifications made necessary by Eleatic criticism. These are two: motion can no longer be assumed as 'eternal' but must be provided with a cause, and the original state of matter cannot be dismissed as simply *apeiron*. Since all things are produced out of it, the questions of whether it was itself one or many, homogeneous or a mixture, and if a mixture what sort of mixture and in what sense it contained the subsequent products— these questions have come into the open and must be answered.

The following doxographic accounts of the cosmogonic process are vouched for as substantially correct where they overlap the fragments, and add information about the origin and nature of the heavenly bodies which is missing from the fragments themselves.

D.L. 2.8: Mind is the cause of the motion, and of bodies the heavy, such as earth,[3] occupied the lower region, the light, such as fire, the upper, and water and *aer* the middle.

[1] ἐκχωρέουσι: 'rush outwards' Burnet, 'tend' KR, 'drängen sich heraus' DK. The commonest meaning of the verb is to give way or withdraw. The stones are less able to resist the drag of the accelerating whirl (p. 303 below).
[2] ἀποκριθῆναι. The word used by Anaxagoras himself in frr. 2 and 4 is the same as occurs in the report of Anaximander's theory (*Strom.* A 10). The close relationship between Anaxagoras and Anaximander is obvious if this report (φησὶ δὲ τὸ ἐκ τοῦ ἀϊδίου [i.e. τοῦ ἀπείρου] γόνιμον θερμοῦ τε καὶ ψυχροῦ...ἀποκριθῆναι καί τινα ἐκ τούτου φλογὸς σφαῖρα περιφυῆναι τῷ περὶ τὴν γῆν ἀέρι) is compared with Anaxagoras fr. 2, καὶ γὰρ ἀήρ τε καὶ αἰθήρ (= πῦρ) ἀποκρίνονται ἀπὸ τοῦ πολλοῦ τοῦ περιέχοντος, καὶ τό γε περιέχον ἄπειρόν ἐστι τὸ πλῆθος.
[3] ὡς τὴν γῆν, corresponding to ὡς τὸ πῦρ a few words further on, is missing from all MSS. except that it has been added by a corrector's hand to one of them (F).

Hippol. *Ref.* 1.8.2 (A42): All things partake in motion, being moved by Mind, and like things come together. Throughout the heavens things have been set in order by the circular motion. Thus what is dense and moist and dark and cold, and all heavy bodies, came together in the centre, and their compaction produced the earth; whereas their opposites, the hot, the bright, the dry and the light, made for the further region of the *aither*.... (6) The sun, the moon, and all the stars are burning stones which have been caught up by the revolution of the *aither*; and below the stars there are certain bodies carried round with the sun and moon, invisible to us.[1]

Aët. 2.13.3 (A71): Anaxagoras says that the *aither* around the universe is fiery in substance. By the vigour of its rotation it has snatched up rocks from the earth, set them on fire and turned them into stars.

The sun, moon and stars, then, mark an exception to the general rule that of bodies caught in a vortex the heavier collect in the centre and the lighter seek the circumference. This applied to the earlier, slower stages, but as the revolution increased in speed and violence it caught up masses of rock from the earth and ignited them, and now keeps them whirling round at a great distance above the earth.[2] This theory evidently owed much to a striking event which happened during Anaxagoras's lifetime and with which his name was connected for hundreds of years afterwards. About the year 467 B.C. a large meteorite fell at Aegospotami in the Thracian Chersonese (Gallipoli peninsula). The ancient testimonies about this are as follows:[3]

(*a*) Pliny, *N.H.* 2. 149 f. (A11): The Greeks tell that in the second year of the 78th Olympiad (467/6 B.C.) Anaxagoras of Clazomenae predicted by his knowledge of celestial lore on what days a rock would fall from the sun, and that this happened in daylight in a district of Thrace near Aegospotami. The stone is still shown, of the size of a cartload and brown in colour. A comet also blazed on those nights.

---

[1] On these bodies see pp. 306f. below.

[2] Burnet (*EGP*, 269) says that this theory 'necessarily implies the rotation of the flat earth along with the "eddy" (δίνη)'. Does it not imply the contrary? If the main mass of the earth was going round with the eddy instead of resisting it, the eddy would hardly have broken off these loose fragments and borne them aloft while the rest remained where it was.

[3] There is also a passing mention in Philostratus's *Life of Apollonius* (1.2, A6). For the date see also *Marm. Par.* in A11 (468–7), Burnet, *EGP*, 252, n. 6. It seems to be beyond doubt, but it is a little surprising that Plutarch should introduce the incident into the life of Lysander after his vivid description of the battle of Aegospotami, on the ground that some people took it for a portent of the Athenian debacle. Granted the coincidence of place, an interval of over sixty years suggests that their credulity was excessive.

(*b*) D.L. 2.10: They say that he foretold the fall of the stone which took place at Aegospotami, which he said would fall from the sun.

(*c*) Plutarch, *Lysander*, 12 (A 12): There fell from the sky, according to general belief, an enormous stone at Aegospotami. It is still shown, for the Chersonites revere it. Anaxagoras is said to have foretold that through a slip or shaking (ὀλισθήματος ἢ σάλου) of the bodies embedded in the sky[1] one of them would be torn off and cast down and fall. Each one of the stars, he claimed, is not in its natural place, for they are stony and heavy, and shine by the resistance and rupture of the *aither*. They are dragged forcibly round, being held tight by the vehement whirl of the revolution, just as at the beginning they were prevented from falling on the earth when cold and heavy things were being separated off from the whole.[2] ... Daimachus also in his work *On Piety* bears out Anaxagoras, recording that for seventy-five days continuously before the stone fell there was seen in the sky an enormous fiery body like a flaming cloud.... When it landed on this spot, and the natives had recovered from their terror and astonishment and approached, what they saw was no fire or trace of fire but a stone lying there, of great size certainly, but nothing to do, as one might say, with that flaming mass.

Plutarch usefully fills a gap in our knowledge of Anaxagoras's theory. The heavenly bodies are masses of rock which naturally belong to the central part of the whirl, but, owing to the excessive speed and violence of the cosmic motion, were carried aloft and heated to incandescence by the *aither* (fire) which, being light, had already taken its station there. (Presumably the rather obscure last sentence of fr. 16 is a reference to this.) This is doubtless why the velocity of the vortex is given such emphasis in fr. 6: 'These things revolve, and are separated by force and velocity. The velocity creates the force, and their speed is unlike the speed of anything that now exists in the world of men, but is assuredly many times as rapid.' Since however they are naturally heavy, it occasionally happens that a piece of one of them breaks off and, defeating the centrifugal force of the whirling *aither*, falls to the earth. The theory was either suggested, or appeared to be confirmed, by the fall of a stone apparently from heaven. Its coincidence with the appearance of a comet led to the idea that it had been a part of the fiery

---

[1] τῶν κατὰ τὸν οὐρανὸν ἐνδεδεμένων σωμάτων. Here again the language is reminiscent of Anaximenes. See vol. I, 135.

[2] D.L. 2.12 quotes the historian Silenus (third century B.C.) as saying that when the stone fell 'Anaxagoras explained that the whole sky was composed of stones. Its coherence was due to the rapidity of its rotation, and if this slackened it would fall.'

body. The belief that Anaxagoras had actually foretold the fall of the meteorite is fairly obviously a particularization, easy in a credulous age, of his general statement that the sun and stars were heavy bodies held aloft by force, so that it was natural to expect that occasionally something of them would fall.[1] It is a fair inference from the theory, as well as from general probability, that the speed of the revolution, which was started by Mind from zero, showed a gradual acceleration. In its earlier stages its effect was to collect the heavier matter at the centre, but as its speed and power increased it caught up some fragments of it and whirled them aloft. Such acceleration, incidentally, would form a parallel to the accelerating revolution initiated by Strife in the cosmogony of Empedocles. There is a further resemblance in that the effect of the revolution in both schemes is to bring like things together in larger masses and to separate unlikes. (Cf. pp. 174, 186 above.) No sure chronological conclusion can be drawn from these comparisons however. If Anaxagoras seems the more 'scientific', this is rather because he adhered to the Ionian tradition whereas Empedocles was closer to the Pythagorean.

(7) *Cosmology and astronomy*

We have noted that most of the extant fragments of Anaxagoras are from the first book and deal with causes, the general structure of matter, and cosmogony. There is enough information to make it clear that he also dealt at length with questions of cosmology, astronomy and meteorology, but our knowledge of his theories on these topics is at best second-hand.[2] Many details of his cosmology confirm the statement of Theophrastus that he inherited much of the philosophy of Anaximenes, but there are fundamental differences of process resulting from the substitution of a pluralistic for a monistic scheme. Thus both men thought of the heavenly bodies as originating from the earth; but Anaximenes, following the monistic hypothesis which sees all things as transformations of one single substance, explained them as formed by vaporization of moisture from the earth, which by further rarefaction

[1] Gilbert, *Meteor. Theor.* 689, n. 1, M. L. West in *Journ. Brit. Astron. Ass.* 1960, 368–9.
[2] The only quotation in this field which seems certainly to reproduce Anaxagoras's own words is a description of the rainbow (fr. 19), though fr. 18 on the moon's light is usually, and perhaps rightly, printed between quotation marks.

turned to fire. The post-Eleatic pluralist, on the other hand, sees the process in much more mechanical terms. The stars are stones, torn from the earth by force and made white-hot by the rapidity of their motion.[1]

Like Empedocles (p. 191 above), Anaxagoras believed that the inclination of the pole was not an original feature of the cosmos, but as reported he offered no reason for this. Nor is any reason recorded for the curious idea that it did not occur until after the beginning of life on the earth.[2]

D.L. 2.9: The stars at first moved as round a dome, so that the ever-visible pole was vertically above the earth, but later took a tilt.

Aët. 2.8.1 (A 67): Diogenes and Anaxagoras said that after the cosmos was formed and had produced animals from the earth, it somehow tilted of its own accord towards the south.

The doxographer adds the conjecture 'perhaps by providence, that some parts might be uninhabitable and others habitable by reason of cold, torrid heat, or moderate temperature', thereby confirming the absence of an explanation in Anaxagoras himself.[3]

It is not always easy to visualize the complete world-picture of a Presocratic thinker. The rotatory process of cosmogony does not inevitably involve a spherical rather than a hemispherical universe. Probably Anaxagoras did think of the cushion of air on which the earth rests as filling the lower half of a sphere, but effectively at least his universe remains hemispherical. The stars fill a sky that is dome-shaped, and if, as Hippolytus says (1.8.8, A 42), their revolution carries

---

[1] For Anaximenes see Hippol. *Ref.* 1.7.5 and Aët. 2.13.10 (A7 and 14, quoted vol. 1, 134). These state definitely that the heavenly bodies are of fire, and contrast them in this respect with the invisible earthy bodies which accompany them. The passage from the *Stromateis* (A6, vol. 1, 133) describes his theory in terms more nearly appropriate to that of Anaxagoras, unless the corruption at the end conceals a different meaning.

[2] Gomperz supposed (*Gr. Th.* 1, 220) that the extraordinary event of the beginning of organic life 'required a complete revision of existing cosmological conditions, and was perhaps better compatible with a permanent spring than with the changes of the seasons'. Zeller (ZN, 1247 n.) conjectures that it was because before the inclination the sun shone continuously on the earth, and Capelle (*N. Jbb.* 1919, 191) also speaks of 'an incomparably stronger action of the sun's rays on the horizontally situated disc of the earth'. But cf. p. 342, n. 3 below. For the tradition that animal life was created in the spring cf. Virg. *Georg.* 2.338. On the ἔγκλισις in Anaxagoras see also Dummler, *Akademika*, 103 ff.

[3] There is a further reference to this in [Plato], *Erastai*, 132a, where Anaxagoras is coupled with Oenopides.

them beneath the earth, the passages just quoted show that this is only the effect of the inclination of the pole: when that was vertically above the earth's centre, they remained above, or level with, its surface, as Anaximenes had believed they still did (vol. 1, 137).[1] There is no question of a complete southern hemisphere of stars. The lack of heat from the stars is explained, as in Anaximenes, by their great distance, though according to Hippolytus (*loc. cit.* 7) Anaxagoras added also (mysteriously, since they are in the *aither*) that they are colder than the sun because they occupy a colder region.

Anaxagoras's claim to an outstanding astronomical discovery is authenticated by Plato, who speaks jokingly of a fantastic etymology of the word *selene* as threatening the priority of 'Anaxagoras's recent assertion that the moon has its light from the sun'. This is repeated (from Theophrastus) in the doxographers, and Plutarch is possibly quoting the philosopher's actual words when he speaks of 'the proposition of Anaxagoras that "the sun imparts the brightness to the moon"'.[2] He seems to have given much thought to this and related questions. Plutarch calls him the man who 'first and most clearly and boldly put into writing an account of the illuminations and shadowing of the moon', contrasting him in this respect with the superstitious fears which lunar eclipses aroused in his contemporaries. He was not, says Plutarch, a figure of the past, and his explanation was still unknown to all but a few.[3] That he explained the moon's eclipses correctly by the interposition of the earth's shadow is implied by Plutarch and stated by Hippolytus. His scientific achievement in this respect is however slightly marred when Hippolytus adds 'and sometimes by the interposition of the bodies beneath the moon', referring to his earlier statement that 'there are beneath the heavenly bodies certain bodies carried round with the sun and moon but invisible to us'. This of course is

---

[1] Heath, *Aristarchus*, 83, is perhaps not a complete answer to the objection of Gomperz that the movement of the stars beneath the earth is inconsistent with the theory that the earth closes the centre of the cosmos like a lid, supported on compressed air. No doubt the stars could pass through air, but if the extent of the earth is sufficient to prevent any of the air from escaping, where is there room for these great fiery rocks to pass beneath its rim?

[2] Plato, *Crat.* 409 a; Hippol. 1 . 8 . 8 (A 42), etc.; Plut. *De facie*, 929 b (= Anaxagoras fr. 18). Later in the same discussion of *De facie*, however (929 d, e), the reflexion of the sun's light by the moon is referred to as 'the theory of Empedocles'. (Cf. p. 197 above.)

[3] Plut. *Nic.* 23, cf. Hippol. *loc. cit.* 10.

simply taken over from Anaximenes, and should have been rendered superfluous by the correct explanation of eclipses if, as is generally thought, that was the original purpose of their introduction.[1] In this connexion Boll made an interesting conjecture. Although the moon was mainly lit by the sun, and was itself mostly of an earthy nature, it had an admixture of fire (Aët. 2.30.2; at 25.9 it is even called a 'fiery solid'). This seemed to be proved by the fact that in eclipse it is usually still visible through the earth's shadow as a red glow which later writers compared to glowing charcoal or embers. Occasionally however eclipses occur in which the moon disappears from sight altogether (e.g. in 1601, 1642, 1816; no examples appear to be recorded from ancient times). Could it be, asks Boll, that since the earth's shadow was not sufficient to blot out the moon completely, it seemed to Anaxagoras necessary to suppose that in these cases a solid body had intervened?[2]

The famous statement that the sun was 'an incandescent stone', which was said to have been the occasion of his prosecution for atheism, is repeated in a number of ancient authors, of whom the earliest are Plato and Xenophon.[3] It was 'larger than the Peloponnese', perhaps 'many times larger',[4] a more cautious estimate than that of Anaximander that it was the same size as the earth. He said correctly that the sun was eclipsed at the new moon when the moon screened it from the earth.

[1] Hippol. *loc. cit.* 9 and 6. For Anaximenes see vol. I, 134, 135. I have omitted the passage on eclipses at Aët. 2.29.6 (A77), which is partly obscure (Diels, *Dox.* 53) and in any case attributes the doctrine to Thales as well as Anaxagoras (to say nothing of Plato, Aristotle and oἱ μαθηματικοί). Translations (with different readings) will be found in Heath, *Aristarchus*, 79 and Cohen and Drabkin, *Source Book*, 94, n. 2.
Burnet alone (*EGP*, 272) thought it unlikely that a man who believed in a flat earth would discover the true cause of eclipses. Heath evidently found this no difficulty, though he does cite the flatness of the earth (and presumed flatness of the moon) as militating against a correct explanation of the moon's phases. On eclipses, he found the evidence 'quite conclusive'. (*Aristarchus*, 80f., 78.)

[2] Boll, *RE*, VI, 2343 f. At Aët. 2.30.2 (A77) it is said that the moon is earthy, but has a mixture of fire with the dark, 'which condition is made visible by the shadowed part', i.e. presumably by the part of the moon shadowed in an eclipse. Cf. Plut. *De facie*, 933 f: 'The moon is not altogether invisible in eclipse, but shows a threatening ember-like tint, which is its natural colour', and other passages cited by Boll. (Others have thought that the object of the invisible earthy bodies was to explain meteorites. Böker (*RE*, 2. Reihe VIII A, 2.2236) calls them meteors.)

[3] Plato, *Apol.* 26d (Socrates says that Meletus, who accuses him of calling the sun λίθος, must be confusing him with Anaxagoras), Xen. *Mem.* 4.7.7 (λίθος διάπυρος). Other phrases are λίθος ἔμπυρος, μύδρος (once μύλος) διάπυρος. μύδρος is defined as πεπυρακτωμένος σίδηρος by Olympiodorus and by the Suda as πύρινος λίθος. See D.L. 2.12 and the passages quoted in DK 59A, 2, 3, 19, 20 a.

[4] 'Larger', D.L. 1.8, Hippol. 1.8.8 (A42); πολλαπλάσιον, Aët. 2.21.3 (A72).

It was generally observed in the second half of the fifth century that solar eclipses could only occur at new moon, and Plutarch remarks that the populace at large already had an idea that they were somehow caused by the moon, and so were not frightened by them as by lunar eclipses.[1] The 'turnings' of the sun (solstices) are explained by 're-sistance of the air in the north, which the sun itself compresses and makes strong by its condensation'.[2]

The moon, like the sun and stars, is an 'incandescent stone'. It is below the sun, nearer to us, and its 'turnings' have the same cause as the sun's, but are more frequent 'because it cannot master the cold'. It is of earthy substance, though with some fire in it, and contains plains, mountains and valleys. It is also said to be habitable, 'with rivers and everything as on the earth', but this statement may well be based on an interpretation of fr. 4 as referring to the moon, which is unlikely.[3] The general impression given by the sources is that Anaxagoras believed the moon to be made of the same stuff as the earth, but hotter. It certainly makes sense (being in fact true) to say that the moon is like the earth with mountains and valleys without implying that it is inhabited.[4]

[1] *Nicias*, 23. For contemporary testimony we have Thuc. 2.28 (referring to the eclipse of 3 August 431 B.C.). For Anaxagoras on the cause of eclipses the authority is Hippolytus (*Ref.* 1.8.9, A42).

[2] Aët. 2.23.2 (A72), explained by Gilbert thus (*Meteor. Th.* 686, n. 1): 'In its passage from east to west, the sun thrusts the air aside northward and southward. This makes the air powerful, so that it opposes further progress to north or south and compels the sun to τροπή.' How exactly the ancients visualized a world in which this action and reaction of sun and air could take place is a question on which someone with a special interest in such matters might well throw some further light. Anaxagoras is following Anaximenes (A15), and a similar view may have been held by Anaximander and Diogenes. (See Lee, Arist. *Meteor.*, Loeb ed., p. 124, n. (a).) Herodotus believed that the sun could be driven off its course by storms (2.24), and the Epicureans thought of air-currents as a possible cause of the motion of the sun through the zodiac, of the moon and of the stars (Lucr. 5.637–49; Epicurus, *Ep.* 2, 93).

[3] Hippol. 1.8.6ff. (A42), and the passages collected in A77. These contain verbal echoes of the same source, namely Theophrastus. The moon has οἰκήσεις according to D.L. 2.8, οἴκησιν ἄλλην ποταμούς τε καὶ ὅσα ἐπὶ γῆς, Achill. *Isag.* 21, p. 49.4M. (A77). On the relevant passage in fr. 4, see p. 314 below.

[4] Kern (*De theogg.* 52 f.) saw in the statement that the moon is inhabited—for such he attributed to Anaxagoras—evidence that he was influenced by the Rhapsodic Theogony of the Orphics. (Cf. his *Orph. fr.* 91.) This is extremely unlikely. (See Guthrie, *Orph. and Gk. Rel.* 232.) He also argues that Anaxagoras used the theogony of Epimenides, on the grounds that Aelian attributes to Epimenides some lines which say that the Nemean lion fell from the moon. But the language of the passages in A77 (δοκεῖ, Schol. Apoll., μυθολογοῦσιν Achilles) in no way implies that Anaxagoras said this.

The belief that the moon is inhabited has a strongly religious, and specifically Pythagorean, flavour. It was attributed to Philolaus (vol. 1, 285); Aristotle said the Pythagoreans believed that

According to Aristotle, Anaxagoras shared with Democritus a curious theory about the nature of the Milky Way. They maintain, he says (*Meteor.* 345 a 25, trans. Lee), 'that the Milky Way is the light of certain stars. The sun, they say, in its course beneath the earth, does not shine upon some of the stars; the light of those upon which the sun does shine is not visible to us, being obscured by its rays, while the Milky Way is the light peculiar to those stars which are screened from the sun's light by the earth.'

Aristotle notes the obvious objection to this that the Milky Way should change with the sun's position. He also attacks it from the standpoint of greater astronomical knowledge, for it demands that the sun be smaller than the earth, whereas he knew it to be greater. It might also be asked how on this theory we can see the stars outside the Milky Way at night any more than in the daytime. Presumably, as Alexander in his commentary implies, what we see is (as with the moon) a reflexion of the sun's light, whereas the stars of the Milky Way are shining with their own.[1] At the least it was a brilliant guess that the luminous band in fact consists of myriads of separate stars.

His opinion about comets (of which he had seen a notable example, p. 303 above and Seneca, *Nat. Qu.* 7.5.3, A 83) was that they were a collection or conjunction[2] of planets, so near one another as to appear to be in contact. Shooting stars are thrown off in the sky like sparks, and quickly quenched (Hippol. 1.8.10, D.L. 2.9, Aët. 3.2.9, A 82). Nothing in the sources suggests that he connected them with the spectacular meteorite that fell in his time.

Pythagoras himself was one of the *daimones* inhabiting the moon (fr. 192 Rose, p. 136 Ross); the Islands of the Blest were the sun and moon in the Pythagorean catechism (Iambl. *V.P.* 82); Proclus attributes to Pythagoras and the *theologos* (i.e. Orpheus) a line which says that the moon has mountains, cities and halls (Kern, *Orph. fr.* 91). Cf. also Plato, *Tim.* 42 d. It is unlikely that Anaxagoras had much sympathy for Pythagorean beliefs. True, no less a scientist than Aristotle speaks of a kind of living creatures whose nature is fiery and who must be sought on the moon (*GA*, 761 b 15–23); but these would scarcely be human beings, and his dismissal of the idea as ἄλλος λόγος suggests that it is perhaps a concession to religious thought which did not greatly interest him.

[1] τὸ τούτων οἰκεῖον φῶς, Aristotle. See Heath, *Arist.* 83 f., Lee, *Meteorol.* 59 n. Briefer statements, taken from Aristotle or Theophrastus, are in Aët. (A 80), Hippol. (A 42, § 10) and D.L. 2.9.

[2] σύμφασιν, Arist. *Meteor.* 342 b 28, σύνοδον D.L. 2.9, σύνοδον...κατὰ συναυγασμόν Aët. 3.2.2 (A 81).

(8) *Earth and sea*

Ignoring or rejecting the different theories of Anaximander, Xenophanes and (if he knew of it) his contemporary Empedocles, Anaxagoras went back to Anaximenes for the view that the earth, which he still believed to have a flat surface like a tympanum, was supported on a cushion of air. This is stated by Aristotle, and the version of Hippolytus is that 'the earth is flat in shape, and remains aloft on account of its size, and because there is no void and the air, being very powerful, carries the earth riding upon it'. The theory is attributed also to Democritus, and its familiarity in the fifth century is attested both by the satire of Aristophanes, who in the *Clouds* makes Socrates pray to 'the lord and master, measureless Air, who holdest the earth aloft', and by a similar prayer in the *Troades* of Euripides to 'the chariot of the earth'. This last phrase is also used of the air in the Hippocratic treatise *De flatibus*. The notion that the air is a divinity which may be the object of prayer is of course foreign to Anaxagoras and Democritus, and must be taken from their contemporary Diogenes of Apollonia.[1]

The surface of the earth is porous, and it is riddled underneath with cavities. According to Aristotle, Anaxagoras said that earthquakes occur when *aither*, coming up from below, gets trapped in these hollows because the pores of the upper surface have become clogged with rain. The earth has both an upper surface (on which we live) and a lower (which presumably has not had its pores clogged, so that the air beneath can penetrate). Aëtius puts it that air gets in under the earth, is compressed and strikes the surface, then makes its surroundings shake because it cannot disperse. It is remarkable that Aristotle should use the word *aither*, which was the term used by Anaxagoras for fire. Even in his own vocabulary it does not mean air, of the dense sort that is underneath the earth, so it is probable that he is using the terminology of the earlier thinker. If this is so, both he and the doxographers are giving a partial account, and the full explanation

---

[1] Arist. *De caelo*, 294b13, quoted vol. I, 133; Hippol. 1.8.3 (A42); Aristoph. *Clouds*, 264; Eur. *Tro.* 884; Hippocr. *De flat.* 3 (VI, 94 Littré; DK 64, C2). Diogenes will have held the same theory, though the positive evidence is slight (a scholium on Basil, DK, 64 A16a).

is that given by Seneca, who describes the theory as involving both air and fire in conflict. Anaxagoras will then, as Gilbert suggested and as is very plausible, have connected earthquakes and volcanic eruptions.[1]

The cavities beneath the earth contain water, and rivers are formed both from these and from rain. The sea is partly fed by rivers, but in origin consists of water which lay on the earth or was drawn up from within it by the heat of the sun. Part of this was vaporized and the rest became salt and bitter. Aëtius seems to imply that this was due to 'burning' by the sun, but Alexander attributes to Anaxagoras and Metrodorus the view that water becomes salt by being filtered through the earth, which contains various salts and sharp-tasting substances. Possibly Anaxagoras combined both explanations.[2]

The cause of the Nile's summer floods aroused much curiosity among the Greeks, and Anaxagoras championed the view that they were due to the melting of snow among mountains further South, in Ethiopia. This is repeated not only by his reputed pupil Euripides but also by the other two tragedians Aeschylus and Sophocles. Since it is not far off the truth, it is a pity that Herodotus found it 'though the most plausible, the most erroneous view'.[3]

(9) *Meteorology*

His account of winds made use of Anaximenes's condensation–rarefaction theory, but (if our sources are to be trusted) in the opposite

---

[1] Arist. *Meteor.* 365 a 19, Aët. 3.15.4, Seneca, *Nat. Qu.* 6.9.1 (DK, A89). See Gilbert, *Meteor. Th.* 298–302. Aristotle himself explains earthquakes as caused mainly by wind trapped beneath the earth, and the winds themselves arise as a result of the heating and drying out of the earth both by the sun and by its own internal fire.

[2] Rivers: Hippol. 1.8.5. Anaxagoras's beliefs about the sea are restored from Hippol. para. 4, D.L. 2.8, Aët. 3.16.2, Alex. *In meteor.* 67.17 (quoting Theophr.: the last two in DK, A90). An Arabic translation of Galen (quoted by DK, A90) gives Anaxagoras as authority for the fact that water, when subjected to a high degree of heat, becomes salty or bitter. The process is explained in greater detail in the Hippocratic *De aere aq. loc.* 8: the heat draws up the finest and lightest parts of the water, and leaves the salty part which is denser and heavier.

[3] Hippol. 1.8.5, where the MSS. have ἐν τοῖς ἄρκτοις so that Aët.'s ἐν τῇ Αἰθιοπίᾳ is the safer reading (4.1.3, A91). The substitution may have been due to confusion with the different theory of Democritus (pp. 424f. below). See Gilbert, *Meteor. Th.* 529, n. 1. So also Seneca, *Nat. qu.* 4a, 2.17 (A91). Cf. Hdt. 2.22.1; Aesch. *Suppl.* 559, fr. 300; Eur. *Hel.* 3, fr. 228; Soph. fr. 797. Further comparative material will be found in Nauck's ed. of the fragments. The fact that Aeschylus (who died in 456) mentioned the theory does not rule out the possibility that Anaxagoras was its originator.

sense, for he said that they occur when the air is rarefied by the sun, not condensed or moistened.[1]

Thunder, lightning, thunderbolts, whirlwinds and the *prester* (for which see vol. 1, 463, n. 3) are all different effects of the downward rush of fire from the upper part of the sky to the colder regions of *aer*, causing a clash of hot and cold. Lightning is this fire as it pierces the clouds, thunder the noise of its being quenched in them, and so on.[2] Clouds and snow, says Aëtius (3.4.2, A85), he explained like Anaximenes. Hail is produced when a cloud is forced upwards and reaches a region where the temperature is lower because the reflexion of the sun's rays from the earth does not reach it. Then the water in it is frozen. Hailstorms are therefore more frequent in summer and in warm districts, because the heat forces the clouds further up from the earth.[3] On the rainbow we have Anaxagoras's own words (fr. 19): 'The reflexion of the sun in the clouds we call a rainbow. It is a sign of storm, for the water flowing round (?) the cloud creates wind or pours down rain.'[4] Empedocles also said that the rainbow brings wind or rain.[5] There is no evidence that Anaxagoras enumerated any of the colours of the rainbow as Xenophanes had done (fr. 32), or tried to explain them like Anaximenes (vol. 1, 139).[6]

[1] D.L. 2.9, Hippol. 1.8.11; contrast Anaximenes, A7 para. 7, A19. Hippol. adds: καὶ τῶν ἐκκαιομένων πρὸς τὸν πόλον ὑποχωρούντων καὶ ἀποφερομένων (ἀποφαινομένων O; ἀνταποφερομένων Usener, DK). Burnet translated: 'and when things were burned and made their way to the vault of heaven and were carried off.' This is not very illuminating. Gilbert (*Met. Th.* 519) thought Anaxagoras is saying that the sun carries off the burnt 'parts' of air to the poles, and supposed him to have had in mind the prevalence of N. and S. winds in Greece. For an explanation based on the more probable view that πόλος means celestial vault in general, see R. Böker in *RE*, 2. Reihe VIII A, 2.2235f., but what precisely was in Anaxagoras's mind remains difficult to grasp.

[2] Arist. *Meteor.* 369b14ff., Aët. 3.3.4, Seneca, *Nat. qu.* 2.12.3 (collected in A84), Hippol. 1.8.11. In the face of the substantial agreement of all these, the hasty jotting of D.L. 2.9 must be either a misunderstanding or a misattribution.

[3] Arist. *Meteor.* 348a15 (identified as Anaxagoras at b12); Aët. 3.4.2 (A85).

[4] On this fr. see now F. Solmsen in *Hermes*, 1963, 251f. Solmsen would read περιεχόμενον for περιχεόμενον.

[5] If indeed it was he. Tzetzes only attributes the line (fr. 50) to Ἐμπεδοκλῆς εἴτε τις τῶν ἑτέρων.

[6] Up to and including Aristotle, ancient science recognized only three colours in the rainbow: red, yellow or green, and blue or violet (πορφύρεον, φοινίκεον and χλωρόν Xenophanes, φοινικοῦν, πράσινον, ἁλουργόν Aristotle); except that Aristotle adds that between the red and the green band there often appears a yellow one (ξανθόν). See *Meteor.* 371b33–372a10.

Meteorology: One World or More?

(10) One world or more?

As with Anaximander, there has been controversy over the question whether Anaxagoras believed our world (*kosmos*) to be unique. It looks at least as if Theophrastus reported that he did. There is, it is true, little value in the lists drawn up by Aëtius of those who believed in one cosmos and those who believed in an infinite number; but his inclusion of Anaxagoras in the former category is supported by Simplicius, who writes:

Those who say that the cosmos is unique, like Anaxagoras and Empedocles, have no need of an infinity of elements, so that Empedocles does better to make them limited.[1]

It is also natural to conclude from a passage in Aristotle's *Physics* (250b 18–27) that he is classing Anaxagoras and Empedocles together as believers in one world only.

It might well be thought that the uniqueness of the cosmos is stated in surviving words of Anaxagoras himself, when he says (fr. 8): 'The things in the one cosmos are not separated from one another nor cut off with an axe.' It has been argued that these words refer only to the internal structure of the universe: it is one, a unity, because nothing in it is separated from anything else.[2] But this, whether true or not, is not in itself evidence of a plurality of worlds. The most that can be said is that, if there is external evidence of plurality, this fragment does not necessarily contradict it. In fact however the external testimony is all the other way.

The question is bound up with an interesting and puzzling passage in fr. 4. After a sentence (quoted on p. 288 above) about the mixture

---

[1] Aët. 2.1.2 (*Dox.* 327), partially quoted in DK, A63; Simpl. *Phys.* 178.25. Gigon, who argues for a plurality of κόσμοι in Anaxagoras (in which he thinks he was following Anaximander, but cf. vol. I, 106 ff.), makes no reference to this passage in Simplicius. He cites instead (*Philol.* 1936–7, 25) *Phys.* 27.17, where, speaking of Mind, Simplicius says that Anaxagoras made it the cause of movement and coming-to-be, 'by which things were separated, and brought into being τούς τε κόσμους καὶ τὴν τῶν ἄλλων φύσιν'. Simplicius has evidently been careless in one of the two passages, and the statement at 178.25 is much more definite and convincing than the vague and imprecise expressions used here. If τοὺς κόσμους means 'worlds', what is τὴν τῶν ἄλλων φύσιν? Of other disputants, Gigon notes that he is siding with Gomperz and Burnet against Zeller–Nestle and Capelle.

[2] So Gigon, *Philol.* 1936–7, 32 f.: 'in diesem einheitlichen Kosmos'.

of many things in all, and the immense variety of 'seeds', Anaxagoras continues with curious abruptness:

And [we must suppose that] men have been formed and all the other animals that have life; and the men have settled cities and cultivated fields as with us, and sun and moon and the rest as with us; and the earth grows all sorts of produce for them, the most useful of which they gather into their houses and use. This is my account of the separating off, that it must have taken place not only where we live, but elsewhere also.

The sudden indication, by the words 'as with us', that Anaxagoras is not describing the part of the world familiar to the Greeks, takes one by surprise.[1] His description of the moon as resembling the earth led some to suppose that it is referred to here, but it seems highly improbable that its inhabitants should have 'sun *and moon* as with us'. Others have therefore assumed that he is speaking of wholly different *kosmoi*, though there is no other hint of these in the fragments, and the external evidence, as we have seen, is strongly against it.

There is a third possibility, the only one which occurs to Simplicius apart from his own Neoplatonic theory of a contrast between the sensible and intelligible worlds. This is that Anaxagoras is referring to other parts of the earth's surface. In Plato's *Phaedo* (109b) Socrates mentions a belief that there are many hollows in the surface of the earth, with water in them forming seas and air above, and the inhabited world as known to the Greeks—'between the Phasis and the Straits of Gibraltar'—is only one of these, in which we live 'like ants or frogs round a marsh; many other men dwell elsewhere in many similar places'. Burnet, though in his *Early Greek Philosophy* he argued that Anaxagoras believed in innumerable worlds, says in his commentary on the *Phaedo*: 'As Wyttenbach saw, this part of the theory comes from Anaxagoras (and Archelaus)', and as Cornford saw, it almost certainly provides the key to fr. 4.[2] It does nothing to contradict the statements

---

[1] It is always possible that Simplicius, to whom alone we owe the fragment, has omitted something. Fränkel (*Wege u. Formen*, 287, n. 1) thinks it probable that fr. 4 is made up of three distinct quotations which do not belong together. Bailey (*Gk. Atomists and Epic.* 542) supposed τοῖς συγκρινομένοις in the first part of the fragment to refer to a plurality of 'compound worlds'!

[2] See further Cornford in *CQ*, 1934, 7f. Kahn (*Anaximander*, 52f.) agrees. I cannot make much of the unsupported statement of Gigon (*Philol.* 1936–7, 26) that Anaxagoras cannot have meant another part of the earth, 'denn die Erde scheidet sich als Eines und Ganzes ab, und nicht hier ein Teil und dort ein anderer'.

Yet another interpretation should be mentioned, though I do not find it convincing. H. Fränkel

of all our authorities that Anaxagoras believed in one cosmos only, which is in any case what his account of cosmogony would naturally lead one to expect, as we follow its progress from the initiation of the revolution by Mind to the formation of natural kinds.

(11) *Origin and nature of living things*

In general Anaxagoras adopted the widespread view that life first arose from moisture, heat and earth.[1] He thus continued the Ionian rationalization of a belief that went back beyond the beginnings of scientific thought, adapting it ingeniously to his own system. *Aer* (air, mist, cloud), as we have seen, was for Anaxagoras not a simple body but an amalgam of all the substances which went to make up plants, animals and inanimate objects. Consistently with this, Theophrastus writes: 'Anaxagoras says that the air contains the seeds of all things and these are brought down together with the water and generate plants.' The second-century Christian bishop Irenaeus says that this applied to animals too:[2] they were created *decidentibus e caelo in terram seminibus*.[3] His authority by itself would not be strong, but this too fits in with the general theory and may be allowed to supplement the bare statement that life arose from the wet, the hot and the earthy.

The way in which this scheme combines originality with an unconscious reflexion of older mythical descriptions of the same belief presents a fascinating paradox. In mythology Sky was the father who impregnated Earth the mother with the rain which was his seed, and it grew in the warmth of her bosom. Alternatively, to make the first woman the fire-god mixed earth and water.[4] For Anaxagoras the atheist,

(*Wege u. Formen*, 286 ff.) argued that the other inhabited region, duplicating 'ours', is a purely theoretical construction: *if* there were another world, it *would be* exactly like this one, even in its social institutions. In this interpretation Fränkel relies heavily on the optative οὐκ ἂν παρ' ἡμῖν μόνον ἀποκριθείη. He regards τῷ ἑνὶ κόσμῳ in fr. 8 as conclusive against the possibility of another cosmos.

The latest champion of a plurality of worlds in Anaxagoras is F. Lämmli, *Chaos zum Kosmos*, 1, 80, 92 ff. He thinks it is 'gesichert' by fr. 4.

[1] D.L. 2.9. Hippol. 1.8.12 simply says that living creatures were first born ἐν ὑγρῷ.

[2] And this, that air contained the seeds of all forms of life, which were washed down from it to the earth, probably accounts for the way that Aëtius (4.3.1, A93) bundles him together with Anaximenes and Diogenes of Apollonia as one of those who said that ψυχή was ἀερώδης.

[3] Theophr. *HP*, 3.1.4 (A117) and *CP*, 1.5.2; Irenaeus, 2.14.2 (A113).

[4] This theme is expounded at greater length, with texts, in Guthrie, *In the Beginning*, chs. 1 and 2. An example is the prayer in Euripides fr. 839: 'Divine *Aither*, Father of men and gods, and Earth who receivest the moist drops of the showers and bearest mortals, bearest plants and the tribes of beasts; whence rightly art thou called Mother of all.' For Anaxagoras cf. Guthrie, 55–7.

seeds are carried down from sky to earth by the rain, and germinated by heat.

Aristotle, not surprisingly, found it difficult to decide whether Anaxagoras identified Mind (*nous*) and life (*psyche*) or distinguished between them.[1] When he says (fr. 11) 'In everything there is a portion of everything except Mind, and in some things there is Mind too', he seems to be distinguishing the whole animate world from the inanimate. At its lowest level, *psyche* was that in living things which gave them the power of self-motion; at higher levels it was the faculty of cognition. By setting Mind at the source of all motion, Anaxagoras blended the two (as indeed they had been assimilated, though less explicitly, in much earlier thought); but for inanimate things it is an external force, for animate beings an internal faculty. Even plants have a degree of sensation and thought, as Empedocles also believed. If we can trust the ps.-Aristotelian *De plantis*, they feel pleasure and pain, and also breathe. They are in fact 'earthbound animals', a notion which was retained by Plato.[2]

'Mind is all alike', so the apparent difference of mental levels between different living things would appear to be due to difference in their bodily structure. This is confirmed by Aristotle in a passage which strikingly points the contrast between the mechanism of Anaxagoras and his own teleological outlook:

Anaxagoras says that man is the wisest of animals because he has hands, but it is reasonable to suppose that he received hands because he is the wisest. The hand is a tool, and nature like a wise man allots each tool to the one who is able to use it.[3]

---

[1] *De an.* 404b1, 405a13. Cf. p. 279 above, and Cherniss, *ACP*, 293.

[2] ζῷα ἔγγεια, Plut. *Qu. phys.* 911d (A116); [Arist.] *De plantis*, 815a15, b16 (A117). For Empedocles see p. 233 above, for Plato *Tim.* 77a, b: a plant is ἕτερον ζῷον and τῆς ἀνθρωπίνης συγγενὴς φύσεως φύσις. Cf. 90a: man is a φυτὸν οὐκ ἔγγειον. He continues: πᾶν γὰρ οὖν ὅτιπερ ἂν μετάσχῃ τοῦ ζῆν, ζῷον μὲν ἂν ἐν δίκῃ λέγοιτο ὀρθότατα. The idea of the kinship of all nature can find a home in two different worlds of thought in the Pythagorean and the Ionian traditions. See further p. 469 below (on Democritus).

[3] *Part. an.* 687a 7. The importance of the hand seems to have become somewhat of a commonplace. Cf. Xen. *Mem.* 1.4.11 and 14. The passage of Plutarch (*De fort.* 98f) given by DK as fr. 21b can hardly be said to add anything to Anaxagoras's opinions about human superiority to the beasts in mental faculties, owing to the difficulty of deciding how much is to be referred to Anaxagoras.

The dependence of mental capacity on bodily forms in Anaxagoras was upheld by Burnet and others, but denied by Zeller. See ZN, 1244f., and the references there.

On the question why men themselves are not all equally clever, Anaxagoras is said to have remarked that though all men have intellect they do not always use it. (See Psellus in A 101 a.)

There is evidence that he too was keenly interested in biological and physiological questions. His general theory that all living things breathed, says Aristotle (*De resp.* 470 b 30), made him turn his attention to fish, and he said correctly that they breathe through their gills. Sleep was a bodily, not a psychic affection, due to bodily exhaustion. There is little evidence of what he said about death, but his general theory left no room for individual survival.[1] Galen raises the question whether blood originates in the body or 'is interspersed with the food', and attributes the latter view to 'those who believe in homoeomers' (*De nat. fac.* 2.8, A 104). It is of course an integral part of Anaxagoras's general theory. Of disease, he said that acute diseases are caused by the gall-bladder overflowing and sending gall to the lungs, blood-vessels and flanks (Arist. *Part. an.* 677 a 5). On reproduction, he held that distinction of sex exists already in the seed, which comes entirely from the male parent, and that males are engendered by seed from the right-hand testicle[2] congealing in the right side of the womb. There is no mention of the effect of temperature as there is in Empedocles, who claimed that both parents provide semen and sex is determined by conditions in the womb.[3] Aristotle (*GA*, 756 b 13) chides Anaxagoras and others for their simplicity in believing that ravens and ibises copulate by the mouth, and among quadrupeds the weasel (*galē*) gives birth through the mouth.

[1] The only information is the sentence in the *Placita* (5.25.2, A 103): εἶναι δὲ καὶ ψυχῆς θάνατον τὸν διαχωρισμόν, which we must translate: 'separation (i.e. of a soul and body) is death to the soul also'. This may be a very crude, even inaccurate, rendering of anything that Anaxagoras himself said. The immediately following references to Leucippus and Empedocles on the same subject are not reassuring. But the survival as such of an individual soul, or portion of Nous, after the dissolution of the temporary bodily concretion which housed it, would contradict all the rest of his theory of reality, and he was no Empedocles to put beside it a doctrine of an indwelling *daimon*. Cf. ZN, 1248, n. 1; Rohde, *Psyche*, 388.

[2] Or perhaps simply the right-hand side of the body. See G. E. R. Lloyd in *JHS*, 1962, 60. The right–left distinction in reproduction is especially associated with the names of Parmenides (fr. 17) and Anaxagoras. For further details see Lesky, *Zeugungslehre*, 39 ff.

[3] Arist. *GA* 763 b 30, D.L. 2.9, Hippol. 1.8.12. Aëtius (5.7.4; DK 28, A 53) links Anaxagoras with Parmenides in the belief about right and left. Censorinus attributes to Anaxagoras, evidently erroneously, the belief of Empedocles and others that children resemble the parent who has contributed more seed (6.8, A 111; cf. pp. 218 f. above). On the association of male with right, female with left, cf. G. E. R. Lloyd, *loc. cit.* in previous note.

He followed Alcmaeon, and differed from Empedocles, in holding that the head, not the heart, was the central organ of perception, and that for this reason it was formed first in the embryo.[1]

(12) *Sensation*

Anaxagoras's notions on the mechanism of sensation, as summarized by Theophrastus,[2] seem rather crude. In general, he was opposed to Empedocles in saying that sensation was due to action between unlikes: if our sense of touch tells us that something is warm or cold, this is because the hand which touched it is colder or warmer. In general we see better by day, because most people's eyes are dark, and the objects are illuminated. Like many others, he thought it sufficient explanation of sight to say that it was due to the reflexion of the object in the eye. He claimed that the powers of sensation depended on the size of the sense-organ: animals with large, clear, lustrous eyes see large and distant objects, and so on. There is no attempt to relate the working of the separate senses to the statement that they all originate in the brain, except in the case of hearing, where it is said that it depends on the penetration of the sound to the brain; 'for the surrounding bone is hollow, into which the sound falls' (i.e. presumably the bone enclosing the brain).[3]

He pronounced that all sensation was accompanied by pain. This he deduced from the assumption that it was the affection of a sense-organ by something dissimilar to it,[4] but the notion not unnaturally met with considerable criticism in antiquity. As empirical evidence he adduced the discomfort caused by excessive or prolonged stimulation of the senses. Presumably the argument was that if sensation in a certain

---

[1] Censorinus, 6.1 (A 108). Cf. p. 219, n. 2 above.

[2] *De sensu*, 27 ff. For further details see Stratton's translation in *Greek Physiol. Psychol.* with notes, and the relevant parts of Beare, *Gr. Th. of Elem. Cogn.*; for the view that Aristotle and Theophrastus misunderstood Anaxagoras, Cherniss, *ACP*, 301, n. 40.

[3] There exists one other statement of Anaxagoras's account of hearing (Aët. 4.19.5, A 106): 'Anaxagoras says that sound occurs when breath [air in motion] collides with stable air, and by recoil from the impact is carried to the organs of hearing, in the manner of an echo.' Cf. Aristotle's remark (*De an.* 419b27) that there is probably an element of echo in all sound.

[4] Theophr. *De sensu*, 29. Aristotle presumably had Anaxagoras particularly in mind when he said in the *Nic. Ethics* (1154b7): ἀεὶ γὰρ πονεῖ τὸ ζῷον, ὥσπερ καὶ οἱ φυσιολόγοι μαρτυροῦσι, τὸ ὁρᾶν, τὸ ἀκούειν φάσκοντες εἶναι λυπηρόν. That was the interpretation of his commentator Aspasius (156.14, A 94).

Sensation and Knowledge

degree is acknowledged to occasion pain, the milder sensation must also cause it in a milder form, even if we are not always conscious of it. Theophrastus objected, among other things, that certain perceptions are accompanied by positive pleasure.

(13) *Theory of knowledge*

He emphasized the inadequacy of the senses, as this passage from Sextus shows (*Math.* 7.90, Anaxagoras fr. 21):

Anaxagoras with his exceptionally scientific outlook says in disparagement of the senses, 'owing to their weakness we are unable to discern the truth', and as proof of their untrustworthiness he adduces the gradual change of colour. If we take two colours, black and white, and pour one into the other drop by drop, our sight will not be able to pick out the gradual alterations although they exist in reality.

Cicero therefore was no doubt right in including Anaxagoras among others of the ancients who denied the possibility of attaining certain knowledge by human faculties alone, like Parmenides, Empedocles, Alcmaeon and Xenophanes.[1] Some of these, contrasting human uncertainty with divine omniscience, could claim to have received the truth from heaven, but this was not in keeping with the rationalistic Ionian tradition of which Anaxagoras was an outstanding representative. Although however he could not use this language (so far as we know, he never referred to Mind as God), he did believe that Mind knew everything, and that our participation in it enabled us to go behind the senses and infer the reality which underlay them. Only Mind can penetrate beyond the coarse organs of sense to become aware of the ultimate constitution of things. They perceive only 'that which predominates', but Mind knows that 'there is a portion of everything in everything'. This is implied by his pronouncement (fr. 21a) that 'phenomena are a sight of the unseen'. Aristotle, after quoting the lines of Parmenides which claim that our perception and understanding depend on the condition of the body, adds: 'There is also related a saying of Anaxagoras to some of his associates, that things would be for them such as they supposed them to be.'[2] 'Sayings' were attached

[1] Cic. *Ac. post.* 1.12.44. See p. 138 above and vol. 1, 398–400.
[2] Parmenides fr. 16, p. 67 above; Arist. *Metaph.* 1009b25.

319

very lightly to any of the great philosophers, and this one sounds more like an echo of one of the contemporary Sophists; but there was considerable mutual influence between the Sophists and the natural philosophers, and on the level of the average sensual man this is something like what Anaxagoras must have believed.[1]

(14) *Conclusion*

In his rationalistic and secular outlook Anaxagoras was a typical Ionian, who knew his Ionian predecessors, especially Anaximander and Anaximenes, and made use of their ideas. But he was an Ionian after Parmenides and Zeno, and his theories had to be adapted to their paradoxical but inescapable conclusions. His achievement is usually summed up as twofold: the idea of Mind as the moving, ordering and ruling force in the universe, and the theory of the structure of matter. The former has acquired special prominence in the light of later philosophy, especially its role in the teleological systems of Plato and Aristotle. Both of these acknowledged its novelty, but complained that Anaxagoras failed to make proper use of it. The role of Mind, in fact, had a recognizable ancestry in the divine substance which in the earlier Ionian systems 'rules over' (κρατεῖ) or 'steers' (κυβερνᾷ) the whole. The great difference was that, owing to the challenge of Parmenides on the subject of motion, the first cause of it has at last been separated from material substance in a clear-cut dualism. One must

[1] F. Lämmli, in the section of his book *Vom Chaos zum Kosmos* which he entitles 'Anaxagoras the "Sophist"' (I, 92–6), argues that Anaxagoras may very well have incorporated in or added to his cosmogony a more or less 'sophistic' doctrine of the origin of civilization. He therefore denies Jaeger's statement (*TEGP*, 164) that 'Anaxagoras's philosophy is physics through and through; it obviously contains no anthropology *in the theological sense* [oddly enough, these italicized words from the original are missing in Lämmli's quotation from the German edition] and completely lacks any centre of gravity of that sort'. In his own support Lämmli refers to Fränkel, *Wege u. Formen*, 285, who writes: 'The inclusion of culture and society in the sphere of things which are produced by a kind of ἀπόκρισις and σύνδεσις marks the system of Anaxagoras as anthropocentric, not physiocentric.' The evidence is mainly fr. 4, but there are of course one or two other passages which may show an interest in the origins of human culture, such as A 102 on the importance of the hands and fr. 21 b on man's use of the lower animals. There is also the general, macrocosm–microcosm point that, as Lämmli says, Nous must work in the same way in both, bringing about διακόσμησις. Nevertheless, though it is impossible to say what we have lost, the positive evidence for an interest in human affairs in Anaxagoras, comparable to that of the Sophists, is meagre. The statement of Favorinus (*ap.* D.L. 2.11) that he 'showed the subject of the Homeric poems to be virtue and justice' probably applies more particularly to his followers like Metrodorus, who 'defended the thesis further'. (I have translated the German of Lämmli and Fränkel.)

distinguish here, as often in the history of thought, between an idea in the mind of the man who first thought of it and its development by those who followed him. With the conception of Mind as the ultimate cause of order and regularity in the material world, and itself something separate from matter, independent and self-governing, the seed of a fully teleological view of nature has been planted, as Plato and Aristotle frankly admitted. Plato's Socrates 'rejoiced and thought that he had found a master after his own heart'; for Aristotle he was 'the first sober man'. The praise is as ready as the subsequent criticism is outspoken. The seed is sown, but it grew and flowered under the hands of others.

His originality and subtlety show themselves more plainly in his theory of matter, which lacked the simplicity of Democritean atomism, but must be given all credit for its ingenuity. The atomists were indebted to him for the notion of infra-sensible reality: 'phenomena are a sight of the unseen' (fr. 21), a saying which Democritus is said to have quoted with approval. It led him also to two other creditable achievements: the idea of the infinitesimal and an advance on the crude Milesian conception of 'opposites'. The hot and the cold are not 'separated or cut off from each other with an axe'—a step towards seeing them as points on a continuous scale.[1] His doctrine of matter carries us a stage further on the road to atomism, from which however it differed in two fundamental ways: in the principle of infinite divisibility, with which 'atomism' is a contradiction in terms, and in supposing that every particle of matter, however small, was endowed with all sensible qualities—including the 'secondary' qualities like colour, taste and smell which for Democritus were purely subjective—although, it might be, to a degree too small to be perceptible.

In one field his mechanistic type of explanation, and refusal to have any truck with contemporary animistic or other religious beliefs, was not altogether an advantage. The Pythagorean hypothesis that the celestial bodies moved according to mathematical laws was much more fruitful for astronomy than Anaxagoras's idea that they were dragged around by the whirling *aither*. But the rationally organized movements of the heavenly bodies were for the Pythagoreans bound up with their

---

[1] This is sometimes seen as polemic against Empedocles. See Vlastos, *Philos. Rev.* 1950, 38.

Anaxagoras

nature as animate, divine beings, and in abandoning what seemed to him a relic of superstition Anaxagoras abandoned also any stimulus towards the discovery of the laws of their motion.[1]

Additional notes

1. Chronology of Anaxagoras's life

D.L. 2.7 reports three accounts. (1) He 'is said' to have been 20 at the time of Xerxes's invasion of Greece and to have lived 72 years. (2) According to Apollodorus, he was born in Ol. 70 (500–497) and died in the first year of Ol. 78 (468, emended by Scaliger to Ol. 88, i.e. 428). Eusebius, DK, A4, similarly thought that his dates were c. 500–460. (3) According to Demetrius of Phalerum he began to 'philosophize' at Athens in the archonship of Callias at the age of 20, 'where also they say that he lived 30 years'. A Callias was archon in 456, but the archon of 480 was Calliades, for which Callias is only an alternative form (ZN, 1197; Taylor, CQ, 1917, 82, n. 1). If we accept with Scaliger that the mention of Ol. 78 is an error,[2] the three sources of Diogenes agree well, and there are many indications that Anaxagoras did not die in his prime and that he was active much later than 468. If he first came to Athens aged 20 'at the time of Xerxes's invasion', the chances are that he was a conscript in Xerxes's army, for as a Clazomenian he would be a Persian subject (Burnet, EGP, 254). Demetrius's report may have meant no more than that he became interested in philosophy as a student at that time.

The difficulties increase when we try to fit in the prosecution which led to his exile and so determine which were the 30 years that he spent at Athens. Diogenes already knew of contradictory versions. The strongest evidence is that the trial took place just before the beginning of the Peloponnesian War, not much earlier than 430. This is said by Diodorus (12.38f.), Plutarch (Pericles, 32) and Sotion (ap. D.L. 2.12). Cleon, whom Sotion names as the accuser, could not have acted thus at

---

[1] This is explained in more detail by B. L. van der Waerden, Science Awakening, 128.

[2] The alternative is to suppose with Davison (CQ, 1953, 40) that by γεγενῆσθαι Apollodorus meant 'flourished', as he plainly did when speaking of Anaximenes (D.L. 2.3), and had placed Anaxagoras about 40 years too early owing to his own mistaken idea (from Epicurean sources) that Democritus was born c. 500 and the statement attributed to Democritus himself that he was 40 years younger than Anaxagoras (p. 386 below).

a much earlier date. Plutarch says the prosecution was brought under the decree of Diopeithes for the impeachment of atheists and 'meteorologists', which must be dated *c.* 433. Diodorus mentions the trial as one of the causes of Pericles's unpopularity which led him to plunge the city into war. According to Sotion, the penalty was a fine of five talents plus exile. The other tradition known to Diogenes is represented by Satyrus, who said that the instigator of the trial was Thucydides, the charge was medism as well as impiety and Anaxagoras was sentenced to death *in absentia*. This would almost certainly have been before the ostracism of Thucydides son of Melesias in 443.

In spite of the championship of A. E. Taylor, the view that Anaxagoras was condemned and left Athens finally about 450 is scarcely tenable. J. S. Morrison (*CQ*, 1941, 5, n. 2) even thinks that it 'runs contrary to the whole weight of the evidence', and his continued presence at Athens at a later date is certainly hard to doubt. A difficulty is caused by the implication of Plato (*Phaedo*, 97b, 98b) that Socrates knew Anaxagoras only through his book and never met him. On this Zeller had something to say (ZN, 1199), but perhaps the most plausible conclusion is that Anaxagoras's thirty years in Athens (doubtless a round figure anyhow) were not continuous. This has been argued by Davison, who suggests that he was twice forced to leave Athens, once by the prosecution of Thucydides perhaps about 455, and then again, after returning under an amnesty some eleven years later, about 432. The alternative is to believe, as some do, that he first arrived in Athens 'in the archonship of Callias', i.e. 456, but apart from the statement that his arrival coincided with Xerxes's invasion, an intermittent sojourn in Athens between the 470's and the 430's certainly makes it easier to fit in the various reports about him, for example, that Themistocles knew him (Stesimbrotus *ap.* Plut. *Them.* 2) and Pericles was his pupil.

For further information and discussion see especially ZN, 1196–201; A. E. Taylor in *CQ*, 1917; J. A. Davison in *CQ*, 1953.

2. *Euripides and Anaxagoras*[1]

The sun a rock or 'golden clod', *Or.* 982ff., fr. 783. The earliest reference to the relationship between the two men is in a line of the poet

---

[1] See p. 269.

and librarian Alexander of Aetolia, who lived in the early third century B.C. (DK, A21). Others occur in Strabo 14.645 (A7), D.L. 2.10 and 45, Diod. 1.7.7 (A62), Schol. Pind. *Ol.* 1.91 (A20a), *Theol. arithm.* 6.18 de Falco (A20b), Cic. *Tusc.* 3.14.30. Allusions to Anaxagoras have also been seen in the following passages:

(*a*) *Hel.* 3, on the cause of the Nile floods. Cf. A91 and p. 311 above. But this occurs as early as Aeschylus (*Suppl.* 559ff.).

(*b*) *Tro.* 886. Cited as Anaxagorean by Satyrus (A20c, probably third century B.C.). But these lines 884–8 refer to the divinity of air which was becoming a commonplace (as is shown by the ridicule in Aristophanes's *Clouds*) and was most probably popularized by Diogenes of Apollonia.

(*c*) *Alc.* 903ff. and fr. 964 have been taken as a reference to the bereavement suffered by Anaxagoras when his son died (see DK, A33), though Nestle thought the reference in fr. 964 was more probably to Pythagoras (ZN, 1203, n. 2).

(*d*) Fr. 910. This is the famous fragment on the happiness of a life devoted to the study of the ageless order of nature. Though some (including Nestle, *loc. cit.*) have taken it as a probable allusion to Anaxagoras, Burnet not unreasonably says that it 'might just as well refer to any other cosmologist, and indeed suggests more naturally a thinker of a more primitive type' (*EGP*, 255).

(*e*) Fr. 484, on the original unity of heaven and earth (quoted in vol. I, 69, n. 2); this is quoted by Diodorus (1.7.7, A62) in connexion with the statement that Euripides was a pupil of Anaxagoras, but its reference is obviously far more general. See vol. I, 69.

(*f*) Fr. 839. This is very generally regarded as dependent on Anaxagoras, but the model may rather be Empedocles. See p. 262, n. 1 above.

(*g*) The papyrus fragments of Satyrus mentioned under (*b*) also quote the opening of fr. 912 as part at least of a rendering of the διάκοσμος of Anaxagoras, but it is not easy to see its relevance.

(*h*) The sense of Eur. fr. 574: 'By things present we judge the things unseen', is very close to the dictum of Anaxagoras that 'phenomena are a sight of the unseen (ἄδηλα)' (fr. 21a), and may well have been modelled on it. The language on the other hand (τεκμαιρόμεσθα

Euripides and Anaxagoras

τοῖς παροῦσι τάφανῇ) recalls rather Alcmaeon. Cf. his fr. 1: περὶ τῶν ἀφανέων...ὡς δὲ ἀνθρώποις τεκμαίρεσθαι.

Euripides entered with zest into all the intellectual excitements of his time, and his plays are full of allusions to the physical theories current in Athens. These are bound to reflect his acquaintance with Anaxagoras, but undoubtedly with others too, and it is not always easy to pin down a line of his verse to one particular philosopher as its source.

I have not seen L. Parmentier, *Euripide et Anaxagore*, Paris, 1893.

3. The words ὁμοιομερής, ὁμοιομέρεια

See Ross's edition of Arist. *Metaph.* I, 132, and Mathewson, *CQ*. 1958, 78 f. The word ὁμοιομερής does not occur in the extant fragments of Anaxagoras, and since later authorities use it to describe the key-conception of his doctrine one would expect it to be quoted at least once. It does not occur at all before Aristotle, and the idea expressed by it is carefully explained by Plato in the *Protagoras* (329 d–e; see Shorey, *CP*, 1922, 350) without the use of the term itself. Mathewson notes that of forty-five compounds in -μερής cited by Buck and Petersen none is pre-Aristotelian; also that the one thing in Anaxagoras that could be called ὁμοιομερής in the sense in which Aristotle uses the word is νοῦς and he does not use it of νοῦς.

Whereas Aristotle uses the adjective ὁμοιομερής with reference to Anaxagoras, the doxographers have more commonly the noun ὁμοιο-μέρεια, a word which is absent from Aristotle and first occurs in Epicurus. (See the word-index to Arrhighetti's ed., p. 646.) Three writers indicate their belief that this term was used by Anaxagoras himself.

(1) Simpl. *Phys.* 1123.23: τὰ εἴδη, ἅπερ ὁμοιομερείας καλεῖ. This is parenthetical, and it seems fair, if we wish, to characterize it with Mathewson (*loc. cit.* 78) as 'a single lapse' and 'not very disturbing'. It is contradicted by another sentence of the same writer, where he follows Aristotle exactly (*Cael.* 603.18): καὶ 'Α. τὰ ὁμοιομερῆ, οἷον σάρκα καὶ ὀστοῦν καὶ τὰ τοιαῦτα, σπέρματα ἐκάλει. (Aristotle has equated ὁμοιομερῆ with σπέρματα in the passage on which Simplicius is commenting, 302 a 29 ff.)

Anaxagoras

(2) Aët. 1.3.5 (DK, A46): ἀπὸ οὖν τοῦ ὅμοια τὰ μέρη εἶναι ἐν τῇ τροφῇ τοῖς γεννωμένοις ὁμοιομερείας αὐτὰς ἐκάλεσε καὶ ἀρχὰς τῶν ὄντων ἀπεφήνατο. This is more circumstantial, and introduces a point of considerable interest. The word ὁμοιομέρειαι here is not used synonymously with the ὁμοιομερῆ of Aristotle. It does not mean things whose own parts are like each other and like the whole thing, but things which are, or whose parts are, like the things of which they themselves are (or become) parts. Food, for instance, is called a ὁμοιομέρεια not as being homogeneous but because when eaten it turns into the bones and tissues of our body and therefore must have contained those 'parts' all the time. This is an accurate description of the material ἀρχαί of Anaxagoras.

(3) Lucr. 1.834 *rerum quam dicit homoeomeriam*. Here the word is given yet another sense, being used collectively of the whole mass of matter according to Anaxagoras's theory of its composition. Bailey (*Gk. Atomists*, 555) calls this use of the singular 'startling' and 'quite unique', but in fact it is used in the same way by Simplicius, *Phys.* 162.31: ἔνεστιν ἄρα ἐν τῇ ὁμοιομερείᾳ καὶ σὰρξ καὶ ὀστοῦν καὶ αἷμα κτλ. Lucretius's 'quam dicit' may well have been a natural, though erroneous, inference from a passage such as this. Bailey, noting that these uses of the noun could not have been developed from Aristotle's adjective, thought that these authors must be believed when they say that Anaxagoras used it himself. His 'surmise' (his own word) is that 'Anaxagoras himself probably used the substantive for the theory, ὁμοιομερῆ σπέρματα for the "seeds", and ὁμοιομερῆ for the substances composed of such seeds. The concrete use of ὁμοιομέρειαι for the seeds by the doxographers and commentators was then a later development.' (Lucr. vol. II, 745.) Perhaps this possibility cannot be ruled out, but the likelihood that the words are inventions of later date, and the doxographers mistaken, seems to me strong. Tannery spoke without further argument of 'le terme *d'homéomères* inventé par Aristote' (*Science Hellène*, 1st ed. 286). Of one thing we may be sure, that Aristotle uses ὁμοιομερῆ in his own sense, simply as a descriptive term to denote 'flesh, bone and other substances of that order'.

Translation of Passages

Selected passages on Anaxagoras's theory of matter

Aristotle, *Metaph.* 984a11: Anaxagoras says the *archai* are infinite, for practically all[1] the homoeomers are generated and destroyed as water or fire are,[2] by aggregation and segregation alone. They are not in any other sense generated or destroyed, but last for ever.

Idem, *Phys.* 203a19: Those who make the elements infinite in number, like Anaxagoras and Democritus (the one producing things from the homoeomers, the other from the totality of seeds of different shapes), say that the infinite is continuous by contact. According to Anaxagoras, every part is a mixture like the whole, because he saw everything coming to be out of everything. This seems to be why he says also that all things were once together: this flesh, this bone, and similarly anything else; everything therefore, and at the same time, for there is an original cause of the division not only in each separate case, but the same for all. For what is generated comes into being from a body of the same kind, and there is generation of all things (though not at the same time), hence there must also be some original cause of becoming. It is a single cause, that which he calls Mind, and Mind begins its work and thought from a certain starting-point. Hence all things must have been once together and set in motion at a particular time.

Idem, *GC*, 314a16: Empedocles posits four elements, or six with the moving causes, but Anaxagoras, Leucippus and Democritus say the elements are infinite in number. Anaxagoras makes the homoeomers elements, such as bone, flesh, marrow and whatever else has parts synonymous[3] with the whole, whereas Democritus and Leucippus... (a25) Anaxagoras plainly says the opposite to Empedocles, for Empedocles claims that the four bodies, fire, water, air and earth, are elements and are simple rather than flesh and bone and similar homoeomers. Anaxagoras on the other hand says that it is the homoeomers that are simple and elemental, and earth, fire, water and air are compounds, being in fact a collection of seeds of the others.

---

[1] σχεδὸν ἅπαντα in Aristotle. Vlastos is probably right in saying that the weakening of the generality of the proposition may be disregarded. Cornford and Mathewson suppose the meaning to be 'Anaxagoras says in effect that'.

[2] See p. 293, n. 2 above.

[3] On this word see p. 283, n. 1 above.

Idem, *De caelo*, 302a28: Anaxagoras is opposed to Empedocles on the subject of the elements. Empedocles's view is that fire and earth and the other substances of the same order are the elements of bodies, and everything is composed of them. According to Anaxagoras, on the other hand, the homoeomers are elements (flesh, bone, and other substances of that order), whereas air and fire are a mixture of these and all the other seeds, for each consists of an agglomeration of all the homoeomers in invisible quantities. That is why everything is generated from these two. (He makes no distinction between fire and *aither*.)

Idem, *Phys*. 187a20: Others say that the contrarieties were in the one and are separated out, for example, Anaximander and those who say that there are one and many like Empedocles and Anaxagoras; for they too separate other things out of the mixture. The difference between them is that one makes the process cyclical, the other once for all, and one posits an infinity of things, the homoeomers and the opposites, the other only the recognized elements. Anaxagoras's assumption of an infinite number appears to have been due to his acceptance of the universal view of the natural philosophers that nothing is generated from what is not. That is why they say things like 'All things were together' and 'To become such-and-such is only alteration',[1] while others speak of mixture and separation. Another reason was that the contraries are generated from each other and therefore must have pre-existed in each other; for if everything which comes to be is generated either from existing things or from the non-existent, and the latter is impossible (all writers on nature agree about that), they supposed the other alternative to be necessary, namely that things come into being from things that exist and are already present, but owing to their minute size are imperceptible to us. For that reason they say that everything is mixed in everything, i.e. because they saw everything coming into being out of everything; but things look different, and are called by different names, according to that which predominates numerically in the mixture of an infinite number of constituents. Nothing is purely and wholly white or black or sweet or flesh or

[1] Zeller (ZN, 1209, n. 1) took the words τὸ γίνεσθαι τοιόνδε καθέστηκεν ἀλλοιοῦσθαι to be a direct quotation from Anaxagoras, and Ross in his note on the passage agrees. But it is plain from the remarks of Simplicius at 163.9ff. (second paragraph of the next passage translated here) that the words ἀλλοίωσις or ἀλλοιοῦσθαι did not occur in the text of Anaxagoras.

bone, but the nature of each thing appears to be that of which it contains most.

Simpl. *Phys.* 162.26: Taking, then, as a prior axiom that nothing comes to be out of what is not, Anaxagoras seems to have put forward some such argument as this. What is generated is generated either from what is or from what is not. It cannot be from what is not, therefore it must be from what is. But if so, it must pre-exist in that out of which it has come, for it clearly cannot come in from anywhere outside, when wasps are generated from horses or vapour from water. Therefore in the homoeomery there are flesh, bone, blood, gold, lead, sweet and white, but in quantities too small to be perceived by us, all being in all. For how could everything be seen to be generated from everything (even if through other intermediaries) if everything was not in everything? But each takes its appearance and is named from that which most strongly prevails. In truth any given thing is not purely white or black or sweet or flesh or bone, but everything contains everything and the manifest nature of something is that of which it contains most. 'Nothing', says Anaxagoras, 'is either generated or destroyed, but they are mixed and separated from existing things.' Wherefore he says at the very beginning of his treatise, 'all things were together'.

The words 'to become such-and-such is only alteration' are said by Alexander to be aimed at Anaxagoras, because in *De generatione* [314a 13] Aristotle finds fault with him for calling aggregation and separation alteration. 'But Anaxagoras', he says, 'failed to understand what he said himself.' At any rate he says [here] that for any kind of thing to come to be or perish is only alteration; for he [Anaxagoras] did not use the actual name of alteration in speaking of aggregation and separation. Porphyry on the other hand refers the words 'all things were together' to Anaxagoras, but 'becoming is alteration' to Anaximenes and 'aggregation and separation' to Democritus and Empedocles. But Anaxagoras in the first book of the *Physica* explicitly calls becoming and perishing aggregation and separation in the words: 'The Greeks have a wrong conception of becoming and perishing. Nothing comes to be or perishes, but there is mixture and separation of things that exist. Thus they ought properly to call generation mixture and extinction separation.' All of these dicta—that all things were together, and that

coming to be is a matter of alteration or of aggregation and separation
—are meant to confirm the belief that nothing comes to be out of
what is not, but things generated are generated from what is; for
alteration is of what is, and aggregation and separation are of things
that are.

Arist. at *Phys.* 187b22 summarizes Anaxagoras's view thus: If all
such things are in each other, and do not come to be but are there and
are separated out, but are called after that of which there is more, and
anything comes out of anything (for example, water separated out from
flesh and flesh from water)....

Simpl. *Phys.* 26.31: Of those who say that the principles are infinite
in number, some make them simple and homogeneous, others compound, heterogeneous and contrary, but characterized by that which
predominates. Thus Anaxagoras son of Hegesibulus of Clazomenae,
after being associated with the teaching of Anaximenes, was the first
to change the doctrine of the principles and supplied the missing cause.
He made the corporeal principles infinite, saying that all homoeomerous
substances like water or fire[1] or gold are ungenerated and indestructible,
but give the appearance of coming into being and perishing through
aggregation and separation alone; for everything is in everything, but
each is characterized by that which predominates in it. That in which
there is much gold appears as gold, though everything is in it. What he
actually says is: 'In everything there is a portion of everything', and
'Those things are and were most plainly each thing, of which there are
most in it.'[2]...'Looked at in this way,' writes Theophrastus, 'Anaxagoras would appear to make the material principles infinite in number,
and the cause of motion and becoming one, namely Mind; but if the
mixture of all things is regarded as a single substance, indefinite both
in form and in size, which is what he appears to mean,[3] it results that he
posits two principles, the *apeiron* and Mind, and so turns out to be
describing the corporeal elements similarly to Anaximander.'

[1] See p. 64, n.2.
[2] I have omitted a few lines here owing to the doubt whether they refer to Anaxagoras or (as
the word ἐκεῖνος would naturally suggest) to Anaximander. McDiarmid (*Theophr. on Presoc.
Causes*, n. 64, pp. 142f.) refers them to Anaximander, Zeller, DK and Kirk (KR, 383, n. 1) to
Anaxagoras.
[3] This clause is added when the quotation from Theophrastus is repeated on p. 154. There are
a few other verbal differences between the two quotations.

Simpl. *Phys.* 460.4 (on Ar. *Phys.* 203a23): Seeing that Anaxagoras assumes the homoeomers, and Democritus the atoms as principles, each making them infinite in number, Aristotle examines the view of Anaxagoras first and teaches us the reason why he came to this opinion. He shows that he had not only to call the whole mixture infinite in size, but also to speak of each homoeomer as having everything in it just like the whole. They are not only infinite but infinite times infinite. To this view Anaxagoras was brought by his belief that (*a*) nothing comes to be out of the non-existent, and (*b*) everything is nourished by its like. He saw (*a*) that everything comes to be out of everything, if not directly then serially (as air from fire, water from air, earth from water, stone from earth, and fire again from stone), and (*b*) that by taking in the same food, for example bread, a great variety of things is brought into being—flesh, bones, veins, sinews, hair, nails, feathers also and horns in certain cases—and like is nourished by like; wherefore he supposed that these things are in the food. Similarly, assuming water to be the nourishment of trees, water contains wood, bark, leaves and fruit. Hence he said that everything is mixed in everything and coming-to-be takes place by separation. With reference to this, perhaps, he also argued that some things persist when others are generated from them, as fire from stone and air from bubbling water.

Seeing then everything being separated out from the things which are now distinct, as flesh and bone and the rest from bread, as if they were all mixed together in it, from this he concluded that all existing things were formerly mixed together before they became distinct. Hence he actually began his treatise thus: 'All things were together', so that everything is a mixture just like the All, for example this bread of this flesh and this bone. From the mixture of each single thing he arrived at the mixture of all things, for individuals are more manifest and more cognizable by sensation than are wholes...(461.7). From what has been said it is easy to see that if everything is separated out from everything and everything is in everything, not only the All but each individual thing will be infinite an infinite number of times over, not only numerically but also in size.[1]

---

[1] If this means that things must be infinitely large, it is a careless statement. Anaxagoras's theory was more subtle. (See pp. 289f.)

Aët. 1.3.5 (A46): Anaxagoras son of Hegesibulus of Clazomenae declared the principles of existing things to be the homoeomers. It seemed to him a baffling problem how anything can come into being out of what is not, or perish into what is not. Yet we take in nourishment which is simple and uniform, bread and water, and from this nourishment grow hair, veins, arteries, flesh, sinews, bones and the other parts of the body. Since this happens it must be admitted that the food which is taken in contains all existing things, and everything is increased from what exists. In that food are particles (μόρια) which can produce blood and sinews and bone and the rest—parts which are discernible by reason. We must not refer everything to sensation, saying that bread and water produce these things; rather, there are in bread and water particles discernible by reason. From the fact that the parts in the food are the same as what is produced, he called them homoeomers and declared them to be the principles of existing things. The homoeomers are the matter, and Mind is the creative cause which set all things in order. He begins thus: 'All things were together, but Mind separated and set them in order.'

Simpl. *Phys.* 155.4: 'Aristotle adds the opposites in Anaxagoras's case,' says Alexander [the reference is to τά τε ὁμοιομερῆ καὶ τὰ ἐναντία at 187a25], 'because the contrarieties are in the homoeomeries as are all qualitative differences.' Yet in the Empedoclean elements there are also contrarieties, of hot and cold, dry and wet, heavy and light and so on, so the words 'and the opposites' are equally appropriate to either doctrine; unless it be that the elements contain *some* contrarieties but the homoeomers embrace them all at once as they do all qualitative differences, and on that account the addition is more appropriate to Anaxagoras. Yet one might say that the elements too contain all the opposites, since they are first principles, only not all immediately as do the homoeomers. Where sweet and bitter are present on the hypothesis of the elements, they are not in the elements directly, but because of heat and cold and dryness and wetness, whereas in the homoeomers they exist primarily and essentially, as also the contrarieties of colour. Yet even in the homoeomers some contrarieties are prior to others and the secondary are brought about by the primary. Anaxagoras himself says in the first book of his *Physics*: 'Water is separated off from clouds, earth from water; and from the earth stones are compacted by cold, and they move outwards more than water.' His view that homoeomers infinite in number become separated off from a single mixture, all things being in everything but each one characterized by that which predominates, he makes clear by what he says at the beginning of the first book of his *Physics*:

'All things were together, infinite both in number and in smallness, for indeed the small was infinite. And when all things were together, none was discernible because of their smallness, for air and *aither* embraced all things, both of them being infinite; for these are the greatest in the collection of all things both in number and in size.' A little later he says: 'Air and *aither* become separated off from the mass surrounding, and the surrounding is infinite in number.' And a little later: 'This being so, we must suppose that there are many things of all kinds in all the things that are being mingled, and seeds of all things with every sort of shapes and colours and flavours. Before they were separated,' he says, 'since all things were together not even any colour could be discerned. This was prevented by the mixture of all things—the wet and the dry, the hot and the cold, the bright and the dark, since there was much earth in it and an infinite number of seeds in no way resembling each other; for not even any of the other things resemble each other.'

That none of the homoeomers is generated or destroyed, but they are always the same, he makes plain in the words: 'Now that these things have been thus separated, it must be recognized that all things are neither less nor more. It is not possible that there should be more than all, but all are for ever equal.'

So much for the mixture and the homoeomers. On Mind he writes as follows:

The rest have a portion of everything, but Mind is something infinite and independent, and is mixed with no thing, but alone and by itself. If it were not by itself, but were mixed with any other thing, it would have had a share of all things if it were mixed with any, for there is a portion of everything in everything, as I have said before. And the things mixed in it would have prevented it from controlling anything as it can when alone and by itself. It is the finest and purest of all things, and has all judgment of everything and greatest power; and everything that has life, both greater and smaller, all these Mind controls; and it controlled the whole revolution, to make it revolve in the beginning. At first it began to revolve in a small part, but now it revolves over a larger field and will include a larger one still. And the things that are being mingled and those that are being separated off and divided, Mind determined them all. Mind set everything in order, what was to be, what was but is not now,[1] and all that now is and shall be, and this revolution in which revolve the stars, sun, moon, air and fire that are being separated off. This revolution caused the separating off. The dense is separated from the rare, the hot from the cold, the bright from the dark, the dry from the wet. There are many portions of many things, and no one thing is completely separated or divided from another save Mind. Mind is all alike, both the greater and the smaller. Nothing else is like anything else, but those things are and were most plainly each thing, of which there are most in it.

That he supposes a twofold ordering, intelligible and sensible, is clear from the foregoing, and also from this:

'Mind, which is for ever, is assuredly even now where all other things are also, in the great quantity surrounding and in the things which have been brought together and those which have been separated.'

Moreover after the words 'there are many things of all kinds in all the things that are being mingled, and seeds of all things with all sorts of shapes and colours and flavours, and men and the other living creatures have been formed', he goes on, 'and the men have settled[2] cities and cultivated fields as with us, and sun and moon and the rest as with us, and the earth grows all sorts of produce for them, the most useful of which they gather into their houses for use'.

At 35.8 Simplicius adds the next sentence of the quotation: 'This then is my account of the separating off, that it cannot have taken place only where we are but elsewhere also.'

Simpl. *Phys.* 164.13 (on Arist. 187b7ff.): Anaxagoras sets out a number of conclusions or assumptions, each of which, as it seems to me

---

[1] Supplied from 177.5.
[2] συνημμένας here, but at 35.4 συνῳκημένας, which seems more likely.

(or almost all), Aristotle now proceeds to counter. That the principles were infinite he says right at the beginning: 'All things were together, infinite both in number and in smallness', and that there is neither a smallest nor a largest among the principles: 'Of the small', he says, 'there is no smallest, but always there is something smaller; for it is impossible that what is should not be. Similarly there is always a larger than the large, and it is numerically equal to the small. In relation to itself everything is both large and small.' For if everything is in everything, and everything is separated out from everything, even from that which seems smallest something smaller than it can be separated out, and what seems largest has been separated out from something larger than itself. He says explicitly: 'Everything contains a portion of everything else except Mind, and some things even contain Mind'; and again: 'the rest have a portion of everything, but Mind is something infinite and independent and is mixed with nothing.' Elsewhere he says: 'And since both the large and the small have portions equal in number, in this way too everything must be in everything. Separate existence is impossible, but everything has a portion of everything. When it is impossible for there to be a smallest, nothing can become separated or by itself, but just as in the beginning, so now also all things are together. Everything contains many things, the larger and the smaller containing an equal number of the things which are being separated off.'

Anaxagoras also believes that each of the perceptible homoeomers comes into being and acquires its character from an aggregation of similars. He writes: 'Those things are and were most plainly each thing, of which there are most in it.' He seems to say too that Mind tries to separate them but cannot.

In combating such assumptions of Anaxagoras, Aristotle starts by contradicting the assertion of an infinite number of principles.

Ibid. 166.10: Anaxagoras, by making his principles infinite not only in number but also in kind, must accept the unreasonable consequence which seems to follow, that the products of these principles also are unknowable.

Ibid. 167.7: It is not possible to have a piece of flesh of any size you like, since flesh is a part of an animal, and the animal itself, of which it is a part, will be of corresponding size. But it is of such homoeomerous substances, according to Anaxagoras, that animals are composed, and into them they are resolved, for in his view there is nothing more ultimate. Therefore their size too is limited to the point to which it can increase without abandoning its own kind. If anyone objects that every magnitude is infinitely divisible and therefore whatever amount you take there is always a smaller, he must understand that the homoeomers are not simply magnitudes but already magnitudes of certain kinds—flesh, bone, lead, gold and so forth—which cannot be divided to infinity and still keep their specific character. As magnitudes, they too are infinitely divisible, but as flesh and bone they are not.

Ibid. 35.13: Hear too what he says a little later [Simplicius has just quoted fr. 4] when he is making a comparison of both [*sc.* the states of mixture or unity and separation]: '...as these things revolve and are separated off by force and swift movement. It is the swiftness that exerts the force. Their speed is like that of nothing that now exists in the world of men, but assuredly many times as fast.'

Ibid. 175.11: Anaxagoras said, 'One thing is not divided or separated off from another', because everything is in everything; and elsewhere, 'Things are not cut off with an axe, neither the hot from the cold nor the cold from the hot', for nothing exists by itself in purity.

Ibid. 176.17: Anaxagoras however did not say outright, so far as I know, that Mind tries to separate the homoeomers but it is impossible for it to do so. He said rather that it is Mind that sets in motion and makes to rotate and is the cause of all separating out; for after saying that Mind is the cause of the revolution, he adds, 'and this revolution caused the separating off. The dense is separated from the rare, the hot from the cold, the bright from the dark, the dry from the wet.' It is a little after this that he goes on, 'No one thing is completely separated or divided from another'. Clearly then when he says 'the dense is separated off from the rare', etc., it is in a different sense from 'one thing is not separated off from another'. And when he speaks of generation from each other, he does not mean from all things (he does not say that a line is separated off from what is white), but from contraries, as when he says elsewhere, 'the things in the one universe are not separated from one another nor cut off with an axe'.

Simpl. *Cael.* 608.24 (after quoting the opening of fr. 1 with its mention of *apeiron* and *apeira*): By *apeira* he probably meant incomprehensible and unknowable to us. This is shown by the words 'so that we cannot know the number of the things being separated off, either theoretically or in practice'. That he believed them to be finite in kind, he makes plain; for he says that Mind knows all things, but if they were literally infinite, they would be altogether unknowable, since knowledge limits and sets bounds to what is known. 'Mind knows all things,' he says, 'both those that are being mingled and those that are being separated, both what was to be and what was.'[1]

Simpl. *Phys.* 300.29: That he uses Mind as an agent of genesis is plain, seeing that he says becoming is nothing but separation and the cause of separation is Mind. What Anaxagoras writes is: 'After Mind initiated motion, it began to withdraw from all that was moved, and all that Mind moved was divided. And as motion and division went on, the revolution caused it to be divided much more.'

Ibid. 178.33 [Empedocles made the elements finite in number, Anaxagoras infinite,] if indeed Anaxagoras was supposing that the compounds, and not the simple and archetypal qualities, were elements when he wrote: 'and this revolution caused the separating off. The dense is separated off from the rare, the hot from the cold, the bright from the dark, the dry from the wet.' And a little later: 'The dense, wet, cold and dark collected here where they are now, and the rare, hot and dry receded to the further region of the *aither*.' These simplest archetypes he says are separated off, and other things more complex than they are, he says, sometimes put together as compounds and sometimes separated off as is earth. He puts it thus: 'From these things as they are separated off, earth is compacted; water is separated off from the clouds, and earth from water, and from the earth stones are compacted by the cold.' By going back to the simple forms in this way Anaxagoras will appear to have brought his philosophy of the elements closer to first principles than Empedocles did. Possibly Aristotle and Plato, and the Pythagoreans before them, came nearer to positing completely elemental

[1] From fr. 12, but cf. p. 273, n. 2 above.

principles, namely matter and form, and even nearer those who assumed variety of shape in a qualityless body to underlie the qualitative differences of the elements, believing it to be close to ultimate matter, and assigned the pyramid to fire and other figures to the other elements. Democritus seems to have grasped this clearly, but falls short of the goal in that he did not go on to analyse the simple bodies into form and matter.

V

ARCHELAUS

Life and range of interests. Our sources are agreed that Archelaus was a pupil of Anaxagoras and teacher of Socrates. His association with Socrates is reported from their contemporary Ion of Chios as well as occurring in later sources, and the fact that he was the older man gives us our only information as to his date.[1] He was an Athenian,[2] and his position between Anaxagoras and Socrates acquired a symbolic significance: he was called the last of the physical philosophers, owing to the over-simple assumption in later antiquity that 'Presocratic' philosophy had been interested in 'the nature of things' whereas Socrates turned it immediately and completely away from that to the problems of human life. Hippolytus for instance writes (1.10) that 'natural philosophy lasted from Thales to Archelaus, whose pupil was Socrates'.[3]

On his writings we have only the statement of the Suda that he 'composed a *physiologia* and considered that right and wrong were not by nature but by convention. He also wrote some other works'. Nothing has survived, save possibly four words in Plutarch (fr. 1a in DK), and on the evidence he seems to have been a distinctly minor, and probably not very clear thinker. The reference to right and wrong may

[1] Wilamowitz (*Glaube*, 2.212) takes Plutarch's statement that he composed a poem for Cimon (*Cim.* 4) as an indication both of his date and of the fact that he belonged to the 'vornehme Gesellschaft'. On the credentials of Plutarch's statement cf. Heinimann, *Nomos u. Physis*, 112, n. 7. (Cimon died in 449.)

[2] The variant ἢ Μιλήσιος occurs only in D.L. 2.16 and the Suda. Both retail also the statement that he was the first to bring philosophy from Ionia to Athens, which favours an Ionian birthplace for him. In fact this distinction belongs to his teacher Anaxagoras, of whom ps.-Galen's *Hist. of Philos.* says that he 'came to Athens and interested Archelaus the Athenian in philosophy' (DK, 59 A 7).

[3] The other authorities for the above paragraph are in the short section 60A of DK. There is one report that he succeeded to the school of Anaxagoras at Lampsacus (p. 268 above). The report of Ion of Chios (D.L. 2.23) is that as a youth Socrates went abroad (ἀποδημῆσαι, a word sometimes used of military service) to Samos with Archelaus. Burnet (*EGP*, 358, n. 5) remarked that if this should refer to the siege of Samos, it is interesting to think of the youthful Socrates serving against a force commanded by Melissus (p. 101 above). The hypothesis is calmly converted into a certainty by Heinimann ('er zog im Jahre 441 mit gegen Samos', *N. u. Ph.* 112), but this oft-repeated embellishment of Ion is vigorously and effectively denied by Jacoby in *CQ*, 1947, 9–11. See also Pohlenz, *Hermes*, 1953, 432, n. 2.

be intended to indicate a separate work on ethical matters. He was commonly called 'the physicist', but Sextus (*Math.* 7.14, A6) says that he pursued both the physical and ethical sides of philosophy, and Diogenes (2.16) that he 'appears to have treated of ethics, for he philosophized about laws and things fair and just', adding the statement about the conventional character of right and wrong. The doxography in Hippolytus (1.9.6, A4) makes it clear that he carried his account of the origins of the world and life down to the beginning of human societies, laws and arts. As a contemporary of the early Sophists, he may well have accepted their favourite antithesis between nature and convention. In view of his comparatively early date, he may even, as the sentences in Diogenes and the Suda seem intended to imply, have pioneered it. From the brief indication in Hippolytus, one can imagine him following the same line as Protagoras in the speech put into his mouth by Plato: morals and law were not an original gift of nature, but acquired in course of time and by bitter experience. More than this one cannot say, but it is useful to be reminded that we are now entering the ferment of the Sophistic enlightenment at Athens, and it is unlikely that any Athenian philosopher was left untouched by it.[1]

Physical principles. The late accounts of his natural philosophy are in parts obscure. This may be due to faulty tradition and confusion with Anaxagoras, but the impression is irresistible that while following his master in many respects, he tried hard also to be original but was incapable of doing so successfully. Theophrastus, recorded by Simplicius, wrote: 'In cosmogony and the rest he tried to make an original contribution, but posited the same *archai* as Anaxagoras. Both assume the homoeomers, making the *archai* infinite in number and heterogeneous.'[2]

Like Anaxagoras he set Mind at the beginning, but he denied its complete purity and separateness: 'even Mind contains mixture' (Hippol. 1.9.1, A4). Mind was the original cause of motion, and, for one of our witnesses, of combination and separation. But it is nowhere

---

[1] Discussions of the subject are in ZN, 1276f., and the authors cited by Nestle, ZN, 1277, n. 1 *ad fin.*; also Heinimann, *N. u. Ph.* 113f., Pohlenz, Hermes, 1953, 431–5. For Protagoras see Plato, *Prot.* 322aff. On the general relation between 'physical' philosophy and humanism see the next chapter.

[2] Simpl. *Phys.* 27.23, A5. Apart from his general history of 'physical opinions', Theophrastus wrote a special work περὶ τῶν ᾿Αρχελάου (D.L. 5.42).

said that it is a source of *order*, indeed in the *Placita* it is expressly denied the title of 'cosmopoeic', and Archelaus seems to have been even more open than Anaxagoras to the charge of leaving the making of the universe to the casual interplay of mechanical natural forces.[1]

Although he used the same *archai* as Anaxagoras (in Hippolytus's version, 'described the mixture of matter as Anaxagoras did, and the *archai* likewise'), he also said that the *arche* or element is *aer* 'and its condensation and rarefaction'. So Aëtius, from whom we also have the brief and surprising pronouncement that he 'called *aer* and Mind the God', and another that 'the cosmos arose from heat and animation'.[2] One can only suppose that, seeing certain affinities between Anaxagoras and earlier Ionian thought, particularly Anaximenes, he tried to bring them even closer by abandoning the pure aloofness of Mind and explaining the animate, self-moving *aer* of Anaximenes as a mixture of Mind and matter—going right back, in fact, to the naïve hylozoism of Anaximenes fr. 2, with its identification of *aer* and life (*psyche*). To identify *aer* with the original 'all things together' was easy, when Anaxagoras himself had said that at this stage '*aer*-and-*aither* embraced all things' (fr. 1, pp. 294f. above). That this is what Archelaus did is the most reasonable conclusion from the doxographers, but although they are seldom models of accurate interpretation, their inconsistency in this case is so excessive as to make one suspect that it goes back to a certain confusion in Archelaus himself. Besides the definite statement that the *arche* and element is *aer*, we are told that the *archai* are hot and cold, or that hot and cold are the two causes of coming-to-be, that the *arche* of motion is the separation of hot and cold from each other, and once that the *arche* of everything is earth![3]

[1] Everything is moved by Mind, Philop. *De an.* 71.17 (A18); 'mentem, quae...particulas coniungendo et dissipando ageret omnia', Aug. *Civ. Dei* 8.2 (A10); οὐ μέντοι κοσμοποιὸν τὸν νοῦν, Aët. 1.7.15 (A12). This sounds like a direct contradiction of Anaxagoras, and hardly an improvement.

[2] ἐμψυχίας. Meineke conjectured the otherwise unknown ἐμψυχρίας to obtain the expected antithesis 'from heat and cold'. (See DK, 10th ed. II, 421.)

[3] ἀήρ is the ἀρχὴ καὶ στοιχεῖον Sext. *Math.* 9.360; the ἀρχή is ἀὴρ ἄπειρος καὶ τὴν περὶ αὐτὸν πύκνωσιν καὶ μάνωσιν, Aët. 1.3.6 (A7). ἀπὸ θερμοῦ καὶ ἐμψυχίας (see previous note) συστῆναι τὸν κόσμον, idem, 2.4.5 (A14). Hot and cold as primary causes, D.L. 2.16, Herm. *Irris.* 11 (A8), cf. Hippol. 1.9.2. On this cf. Reinhardt's note, *Parmenides*, 225, n. 1. Only Epiphanius (*Adv. haer.* 3.2.9, A9) accuses Archelaus of saying ἐκ γῆς τὰ πάντα γεγενῆσθαι, αὕτη γὰρ ἀρχὴ τῶν ὅλων ἐστίν. This was probably a mistaken transference to the origin of the universe of what Archelaus said on the origin of life, as happened with Xenophanes (vol. 1, 383–6).

Cosmogony. The original mixture, we may conclude, resembled a
dark mist, and from this the hot and the cold were the first to be
separated out, as from Anaximander's *apeiron* but by Anaximenes's
process of condensation and rarefaction. This is essentially a repetition
of Anaxagoras (p. 301 above). They took the form of fire and water
(Aët. 1.3.6, A7). The water, 'melted' by the hot, flowed to the centre,
and by further cooling condensed into earth.[1] The earth is 'mastered'
(kept in position) by the air, and the air in turn by the revolution of the
fire outside it. Thus the earth is at rest in the centre (for it is a property
of the hot to move and the cold to stay still), and is a very small part
of the whole.[2]

The air (not the original air, but that produced by the 'fire-process',
i.e. presumably by the action of heat from the water condensed out of
the primal air), as it is further burned up, becomes the stars, of which
the sun is the largest, the moon second, and the others of varying sizes.
They are described in the words of Anaxagoras as fiery lumps of stone
(Aët. 2.13.6, A15). Before the tilting of the heavens the sun did not
shine upon the earth: only afterwards did the sun give it light, dry it
up, and make the air transparent.[3] Earlier the earth was a watery swamp,
high round the rim and hollow in the middle. This concavity explains

---

[1] This is supported by the only words which may be a direct quotation from Archelaus:
'coldness is the bond of the earth', or that which holds it together (Plut. *De primo frig.* 954f,
fr. 1a). It is here, however, that our sources, or Archelaus himself, show the greatest confusion.
D.L. 2.16 is corrupt, but at least agrees with Hippolytus that water changes not only into earth
but also into *aer*, which, cosmogonically speaking, is unnecessary since *aer* was there at the
beginning. Of course once the cosmos was formed, evaporation continues to take place so that
some water is continually changing back into vapour. Hippolytus says that the water becomes
not only air but also earth 'by being burned'. τηκόμενον τὸ ὕδωρ (Hippol. 1.9.2, A4) apparently
means 'came into being by the melting (of something else)', a curious use of the word. At Plato,
Tim. 49c, water is more naturally said τήκεσθαι when it dissolves into air.

[2] Hippol. 1.9.3 (A4), D.L. 1.17. In view of D.L.'s words ἡ μὲν (*sc.* γῆ) ὑπὸ τοῦ ἀέρος κρατεῖται
it would seem more likely that the missing words in the passage of Hippolytus are τὸν δ' ἀέρα
κρατεῖν τῆς γῆς, rather than τοῦ παντός. The latter is supplied by Roeper and DK, no doubt
because the omission of the clause can then be explained by haplography. The previous
sentence ends with τοῦ παντός.

[3] So Hippol. 1.9.4. Originally, says Zeller (ZN, 1274), the stars 'revolved sideways round the
earth, which therefore lay in continuous shadow behind its raised rim'. So also Dümmler,
Akademika, 106: before the ἐπίκλισις the sun, circling round the horizon, was invisible on
account of the raised edges of the earth, and the earth was dark and miry. Anaxagoras with his
flat earth is supposed by Zeller to have drawn the opposite conclusion when he said the same thing,
namely that the cosmos became inclined relatively to the earth at a late stage of the creative
process (p. 305, n. 2 above): he brought animals to life before this event 'because the sun could
still shed its influence continuously on the earth' (ZN, 1247 n.).

why the sun does not rise and set at the same time in different parts of the inhabited world. It represented a departure from Anaxagoras, but was adopted by Democritus.[1]

Living creatures. There are two accounts of what Archelaus said about the origin of animal life:

(*a*) D.L. 2.17: He says that the animals were born from the earth when it was warm, and it sent up an ooze resembling milk to serve as nourishment: it produced men in the same way.

(*b*) Hippol. 1.9.5 (A4): Concerning animals he says that when the earth grew warm first of all in its lower part, where hot and cold were blended, many kinds of animals appeared, including man. All had the same diet, being nurtured on the ooze, and they were short-lived. Later on they were engendered from each other.

The origin of animals and men from the earth, under the action of heat, reflects once again a very old belief which had already been rationalized by several philosophers, including Anaximander and Empedocles (pp. 59, 200, 207 above). Moisture as well as heat is necessary, and though that is not mentioned in these brief statements we know that for Archelaus the earth started as a swamp or lake (λίμνη). The analogy between the procreative earth and a human mother was taken seriously,[2] and here it is carried a stage further in that the earth provides a milky fluid to nourish its offspring. This is the first appearance of this strange notion, which was taken up later by the Epicureans.[3]

Archelaus copied Anaxagoras in saying that Mind is present in all animals alike, though some are slower and others quicker to use it (Hippol. 1.9.6). Theophrastus did not think his theories of sense-perception worthy of mention in his own history of the subject, so they were probably not original. We know nothing of them except

---

[1] 68A94, cf. 59A42 §3 and A87.

[2] E.g. Plato, *Menex.* 238a: 'In pregnancy and childbirth it is a woman who imitates the earth, and not the other way round', and the quotation from *De nat. pueri* on p. 299, n. 2.

[3] In the zoogony of Diod. 1.7, which contains much early material (see p. 210, n. 1 above) the embryo animals in the 'wombs' that formed on the surface of the earth are nourished by a kind of dew or mist (ὀμίχλη) which fell at night. For the theory in Epicureanism see especially Lucr. 5.805–15. It became a commonplace, and is vividly described by Dio Chrysostom, *Or.* 12.29–30: 'The first of them, those who were born from the earth, had the earliest kind of food, that which comes from the earth, for the ooze was then soft and rich and they lapped it from the earth as from a mother, in the same way as plants draw the moisture from it now.'

for the erroneous statement in Diogenes (2.17) that he 'was the first to say that sound is produced by concussion of the air'.

Conclusion. Archelaus was a pupil of Anaxagoras who accepted his teacher's theory of matter, but, it would seem, said little about it and concentrated on the development of the cosmos from the hot and cold which first separated out from the original *aer*-like mass and might be considered as the *archai* of the present world. It is natural that he should have passed quickly over the 'homoeomerous' theory of matter, since that had been dealt with in masterly fashion by its originator and could only have been coarsened in the hands of his less gifted pupil.

In his cosmogony he carried further the tendency to hark back to earlier Ionian models wherever possible. This appears for instance in his abandonment of the purity and aloofness of Mind, and in his Anaximenean theory of the heavenly bodies as produced from air by rarefaction, in contrast to his master's idea that they had been forcibly torn from the earth and ignited by the whirling of the heavens.

He carried his speculations down to the origins of human society, laws and arts, right and wrong. If it is true that in this part of his work he deserves to be singled out as the original formulator of the convention–nature antithesis, and the statement that right and wrong are a matter of convention and have no place in the nature of things, that is perhaps his best claim to fame. It was the favourite catchword of Athenian thought in the second half of the fifth century, and the chief bone of contention between the Sophists on the one hand and Socrates and Plato on the other.[1]

---

[1] Some scholars have detected a strong influence of Archelaus on contemporary and later medical writers, e.g. Petron of Aegina and the π. διαίτης. The point of comparison is the assumption of two elemental substances, the hot and the cold. See ZN, 1276, n. 3 and references there, especially Fredrich, *Hippokr. Unters.* 129, 135 ff. Euripides is also supposed to have followed him in this dualism (Nestle, *Euripides*, 158 f.). A more adventurous account than that here given of Archelaus's philosophical character and achievements may be found in Lämmli's *Chaos zum Kosmos*, section II. For instance, II. 15 ('Archelaos incognito?') attempts a reconstruction of his cosmogony from passages in Euripides, Aristophanes and others.

VI

PHILOSOPHY IN THE SECOND HALF
OF THE FIFTH CENTURY

In Archelaus we have found united the two strands of cosmogonical speculation and ethical and sociological theory. It is a good moment to pause and consider the relations of these two spheres of interest at this juncture in the history of Greek thought. The term 'Presocratic' is commonly used to cover all the 'physical' philosophers of the sixth and fifth centuries, as opposed to Socrates himself and the Sophists as well as to later thinkers.[1] This goes with the traditional view that up to a certain point of time the interest of serious thinkers was centred in the world of external nature, cosmogony and cosmology with animal and plant life in its physical aspect, and that at this point a change in the climate of thought took place. Man replaced the universe as the focus of interest, moral and political theory was developed while natural philosophy dropped into the background. It was a matter of chronological succession, and the shift was in large measure due to one man, Socrates. This view takes its origin from Aristotle, who with a love of tidiness and system less appropriate to his historical than to his logical pronouncements, said roundly that with Socrates the investigation of nature ceased, and philosophers turned their attention to practical and political excellence; but it goes further back, to the autobiographical passage in Plato's *Phaedo*, which describes the disillusionment with physical investigations as taking place in Socrates's own mind.[2]

[1] Diels–Kranz actually include a number of fourth-century figures, as well as the Sophists, in the *Fragmente der Vorsokratiker*. In the preface, Kranz explains the principle that underlies the book. 'Presocratic' is intended to mean, not (as it is often taken) 'before Socrates', but 'before the Socratics'. Its unity lies in the presentation of a philosophy (the singular, rather surprisingly, is used) which has not been through the school of thought of Socrates and Plato. It gives in fact the non-Socratic, rather than the pre-Socratic part of ancient philosophy, and its character is determined by content rather than chronology. Without this explanation the title is somewhat misleading.

[2] Arist. *Part. an.* 642a28; Plato, *Phaedo*, 96af. (Cf. Arist. *Metaph.* 987b1.) Some weight should also be allowed to passages in Xenophon like *Mem.* 1.1.11–16, 4.7.5. Such opinions taken together rule out the idea that Socrates's abandonment of science for ethics was a 'later view' which may be credited to Panaetius. It was of course made much of in Hellenistic times. See especially Cicero, *Tusc.* 5.4.10, *Ac. post.* 1.4.15.

Though not devoid of truth, this thesis in its simple form tends to give a false impression of the sequence of events in the latter part of the fifth century. It also perhaps does less than justice to the interlocking of microcosm and macrocosm, the interpretation of the universe in terms of human relations, which can be detected even in earlier thinkers. Foremost was the concept of *diké*, justice, whether as abstract principle or powerful goddess. Anaximander saw it at work in the great cosmic processes. In Heraclitus it guarded the measures of the sun's course and was identical with the cosmic strife on which the existence of the world depended, as well as being powerful against human sinners. The same is true of *nomos*, law, a single divine ordinance governing man and the world alike.[1] For Parmenides it is Diké who forbids the coming into being or perishing of anything. Xenophanes was more openly interested in human affairs, and to quote Jaeger again, his 'daring attempt to found human areté on the knowledge of God and the universe did actually establish an immanent connexion between cosmological science and education'. In the Italian tradition the connexion was even more obvious and essential. The Pythagoreans studied the cosmic order for the purpose of reproducing its harmonies in the individual soul and in society. The use made of the word *kosmos* itself is an integral part of this. It should not be overlooked that in addition to its other uses,[2] it had an established political significance in the fifth century. When Herodotus speaks of the Lycurgan constitution of Sparta, and Thucydides of a Boeotian party which wished to change the constitution to a democracy, or of an oligarchic constitution, the noun they use is *kosmos*.[3]

There are then certain considerations which forbid one to speak of a change among philosophers in the fifth century from an exclusive interest in the physical world to a concern for human affairs. Yet an intellectual revolution took place all the same. Even in the use of *diké*

---

[1] 'Only Heraclitus was a great enough thinker to construct upon one single principle a theory of the cosmos under the government of law, which included man as an essential part of it.' (Jaeger, *Paideia*, I, 291. Cf. fr. 114, and for *diké* frr. 28, 80, 94.)

[2] For which see vol. I (index, s.v. *kosmos*).

[3] Hdt. 1.65, Thuc. 4.76, 8.72. The close connexion between this and the more general sense of 'order' is brought out by the use in Plato, *Prot.* 332c. In Cretan cities the highest magistrates were called κόσμοι and the singular was used collectively to mean 'the government' (*RE*, XI, 1495).

by an Ionian like Anaximander, and still more in Heraclitus and the Western Greeks Parmenides and Empedocles, one can detect religious overtones inherited from a mythopoeic past. Parmenides, Xenophanes and Empedocles were themselves poets and heirs of the poetic tradition. This was a tradition steeped in ethical as well as religious lore, the tradition of Solon and Theognis, going back to Homer and Hesiod. The new spirit which we meet in fifth-century Athens is one of conscious reaction against religion, of humanism in the full sense. It sees human nature as autonomous, and the existence of higher powers either as doubtful or frankly as a man-made fiction. At the same time the gnomic wisdom of the poets is being transformed into systematically argued ethical and political theory. This is the revolution in which the Sophists took a leading part.

As to chronology, the table given on p. 348 yields a few interesting facts which are sometimes forgotten. Many of the dates are only approximately known, but if we confine ourselves to decades we may speak with some confidence. Where there is a chance of being correct to within a year or two, the most likely date is mentioned in brackets. It emerges that the most influential of the Sophists, Protagoras and Gorgias, were almost exact contemporaries of Empedocles and Anaxagoras, older than Zeno of Elea and Archelaus, and 30–40 years older than Democritus. Prodicus too was older than Democritus, and roughly contemporary with the Eleatic philosopher Melissus. Exactly when these men wrote their works is even more difficult to determine than the dates of their births and deaths, but we must evidently allow for an influence not only of the 'physicists' on the Sophists (which is universally recognized), but also in the reverse direction. We are dealing with contemporaries, who read each others' works and were in many cases personally acquainted.

The common meeting-ground was Athens. Only Socrates and Archelaus were natives of the city, but the Athens of Pericles was an intellectual magnet of extraordinary power. Here the youthful Socrates could sharpen his wits against Parmenides and Zeno about the year 450. Anaxagoras from Clazomenae spent some thirty years there. Socrates read his book and was taught by his pupil Archelaus. Protagoras set up as a professional teacher and practised there for more than ten years. He was entrusted by Pericles with the legislation for his

DECADE	'PRESOCRATICS'	SOPHISTS	OTHERS	EVENTS
500–490	Pythagoras died.[1] Parmenides a youth. Empedocles born (c. 492) Anaxagoras born (c. 500).	Protagoras born (490 or earlier).	Aeschylus's first production (499). Herodotus born (495). Sophocles born (496). Pindar a young man (b. 518). Pericles born.	
490–80	Zeno born. ? Archelaus born (younger than Anaxagoras but older than Socrates).	Gorgias born (483).	Euripides born (484).	Persian Wars.
480–70	Xenophanes died.	Prodicus born (probably about 20 years after Protagoras).		
470–60	Anaxagoras and Diogenes of Apollonia wrote after 467. (See col. 5.)	? Antiphon born (roughly contemporary with Socrates).	Socrates born (469). Sophocles's first production (468).	Fall of meteorite mentioned by Anaxagoras and Diogenes of Apollonia (467).
460–50	Democritus born (c. 460).	Critias born (455). **Antisthenes born (455)**.	Aristophanes born (450). Thucydides born. Euripides's first production (c. 455)	Parmenides, Zeno and Socrates met in Athens c. 450.
450–40	Melissus in command at Samos (441).			Founding of Thurii 443 attended by Protagoras, Herodotus and possibly Empedocles.
440–30	Leucippus fl. Empedocles died.			Meeting of Socrates with Protagoras, Prodicus, Hippias in Athens (? 433). Outbreak of Peloponnesian War (431).
430–20	Diogenes of Apollonia wrote before 423. Democritus writing. Anaxagoras died (428).		Pericles died (429). Aristophanes, Clouds (423). Herodotus died (? 425). Plato born (427).	
420–10		Protagoras died (420).		
410–400		Critias killed (403).	Sophocles died (406). Euripides died (406). Thucydides died (? c. 400).	End of Peloponnesian War (404). Rule of the Thirty Tyrants (404) and restoration of the democracy (403).
400–390	Democritus died. (p. 386 n. 2).		Socrates executed (399).	

colony at Thurii in Italy, at the foundation of which he would meet Herodotus and probably Empedocles.[1]

Democritus the atomist, from the same northern city as Protagoras, also came to Athens and according to one source spent several years there.[2] Gorgias was sent to Athens in 427 at the head of an embassy from his native Leontini in Sicily, and his oratory made a tremendous impression. Besides being the leading orator of the day, he knew and adopted the theories of sensation taught by his fellow-islander Empedocles, and was capable of writing an exercise in Eleatic logic. It is unlikely that his official embassy to Athens was his only visit. Prodicus and Hippias talked with Protagoras and Socrates in Athens shortly before the outbreak of the Peloponnesian War. Prodicus, says Plato, frequently came there, and Hippias more than once. There is no record of a visit to Athens by Diogenes of Apollonia, but his views were well known to Euripides and Aristophanes. These and other Athenian writers of the time, like Sophocles and Thucydides, and Herodotus who came to Athens and settled in its colony Thurii, bear witness to the wide dissemination of the ideas both of the natural philosophers and the Sophists. Aristotle indeed said rather unkindly of Empedocles that he was more of a natural scientist than a poet (*Poet.* 1447b 19).

[1] Morrison says (*CQ*, 1941, 5) that Empedocles attended the actual foundation ceremonies. Presumably this depends on the evidence of the contemporary poet Glaucus that he went to Thurii νεωστὶ παντελῶς ἐκτισμένους (D.L. 8.52), which may however mean that his visit was very soon after, rather than at, the foundation. On action and reaction between thinkers of this period Fredrich in his *Hippokr. Unters.* has some useful observations (§5, 'Die griechischen Philosophen in der zweiten Hälfte des fünften Jahrhunderts').

[2] 'Athenis annis compluribus moratus', Val. Max. 8.7 extr. 4 (DK, 68, A11). The remark of Democritus quoted by Demetrius of Magnesia (*ap.* D.L. 9.36), 'I came to Athens and no one knew me', sounds like one of the apocryphal sayings of which Diogenes was fond. It is quoted similarly by Cicero (*Tusc.* 5.36.104, see DK, 68 B116), though Valerius—not the most critical of sources—says that Democritus stated it 'in some book'. If it is genuine, the context in all three places shows that it was not intended as a complaint, nor 'ironical' as Jaeger calls it. It is quoted expressly to illustrate Democritus's dislike of notoriety and the success of his determined effort to be left in peace to pursue his researches.

NOTE TO TABLE

[1] The chronology of Pythagoras's life presents an extremely complicated problem. See now von Fritz in *RE* xxiv (1963), 179–87, and J. P. Barron's re-dating of Samian history in *CQ*, 1964, esp. pp. 226f. Timaeus appears to have put his death as late as 480, but Barron's work suggests that it may have been earlier than 500. I hope it is not misleading to include it here and so draw attention to the fact that, even if Pythagoras died before 500, not much more than a century separates his death from that of Socrates.

A striking instance of the error of supposing that the era of cosmological and physical speculation was entirely prior to the humanism of
Socrates and the Sophists is provided by the relation of Democritus
to Protagoras. Democritus, 'un Presocratico in ritardo' as Alfieri
rather happily calls him, mentioned Protagoras (D.L. 9.42), indeed
attacked and 'wrote persuasively and at length' against his subjective
theory of knowledge (Plut. *Colot.* 1109a). Sextus couples him with
Plato in this activity, and with the fact assured, one can feel justified
in taking his assertion that 'for all men the same thing is good and true'
(fr. 69) as directed intentionally against this subjectivity.[1] Similarly his
high moral precept (fr. 264) that 'one should feel shame before oneself
no less than before others, and behave no more wickedly if no one is
going to know about it than if everyone is' sounds like a deliberate
rebuttal of the immoralist idea of Antiphon and Critias that the only
reason for not doing wrong is the fear of being found out.

One reason why one cannot speak of humanism as simply replacing
natural science is that the interests of both to a considerable extent
overlapped. Some of the Sophists were polymaths who included
astronomy and other special subjects in their instruction. Conversely
Democritus, chiefly known now for his atomic theory of matter, wrote
extensively on ethics. There was no dividing line between 'nature' and
'man', as was particularly evident in Archelaus. Cosmologists had
always included in their speculations the origin of animal and human
life. It seemed a part of the same continuous story to theorize about the
beginnings of civilization and the arts, and one's views on the origin of
social and political institutions decisively colour (or are coloured by)
one's conception of their nature and use at the present day. Speculations of this universal scope may go right back to Anaximander, and
it was certainly assumed by Anaxagoras, as Vlastos puts it, that 'civilization is a cosmic episode'.[2] So it happens that the account of the
origin of the useful arts, of societies and of morality which Plato puts

---

[1] So Vlastos in *Philos. Rev.* 1945, 591, referring to the expressions attributed to Protagoras in
Plato's *Theaet.* (167b). On the relations between Democritus and Protagoras cf. also A. L.
Peck's note (c) on p. 76 of the Loeb ed. of Arist. *Part. an.*, C. J. Classen in *Proc. Afr. Class.
Assns.* 1959, 41.
[2] For Anaximander cf. the opinions of Cherniss and Heidel (vol. 1, 75). For Anaxagoras see
fr. 4, and Vlastos, *Philos. Rev.* 1946, 53.

into the mouth of Protagoras, the Sophist who despised useless knowledge and claimed to teach the political art, is paralleled in Democritus and in the cosmology preserved by Diodorus. His point that the physical superiority of the beasts is outmatched by the intelligence of man recurs in Anaxagoras (fr. 21b). Democritus on the other hand, also interested in the origin of the arts, attributed them to observation and imitation of the animals: the spider taught us weaving, the swallow housebuilding. Accounts of the origin of the arts, with the emphasis on human intelligence, are put into the mouths of their characters by all three tragedians.[1]

That is one link between physical and humanistic philosophy at this time. Another is the word *physis* ('nature') itself. The Ionian scientists had used it in a general sense, for the sum-total of reality, or its origin and present constitution; but of course it had also been applied from an early date to the constitution or form of particular things or species, like the plant moly in the Odyssey.[2] In the fifth century it began to be used especially of *human* nature, and in the plural, of the nature of individual human beings. We read in Euripides of 'the natures of mortals'. 'Such natures' (as that of Oedipus), says Creon in the *Oedipus Tyrannus*, 'are a burden to themselves'. In Aristophanes we hear of 'learning of oneself, without a teacher, from a clever nature', which is closely matched by Thucydides's characterization of Themistocles as 'displaying a remarkable power of *physis*' because he reached sound conclusions 'by his native wit without learning'. *Physis* as inborn genius was already contrasted with learning by Pindar.[3] This application of the word to human nature, and particularly to its distinctive characteristic of intelligence, is described by Jaeger (*Paideia*, I, 303) as 'a momentous departure.... The concept of *physis* was transferred from the whole universe to a single part of it—to mankind.' To speak of a transfer from whole to part is an exaggeration. Ever since Homer the word *physis* had been used of a single thing or species as well as of the whole universe. (Parmenides wrote of the *physis* of

---

[1] Aesch. *P.V.* 442 ff., Eur. *Suppl.* 201 ff., Soph. *Ant.* 332 ff. For a parallel between the Diodoran account and Archelaus see p. 343, n. 3 above, and for further details Guthrie, *In the Beginning*, ch. 5.
[2] See vol. I, 82 f.
[3] Eur. *El.* 368, Soph. *O.T.* 674 f., Arist. *Wasps*, 1282, Thuc. 1.138.3, Pindar *Ol.* 2.86.

the moon.) This was so common that 'the *physis* of something' need be no more than a periphrasis for the thing itself, as when Oedipus tells Teiresias that he would move a rock to anger (literally 'the *physis* of a rock', *O.T.* 334f.), and it would be strange if it were not applied to human nature along with the rest.

It is true, however, that at this time the study of human nature was receiving an increasing amount of attention. This process was assisted by the Hippocratic treatment of man as a physical organism.[1] 'The nature of man' and 'human nature' are both Hippocratic phrases, the latter occurring in the treatise of which the former is the title. It was also used as a title by Diogenes of Apollonia and Democritus. To understand and cure diseases it was essential to be familiar both with the *physis* of man in general and with the various *physeis* of individual patients. *Epidemics* I says that in diagnosis we learn 'from the common *physis* of all and that peculiar to each individual', *Epidemics* VI that 'natures' are the real physicians; nature finds ways for herself and does what is necessary without instruction. According to *De humoribus*, different natures do better in different climates and places. An aphorism says that diseases are less dangerous if the *physis* of the patient suits them, and *De arte* speaks of the *physis* both of the patient and of the disease.

The individuality of each man's 'nature' was already recognized by Empedocles (fr. 110.5, p. 352 above), and is repeatedly emphasized in the Hippocratic corpus. Another example is in *De flatibus*: 'One body differs from another, one *physis* from another, one diet from another.' To write correctly about regimen (says the treatise on that topic), 'one must first recognize and distinguish the *physis* of every man'.[2] Together with Empedocles and the epistemology of Parmenides fr. 16 (p. 67 above), this fits in well with the relativist theory of knowledge of a Protagoras. The Hippocratic treatises extend through the fifth and fourth centuries, and the precise date of each is uncertain. But Hippocrates himself was roughly contemporary with Socrates (b. 469), and the

---

[1] As Jaeger (*ibid.*) also saw, though here again his claim that 'this is the first recognition of the fact that the *physis* of man is a physical organism' might be hard to substantiate.

[2] The passages quoted above are (Littré's pages in parentheses): *De nat. hom. init.* (VI, 32), *Epid.* I (II, 668–70), 6 (V, 314), *De humor.* 16 (V, 496), *Aph.* 2.34 (IV, 480), *De arte* 11 (VI, 20), *De flat.* 6 (VI, 98), *De victu* 1, 2 (VI, 468). Also relevant are *De victu* 1, 6 (VI, 478), 11 (VI, 486), 15 (VI, 490), *De virgin.* 1 (VIII, 466), *De diebus iudic.* 2 (IX, 298).

doctrines of human nature here quoted evidently belong to the intellectual milieu of fifth-century natural and humanistic philosophy. Needless to say, the more general sense of *physis* is not lacking: we find criticism of those who have written on nature, reference to the ordering of things by nature, and so forth.[1]

This leads to another link between the natural philosophers and the humanists, namely the contemporary excitement over the question of the relations between *physis* and *nomos* (usage, custom, convention, law). This will be dealt with fully later on. Here one may simply mention that in earlier times, law had been regarded as immutable because of divine origin. As Heraclitus said (fr. 114), 'All human laws are nourished by one, the divine'. The antithesis between *physis* as divine and unalterable, and *nomos* as man-made and shifting, appears in the Hippocratic writings.[2] For the Sophists it was a basic tenet. The *locus classicus* is the long papyrus fragment of Antiphon, in which the differences between natural and conventional morality are worked out in detail, and it is constantly held up in the pages of Plato as the arch-enemy of his own world-view. In its sophistic form it was a translation into moral terms of the distinction between appearance and reality which haunted philosophy since Parmenides. Empedocles said that though birth and death are unreal, he will conform to *nomos* by speaking of them (fr. 9, p. 156 above). The climax comes with Democritus, who taking phenomena simply as a signpost to unseen reality, concluded that the homogeneous atoms alone constituted reality (i.e. *physis*, fr. 168): perceptible qualities like flavour, warmth and colour only had that title by *nomos* (fr. 125). They are the subjective result of interaction between the atoms making up external objects (or films of atoms discharged from them) and those in our own bodies; and since no two men's atomic constitutions were identical, no two men's sensations could be identical either. Diogenes of Apollonia agreed that what we perceive is a matter of *nomos* not *physis*. A relativistic theory of

---

[1] Examples could be cited indefinitely. Aristophanes refers to sexual impulses as 'compulsions of nature', Plato speaks a little later of philosophic, prudent, tyrannical and acquisitive natures, and so on. Instead of multiplying them, it would be preferable simply to say that, both in ordinary and in philosophic language, φύσις covers the same ground as 'nature' in English; but some scholars are hard to convince of this.

[2] See *De victu* 1.11 (vi, 486 Littré, a passage imitating Heraclitean style).

knowledge was also being preached by the Sophists. One cannot say that they learned it from the atomists or Anaxagoras (p. 319 above) nor the physical philosophers from them. It was part of the spirit of the age, which had caused Pindar to sing of '*Nomos* King of all'. More generally it appears in the relish with which Herodotus discovers and narrates the incompatible customs and beliefs of different races, and it had a forerunner in the Ethiopian and Scythian gods of Xenophanes (vol. 1, 371). Closely connected with this was the question of the part played by natural endowment and teaching respectively in the acquisition of various skills, and especially of the *areté* which brought success in social and political relations. It derived a practical urgency from the claim of the Sophists to impart these accomplishments, and the question 'Is virtue teachable?', which figures in the Platonic dialogues, can be detected already in fifth-century literature.

The Ionians had begun the tradition of free inquiry, bringing everything to the bar of rational criticism and discussion. In the fifth century this tradition established itself firmly at Athens among natural philosophers and humanists alike, justifying the title of 'enlightenment' which is commonly given to that age and place, and leading to the most fundamental and universal of the tenets which they held in common: the substitution of natural for divine causation everywhere.[1] Among the physicists a reaction towards earlier Ionian thought is noticeable in specific doctrines: Diogenes of Apollonia, Idaeus of Himera, and in his own way Archelaus go back to Anaximenes in choosing air as primary substance and rarefaction and condensation as the basic process of cosmogony. Hot and cold continue at this time, in both cosmological and biological theory, to play the vital role which was first given to them by Anaximander.

APPENDIX

Some minor figures of the period

Hippon[2] was a typical eclectic of this period, a natural philosopher of no great originality with, like others of the time, a strong interest in physiology. He was satirized by Cratinus, the contemporary of

---

[1] It may be worth while referring back to Plato's statement of this outlook in *Laws*, 10 (vol. 1, 144).   [2] Already occasionally mentioned in vol. 1. See index.

Aristophanes, in a play called the *Panoptai* or *Omniscients* produced some time before Aristophanes's *Clouds* (423 B.C.). The label 'atheist' which he commonly bears, and for which no cogent reason is given, may have stuck to him as a result of the play, for Cratinus is said to have represented him as irreligious, and we know the harm that was done to Socrates by a similar characterization in the *Clouds*.[1] That he wrote after Empedocles is reasonably inferred from Aristotle's note (*De an.* 405 b 3) that he criticized those who said that the soul was blood.[2] He is variously said to be from Samos, Metapontum, Rhegium and Croton, a mixture with a Pythagorean flavour, and he was probably at one time a member of the Pythagorean brotherhood, as Iamblichus (on the authority of Aristoxenus) says.[3]

Aristotle had a low opinion of him: the 'cheapness' or 'worthlessness' (εὐτέλεια) of his thought makes him unworthy to be included in the succession of philosophers (*Metaph.* 984 a 3); he belongs to the coarser or more vulgar (φορτικώτεροι) thinkers (*De an.* 405 b 1). The evidence supports this verdict. On the *arché* of the universe he tried to revive the oldest theory of all, that of Thales that it was water or 'the moist'. He appears, says Aristotle, to have had in mind its generative power, arguing from the liquid nature of semen.[4] Hippolytus reports more precise information (*Ref.* 1.16; DK, A3): water produced, or gave birth to, fire, which then 'overmastered its parent' to form the cosmos. This would account for other late statements that he posited two *archai*, fire and water. It looks like an attempt to conflate early monism with a theory like that in the Way of Seeming of Parmenides,

[1] A scholiast on *Clouds*, 94 ff. (DK, A 2) says that Cratinus had earlier made similar remarks about Hippon in the *Panoptai*. The information that he called him ἀσεβής comes from a scholiast on Clement's *Protrepticus* also quoted by DK. Philoponus and ps.-Alex. in their commentaries on Aristotle (*De an.* 88. 23 and *Metaph.* 462.29, DK, A 8 and 9) attribute the title 'atheist' to his materialism, but he was by no means alone in this.

[2] Cf. Empedocles, fr. 105, p. 229 above and Theophr. *De sensu*, 10 on p. 228. Reiche's complex argument against this supposition has not convinced me (*Emped.'s Mixture*, 15).

[3] Iambl. *V.P.* 267 and other passages in DK, A 1. The homes of Hippasus and Philolaus are also variously given. One remembers that enforced changes of residence were part of the Pythagorean lot.

[4] Commenting on the *Metaphysics* passage, Alexander (DK, A6) says that Hippon used the general term 'the moist' without specifying whether he meant water like Thales or *aer* like Anaximenes and Diogenes; but Simplicius (*Phys.* 23.22, A4) couples him directly with Thales as speaking of water.

One may presumably ignore the isolated and incredible remark of Johannes Diaconus (? ninth century A.D.: DK, A6) that he made earth the ἀρχή.

though how water alone (also called 'the cold') could produce fire ('the hot') is not explained. It is all very well for Simplicius to say that 'the hot lives on the moist' (*Phys.* 23.24; DK, 11 A 13) in the present world, but this is only possible because they have always existed together in a state of parity, as Parmenides saw.

The universal *arché* was, as always, the life-substance or *psyche*. Hippon said that the *psyche* was the brain, watery in substance and arising from the semen, which flows from the marrow. For the Greeks brain and marrow were identical, the brain being a continuation of the spinal 'marrow', and brain and semen had been identified by Alcmaeon and probably more generally.[1] Into this system Hippon fitted another Greek commonplace, the association of youth and suppleness with moisture, old age and death with dryness.

His view is that there is within us our own moisture, by which we are sentient and by which we live. When this moisture is in its proper condition, the living creature is healthy, but when the moisture dries up, it loses sense and dies. This is the reason why old men are dry and enfeebled in their senses, namely that they are without moisture. Similarly the soles of the feet are insensitive because they lack moisture....In another book the same writer says that the aforesaid moisture changes through excess of heat and cold, and so brings on diseases. It changes to greater moisture or dryness or to a coarser or finer texture or into other substances, and so he explains the causes of disease. He does not however name the diseases so caused.[2]

---

[1] Hippolytus, 1.16 (DK, A3), Aët. 4.3.9 (A10), Censorinus 5.2 (A12) and 6.1 (A15). For μυελός (marrow) as brain (ἐγκέφαλος) see Soph. *Trach.* 781, Hom. *Il.* 20.482, Onians, *Origins of Eur. Thought*, 118 (also *ibid.* 109–10 and 115 for marrow as source of semen). According to LSJ ἐγκέφαλος is an adjective with μυελός for its noun. For Alcmaeon see vol. 1, 349, n. 1. If Censorinus is to be believed, Hippon 'proved' the origin of semen from the marrow by experiment: if male animals are killed after serving a female, it will be found that the marrow is drained away. Hippon's theories of reproduction are fully dealt with by Erna Lesky, *Zeugungslehre*. (See her index.)

[2] *Anon. Londinensis*, 11.22; DK, A11 (based on the *Iatrica* of Aristotle's pupil Menon). The papyrus was in a sorry state at this point, and only the first three letters of Hippon's name are preserved, but no other is possible (Diels, *Hermes*, 1893, 420–1). The author of this passage calls Hippon a Crotoniate, and if he were at any time an adherent of the Crotoniate medical school he would naturally know the work of Alcmaeon. Alcmaeon's anatomical researches showed the 'passages' from eye to brain, and he considered the water in the lens an essential instrument of the power of sight. Diels suggests that Hippon with his more limited intellect was led into a clumsy generalization of Alcmaeon's discovery. However, the association of life with moisture was, as I have said, a commonplace, and from that to holding it responsible for sensation is surely an easy step.

On the controversial question of whether both parents contribute seed in reproduction, on which Empedocles and Anaxagoras had differed, Hippon made the uninspired suggestion that females produce seed but it is discharged from the womb and contributes nothing to the birth.[1] He also said that the sex of the offspring depends on the consistency of the semen (Aët. and Censorinus, A14). Another passage of Censorinus represents him as emphasizing the importance of the number seven in the cardinal stages of human life in the same way, and almost in the same words, as Alexander of Aphrodisias ascribes to the Pythagoreans. That the number ten is also given special significance certainly does not lessen the case for his Pythagorean affinities.[2] Like Diogenes of Apollonia and Democritus he supposed embryos to be nourished by sucking a breast-like growth on the womb (Cens. 6.3, A17).[3] He also wrote on botany, and his remarks on the distinction between wild and cultivated plants are quoted and criticized by Theophrastus in his *Historia Plantarum* (1.3.5, A19).

A single fragment of his actual writing was discovered in 1885, quoted by Crates of Mallus (second century B.C.) and repeated in a scholiast on the *Iliad* (DK, 11, pp. 387 f.). It says that all sweet water comes from the sea, because the sea is deeper than any well, and what is at a higher level than the sea must have come from it. Zeller (ZN, 336, n. 1) thought this showed that Hippon accepted Thales's idea that the earth floats on water, which no doubt he did. The sea-water is sweetened by filtering as it rises through the porous earth. This would be the opposite of what Anaxagoras supposed to happen (p. 311 above). In any case the fragment is hardly exciting.

---

[1] Aët. 4.5.3 (A13). Hence, he says, some widows and women separated from their husbands discharge seed. There is no explicit mention of the menses, which Aristotle regarded as 'analogous' to semen in males (*GA*, 727a3). For Empedocles and Anaxagoras cf. pp. 217, 317 above. According to the *Placita* (5.5.1–3), Pythagoras and Democritus were of Empedocles's opinion.

[2] Cens. 7.2 (A16): 'Hippon of Metapontum reckoned that men could be born from the 7th to the 10th month.... This maturity beginning from 7 months is prolonged until 10 because this is the natural way with everything, that to 7 months or years 3 should be added for the consummation to be reached. Teeth begin for an infant of 7 months and are complete in the 10th at most, in the 7th year the first of them fall out, in the 10th the last', etc. Cf. what Alexander has to say about Pythagorean number-mysticism, vol. 1, 303.

[3] On this theory see also pp. 378 and 468 below.

Such interest as Hippon has to offer arises in a left-handed way from his lack of distinction and originality, which makes him a mirror of the current ideas of his time. In particular one may notice once again the tendency to hark back to the Ionians, the capital importance of heat and cold,[1] and the intimate connexion between the universe and the human body, cosmology and physiology. This parallel between macrocosm and microcosm pervaded many of the Hippocratic writings too, though strenuously combated in the more empirical and strictly medical treatises, and reaches a height of absurdity in the treatise *On Sevens*. There it is said that animals and trees on the earth have a constitution resembling that of the universe: the stony parts of the earth resemble the bones, what is around them the flesh, rivers the blood in the veins and so on. The importance of the number seven in human life goes back at least to Solon, but he would hardly have proceeded to the grotesque comparison of the Peloponnese to the head (because 'a seat of high-minded men'), Ionia to the diaphragm, Egypt to the belly and so on up to seven.[2] The identification of macrocosm and microcosm, in one form or another, reaches back to pre-philosophical man. It goes with the conception of the earth as mother, and the idea that the rocks are her bones is central to the myth of Deucalion. What is fascinating, as an instance of the persistent dominance over the Western mind enjoyed by certain basic forms of myth, is to find it flourishing in the full light of fifth-century rationalism (as it flourished still at the Renaissance), and to trace the variations of which it was capable in the maunderings of *On Sevens*, in a would-be rationalist like Hippon and a superior mind like Alcmaeon's.

A few other names of the time may be briefly noticed. *Cratylus* is chiefly known for having carried the Heraclitean doctrine of flux to such an extreme that he was finally led to abandon the use of language and simply move his finger. In the dialogue called after him Plato represents him in conversation with Socrates, though he may well have

---

[1] Cf. Fredrich, *Hippokr. Unters.* 134f.

[2] *De septiman.* 6, 11 (VIII, 637, 638 and IX, 436, 438 L.); Gomperz, *Gr. Th.* I, 294f. This part of the work survives only in a barbarous and mutilated Latin translation, but the original is at least as early as the fifth century. (Wellmann, *F.G.Ä.* I, 43, assigned it to the fifth, Roscher in his edition of 1913 argued that the theories in the work went back to the sixth. See also Kranz in *Nachr. Gött.* 1938 and *Philol.* 1938–9.)

been a younger man. Here too he is made to express agreement with the opinions of Heraclitus (though not to go beyond him), and to believe that names have a natural appropriateness to the objects named. Perhaps, as D. J. Allan has suggested, this represented an earlier stage of his thought than that to which, in Aristotle's words, he came 'in the end'.[1] The views of *Cleidemus* on sensation are mentioned by Theophrastus between those of Anaxagoras and Diogenes of Apollonia, which may be a clue to his date, since Theophrastus seems to proceed in chronological order.[2] He grants him originality on the subject of sight, which he said was due solely to the fact that the eyes were transparent. All the senses except hearing were autonomous, whereas the ears had no power of discrimination themselves but must remit the stimulus to the mind. He said that lightning was only an appearance, like phosphorescence, and he figures in Theophrastus's botanical works with remarks on plants, their general nature (composed of the same elements as animals but more turbid and colder), their diseases, and the best time to sow. *Idaeus of Himera* is grouped by Sextus (*Math.* 9. 360; DK, 63) with Anaximenes, Diogenes of Apollonia and Archelaus as holding that air is the *arché*. This mention of (presumably) some 600 years after his time occurs in a sketchy and partly inaccurate list of all who have posited corporeal elements. (It says that Xenophanes posited both earth and water as *archai*, quoting in support the statement of fr. 33 that '*we* are all born out of earth and water'.) Nothing else is known of him, though it has been conjectured, on no very obvious grounds, that he may have been the philosopher of the mysterious

---

[1] See vol. I, 450, n. 3. The more factual statement is Aristotle's, and it is extremely improbable that it could have been founded on anything in Plato's dialogue as Kirk suggested in *AJP*, 1951. His arguments were answered by Allan in *AJP*, 1954, though Allan's own attempt to make Cratylus primarily a fourth-century figure, no older than Plato, depends partly on giving an unlikely sense (logical, not temporal) to πρῶτον at Arist. *Metaph.* 987 a 32, as Cherniss showed (*AJP*, 1955, 184–6). No doubt the relation of the historical Cratylus to Plato's presents some problems. Since parts of the dialogue (the etymologies proposed by Socrates) are obviously not serious, it is difficult to be sure about the rest, but Cratylus's statement in 440d–e, that after considerable mental effort he thinks Heraclitus was right, can hardly be explained away.

[2] A historian of Attica named Cleidemus was writing in the middle of the fourth century (Jacoby in *RE*, XI, 591), and the philosopher mentioned by Theophrastus has sometimes been thought to be the same man, though his place in the *De sensu* tells against this. References for the discussion are collected by Regenbogen in *RE*, Suppl. VII, 1457 f. The sources for Clidemus are in DK, 62.

'intermediate substance' between water and air or air and fire, occasionally mentioned by Aristotle.[1]

Oenopides of Chios is included by Sextus in another list as having posited two *archai*, fire and air, and appears in Aëtius among those who said that God was the soul of the world.[2] Presumably therefore he wrote on cosmology, but we cannot claim to know what he said except on astronomy. This and mathematics were his special interests. His activity can be approximately dated early in the second half of the fifth century by (*a*) a statement of Proclus that he was a little younger than Anaxagoras, (*b*) a report that he was a contemporary of Democritus and mentioned by him; and more precisely by (*c*) the fact that his estimate of the solar year must have preceded that of the astronomer Meton, which is fixed by its reference to the summer solstice of 432.[3] Eudemus is quoted as saying that he discovered the obliquity of the ecliptic. This is elsewhere credited to Anaximander, and it is difficult to believe that it could have remained unobserved as a fact until this date. Probably he calculated its angle. The feat would have been within his mathematical capacity, and Proclus hints that he valued mathematics as an astronomical tool.[4] The Milky Way, he held, marked a former path of the sun, which later turned aside to its present course through the Zodiac. This is a theory which Aristotle attributed to a section of the Pythagoreans.[5] He spoke of a 'Great Year' (the shortest

---

[1] Zeller in ZN, 337. Burnet preferred to follow the general opinion of ancient commentators that Aristotle was referring to Anaximander's *apeiron*. (See *EGP*, 55 f., 65, and for the Greek text DK, 63.) The best discussion of the question is in Ross's edition of the *Physics*, 482 f. The attribution to Anaximander is made particularly difficult by *Phys.* 187 a 12–21, where the reference to condensation and rarefaction suggests rather Anaximenes, and Anaximander himself is mentioned in a different connexion. Ross concludes that 'we must be content to refer the belief in an intermediate substance to some other member or members of the school of Anaximenes'.

[2] Sextus, *Pyrrh. hyp.* 3.30, Aët. 1.7.17 (DK, 41, 5 and 6). Sextus's list is not consistent with the one at *Math.* 9.360 already mentioned, nor is that in Aëtius of much historical worth.

[3] (*a*) Procl. *Eucl.* 65.21 Friedl. (DK, 1), (*b*) D.L. 9.41, (*c*) see von Fritz in *RE*, XVII, 2258 f. The earliest extant mention of Oenopides is in the pseudo-Platonic *Erastai* (of the third or early second century B.C.). It introduces his name with Anaxagoras's in a geometrical context.

[4] Theo. Sm. p. 198. 14 Hiller, Diod. 1.98.2 (DK, 7). Against Heath, *Aristarchus*, 131, see von Fritz in *RE*, XVII, 2260. Oenopides investigated a geometrical problem χρήσιμον αὐτὸ πρὸς ἀστρολογίαν οἰόμενος, Procl. *Eucl.* 283.4 (DK, 13). Aelian called him ἀστρολόγος (*V.H.* 10.7; DK, 9).

[5] Achilles, *Isag.* p. 55.18 Maass, cf. Arist. *Meteor.* 345 a 13 (DK, A 10). The cause of the sun's swerve was said by some, including apparently Oenopides, to be horror at the banquet of Thyestes. As von Fritz says, a curious mixture of Pythagorean and mythical elements with Ionian physics!

number of years which will contain an exact number of lunar months) of fifty-nine ordinary years, and calculated the length of the year at $365\frac{22}{59}$ days.[1] In mathematics, we learn from Eudemus in Proclus's commentary on Euclid that he investigated the problem of drawing a perpendicular to a given straight line from a point outside it and discovered how to construct at a point on a given straight line an angle equal to a given rectilineal angle (Euclid 1.12 and 23).[2] His theory of the Nile floods was at least original. Subterranean water (as in wells) is warmer in winter than in summer, therefore it dries up more in winter and flows more freely in summer. Since (unlike e.g. Greece) Egypt has little rain winter or summer, this fact accounts for the summer flooding of the river (Diod. 1.41.1; DK, 11).

These examples, which exclude the men usually known as Sophists, may help to consolidate our picture of the range of interests of this intellectually intensely active period. The Sophists included many of the same subjects in their teaching, along with the human studies of ethics, politics, linguistics. Others like Meton the astronomer or Hippocrates of Chios the mathematician[3] specialized in a single branch of learning. One who, as much as any other, might be called a fashionable philosopher of the time was Diogenes of Apollonia, but his ideas are worth considering by themselves at greater length.

[1] Aelian, *V.H.* 10.7; Censorinus, 19.2 (DK, 9 and 8).
[2] Procl. *Eucl.* 80.15, 283.4 (DK, 12 and 13). See Heath, *Aristarchus*, 130, and for this and the general importance of Oenopides in the history of mathematics von Fritz, *loc. cit.* 2264ff.
[3] Vol. I, 219, 335.

VII

DIOGENES OF APOLLONIA

As a younger contemporary of Anaxagoras, whose views were parodied by Aristophanes, Diogenes is in the centre of the intellectual activity described in the last section. In an attempt to revive monism and even the hylozoism of Anaximenes in a post-Parmenidean age, he made considerable use of earlier theories, and he had strong physiological and medical interests. Apart from the heroic effort to reconcile Ionian monism with contemporary currents of thought, his greatest significance lies perhaps in his explicit statement and defence of the teleological explanation of nature,[1] which underwent such remarkable and influential developments in the hands of Plato and Aristotle.

(1) *Life and writings*

Diogenes Laertius (9.57) says that he lived in the time of Anaxagoras, and this is made more precise by the statement of Theophrastus (*ap.* Simpl. *Phys.* 25.1, A5) that he 'was pretty well the latest of those who studied these matters [i.e. the *physis* of things and the problem of change], and wrote for the most part eclectically, in some things following Anaxagoras, in others Leucippus'.[2] Considering the parody of his

---

[1] F. Hüffmeier has argued against this in an article 'Teleologische Weltbetrachtung bei Diog. Apoll.?' in *Philologus*, 1963. On p. 134 he writes: 'Es steht einfach nicht im Text, dass die Ordnung der Welt die αἰτία οὖ ἕνεκα der Kosmogonie war.... Die von Theiler benötigte Voraussetzung, dass Diogenes hierin über Anaxagoras (besonders 59 B 13 und 14) hinausging, ist also nicht gegeben.' But is it not unreasonable to deny the epithet teleological to the doctrine that an intelligent being existed prior to the cosmos as *arché*, was its efficient cause, ordered it in the best possible way and is still active in the world? All this is in the text. Where Diogenes went beyond Anaxagoras was in removing Mind from its position of proud but inefficient isolation, 'mixed with no other thing', and bringing it into continuous living contact with the world.

[2] It might therefore be thought more logical to consider Diogenes after the atomists, as KR do, rather than before them as here. I confess that in choosing the present order I have acted from a feeling that the atomists are the climax of Presocratic thought and therefore form the most fitting conclusion to an account of it. So far as Diogenes's debt to Leucippus is discernible from the evidence, it consisted mainly in the admission of void (pp. 367 f. below), and this is not a conception which should cause difficulty. On the other hand Diogenes probably wrote before Democritus. The important thing to remember is that all these thinkers, including Melissus, were contemporaries. Most scholars would say that both Leucippus and Diogenes wrote with knowledge of the work of Melissus, yet it has also been argued that *his* work was a criticism of *theirs* (p. 368, n. 1 below). We shall not go far wrong in thinking of all three as active together in the decade 440–30.

views in the *Clouds* of Aristophanes (produced 423 B.C.), one may say with a high degree of probability that he was writing between 440 and 423.

Jaeger (*TEGP*, 165) took the attentions of the comic poets, Aristophanes and Philemon, as proof that he 'lived for a long time in Athens'. His views seem to have been well known there, but otherwise we have no clue to the events of his life.[1] It is not even certain where he was born, for there existed a large number of cities called Apollonia. Aelian mentions 'Diogenes the Phrygian' in a list of 'atheists', and Stephanus of Byzantium (fifth century A.D.) 'Diogenes the natural philosopher' as coming from Apollonia in Crete, the former Eleuthernae. It is generally supposed that he is 'the Phrygian', and came from the Milesian colony of Apollonia on the Black Sea.[2]

Of his writings Simplicius gives the following description (*Phys.* 151.24, DK, A4):

One must know that this Diogenes wrote a number of treatises, as he himself mentions in the book *On Nature*, where he says that he has written something against the natural philosophers (whom he himself calls sophists), and a *Meteorology* (in which, he adds, he discusses the *arche*), and moreover a work *On the Nature of Man*. However, in *On Nature*, the only one of his works that has come into my hands, he sets out to demonstrate at length that in the *arche* which he posits there is much intelligence.

(Simplicius then proceeds to quotation.) From a second-hand statement in Galen (see Diogenes fr. 9), who frankly admits that he himself has not seen the work, we learn that *On Nature* contained at least two books. This is the sum of our information about the number and nature of his works.[3] The opening sentence of his 'treatise' (i.e.

---

[1] Kahn (*Anaximander*, 106) criticizes those who connect the references to air-theories in Aristophanes and Euripides with Diogenes's supposed visit to Athens, the evidence for which is, as he says, tenuous; but the familiarity of his views did not necessarily depend on his physical presence. On the other hand it is possible that his influence has been exaggerated. See p. 380 below.

[2] See DK, A3 and Burnet *EGP*, 352, n. 3.

[3] Further speculation is perhaps not very profitable. Diels claimed that the titles mentioned by Simplicius as cited by Diogenes himself all refer to the same work, the π. φύσεως. Relying on fr. 9, he suggested that, since in Hellenistic times it was evidently divided into at least two books, π. ἀνθρώπου φύσεως refers to the second. He adds, purely conjecturally, that the μετεωρολογία, which 'no one will take for the title of an ancient book', was either the beginning of π. φύσεως 2, or a separate third book. (See DK, II, 59, 52 n.) Wellmann (*RE*, v, 764), though with more caution, inclined to the same view, which involves the assumption that Simplicius only possessed

presumably *On Nature*) is quoted by Diogenes Laertius (9.57, fr. 1), and gives his creed as a writer:

I hold that whoever undertakes an exposition ought to make the starting-point (or first principle, *arche*) indisputable,[1] and the explanation simple and dignified.

(2) *The fundamental thesis: air as the* arché *of nature and life*

Fortunately for our knowledge of Diogenes, Simplicius not only possessed his book *On Nature* but quotes freely from it. Apart from a highly specialized passage on the veins, all our extracts come from the same place in his commentary on Aristotle's *Physics*, and it will be as well to begin by translating them in their setting in Simplicius's text. The passage is an immediate continuation of that just quoted (*Phys.* 151.28):

Immediately after the introduction Diogenes writes as follows (fr. 2):

'My view is, in sum, that all existing things are modifications of the same thing, and are the same thing. This is obvious; for if the things now existing in this cosmos—earth, water, air, fire and all the other things which manifestly exist in this cosmos—if one of these was different from another, different, that is, in its own proper nature, and not the same thing changed and altered in many ways, they could in no way mix with one another, nor affect one another for good or ill. Not even a plant could grow from the earth, nor could any animal or anything else come into existence, if everything were not so constituted as to be the same. But in fact all these things are variations of the same thing: they became different at different times and revert to the same thing.'

Happening upon these words first, I too thought he meant that besides the four elements there was something else to serve as common

bk. 1 of the π. φύσεως though he thought he had the whole. Simplicius's statement was defended by Theiler (*Teleol. Naturbetr.* 6) and Burnet (*EGP*, 353). It is interesting, as Burnet notes, that Simplicius should have preserved the detail that, where he himself would speak of φυσιολόγοι, Diogenes said σοφισταί, reflecting the usage of an earlier day. Kirk sums up the question judiciously (KR, 428 f.). He points out that Aristotle's long extract from Diogenes on the veins (*HA*, 511b31) seems to give exactly what Simplicius claims (153.18) to have found in *On Nature*, rather than coming from a separate work *On the Nature of Man*. Nevertheless he quotes a passage from Galen which, if the Diogenes there mentioned is our Diogenes, speaks of a separate treatise by him on medicine. (Walzer's edition of the Arabic version of *On Med. Experience*, 1944, 22.3.)

[1] The same methodical principle is enunciated by contemporary medical writers: Hippocr. *De arte*, 4 (VI, 6 L.) ἔστι μὲν οὖν μοι ἀρχὴ τοῦ λόγου ἣ καὶ ὁμολογέεται παρὰ πᾶσιν; *De carn.* 1 (VIII, 584 L.) ἀναγκαίως γὰρ ἔχει κοινὴν ἀρχὴν ὑποθέσθαι τῇσι γνώμῃσι.

substratum,[1] seeing that he says the elements would not mingle nor change into one another if some one of them was the first principle with a nature of its own instead of the same thing underlying them all, of which they were all variations. However, he goes straight on to show that this first principle possesses a high degree of intelligence, 'for', he says (fr. 3),

'without intelligence it would not have been possible for a division to be made in such a way as to keep the measures of all things—winter and summer, night and day, rain, winds and fair weather; and all else too, if one is willing to reflect, one will find arranged in the best possible way';

and then he argues that men and the other animals owe their life, soul and intelligence to this principle, which is air. His words are these (fr. 4):

'Moreover there are in addition these important indications. Men and the other animals live on air, by breathing, and this is to them both soul and mind, as will be clearly demonstrated in this treatise; and if this leaves them they die and their mind fails.'

A little after this he goes on plainly (fr. 5):

'And I hold that that which has intelligence is what men call air. All men are guided by it, and it masters all things. I hold that this same thing is God,[2] and that it reaches everything and disposes all things and is in everything. There is not one thing that does not have a share of it. Yet no one thing shares in it just as another does, but there are many forms both of air itself and of intelligence, for it is multiform—hotter and colder, drier and wetter, more stable and more swift-moving, and there are many other varia-

---

[1] 'I too'. Simplicius is refuting the opinion of Nicolaus of Damascus and Porphyry that when Aristotle speaks of believers in a basic substance separate from all the elements, something 'denser than fire but rarer than air' (*Phys.* 187 a 14), he is referring to Diogenes. That is his purpose in quoting the passages which make it clear that for Diogenes the ἀρχή was in fact air itself. Cf. also 25.4ff. For Simplicius as a good Aristotelian it seemed natural that any explanation of change should satisfy the Aristotelian demand for a neutral substratum distinct from the changing substances or their qualities (e.g. Arist. *Metaph.* 1069b3ff.).

In spite of Cherniss, *ACP*, 54, n. 215, I cannot reconcile these two passages in Simplicius with 203. 2–3, where he contrasts Diogenes with Anaximenes as making τὸ μεταξύ the ἀρχή *as opposed to* air. He is giving a quick list of examples of monists (Thales water, Heraclitus fire, Anaximenes air, Diogenes the intermediate body), and since the attributions are at the moment unimportant, allows Nicolaus's conjecture to slip in. ὡς before Thales is almost 'as it might be'. (Cherniss does not even mention Simplicius's strenuous denial of Nicolaus in two places.) That Simplicius should seriously have supported Nicolaus in this is all the more unlikely in that Aristotle himself expressly couples Diogenes with Anaximenes as making air μάλιστ' ἀρχὴν τῶν ἁπλῶν σωμάτων (*Metaph.* 984a5).

[2] The mistake in the MSS. of Simpl. ἔθος for θεός (which goes with other minor corruptions) is strange, but the correction seems certain, though a valiant attempt to defend the MS. reading was made by Weygoldt in *Archiv.* 1888, 165. Cf. Burnet, *EGP*, 354, n. 1. The supremacy of air justifies the use of the capital letter in preference to the translation 'a god'. What Diogenes thought of the popular gods is not known.

tions and an infinite variety both of scent and colour. Moreover the soul of all animals is the same thing, namely air, warmer than the air outside in which we are, but much colder than that near the sun. No animal has the same heat as any other, nor even one man the same as another, but the difference is not great, no more than is compatible with their being similar. None of the things subject to change can become exactly like another, without becoming the same thing.[1] Since the differentiation is multiform, living creatures are also many and various, not resembling one another either in appearance or in manner of life or in intelligence, owing to the multitude of differentiation. Yet all owe their life and sight and hearing to the same thing, and get the rest of their intelligence from the same thing.'

After this he shows that the seed of animals also is aeriform, and mental activities[2] take place when the air with the blood pervades the whole body through the veins, in a passage in which he gives a precise anatomical account of the veins.

In these sentences, then, he says quite plainly that what men call air is the *arché*. It is remarkable that while maintaining that everything else is generated by differentiation from air, he nevertheless calls it eternal, saying (fr. 7):

'and this itself is a body both eternal and immortal, but by it some things come into being and others perish.'[3]

And elsewhere: 'But this seems to me evident, that it is great and strong and eternal and immortal and knows many things.'

Theophrastus's statement that Diogenes owed much of his doctrine to Anaxagoras and Leucippus does not of course refer to the two fundamentals, the choice of primary substance and the process of generation. It occurs at the end of a rapid review of the monist philosophers in Simplicius, and he continues (still quoting Theo-

---

[1] Kranz in the *Nachtrag* to DK, II (10th ed. 1962, p. 421) remarks that this appears to be the earliest statement of Leibniz's principle of the identity of indiscernibles. A similar statement was quoted by Porphyry as an argument for the Parmenidean thesis of the unity of all being (*ap.* Simpl. *Phys.* 116.14): τὰ ὅμοια ἦ ὅμοια ἀδιάφορα καὶ οὐχ ἕτερα τυγχάνει ὄντα, τὰ δὲ μὴ ἕτερα ἕν ἐστιν. It is interesting to know that this principle cited by a Neoplatonist does go back to Presocratic times (noted by Reinhardt, *Parmenides*, 105). Sambursky, commenting on the application of the principle by the Stoics, notes that in Greek philosophy it was a feature of continuum as opposed to atomic physical theory (*Phys. of Stoics*, 47), and that this too is in accordance with Leibniz.

[2] νοήσεις, the plural of the word hitherto translated 'intelligence'. Its range of meaning is wide, and here 'perceptions' might be more appropriate. In the previous sentence one might well render: 'the rest of their power of apprehension'.

[3] Or 'but of the rest some come into being and others perish'. The MSS. vary between τῶ δὲ and τὸ δὲ. In printing τῶν DK follow the Aldine ed., but Diels in his text of Simplicius has τῷ, with the comment 'i.e. τῷ ἀέρι'. I feel a slight preference for this.

phrastus): 'But as to the nature of the whole, he too [*sc.* like Anaximenes] says that it is infinite and everlasting air, out of which other things take shape as it thickens and thins and changes its condition.'

The downright assertion that everything that exists is a modification of one and the same basic substance, and that substance one of the recognized elements, is a deliberate invitation to return to earlier modes of thought and a challenge to contemporary philosophy. To maintain it, Diogenes had to argue on two fronts: first he must show that recent attempts to escape the Eleatic arguments by assuming an ultimate plurality of elements were unacceptable; and secondly he must himself meet the Eleatic argument that what was one could never become many.

In fr. 2 he attacks the four 'roots of all things', which Empedocles, in deference to Eleatic principles, had assumed to be incapable of transmutation into one another, and to produce the variety of the natural world solely by mixture in different proportions. Without an underlying unity of substance, says Diogenes, to allow of their mutual transformation, the kind of interaction necessary to produce such complex organisms as plants and animals could not take place. This difficulty had also been felt by Anaxagoras. Everything that we see existing, he had said, must have grown out of something identical with it. His own solution had been to extend pluralism to its ultimate limits with his idea of 'a portion of everything in everything'. The complexity of the resulting theory was formidable, and Diogenes saw the way out in a return to the simplest meaning of the hypothesis on which all alike agreed, that whatever exists, in spite of apparent changes, must remain essentially what it was: substantial change is inconceivable because it would mean the actual coming-into-being and perishing of 'what is'. The obvious inference from this inescapable Parmenidean tenet, he said, is not the infinite plurality of the real, but its unity.

Here however he had to meet the further consequence of Eleatic logic, which had made the theory of ultimate pluralism seem inevitable, namely that there was no means by which a world of change and motion could be produced from unity. But the stumbling-block here had been the denial of empty space, which the Eleatics equated with non-being. Both Empedocles and Anaxagoras had felt bound to accept this, but Leucippus had already removed it from the path of Diogenes. That he believed in an *infinite* void is stated only by Diogenes Laertius (9.57), but the statement receives strong circumstantial support, and his belief in the existence of void is vouched for by Aristotle, who explicitly contrasts him with Anaxagoras in this respect (*De resp.* 470b30, p. 379 below). We know from Theophrastus that Diogenes adopted some of Leucippus's ideas, and it is impossible that anyone in his day could fail to be aware that condensation and rarefaction (the process by which air took on its manifold disguises) demanded void as a pre-condition. The contemporary Eleatic Melissus drew this conclusion explicitly.[1] If our other authorities for Diogenes do not mention it, this is probably because in anyone writing after Leucippus and accepting the two facts of change and basic unity, it could be taken for granted. Had Diogenes *not* seen that his system demanded a void, Theophrastus would probably have criticized him for inconsistency as he did the Empodoclean theory of 'pores'. The denial of void is reported for Zeno, Melissus, Empedocles and Anaxagoras, so that even the silence of our authorities lends some support to the one definite statement that Diogenes accepted it. Diogenes was not an atomist, but he had read Leucippus and agreed with him on two fundamental points: the material uniformity of all body and the existence of empty space.

(3) *Air is intelligent and divine*

A system deliberately combining Ionian monism with the recent recognition of the concept of void, even though the one came from Anaximenes and the other from Leucippus, cannot be said to lack all originality. It was a serious philosophical attempt to rival the fashionable pluralistic worlds as a defence of phenomena from Parmenides, and it is hardly fair to say with Jaeger (*TEGP*, 166) that Diogenes's motives for the return to monism were primarily theological. Theological considerations may, however, have played their part in the choice of the single *arché*. In the course of this history we have more

---

[1] Priority between Diogenes and Melissus cannot be determined with certainty. Diller in *Hermes*, 1941, tried to prove that Melissus wrote later and in criticism of Diogenes, but his arguments, based on verbal similarities, are by no means conclusive (cf. Kirk in KR, 430f.). The two were contemporaries, and the main point is that no one at this time could have revived the theory of condensation and rarefaction without recognizing the problem of void, of which its original author Anaximenes was happily unaware.

than once had occasion to notice the ancient connexion between air, life and divinity, which had already been exploited by Anaximenes (vol. I, 127 ff.). This connexion Diogenes developed under the influence of Anaxagoras's concept of Mind as the first cause. It enabled him to account for the influence of Mind on material events without contravening his principle that what is essentially different from anything can have no effect upon it. The aloofness of Mind from the world, as we saw, had prevented Anaxagoras from fulfilling the hopes of a theological explanation of nature to which the concept of Mind as first cause gave rise.

In Diogenes the theological explanation is paramount. The air from which all things come is also an omnipresent and omniscient god, whose conscious wisdom ensures the regularity and order of the cosmos. (The emphasis on 'measures' is probably an echo of Heraclitus.) For its activity he revived the old word κυβερνᾶν, 'guide' or 'steer', a keyword of the Milesians and Heraclitus, and Parmenides in the Way of Seeming (vol. I, 88). Jaeger (*TEGP*, 204, 243) has rightly drawn attention to the traditional religious, even hymn-like character of the language which Diogenes bestows on the god, once his existence has been assured on rational grounds. Still developing older ideas, Diogenes followed Anaximenes and certain religious teachers (vol. I, 201) in identifying the divine air in the world with the life-giving principle in animals and men, which is drawn in with the breath. The air in our bodies was 'a small portion of the god' (p. 374 below). We also notice from fr. 5 the infinite variety of the forms of air and the special importance of differences of temperature. All these variations could have been ultimately reduced by Diogenes, as heat and cold were by Anaximenes, to differences of density; but it sounds as if he paid more attention to the many derivative changes of quality, as is perhaps implied also in the words of Theophrastus that things are produced by air, 'thickening and thinning and changing in its qualities (πάθη)'. Finally, it is natural to infer from fr. 5 that the purest form of air, which is sheer intelligence and God, is warmer than that which gives life and less perfect powers of cognition to the animals and ourselves.

Diogenes of Apollonia

(4) Physical theories (cosmogony and cosmology, meteorology, magnetism)

Not much information and no fragments are preserved on these topics, evidently because Diogenes was not thought to have contributed much that was interesting or original. Thus the *Stromateis* record (A6):

Diogenes postulates air as the element. Everything is in motion and there are innumerable worlds. He constructs the cosmos thus: the whole is in motion and becomes thin in one place and dense in another, and where the dense comes together it has formed a close mass,[1] and so on with the rest in the same way: the lightest parts took the uppermost station and produced the sun.

From Aëtius we have (2.13.5 and 9, A12):

Diogenes says that the stars are like pumice-stone, and he regards them as the breathing-holes of the world. They are fiery. With the visible stars revolve stones which are invisible, and for that reason nameless. They often fall on the ground and are extinguished, like the stone star that came down on fire at Aegospotami.

Aëtius also reports that the sun is pumice-like, 'and the rays from the *aither* are fixed in it'. This suggests a combination of Empedocles's sun, which was purely a concentration of light-rays, and the 'fiery stone' of Anaxagoras. It is quenched (every night presumably; we are not told) by cold attacking the heat. The moon also is an ignited mass of pumice-like material. (Aët. 2.20.10, 25.10; DK, A13 and 14.) 'Comets are stars' (Aët. 3.2.8, A15), no doubt a condensed expression of the same view that Anaxagoras held, that they are chains of planetary bodies (p. 309 above). In fact we learn little from these snippets save that Diogenes had read Anaxagoras's book, in which he would find the impressive story of the Aegospotami meteorite. He is also coupled with Anaxagoras as believing that the cosmos took a tilt after animals had appeared on the earth (p. 305 above). He did indeed refine the 'incandescent stones' into pumice, whose obvious qualities are lightness and porosity. The latter would allow internal fire to shine through, but is also brought into connexion with a possibly interesting idea that the

[1] I.e. the earth. Diels and Kranz emended in different ways to bring this into the text: συστρο-φὴν ποιῆσαι MSS., συστραφὲν γῆν ποιῆσαι D., συστροφῇ ⟨τὴν γῆν⟩ K.

world has breathing-holes. Diogenes may have put to a new use the breathing-holes in Anaximander's star-wheels[1] and also remembered something of the Pythagorean notion that the cosmos breathes in from the 'void' outside. Those who had said this identified 'void' with breath (vol. I, 280). For Diogenes too the world was surrounded with infinite air or breath, though this was interspersed with true void to allow of its expansion and contraction.[2] The ingenuity with which he adapted the various conceptions of his predecessors to a system in keeping with the most recent advances of thought compels an admiration which is scarcely conveyed by the word 'eclecticism'.

For Anaxagoras the whole sum of matter had once been motionless, and the action of Mind was needed to set it in motion. Since Diogenes identified the ruling mind with matter itself, he naturally took the opposite view. The present cosmos has had a beginning and will in due time disappear again. On the question whether other worlds exist simultaneously or there is only a temporal succession of one at a time, the evidence is conflicting, nor can we be certain what Theophrastus recorded. Aëtius (2.1.3; DK, 12 A 17) and the *Stromateis*, already quoted, credit Diogenes with innumerable worlds, but Simplicius, expanding with examples a passage in which Aristotle contrasts those who believed in innumerable worlds with those who believed in one only, puts him among those who believed in one world at a time, perishing and renewed periodically. Seeing that he wrote after Leucippus, and accepted from him the existence of void and the infinite extent of matter, it seems more likely that he also took over the innumerable worlds, coexistent as well as successive.

He followed Anaxagoras in supposing the earth to be supported on air, and in the theory of its porous consistency, full of inter-communicating channels. For the origin of the sea he is said to have gone back to Anaximander. It is what remains of a layer of water on the earth, which the sun is gradually drying by evaporation. This evaporation is also the cause of its saltness, for it is the sweet water that

---

[1] Aët. uses διαπνοαί of Diogenes's stars, Hippolytus ἐκπνοαί of the star-wheels of Anaximander.

[2] This ignores a problem to which our sources do not provide the answer, namely the composition of the cosmic envelope. If the cosmos needed the stars as openings through which to draw in the life-giving breath from outside, it was presumably impenetrable elsewhere. Perhaps Diogenes borrowed the idea of a 'membrane' from Leucippus, but there is no information.

24-2

is evaporated out of it first. On the Nile floods he seems to have attempted originality, with a curious theory based on evaporation from the earth. As reported by Seneca he said that this takes place especially in the South. Because of the subterranean perforations, one part cannot be dried up while another overflows with water. The dry parts draw on the moist, so there is a rush of water from north to south. Seneca finds this explanation inadequate, and if he has reported it fully one can only agree with him.[1]

Some of his predecessors had made wind the agent of thunder, others fire. Diogenes hospitably suggested that there were two kinds: thunder preceded by lightning was caused by the fire, other thunder-claps by wind. So at least Seneca reports, and this can be reconciled with the version of Aëtius that thunder is 'an incursion of fire into a moist cloud, which causes thunder by its quenching and lightning by its brilliance; but he also adduces wind as a part-cause.'[2]

Diogenes had an elaborate and rather fantastic theory of magnetic attraction. We may consider it briefly in relation to the other Presocratic theories on this subject of which anything is known, namely those of Empedocles and Democritus (pp. 232, 426). Our knowledge of all three comes from a chapter on magnetism in the *Natural Questions* of Alexander of Aphrodisias, and is mainly interesting for the ingenious way in which all alike tried to apply the general principles of their systems to this as to other physical phenomena.

[1] Seneca, *Qu. nat.* 4a2, 28 ff. According to Seneca he used the analogy of the oil in a lamp, which is drawn up the wick to the burning tip. Under A 18 DK also quote the version of a scholiast on Apollonius Rhodius, which runs: 'Diogenes of Apollonia says that the sea-water is drawn up by the sun, and then brought down to the Nile. He thinks that the Nile floods in summer because the sun turns towards it the moisture of the earth.' For comparisons with Anaxagoras on earth, sea and Nile see pp. 310 f. On the shape of the earth we have only the ambiguous word στρογγύλη ('round') in D.L. 9.57, i.e. presumably disc-shaped as in Anaxagoras.

One must not forget the dubious nature of some of the sources. The statement that according to Diogenes the earth was supported by air occurs only in a scholiast on St Basil (DK, A 16a), but the extent to which he followed Anaxagoras in cosmological matters gives every reason for believing it.

[2] Texts in DK, A 16. This rather minor matter caused a thundering of giants in the last century, part of a clash between Diels and Natorp which is still worth reading (*Rh. Mus.* 1887, 1–14 and 374–86), especially pp. 10 f. and 381 f.). Diels chose it as an illustration of Diogenes's eclecticism: thunder was caused by fire for Leucippus, by wind for Anaximenes and Anaxagoras. He also drew attention to the use of ἔμπτωσις for ἔκπτωσις, making the thunderclap occur at the entry of fire into the cloud, as another borrowing from Anaxagoras. Natorp showed that Diogenes is in part closer to Empedocles, and that the variation between ἔμπτωσις and ἔκπτωσις is only accidental: Aristotle (*Meteor.* 370a5) uses ἔκπτωσις with reference to Empedocles and Anaxagoras.

Diogenes, with his belief in air—warmer or colder, wetter or drier—
as the basic form of matter, tended to explain a great deal on the
analogy of breathing. Even inanimate substances like metals inspired
or expired, not atmospheric air but a dampness or moisture, so that the
expulsion of it was a kind of sweating. We shall see in relation to his
psychology what a key position the two words moisture (ἰκμάς) and
drawing in (ἕλκειν) had in his system. Both iron and the lodestone
are subject to this process, but because the lodestone is 'more earthy
and of looser texture' it draws in more moisture than it expels. Applying also the principle of like acting on like, he explains that it draws in
the sweat (as one might call it) of iron but not of other metals. Since
its more open texture enables it to suck it in 'all at once', this action is
powerful enough to drag the iron with the moisture that it exudes.

This is an adaptation of the Empedoclean theory of pores and
effluences, which Empedocles had already applied to magnetism.
According to him, effluences from the magnet fit the pores of the iron
and by entering them drive out the air which they contain. This increases the flow of effluences from the iron so powerfully that as
they press into the pores of the magnet the iron itself is drawn after
them. Alexander complains that on this theory there is no reason why
the iron should be drawn to the magnet rather than *vice versa*, and
Diogenes's suggestion of the looser texture of the lodestone seems a
refinement designed to overcome this objection. The theory of Democritus is essentially that of Diogenes with the necessary modification
that the effluences are streams of atoms.[1]

(5) *Life, thought and sensation*

In Greek thought the soul (*psyche*) which animates living creatures has
two main functions: it gives the body its power of movement and makes
it aware of its surroundings through sensation and (in the case of
human beings) thought. Some laid more stress on one of these functions, some on the other. Diogenes was classified by Aristotle as one of
those who tried to explain both. For him the *psyche* was air (fr. 4), and
it acts in this dual way by being at once the basic substance of which all

[1] The relevant extracts from Alexander, *Quaest.* 2.23, are in DK, 31 A 89, 64 A 33, and
68 A 165.

existing things are modifications, and in its typical form the lightest, finest and hence most mobile form of body, corresponding to the tiny smooth soul-atoms of Democritus.[1] As such it imparts motion to the body, and as the common element it can cause awareness on the widely accepted principle that like is known by like, crudely applied by Empedocles in the line that 'with earth we see earth, with water water'.

This air which is soul, says Diogenes (fr. 5), is warmer than the atmosphere but much colder than that in the neighbourhood of the heavenly bodies. There its divinity is unalloyed, but even 'the air within us has perception because it is a small part of the God'. This sentence comes from Theophrastus's *De sensu*, as does practically all our information about Diogenes's views on thought and sensation except what is in the actual fragments.[2] Since God is mind, what perceives is essentially intelligence. That is why when the mind is distracted we do not perceive though sights and sounds may be presented to our eyes and ears.[3] To be the agent of thought the air must be pure and dry, for moisture impedes intelligence. Like Heraclitus, Diogenes mentions drunkenness in this connexion. Sleep is also caused by a moistening of the air-soul. (More specifically it is said to occur when blood fills the veins and drives the air in them to the chest and stomach, Aët. 5.24.3, A29.) The detail of these materialistic explanations verges on the fantastic, and it is not surprising that they appealed to Aristophanes's sense of the ridiculous.[4] Animals are less intelligent than men because they breathe air closer to the earth and eat moister food. Since this argument cannot apply to birds, a physiological explanation is found for their lack of reason: their breath is confined to the belly where it is all used up in the digestion of food. (Hence also the rapidity of this process in birds.) He added more perceptively that the formation of tongue and mouth, by precluding speech, makes mutual under-

---

[1] Arist. *De an.* 403b25 ff., 405a21.

[2] *De sensu*, 39–45 (DK, A19): full translation in Stratton, 101–7, partial in KR, 440f.

[3] *De sensu*, 42. This is also quoted by Cicero, *Tusc.* 1.20.46, who adds the corollary explicitly: 'ut facile intelligi possit, animum et videre et audire, non eas partes quae quasi fenestrae sunt animi.'

[4] The word ἰκμάς (rather than ὑγρόν) for moisture is Ionic, and when Aristophanes makes Socrates say that he must be swung up into the air to do his thinking because 'the earth draws to itself the ἰκμάς of the mind', we can be sure that in this travesty of Diogenes's theory he is using the philosopher's own word.

standing between the birds impossible. The intellectual immaturity of children is due to the fact that they have more moisture in their bodies than adults, which prevents the drier air from permeating the whole, and forgetfulness has a similar cause.

Within his materialism Diogenes seems to have come nearer than any other fifth-century philosopher to the distinction between a physical and a psychological event which was clearly drawn by Aristotle. Democritus explained vision simply as the reflexion of the object in the eye. Why then, asked Aristotle, has not every reflecting surface the power of sight? In an act of sensation, alteration of the bodily organ is only a precondition, not the sensation itself. One must distinguish between organ and faculty, the latter being an aspect of the *psyche*. The perception of warmth is something different from the material affection of becoming warm.[1] Some inkling of this meets us in Diogenes when he notes that mental distraction can prevent perception of what is physically present to the sense-organs. The mind is pure, dry air, and in his theory of sight, for instance, Theophrastus reports him as saying that while objects must be reflected in the pupil, they are only seen if the pupil 'is mingled with the internal air' which is the mind. When the vessels or ducts of the eye are inflamed, he adds, sight is impaired because the passage of air is interrupted, although the image appears in the pupil just the same. Thus, as Theophrastus admits, he to some extent refutes those who equate sight with reflexion, 'though without assigning the right cause himself' (*De sensu*, 47). That an Aristotelian should allow so much to a materialistic theory is evidence of the ingenuity with which it was applied.

Diogenes followed Empedocles in holding that black eyes see better by day (and with bright objects), others by night, giving as his reason that the contrary colour is better reflected. Keenness of sight depends on purity of air and fineness of the ducts, as with the other senses, and also on a lustre in the eye promoting reflexion. Hearing takes place when air within the ear is stirred by that outside and transmits the motion to the brain. Large, erect ears are desirable, and short, fine, straight ducts. 'Air around the brain' is made responsible for the sense of smell, because it is 'massed' there, and in Theophrastus's termino-

[1] On this distinction in Aristotle see especially Cassirer, *A.s' Schrift von der Seele*, 153.

375

logy so blended as to be 'commensurate' with the odour. At the same time keen scent is associated with a small amount of air in the head, because it and the odour then 'blend most quickly', as well as with the length and narrowness of the passage through which it is drawn in, giving the opportunity for its detection. This is alleged as the reason why some animals have keener scent than man, though our scent is also keen when odour and cephalic air are of a composition to mingle easily.[1] The tongue is the organ of taste because of its sponginess (softness and porosity) and the number of vessels which lead into it. From it the flavours can be dispersed through the body and reach the central organ of sense.[2]

Diogenes appears to have followed Alcmaeon and Anaxagoras in regarding the brain as the central organ of sensation and thought, rather than making it the heart like Empedocles and his Sicilian followers. We have noted that hearing requires that the motions should be transmitted from the ear to the brain, which also figured in smelling. That the air should be 'massed' there (ἄθρους) is a hint in the same direction. A passage in the Hippocratic treatise on the Sacred Disease begins: 'I hold that the brain has most power in man', and continues in a way that shows clear dependence on Diogenes: 'For the brain, if it is healthy, is the interpreter of the things that come into being from air; and air provides intelligence.' When a man draws breath it goes first to the brain and then to the other parts of the body, leaving in the brain its best part, that which is wise and understanding. Otherwise it would absorb moisture from the flesh and blood and reach the brain

---

[1] Some details of Diogenes's theories of hearing and smell are obscure owing to textual difficulties. See the apparatus in DK, notes *ad loc.* in Stratton, and Beare, 105, 140f.

[2] Combining Theophr. *De sensu*, 40 and 43 with Aët. 4.18.2 (DK, A22). If by ἡδονή in 43 Theophrastus simply meant 'pleasure', I am sure Beare (169, n. 3) is right in holding that this is a misunderstanding and that the word in Diogenes meant 'taste', as in fr. 5 and Anaxagoras fr. 4. Yet to call it a misunderstanding may be an over-simplification. To suggest that Theophr. himself was thinking of taste may seem to accuse him of clumsy arrangement, since the words apparently come in a discussion of pleasure and pain. In fact however the undoubted use of ἡδονή for flavour is evidence that there was a peculiarly intimate connexion in the Greek mind between taste and pleasure or its opposite. Thus Aristotle says (*De an.* 414b13) that hunger is a desire for the dry and warm, thirst for the cold and wet; and flavour is a kind of ἥδυσμα of these. In Hippocr. *De victu*, 1.23 (quoted DK, 22 c 1) the author is relating the senses (or sense-organs) to their objects, and says that hearing is of sound, sight of the visible, the nostrils of smell, the body in general of touch, and γλῶσσα ἡδονῆς καὶ ἀηδίης. Cf. Xen. *Mem.* 1.4.5 τίς δ' ἂν αἴσθησις ἦν γλυκέων καὶ δριμέων καὶ πάντων τῶν διὰ στόματος ἡδέων, εἰ μὴ γλῶττα τούτων γνώμων ἐνειργάσθη; (See also Vlastos, *Philos. Rev.* 1945, 586, n. 48.)

dulled and impure.[1] Moreover Aristotle, after quoting at length the detailed description of the course of the veins in Diogenes, Syennesis and Polybus, says (*HA*, 513a9): 'There are other writers on nature who have described the veins in less meticulous detail, but all alike trace their origin from the head and the brain.' The starting-point of the blood was also the seat of consciousness, both in Aristotle himself and earlier writers; and particularly for Diogenes, who emphasized the part played by the veins in carrying air as well as blood. 'Perceptions take place when the air with the blood pervades the whole body through the veins.' (Simpl. *Phys.* 153.13; see fr. 6.)[2]

Diogenes agreed with the atomists in holding that sensations were subjective and relative.[3] He is classed with them by Aëtius (4.9.8, A23), and fr. 5 shows that perceptions will differ according to the constitution, and in particular the temperature, of the air in each individual. Pleasure, pain and emotions have similar physical causes. Pleasure attends on a rich mixture of air lightening the blood, pain on a pathological condition in which the blood is sluggish and thick through lack of air uniting with it (Theophrastus, *De sensu*, 43). Should the air leave the blood altogether, death occurs (Aët. 5. 24. 3, A 29).

---

[1] *Morb. sacr.* 16 (DK, 64c3a). Much of it is translated in KR, 442.

[2] The statement at Aët. 4.5.7 that for Diogenes the ἡγεμονικόν is in the heart must be a mistake. There is a similar mistake about Democritus: at 4.4.6 it is said that the reasoning part of the soul is in the breast, at 4.5.1 that the ἡγεμονικόν is in the brain. Aristotle in the passage quoted clearly includes Diogenes among those who traced the origin of the veins to the head. It must be admitted, however, as Littré noted (1, 220), that this does not emerge at all clearly from the description of the system in Diogenes which he actually quotes. Burnet (*EGP*, 358) wrote that 'no special seat, such as the heart or the brain, was assigned to the soul; it was simply the warm air circulating with the blood in the veins'. Similarly, Wellmann (*FGÄ*, 1, 15, n. 4) says that Diogenes 'der Seele kein bestimmtes Organ als Sitz anweist'. This of course is true for ψυχή as a whole, as with the atomists. But that would not prevent Diogenes from supposing, like them, that there was a concentration of it in a particular part of the body which served as a central organ of cognition or common sensorium. Weygoldt (*Arch. f. Gesch. d. Phil.* 1888, 165 f.) claims that *De morb. sacr.* 3 (VI, 366 L.) reproduces Diogenes's account of the veins more accurately than Aristotle; and this does say that φλέβες ἐς αὐτὸν [sc. τὸν ἐγκέφαλον] τείνουσιν ἐξ ἅπαντος τοῦ σώματος.

[3] This subjectivity however did not for him carry with it the denial of sensible qualities to the primary substance itself, as the atomic theory demanded. This too is clear from fr. 5, and need not involve the blatant contradiction which Natorp saw in it (*Rh. Mus.* 1887, 383). Actual sensations are still due to the interaction between the object of sense and the human body, the constitution of which varies from one individual to another.

(6) *Physiology*

Since Diogenes's explanations of sensation and thought were entirely physiological, something has already been said on this subject; for the rest, he had a physician's interest in the body, and there are one or two references to the diagnosis of disease, mentioning colour and the state of the tongue as particularly useful indications. Colour, says Galen, was reckoned by 'Diogenes and the pundits of his time' to be the most accurate sign. They classified diseases by it, matching different complexions with amount of blood and prevalence of the different humours.[1]

Some reports of his views on reproduction and embryology have been preserved. They say that he accepted the etymology of *aphrodisia* from *aphros*, 'foam', holding that semen was a foam or froth formed from the blood by the heat of the male in copulation. Being the vehicle of life, it naturally contains a high proportion of air. Embryos are nourished not through the umbilical cord but by fleshy cup-shaped growths ('cotyledons') on the sides of the womb.[2] Only the male parent contributes seed, not the female, a contradiction of Empedocles (p. 217 above). The formation of the male body takes four months, of the female five. Flesh is formed first, out of moisture, then bones, sinews and the other parts from flesh. Infants are born lifeless, but 'in heat' (or 'warm'): hence the innate heat, as soon as the babe is delivered, draws the cold into the lungs.[3]

[1] Theophr. *De sensu*, 43; Galen, *De humor.* XIX, 495 Kühn (A29a).

[2] Aristoph. *Epit. hist. an.* 1.78 (*Suppl. Arist.* I, 1.23.13), A25. Nourishment through the cotyledons was refuted by Aristotle, *GA*, 746a19ff., who perhaps was criticizing his contemporary Diocles rather than the fifth-century Diogenes (fr. 27 Wellmann; Jaeger, *Diokles*, 166). See further pp. 357 and 468. Semen is πνευματῶδες Simpl. *Phys.* 153.13.

[3] For sources of this paragraph see A26–8 (Censorinus and Aëtius). The account of the infant's first breath may be compared with those of Empedocles and Philolaus (pp. 219f. above and vol. I, 278f.). There is no suggestion in these that it is lifeless until this takes place. Diller (*Hermes*, 1941, 373) explains Diogenes thus: ἀήρ in Greek usage is cold and damp. Hence the warmth, which is to be characteristic of the *vital* air, exists within us before birth. Nevertheless the embryo is lifeless. Only by breathing, which is contemporaneous with birth, is the life-giving coolness of the outer air drawn into us by the warmth. In breathing not only is the internal warmth cooled, but the air that enters is warmed, and only by this mingling does it become specifically soul. The warmer air is higher and more divine (Diller sees Heraclitean influence here), whereas Diogenes's physiological interests made him realize that the air we breathe is cold. (One may compare fr. 5: the soul is air warmer than that outside us. So far as it goes this accords with Diller's explanation.)

The order of formation of the various bodily tissues is described similarly and in greater detail in the Hippocratic *De nat. pueri*, 16f. (VII, 496f. L.), no doubt following Diogenes. See Weygoldt, *Arch. f. Gesch. d. Phil.* 1888, 170.

To explain breathing Diogenes made use of the newly vindicated concept of void. Like Anaxagoras he maintained that fish breathed, but, says Aristotle, whereas Anaxagoras had had to explain this on the assumption that there was no void, Diogenes said that when they expel water through their gills they suck air out of the water round the mouth by means of the vacuum formed in it (*De resp.* 470b30–471a5). Plants cannot breathe because they have no hollow parts in which a void can be created.[1]

If we agree with those who have claimed to recognize Diogenes as the source of certain passages in Xenophon, we find him working out his teleological interpretation of nature in a systematic series of parallels between parts and organs of the body and human technical devices. The eyelids are doors, the eyelashes sieves, the eyebrows like the cornices of a building to keep away sweat, the excretory system corresponds to drains, conveniently placed where the effluent will least offend the senses.[2]

(7) *Conclusion*

There is no mention of Diogenes by name in any writer before Aristotle, yet his theories seem to have made a great impression on his contemporaries and immediate successors, in so far as we may assume that he was the originator of them. The idea of air as both God and the mind of man appears in the prayer of Hecuba in Euripides's *Troades* (884ff.):

O thou on whom earth rides and who hast thy station above the earth, whosoever thou art, hard to divine or know, Zeus,[3] be thou nature's compulsion or mind of man, to thee I pray; for treading thy noiseless way thou leadest aright all the things of mortals.

In the *Clouds* of Aristophanes (264), Socrates prays to the 'Lord and Master, measureless Air, who holdest the earth aloft', and swears by

---

[1] Theophr. *De sensu*, 44. One other observation about plants is recorded for Diogenes, also in contrast to Anaxagoras. Whereas the latter spoke of seeds falling from the air and generating plants, Diogenes attributed their origin to water 'rotting' and mixing with earth. (Theophr. *HP*, 3.1.4. The subject of γεννᾶν would seem to be grammatically σπέρματα, not ἀήρ as DK say at A32.)

[2] Xen. *Mem.* 1.4.6. For the identification see Jaeger, *TEGP*, 167f.; Theiler, *Teleol. Naturbetr.* 18ff. It is by no means certain. Vlastos is sceptical in *Philos. Quart.* 1952, 115, n. 84, and cf. Solmsen's remarks in *JHI*, 1963, 479, n. 33; F. Hüffmeier in *Philologus*, 1963, 131–8.

[3] Diogenes is said to have praised Homer for saying that the air was Zeus, a fact which he deduced from the poet's pronouncement that Zeus knew everything (Philodemus, *De piet.* c. 6b, A8).

Respiration, Chaos and Air instead of by the Olympians (*v.* 627). He philosophizes from a basket suspended aloft, in order to 'mingle his fine (λεπτήν) wit with the *kindred* air', and explains that if he were down on the earth it would draw to itself the moisture of his mind (226ff.). More seriously, in Plato's *Phaedo* (96b), among the theories which Socrates studied as a young man was the one which said that we think by means of air (as well as those of Empedocles and Heraclitus that blood and fire respectively are the vehicles of thought). An obvious parody of the same ideas occurs in a rather later comic poet, Philemon (born *c.* 361 B.C.; fr. 91, DK, 64C4):

I am he from whom none can hide in one single thing that he may do, or be about to do, or have done in the past, be he god or man. Air am I, whom one might also call Zeus. I am everywhere, as a god should be—here in Athens, in Patrae, in Sicily, in all cities and in all homes, in every one of you. There is no place where is not Air. And he who is present everywhere, because he is everywhere of necessity knows everything.

There is no need to argue the identity of Philemon's air-god with that of Diogenes frr. 5 and 7. At the same time it must be remembered that many of Diogenes's ideas were part of the intellectual climate of the fifth century, and did not originate with him. The supporting of the earth by air, mentioned by both Euripides and Aristophanes, goes back to Anaximenes and was retained by Anaxagoras and Democritus and the author of the Hippocratic *De flatibus* (p. 310 above). Probably the last-named was indebted to Diogenes, for there is other evidence in the Hippocratic writings of his influence on medical science. The connexion between the moisture in the earth and that in a living creature occurs in the treatise *On the Nature of the Child* (p. 209 above), and might have been borrowed by Aristophanes from Hippocrates or one of his school as easily as from Diogenes himself, and the philosophic author of *The Sacred Disease* owed him a pretty obvious debt.[1]

Serious attempts have been made, by diligent comparison of passages, to estimate the influence of Diogenes in particular matters. The details must remain in part debatable,[2] for it is difficult to be certain about the

---

[1] See most recently H. W. Miller in *TAPA*, 84 (1953), 1–15.
[2] Fredrich (*Hippokr. Unters.* 132) issued a caveat against exaggerating his influence on the Hippocratic writers.

originator of some theories which were obviously common ground among a number of investigators at the same time. It may be said, however, that he both developed and popularized three doctrines, all interrelated: the idea of air as *arché*, the essential identity of microcosm and macrocosm (the human soul and the divine, omnipresent, controlling mind), and the teleological interpretation of nature. The importance of this outlook on the world for medical theory, for Plato, Aristotle and Hellenistic thought fully justifies his position in the main stream of Greek philosophy, and his restoration of a physical monism in the face of Eleatic argument and the pluralistic tendencies of his time was a *tour de force* which must not be underestimated.[1]

Two additional points may be singled out as being of some philosophical interest. First, Diogenes was led to distinguish between sense-organ and perceiving mind by the observation that it is possible not to perceive although suitable objects are presented to the senses.[2] Secondly, there is his suggestion that a subjective or relativist theory of perception was not incompatible with the assumption of a common object of sense endowed with all sensible qualities.[3]

[1] On the influence of Diogenes in general see Theiler, *Teleol. Naturbetr.* 6–36, 57–61 (the Stoa). For the medical writers Theiler refers to F. Willerding, *Stud. Hippocratica*, 1914, to which may now be added K. Deichgräber, *Hippocr. über Entstehung u. Aufbau des menschl. Körpers* (1935), 27 ff., and Pohlenz, *Hippokrates*, 1938, pp. 9, 39, 73. The spread of his influence in the Hellenistic age must have been made easier by the fact that Theophrastus wrote a *Collection of the Opinions of Diogenes* in one book (D.L. 5. 43).

[2] P. 374. The permanent interest of this for philosophers and psychologists may be seen from a history of the subject like D. W. Hamlyn's *Sensation and Perception*; e.g. on p. 160 Hamlyn notes that James Ward 'lays emphasis upon the notion of "attention", stressing the point that the mind must *attend* to presentations as well as receive them'.

[3] P. 377, n. 3. *Philos. and Phenom. Research*, 1962–3, 533 f. may be mentioned as an example of modern discussion of the question whether, if different people claim to perceive different colours (or shapes, tastes or odours) in the same object, some must be sensing or imagining colours, etc. which do not characterize the object. A. O. Lovejoy had maintained that this was so, but in the author's view (C. A. Baylis), if, say, a theatre-curtain has a succession of different-coloured lights played on it, and some of those looking at it suffer from red–green or blue–yellow colour-blindness, the fact that some people see different colours successively on the surface of the same curtain, and some simultaneously see different colours from others, should not be explained by saying that the curtain cannot be characterized by these incompatible colours. 'Why not say that its surface has all the corresponding colour qualities, though for these to be seen requires special combinations of a light ray of a certain sort with a perceiver of a certain sort?' The two points of view here represented bear some relation to those of Democritus and Diogenes respectively. (Sext. *Pyrrh. hyp.* 2.63, DK, 68 A 134: because honey tastes sweet to some and bitter to others, Democritus said it is neither sweet nor bitter.)

VIII

THE ATOMISTS OF THE
FIFTH CENTURY

The atomic theory was the work of Leucippus and his pupil Democritus, and it is with this pre-Platonic atomism that we are here concerned. It was continued and modified, from different motives, by Epicurus at the end of the fourth century,[1] but this belongs to a later chapter of our history. Diogenes Laertius gives a fairly full account of general principles, cosmogony and cosmology according to Leucippus, but in other sources the atomic theories are most commonly attributed either to both men together or to Democritus. Evidently Democritus, who was a most prolific writer, followed his master in essentials, but developed and elaborated his theories considerably from (it would seem) a more empirical and less deductive viewpoint. He also displayed an interest in ethical questions which there is no evidence that Leucippus shared. It will be best to treat the atomic world-view of this period as a single whole (except for a few points of detail on which a difference is recorded), after first saying something about the two men who were its authors.[2]

[1] Alfieri (*Estudios Mondolfo*, fasc. 1, 149 ff.; *Atomos Idea*, ch. 2) suggests that the name 'School of Abdera' would be better than 'Atomists' if one wishes to exclude Epicureanism, as avoiding the necessity of speaking of 'older atomism'. It is justified, he claims, if (as with the Eleatics) one means by 'school' not a *thiasos* like the Pythagorean or a community in a *gymnasion* like the Academy or Lyceum, but a succession of philosophers of whom one was the disciple of the other. Leucippus must have written his works, and taught Democritus, at Abdera. Democritus, Anaxarchus and Bion were Abderites. Hecataeus and Nausiphanes came from Teos, the mother-city of Abdera which maintained close relations with it. Metrodorus of Chios must have come to Abdera to be Democritus's pupil. From Abdera issued all those works of Democritus which constituted an encyclopaedia of knowledge unparalleled until Aristotle. The readers and disseminators of these books constitute the School of Abdera; they are disciples of Democritus whether or not he gave them oral instruction. It is possible to name eleven who were more or less certainly members of this school, which covered a century and a half, roughly from Cimon and the building of the long walls of Athens to Ptolemy Lagus, in whose reign lived Nausiphanes.

Here, however, we shall not be concerned with Nausiphanes nor with any other of the epigoni of Democritus, some of whom there is no evidence to connect with the atomic theory of reality. Nor has Protagoras a place in a discussion of atomism, though his omission would be unpardonable in any chapter claiming to deal with the philosophers of Abdera.

[2] Bailey (*Gk. Atomists*, 68) claims that this is an unsatisfactory procedure. Yet much that he assigns to the section on Leucippus alone is attributed in the sources to Leucippus and Democritus

Authors of the Atomic Theory

A. LEUCIPPUS

Epicurus, who adopted the atomic system a century after Democritus, is reported as having said that there never was such a philosopher as Leucippus.[1] This statement gained surprising credence among some scholars, but the matter has now been thoroughly thrashed out and need not detain us long.[2] It is quite incredible in face of the repeated mentions of him, both alone and with Democritus, by Aristotle and Theophrastus (or those who quote him). Epicurus was notoriously touchy on the subject of predecessors. He claimed (manifestly falsely) complete originality, and heaped contempt and ridicule on those from whom he might be supposed to have learned.[3] In Hellenistic times the greater fame of Democritus certainly relegated Leucippus to the background. This would be not only because Democritus was a greater philosopher with more universal interests, but also because he wrote a large number of published works which were carefully edited and highly praised for their purely literary merits. In this respect ancient critics, including Cicero, coupled his name with Plato's. What Leucippus wrote, on the other hand, was probably more in the nature of school literature, disseminated by being read aloud as lectures, and, as Stenzel says, where recognition by posterity is in question, the contest between works like these and brilliant literary productions on the same subject is an unequal one.[4]

together. No doubt Leucippus as the older man deserves the credit due to a pioneer, but in default of more rigid separation in the sources we cannot say how far he went, and nothing is lost by taking the system of the two men as a whole. A more detailed attempt to separate them was made by Dyroff, *Demokritstudien*, 3–49, but though this work offers much of interest, it is not free from dubious argument and questionable statements and must be used with caution. See also von Fritz, *Philos. u. Sprach. Ausdruck*, 12 ff., 24 f.

[1] D.L. 10.13. It has been suggested that the sentence means only that Epicurus denied that Leucippus was a philosopher, but the word τινα is against this.

[2] The existence of Leucippus was denied by Rohde, and his view, though strenuously contradicted by Diels, was revived by Nestle (ZN, 1040–3). Diels returned to the attack in the preface of the 4th ed. of the *Vorsokratiker*, and there is an excellent discussion of this 'unerhört kühne These' by Stenzel in *RE*, XII, 2267–9. For fuller references to the controversy see besides this article (col. 2268), DK, II, notes to pp. 71–2. and Kerschensteiner, *Kosmos*, 150, n. 1. The arguments are conveniently summarized by Ameri, *Atomisti*, 8, n. 27.

[3] Burnet suggested (*EGP*, 330, n. 2) that the story in Diogenes might have arisen from a misunderstanding of a sally of this kind. Epicurus might have said of Leucippus οὐδ' εἰ γέγονεν οἶδα, meaning (like Demosthenes in *De cor.* 70) that he had not the slightest interest in him.

[4] *RE*, XII, 2270. Stenzel notes that the same thing happened within the corpus of Plato's writings. The case of Aristotle, which Stenzel does not mention, might be thought to be a contrary instance, but it must be granted that the early history of his writings is unique, and by all accounts owed much to sheer accident.

Even so, Cicero cites Leucippus twice, noting in one place (*N.D.* 1.24.66) that he came before Democritus.

Some said that Leucippus was from Miletus, others from Elea, others from Abdera. The three places epitomize his chief philosophical associations: essentially Ionian in outlook, he was well versed in Eleatic philosophy, and he taught Democritus the Abderite. It is therefore easy for the sceptic to say that the traditional localizations have no basis in fact, but are simply projections from the philosophy. The less sceptical prefer to account for the philosophical history by sojourns in each place. So Kranz held (*Hermes*, 1912, 19) that he was certainly born at Miletus, went to Elea and studied under Zeno, then turned back eastward and founded his school at Abdera. Since the statements are there, but there is no means of checking them, the choice in this not very important matter is free.[1]

Of his date one can say that he was older than Democritus, who was born about 460, old enough too to have influenced Diogenes of Apollonia whose teaching was satirized by Aristophanes in 423 (pp. 362 f. above), but young enough to be acquainted with the doctrines of Zeno and Melissus as well as Parmenides. He is said to have been Zeno's pupil, and there is no reason why this should not be true. Theophrastus's testimony is likely to be the most accurate, but is not unequivocal: 'Leucippus of Elea or Miletus (both accounts of him are current) was associated with Parmenides in philosophy, but did not go the same way as Parmenides and Xenophanes in his explanation of reality, indeed it would seem he went the opposite way.' The statement that he was 'associated with Parmenides' is ambiguous in the Greek, but if we agree that it implies personal association it could still be true, and need not conflict with calling him a pupil of Zeno, since if Parmenides was alive when Leucippus went to Elea he must have been an old man and Zeno already mature. It cannot be far wrong

---

[1] Elea, Abdera or Melos (which must be a copyist's error for Miletus), D.L. 9.30; Elea or Miletus, Simplicius, *Phys.* 28.4 (A8); Miletus, Aët. 1.3.15 (A12), Epiphanius *Adv. Haer.* 3.2.9 (A33). Nestle (ZN, 1039 n.) thinks 'possible' the same sequence as Kranz, which is also upheld by Alfieri (*Estud. Mondolfo*, 150, 165). Stenzel (col. 2267) thought Abdera a later invention resulting from Leucippus's disappearance behind Democritus in Hellenistic times. (But where then did the two men associate?) To Gomperz (*Gr. Th.* 1, 567) it appeared most likely that he was a Milesian 'because in the two other cases of Elea and Abdera his relations with Zeno and Democritus respectively might be regarded as probable sources of error'.

to date the promulgation of his theory round about the year 430 or a little earlier.[1]

Of his works there is mention of a *Great World-System* and a treatise *On Mind*. In Hellenistic times the former was attributed to Democritus, as well as a *Little World-System*, but Diogenes Laertius in the list of Democritus's works notes against the *Great World-System* that Theophrastus and his school assign it to Leucippus. Theophrastus was in a better position to know than Thrasyllus, whose catalogue, of the first century A.D., Diogenes is reproducing. By that time there existed a kind of corpus of the literature of atomism under the name of Democritus, its most famous representative. The existence of two works with the same title, distinguished as 'Great' and 'Little', makes the difference of authorship all the more likely. The epithets probably do not refer to size. Democritus may have called his cosmology 'the Little' out of modesty, and Leucippus's could have been dubbed 'the Great' in consequence.[2] Others have assumed a difference of content, the work of Leucippus being cosmological (covering the ground later traversed by Lucretius in books 1 and 2) whereas Democritus supplemented this with an account of the origin and development of human life and civilization (corresponding to Lucretius 5). This suggestion[3] is sup-

---

[1] Simpl. *Phys.* 28.4 (A8 = Theophr. *Phys. op.* fr. 8). Burnet (*EGP*, 332, n. 2) and Zeller (ZN, 1039 n., 1202 n.) thought that the dative in κοινωνήσας τῷ Παρμενίδῃ τῆς φιλοσοφίας implied a personal relationship absent from the κ. τῆς 'Αναξιμένους φιλοσοφίας which Theophrastus said of Anaxagoras. For Leucippus as pupil of Zeno see D.L. 9.30, Clem. *Strom.* II, 40 St. (A4, a weak testimony), ps.-Galen, *Hist. phil.* 3 (A5).

If we wish to speculate, there is something attractive about the suggestion of Alfieri (*Estud. Mondolfo*, 165), based on the three places with which his name is connected, that he left Miletus at the revolution of 450, moved to Elea, then came to Abdera about 440 and taught his new doctrine to Democritus who would be about 20. In this way the atomic theory in general would be the result of collaboration between the older and younger man rather than of successive developments.

[2] See DK, II, 80 n.; ZN, 1040 n.; Bailey, *Gk. Atomists*, 113. Ch. Mugler (*Rev. de Philol.* 1959, 11) assumes without argument a distinction of substance different from that mentioned in the text. The Μικρὸς διάκοσμος (by Democritus) was the study of a single world (our own for example), whereas the Μέγας δ. (by Leucippus) described the process of selection whereby certain of the infinitely various atoms in the infinite void came together and were formed into a world. It is difficult to see any particular justification for this, but even if Democritus's main subject was the microcosm he would preface it with a summary of the cosmogony evolved by Leucippus and himself. For Ionians anthropology was only a continuation of the same cosmic study.

[3] In which Alfieri has followed Reinhardt: see *Atomisti*, 37 n., 150 and *Atomos Idea*, 108, 116 f.; also Schmid, *Gesch. gr. Lit.* 1.5.2.2, 256 f. Kerschensteiner, however (*Kosmos*, 155, n. 1), thinks that to suppose a difference of theme goes against linguistic usage. In view of the confidence with which some modern scholarship has assumed that Μικρὸς διάκοσμος and the development of civilization are synonymous (see especially Schmidt, *op. cit.* 1.5.2.2, 264), it must be emphasized that this is conjectural even if likely.

ported by the consideration that Democritus is the first in history, so far as we know, to have given the name 'little world' or microcosm to man (fr. 34).

Of the treatise *On Mind* there survives the one famous sentence: 'Nothing comes to be at random, but all things for a reason and of necessity.'[1]

B. DEMOCRITUS

Date and life. Democritus himself said in the *Little World-System* that he was young in the old age of Anaxagoras, probably adding that the difference in their ages was forty years. He was, then, born about 460, and though the date of his death is not known, he is said to have reached an advanced old age, some even putting it at over a hundred.[2] He was, like Protagoras, a native of Abdera in Thrace, a colony established from Teos in this remote north-eastern region about the middle of the sixth century, after an earlier unsuccessful attempt by Clazomenae. In his curiosity and zest for travel he resembled a more scientific Herodotus. Visits to Egypt, Persia and Babylon, and instruc-

[1] Thrasyllus's catalogue of the works of Democritus also includes a Περὶ νοῦ, and those who did not believe in the existence of Leucippus naturally thought that this was the work which Theophrastus had attributed to him. It may have been general rather than psychological in content, containing a refutation of the νοῦς of Anaxagoras as a cosmological principle; but this can only be a guess. See Stenzel, *RE*, XII, 2273 f.; Alfieri, *Atomisti*, 9 f.; Kerschensteiner, *Kosmos*, 155.

[2] D.L. 9.41 and 34. The phrase ἔτεσιν αὐτοῦ νεώτερος τετταράκοντα occurs in both places, and some have thought it a suspiciously Apollodoran number. Apollodorus, who liked to space out the generations of philosophers at forty-year intervals (cf. p. 2 above), is mentioned in the next sentence of ch. 41 as dating Democritus's birth in Ol. 80 (460–57). The number may however be a coincidence, and the quotation from Democritus himself continues further as if the phrase were a part of it. Thrasyllus (D.L. *ibid.*) gave the third year of Ol. 77 (470–69), adding that he was older than Socrates, though the date makes him exactly the same age. Passages in Aristotle (*Part. an.* 642a24; *Metaph.* 1078b17ff.) have also been thought, unjustifiably, to imply the temporal priority of Democritus to Socrates. Later stories that Protagoras was his pupil cannot be reconciled either with his own statement that he was much younger than Anaxagoras or with the dating of Apollodorus or Thrasyllus, nor is there much temptation to believe them. They go with anecdotal matter, their source is Epicurus (*ap.* D.L. 9.53 and Athen. 8.354c, DK, A9), and they conflict with the better-attested fact that Democritus in his own writings attacked Protagoras's teaching (p. 350 above). See also ZN, 1302, nn. 2 and 4. The only sure testimony is that of Democritus himself.

For an introduction to modern controversy on the subject see ZN, 1044–6 n.; Alfieri in *Estud. Mondolfo*, 149–67 (who argues cogently on pp. 156f. against the very early dating of Stella); Davison, *CQ*, 1953, 38f. The arguments of Diels against Rohde, *Rh. Mus.* 1887, 1–5, are still worth reading. Davison notes that since the Epicureans put his birth about forty years too early, they were probably responsible for the reports that he lived to over a hundred, if he was known to have died between 400 and 390. These reports come from Antisthenes of Rhodes and Hipparchus (*ap.* D.L. 9.39, 43) and ps.-Lucian, *Macrobioi*, 18 (DK, A6).

tion from priests, magi and 'Chaldeans', are widely attested. One or two late sources add Ethiopia and India. Clement quotes as from his own pen the claim: 'I covered more territory than any man in my time, making the most extensive investigations, and saw more climes and countries and listened to more famous men.'[1] These voyages of study may have taught him much about special subjects like mathematics and astronomy, but the atomic theories themselves seem to spring entirely from the contemporary state of philosophical questions in Greece itself.[2]

He was the subject of a number of anecdotes, none of which can claim much relation to fact or even serve very well as indicators of the character he bore in antiquity. Some he shares with other famous philosophers, Thales, Anaxagoras or Protagoras. However, the general impression is one of serenity, good humour and fortitude which accords well enough with his surviving ethical precepts.[3] His sobriquet of the Laughing Philosopher, moved to mirth by the follies of mankind as Heraclitus to tears, is first alluded to by Cicero and best known from Horace.[4]

His only undoubted teacher was Leucippus. Some said he was also a pupil of Anaxagoras, and his contemporary Glaucus of Rhegium that he 'heard' one of the Pythagoreans, whom Apollodorus of Cyzicus[5] later identified with Philolaus. A book on Pythagoras was included among his works, and was said to be laudatory. These contacts are chronologically possible, and the man who travelled as far as Egypt and Persia to meet the world's most famous teachers is not likely to have neglected the opportunities that lay nearer at hand.

[1] Fr. 299. Opinions on its genuineness have differed widely. See ZN, 431, n. 1, 1049n.; Alfieri, *Atomisti*, 278, n. 706, and DK, ii, 209. Regenbogen was 'not convinced that it is spurious' (*RE*, Suppl. vii, 1541). For other references to Democritus's travels see DK, A1 (ch. 35), 9, 12, 13, 16 and Diod. 1.98.3, who says that he is believed to have spent five years in Egypt, where he learned much astronomy. He spoke from his own experience when he said (fr. 246): 'Foreign travel teaches the self-sufficient life: barley bread and straw to lie on are the best cures for hunger and weariness.'

[2] For the later legend of a prehistoric Phoenician Mochus as originator of the atomic theory, and for comparison with Indian thought, see Bailey, *Atomists*, 64f.; R. A. Horne in *Ambix*, 1960, 98–110, and H. V. Glasenapp in Schmid, *Gesch. gr. Lit.* 1.5.2.2, *Nachtr.* p. 350. On the growth of the legend of Democritus as skilled in the arts of the magi, see Schmid, *ibid.* 236, n. 11, and for possible parallels between the two, the references to Bidez and Cumont in 241, n. 4.

[3] Some of them are in Bailey, *op. cit.* 109 ff.

[4] Cic. *De or.* 2.58.235; Hor. *Ep.* 2.1.194: the contrast with Heraclitus in Sotion (the teacher of Seneca). Passages collected in DK, A21, also Hippol. *Ref.* 1.13.4 (A40) and the Suda (A2). But fr. 107a, whether genuine or not, suggests a different tradition.

[5] For whom see DK, ii, p. 246; Schmid, *Gesch. gr. Lit.* 1.5.2.2, 335f.

Writings. He was an encyclopaedic writer, whose works anticipated Aristotle's in their volume and variety, but unfortunately suffered a different fate. Their loss forbids the comforting theory that time has spared or overwhelmed the works of antiquity according to their merits. In any case, no scholastic ingenuity could have used his system, as it did Aristotle's, as a model for the orthodox Christian world-view. Diogenes Laertius (9.45–9) reproduces an Alexandrian catalogue of over sixty works arranged in groups of four, like the ancient editions of Plato whose order is still preserved in our printed texts.[1] These are divided into five main sections,[2] ethical, physical, mathematical, musical (in the wide Greek sense of the term), and technical, together with a few unclassified works. Even allowing for the intrusion of some spurious titles, the total is impressive both in amount and in scope, and puts him in a different class from any of his predecessors. It includes treatises on theory of substance (*physis*), cosmology, astronomy, geography, physiology, medicine, sensation, epistemology, mathematics, magnetism, botany, musical theory, linguistics, agriculture, painting (cf. p. 270 above) and other topics. Pronouncements from many of these works are cited by later writers, but the works themselves have not survived, in spite of Cicero's eulogies of their style.[3] In Graeco-

---

[1] Thrasyllus (time of Tiberius), from whom Diogenes took it, will not have been its originator. Callimachus, as librarian at Alexandria, compiled a catalogue together with a glossary of terms used by Democritus (Suda, DK, A32 and note *ad loc.*). It seems however that Thrasyllus's list contains some of the works of Bolus of Mendes, a Hellenistic writer of uncertain date who usurped the name Democritus for his books on medical, magical and other topics, so that not all of its contents go back to the time of Callimachus. See the summing-up in Alfieri, *Atomisti*, 71, n. 113 (and cf. *Atom. Idea*, 195), and Hammer-Jensen in *RE*, Suppl. IV, 219–23, where references to the work of Wellmann and others will be found. On Usener's attempt to trace the tetralogical arrangement to Tyrannio, mentioned with approval by Zeller (ZN, 1054 n.), see now Wendel in *RE*, 2. Reihe VII, 1818. K. Freeman gives a general review of the works attributed to Democritus in *Companion*, 295–9.

It is impossible to be certain just how long his writings survived, and which of the commentators were directly acquainted with them. Schmid wrote (*Gesch. gr. Lit.* 1.5.2.2, 247) that, among others, the 'sehr gelehrter' Simplicius may have read them directly, but the honest avowals in his commentary on Aristotle's *De anima* suggest that he knew them only at second hand. At 25.30 he refers the reader to book I of Aristotle's *Physics* for a clear statement of Democritus's theory of the elements (a strange book to choose, incidentally), and a little later (26.11) he confesses that he cannot choose between two possible ways in which Democritus might have produced life from the atoms, because Aristotle's account is only in general terms.

[2] This is presumably the reason why Thrasyllus wished to identify him with the unnamed speaker in the ps.-Platonic *Erastai* (136c) who approves the comparison of the philosopher to a πένταθλος (D.L. 9.37).

[3] *De or.* 1.11.49, *Orat.* 20.67 (DK, A34).

Roman times Democritus became a legendary figure, the typical investigator of natural products (herbs, precious stones and so forth) for their practical effects. Not only medical, but magical and alchemical discoveries and writings were attributed to him, and this has considerably complicated the question of the authenticity of our quotations. The accounts of his philosophy in Aristotle and others are therefore in many cases more trustworthy records than passages which profess to give his actual words.[1]

C. THE ATOMIC THEORY

(1) *Fundamentals*

Atomism is the final, and most successful, attempt to rescue the reality of the physical world from the fatal effects of Eleatic logic by means of a pluralistic theory. To its proponents, the infinite divisibility and qualitative differences of Anaxagoras's 'seeds' seemed an evasion of the question, and they found the solution rather in a reformed and corrected version of Pythagoreanism. Aristotle, in one of his less fair-minded moods (*De caelo*, 303 a 8), says that in a way they too claim that everything that exists is numbers or evolved from numbers: 'they may not show it clearly, but this is what they mean'.[2] He is right to direct our thoughts back to the Pythagoreans, but with the clarity owed to Parmenides (p. 49 above), the atomists perceived that these had overlooked the unbridgeable gap between mathematical figures and the world of nature. If this world was constructed out of units, they must be units of solid physical substance.

Aristotle, after praising Leucippus and Democritus for their consistency and for beginning at the natural starting-point, explains how their theory originated in a reaction from those who held that 'what is'

---

[1] A warning is particularly necessary concerning the lengthy passages of Diodorus printed by DK (II, 135 ff.) with extracts from Tzetzes and Johannes Catrares as reproducing the content of the Μικρὸς διάκοσμος of Democritus. Their inclusion depends on a confident attribution by Reinhardt in 1912, which however was already seriously impugned by Dahlmann in 1928, since when an extensive literature has accumulated around the subject. Although scholars differ in their positive conclusions, almost all agree that Reinhardt's thesis is condemned by the absence of any trace of the atomic world-view. See p. 210, n. 1 above. Alfieri however (*Atom. Id.* 120, n. 3) defends Reinhardt's view.

[2] See note *ad loc.* in Loeb edition. Aristotle knew very well the difference between Pythagorean and Democritean units.

must be one and immovable: void 'is not', and without a void separate from it reality cannot move, nor can things be more than one if there is nothing to keep them apart. He continues (*GC*, 325 a 23):

But Leucippus thought he had a theory which would agree with the senses and would not abolish coming-to-be or destruction or motion or the plurality of existing things. So much he conceded to the phenomena, whereas to the proponents of unity he granted that there could not be movement without void, that the void was 'not being', and nothing of what is is not being; for what, strictly speaking, *is*, is completely full. But such being, he claimed, is not a unity. It consists of a plurality of things infinite in number and too small to be seen. They move in the void (for there is void), and their combination causes coming-to-be, their separation dissolution. They act and are acted upon as they happen to touch (for in this way they are not one) and generate by coming together and interlocking. A true unity can never give rise to multiplicity, nor a true plurality produce unity. That is impossible, but as Empedocles and others say that things are acted upon by means of pores, so he claimed that alteration and every form of being-acted-on takes place in this way: dissolution and destruction occur by means of the void, as also does growth when solid bodies slip in [*sc.* to fill empty spaces].

Leucippus is here represented as insisting on the strict fulfilment of the Eleatic conditions of being. What is must be a plenum (cf. Parm. 8.22–5). Generation and destruction in a literal sense are impossible. What is one cannot become many, nor many things one. Hence the insistence that what is built up out of atoms in contact is not a unity; no new single being is generated by this means.[1] Only one thing is

[1] 'As they happen to touch, for in this way they are not one.' ἢ and ταύτῃ at 325 a 33 have been translated locally ('where...for there they are not one') by Joachim and Forster, which sounds as if a plurality of atoms *were* 'one' when *not* in contact. The point is, I think, that a number of bodies cannot properly be said to have become a unity simply by contiguity or inter-locking with each other. Leucippus and Democritus seem to have attached great importance to satisfying this particular Eleatic condition, and Aristotle mentions it several times: *GC*, 325 b 31, according to Leucippus generation is from the atoms 'by means of the void and through contact, for by this each thing is divisible' (i.e. each composite body is divisible—is not a unity—because it is only an aggregate of tiny units in contact); *On Democritus, ap.* Simpl. *Cael.* 295.11, 'As they move they collide and become entangled in such a way that while they touch and lie close to one another, no single nature is ever truly generated from them; for he [Democritus] held that it was simply foolish to suppose that two or more could ever become one. The fact that they hold to-gether for a certain time he attributed to their interlocking and catching hold of each other' (by reason, as Aristotle goes on to explain, of their irregular shapes); also *De caelo*, 303 a 6; *Metaph.* 1039 a 9.

Alfieri's note on the words φύσιν μέντοι μίαν ἐξ ἐκείνων κατ' ἀλήθειαν οὐδ' ἡντιναοῦν γεννᾷ (*Atomisti*, 80, n. 154) seems to me misleading: Aristotle is expressing the atomists' point of view very accurately.

necessary if we are simultaneously to satisfy the Eleatic conditions of being and allow for a physical world: empty space. The nature of being according to Parmenides does not demand, as he thought,[1] that void is inconceivable. The way in which Leucippus met this difficulty, the assertion that 'void is not being yet exists', is less paradoxical than it sounds, when we remember the universal assumption hitherto that whatever exists exists in bodily form.[2] Hence the Pythagoreans, believing that geometrical figures exist, saw no difficulty in constructing a physical world from them. Parmenides detected the flaw in this, but himself described his non-sensible reality as a sphere and 'full', language which led Burnet to regard it as corporeal, though we have seen reason to doubt his judgment (p. 25 above). Leucippus seized on this aspect of it. He clarified and made explicit the assumption that what has real existence must be corporeal. But to say this does not imply that it is continuously present everywhere. There can be places[3] which it does not occupy, though obviously it would be wrong to call these spaces themselves 'being' or 'an existing thing'. Anyone today who looked in a box and reported 'there's nothing in it', would similarly claim to be misrepresented if told that he was denying the existence of emptiness. Here then, Leucippus thought, was a misunderstanding which alone had prevented philosophers from constructing a physical world on Eleatic principles of being. Empedocles and Anaxagoras had not done this. They had transgressed by admitting motion without void, by attributing sensible qualities to 'what is' (Parm. 8.38–41) and in Anaxagoras's case by making 'what is' divisible (Parm. 8.22).

The admission of void brought with it the possibility of plurality and motion. Nothing else was needed for the construction of a cosmos

---

[1] I believe that Parmenides himself was responsible for the denial of void (pp. 33 f. above). If however one prefers to substitute Melissus here, or speak of the Eleatics generally, the present account is not affected.

[2] Zeno's pronouncements that 'if what is had no magnitude, it would not even be' (frr. 1 and 2) have more than mathematical significance. They show how inextricably existence was tied up with corporeality at that time. (σῶμα and μέγεθος are synonymous in the argument of Democritus reproduced at Arist. *GC*, 316a15 ff.)

[3] Democritus drew no distinction between place (τόπος) and void (κενόν). See Aristotle *ap.* Simpl. *Cael.* 295.3 (A37), Simpl. *Phys.* 394.25, 533.18. Once, at *Phys.* 571.22 ff., Simplicius attributes a distinct definition of τόπος to Democritus, Epicurus and the Stoics alike. It looks like an Epicurean one, written in the light of Aristotle's investigation of the notion of space (ZN, 1069, n. 1).

out of elementary realities each of which satisfied the Eleatic conditions of existence: for Being (ὄν) is substituted Beings (ὄντα). From these intellectual origins sprang the first European theory of the atomic structure of matter.

(2) *General nature of atoms*

It is sometimes said[1] that Leucippus took up the challenge of Melissus: that if, *per impossibile*, there were many things, each would have to have the character of the Eleatic One as he saw it. Leucippus said, in effect, 'Why not?', and gave each of his atoms the same properties. This needs qualification. Melissus said that the One was infinite, unmoved, and without density. An atom is none of these. Leucippus looked rather to Parmenides, whose theory he modified only in the minimal ways just mentioned. What exists must still be ungenerated and imperishable, unchangeable, incapable of being added to or subtracted from, homogeneous, finite and a plenum, continuous and indivisible. 'What is' may have void outside it, but none (and hence no movement) within. All these conditions can be satisfied, thought Leucippus, and the sensible world accounted for, on the supposition that there are millions of such solid, imperishable entities of microscopic size, surging around in infinite space.

A second account of the principles of atomism occurs in Aristotle's historical review at the beginning of the *Metaphysics* (985 b 4). Here he says:

Leucippus and his associate Democritus name plenum and void as elements, calling them 'being' and 'not-being': the full and solid is being, the empty and rare[2] is not-being. Hence they say that being exists no more than not being,[3] because void exists no less than body. These are the material causes

---

[1] E.g. by Burnet, *EGP*, 335, repeated in different words by Bailey, *Atomists*, 71 and KR, 406. This has already been mentioned on pp. 117f. above.

[2] Presumably Aristotle thought that the addition of the word μανόν would make clearer what was meant by κενόν. In fact it is rather confusing, since elsewhere it does not mean completely empty but only rare or loose in texture as opposed to tightly packed. Bailey (*Atomists*, 77) calls it 'one of those quaint terms which he [Leucippus] invented for the atomic theory, "porous"'; but in the first place he did not invent it (it was probably used by Anaximenes, and occurs in a line of Empedocles, fr. 75.1), and secondly Aristotle does not seem to be giving Leucippus's terms in this sentence; otherwise he might be expected to have said ναστόν for στερεόν.

[3] This is borne out by a passage in Plutarch reproducing Democritus's own terms (*Adv. Col.* 1108f, fr. 156 DK), μὴ μᾶλλον τὸ δὲν ἢ τὸ μηδὲν εἶναι, 'the *hing* exists no more than the *nothing*' as Raven rendered them (KR, 407; 'das Ichts um nichts mehr als das Nichts', ZN, 1056). The

of things, and just as those who posit a single underlying substance generate everything else by its affections, so they too say that the differences [sc. in the atoms] are responsible for everything else.[1] These according to them are three: shape, arrangement and position, for they say that they differ in 'rhythm','touching', and 'turning'. 'Rhythm' is shape,'touching' is arrangement, and 'turning', position. For instance, A differs from N in shape, AN from NA in arrangement, Z from N in position.[2]

With differences of shape went differences of size, not mentioned here but added by Aristotle elsewhere: (*Phys.* 203 a 33) 'But Democritus [sc. in contrast to Anaxagoras] claims that no elementary particle arises from any other. Nevertheless their common body is the source of everything, differing from part to part in size and shape.'[3] These are the only intrinsic differences between atoms. 'They are differentiated by their shapes, but their substance (φύσις) is one, just as if each were a separate bit of gold' (*De caelo*, 275 b 31). They differ, however, from a familiar substance like gold in being qualitiless, or at least without *sensible* qualities.[4] In this the atomists contradict Anaxa-

---

word δέν, also quoted as Democritus's by Aristotle (*ap.* Simpl., DK, A 37), was apparently not his invention, as it occurs in a brief fragment of Alcaeus (23 Diehl). Matson's article (*CQ*, 1963) should be read in conjunction with those of Moorhouse in *CQ*, 1962 and 1963. I do not find it convincing, but others may.

[1] The mention of material cause and underlying substance, like the description of plenum and void as στοιχεῖα, can be ignored as restatements in terms of Aristotle's own theories.

[2] Aristotle's example is Ⲍ (the older form of zeta) and H. The atomists developed a technical vocabulary of their own, of which we see some examples here. In naming the differences in shape, order and arrangement of the atoms, their aim seems to have been (as I have tried to bring out in the English equivalents) to emphasize the dynamic aspect and indicate the ceaseless movement, the shifting of atoms in relation to each other, on which the nature of the phenomenal world depends. Cf. the remarks of von Fritz in *Phil. u. spr. Ausdr.* 25–8. τροπή for instance would be chosen rather than θέσις because the atoms, continually moving ἀπὸ ταὐτομάτου in an infinite space which is 'nothing', cannot be said to be *situated* anywhere. Rather an atom *turns* one side to another atom. Similarly the neologism διαθιγή means, not a state of being in contact, but a *coming* into contact. Jaeger (*Paideia*, Eng. tr. 1, 1939, 123) denied the connexion of ῥυθμός with flowing, but see on this Mansfeld, *Offenbarung*, 21, n. 1.

The terms as given in Aëtius (1.15.8, 68 A 125) are ῥυθμός, διαταγή and προτροπή, which at least argues a certain independence of Aristotle.

The examples of the letters A, N and Z to illustrate differences in the shape, order and position of atoms were repeated by Boyle (Van Melsen, *From Atomos to Atom*, 100).

[3] Also in the passage from his lost work on Democritus quoted by Simpl. *Cael.* 295.7 (DK, 68 A 37).

[4] The atoms ἄποια, Plut. *Adv. Col.* 1110 f (68 A 57), Aët. 1.15.8 (A 125); ἐξ ἀποίων δὲ τῶν λόγῳ θεωρητῶν τὰς αἰσθητὰς ἀποφαίνονται γίνεσθαι ποιότητας [sc. οἱ τὰ ἄτομα], Aët. 1.15.11 (A124); χωρὶς ποιοτήτων, Galen, *De elem. sec. Hippocr.* 1.2 (A49); πάσης αἰσθητῆς ποιότητος ἔρημον ἐχουσῶν φύσιν, Sext. *Math.* 8.6 (A59). The necessity for a neutral substratum, like the odourless oil which must be the basis for the perfumer's art, was taken up by Plato, *Tim.* 50e.

goras (as also in their denial of infinite divisibility), and revive the concept of Anaximander's *apeiron* in a more sophisticated form: that which serves as the underlying matter of all things—with every kind of colour, taste and smell—must itself be without any of the various colours, flavours or scents.

Not only is the number of the atoms infinite, but they represent an infinite variety of form. They are 'infinite both in number and in shapes'. (So *GC*, 314a22, also 325b27. The reason which Aristotle gives for this, that 'they saw reality in appearance, and the phenomena are mutually contrary and infinite' is probably his own inference. See *GC*, 315b9; *De caelo*, 303a10.) Connected with this is a certain doubt of what Democritus said about their size. For Leucippus there is no problem. Nothing contradicts the statement that they were 'invisible owing to their small size' (*GC*, 325a30). Aristotle says the same for Democritus (*ap.* Simpl., DK, A37): the atoms are 'so small as to escape our senses', and out of them he 'generates and constructs the visible and sensible masses'. Similarly when Aristotle quotes the comparison of the atoms (or a particular class of them, *De an.* 404a3) to motes dancing in a sunbeam, Simplicius (*De an.* 25.33) is careful to point out that it is only an analogy: the visible motes are not the microscopic atoms themselves.

Later sources hint at something different. Dionysius, a third-century Bishop of Alexandria quoted by Eusebius (*P.E.* 14.23; DK, 68A43), distinguishes Epicurus from Democritus on the grounds that his atoms were 'very small and for that reason imperceptible', whereas Democritus 'assumed also very large atoms'. Aëtius (1.12.6, A47) even credits him with saying that there could be an atom as large as the cosmos. Such sources can hardly be used to discredit Aristotle. It is possible that the early atomists allowed themselves to say that the atoms varied infinitely in shape *and in size*,[1] without perceiving that, since their size had a lower limit, this would demand that there be no upper limit;[2] and Epicurus criticized them for this on the grounds that some atoms would have to be large enough to be visible. He may even have

[1] This is probably the meaning of D.L. 9.44 καὶ τὰς ἀτόμους ἀπείρους εἶναι κατὰ μέγεθος καὶ πλῆθος.
[2] Mugler (*R. de Philol.* 1959, 9) says this is not necessary 'puisqu'il peut y avoir une infinité d'espèces d'atomes de grandeurs différentes comprises entre deux valeurs finies'; but since atomic theory ruled out the notion of the infinitely small, this would surely be impossible.

said that logically Democritus's theory demanded an atom as big as the cosmos. These criticisms could easily mislead the Christian writer, who is explicitly contrasting the two systems and no doubt had Epicurus to read but not Democritus.[1]

The importance of the shapes of atoms in accounting for the variety of perceptible nature was emphasized by actually calling them 'shapes' or 'forms' as well as atoms. Democritus wrote a work *On Forms*.[2]

As the name 'shapes' emphasizes their variety, so the name *atom* calls attention to an essential characteristic, *indivisibility*.[3] This followed from their faithfulness to the pattern of the One of Parmenides, its

---

[1] Cf. Epicurus, *Ep.* 1.55 f.: Atoms vary in size, but 'we must not suppose that every size exists....Every size is not required to explain the differences of qualities in things, and at the same time some atoms would be bound to come into our ken and be visible; but this is never seen to be the case, nor is it possible to imagine how an atom could become visible.' (Trans. Bailey.) This sounds as if Democritus posited atoms in an infinite variety of sizes, but that it was Epicurus who pointed out that this would inevitably involve visible atoms, in which neither he nor Democritus believed.

The best discussion of the question is Alfieri's in *Epicurea in mem. Bignone*, 62 (also *Atomos Idea*, 62 f., 129). Mugler (*R. de Philol.* 1959, 9 f.) accepts Dionysius and Aëtius without question, and regards them as having preserved a fundamental difference between Leucippus and Democritus which had escaped all commentators beginning with Aristotle! Kerschensteiner (*Kosmos*, 165, n. 3) is in doubt whether the idea of cosmos-sized atoms was the statement of a theoretical possibility (so also ZN, 1066 n.) or originated in an Epicurean *reductio ad absurdum* of the Democritean theory. Freeman (*Companion*, 299 f.) regarded it as a misunderstanding, but her discussion is vitiated by the suggestion that 'infinite in size' in D.L. means 'infinitely small'.

It is probably a mistake to take Eusebius's quotation of Dionysius seriously at all. It begins by attributing to both Democritus and Epicurus a view of the atoms as ὡς ἔτυχεν ἐν τῷ κενῷ φερομένας αὐτομάτως τε συμπιπτούσας ἀλλήλαις διὰ ῥύμην ἄτακτον, which is flatly untrue for Epicurus.

For a different view see Mugler in *REG*, 1963, 397 ff. From the statement that a single atom is without sensible qualities (e.g. Sext. *Math.* 8.6, A59) he draws the conclusion that even if a Democritean atom were as big as the world it would still be invisible. It could not, after all, emit effluences (p. 442 below). His apocalyptic vision of the destruction and suffering caused by the impact on a world like ours of one of these huge, silent and invisible visitors from outer space is impressive. (He links it with Hippol. 1.13.3, A40.)

[2] τὰς ἀτόμους ἰδέας ὑπ' αὐτοῦ [Democritus] καλουμένας Plut. *Adv. Col.* 1111 a (68 A 57), cf. Hesych. (fr. 141), Simpl. *Phys.* 327.24 (fr. 167), and for the περὶ ἰδεῶν Sext. *Math.* 7.137 (fr. 6). This characteristic the atoms shared with Anaxagoras's σπέρματα (ἰδέας παντοίας ἔχοντα, fr. 4). σχήματα was probably also used (Arist. *Phys.* 203 a 22; *GC*, 315 b 7). The fact that both Democritus the materialist and Plato the idealist called their ultimate imperceptible realities ἰδέαι has often been commented on. Both were in their different ways making use of Pythagorean theories, but the notion of geometrical regularity, so essential both to Pythagoreanism and to Plato, was abandoned by the atomists.

[3] The name ἄτομος (fem.) or ἄτομον, though frequent in our authorities, does not occur in any actual fragment of Democritus, but must have been used by him and probably by Leucippus as well (ZN, 1058, n. 3). It is of course regular in Epicurus. The feminine form suggests that ἰδέα is still understood (DK, II, 99 n.; οὐσία would be an anachronism, as Alfieri points out, *Atom. Id.* 52 f.). Other words for the atom were δέν, ὄν and (in opposition to the void) ναστόν. These are attested for Democritus by Aristotle (*ap.* Simpl. *Cael.* 295.5; DK, A37), and the last for Leucippus by Theophrastus (*ap.* Simpl. *Phys.* 28.13, A8; cf. ZN, 1057, n. 2).

homogeneity and fulness. 'That which strictly *is*, is completely full', said Aristotle, and Philoponus adds a comment which suggests once again that it was to 'father' Parmenides rather than to his followers Zeno and Melissus that Leucippus looked for his arguments. Leucippus proved the indivisibility of the atoms thus: each of the things that is, *is* in the proper sense. In what is there is nothing that is not, hence no void. Division cannot occur without void, therefore it is impossible for them to be divided (Philop. *GC*, 158. 22). In any case 'what is' can suffer no change (hence the atoms are impassible, ἀπαθεῖς) nor have any parts (which would destroy its absolute unity). Going beyond his Eleatic model, Leucippus also alleged the smallness of his atoms as a reason for their indivisibility, a more vulnerable argument than the purely logical one.

The question whether the atoms were not only physically but also theoretically or mathematically indivisible has naturally aroused great interest among historians of mathematics. Burnet wrote (*EGP*, 336) that 'the atom is not mathematically indivisible, for it has magnitude; it is however physically indivisible, because, like the One of Parmenides, it contains no empty space'. This sentence correctly puts the emphasis on the logical consequences of unity as seen by Parmenides: each atom was to be a reproduction of the One. Recent work, however, tends to confirm that Democritus held, and was prepared to argue, that his atoms, being not only very small but the smallest *possible* particles of matter, were not only too small to be divided physically but also logically indivisible. To suppose otherwise would admit the principle of infinite divisibility, which to Democritus was inconceivable.[1]

(3) *Motion and its cause*

Any study of the cause and nature of motion in the atomic system must start from the complaints of Aristotle that it was left unexplained.[2] The historical summary quoted above on pp. 392f. continues immediately (985 b 19): 'But the question of movement, whence or how it belongs to things, they too, like the others, carelessly neglected.' In *De caelo*

---

[1] The most important evidence is the Democritean argument preserved by Aristotle, *GC*, 316a 14ff. For further details see appendix, pp. 503 ff. below.

[2] Zeller, whose view of the matter is now generally rejected, provides an object-lesson: he brings in Aristotle's statements only at the end, and his attempt to fit them to his preceding discussion reads very like special pleading.

(300b8) he says: 'Leucippus and Democritus, who say that the primary bodies are always in motion in the infinite void, ought to tell us what sort of motion and what is their natural motion.' Similarly *Metaph.* 1071 b 31, where Leucippus is coupled with Plato as saying that motion is everlasting, 'but from what cause, or what kind it is, they do not say, nor the reason why it is in this direction or in that'. The inclusion of Plato in this condemnation may raise a doubt whether the atomists in fact 'carelessly neglected' the question, or simply failed to provide an answer to satisfy Aristotle's own particular requirements; and other remarks of his own suggest that he may have found a little more on the subject in their writings. Thus he says (*GA*, 742 b 17; more briefly *Phys.* 252 a 32):

Those are wrong, and fail to state the causal necessity, who say that things have always happened so and think this explains their origin. So Democritus of Abdera says that there is no beginning [or origin, *arché*] of the infinite,[1] that a cause is an origin and what is everlasting is infinite; therefore to ask 'why?' in a case like this is to look for an origin for the infinite.

This tight little argument has an Ionian sound, and an Ionian reminiscence of the *apeiron* as *arché*. It is certainly Democritus's, and many will agree with Sambursky that it was 'a sound instinct' that led the atomists to accept movement as a given fact rather than raise the problem of the first cause.[2] It is more relevant to remember how much of their stimulus came from the Eleatics. Eleatic standards must be upheld to the greatest degree compatible with allowing for the obvious fact of motion. The answer lay in the prime discovery that the notion of empty space was not an illogical one. This immediately admitted both plurality and movement. Looking back, it is not easy to appreciate the complete *novelty* of the idea, though the fact that the atomists had to clothe it in such paradoxical terms should help. Earlier thinkers had never clearly conceived a vacuum: their primary substance or substances had filled the whole. Only the Pythagoreans had spoken of void, and they were so far from understanding its strict meaning that they had identified it with air, which the universe could 'breathe in' (vol. 1, 280, 340).

---

[1] I agree with Platt *ad loc.* (Oxford trans.) in wishing to expunge ἀεὶ καὶ before ἀπείρου.

[2] *Phys. World of Gks.* 112f. He adds: 'The picture drawn by Democritus reminds us of the ideal gas in the modern kinetic theory of gases, which are kept in perpetual motion characterized by constant collisions.'

Parmenides had condemned for ever any system which, like the Milesian or the Pythagorean, combined the notions of a one and a many. One could never become many, indeed all change and motion were impossible because, among other reasons, void was an inadmissible concept. Empedocles and Anaxagoras had tried to save the phenomena by abandoning the original unity. Positing an initial plurality, they thought to retain the possibility of locomotion by a kind of reciprocal replacement.[1] Given such a plenum, an external cause of motion seemed necessary if it was not to remain a static, frozen mass. Hence the Love and Strife of Empedocles and the Mind of Anaxagoras. But to an age for which only corporeal being was real, the introduction of Mind over the mixture must have seemed suspiciously like the reintroduction, by a back door, of the One behind the Many, laying Anaxagoras's system open once more to criticism of the Eleatic type.

These considerations may lead us to think that the atomists had consciously faced the problem of motion and its origin, and considered that they were providing not only a necessary but a sufficient reason by attributing it to the existence of void. Melissus, after all, had argued directly from the non-existence of void to that of motion (fr. 7.7, p. 104 above). Earlier pluralist attempts to rescue phenomena from Eleatic logic had been baulked by the difficulties of accounting for a beginning of motion in a mass of matter heterogeneous indeed, but locked together with no chink of empty space between its parts. Substitute for this the alternative picture of an infinite number of microscopic atoms let loose, as it were, in infinite empty space, and it is as reasonable to ask 'Why should they stay still?' as 'Why should they move?' Indeed Aristotle speaks in the *Physics* of those who 'make the void the cause of motion'.[2] It does not in his eyes absolve them from

---

[1] Probably if not certainly. See p. 147 with n. 1 above, as well as Solmsen, *Arist.'s System*, 142. That both upheld the denial of void may be taken as certain. (Pp. 139, 271, n. 2 above.)

[2] *Phys.* 214b16 δοκεῖ γὰρ αἴτιον εἶναι [sc. τὸ κενόν] κινήσεως τῆς κατὰ τόπον. At 265b23 he speaks of ὅσοι τοιαύτην μὲν οὐδεμίαν αἰτίαν λέγουσιν διὰ δὲ τὸ κενὸν κινεῖσθαί φασιν, where τοιαύτην αἰτίαν refers to external motive causes, the Love and Strife of Empedocles and the Mind of Anaxagoras. The void was not a cause in that sense: it was only αἴτιον κινήσεως οὕτως ὡς ἐν ᾧ κινεῖται (214a24), for as he explains it at 213b5, οὐ γὰρ ἂν δοκεῖν εἶναι κίνησιν εἰ μὴ κενόν. τὸ γὰρ πλῆρες ἀδύνατον εἶναι δέξασθαί τι. Such expressions have led scholars in the past to describe the void as a *conditio sine qua non* of movement, a necessary but not a sufficient cause (e.g. Brieger and Liepmann, see Liepmann, *Mechanik*, 37); and so, from their point of view, it had to be. I would nevertheless doubt whether it appeared so to Leucippus and Democritus.

the charge of neglecting the question, since from his point of view it was obvious that empty space was only a *sine qua non*, not a positive or sufficient cause such as his own (erroneous) mechanics required. But it may put us on the track. Coming at a stage in the history of thought when the need for a positive cause of motion was entangled with the lack of a true conception of void, the setting free of the atoms may well have seemed a sufficient explanation of their motion, combined with the assertion (a contradiction of Anaxagoras) that it had had no temporal beginning. In rejecting the demand for a first active agent of motion, Leucippus and Democritus are nearer than Aristotle to the views current among European scientists since Galileo and Descartes.[1]

There is another point of interest. Pre-Parmenidean Ionians had also said that motion was eternal, but for them this conception was inevitably linked with that of life. What owed its motion to no cause outside itself was alive; if its motion was eternal, as that of the *arché* must be, it was not only alive but divine. The materialism of Leucippus and Democritus has restored the idea of motion as natural to matter and hence belonging to it from all time, but from this conception they have removed the last traces of animism. The motion is purely lifeless and mechanical. It happened 'automatically' or 'of necessity' (concepts of which there will be more to say later). Is this perhaps one of their most original and influential contributions to thought? And was it not made possible by one thing only, the conscious postulation of an absolute void?

[1] The last two paragraphs are taken with little change from my article in *JHS*, 1957 (i), 40f. On the atomists' achievement in this respect cf. the quotation from Heisenberg in Alfieri, *Atom. Id.* 77, n. 1.

Alfieri (*op. cit.* 80) suggests another reason why the atomists were shy of offering a more positive explanation of motion. He claims that they could have had no reply to the Eleatic ἀπορίαι about it because, since they denied infinite divisibility, they were wide open to Zeno's arguments against it. Body consisted of discontinuous atoms, and time must consist of discontinuous instants. Yet they did not consider how the same body could occupy different parts of space in successive instants and so get from *A* to *B*. Thus, he suggests, they had no mathematical or philosophical theory of movement, but a physical and empirical conception of it. On the atomists' conception of time see also Luria, *Infinitesimaltheorie*, 163–6 (who takes a more favourable view), and pp. 427 ff. below.

(4) Nature of the original motion: the question of weight

Accounts of the cosmogony of Leucippus start from the picture of countless atoms of various shapes and sizes in motion in empty space. They jostle, collide and become entangled, and here and there a complex of them sets up the kind of vortex-like motion which was believed necessary to create a world. The formation of the cosmos is then explained as flowing from the action of the vortex and its effect on the subsequent motion of the atoms. From the inception of a cosmic system, therefore, their motion is accounted for, but this was not, as it had been for Anaxagoras, the beginning of motion altogether. Hence from Aristotle down to the present day, the question has been put: what caused the original motion, and what sort of motion was it? Since Aristotle could read Leucippus and Democritus and we no longer can, we are not likely to get much further than he did: and on the cause of motion he tells all that we need. Anaxagoras, they said, was wrong to suppose that things were once at rest, and then began to move at a particular point in time;[1] and if motion is eternal, it is idle to seek for its cause. This argument would come particularly easily to a fifth-century Greek, for whom the notions of beginning, origin, governing principle and cause were closely united in the single word *arche*.[2] Alexander of Aphrodisias elaborates Aristotle's criticism slightly (*Metaph.* 36.21; DK, 67 A 6): 'Leucippus and Democritus say the atoms move by striking and knocking against one another, but whence comes the beginning of motion for the natural world, that they do not say.'

Of the *cause* of the original motion there is no more to be said. Of its *nature*, there have in the past been two contending views: one, that it was a confused and aimless motion in all directions, the other, that it

---

[1] It is remarkable how much more strictly than the earlier pluralists Leucippus obeyed the dictates of Parmenides, while succeeding in drawing opposite conclusions from them. What he said of motion reminds one of Parmenides's question about γένεσις: Why should it have started at one time rather than another?

[2] The case of the Latin *principium* was similar, as when Cicero writes (*Fin.* 1.6.17): 'eumque motum atomorum nullo a principio sed ex aeterno tempore intellegi convenire.' Cf. *Tusc.* 1.23.54: 'origo principii nulla est, nam ex principio oriuntur omnia.' For Aristotle too ἀρχή and αἴτιον were inseparably united (e.g. *Metaph.* 1003 b 24), and it was only as a consequence of his own teleological doctrine of potentiality and actuality that a world which was everlasting nevertheless needed an eternally active ἀρχή to sustain its operations.

was a downward fall, or rain, of atoms due to weight. The evidence must be considered here, but since the first view is not only pretty certainly correct, but now generally accepted, we may be excused from any detailed consideration of the rival views of the past.[1]

Against a downward fall as the original motion are all those passages in which Aristotle blames the atomists for neglecting to state *either* what causes it *or* what kind of motion it is, and especially two of them. At *De caelo*, 300b11 he follows up this criticism by saying that every element must have a natural motion. This was his own belief, and it was therefore in his eyes a basic fault that the atomists assigned no natural motion to their own elements. But motion downwards *was* a natural elemental motion for Aristotle, and if they had posited it he could not have brought this charge. *De caelo*, 275b29ff. makes the point even clearer: the atoms being all of the same substance ought to have a single proper motion, and if, he continues, this were a motion due to weight, the whole would have a centre and a circumference, which the space of the atomists, being infinite, cannot have. The argument is hypothetical. Neither here nor anywhere else does he criticize the atoms for the absurdity of moving downwards in an *apeiron*.

More positively, in the extract from his work on Democritus (*ap.* Simpl. *Cael.* 295.9, 68 A 37) he describes the original motion of the atoms by the verb στασιάζειν—to quarrel, be at odds or in a state of discord —a metaphor from the all-too-familiar phenomenon of civil strife in Greek states: 'they are at odds and move in the void owing to their dissimilarity and the aforementioned differentiae'. The image of a *mêlée* is made more concrete by the explanations of his commentators: 'these atoms...are in motion in the void, and catching up with one another they collide, whereupon some rebound at hazard and others become entangled' (Simpl. *Cael.* 242.21, 67 A 14). Alexander's description is similar (see previous page). So also Aët. 1.12.6 (68

---

[1] The chief upholder of uniform downward motion was Zeller (ZN, 1084). The other view, which Brieger had put forward in 1884 (in his *Urbewegung*) and Liepmann independently in 1886 (in his *Mechanik*), was vigorously reinstated by Brieger against Zeller in *Philologus*, 1904. Both these scholars however complicated their position by trying to maintain that Leucippus and Democritus did assign weight to the atoms as an original property while at the same time denying that it was the cause of their original motion. Of recent scholars taking a similar view to that taken here it will suffice to mention Burnet (*EGP*, 344f.), Bailey (*Atomists*, 83 Leucippus, 129ff. Democritus), Alfieri (*Atomisti*, 2, n. 6, 3, n. 10 *et al.*; *Atom. Id.* 83) and Kirk (KR, 416).

A 47): 'Democritus says that the primary bodies, or solids, have no weight but move according as they strike one another in the infinite.' This is one of two passages in the *Placita* which expressly deny weight to the atoms. The other is 1.3.18 (A 47), where a distinction is made on this score between Democritus and Epicurus: 'The atoms have these three properties, shape, size and weight. Democritus gave them two, size and shape, but Epicurus added weight to these as a third; for he said that bodies must be carried on by the impact [πληγή, lit. "blow"] of weight: otherwise they would not move.'

Epicurus, according to this, spoke of weight as a *blow*, an unusual expression which sounds like a deliberate corrective use of the earlier atomists' terminology. A speaker in Cicero's *De fato* (20.46, 68 A 47) asks what need the Epicureans have for the innovation of an 'atomic swerve': 'the atoms had another motive force, from Democritus the impulse which he calls *plagam* [a blow], from you,' Epicurus, the force of gravity or weight'. Aëtius (1.26.2, 68 A 66) speaks of the 'repercussion, motion and blow (πληγή) of matter' in Democritus, and Simplicius says that Democritus 'made his atoms naturally motionless [i.e. they had no 'natural motion' in the Aristotelian sense] but said that they moved by impact [blow, πληγῇ]'. This is in keeping with the verdict of Aristotle (*De caelo*, 300b11, and Simplicius in his comment on the passage) that the motion of atoms was 'enforced' (βίᾳ), which according to his own doctrine ought to presuppose a prior natural motion. The difference on this point between Democritus and Epicurus seems to have been well known. In Cicero's *De finibus* we read (1.6.17): 'Democritus believed that the atoms move in infinite void, in which there is neither top nor bottom nor centre nor extremity, in such a way that they collide and cling together.' Not only does this, like Aristotle at *De caelo*, 275b29, appear to exclude downward motion as inconceivable, but the speaker goes on to mention 'errors peculiar to Epicurus', of which the first is to suppose that they are borne perpendicularly downwards by their weight.[1] The influence of Aristotle

---

[1] Epicurus realized that bodies of different weights would fall through a vacuum at equal speeds, and to account for their collisions endowed the atoms with the independent power of occasionally swerving minutely from their courses. We may agree that if Democritus *had* conceived of the pre-cosmic motion as a fall, he would have been unaware of this point. Whether Epicurus accused him of doing so, and was claiming to correct him, is disputed. (Contrast

and the Peripatetic tradition made it impossible to ignore the demand for a 'natural' motion of the atoms, logically even if not chronologically prior to the motions which they imparted to each other by their impact. No such demand presented itself to Democritus.

In *Gen. et Corr.* (326a9) on the other hand Aristotle says: 'Each atom is heavier, the bigger it is.'[1] This is the only sentence in which Aristotle unambiguously attributes weight to the atoms,[2] but if he had not thought it right to do so, he would certainly have charged them, as he did the Pythagoreans and Plato, with producing weighty bodies from weightless elements, and this he never does. Moreover the sentence in Theophrastus, *De sensu*, 61, 'Democritus distinguishes heavy and light by size' also refers to the atoms. This apparent contradiction with the evidence considered so far is explained by a sentence in Simplicius (*Cael.* 569.5, 68 A 61) which also says that the atoms have weight, but in a context which puts it beyond doubt that he is describing the state of things within a cosmic vortex, not the behaviour of atoms floating freely in the void.[3]

Bailey, *Atomists*, 313, with Alfieri, *Atom. Id.* 81, n. 1.) If he did, we may be sure that he misunderstood him. (See Alfieri, *loc. cit.*) Dyroff (*Demokritstud.* 38) argues that if each atom had weight, the 'full' must continually fall into the bottomless, and the upper regions form an ever-increasing void. Since not only space but also the number of atoms is infinite, this objection seems invalid. But the evidence against an original downward rain of atoms is so overwhelming that we need not trouble to invent hypothetical arguments on Democritus's behalf.

[1] καίτοι βαρύτερόν γε κατὰ τὴν ὑπεροχήν φησιν εἶναι Δημόκριτος ἕκαστον τῶν ἀδιαιρέτων. The translations of Joachim (adopted by Sambursky, *Phys. World*, 111), Kirk and Forster are substantially the same. I cannot see that the words, taken in their obvious sense, convey the nonsensical 'every atom is heavier than every other', which made Dyroff (*Demokritstud.* 33, n. 2) want to alter the text and Cherniss (*ACP*, 97, n. 412) propose a somewhat artificial explanation. See also Burnet, *EGP*, 342, n. 1.

[2] *De caelo*, 309a2 τὸ μεῖζον εἶναι βαρύτερον αὐτῶν is usually quoted as a second example, but I think Cherniss has shown conclusively (*ACP*, 97, n. 412) that these words refer to compounds. The immediately following τῶν δὲ συνθέτων makes this seem unnatural, but the whole of Aristotle's argument demands it, and it is not the first time that he has been caught out in careless or inelegant composition. (This note may be taken as a correction of my own rendering in the Loeb edition.)

[3] This and related passages will therefore be dealt with under cosmogony, p. 410 below. In any case the passage shows a somewhat uncritical juxtaposition of Epicurus and Democritus. At *Phys.* 1318.35 (68 A 58) he shows a similar confusion: the atoms are said to move through the unresisting void by reason of their weight (as they certainly did for Epicurus), but this motion is then described by a word which cannot apply to a consistently downward fall. (This must be true whatever correction is to be made to the corrupt περιπαλαίσεσθαι. I do not put it more positively, nor translate the conjecture περιπαλάσσεσθαι, since McDiarmid has cast legitimate doubt on this emendation in his article in *Hermes*, 1958, 291–8. In general, however, it is still accepted (as in KR), and was defended by Alfieri, *Atom. Id.* 87.)

We may conclude, then, that Leucippus and Democritus saw no reason to offer a positive cause for the motion of the atoms save the fact that they were free in infinite void, and that they did not assign to them any of the motions which Aristotle called 'natural'. Motion was to be accepted as an inherent and eternal characteristic of matter when unimpeded by any obstacle. It was a confused and irregular motion in all directions, and since it was eternal and without beginning, it was as reasonable to say that the collisions and rebounding of the atoms determined their direction as that the random nature of the motion caused the collisions. 'They move according as they strike one another.'[1] The 'necessity' which governs their motion and from time to time produces a cosmic vortex is 'the repercussion and motion and impact of matter'.[2]

These are the sole data required for producing (among countless other systems) a world like our own with its rocks and trees, men and animals, births, changes and deaths, and all our sensations of sight and sound, smell and taste. Atoms in motion account for it all. 'They say that nature is subject to local motion,... but that the first bodies undergo none of the other forms of change. These only affect their products, which grow and waste away and alter by combination and separation of the atoms' (Arist. *Phys.* 265 b 25).

(5) *Innumerable worlds: cosmogony*

Phenomena in general—'animals, plants, cosmic systems and in short all perceptible bodies'[3]—are produced because some of the atoms in their eternal jostling of each other do not recoil and separate again, but being of suitable shape for combination cling together and become

---

[1] Aëtius (1.23.3, 68 A 47) says that the only kind of motion admitted by Democritus was παλμός, a word applied later by Epicurus (*Ep.* 1.43) to the oscillation of atoms when entangled or confined in complex bodies, and Kirk (KR, 418) thinks that Aëtius is 'reading an Epicurean idea into Democritus'. παλμός however does not seem too unsuitable a term for the kind of motion described above. It is the verbal noun from πάλλω, which means to shake, sway or brandish, and in the passive to quiver, pulsate or vibrate, a good description of the clashing and recoiling of the atoms. It must always be remembered that, as there was no beginning of their motions, so there was no beginning of collisions, recoil and entanglement. (πάλλω is as old as Homer, and παλμός occurs in the Hippocratic Corpus and Aristotle as a medical term meaning throbbing or palpitation. See LSJ.)

[2] With this definition of ἀνάγκη at Aët. 1.26.2 (68 A 66) cf. Sext. *Math.* 9.113 (A 83).

[3] Simpl. *Cael.* 295.21, probably still citing Aristotle's Περὶ Δημοκρίτου.

entangled (περιπλέκεσθαι), thus generating perceptible bodies. Aristotle's brief statements of this (*GC*, 325 a 31 and 34; 315 b 6)[1] are elaborated a little by Simplicius (*Cael.* 242.21, 67 A 14, partly quoted already, p. 401 above): 'These atoms, separate one from the other in the void which is infinite, and differing in shape, size, position and order, are in motion in the void, overtake one another and collide. Some rebound at hazard, others become entangled when their shapes, sizes, positions and order are favourable, and thus it happens that they bring about the generation of composite things.' Some of these shapes are enumerated in Simplicius's quotation from Aristotle (68 A 37): 'some are irregular, some hooked, some hollow, others convex, and others have innumerable other differences'.

Since there is no limit either to the atoms or the void, many and various systems have been formed, of which our cosmos is only one. Some have dissolved again, others coexist with ours. As a follower of Democritus picturesquely expressed it, it is as unlikely that a single world should arise in the infinite as that one single ear of corn should grow on a large plain.[2] Democritus himself, according to Hippolytus (*Ref.* 1.13.2, A 40), said that

there are innumerable worlds of different sizes. In some there is neither sun nor moon, in others they are larger than in ours and others have more than one. These worlds are at irregular distances, more in one direction and less in another, and some are flourishing, others declining. Here they come into being, there they die, and they are destroyed by collision with one another. Some of the worlds have no animal or vegetable life nor any water.

One cannot but admire a man whose scientific imagination reached so far beyond the limited experience of his time as to paint this picture of an infinite variety of cosmic systems, in some ways so suggestive of modern cosmological knowledge. We note also the complete emancipa-

---

[1] Aristotle credits Leucippus and Democritus (the latter, he says admiringly, 'seems to have thought of everything') with having, alone among his predecessors, distinguished between γένεσις καί φθορά and ἀλλοίωσις: γένεσις and φθορά are a matter of the combination and separation of atoms (i.e. the formation and dissolution of compounds), whereas ἀλλοίωσις is an alteration of their order and position in a compound (*GC*, 315 a 35, b 6).

[2] Metrodorus of Chios, as reported by Aëtius (DK, 70 A 6).

tion from any trace of animistic or teleological explanation. The contrast with Anaxagoras, for whom 'Mind came and ordered all things', is no doubt deliberate.[1]

Diogenes Laertius alone has preserved an exposition of the origin of the cosmos according to Leucippus (9.30ff.). Beginning with a 'summary statement', he proceeds to 'details' as follows:[2]

The whole is infinite, as aforesaid. Part of it is full and part empty, and these[3] he calls elements. Worlds unlimited in number are formed from these and dissolved into them. The manner of their formation is this. Many bodies [atoms] of all sorts of shapes are cut off from the infinite[4] and stream into a great void, and these when collected in a mass produce a single vortex,

---

[1] The existence of innumerable worlds for both Leucippus and Democritus is briefly mentioned by Diog. Laert. (9.31 and 44), Simplicius, *Cael.* 202.16 (67 A 21), and for 'the atomists' in general by Dionysius *ap.* Eus. *P.E.* 14.23 (68 A 43). Cicero (*Ac. pr.* 2.17.55) adds that some of them are absolutely indistinguishable from each other. This may well be right, for it is logical that infinite space, time and number of atoms should have given rise to identical as well as to different combinations. (Cf. Kerschensteiner, *Kosmos*, 166 with n. 2.) It may on the other hand be due to a misunderstanding. Simplicius (*Cael.* 310.15, 68 A 82) says, using Peripatetic language, οἱ δὲ Δημοκρίτου κόσμοι εἰς ἑτέρους κόσμους μεταβάλλοντες ἐκ τῶν αὐτῶν ἀτόμων ὄντες οἱ αὐτοὶ τῷ εἴδει γίνονται εἰ καὶ μὴ τῷ ἀριθμῷ. This of course only means that they are of the same species, but a similar remark might have led an unwary reader to suppose that they were formally identical.

[2] The purely Theophrastian origin of this account was noted by Diels (*Dox.* 165), and its freedom from Epicurean accretions is emphasized by Alfieri (*Atomisti*, 2, n. 4). One cannot however follow the latter when he claims this freedom also for the passages from Aëtius which DK reproduce in A24 as extracts from the Μέγας διάκοσμος of Leucippus. (Contrast his *Atom. Id.* 108. That this was an Epicurean extract was argued long ago by Liepmann, *Mechanik*, 19ff. See also Burnet, *EGP*, 339, and in more detail Spoerri, *Späthell. Berichte*, 7f.) In the same note Alfieri praises the reconstruction of early atomic cosmogony by Hammer-Jensen, which she achieved by elucidating the partially confused account of Diogenes in the light of the cosmogony in Plato's *Timaeus*. Although she has been followed by many later scholars, the Democritean origin of the *Timaeus* motifs cannot be taken as proved. See DK, II, 83n., where the conclusion that 'the whole question needs to be gone into afresh' is undoubtedly correct, as is Nestle's that her thesis 'rests on a rather shaky foundation' (ZN, 1099). It involves believing that Plato had already started the *Timaeus*, and reached the section on vision, when he 'plötzlich auf irgend Weise' became acquainted with Democritus and had to write some of the rest from a quite different standpoint. Her argument is often superficial and sometimes plainly mistaken, as when she says (*Arch. f. Gesch. d. Philos.* 1910, 103) that Plato's denial of *up* and *down* has as its background the atomistic infinity of space. His reason for abandoning the concepts of *up* and *down* is τοῦ παντὸς οὐρανοῦ σφαιροειδοῦς ὄντος, i.e. the same as Aristotle's. Immediately after this comes her conclusion, that 'if one admits that the atomic theory lies behind the later one in the *Timaeus*, the *Timaeus* becomes a source from which to increase our scanty knowledge of atomism'. A somewhat clouded source!

[3] I.e. the full and the empty. This is simply a repetition of Aristotle, *Metaph.* 985 b 4 (p. 392 above), and there is no suggestion that Leucippus applied the word στοιχεῖον to them.

[4] ἐκ τῆς ἀπείρου, fem. No doubt χώρας is to be understood; cf. Galen (DK, 68 A 49) τὸ δὲ κενὸν χώρα τις. (So DK *ad loc.*)

following the motion of which they collide and revolve in all sorts of ways and begin to be sorted out, like to like. But when owing to their numbers they can no longer be carried round in equilibrium,[1] the small atoms pass to the void without, as if through a strainer.[2] The rest hold together, become entangled and move in conjunction with one another, so forming a first spherical complex.[3] From this complex[4] a kind of membrane becomes detached, containing within itself bodies of every kind. These whirl round in proportion to the resistance of the centre,[5] and the membrane becomes thin as the contiguous bodies continually flow together by contact in the vortex. In this way the earth was formed, by the cohesion of the bodies which had moved to the centre. The enclosing membrane in turn is augmented by the influx[6] of atoms from outside; and as it whirls around, it adds to itself those that come into contact with it. Some of these become interlocked and form a complex that is wet and muddy at first, but drying out as they are carried round in the universal vortex they finally catch fire and form the substance of the stars....All the stars are ignited by the speed of their motion....Just as a cosmos is born, so also it grows, declines and perishes by some sort of necessity, the nature of which he does not specify.

[1] Brieger, Burnet and Bailey referred ἰσορρόπων to pre-cosmic motion. Only when the atoms could *no longer* move 'in equilibrium' (i.e. in all directions alike) are they drawn into the δίνη. I agree with Alfieri (*Atomisti*, 4, n. 13) that their ἰσορροπία is the *result* of their being drawn into the δίνη. This is indicated mainly by the position of the sentence but also by the verb περιφέρεσθαι. I do not feel so certain that Alfieri is right in joining διὰ πλῆθος with ἰσορρόπων rather than with the following words ('sono in equilibrio per la loro quantità').

[2] ὥσπερ διαττώμενα. The verb means (1) to filter or strain, of a liquid (Plato, *Crat.* 402c); (2) to rub or grate a solid through a mesh to reduce it to powder or purée, as in Hippocr. *Ulc.* 21 (VI, 424 L.), Theophr. *HP*, 3.18.5, and probably Plato, *Soph.* 226b; (3) to sift, as flour (Plato, *Tim.* 73e, where see Taylor's note); (4) to winnow grain, assuming διηττήσεις to be correct in Plut. *Qu. Conv.* 693d. I do not think that this range of meaning allows us to draw any conclusion from the word as to the kind of motion performed by the atoms, as Hammer-Jensen and Mondolfo do.

[3] Kerschensteiner has a useful note on the word σύστημα in *Hermes*, 1959, 441, n. 4.

[4] τούτου for τοῦτο as suggested by Kerschensteiner. On the formation of the membrane see her remarks, *loc. cit.* 441–6, where the interpretations of others are criticized. It is difficult to see how the whole structure itself can 'stand apart like a membrane' (KR), since it appears to consist of all the atoms in the cosmic vortex, from centre to circumference. Nevertheless, considering the imperfections of this account it is not impossible that σύστημα σφαιροειδές is intended to refer only to the outer spherical envelope formed by the linkage of hooked atoms (67 A 23).

[5] κατὰ τὴν τοῦ μέσου ἀντέρεισιν. A difficult phrase, as Alfieri recognizes (*Atomisti*, 6, n. 14). The atoms can hardly whirl round *owing to* the resistance of the centre (i.e. presumably a solid mass already formed at the centre); rather, as Bailey says (*Atomists*, 96), as things approach the centre their motion must become weaker and slower. See also Burnet's explanation, *EGP*, 346. According to Democritus the heavenly bodies revolve more slowly the nearer they are to the earth, because less affected by the motion of the vortex (Lucr. 5.623f.; for further details see Löwenheim, *Wissenschaft D.s*, 97).

[6] Like Kerschensteiner I see no reason to alter the ἐπέκρυσιν of the tradition. See her remarks *loc. cit.* 446, n. 4.

Lacking the work of Leucippus, we must make what we can of this compilation from an epitome of Theophrastus's version of what Leucippus said. The reminder should be a check to dogmatism. One obstacle to understanding might still have faced us if we were reading the atomist himself. From this and other passages it is obvious that he and Democritus described the formation of a world in terms appropriate to the birth of an animal, and this may well have led to the omission or blurring of certain links which we should expect to find in a chain of mechanical processes. That the process was in their eyes a mechanical one we need not doubt. If Democritus called man a miniature cosmos (fr. 34), his intention was to assimilate the processes of organic to those of inorganic nature, not *vice versa*. Yet the assimilation was made under the influence of earlier cosmogonies, like that of Anaximander, which saw the world as a living and growing organism, and this mode of thought was not completely outgrown. The world's outer envelope is a membrane (ὑμήν, *hymen*) such as encloses the foetus in the womb.[1] Worlds grow to maturity,[2] then become senile and finally die.

A world, then, is formed thus. From all eternity there is an infinite number of atoms of different shapes moving in infinite space with an irregular and aimless motion, and so at irregular distances. Where a large interval of space happens to be empty of them, a whole lot of atoms pours in and for a reason not stated sets up a circular eddy. It may be simply that with an infinity of space and of atoms and all eternity for them to move in, *every* variety of motion must have resulted from their contact somewhere, sometime. Only when it takes this circular form does a cosmos result. Though all atoms within reach are drawn into the general pattern of the whirl, they are still constantly tumbling over one another and performing all sorts of gyrations within

---

[1] The word χιτών, which Leucippus and Democritus are also said to have used in this connexion (Aët. 2.7.2, 67 A 23), had the same meaning. See Kerschensteiner, *loc. cit.* 444 and cf. p. 254, n. 1 above. ὑμήν was also used of the skin or membrane immediately inside the shell of an egg, and in spite of the lateness of our immediate source it is suggestive that an Orphic account compares the order of the universe to that in an egg: as the shell is to the egg, so is the outermost heaven to the universe, and as the *aither* is suspended all round from the heaven, so is the ὑμήν from the shell. (The source is the *Isagoge* of Achilles. See DK, 1, p. 11 or Kern, *Orph. Fr.* 70, p. 150, p. 190 above. ὑμήν could also mean the shell itself before it had hardened, Arist. *GA*, 752 a 32.) These notions are older than Leucippus.

[2] Hippolytus (*Ref.* 1.13, 68 A 40) twice uses the word ἀκμάζειν as Democritean in this connexion.

it.[1] At this point a cardinal law of atomism begins to operate: like tends towards like, and like acts upon like. This law, originating in the motion of atoms, and so limited to resemblances in size and shape, can be seen to operate in both the organic and the inorganic worlds. The chief *locus* is Democritus fr. 164, where Sextus quotes him as illustrating the law in the animal world by the tendency of creatures of the same species to herd together, and in inanimate things by the action of sieving and the disposal of pebbles washed up by waves on the beach. Although in the analogy of the sieve he mentions lentils, wheat and barley grains, the essential differences are not those of kind, but of shape, as the pebbles indicate ('the long pebbles are brought to the same place as other long ones, and round to round, as if their similarity had some attractive power') and as Aëtius in his paraphrase says.[2] That like acts on like is attested by Aristotle (*GC*, 323 b 10):

Democritus...says that agent and patient are the same or similar: it is impossible for disparate things to act on each other, but if, though different, they should nevertheless have some mutual effect, this occurs not because they are different but in so far as they have some common characteristic.

Aristotle calls this a doctrine peculiar to Democritus alone, which is at first surprising, for it appears prominently in Empedocles and in the separation of unlikes in the cosmogonic revolution of Anaxagoras. The explanation may be that for the atomist the claim that there is no

[1] So I interpret προσκρούοντα καὶ παντοδάπως κυκλούμενα, which Hammer-Jensen, and following her Alfieri (*Atomisti*, 4, n. 12), regard as evidence that the δίνη is not a circular vortex but an irregular shaking as of a sieve (or rather of a winnowing-fan, since these scholars argue from the πλόκανον of Plato's *Timaeus* to the κόσκινον of Democritus). Since its product is the present world with its revolving sky set with the heavenly bodies, we should have to suppose two sorts of δίνη, ἡ τοῦ ὅλου δίνη which carries the circling stars having quite a different motion from the δίνη set up at the birth of the cosmos. This is surely impossible. Its chief support is the quite unproven assumption that the atomists' δίνη was the model for the chaotic motion of Plato, *Tim.* 52e. But Plato is describing *pre-cosmic* motion, and if, as is possible, he had the atomists' system in mind, it is surely with their pre-cosmic motion that his own should be compared, not with the δίνη that is the beginning of a cosmos.

No doubt, as Sextus says (Democr. fr. 164), to illustrate the doctrine of 'like to like' Democritus used the metaphor of sieving, but it is no more necessary to suppose on this account that the cosmic δίνη resembled the motion of a sieve than that it undulated like the waves of the sea, which, says Sextus immediately after, Democritus instanced as having a similar effect.

[2] Aët. 4.19.3 (68 A 128, where 13 is a misprint) καὶ ἐπὶ τῶν κοσκινευόντων δὲ ἐπὶ τὸ αὐτὸ συναγελίζεται τὰ ὁμοιοσχήμονα ὥστε χωρὶς εἶναι τοὺς κυάμους καὶ ἐρεβίνθους. The analogy might seem easier if the process envisaged were winnowing rather than sieving or riddling (as Gomperz happily assumed without question, *Gr. Th.* I, 336), but I see no evidence that κόσκινον could = πλόκανον.

difference between agent and patient, but everthing happens by mutual influence of similars, excludes the possibility of external agents like the Love and Strife of Empedocles and the Mind of Anaxagoras. The interaction, springing as it does from the eternal motion of the atoms, is without external cause.[1] Its reality is argued from observation of what happens in the macroscopic world.

In accordance with this law atoms of similar shape and size draw together, and as more and more crowd into the vortex disturbances occur and those with less resistance are forced to the outer reaches and even beyond. Diogenes may be supplemented here by the Epicureanizing exposition of Aëtius (1.4.2, 67 A 24):

As these atoms crowded together in the same space, the larger and heavier sank down in all sorts of ways, while the small, round, smooth and slippery were squeezed out in the concourse of atoms and carried to the upper regions.

Shape as well as size is a factor, and with size goes weight as the atomists conceived it; that is, a tendency to seek the centre of the eddy, and a power of resistance to the impact of other atoms by which smaller and less heavy atoms could be displaced to great distances.

The atoms are of the same substance and have weight, but because some are heavier the lighter ones are forced out by these as they sink down, and are borne upwards. This, they say, is how some bodies seem to be light and others heavy.[2]

The model for the vortex was an eddy of wind or water, in which heavier bodies do gather in a heap at the centre while lighter ones are carried away.[3]

At the circumference of the spherical whirling mass which is an embryo universe, a skin is formed comparable to the caul round a foetus, being 'woven together out of the hook-shaped atoms' (Aët.

[1] This point is well made by Kerschensteiner, *Kosmos*, 162f. Cf. also Gomperz, *Gr. Th.* 336 (with the reservation made in the previous note).
[2] Simpl. *Cael.* 569.5. Simplicius writes in the Peripatetic belief that some elements (fire and air) are absolutely light, i.e. have a natural motion away from the centre of the universe. This is the belief which he represents Democritus as denying. Cf. *ibid.* 712.27: fire according to Democritus has *less* weight, hence gets squeezed out and *appears* to have actual lightness. (Both passages in DK, 68 A 61.)
[3] So also in Anaxagoras. See pp. 300 f. and the quotation there from Arist. *De caelo.* For a defence of the atomists' generalization of this phenomenon see Burnet, *EGP*, 346.

2.7.2, 67 A 23). Its formation is assisted by the addition of similar atoms from outside, and although small atoms are being constantly extruded from within, these presumably do not assist its growth to any great extent since the atoms subject to extrusion are primarily smooth and round, not hooked. The idea that the world is surrounded by a skin or membrane is strange to us and not particularly helpful to the atomists' own scheme. It was of course an inherited and deeply seated belief. To stop short of mythical cosmogonies which thought of it as a huge egg, the outer sphere of flame in Anaximander was described by a word which can mean either bark or skin, and either a skin or a hard surface is assumed by Anaximenes, Parmenides and Empedocles.[1] In the atomic picture there are of course interstices between the linked atoms,[2] and the snatching up of atoms from outside is also a peculiar feature.

The formation of the heavenly bodies, as Diogenes relates it, is not very clear. Some of the atoms which are caught up in the whirl cling together and form sizeable concentrations. Why these should be wet and muddy is not stated. In the system of Anaxagoras there was a good reason, for they were lumps of the earth which had been flung into the sky at an early stage in its formation, and it looks as if they have retained the property without the justification for it. Anaxagorean also is the explanation of their catching fire from the rapidity of their rotation.[3] All this is not very easy to explain in atomic terms. What is wet and earthy is composed of large atoms, whereas fire is a body consisting of spherical atoms of the smallest size. These are just the kind to be 'squeezed out' by the others, and their squeezing out is no doubt intended to explain the universally accepted fact that the bulk of fire in the universe is located in its outer regions. Presumably a large number of these become incorporated in the formerly muddy bodies as they whirl around, but from the meagre statement offered here we can

---

[1] Vol. I, 91, 135 ff., and pp. 61, 188 above.

[2] As between any contiguous atoms. This was important for Eleatic reasons, to show that a compound was not 'one'. (Cf. p. 390, n. 1 above.) Philoponus (*GC*, 158.26, 67 A 7 *ad fin.*) says that Democritus did not use the word 'contact' of atoms in its strict sense, 'but what he called contact was proximity, for they were in every case separated by the void'. Unless this is entirely erroneous (as Zeller thought, ZN, 1069, n. 5 *ad fin.*), it refers to the fact that owing to their irregular shape atoms could never be more than partially in contact.

[3] Though this by itself goes back to Anaximenes (vol. I, 133).

only guess at Leucippus's explanation. As it is, the novel idea that the matter of the stars is of extra-cosmic origin seems to sit rather uncomfortably on the Anaxagorean conception of it as earthy and wet. In general such material collected at the centre, as in other cosmogonies, and gradually built up the earth.[1] This, at least in the system of Democritus, was formed before the stars (Hippol. *Ref.* 1.13.4, 68 A 40).

Democritus may have tried to introduce more consistency into Leucippus's account at this point. Diogenes states explicitly (9.44) that the fiery nature of the sun and moon is due to the presence in them of atoms of the appropriate type, round and smooth, but the only other information, in a passage of the *Stromateis* (68 A 39), is not altogether clear. After affirming that, as in Leucippus, the sun and moon at their birth were neither hot nor bright but like earth, it goes on to say that 'as the sun's circle increased in size fire became incorporated in it'. Perhaps then the sun and moon were not, in Democritus's system, formed from extra-cosmic matter, and their originally cold and earthy nature was connected with their moving in smaller orbits, nearer to the earth, and only becoming ignited as they swung further into the outer regions where they would meet with the small round fire-atoms.[2]

The destruction of worlds by collision has already been mentioned. In the same section Hippolytus adds a little about their acme and decline: 'They flourish until they are unable to take in any more from outside.' Here again one can detect an echo of other cosmogonies based on the conception of the world as a living and growing organism, for it recalls the idea of the 'nourishment' of the stars in Heraclitus, and

---

[1] The connexion of 'fine' and upward-moving bodies with fire and air, and of the 'dense' and downward-sinking with water and earth, is alluded to by Hermeias, *Irris.* 12 (67 A 17).

[2] The same passage includes the strange statement: γεγονέναι γὰρ ἑκάτερον τούτων πρότερον ἔτι κατ' ἰδίαν ὑποβολήν τινα κόσμου, which Bailey and Alfieri both translate without apparently thinking it calls for explanation. ('Each of them was brought into being by a separate foundation of the world', B.) Zeller (ZN, 1106), whom Heath followed, took it to mean that sun and moon were originally the centres of independent world-systems as the earth is of ours. This, and the supposition that the sun became fiery as its orbit increased, can, he thought, be reconciled with the rest of the atomic cosmogony on the assumption that sun and moon were at an earlier stage of their formation caught up by the masses whirling round the earth as centre and so brought into our own system. I cannot understand this, nor see how his final assumption fits with the originally smaller orbit of the sun. (It surely cannot have been a *different* orbit, not concentric with the present one.) I have no solution, but I am doubtful whether ὑποβολή can have the same sense as καταβολή in the N.T. phrase καταβολή κόσμου.

of the cosmos in Philolaus.[1] Nevertheless, the persistence of this pattern of the world's growth must not make us forget that for the atomists it was no longer a living thing.[2] It was an undesigned combination of atoms subject to an apparently random motion which had happened to take certain directions under a purely mechanical compulsion. The various kinds of movement which worked together to produce it may be summarized as follows: (1) a universal vortex to which minor movements are subordinate; (2) within this, a continuance of the original irregular motions of individual atoms resulting from their collisions and recoil; (3) a tendency of larger and heavier bodies to seek the centre of the vortex and smaller and lighter ones to be squeezed outwards;[3] (4) more generally, the attraction of like to like, a law applicable both to single atoms and to their compounds. All this Leucippus and Democritus attributed to 'necessity', a concept which, so their ancient critics say, was left unexplained but was in effect no different from chance. The relation between these two concepts is worth a somewhat closer study. (See §7 below.)

(6) *The four elements*

The prominence of the four elements in Greek philosophy has made it seem important to many scholars to consider their status in atomism. Obviously there can be no question of truly elemental bodies except the atoms. Moreover, since the atoms are of infinitely different shapes and sizes, they cannot build up into four primary kinds of bodily substance which were the basis of all others, as did Plato's elementary particles which were confined to the shapes of four of the regular solids. Nevertheless, since earth, water, air and fire always held a special place in the Greek mind and had recently been given elemental status by Empedocles, Leucippus and Democritus would presumably make some attempt to explain their differences by atomic composition.[4]

That their atoms differed in size is obvious from the way the universe

---

[1] Philolaus, A 18. For Heraclitus see vol. 1, 484. Cf. also τραφέντα in Parmenides fr. 19.2.

[2] Aët. 2.3.2 (67 A 22): Λεύκιππος δὲ καὶ Δημόκριτος καὶ Ἐπίκουρος οὔτ' ἔμψυχον οὔτε προνοίᾳ διακεῖσθαι [*sc.* τὸν κόσμον], φύσει δέ τινι ἀλόγῳ ἐκ τῶν ἀτόμων συνεστῶτα.

[3] For the flying upward of the latter Democritus used the word σοῦς (Arist. *De caelo*, 313 b 5), apparently a Laconism. (Cf. Plato, *Crat.* 412 b.)

[4] In what follows I have had particularly in mind the views of Zeller (ZN, 1075), Hammer-Jensen (*Archiv.* 1910, 212), Alfieri (*Atom. Id.* 177 f.) and Kerschensteiner (*Kosmos*, 164 f.).

was formed: large and heavy atoms form the earth, specially light and mobile ones fly outward and become fire, and the atoms of the intermediate bodies water and air must be of correspondingly intermediate size. Only of fire, so far as we know, did Democritus specify a shape, namely round and smooth,[1] and even then it must be remembered that the atoms of soul, and of anything sweet-flavoured, are also round. Yet one may assume that the atoms of a stable substance like earth must have been hooked or burr-like in comparison with fluids or vapours. The two points that only fire was allotted a special shape, and that there was no essential distinction between the 'elements' and other atomic compounds, are borne out by several passages. Aristotle says that, while assigning the sphere to fire, the atomists did not define the shapes of the atoms forming the other elements: 'air, water and the rest they distinguished by size, considering their nature to be a *panspermia* (seed-collection) of all the elements [i.e. atoms]'. Plutarch, after describing the atoms of Democritus, continues: 'and when they approach each other or collide or get entangled, the result of the concourse appears in one case as fire, in another water, in another a plant or a man'. Aristotle may have used the word *panspermia* somewhat carelessly (it seems more appropriate to the theory of Anaxagoras), but it is a reasonable conclusion that the atomists did not assign a definite shape to the atoms of the other three 'elements' and that they spoke of air and water, plants and men, as compounds on much the same level.[2]

(7) *Causality in atomism: necessity and chance*

No cause or force was required to set the atoms in motion originally, for their motion is eternal. For the course which their movement takes (on which depends all that happens in the world), both necessity and chance are alleged as causes.[3] They are clearly very similar conceptions,

[1] Even after Newton it was possible for his follower Boerhaave to think of fire as a body, composed of especially fine, round, smooth and polished particles, without hooks, projections, or indentations (Toulmin, *Arch. of Matter*, 211).

[2] Arist. *De caelo*, 303 a12 (and *De an.* 404 a4); Plut. *Adv. Col.* 1110 f (68 A 57). For *panspermia* and Anaxagoras cf. Arist. *GC*, 314 a 24–b 1 and p. 282, n. 2 above. It may well have been Anaxagoras who put the idea into the atomists' heads, as Kirk points out (KR, 421).

[3] ἀνάγκη and τύχη or αὐτόματον. That our sources from Aristotle onwards use the latter two as synonymous in speaking of the atomists is clear from Arist. *Phys.* B ch. 4 and Simpl. *ad loc.* 327.25–6. It is not certain that αὐτόματον was a technical term of atomism: it occurs only once in a fragment of Democritus, as an adjective and in an ethical context (fr. 182).

and this may cause surprise at first sight, since we tend to contrast them strongly as what produces invariable results with what is unpredictable and haphazard in its effects. Yet although 'necessity' and 'chance' are reasonable translations of the relevant Greek words, the Greeks saw things so differently that to them the expression 'necessary chance' was perfectly natural.[1] Aristotle was not cheating when he at the same time spoke of the earlier natural philosophers as disallowing a teleological view of nature by attributing everything to *necessity* ('rain falls because vapour when drawn up *must* cool, and when cooled *must* become water and descend again') and criticized this position by an argument designed to show that natural events are not at the mercy of *chance*, but exhibit a certain constancy and regularity. How this could be so we shall see.

Necessity was all-potent for Leucippus and Democritus. In a sentence hard to transpose into another tongue, Leucippus said: 'Nothing occurs at random,[2] but everything for a reason and by necessity.' 'Democritus,' said Aristotle, 'ignoring the final cause, refers all the operations of nature to necessity.'[3] The origin, development and decay of worlds is due to necessity, with which are equated all the myriad collisions and recoils of atoms among each other, and in particular the cosmic vortex into which they are drawn.[4] Chance as a cause of physical events in atomism is mentioned only by commentators and critics.[5] In an obvious reference to Leucippus and Democritus,

[1] ἀναγκαία τύχη Soph. *Aj.* 485 and 803, *El.* 48; Eur. *I.A.* 511. Cf. ἀνάγκη τῆσδε...τύχης, Aesch. *Ag.* 1042, and the phrase κατὰ τύχην ἐξ ἀνάγκης, Plato, *Laws*, 889c.

[2] μάτην may mean one of two things in Greek: (*a*) in vain, failing to accomplish an intended purpose (Lat. 'frustra'); (*b*) without any reason or purpose (Lat. 'temere'), as in Soph. *O.T.* 609 τοὺς κακοὺς μάτην χρηστοὺς νομίζειν. Leucippus is evidently using it in the second sense.

[3] Leucippus fr. 2 (Bailey's translation, adopted also by KR); Arist. *GA*, 789b2. In Democritus himself the word ἀνάγκη is only preserved in the ethical fragments, where it signifies a lack of freedom of action, whether due to compulsion of others (as opposed to persuasion, fr. 181) or pressure of external circumstances (frr. 144, 289).

[4] ἀνάγκη and the vortex, D.L. 9.33 and 45, Sext. *Math.* 9.113 (68 A 83). According to Democritus, it is the ἀντιτυπία καὶ φορὰ καὶ πληγὴ τῆς ὕλης, Aët. 1.26.2 (68 A 66). Cf. Cic. *De fato*, 10.23: Epicurus introduced the swerve to avoid determinism, but 'id Democritus, auctor atomorum, accipere maluit, necessitate omnia fieri, quam a corporibus individuis naturales motus avellere'.

[5] τύχη in the fragments of Democritus occurs mostly in ethical maxims, i.e. as 'fortune' in human affairs. 'Fools are shaped by the gifts of fortune, but men who understand such things by those of wisdom' (fr. 197). 'Fortune provides a rich table, self-control a sufficient one' (fr. 210). 'Courage initiates action, but fortune is mistress of the end' (fr. 269). 'Those who take pleasure in the misfortunes of their neighbours do not understand that what fortune sends is common to all' (fr. 293). And so on.

Aristotle speaks of some who 'allege chance (τὸ αὐτόματον) as the cause of this heaven and all the worlds; for they say that the vortex, the movement which separated and brought the whole to its present order, arose by chance'. This, he comments, is odd: they cannot ascribe the smaller details of nature to chance (τύχη; it is not a matter of chance what kind of plant will grow from a particular seed), and it is illogical to suppose that chance produced the universe at large but regular causation governs the sphere of plants and animals which are dependent on the larger cosmic motions (*Phys.* 196a24 ff.).

To understand the atomists' conception of necessity we must take account of the point of view from which Aristotle was criticizing it. He wrote as a teleologist, who sees natural processes in the light of their ends, to which the earlier stages must be thought of as means. Even if one cannot identify a designing mind at work, yet all the stages of growth from a seed to an oak-tree can only be understood in the light of the 'form' of the tree regarded as pre-existing and governing their direction, just as as the pre-existing plans in the mind of an architect, or committed by him to paper, must control the subsequent process of building. To this view the blind necessity of atomic motion, seeing events as determined by the inchoate and not the final state, was in direct opposition. For the mechanists, says Aristotle, nature does not act in a particular way because it is better, and subserves an end, but as rain falls, that is, by the necessity inherent in the properties of moisture, heat and so on, not in order to make crops grow. Indeed, it may sometimes destroy them. Whichever it does, the result is only accidental: the cause is blind, mechanical necessity.[1]

Against this he appeals to the constancy of nature. Natural events follow certain laws, either invariably or at least with a prevailing regularity. A poppy-seed always produces a poppy, never a thistle. In Greece it is regularly hot and dry in July, cool and wet in the winter. Hence natural events cannot be due to chance. If there is a rainstorm in July we do attribute it to chance, just because it is exceptional. The arguments of those who attribute everything to necessity 'cannot be

---

[1] Schumacher's contention (*Ant. Medizin,* 141) that the aetiology of the atomists does not exclude final causation has little to recommend it and would be refuted by Aristotle's opposition alone.

true, because natural events happen always or usually in the same way, and this cannot be true of [necessary events? No, but] *chance* events.' (198 b 32 ff.)

This looks like a blatant shifting of ground. How can one quote the view that all nature is governed by *necessity* and claim to refute it on the ground that its working does not seem to be governed by *chance*? Such a shift offers a temptation to the teleologist, since for him there are only two alternatives: things either happen at random, in which case they are ruled by chance, or with regularity, which for him is tantamount to proof that they are purposeful. The third hypothesis, of a purposeless but unvarying force called necessity, does not exist. (Cf. 199 a 3.)

Yet the existence of phrases like 'necessary chance' in Greek suggests that there is more to it than mere misunderstanding. The early natural philosophers conceived of necessity as an internal cause rather than a cause relating two or more events to each other. To us, problems of causation in science are concerned with the explanation of sequences, chains of cause and effect linking together x and y and z. The Greek on the other hand investigated what he called 'the nature of things', and asked himself 'what is it *in* x that causes it to behave as it does?' He would ask a similar question about y and z, but they would be separate questions. There is a necessity governing the behaviour of fire and causing it to fly upwards (it is the same as the *physis* of fire), and a necessity governing the downward movement of earth. Hence the direction each takes is invariable. But whether a particular portion of fire will meet a particular piece of earth, and what will happen if it does, this doctrine does not say. Such events it appears that the atomists referred to chance. By this they did not mean that their coming-to-pass had no relation to necessary causes, but only that it owed its origin to a nexus of necessary causes so complex that it was beyond human powers ever to comprehend it. Chance was something subjective, exceeding our powers of prediction, because the necessary causes involved were (not non-existent, but) indefinite in number. Obviously if we had complete understanding of the motions of fire in general and every portion of fire in particular, and an equally complete understanding of the necessity governing, in general and in particular, every portion of every natural body with which fire ever comes into contact, we could predict accurately the moment and the spot at which a forest fire would start in the Australian bush. But equally obviously, such omniscience is beyond our reach.

In *Physics* B, chapter 4, Aristotle describes three conceptions of chance which were current among his predecessors. Curiously enough, there are good grounds for thinking that all three are different aspects of the view held by Democritus.[1] First comes the view that there is no such thing and that everything that is said to happen by chance has in fact its own determinate cause. Aristotle's pupil Eudemus, whom Simplicius quotes on this passage, referred this to Democritus on the ground that, even if he appears to employ chance as a cause in his cosmogony, in detail he ascribes all events to other causes (Simpl. *Phys.* 330.14, 68 A 68). Take the analogy of a man who, wishing to plant an olive tree, digs a hole and comes upon a treasure. This, said Democritus, we call chance or luck, but it had its cause in the need to plant the tree, and (we may add) if we knew also the reason why the owner of the treasure buried it there, we should have a full explanation.

The second view, already quoted, is vouched for as Democritean by its references to the cosmogonic vortex and the plurality of worlds. It is the view that the origin of the world seems due to chance but the growth of things on earth exhibits regularity.

From these hints, given with a teleologist's bias, we may reconstruct the atomists' notion of causation. Objectively there is no such thing as chance, but everything is subject to a strict law of mechanical necessity, as Leucippus said. Within this universally operating necessity, the human investigator distinguishes between what are *to him* two different kinds of causation, that which brought about 'this heaven and all the worlds' and that which operates in the germination of a seed. Germination does not seem to be a chance or haphazard process because when we examine the seed we can safely predict what it is going to become. The difference between such an event and the great cosmic events which, it seems, the atomists did attribute to chance, is that the

---

[1] Some may feel difficulty in believing this on the formal ground that when Aristotle writes ἔνιοι γάρ at 195 b 36 and εἰσὶ δέ τινες at 196 a 24, he can hardly have meant the same set of people. But the φυσικά ἀκροάματα were not carefully composed for publication; they are rather a series of notes. Rough and unfinished writing can be found in other places too.

latter contain features which make them unpredictable by man. The whirl is created by necessity, and as the millions of atoms move in space and collide, there is in reality a strict mechanical cause for the behaviour of each one. Yet we could never predict the fate of an individual atom, whether it will be drawn into the whirl or not, as we can predict the development of a seed. Chance as a subjective notion can take its place in the system without prejudice to the ruling idea of an all-pervading necessity.

In this way it approximates to the third of the views reported by Aristotle in this chapter, that chance is 'a cause obscure to human understanding'. True, he adds 'as being something divine and miraculous', which must refer not to the atomists but rather to popular beliefs about fortune.[1] But the definition of chance as simply a cause that is beyond human understanding is ascribed to Democritus (along with Anaxagoras and the Stoics) by Aëtius in practically the same words.[2]

We conclude that Democritus's theory of causality comprised the following three points:

(1) Every event is determined. There is no such thing as chance if the term is used in an absolute or objective sense.

(2) The notion of chance may be retained and used in a qualified sense to mean a cause which is, and must remain, obscure to us.

(3) The incomprehensibility of such a cause lies in the fact that it is always, so far as we are concerned, one of an indefinitely large number of possibilities.

(8) *The heavenly bodies; the earth; other natural phenomena*

Astronomy. The shape and general arrangement of the cosmos, and the composition of the heavenly bodies, have emerged from the account of its formation. On the relative distances of the heavenly bodies from

---

[1] Simplicius refers it to the cult of Tyche as a goddess, and quotes the Delphic invocation 'O Tyche and Loxias' and the remark in Plato's *Laws* (709b) that 'God, and with God *tyche* and opportunity direct all human affairs'. The phrase θεία τύχη was common in tragedy.

[2] Aët. 1.29.7 (DK, 59 A 66) ἄδηλον αἰτίαν ἀνθρωπίνῳ λογισμῷ. (Similarly in Theodoret, Diels, *Dox.* 326 n., with λόγῳ for λογισμῷ.) Aristotle's words (*Phys.* 196 b 6) are αἰτία ἄδηλος ἀνθρωπίνῃ διανοίᾳ. The meagre remains of Democritus himself include the maxim that 'men have invented an image of chance as an excuse for their own folly'. This occurs in a practical context, but is only the ethical counterpart of his physical doctrine. In human affairs it is man's intelligence (or the lack of it) that is the determining factor, in the rest of nature it is necessity.

the earth, the two atomists differed. Leucippus (D.L. 9.33) went back to Anaximander in supposing that the sun's orbit was outermost, but put the fixed stars next, and the moon nearest the earth. The reason for the position of the sun may have been (though it is not mentioned in any ancient authority) that as the brightest and hottest body it must be where the speed of the revolution is greatest.[1]

Democritus on the other hand is reported to have adopted the normal order, putting the fixed stars furthest away, and also to have distinguished the various orbits of the planets. For him 'the planets themselves are not all at the same height', says Hippolytus (*Ref.* 1.13.4, A 40), and another version of his order is 'first [i.e. outermost] the fixed stars, then the [other] planets, and after them sun, Venus, moon' (Aët. 2.15.3, A 86). The titles of Democritus's works include one devoted to the planets, which indicates a special interest, and on the most likely interpretation of a passage in Seneca (*Nat. qu.* 7.3.2, A 92) he knew their names and order and suspected the existence of others as yet undiscovered. The clear distinction between planets and fixed stars, and attribution of differing orbits to the former, was ignored by Leucippus, though the advance can scarcely have been due to Democritus himself.[2]

The order of the heavenly bodies, together with the fact that a body moves more slowly the nearer it is to the earth (p. 407, n. 5 above),

---

[1] So Bailey, *Atomists*, 98, and Kerschensteiner, *Kosmos*, 159, n. 2. Anaximander was alone in questioning the proximity of the moon to the earth. For a possible Persian origin of these unusual speculations about the arrangement of the heavenly bodies, see the references in W. Burkert, *Rh. Mus.* 1963, 104, n. 22.

[2] Anaximander did not distinguish the orbits of the planets from those of the fixed stars (vol. 1, 94). Anaximenes probably did (see now Burkert, *Weisheit u. Wiss.* 290, n. 71), but if so it was in the context of an extremely childish astronomy (vol. 1, 135). According to Eudemus the order of the planets was first determined by 'the Pythagoreans' (*ibid.* 93, 298), which is vague as to date, but it may be thought to go with the doctrine of the harmony of the spheres (*ibid.* 296). However, see *ibid.* 300 on the original form of this doctrine. Parmenides's theory of the στεφάναι (pp. 62f. above), though inadequately and obscurely described in our sources, no doubt involves the distinction between fixed stars and planets, which is also recorded for Empedocles (A 54, p. 192 above). For Anaxagoras we have no information except for his use of the word 'planets' in connexion with comets. (See p. 309 above and Burkert, *loc. cit.* n. 74.) On the passage in Seneca see now Burkert, *op. cit.* 292f. It seems probable that Seneca misunderstood his source in supposing that the number and names of the five planets were not known in Democritus's day. (This was first suggested by Zeller, ZN, 1107, n. 2 *ad fin.*). They had of course long been known in the eastern lands in which he is said to have travelled. Burkert from his anti-Pythagorean viewpoint conducts a spirited defence of Democritus's astronomy against those who, like Burnet and Heath, have dismissed it as childish and reactionary.

means that the sun is outstripped by the stars and the moon by the sun, and this gives us the illusion that sun and moon are moving in the reverse direction through the zodiac, at different speeds, while the fixed stars remain still.[1]

The stars according to Leucippus are ignited by the rapidity of their movement, 'and the sun', adds our source (D.L. 9.33), 'is also ignited by the stars', i.e., presumably, as well as by its motion. Bailey suggests that the dual causation was intended to account for its superior brightness. Leucippus's ideas on these matters seem to have been remarkably naïve, though we must allow for the inadequacy and inferiority of our source. The moon, we are told, 'has only a little fire'. Such as it has appears to be its own, and Leucippus either did not know or disbelieved the discovery of Anaxagoras that it derived its light from the sun.[2] Democritus accepted from Anaxagoras the view that the moon resembled the earth in containing 'glens and valleys', and said that we see in it the shadows of the higher parts (Aët. 2.25.9, A 90); and a passage in Plutarch, which is otherwise not free from obscurity, at least makes plain that he knew it to be illuminated by the sun.[3] He is

---

[1] This is explained as Democritus's teaching, at some length, by Lucretius, 5.621 ff. See also ZN, 1107, n. 2.

[2] Cf. Plutarch's remark (*Nic.* 23): Ἀναξαγόρας οὖτ' αὐτὸς ἦν παλαιὸς οὔτε ὁ λόγος ἔνδοξος ἀλλ' ἀπόρρητος ἔτι καὶ δι' ὀλίγων καὶ μετ' εὐλαβείας τινὸς ἢ πίστεως βαδίζων. To promulgate such doctrines at Athens in the climate of the time was dangerous, he adds. It is however just possible that Leucippus did follow Anaxagoras here, for our information is meagre, and Anaxagoras, even though he knew the moon got its light from the sun, still held that it contained some fire itself. (See p. 307 above.)

[3] *De facie*, 929 c. The speaker is refuting the notion (which he does not ascribe to any authority by name) that the moon is transparent, 'like glass or ice', and lets the sun shine through it. After stating one objection he goes on (trans. Cherniss): 'Certainly her deviations or aversions cannot be alleged as the cause of her invisibility when she is in conjunction, as they are when she is at the half and gibbous or crescent; then rather, "standing in a straight line with her illuminant", as Democritus says, "she sustains and receives the sun", so that it would be reasonable for her to be visible and to let him shine through.' This, as he goes on to point out, is the reverse of what happens, so once again the hypothesis of a transparent moon is defeated. Bailey (*Atomists*, 151) is entirely wrong in supposing all the rest of the sentence to belong to Democritus, and so making him responsible for the 'extraordinary notion' that the sun's light is seen through the moon. The man who thought of the moon as earthy in appearance, with glens and valleys, can hardly have believed that, nor does Plutarch say he did.

For the meaning of κατὰ στάθμην cf. Sosigenes *ap.* Simpl. *Cael.* 505.3. Eisler (*Archiv*, 1917, 52 ff.) thought this expression, and the words ὑπολαμβάνει and δέχεται, were borrowings from Babylonian. Alfieri (*Atomisti*, 118) translates ὑπολαμβάνει as 'intercepts'. But parallels cited by Cherniss (Loeb ed. XII, 103) show that the verbs have a sexual meaning.

D.L. 9.33 has a report on Leucippus's explanation of eclipses, but the text is incomplete and its meaning doubtful. Diels suggested ἐκλείπειν δὲ ἥλιον καὶ σελήνην ⟨...τὴν δὲ λόξωσιν τοῦ

also said to have shared Anaxagoras's explanation of the Milky Way and of comets. He defended the theory of comets as an apparently contiguous collection of planetary stars by maintaining that at their dissolution the separate stars have sometimes been seen to appear.[1]

The earth. Leucippus retained the familiar flat round ('drum-shaped', D.L. 9.30 and Aët. 3.10.4, A 26) earth, but Democritus had the original idea that it was 'elongated, of length one and a half times its breadth'.[2] He also said, like Archelaus (p. 342 above), that it was concave, in which respect he is contrasted with Anaxagoras. (See DK, 59 A 87, 68 A 94.) Leucippus said that it was 'borne rotating about the centre' (D.L. 9.30), whereas according to Democritus (Aët. 3.13.4, A 95) 'at first it strayed about, being small and light, but as in time it grew thicker and heavier, it came to rest'. Any rotatory movement must have been slow, for all bodies, as we have seen, move more slowly as they near the centre owing to its 'resistance' to the cosmic whirl; and so far as our sketchy reports go, it is possible that Democritus visualized a revolving earth as did Leucippus. Its settling at the centre of the universe is contrasted with its 'straying about' in the earlier stages of cosmogony, when it had not collected so much

---

ζῳδιακοῦ γενέσθαι⟩ τῷ κεκλίσθαι τὴν γῆν πρὸς μεσημβρίαν: i.e. he thought that the explanation of eclipses was lost and the tilting of the earth intended to explain the inclination of the ecliptic. Bailey rather surprisingly accepts the added words, but supposes no lacuna before them, so that the tilting of the earth towards the south explains both phenomena: eclipses are 'due to the passing of sun and moon behind the raised northern parts of the world', their orbits being horizontal. If this is so, it makes the conjectured reference to the ecliptic unnecessary. Leucippus also noted that the moon was eclipsed more often than the sun, and attributed this to 'the inequality of their orbits'.

[1] Arist. *Meteor.* 343 b 26. Cf. p. 309 above, and Democritus A 91 and 92.

[2] Fr. 15. The evidence is, as so often, rather dubious, but I have adopted the more circumstantial account. It depends on Agathemerus (a geographer of quite uncertain date who seems, however, to have got much of his information from Eratosthenes), and the word προμήκης alone in Eustathius. (See Democritus fr. 15 and A 94.) The former contrasts Democritus with the earlier writers who wrote of the earth as round, with Delphi as its centre. Aëtius on the other hand (3.10.5, A 94) uses the word δισκοειδής.

Bailey (*Atomists*, 151 f.) suggests that Democritus was influenced by the theory about the Milky Way which he shared with Anaxagoras, making the earth conform more to its contours. Löwenheim (*Wissenschaft D.s*, 98 f.) argues with some plausibility that Democritus knew of the doctrine of a spherical earth and consciously rejected it. This would be in keeping with his Ionian, un-Pythagorean leanings, and Aristotle, *Cael.* 293 b 32 ff., shows that the two views were rivals. The flat-earth party adduced the fact that the sun at its setting and rising shows a straight, not curved, line, where it is cut by the horizon. But Löwenheim's general reasoning is weakened by his translating τύμπανον as 'Kesselpauke' and assuming it to be hemispherical. He does not mention the flat tambourine, which appears on vase-paintings, bas-reliefs, etc. and was the commonest, if not the only, form of the instrument.

matter: after it 'came to rest' there, there is no reason why it should not revolve.[1] Whether this hypothesis of an earth still rotating under the residual influence of the vortex is solely Leucippus's or adopted by Democritus, neither of them believed the earth to be a sphere, and there is nothing to suggest that they related the fact to the apparent motions of the heavenly bodies. One cannot credit them with the brilliant notion, propounded by the early fourth century, that the apparent movement of the stars could be explained on the hypothesis of a rotating earth and motionless heavens (vol. 1, 327 f.). This information about the earth raises two incidental points of interest. It illustrates the atomists' conception of weight as a tendency towards the centre of the vortex and a power of resistance to external disturbance, and it shows that the vortex is in a horizontal plane relative to the earth.

Empedocles, Anaxagoras and Archelaus had explained the angle between the zenith and the celestial pole by the supposition that the outer shell of the cosmos had at some time taken a tilt. Leucippus and Democritus on the other hand taught that it was the earth that had tilted. The cause of this phenomenon, as reported, shows a lively imagination on Democritus's part: 'Because the southerly part of the surrounding [atmosphere] is weaker, the earth as it grew tilted in that direction; for the northerly parts are intemperate, the southern temperate, hence it grew heavier in the latter quarter where it is abundant in fruits and produce.'[2] The warmth rarefies the air (a connexion of thought that goes back to Anaximenes), and makes it less able to sup-

[1] Cherniss (*ACP*, 202, n. 230) thinks it likely that 'all who believed the cosmos to be a whirling eddy with earth at the centre (Anaximander, Anaximenes, Anaxagoras, the Atomists) thought of the flat earth as rotating about its short axis which is the centre of the eddy (cf. Burnet, EGP³, p. 66, n. 3; p. 300, n. 1), so that strictly they did not think the earth immobile save in so far as it does not move away from the centre of the whirl'. I have my doubts about Anaximander and Anaxagoras (p. 302, n. 2 above and vol. 1, 99), and unfortunately he does not discuss our present passage from Aëtius. But it may well be true about Democritus, and if the notion of the δίνη originated from observation of eddies in water (p. 410 above), the belief that matter collected at the centre still revolved, though slowly, would be a natural one.

[2] Aët. 3.12.2, A96. The explanation given for Leucippus in the same section (67 A 27) is similar in essentials: the air in the south is 'thin' because of the earth's intense heat there, in contrast to the frozen north. But there is no mention of vegetation, and πεπυρωμένων seems to exclude it. Did Democritus not share the common belief that the torridity of the extreme south was as 'intemperate' as the cold of the North? For the tilting of the sky in Empedocles and the others see pp. 191 f., 305, 342 above. It seems the better explanation, since as Zeller remarked (ZN, 1108, n. 6), on the atomists' view it is hard to see why all water does not flow south and flood the southern lands.

port the southern half of the earth, which accordingly sinks. This confirms Aristotle's statement that for Democritus, as for Anaximenes and Anaxagoras, the earth owed its support in the centre of the cosmos to the air, on which, owing to its flatness, it 'settled like a lid'.[1] The brilliant conjecture of Anaximander, that it remained there in equilibrium simply because, being equidistant from all points on the circumference of the cosmos, it had no reason to move in one direction rather than another, is attributed to him along with Parmenides by Aëtius; but the testimony of Aristotle must be preferred, and it is likely that the passage in Aëtius contains some confusion.[2]

As recorded by Aristotle, Democritus's account of earthquakes seems to be based on Anaximenes, for they are caused by heavy rain or drought. The earth, as for Anaxagoras, contains cavities (κοιλίαι Aristotle, *concava* Seneca) full of water. When rain overfills them, the water breaks out and causes the earthquake. Conversely, a rush of water causing an earthquake may be brought about when the earth dries out and the water is drawn from the fuller to the empty parts.[3]

Another return to the previous century is seen when Democritus maintains Anaximander's theory that the sea is getting smaller and will finally dry up.[4]

On the much-talked-of question of the Nile's summer floods, Democritus is said to have written that when the snow melts in the North in summer, clouds collect from the vapour formed. These are driven south to Africa by the etesian winds (north winds which blow in summer in the Mediterranean) until they come up against the excep-

---

[1] Arist. *De caelo*, 294 b 13. See also p. 310 above.

[2] Cf. Kahn, *Anaximander*, 79, n. 4. Cherniss thinks the words ὀχεῖσθαι περὶ τὸ μέσον δινουμένην in D.L. 9.30 imply that Leucippus attributed the earth's position at the centre to the force of the cosmic whirl, and would extend this to Democritus also (*ACP*, 202, n. 230).

[3] Arist. *Meteor.* 365 b 1 (a 1 erroneously in DK, 68 A 97). Cf. b 6 of Anaximenes: 'When the earth is becoming wet or dry it breaks... which is why earthquakes occur in droughts and again in heavy rains.' (More fully, vol. I, 139.) Seneca (A 98) gives a fuller account, according to which the prime force is *spiritus* (πνεῦμα) driving the water.

[4] Arist. *Meteor.* 356 b 9, cf. vol. I, 92. On the sea there is also a fragment of papyrus from El-Hibeh in Egypt, discovered in 1902, which speaks of its formation from homogeneous atoms by the law of like to like. It is probably from a work of Theophrastus, to whose account of the atomic theory of sensation it contains a striking parallel, and if so it was written little if at all after the death of its author. (Grenfell and Hunt, *Hibeh Pap.* 16, p. 62; DK, 68 A 99a.) Democritus also believed (like Empedocles, p. 199 above) that the sea contained a certain amount of fresh water, on which the fish lived. See Aelian, *Nat. an.* 9. 64 (A 155a)

tionally high mountains of Ethiopia, where they break and cause violent rains at the Nile's sources. This solution avoided the difficulty that was felt in believing that enough snow could fall, even on mountains, in the torrid climate of Ethiopia, and it was endorsed later by Aristotle.[1]

Meteorology: magnetism. Most theories of wind of which we have any record, down to and including Aristotle, speak in terms of the effect of heat on moisture, or of warming or cooling of the air causing condensation or rarefaction; but Democritus, it seems, offered an extremely simple explanation based directly on the restless dance of the atoms: where there are few in a large space, the air is still, but a multitude crowded into a small space collide, rebound, stick together, get compressed, and this disturbance generates wind when the originally confused motion sets in a particular predominating direction (Seneca, *Nat. qu.* 5.2, 68 A 93a).

The statement of Leucippus's theory of thunder ('the violent breaking out of fire enclosed in very thick clouds') reads like a conflation of Anaximander with Anaxagoras.[2] Democritus differed. A scanty summary of his views on some meteorological phenomena is preserved in Aëtius (3.3.11, A93), from which it would appear that he was at pains to restate earlier Ionian theories in terms appropriate to atomism. The general basis seems to be Anaxagoras's downward rush of fire (p. 312 above).

Thunder is caused by an uneven combination of atoms forcing the cloud which encloses it in a downward direction: lightning is a collision of clouds owing to which the fire-producing particles gather together as they rub one another through the many void apertures into a single spot and filter through. A thunderbolt is produced when the downward motion is forced in a cloud by fire-producing particles which are purer and finer and more even and, as he says himself, 'close-fitted' (πυκνάρμονα). Waterspouts (*presteres*) occur when combinations of fire with more void are caught in places full of void and in a kind of peculiar membrane which surrounds them, and then forming into bodies owing to this mixture of many elements, swoop down upon the deep.[3]

[1] Aët. 4.1.4 (A99); Diod. 1.39; Lucr. 6.729–31. For Aristotle see frr. 246, 247 Rose.

[2] Aët. 3.3.10 (67 A 25). Anaxagoras used the agency of fire, but in a different way, and for Anaximenes it was wind (πνεῦμα) whose breaking out caused the thunder. See p. 312 above and vol. I, 106. The explanation of thunder is all that survives of Leucippus's meteorology.

[3] Bailey's translation. Democritus also took the opportunity to point the atheistic moral which was made so much of in Aristophanes's *Clouds*, by saying that the thunderbolt was 'no Zeus-sent thing' (Plut. *Qu. conv.* 665f, Democr. fr. 152).

With Democritus the Empedoclean 'pores and effluences' explanation of magnetism acquires consistency, now that for the first time a true void has been unambiguously posited. He also forestalled Alexander's question why the iron followed the magnet and not *vice versa*. The latter's statement affords a good example of the extraordinary contortions to which Democritus was prepared to resort in applying his general principles to minor phenomena (Alex. *Quaest.* 2.23, A165):

Democritus also says that there are effluences and that like bodies are attracted to like, but adds that all are attracted to a void. Having made these hypotheses, he supposes that the lodestone and iron consist of similar atoms, but those of the stone are smaller and it is of rarer texture than the iron and contains more void. For this reason, its atoms being more mobile are attracted more quickly to the iron (for they are moving to their similars), and entering the pores of the iron disturb the atoms in it as they pass between owing to their small size. The atoms of the iron, thus disturbed, stream outside towards the stone because of their similarity and because it has more void. The iron [as a whole] follows them in their wholesale expulsion and movement and is itself drawn towards the stone. The reason why the stone does not move any more towards the iron is that the iron does not contain so much void.

After all that, the only objection left to the (one imagines) rather breathless but persevering commentator is that, if the attraction is caused by similarity of atoms, the atoms of chaff and other things attracted by amber must be similar to those of the amber and of each other. Why then do they not attract each other?

The general impression gained from our scrappy information about the atomists' account of cosmology and natural phenomena is that they were highly conservative and entirely in the Ionian tradition, though Democritus took some pains to ensure that his explanations were consistent with the general atomic theory, and in doing so produced a few original ideas. Leucippus placed the sun beyond the fixed stars: so had Anaximander. Anaximander had said long before Democritus that the sea was contracting and would one day dry up. To Anaximenes Democritus owed his explanation of earthquakes and (through Anaxagoras) the belief that the earth floated on a cushion of air. The ignition of the stars by their rapid motion was Anaxagorean and did not fit very easily into Leucippus's cosmogony; so were Democritus's ideas of valleys in the moon and of the Milky Way and comets.

Equally marked is the absence of all trace of earlier or contemporary Pythagorean or related Greek notions. The contrast is seen particularly in the attitude to the heavenly bodies, divine for Pythagoras, Alcmaeon and their like, but for Xenophanes ignited clouds, ephemeral and at no great distance from the earth, for Anaxagoras and Democritus lifeless lumps of matter carried round passively by the universal vortex and rendered incandescent by the speed of their revolution. Both schools of thought defended their belief with rational arguments. Why were the motions of sun, moon and planets different from those of the fixed stars? Democritus offered an explanation based entirely on the mechanical action of the vortex (pp. 420 f. above): for the Pythagoreans the aberrations seemed evidence of an independent motion, and to any Greek the idea of independent motion was inseparable from that of life.

(9) *Time*

An atomic theory of time as a series of discrete instants was evidently current when Zeno wrote, since he took such pains to refute it; and it has been plausibly connected with the Pythagoreans. It is strange that Democritus, the first to work out an atomic theory in comprehensive detail, should not have produced counter-arguments to Zeno's, yet there is no evidence that he did. The atomists, says Alfieri,[1] attempted no mathematical or philosophical analysis of either time or motion, such as would have enabled them to stand up to Zeno's thesis that if time was discontinuous motion was impossible. This is probably true. They may have believed that units of time, as of body, existed below the threshold of sensation, but if so they relied for proof simply on experience, the 'bastard' knowledge which points the way to the 'legitimate'. This will be true if Democritus's theory of vision was basically the same as that mentioned by Aristotle in *De sensu*, 440a20 (pp. 444 f. below) and denied by him at 448a24.[2] In general Aristotle's

---

[1] For his criticism of the atomists' views on time see *At. Id.* 78–80.

[2] Cf. also his phrasing of it at b 2, εἴπερ ἔστι τι μέγεθος καὶ χρόνου καὶ πράγματος ἀναίσθητον ὅλως διὰ μικρότητα.

own arguments against the conception of time as made up of atomic 'nows' suggest that it survived Zeno's criticism and was still seriously maintained, though he does not say by whom.[1] None of our evidence is sealed with the name of Leucippus or Democritus, and we must leave it an open question whether they ever said in so many words that time was made up of atomic instants.[2] Yet if they failed to make this point clear, and brought no mathematical arguments to bear on it, in another direction they must be given credit for a considerable achievement in originality and independence of thought. With the exception of the Eleatics who denied the reality of the temporal altogether, the prevailing view of time before Leucippus was cyclical. It might be more or less conscious and more or less strict, but in one form or another it is a view which goes back to the most primitive modes of thought, being based on elementary observation and crystallized in magical and religious practices. Starting from the annual recurrence of the seasons, it extended to the 'Great Year' based on astronomical data and sometimes connected with natural catastrophes like the flood (vol. 1, 458, n. 4). Among the Ionians a cyclical conception is indicated by the sole extant fragment of Anaximander. The Pythagoreans believed in a strict repetition of history. The cyclical rise and fall of civilizations, marked by natural disasters falling short of the complete dissolution of the world, was probably taught by Xenophanes and reappears after the atomists in Plato and Aristotle. A cyclic scheme involving periodic destruction and rebirth of the cosmos appears in Empedocles and later in Stoicism.[3] The circle of time turns up in non-philosophical literature too, reflect-

[1] He denies it in connexion with Zeno's paradox of the arrow at *Phys.* 239 b 8, but again in book 8 at 263 b 27; and Zeno after all was not maintaining the thesis himself. He was equally prepared to assume the contrary in the Achilles paradox, being concerned with the impossibility of motion on any hypothesis.

[2] Epicurus of course did: see especially Simpl. *Phys.* 934.23, 938.21, Sext. *Math.* 10.142. It may also seem probable, if not inevitable, *a priori*. But a different view is possible, as Strato showed by maintaining that time was composed of indivisible parts but matter and space were infinitely divisible (fr. 82 Wehrli, Sext. *Math.* 10.155); and Sextus mentions Epicurus alone, though his name was commonly and lightly coupled with that of Democritus by commentators.

[3] Vol. 1, 76, 281 f., 352, 388 f., 452, 458. There is no evidence that Anaxagoras gave much consideration to the character of time. He believed motion to have started at a given moment after an indefinite period of immobility. If he expressed this in anything like the terms in which Aristotle reports it (πάντων ἠρεμούντων τὸν ἄπειρον χρόνον, p. 296 with n. 1 above), this suggests that he had thought little about it. The notion of time divorced from any kind of motion is a strange one, both in general and for his period.

ing in fact the current mode of thought.[1] In face of all this it is remarkable to find in Leucippus and Democritus a conception of the infinity of time with no trace of cyclical return in any form.[2] Worlds come into being and pass away, but there is no repetition of *this* world. As the infinite millions of atoms jostle in infinite space through infinite time, all sorts of formations will occur. Some may even be identical, but if that happens it is purely by chance (68 A 40 and 81, pp. 405 f., 406 n. 1). This has wider implications. In Greek thought the notions of circular motion and rational activity were intimately connected (vol. 1, 353 f., 356), and in Plato's *Timaeus* the circular paths of the heavenly bodies were permanent and essential to their nature as the creations of a superior intelligence. In Democritus they are purely accidental and temporary. The sun and stars will disintegrate, and their constituent atoms may be pushed into quite different paths. The dethronement of the cyclical conception of time went with the banishment of reason from the making of the world. It corresponds to the infinite irregularity of atomic shapes which Plato's creator-god reduced to limit and order in the form of the regular geometrical solids.

If Democritus did not trouble to argue about the nature of time, this may have been because of its unreality. Sextus says: 'There appears also to be ascribed to the natural philosophers who follow Democritus and Epicurus some such conception of time as this: "Time is an appearance resembling day and night."'[3] Caution is enjoined by the extreme vagueness of the reference, but the doctrine seems to be that of Epicurus that time is 'an accident of accidents', i.e. something that we associate not with concrete things themselves but with their actions and sufferings, under which he includes days and nights as well as feelings, movements and states of rest.[4] If Sextus is right in saying that this, like so much of Epicurus, originated with Democritus, then time for him, so far from being a reality like atoms and void, was not even

---

[1] Examples are hardly necessary. Aristotle was quoting the general belief when he wrote (*Phys.* 223 b 28) καὶ γὰρ ὁ χρόνος αὐτὸς εἶναι δοκεῖ κύκλος τις...τὸ λέγειν εἶναι τὰ γιγνόμενα τῶν πραγμάτων κύκλον τὸ λέγειν ἐστὶν τοῦ χρόνου εἶναί τινα κύκλον· τοῦτο δὲ ὅτι μετρεῖται τῇ κυκλοφορίᾳ. It was of course intimately connected with reincarnation, the κύκλος γενέσεως.

[2] Mondolfo has commented on this in *L'Infinito*, 89.

[3] χρόνος ἐστὶν ἡμεροειδὲς καὶ νυκτοειδὲς φάντασμα, *Math.* 10.181, DK, 68 A 72.

[4] *Ep.* 1. 72 f., Sext. *Math.* 10.219. See Luria, *Infinitesimaltheorie*, 164.

a first-degree sensible like a physical object[1] or its attributes. The light and darkness, which we call day and night, are themselves 'accidents' of earth, sky, sun, moon and so forth, and time is only a peculiar kind of accident of them,[2] of which we are aware by some kind of immediate intuition. It should also be noticed however that if Democritus made this remark of time in general, it could only have been as an analogy, for he believed that time had never had a beginning,[3] whereas this world with its rising and setting sun has not always existed. For Plato time *was* the motion of the heavenly bodies and had no existence before them,[4] since he would only apply the term to a succession that was regular and ordered. This had no meaning in the mindless universe of Democritus, and the definition 'a day-like and night-like appearance' sounds suspiciously Platonic. If Democritus used it, it is interesting as a further illustration of the paradoxical tension between the two philosophies.

(10) *Soul, life and death*

The atomists were least of all likely to depart from the consensus of their period that soul (*psyche*, that which distinguished living from lifeless) was a tenuous form of material substance. In their system both soul and fire (or heat) consisted of especially small, round atoms, and Aristotle regularly says that Leucippus and Democritus actually identified all three. Typical is *De an.* 403b31: 'Democritus says the soul is fire, and hot, for of the infinite shapes and atoms existing he says the spherical are fire and soul.... Similarly Leucippus.... The round ones are soul, because shapes[5] of this kind are best able to slip through anything and to move other things by their own movement.' He com-

---

[1] Even the idea that time is a body is apparently not completely inconceivable! It is said to have been the opinion of Aenesidemus in the first century B.C. (Sext. *Math.* 10.216).

[2] ἰδίωμα, ἴδιον σύμπτωμα, Epicurus, *Ep.* 1. 72, 73.

[3] According to Aristotle and Simplicius, he even used this, as a self-evident fact, to prove that there were some ungenerated entities and so make more reasonable his Eleatic postulate that atoms and void were not subject to generation or decay. (Arist. Phys. 251b16, Simpl. *ad loc.* 1153.22. Alfieri, in *At. Id.* 79, perhaps exaggerates the circularity of this argument, which does not in itself claim that *nothing* is γενητόν.)

[4] *Tim.* 38b–39e. Cf. vol. I, 338f.

[5] Aristotle uses Democritus's word ῥυσμούς, which suggests first-hand information. In one of the passages where Aristotle says that 'soul and mind (νοῦς) are the same' (*De an.* 405a9), he brings fire into connexion with both: they are composed of atoms that are mobile owing to their small size and their shape, which is spherical. 'Such are mind and fire.'

pares Democritus to Daedalus as he was described in a comedy, making wooden images of Aphrodite move by pouring quicksilver into them (406b 15); 'for he says it is the nature of the atomic spheres never to be at rest and by their movement to draw the whole body into motion with them.' Thus Democritus belongs for Aristotle to that school which thought of motion as the primary characteristic of life (403 b 28). The connexion with heat is brought out again in *De respiratione* (472 a 3): 'He says the soul and the hot are the same, namely the primary forms of spherical particles.' We remember too that, again according to Aristotle, fire was singled out from the other elements by Leucippus and Democritus as consisting of spherical atoms (*De caelo*, 303 a 14, p. 414 above). Later, in Diogenes (9.44), we are told that for Democritus soul was made of the same smooth, round atoms as the sun and moon.

Did Democritus actually identify soul with fire? The question is not altogether simple. One is inclined to say that, on atomic principles, a single atom, whether spherical or otherwise, could not be either, for the atoms are without qualities (p. 393, n. 4 above). Aristotle has inferred the identity from the fact that both are composed of atoms of the same shape, but as Cherniss pointed out (*ACP*, 389, n. 3), 'a single spherical atom is neither fire nor soul: the specific characteristics of both of these as of all complex bodies were considered to be merely epiphenomena of the combination of atoms'. Aëtius retains the relationship to fire, but says that soul is 'a fire-like *compound* of atoms spherical in shape and having the potency of fire' (4.3.5, A 102). Of the atoms of which fire is composed he says, not that they *are* fire, but that they *produce* it.[1] Amplifying the absence of sensible qualities in the atoms, Galen specifies that they grow neither hot nor cold (*De elem. sec. Hipp.* 1.2, 68 A 49). (To Aristotle this may have seemed a little absurd, just as Theophrastus in *De sensu*, 69, said it was unreasonable to make sense-data at the same time affections of the senses and due to atomic shapes, because shape is something absolute whereas sense-data are relative to the perceiver.) Moreover the character of the compound is not determined by shape of atoms alone, but also by size and arrangement. The atoms of sweet-tasting substances also were round, but 'not very small'

---

[1] τὰ γεννητικὰ τοῦ πυρός, 3.3.11 (A 93).

The Atomists of the Fifth Century

(Theophr. *Sens.* 65); and things are hot and fiery 'when formed of mobile and tiny bodies evenly spaced'.[1]

Yet although the atomic theory may not have demanded that two things composed of spherical atoms should have the same character, all previous and contemporary thought would influence Democritus towards associating life with heat,[2] and all authorities agree that he did so. For thought to take place, the soul must be rightly tempered; and this means that if we become *too hot or too cold*, the mind wanders (Theophr. *Sens.* 58). Fire (= 'the hot') is not all visible as a glow or flame. The invisible kind has atoms smaller than those of visible fire, as one may see from Theophr. *Sens.* 75, where the colour red is said to consist of atoms like those of heat but larger: 'compounds of larger atoms are redder, as the flame and charcoal of green wood compared with that of dry.'[3] Soul, or vital heat, one may assume, has the finest texture and smallest atoms of all, being neither visible nor even perceptible as heat at all.

Even the point that a single atom, whatever its shape, cannot have the qualities of soul—which might seem to be demanded by the general atomic theory—is rendered doubtful when we go on to consider the distribution of soul-atoms in the body. They are dispersed throughout it in such a way that single atoms of soul and body alternate.[4] By this device Democritus thought that the soul could best carry out its primary function of imparting motive power, and it means that, so far as it discharges that function, there are no aggregates of soul-atoms anywhere. This does not, however, constitute a breach in the monism of atomic theory by ascribing 'qualities', i.e. sensible qualities, to single

[1] ἐξ ὀξυτέρων καὶ λεπτομερεστέρων καὶ κατὰ ὁμοίαν θέσιν κειμένων, Simpl. *Phys.* 36.4. I take it that ὀξυτέρων means 'swift' rather than 'sharp' (instead of round), which would contradict all other testimony. For Plato on the other hand the atoms of fire had a piercing quality from their pyramidal shape.

[2] The role of heat as the active element in the production of life has often been alluded to in the present work. See vol. 1, 61, 101 f., 291, and pp. 59, 207 above.

[3] There is some difficulty over this passage as a whole, but even if at the beginning of the section it is larger *aggregates* of atoms that are in question, τὰ ἐκ μεγάλων ὄντα σχημάτων can only mean 'compounds of larger atoms'.

[4] Lucr. 3.370–3:   Illud...
                   Democriti quod sancta viri sententia ponit,
                   corporis atque animi primordia singula privis
                   apposita alterius variare ac nectere membra.

Aristotle simply said that soul is present throughout the whole body, *De an.* 409a32.

atoms.[1] All atoms are naturally, and if left to themselves, in motion. In the cosmic vortex the larger and heavier of them, and those whose shape makes them liable to entanglement, interfere with each other and their motion is retarded or stopped. Smooth round atoms are least liable to entanglement or clogging, the less so the smaller they are. They can become entrapped in the larger conglomerations, but continue to move freely within them and by this means impart their motion to the others, making of the body as a whole a self-moving (i.e. living) creature. No properties are involved other than the shape, size and arrangement which are basic to all atomic theory. There is some element of absurdity in this audacious attempt to explain the phenomena of life on such simple materialistic and mechanistic principles, and Aristotle's jibe about the quicksilver is not unjustified; but so far it is perfectly consistent.

The mind, or thinking portion of the soul, is an exception to the general rule that soul-atoms alternate with body-atoms throughout the body. The evidence is late and conflicting, but leaves little room for doubt. The *Placita* in contiguous sections (*a*) link Democritus with Epicurus as holding that 'the soul has two parts, that which has reason being situated in the heart while the unreasoning part is dispersed throughout the whole body', and (*b*) say that though Epicurus placed it in the heart, Democritus like Plato put it in the head.[2]

These reports agree that the mind is a concentration of soul in a particular part of the body, and there is no evidence of any weight to set against them.[3] We may take it that this location is in the head, as it

---

[1] As is claimed by Schmid, *Gesch. gr. Lit.* 1.5.2.2, 272: 'the soul-atom with its effects is something essentially different from the other, qualitiless atoms, it is irreconcilable with the monistic theory of matter'.

[2] 4.4.6 and 5.1 (A 105). The brain also in Theodoret's version (5.22, Diels, *Dox.* 391 n. Both the passages that assign reason to the head use the Stoic term ἡγεμονικόν for it.

[3] Philoponus (*De an.* 35.12, A 105) attributes to Democritus the statement that the soul is undivided (ἀμερῆ) and not many-powered, adding that thought is the same as sensation and both proceed from the same δύναμις. He however is commenting on Aristotle's *De anima* and basing his explanation on Aristotle's that for Democritus ταὐτὸν ψυχὴν καὶ νοῦν, which implies no more than that both are of the same atomic composition and work in the same materialistic way: neither can occur without external stimulation (Aët. 4.8.10, 67 A 30). ἀμερῆ in Philoponus is not contrasted with the διμερῆ of the *Placita*, but with πολυδύναμον. The same may be said of the vague reference in Sextus (*Math.* 7.349, 68 A 107) to τινες κατὰ Δ. holding that διάνοια pervades the whole body: Democritus said soul is dispersed throughout the body, Aristotle makes him say soul and mind are the same, therefore mind must be dispersed throughout the body.

was for Alcmaeon, Anaxagoras and Diogenes of Apollonia, and later for Plato. For Epicurus it was the heart, and the testimony which links the earlier atomist with the later is more likely to be from an Epicurean source, and incorrect, than the one which distinguishes between them.[1]

The atomic explanation of the mechanism of life and the cause of death has been preserved by Aristotle. Leucippus and Democritus taught that life is maintained in our bodies by breathing. The tiny, mobile soul-atoms are under constant pressure from the atmosphere outside, which extrudes them from the body, just as the smaller and smoother atoms were squeezed out by the larger in the formation of the universe. But the air itself contains 'many of those particles which Democritus calls mind and soul. Hence, when we breathe and the air enters, these enter along with it, and render the pressure ineffective, thus preventing the dispersal of the soul within the animal.' 'Death occurs when the pressure from the environment gets the upper hand, and the animal being unable to respire, the air from outside can no longer enter and counteract it. Death is the outflow of soul-atoms from the body owing to pressure from the environment.' In a milder and reparable form the preponderance of outflow over inflow induces sleep.[2]

It is obvious that for Democritus, as later for Epicurus, the individual soul is dispersed at death, and its component particles scattered throughout the universe: 'Democritus and Epicurus say that the soul is mortal, and perishes along with the body.' Consequently no man need make himself miserable by fears of torments and punishments after death — the message which Epicurus and Lucretius were later to preach with

---

[1] Aët. 4.5.1 and 5: Πλάτων Δημόκριτος ἐν ὅλῃ τῇ κεφαλῇ...Παρμενίδης καὶ Ἐπίκουρος ἐν ὅλῳ τῷ θώρακι. In view of its freedom from Epicureanism, one may also adduce the spurious letter of Democritus to Hippocrates (Hippocr. *Ep.* 23, IX. 394 L.) in which he calls the brain φύλακα διανοίης, assigns anger to the heart, and desire to the liver. For the brain as central organ of cognition in Diogenes and the Hippocratic *De morbo sacro* see above, p. 376. According to Jaeger (*Diokles*, 214) it represents the doctrine of the Coan as opposed to the Sicilian school of medicine. Empedocles located it in the heart (p. 229 above).

[2] Arist. *De resp.* 471 b 30 ff. In a similar account in *De Anima* (404 a 9) he mentions both Leucippus and Democritus. It is interesting to notice how once again an old and popular belief (in this case the connexion of soul with air) is retained and given scientific clothing. Cf. vol. I, 128–30. For sleep see Aët. 5.25.3 (67 A 34). (The 'indispensable word' ὕπνον, which Zeller says is missing, can be safely supplied from the previous paragraph on Anaxagoras and the title of the section.)

evangelical fervour.[1] Nevertheless, Democritus taught that this did not happen all at once, just as the body does not immediately disintegrate. Indeed he is said to have maintained that the precise moment of death is difficult to determine. The following passages are relevant:

(*a*) Alex. Aphrod. *Top.* 21.21 (68 A 117; the same in Aët. 4.9.20): Dead bodies have sensation, so Democritus thought.

(*b*) Aët. 4.4.7 (A 117): Democritus says that all things share in some sort of soul, even dead bodies, because they plainly retain some portion of warmth and sensitivity when most of it has been breathed out.

(*c*) Tertullian, *De an.* 51 (A 160): Democritus draws attention to the growth of nails and hair for a certain time in the tomb.

(*d*) Celsus, 2.6 (A 160): Democritus, so far from allowing that there were any certain symptoms of approaching death, declared that there were no completely certain indications by which medical men could satisfy themselves of the actual cessation of life.

With the cessation of breathing, then, most of the soul-atoms are expelled from the body and dispersed, but since life and warmth are closely associated (or even identified) and the body only gradually · grows cold, and from certain other observations, Democritus concluded that some vital functions, including even a minimum of sensation, were temporarily prolonged by a few remaining soul-atoms.[2]

---

[1] Aët. 2.7.4 (68 A 109) Δημόκριτος Ἐπίκουρος φθαρτήν [*sc.* τὴν ψυχήν], τῷ σώματι συνδιαφθειρομένην. The rest comes from Stobaeus's collection of fragments (297 in DK), and is as likely to be genuine as most of that collection, at least in content. Since it contains what would be the first known occurrence of both συνείδησις and μυθοπλαστεῖν—the latter dubbed by Rohde 'a late monstrosity'—it is probably not verbally accurate. It runs: 'Some men, not understanding the corruption of our mortal nature, and conscious of their own wicked deeds, drag out their lives in fear and confusion of mind, imagining lying myths about the time after death.'

[2] It will be remembered that Parmenides too taught that corpses retained a certain sensitiveness (p. 67 above). Whether the πάντα in Aët. 4.4.7 means literally everything, including the inanimate world, is perhaps doubtful in view of the words '*even* dead bodies' which follow. Probably however Democritus did believe that there was some small measure of soul in everything. Not only would he be following Empedocles (fr. 110.10, p. 233 above) and (if Theophrastus is to be trusted here) Parmenides—which would accord with his general conservatism—but it would agree well with his general theories if the tiniest and most mobile of all atoms should find their way everywhere. We know already that the atmosphere contains them.

Mention should perhaps be made of Cicero, *Tusc.* 1.34.82: 'Fac enim sic animum interire ut corpus: num igitur aliquis dolor, aut omnino post mortem sensus in corpore est? Nemo id quidem dicit, etsi Democritum insimulat Epicurus: Democritii negant.' The speaker is countering the objection that the Epicurean denial of immortality robs us of the hope of future happiness. Since all consciousness ends with death, the loss will not worry us. The most probable interpretation of the passage quoted is that Epicurus (always ready to belittle his predecessors in the atomic theory) misrepresented Democritus's scientific caution as allowing a loophole for immortality. Contemporary *Democritii* would naturally rebut such a charge.

In the collections of ethical sayings attributed to Democritus the *psyche* appears as naturally superior to, and in control of, the body, which is called its tent, hut or tabernacle (σκῆνος, the word which survived to represent a very different relationship between soul and body in the New Testament).[1] The soul deserves the higher consideration, for its perfection can correct bodily defects but not *vice versa*, and its goods are 'more divine' than bodily goods; in its domain lie happiness and unhappiness, and so forth. This must be considered in another context, together with the question of the authenticity of the ethical fragments. Despite the soul's superior dignity, Zeller was right to emphasize that nothing is said about it to contradict the out-and-out materialism of the atomists.[2] Cicero twice speaks of the 'concursio fortuita' of atoms that goes to produce soul and mind in Democritus.

Additional note: Democritus 'On the Next World'

A work of this name (περὶ τῶν ἐν Ἅιδου) is listed among the ethical (not physical) writings of Democritus in the catalogue of Thrasyllus. Athenaeus (168b, DK, fr. o c), telling the story of how Democritus escaped prosecution by reading his own writings, says that the writings in question were this one and the *Great World-System*, though Diogenes (9.39) mentions only the latter in this connexion. Proclus (*In Remp.* 2.113 Kroll, DK, fr. 1) again cites the work (with the slight variation περὶ τοῦ Ἅιδου in the title) as authority for giving credit to stories of the resuscitation of the apparently dead. 'Death', he says, 'is not, it seems, according to this book the extinction of all life whatsoever in the body. It is weakened, perhaps, by some blow or wound, but the bonds of the soul remain rooted in the marrow and the heart retains the spark of life buried in the depths. So long as these remain, the body is fit for animation and recovers the life that has been quenched.' Proclus is commenting on the myth of Er in the tenth book of Plato's *Republic*. Democritus, he says, 'like many other writers of

---

[1] Vlastos notes its recurrence in two passages of the Hippocratic Corpus (*Ph. Rev.* 1945, 579, n. 11).

[2] ZN, 1120. The superiority of soul to body is equally rightly insisted on by Havelock, *Preface to Plato*, 211, n. 3, though he cites fragments (especially 31) whose authenticity is even more doubtful than that of the others. Those mentioned in the text above are 187, 37 and 170. See further p. 494 and fr. 159 on p. 470, and compare the remarks of Vlastos, *Ph. Rev.* 1945, 581 f.

antiquity', has collected stories of such resuscitations, and this is his explanation of them. It is a rational explanation fully in keeping with what we have just seen of his theories about death, and Proclus's words do much to allay suspicions which may arise from the fact that works with the same title are ascribed by Diogenes (9.55 and 5.87) to Democritus's older contemporary Protagoras and to Heraclides Ponticus. Stories of miraculous resuscitations were told of a number of semi-mythical figures, notably Abaris, Epimenides and Hermotimus (the stock examples, mentioned here by Proclus). That of Abaris appears in Herodotus, Epimenides was well known to both Plato and Aristotle and so no doubt was Hermotimus also, though Aristotle is the first to mention him. These facts must be set against the argument of M. Wellmann that the passage comes from Bolus (p. 388, n. 1 above) and belongs to an alleged 'ἀναβίωσις-literature' initiated by Heraclides, Chrysippus and others. Wellmann's arguments are summarized by Alfieri (*Atomisti*, 180, n. 461), who is convinced by them and adds others which seem no more compelling, e.g. that there are traces of Pythagorean language and no mention of atoms. Of other scholars one may mention that Rohde (*Psyche*, 408, n. 103) thought it 'difficult to be certain that Democritus was the author of the work', but Wilamowitz (*Glaube*, 1.304, n. 1) assumed its authenticity and Schmid (*Gesch. gr. Lit.* 1.5.2.2, 248, n. 7) thought the doubts of Wellmann unjustified.

In view of stories like those of Aristeas (Hdt. 4.14) and Er the Armenian (for Plato was clearly not the first to tell such a tale), one must accept the fact that 'ἀναβίωσις-literature' has a long history, and that a work in the course of which Democritus is reported to have investigated its scientific credentials is very likely to have been genuine. The general purport of the work was no doubt to disprove the possibility of the soul living on in another world after the dissolution of the body, and in all probability fr. 297 (p. 435, n. 1 above) came from the same source. On the other hand in the particular passage which we have been considering Proclus makes no claim to be giving a literal quotation, and some of the language, and even other details (e.g. the prominence of marrow and heart), may be un-Democritean. All one can take from it is that Democritus upheld the credibility of stories about recovery from apparent death by reference to his theory that the body is not robbed of every spark of life at the moment of death, and indeed that the 'moment of death' is not determinable with certainty.

(11) *Sensation*

The atomists' theories of sensation are attributed either jointly to Leucippus and Democritus or to Democritus alone. From the long and elaborate account which Theophrastus gives of the views of Democritus, we may conclude that he added a great deal of detail to a comparatively simple outline provided by Leucippus. In general, sensation is the result of an alteration in our own bodies, or parts of them, caused by the impact of atoms from without. Sensible qualities are 'affections of the sensitive part undergoing alteration, from which comes the perception: not even cold and heat have an objective character, but the atom as it moves brings about an alteration in us also'.[1] Every act of sensation must involve actual physical contact, so that all sensation becomes a form of touch, as Aristotle noted and Lucretius later proclaimed with an emotional insistence:

> Tactus enim, tactus, pro divom numina sancta,
> corporis est sensus.[2]

As evidence that sensations are not solely determined by the atomic composition of the sensa, but by an interaction of this with the body of the perceiving subject, Democritus adduced the relativity of sensations: what is sweet to one is bitter to another, and so on (63).[3] 'The perceiving subjects alter in composition according to their condition and age, whence it is clear that their physical state is a cause of their sense-impressions' (64). After explaining that every sensible object contains atoms of many different shapes but takes its character from those that preponderate, Theophrastus continues: 'it depends also on

---

[1] Theophr. *Sens.* 63. αἴσθησις, usually abstract (power or faculty of sensation), becomes concrete in the materialistic context of atomism. φαντασία is used as in Plato, *Theaet.* 152c φαντασία καὶ αἴσθησις ταὐτόν. τὸ σχῆμα μεταπῖπτον has been translated differently, but σχῆμα for 'atom' and μεταπίπτειν for 'to change place' are frequent, and thus rendered the words give the best sense here. For the doctrine cf. also 60 Δ. δὲ πάντα [τὰ αἰσθητά] πάθη τῆς αἰσθήσεως ποιῶν; Aët. 4.8.5 (67 A 30) ἑτεροιώσεις τοῦ σώματος. It is mentioned already by Aristotle, *Metaph.* 1009b13.

[2] Lucr. 2.434. As Aristotle also notes (*De sensu*, 442a29) this is a necessity not only for Democritus but for all the early *physiologi* who had no conception of non-material reality. But none of the others followed it up so consequentially as did Democritus.

[3] These numbers in brackets refer to sections of Theophr. *De sensu*.

the condition of the body which they enter; this too makes no little difference, because the same object can sometimes produce contrary effects and contrasting objects the same effect' (67).

Theophrastus claims to see a glaring contradiction in a theory which calls sensations affections of the sense-organ and at the same time accounts for them by atomic shape, so that heat for example is said to have no 'nature' of its own but to be a purely relative and subjective impression, and yet one can speak of the 'shapes' of heat as spherical (68 and 69: this is 'the greatest inconsistency and affects all instances alike'). There does not seem any inconsistency in supposing that the effect on a subject of atoms of a certain shape varies according to the state of the atoms in the subject itself; yet since Democritus apparently committed himself to definite statements like 'sweet flavour consists of round atoms', one wonders whether, when the same substance tastes sweet to one and bitter to another, it is round atoms that are actually the cause of bitterness. Whether or not Democritus was explicit on the point,[1] the explanation in his mind was probably that every physical substance contains atoms of many different shapes and takes its sensible qualities from those which predominate. This he did say (67), so that honey, for instance, whose larger and smooth-surfaced atoms entering our bodies produce sweet taste, also contains rough and smaller ones which produce bitter. Which of these objective factors becomes effective would then depend on the state of the passages (*poroi*) in the perceiver's body. There is some evidence that Democritus, like Empedocles, in his theory of sensation made use of *poroi* which must be of the right size for the sensa to fit them.[2]

[1] There seem to have been gaps in his exposition. Even in the case of a bitter juice turning sweet, where an explanation on atomic lines is easy, Theophrastus has to choose between the possibilities himself because he has not found one in Democritus (*CP*, 6.7.2, A132). On the question of relativity it may just possibly be significant that atoms causing bitterness and sweetness are said to be basically of the same shape: the former too are smooth and round, but small, and with 'curvatures' (καμπαί) on the surface which make their compound sticky (66). They are not sharp and angular like those producing astringency (στρυφνόν), so might perhaps taste sweet to an unusually constituted tongue. This of course is sheer guesswork.

[2] A suspiciously comprehensive catalogue in Aëtius (4.9.6, DK 28 A 47) lists him along with Parmenides, Anaxagoras and Heraclides as well as Empedocles and Epicurus as giving this explanation. Plutarch (*Qu. conv.* 735 a, 68 A 77) speaks of εἴδωλα entering the πόροι in Democritus's theory of dreams. Cf. the mention of Democritus and πόροι by the comic poet Damoxenus, fr. 2.29–32 (68 c 1). They also figured in his explanation of magnetism (p. 426 above). The point made in the text (and previously by Brieger, *Hermes*, 1902, 64 f.) is very clearly put by Lucretius, 4.649–72.

There is perhaps more substance in another of Theophrastus's criticisms, that it was unreasonable to assign objective existence not only to shape and size, which are primary because properties of single atoms, but also to weight and lightness, hardness and softness, in compound bodies.[1] These Democritus explained as dependent on the proportion of atoms to empty space in the perceived body. Light, and also soft or yielding, bodies contain more void; heavy, and hard or resistant, more solid.[2]

The general theory may be summed up in the saying of Democritus which was often quoted, most fully by Sextus: 'In our belief there are sweet and bitter, hot and cold, in our belief there is colour; but in truth there are atoms and void.' To this Sextus adds another direct quotation: 'In reality we grasp nothing precisely, but as it shifts according to the disposition both of our body and of the things that enter into and press upon it.'[3] Simplicius was no doubt right in seeing a reference to Democritus when Aristotle attributes to 'earlier scientists' the Berkeleian-sounding view that 'there is no black or white without sight, nor flavour without tasting'.[4]

[1] 68, 71. Within the cosmic whirl single atoms themselves differ in weight, which, since they contain no void, depends directly on their size. In this connexion weight is simply a greater or lesser tendency to move in a particular direction. Similarly the hardness and softness of compounds may be described only in terms of capacity to resist pressure. But if Theophrastus is right, when speaking of compounds Democritus treated all these as sensible properties (αἰσθητά, 63): things 'feel heavy' or 'feel soft'. (Baeumker goes into this question in considerable detail in *Probl. d. Materie*, 92, n. 5, 93 f.)

[2] He did not overlook the fact that a soft substance (e.g. lead) may be heavier than a harder one (iron), but explained this as a matter of position and grouping of the internal spaces (62). Lead contains a greater total of solid than an equal volume of iron, but has solid and void evenly distributed throughout: the hardness of the iron is due to its having patches of greater density occurring irregularly among larger spaces. See further on this Sambursky, *Phys. World*, 120 f., who discusses the matter in modern terms of solid state and lattice-structure, and von Fritz, *Philos. u. sprachl. Ausdr.* 20. Von Fritz makes sense of the explanation by what is perhaps a rather conjectural expansion of Theophrastus's words.

[3] Sext. *Math.* 7.135–6 (Democr. fr. 9). Cf. Galen, *De medic. empir.*, Democr. fr. 125 and Walzer's ed. p. 113; idem, *De elem. sec. Hipp.* 1.2 (68 A 49), D.L. 9.72. νόμῳ, which is glossed by Sextus with the words νομίζεται καὶ δοξάζεται and by Galen with πρὸς ἡμᾶς, is not far from Locke's phrase 'in idea' in the sentence 'What is sweet, blue or warm in idea, is but the certain bulk, figure and motion of the insensible parts of the bodies themselves, which we call so' (*Essay Concerning Human Understanding*, Bk. II, viii, 15). It signifies belief rather than custom or convention, and may well owe its use (as Reinhardt supposed; see Alfieri, *At. Id.* 127) to νενόμισται of Parmenides 6.8 rather than to the Sophists. Aëtius says it was already used by Leucippus (4.9.8, 67 A 32). For various opinions on the relation of Democritus's theory to those of Locke, Galileo and Descartes see ZN, 1071, n. 2.

[4] Arist. *De an.* 426a20, Simpl. *ad loc.* 193.27. So Bonitz, *Ind. Ar.* 175 b 48, and Ross, *Arist. De an.* (1961), 276. At *GC*, 316a1 Aristotle simply says that according to Democritus 'colour does not exist; it is a matter of position [of the atoms]'.

Individual sensations and their objects. For our knowledge of what Democritus wrote on these topics we depend almost wholly on Theophrastus, from whom we learn that he only gave a partial account: of the senses he had his own views on sight and hearing, but 'treats the rest much as most other thinkers have done' (57); and whereas he explained all objects of sense by their atoms, 'he does not recount the shapes of all of them, but concentrates on flavours and colours' (64).

All sensation is the result of physical contact, yet this does not seem to have given any universal primacy or authority to the sense of touch itself. It is consigned, along with the other senses, to the realm of 'bastard knowledge' in fr. 11.[1] We have seen some examples of tactual sensations, and a little more may be added on that of warmth. Theophrastus associates the atomism of Democritus with that of the Pythagoreans as maintaining that 'bodies which separate and divide give the sensation of warmth, whereas those that draw together and condense give the sensation of cold'. Again, after saying that rough and angular atoms cause sour tastes by their power of 'drawing together and contracting', he adds: 'wherefore sourness also heats the body, by creating empty spaces within it; for that grows hottest which contains most void.'[2] This is the familiar connexion of heat with expansion and cold with contraction, established by Anaximenes and here transmuted into atomic terms. In these terms, however, it means that the rough and angular atoms bring about indirectly the same result as the tiny spherical fire-producing atoms achieve by their smallness and rapid motion. This was noted by Hammer-Jensen, who also draws attention to a passage in Aristotle in which Democritus is said to have explained the freezing of liquids by the position and arrangement of the atoms, and concludes that the atomists were the first Greeks to distinguish heat from fire.[3]

Vision and colour. The atomic theory of vision is reported in a simpler and a more complex form. In the former it is attributed to Leucippus and Democritus together, in the latter to Democritus alone. It looks

[1] See further on this Alfieri, *Atom. Id.* 128.
[2] Theophr. *Phys. ap.* Simpl. *Cael.* 564.24 (68 A 120); *De sens.* 65.
[3] I. Hammer-Jensen, *Archiv.* 1910, 226; Arist. *GC*, 327a18. Aristotle uses the atomists' technical terms τροπή and διαθιγή for which see p. 393, n. 2 above.

therefore as if here too Democritus had elaborated a theory of Leucippus, and in a way which raises serious difficulties.

In its first form the theory takes over the Empedoclean doctrine of effluences, with the eye performing a purely receptive role. External objects are constantly giving off films of atoms which retain the approximate form of their surfaces and so constitute 'images' of them. These actually enter the eye, where they appear as the reflexion of the object, and stimulate the sensation. The laconic expression of Aristotle (*De sens.* 438a6) that 'Democritus thinks sight is the reflexion' is thus expanded by his commentator Alexander (p. 24.14, 67 A 29):

Democritus says that to see means to receive the reflexion from what is seen. The reflexion is the shape which appears in the pupil, just as it does also in any other bright things which are capable of retaining a reflexion. He believed (like Leucippus before him and the Epicureans after) in certain images emanating from things and similar in shape to the things from which they emanate (i.e. the objects of vision), which enter the eyes of the beholder, and that this is how vision occurs.

Similarly, Theophrastus begins his account with the words (§ 50): 'Vision he explains by the reflexion', and in 80 observes: 'He says that our seeing is due to the effluence and to the reflexion falling upon the eye.'

This at least has the merit of simplicity, and upholds the requirement of atomic materialism that all sensation, like every other form of action, must involve direct physical contact. In the transit of the images through the air it also allows for the possibility of distortion and hence of errors in identification. Aristotle's criticism, that if sight involves nothing further than reflexion all reflecting surfaces ought to see, is only pertinent from the point of view of a more advanced period of thought when the difficulties of any purely materialistic explanation of psychical phenomena were becoming apparent.[1] The theory did indeed lead to difficulties. There was the question how two people could see each other without their 'images' colliding, though the atomists may have thought that these were tenuous enough, and with sufficient interstices of void, to pass through one another; and there seems to be no explanation of how the effluences from an elephant shrink sufficiently to enter the eye as a miniature picture of him.

[1] Cf. however what is said of Diogenes on p. 375 above.

It may have been this sort of consideration that led Democritus to introduce an ingenious complication into the theory, about which one is tempted to echo the words of Theophrastus (55) that 'in trying to say something original about vision he has left the problem even farther from solution'. As Theophrastus explains it (50), the reflexion, that is, the image of the object seen, is not formed directly in the eye. There are effluences from everything, including the eye itself,[1] and those from eye and object meet somewhere in the air between them, compress and even solidify it, and stamp on it the image of the object 'as if moulded in wax' (a phrase which Theophrastus claims to be taking from Democritus himself). This image[2] enters and shows up in the eyes, being described as solid in contrast to their moist consistency. There follow some details of the sort of eyes which are best adapted to receive the images and so enjoy the clearest vision: they must be moist and spongy rather than hard, and in particular must have 'ducts' (φλέβες, lit. 'veins') that are straight and of a formation corresponding to that of the impressions, as the Empedoclean and atomic theories demanded. To explain why we see by day and not in the dark, Democritus felt compelled to suppose that the sun drives air away from itself and in so doing condenses it, thus making it more capable of receiving and retaining an impression. The actual sensation of sight (Theophrastus informs us) is a function not only of the eyes but of the whole body (that is, presumably, of the soul-atoms in it), to which the eyes 'transmit' the image or reflexion.

An isolated assertion of Democritus, that 'if the space between were void, one could even see clearly an ant on the vault of the sky', does nothing to decrease our bewilderment about these strange theories. Aristotle, who quotes it, criticizes it on the ground that sight requires a medium; but that is precisely what Democritus believed, indeed his medium, air, was something which filled space even more obviously than Aristotle's, which was light. If Democritus really said this, he

---

[1] This is also taken over from Empedocles: see pp. 234 ff. above. A wish to do justice to Empedocles's theory of fire streaming from the eye may have been one of the motives for introducing the complication.

[2] Aristotle and Theophrastus use the familiar word εἴδωλον, but according to the *Etym. Gen.* (Dem. fr. 123) Democritus had his own special term δείκελον, perhaps to distinguish these imprints from films coming directly from the objects.

must have been using the word 'void' for once in a loose sense to mean void of anything non-transparent to obstruct the view.[1]

If we had Democritus's own writings on vision, they might have enlightened us on many points. Seen through the unsympathetic eyes of Theophrastus, the theories contain absurdities which there is little point in trying to remove by guesswork. How, asks Theophrastus, can so unstable a substance as air have permanent impressions stamped on it? Why are they necessary in any case, when we are already provided with emanations which convey the object's form? What is meant by the sun's condensing the air? Its normal effect is to disperse it. Why do we not see ourselves, and, in general, how do all the thousands of imprints in the air avoid crossing each other's paths and interfering with each other? And so forth. If Democritus had answers to all these queries, we do not know what they were. One point of interest may be added.[2] There is evidence, mainly from Alexander's commentaries on Aristotle, that just as a single atom is below the level of perception, so also is a single film or 'image', which is probably only one atom thick. The films are, however, thrown off from their objects in rapid succession, and they (or the air bearing their imprints), entering the eye without interruption, give an effect of continuity. Otherwise there would be no continuity in sensation or unity in the object perceived, any more than in an object whose individual atoms could be perceived singly. It follows that there is not only a threshold of size

---

[1] Arist. *De an.* 419a15. Mugler (*Rev. de Philol.* 1959, 22, n. 3) suggests that the remark was intended to anticipate criticism such as that of Alexander (*De sensu*, 28.18 and *De an., scr. min.* 138.20) that the continuous giving-off of films of atoms by the objects of sight must in time have reduced them to nothing, especially considering that we see things as far distant as stars in the sky. (This objection was also put forward by Gomperz, *Gr. Th.* 1.358.) The quantitative disproportion between a visible body and the εἴδωλα it emits (says Mugler) is so great that even something so small as an ant contains enough substance to send out, without endangering its consistence, material images across the whole distance between earth and stars. This is conjectural, and in fact Zeller took a contrary view (ZN, 1127, n. 1): the possibility of seeing an ant in heaven, he says, explains why Democritus said it was not the εἴδωλα themselves that fall on the eye but only their imprint. If I understand the point, he means that it was impossible for Democritus to conceive of the actual films of atoms from the creature's body performing the whole journey. In the same note Mugler asserts (without argument or evidence) 'Démocrite n'a jamais enseigné l'émission, par l'œil, de rayons visuels'. This is contrary to the evidence.

[2] I owe the following observations to Mugler's article in *Rev. de Philol.* 1959, pp. 23 ff., where the passages from Alexander and others will be found. It is Democritus and Leucippus, rather than Epicurus, whom Alexander has taken as authorities for the theory of visual effluences, though he mentions Epicurus as their follower (*De sensu*, pp. 24 and 56 Wendland).

below which bodies are imperceptible, but also a lower limit of perception in time. Aristotle mentions the possibility of imperceptible time in connexion with an atomic theory of colour in the *De sensu*.[1]

This brings us to colour, which we already know to be a purely 'secondary' and subjective quality. The sensation of colour is produced in the soul by the shape and position of the atoms on the surface of objects, and the amount of space between them. There are four primary colours—white, black, red and yellow—and the others are combinations of these. Atoms producing the effect of white are smooth on hard surfaces, round on those that are loose and friable. These cast no shadow and are easy to penetrate, thus giving the effect of brightness and translucency. (Theophrastus complains that Democritus writes as if he were talking of these qualities rather than of white colour.)[2] Black results from rough and irregular atoms which cast shadows and from *poroi* that are crooked and not easy to penetrate; red from atoms 'similar to those which produce heat but larger'. Concerning yellow Theophrastus could find no mention of the shapes of atoms, but only that it results from 'the solid and the void, being mixed of both, and its colour varying according to the position and order of these constituents'. It seems natural to suppose from what we are told that colour varies according to the ways in which the atoms, by their different shapes and the different angles at which they lie to one another and to the beholder, throw back, absorb or let through the light that falls upon them. Unfortunately the sources tell us nothing about Democritus's views on the nature and behaviour of light, which like everything else must have been corporeal and atomic in structure. Aristotle contents

---

[1] 440a20. This is quoted by Mugler, who does not however add that the theory in question, though it offers an atomic explanation of colour, is different from that of Democritus as described in detail by Theophrastus. The one which Aristotle is criticizing derives all other colours from black and white, affirming that they are only an effect produced when these two are juxtaposed in quantities so minute that either separately is invisible. Each sends out emanations which reach the eye in such rapid succession that they seem to arrive simultaneously, and give the effect of a colour which is neither white nor black. Democritus, however, taught that red and green are equally primary with black and white. The primacy of black and white only was said by Theophrastus (59, 79) to have been commonly accepted by earlier thinkers, and was retained with a different explanation by Aristotle himself, but Democritus was an exception. (Possibly also Empedocles, see p. 148, n. 1 above.)

[2] *De sensu*, 80. In the *Timaeus* Plato writes as if λαμπρόν were itself one of the simple colours entering into compounds with others like white and red. (68b λαμπρόν τε ἐρυθρῷ λευκῷ τε μειγνύμενον ξανθὸν γέγονεν.)

himself with the condescending remark, in connexion with the theory of vision, that at that period, evidently, there was no scientific knowledge of the phenomena of image-forming and reflexion (*De sens.* 438a9).

The production of other colours by mixture of the primaries was described by Democritus in loving detail, some of which is reproduced in Theophrastus. One is inevitably reminded of the simile of the painter's palette in Empedocles, and whether or not Democritus was drawing on experience of the actual mixing of pigments,[1] he certainly shows a genuine delight in the rich variety of colour. An example will suffice (76):

Gold, bronze and all similar hues are composed of white and red: from the white comes their brightness and from the red their ruddiness, for in combination the red sinks into the empty interstices of the white. If to these be added yellow,[2] it produces the most beautiful colour, but the additions of yellow must be small, for the white and red are so combined as not to allow of a large admixture. The tints will vary according to the amounts added.

Democritus gave similar descriptions of blue (woad), leek-green, cyanus and nut-brown, adding that the number of colours which can be produced by mixture is infinite.[3]

Hearing and sound. Theophrastus found Democritus's explanation of hearing 'similar to that of others', and gives a brief general statement of it (55), namely that it is caused by air entering the empty hollow

[1] The difficulty about the present passage is, as Dyroff pointed out long ago (*Demokritstud.* 179), to see how the composite colours could ever in practice be produced from paints of the colours which Democritus names as their components. This did not worry Plato (*Tim.* 68d), but ought to have worried Democritus, who could not, like Plato, shift the onus on to God! Kranz, in his article on early Greek teaching about colour (*Hermes*, 1912), believed that Democritus could not have been speaking from any practical experience, but the personal ἐάν τις τὰ μὲν ἀφαιρῇ τὰ δὲ προστιθῇ in 78 is striking. One is reminded also that Democritus, like Anaxagoras, is credited with a treatise on scene-painting and perspective (p. 270 above). Does the mysterious title ἀκτινογραφία in Thrasyllus's catalogue (under μαθηματικά) really mean a treatise on the radiation of light, as Stephanus and LSJ suppose, or might it be a parallel formation to σκιαγραφία and refer to a form of drawing or painting? (Cf. fr. 15bDK.)

[2] It is notoriously difficult to determine the exact value of Greek words for colours. This one (χλωρός) seems to have meant sometimes a fresh green with a fair amount of yellow in it, and sometimes yellow. It is applied on the one hand to fresh foliage, growing corn and emeralds, and on the other to honey, egg-yolk and sand. It is also used as a general word for pale, and metaphorically it means young or fresh.

[3] In addition to the article of Kranz already mentioned, the following will be useful to any interested in further discussion of Democritus's and other ancient Greek theories of colour: Dyroff, *Demokritstudien*, 176–84 (*Exkurs, Zur Farbenlehre des Demokrit*); W. Capelle in *Rh. Mus.* 1958; C. Prantl, *Aristoteles über die Farben*; W. Schultz, *Farbenempfindungssystem der Hellenen* (details in bibliography).

of the ear. In general terms this was the explanation of Alcmaeon, Empedocles and Anaxagoras. Democritus added that of course this air can enter the body at all points, but not through passages large enough to make the sound perceptible. On the other hand, once the sound has entered, the ear (like the eye in sight) acts only as a channel through which it is dispensed all over the body. In both sight and hearing, we perceive (as Plato later put it) not *with* but *through* the sense-organs: the sensitive soul is ubiquitous in the body (p. 432 above).

Aëtius, in an extract which is independent of Theophrastus and may come from Posidonius, describes the theory as more complex. It is best seen in the context of that of Epicurus which precedes it:[1]

Epicurus says that sound is a stream [*sc.* of atoms] emitted by whatever gives tongue or produces a noise of any kind. This stream is shattered into particles of similar shape, that is to say, round going with round and irregular and triangular with their like. When these enter the ears they effect perception of the sound....Democritus says that the air also is shattered into particles of similar shape and rolled along with the sound.

The rest of the passage consists of illustrations of the law that like is drawn to like (p. 409 above), in justification of the segregation of particles into groups of similars.

The two theories form a parallel to those of sight. In both cases Epicurus has rejected Democritus as over-subtle and adopted a simpler view which perhaps goes back to Leucippus. For both of them sound, like everything else, was a material body of particulate structure ('breath-like' according to Epicurus);[2] but whereas Epicurus taught that these sound-particles themselves, emitted by the sources of sound, impinged on the ear of the hearer, Democritus added an intermediate stage. The sound-particles first strike the intervening air and conform it to their own likeness. Presumably then, as with sight, it is not the actual effluence from the object, but an 'image' of it 'stamped upon' the air, which enters the organ of the perceiver. Perhaps (we do not know) the motive of this awkward theory was to explain the diffusion

---

[1] Aët. 4.19.2–3 (*Dox.* 408; §3 only in DK, 68 A 128). Posidonian origin is suggested by DK, n. *ad loc.* Bailey thought with some reason that part of the unusual expression must be Democritus's own (*Atomists*, 170).

[2] *Ep.* 1.53. In 52 and 53 we have the original of Aëtius's paraphrase, and it contains an explicit rebuttal of the more complex view.

of sound over a wide area, or to account for its distortion and weakening. Whatever the reason, its form may well have owed something to a hint in Anaxagoras, who in his explanation of sound distinguished between 'breath' and 'air' and spoke of the impact of the one upon the other (p. 318, n. 3 above). Empedocles took the simpler view, though here as in general Democritus followed him in supposing that sensation could only take place through passages of the right size to fit the appropriate effluences. Theophrastus concludes with a description of what Democritus thought was the best physical condition of ears and head to ensure keen hearing.[1]

Taste, flavours, odours. In the discussion of flavours in his treatise *De causis plantarum* (6.1.2ff.), Theophrastus suggests that there are two main types of explanation, in terms of the effect on the sense-organ and in terms of the intrinsic properties of the flavoured substance. One may for instance describe what is sweet as penetrating the moisture of the tongue, or as having a relaxing or smoothing effect, or say that pungent things heat the tongue, astringent dry it and so forth. Alternatively one may say that the particles of sweet substances are large and round, those of astringent large, rough and polygonal, and so forth. Democritus chose the latter way. In fact however the two ought not to be separated, since the purpose of ascribing shapes to the particles can only be to explain how they come to have the sensible effects which they do; and that being so, some account of the body acted upon is called for as well as of the body acting, of the subject as well as the object of taste. This applies particularly to the theory of Democritus, because he held that the same object might produce the effect of different flavours in different people.[2] Yet this side of the question, Theophrastus claims, was neglected by Democritus in the case of taste (*De sensu*, 72).

The fullest description of the atomic shapes accounting for flavours and their effects is given by Theophrastus in *De sensu*, 65–7. They are summarized thus in *De causis plantarum* (6.1.6, A129):

Democritus assigns a shape to each flavour. Sweetness is round and large; astringency large, rough, polygonal, not rounded; sharp [sour] taste as its

---

[1] *De sensu*, 56. For details see Stratton's translation and notes.
[2] This part of the criticism is printed in DK, A130. Cf. the further remarks of Theophrastus in *De sensu*, pp. 438 f. above.

name indicates has a sharp body, angular, bent, small, not rounded; pungency is round, small, with angles and bends; saltiness angular, large, crooked, with equal sides; bitterness round and smooth but with irregularities and small in size; oily flavour is fine, round and small.

In its details, this reduction of flavours to the effects of atomic shape becomes somewhat fantastic, yet it has had a long history. The French chemist Lémery wrote in 1675:

The hidden nature of a thing cannot be better explained than by attributing to its parts shapes corresponding to all the effects it produces. No one will deny that the acidity of a liquid consists in pointed particles. All experience confirms this. You have only to taste it to feel a pricking of the tongue like that caused by some material cut into very fine points.[1]

On odour and smelling we have only one sentence from Theophrastus, designed to exemplify how much Democritus left out (82):

He omitted to add any definition of odour except for this, that it is produced by something subtle emanating from heavy substances. But he does not go on to say what its nature is, or what is the agent, though that is perhaps the most important point.

Additional note: the number of the senses in Democritus

Section 4.10 of Aëtius summarizes opinions on the number of the senses: in Stoic belief there are five, in Aristotle five plus the 'common sense', which however is not a sixth sense but a mode of joint operation of the others. It continues:[2]

Democritus says there are more [i.e. more than five, as the context makes clear] in irrational animals, in wise men, and in the gods.

Democritus says that there are more senses than objects of sense, but because the objects do not correspond in number [i.e. presumably to the senses] they are not noticed.

Δ. πλείους εἶναι αἰσθήσεις περὶ τὰ ἄλογα ζῷα καὶ περὶ τοὺς σοφοὺς καὶ περὶ τοὺς θεούς.

Δ. πλείους μὲν εἶναι τὰς αἰσθήσεις τῶν αἰσθητῶν, τῷ δὲ μὴ ἀναλογίζειν [?] τὰ αἰσθητὰ τῷ πλήθει λανθάνειν.

I see no difficulty in the first sentence. Observation of the instinctive behaviour of animals can easily lead to the supposition of a sixth sense,

---

[1] See Cornford, *Before and After Socrates*, 26. The appeal to experience, but in an entirely naïve and superficial form, is particularly characteristic of Presocratic thought.
[2] Subsections 4 and 5, reversed in DK, A115 and 116.

and it is equally natural to suppose that the gods possess senses lacking to ordinary men. Scholars have been puzzled by the inclusion of 'wise men', and Rohde was driven to the expedient of supposing that their extra sense was to be identified with reason, the 'genuine cognition' which Democritus expressly contrasted with the 'bastard cognition' of the senses (p. 459 below). This is impossible, but the word used (*sophoi*) is one which included poets, prophets and religious teachers and sometimes referred primarily to such figures. These in common belief were men who had direct access to superhuman sources of cognition, and it was sometimes suggested that to arrogate to oneself the title of *sophos* was to lay claim to divine powers. There is the story that Pythagoras would only call himself *philo-sophos*, lover of wisdom, for 'no one is wise save God' (vol. I, 204); and in Plato's *Phaedrus* (278 d) Socrates repeats that the word 'befits a god alone'. Now Democritus believed that poets wrote 'under divine inspiration and by a holy spirit' and that prophetic dreams, voices and visions were a reality (frr. 17, 18, 166, A 77; see pp. 477, 482 below). Neither poets nor prophets were thinking things out intellectually; they were undergoing a direct experience, and the capacity to do so may well have appeared to Democritus (or at least been interpreted by his expositors) as an extra sense.

The second sentence is obscure. I can find no certain explanation of it, and I suspect that the text may have got corrupted. Zeller, after paraphrasing it 'that many impressions arouse no sensation', states frankly in a footnote (ZN, 1125, n. 2) that to give it this sense 'is pure conjecture'. Diels connected it with Lucretius 4.802:

> quia tenuia sunt [*sc.* simulacra], nisi quae contendit acuta,
> cernere non potis est animus.

It has been usual to translate αἰσθήσεις here (as the Lucretian parallel demands) as 'individual acts of sensation' instead of 'senses'. Thus Mugler (*R. de Philol.* 1959, 35) says: 'Démocrite, d'après Aétius, considérait le nombre de sensations possibles comme supérieur à celui des objets effectivement perçus.' According to him, the soul exercises choice over what it will perceive and can let other objects or 'images' slip by, otherwise the organism would be at the mercy of an excessive number of stimulations from its environment. This, it seems to me, would require that αἰσθητά should be more numerous than αἰσθήσεις, not *vice versa*. (The shift of meaning produced by the addition of 'possibles' and 'effectivement' is scarcely legitimate.) Apart from this, the use of the word to mean a single act of sensation is rare,[1] and in the context of Aët. 4.10 practically impossible. If the sentence reflects anything that Democritus actually said, a possible meaning might be that because (as the previous sentence has told us) some living creatures have more than five senses, there must be more senses than there are classes of the things commonly recognized as sensibles (αἰσθητά). These are sights, sounds, flavours, odours and tactile sensa. An extra sense will have none of these as its object, hence there are more senses than αἰσθητά in the ordinary sense of the word. This however cannot be said to be certain, and the possibility remains that the sentence has suffered damage and is inherently confused. For other opinions see Zeller and Mugler, *locc. cit.* and Alfieri, *Atomisti*, 134, n. 337 (for A115) and 135, n. 339 (for A116).

(12) *Thought*

The materialism of Leucippus and Democritus allowed of no exceptions. Thought as well as sensation had to depend on a physical mechanism. The report of Aëtius is (4. 8. 5 and 10, 67 A 30):

Leucippus and Democritus say that sensations and thoughts (νοήσεις) are alterations of the body.

Leucippus, Democritus and Epicurus say that sensation and thought take place by the impact of images from outside. Neither occurs to anyone without the impact of an image.[2]

A more complex, and in parts obscure account is given by Theophrastus in *De sensu* (58):

Concerning thought (τὸ φρονεῖν) Democritus said this much, that it occurs when the soul is in a balanced condition after the movement;[3] but if

---

[1] LSJ can cite only one instance, and that only by mistranslating it (Arist. *Metaph.* 980a22, where ἡ τῶν αἰσθήσεων ἀγάπησις surely means 'the pleasure that we get from exercising our senses'). The only clear example that occurs to me is Plato, *Phcedrus*, 249b.

[2] It must be remembered throughout that 'image' (εἴδωλον) is a technical term meaning a purely material film of atoms thrown off by an object and travelling to the perceiving subject.

[3] μετὰ τὴν κίνησιν. The MS. reading has been emended into κατὰ τὴν κίνησιν (Brieger, Nestle) and κατὰ τὴν κρῆσιν (Schneider, Diels, retained in DK); but Zeller, Philippson, and Alfieri have thought alteration unnecessary. According to Alfieri it means 'after the agitation of sensation'. See ZN, 1129, n. 3; Philippson in *Gnomon*, 1930, 466; Alfieri, *At. Id.* 137.

the subject is too hot or too cold, it is disturbed [or altered, μεταλλάττειν]. Hence the ancients were right in thinking of it [i.e. mental derangement] as 'being of altered mind'.[1] It is evident then that he derives thought from the composition of the body, which no doubt is only logical since he regards soul as a form of body.

In Aristotle's view, 'soul and mind are the same' for Democritus, and 'truth is what appears'. This is true in so far as both soul and mind are material and of the same atomic composition, and since all reality must have a physical form there are no objects of cognition which Aristotle would class as 'intelligibles' (νοητά). All forms of physical existence are for him objects of sensation. So he says elsewhere that Democritus is one of those who hold that thought is a form of sensation, and sensation a physical alteration, and that therefore what appears to the senses is necessarily true.[2]

Thought, then, is exactly parallel to sensation in that it results from a disturbance of the soul-atoms by atomic complexes from without; and it varies according to the internal condition of the thinking subject. For the best results the bodily 'mixture' (κρᾶσις) must be 'duly proportioned' (σύμμετρος). Remembering that the organ of thought is a concentration of soul-atoms in a particular part of the body, one may assume that it is capable of being stimulated by complexes that are too subtle to affect the sense-organs as they traverse their 'passages', or the thinly spread soul-atoms elsewhere; for as Theophrastus puts it (63), 'what is massed together has a powerful effect, but what is widely

---

[1] ἀλλοφρονεῖν. The word is used by Homer (Il. 23.698), and its approving citation by Democritus is vouched for also by Aristotle in the words (De an. 404a29) διὸ καλῶς ποιῆσαι [sc. λέγει Δ.] τὸν Ὅμηρον ὡς ὁ Ἕκτωρ 'κεῖτ' ἀλλοφρονέων'. (Cf. Metaph. 1009b28.) Actually this phrase does not occur in our texts of Homer, and either Democritus or Aristotle seems to have suffered a lapse of memory. The word ἀλλοφρονέοντα is applied to Euryalus. Il. 22.337 says of Hector τὸν δ' ὀλιγοδρανέων προσέφη, but although the participles are metrically equivalent, the unsuitability of ἀλλοφρονέων to the context makes it unlikely that it could have stood in the text available to Democritus or any other. Kranz (Phil. u. sprachl. Ausdr. 29, n. 1), following Fick and Leumann, says that the Greeks were ignorant of the true etymology of the word, which has no connexion with ἄλλος but is an Aeolicism from ἠλεός, 'crazy'. Frisk however is more cautious in Gr. etym. Wörterbuch s.v. ἠλεός, and Dr John Chadwick informs me that Sanskrit anya, 'other', has compounds such as anyacetas meaning 'thinking of another: distraught'.

[2] Arist. De an. 404a27, 405a9 (quoted on p. 430, n. 5 above); Metaph. 1009b12. These passages will receive further consideration in connexion with the atomists' theory of knowledge in general.

diffused is imperceptible'. This point has been most clearly expressed by Bailey (*Atomists*, 173):

Certain 'idols', then, which are too fine to stir the more distributed soul-atoms on the surface of the body and in the organs of sense and so produce sensation, pass on within the body until they reach the mind. There, as the soul-atoms are so closely packed, the 'idols' cannot pass by without moving them and the result of this motion is the peculiar kind of sensation which we call thought: it is in its nature exactly parallel to the movements which produce sight or hearing.

This I believe is true, but probably not the whole truth. It suggests complete independence, whereas thought is in some sense derived from sensation; it receives its data from the senses as Democritus said in what is apparently a direct quotation (fr. 125). It looks therefore as if the experience of sensation may so disturb the whole soul that its agitation reaches the mind and can affect its capacity for thought. If the reading is correct, this will be the meaning of the words 'after the movement' in the passage quoted from Theophrastus 58. Here however we touch on the whole theory of knowledge, which had best be reserved for separate treatment.

Democritus's explanation of thought reminds us of that of Parmenides in the Way of Seeming. He too said that the mind varied according to the condition of the body, and in particular according to the prevalence of hot or cold, a close parallel to what Theophrastus says of Democritus in 58. The same dependence on changing physical condition was emphasized by Empedocles.[1] These resemblances were noticed by Aristotle, who summed up what was for him their common philosophical failure in the words (*Metaph.* 1010a1): 'They sought the truth about reality, but on the assumption that the only real things were the sensibles.' For Aristotle, trained by Plato, reality was divided into sensible (corporeal) and intelligible (incorporeal), and he put all his predecessors on a level because they were incapable of recognizing this distinction.[2] The truth seems to be that all philosophers hitherto (with the exception of the unique arguments of Parmenides in the Way of

---

[1] Parm. fr. 16 and Theophr. *Sens.* 3; Emped. frr. 106 and 108. See pp. 67, 228 and 243 above.

[2] Cf. *De an.* 427a21 ff. 'Early thinkers identified thought and sensation.... All these suppose thought to be a bodily process like sensation.'

Truth) had given an explanation of knowledge in what to a more sophisticated mind are materialistic terms, but only now that the atomists have gone further in sharpening and making explicit the concept of materialism, have the problems of explaining intellection and knowledge in these terms become acute. Indeed they have come into sight for the first time. By the uncompromising clarity of their materialism, the atomists made it very difficult indeed for themselves to answer questions about the relation between sensation and thought, or to meet a jibe like that of Cicero, who asked whether, whenever he thought about Britain, an 'image' had detached itself from that island to come and hit him in the chest (*Ad fam.* 15. 16. 2). It is not surprising if the first serious attempt to reduce all intellectual activity to purely material contact was not entirely successful. We may still admire its boldness and consistency.

(13) *Theory of knowledge*

Nowhere does one feel so keenly the loss of Democritus's own writings as in trying to discover what the atomists thought about how, and to what extent, we can know the truth about the world around us, by what means our minds can be put in contact with reality and comprehend its nature. For this we must rely on some quotations and comments in Sextus and a few remarks in Aristotle, and these have been thought by many to be flatly contradictory. Before considering them directly, some preliminary points must be borne in mind.

First, epistemology, which has bulked so large in later philosophical investigation, occupied a much humbler place in the mind of a fifth-century thinker, where it was completely overshadowed by the search for being, or ontology. We must not expect to find it discussed for its own sake, or with the concentration and clarity bestowed on it in later centuries.[1] For Sextus on the other hand, in his writings on Scepticism, the problems of cognition and the criteria of truth were already central.

---

[1] 'The search for being, which even as a problem is hardly understandable in later centuries, was the chief endeavour of Greek philosophers from Parmenides to Aristotle.... [They] primarily and essentially investigated being and only secondarily the human faculties of grasping being' (Weiss, *CQ*, 1938, 49 and 52). This is an important and too often neglected truth, and it means that for them degrees of knowledge are intimately connected with, and dependent on, the degrees of reality in its objects.

Secondly, we must bear in mind the philosophical situation which the atomists had inherited. This has been graphically described by S. Luria. Democritus began to work in an atmosphere of ruin, which he could not ignore. He must first explain the hopeless state of the quest for truth, and try to find a way out.[1] In the mathematical sphere Zeno had shown that the assumption that bodies were divisible at all implies that any body is infinitely great, and infinite divisibility means that a body has no magnitude at all. Yet no one can deny divisibility. In the physical sphere he and Parmenides had shown that the objective world in no way corresponds to the unreal and contradictory world of sense-perception. On the other hand the outlook for the construction of an independent world of being by the *physici* was poor, because by arguments of approximately equal cogency they had reached different and mutually exclusive results. Protagoras had denied that there are any criteria by which to recognize an external world of being. He was content with a 'collectively subjective' world reached by comparing the subjective worlds of individuals, which could be relatively and temporarily valid for particular communities of men. Even this compromise was impossible if one adopted the standpoint of Gorgias or Xeniades[2] that 'nothing exists'. Even individual subjective worlds cannot exist, for they too are thoroughly contradictory: the rules of logic, whereby we test the rightness of our sensations, are as arbitrary as the sensations themselves. To undertake in these circumstances to rebuild the house of truth as it lay shattered by such an earthquake demanded scientific passion and an unshakable faith.

This leads to a third point, that the aims of the atomists were not those of empirical scientists. They had the contemporary philosophical purpose of rescuing reality and showing in which direction it was to be sought. Democritus refuted Protagoras, but in origin the atomic doctrines, like their immediate predecessors, were designed to meet the

---

[1] Luria, *Anfänge d. gr. Denkens*, 144f. This in Luria's view is the meaning of fr. 117, ἐν βυθῷ ἡ ἀλήθεια. It does not reflect genuine scepticism, but only a lament for the pass to which philosophy has come. It is a 'propaedeutic aporia'. To connect it with the contempory state of philosophy is extremely far-fetched, but I would agree that it means no more than that truth is hard (though not impossible) to discover. In *Infinitesimaltheorie* (140, n. 81) Luria more aptly confronts the ἐτεῇ δὲ οὐδὲν ἴσμεν of fr. 117 with ἐτεῇ δὲ ἄτομα καὶ κενόν in fr. 125.

[2] The latter is known only from two passages in Sextus, *Math.* 7.53 and *Pyrrh. hyp.* 2.76 (DK, II, 271). See also ZN, 1369, n. 2.

Eleatic challenge. Leucippus too would 'judge by *logos*' as Parmenides demanded, but claimed that *logoi* themselves could be reconciled with the existence of a sensible world including motion, plurality and the impermanence of individual physical things.[1]

Fourthly, statements which are superficially contradictory may be reconciled by taking into account the different philosophical standpoints of those who made them. To take the most obvious example, Aristotle says that for Democritus 'what is true is the phenomenon', Sextus that he 'did away with', 'denied' or 'discarded' phenomena. Aristotle is judging from his own dichotomy of existence into sensible and intelligible. The *archai* of all things must be intelligible in his sense, that is, incorporeal and apprehended intuitively and directly by *nous*, which is not discursive reason but the soul's power of immediate apprehension comparable to that of sense-perception in the material world. The first principles of Democritus were still a part of the sensible world, empirically imperceptible owing to the accident of smallness (*GC*, 325 a 30) but substantially the same as perceptible bodies, which are in fact only aggregates of them. For Democritus there is no noumenal world to set over against the phenomenal. When Sextus maintains that Democritus denied or abolished phenomena and said that only the intelligible exists, he is not using the word in its Platonic–Aristotelian sense but simply referring to the basic atomic doctrine that sensible properties are subjective impressions resulting from alterations in our own make-up; only atoms and void have objective existence, and they are deduced by the mind, not directly perceived by the senses.

On a superficial view, the ancient evidence involves Democritus in the following doctrines: (*a*) what appears to the senses is true, (*b*) what appears to the senses must be rejected, (*c*) sensible phenomena lead to knowledge indirectly, (*d*) knowledge is altogether impossible, (*e*) complete scepticism about the possibility of knowledge is unjustified. The relevant passages cannot however simply be grouped under these five heads separately, because Sextus makes a genuine effort to understand Democritus and place his various statements in relation to one another; and to dismember in this way a long passage (like *Math.* 7.135–7) in

---

[1] Arist. *GC*, 325 a 23, translated on p. 390 above.

which he brings the several strands of thought together would be highly misleading. With this proviso I give the evidence first.

The following passages of Aristotle speak for doctrine (*a*), that what appears to the senses is true:

(i) Arist. *De an.* 404a27: For Democritus soul and mind were simply identical, for what is true is the phenomenon (or 'that which appears').

(ii) Idem, *GC*, 315b9: But since they [Leucippus and Democritus] held that truth was in appearance, and the phenomena were infinitely numerous, they made the atomic shapes infinite, so that by changes in the compound the same thing makes a contrary impression on different people; it is shifted by a minute addition to its composition and by the transposition of a single atom appears utterly different; for tragedy and comedy are composed of the same letters.

(iii) Idem, *Metaph.* 1009b12 (where Democritus is being included in a generalization with other pre-Platonic thinkers): in short, because they identify thought with sensation and that with bodily alteration, they necessarily say that what appears in sensation is true. It is on these grounds that Empedocles and Democritus and most of the others have become ensnared by such beliefs.

Note that in these passages the statement that what appears is true is evidently Aristotle's own. In passage (ii), what he cites from Democritus in its support is taken by others (and with more justification) as implying the opposite. In the same passage he admits the distinction between sensible appearances and the imperceptible atoms alongside the statement that truth is in appearance. Evidently he saw no incompatibility between the two, and this can only be because he was using 'appearance' in the wide sense, to include all bodily existence.

In the next two passages Sextus concludes that Democritus rejected sensible appearances as false:

(iv) *Math.* 7.369 (DK, A110): Some have abolished all phenomena, like Democritus.

(v) *Ibid.* 8.6 (DK, A59): Plato and Democritus considered that only the objects of thought exist: but Democritus's reason was that nothing perceptible by sense existed in nature, whereas Plato's was that sensible things were always becoming but never being.

(vi) *Ibid.* 8.56 (not in DK): Democritus and Plato throw things into confusion by rejecting the senses, annihilating their objects, and holding only to the intelligibles.

In the next passage Sextus attempts to correlate the various statements of epistemological import which he has found in Democritus. Here too he begins with the rejection of appearances.[1]

(vii) *Math*. 7.135 (DK, fr. 9): Democritus in some places abolishes the things that appear to the senses and asserts that none of them appears according to truth but only according to opinion: the truth in things that exist is that there are atoms and void.

After supporting this by direct quotation from Democritus (already given on p. 440 above), Sextus continues (136):

And in his *Confirmations*, although he had promised to assign the power of conviction to the senses, he is none the less found condemning them, for he says, 'In reality we know nothing for certain, but what shifts according to the condition of the body and of the things which enter it and press upon it'.

In this sentence from Democritus himself the relativity of sensations seems to be made the basis of a complete scepticism, or disbelief in the possibility of knowledge about reality, and Sextus proceeds to add several other quotations of the same tenour.

And again he says (fr. 10): 'That we do not comprehend what is or is not the true character of each thing has often been made clear' (137); and in the work *On Forms* (fr. 6): 'Man must learn on this principle that he is separated from reality', and again (fr. 7), 'This argument too shows that we know nothing truly about anything, but each man's opinion is a reshaping',[2] and further (fr. 8), 'Yet it will be clear that it is impracticable to get to know the true character of each thing'.

Elsewhere, however, Democritus offered a way of escape from this complete pessimism as to the possibility of knowledge. Sextus proceeds

---

[1] The same point is repeated at *Math*. 8.184 and 355, which add nothing of substance to what is here quoted.

[2] ἐπιρυσμίη ἑκάστοισιν ἡ δόξις. This phrase has become famous in critical literature, and Langerbeck chose it for the title of his monograph. The words are Democritus's own, and ἐπιρυσμίη must be connected with ῥυσμός (ῥυθμός), which as we know from Aristotle was his term for the shapes of the atoms. This, and the use of the verb ἐπιρρυθμίζειν in Plato's *Laws* (802b), suggest that the word (whether adjective or noun) means remoulding or reshaping. It refers once again to the fact that all our impressions are the result of changes in our atomic composition caused by the impact of complexes of atoms from without. Hesychius glossed it ἐπιρρέον whence presumably Bury's 'due to influx' (in Loeb ed.). (So also Bailey, *Atomists*, 178.) Effectively the sense is little altered. Other renderings are: 'Opinion for everybody is what is formed in his mind (by the atoms which move in it or into it)' (von Fritz, *Phil. u. sprachl. Ausdr.* 37); 'jedem seine Meinung durch das herankommen der Gestalten entsteht' (Dyroff, 84); 'L'opinione è in ciascuno una (sorta di) nuova configurazione' (Alfieri, *At. Id.* 162).

to show how, without abandoning his conviction that the truth is not in sense-impressions themselves, Democritus suggested that through them the mind might ultimately be led to it. He continues:

Now in these passages he practically does away with all apprehension, even though it is only the senses that he singles out for attack. But (138, DK fr. 11) in his *Canons* he says that there are two kinds of cognition, one through the senses and the other through the intellect. Of these he calls that through the intellect 'legitimate', and attests its trustworthiness for the judgment of truth, and that through the senses 'bastard', denying that it is free from error in the discernment of truth (139). To quote his actual words: 'There are two forms of cognition, one legitimate, one bastard. To the bastard belong all these: sight, hearing, smell, taste, touch. The other is legitimate, and separate from these.' Then in preferring the legitimate to the bastard he adds: 'When the bastard cognition cannot see any further in the direction of smallness, or hear or smell or taste or perceive by touch, but [we advance?] to the more minute....'[1]

So Democritus too makes reason [*logos*, cf. p. 456 above] the means of judging, and calls it 'legitimate cognition'. (140, A111) Diotimus[2] used to say that according to Democritus there are three criteria: (1) for the apprehension of unseen things, the phenomena, for as Anaxagoras says (and Democritus commends him for it), 'phenomena are the sight of the unseen'; (2) for investigation, the conception, 'for on every topic, my child, there is one starting-point, to know what the subject of investigation is'; (3) for choice and avoidance, the feelings, for what we feel at home with is to be chosen, but what we feel alien to is to be avoided.

This is an interpretation of Diotimus, who has recast Democritus's thought in a post-Aristotelian mould. His threefold classification relates it to the later division of philosophy into physics, logic and ethics. The distortion however is mainly confined to the second criterion, for which the only documentary support which we are offered is a garbled quotation not from Democritus but from Plato (*Phaedrus*, 237b). The first includes a valuable piece of information about Democritus himself and can be fitted in with other testimony, and the third is borne out by sayings attributed to Democritus like fr. 188, that the mark of

---

[1] The sentence breaks off here and presumably some words have fallen out, but the sense is not in doubt. The senses give us our impressions of the macroscopic world, but when it is a question of understanding the microscopic (where alone reality is to be grasped), the intellect takes over.

[2] Little is known of this man. For what there is see DK, 11, 250, *Dox*. 346 n., *RE*, v, 1150.

what is profitable or harmful is the enjoyment or lack of enjoyment that we feel.

The idea that the mind attains knowledge through the media of the senses is strongly supported by another quotation from Democritus which we owe to Galen:

(viii) Galen, *De medic. empir. fr.* Schöne, 1259, 8 (DK, fr. 125, now incorporated into the text in Walzer's edition of the Arabic version, p. 113). After quoting the well-known fragment about the arbitrary nature of colour and flavours and the reality of atoms and void only, Galen continues that after thus abusing the senses Democritus represents them as saying to the mind: 'Wretched mind, do you take your evidence from us and then throw us down? That throw is your overthrow.'

In support of a sceptical interpretation we have the following, which however can now be read in the light of the full text of Sextus on the subject:

(ix) Democritus fr. 117 (D.L. 9.72): 'In reality we know nothing, for truth is in the depths.'

(x) Arist. *Metaph.* 1009b2ff. Earlier philosophers, says Aristotle, have argued that truth is not to be discovered by counting heads. A sick man experiences as bitter what to others is sweet, but if most men were sick or mad it would be the few who found it sweet who would be called ill or crazy. 'Therefore (b9) which of these sensations is true or false is obscure: they are equally true, none more than another. Hence Democritus says that either truth does not exist or else it is hidden from us.'

To stop here however is cheating, and shows what mischief can be done by quoting sentences without their full context; for the next sentence is no. (iii) above, to the effect that these same philosophers are compelled to say that all sense-impressions represent the truth. Evidently Aristotle saw no contradiction between the two.

(xi) Theophr. *Sens.* 69: [Democritus said that] things appear different to people in different condition, and again that no one person attains the truth more than any other. This is unreasonable, for it is likely that the better man would see it more clearly than the worse, and the healthy than the sick, for his condition is closer to nature.

Here Theophrastus seems to apply to Democritus the sort of criticism that was levelled at Protagoras, with whom we know Democritus disagreed. He has already shown himself captious in this section (p. 439 above), and in the last sentence is introducing a specifically Peripatetic notion, that everything has its proper 'nature' (*physis*) which is its best state. All that Democritus will have meant is that no one attains the truth by sense-perception alone, which cannot reveal things for what they are, namely aggregates of atoms and void.

Finally there are one or two passages where the complete scepticism as to the possibility of knowledge, which some of Democritus's fragments might suggest, is expressly denied.

(xii) Plutarch, *Adv. Col.* 1108f (DK, fr. 156): Colotes alleges against Democritus, first, that by saying that each thing is no more this than that he threw life into confusion. But in fact he was so far from saying that each thing is no more this than that that he did battle with Protagoras the Sophist for saying so and brought many convincing arguments against him. Colotes, never having so much as dreamed of these, misunderstood the philosopher's language when he wrote that 'the *hing* exists no more than the *not-hing*',[1] calling body 'hing' and void 'nothing', to bring out the point that it too had its own nature and reality.

(xiii) Sextus in his *Outlines of Pyrrhonism* (1.213) also comments on Democritus's use of the phrase 'not more'. Since it is a sceptic formula[2] it had been thought to show that he shared the sceptics' views. But, says Sextus, when we sceptics say that honey is no more sweet than bitter, we mean only to express our ignorance of whether both, one, or neither of the sensations is real, whereas Democritus meant to affirm the unreality of both.

A reading of the foregoing passage forbids us to interpret Democritus as a complete sceptic, denying altogether the possibility of attaining knowledge of reality. Truth is indeed in the depths. If we look only on the surface, as most men do, we remain unaware of the true character of things. We are 'separated from reality' by the barrier of the senses, which seem to tell us what things are but in fact give a false picture. This must be the meaning of those fragments (6–8, 9, 10, 117) which if taken in isolation seem to declare that knowledge is altogether

---

[1] See p. 392, n. 3 above. Plutarch's quotation of the sentence in this argument does not seem particularly apt. From Simpl. *Phys.* 28.10 and 25 (DK, 67 A 8, 68 A 38) it is probable that some such phrase as οὐδὲν μᾶλλον τοιοῦτον ἢ τοιοῦτον εἶναι was used by the atomists themselves. It is tempting to associate it with the fact that the atoms were ἄποια, but Brieger was probably right in maintaining against Zeller that it refers in Simplicius to composite bodies, not the atoms.

[2] *Pyrrh. hyp.* 1.14 σκεπτικὰς φωνὰς οἷον τὴν 'οὐδὲν μᾶλλον' ἢ τὴν 'οὐδὲν ὁρίζω'.

impossible of attainment. When Aristotle in passage (x) above credits Democritus with the belief that either nothing is true or what is true is hidden (or unseen), the word for 'hidden' (ἄδηλον) is one which is frequently used to mean 'hidden from sense, imperceptible'.[1] Democritus did not subscribe to the thesis of Gorgias that if anything exists we have no possible means of knowing it. What he did say was that the truth must lie somewhere beyond sense-perception. So Sextus can even class him with Plato as believing that only intelligibles (νοητά) are real.[2] Plato would have vehemently repudiated the comparison. From the point of view of his own distinction between bodiless forms and physical objects, the atoms of Democritus belonged essentially to the sensible world. Yet who can estimate his unacknowledged debt to his great predecessor? Democritus, after all, taught that reality is only comprehensible by the mind, not the senses, that it is opposed to the world of the senses as what is stable, everlasting, unchanging to what is in a constant flux of change (the contrast of being and becoming), and even that the best name for these real, unchanging, intelligible objects was 'forms' (ἰδέαι, p. 395, n. 2 above). The materialism of Democritus and the idealism of Plato present a truly Heraclitean 'harmony of opposites', reflected in a kind of love–hate relationship. The *Timaeus* is constantly reminding one of Democritean doctrine, and it can hardly be accidental that neither there nor anywhere else does Plato ever mention his name. He was the arch-enemy, for to Plato being and value were essentially linked in a teleological scheme, utterly irreconcilable with the soulless mechanical origin of the atomic universe. Yet he must sometimes have seen in him as it were the negative by reversal of which his own picture of beauty, goodness and order was printed off.

No extant text explains for us exactly the relationship between sensible experience and rational thought in Leucippus or Democritus. Moreover, since they were clearly determined to admit no account but a purely materialistic one, no causal factor other than physical contact,

---

[1] At *PA*, 665a30 Aristotle says that bloodless animals have no viscera. Democritus was wrong in thinking that they were there, but διὰ μικρότητα ἄδηλα. Similarly the atoms were ἀόρατα διὰ σμικρότητα τῶν ὄγκων, *GC*, 325a30. Cf. the contrast between φαινόμενα and ἄδηλα in Sextus, e.g. *Pyrrh. hyp.* 1.20, and of course Anaxagoras's ὄψις τῶν ἀδήλων τὰ φαινόμενα.

[2] Alfieri, *L'atomo come principio intelligibile*, is interesting on this point.

it is unlikely that they were completely successful in relating the two. By saying that 'truth is the phenomenon', Aristotle conveys to us the conviction of Democritus that all reality is physical body, there is no *super*-sensible reality, and it is by starting from sense-impressions that the truth has somehow to be reached. The denial of objective existence to secondary qualities gives plenty of justification for those who say that Democritus 'sometimes does away with phenomena', but even through sensation (which is after all only one form of atomic action) we receive our first awareness not only of secondary qualities but also of size, shape, solidity, hardness and other properties which are possessed by the real itself.[1] Here the distinction between the two sorts of cognition comes to our aid (passage (vii), §138 above). The senses take us as far as they can go, and when we pass beneath the threshold of perception the mind takes over. This does not suggest a radically different process but only a continuation to a new level of the same process, as indeed it must be if the materialistic hypothesis is to be maintained.

No scholar, so far as I can see, has attempted to show how the atomists' epistemology was to be explained in atomic terms. Even Helene Weiss, whose account I have found much the most illuminating, speaks of human understanding reaching the atoms and the void 'by a way of thinking which starts from the appearances and refers back, i.e. a discursive thinking.... The *logoi* are an indirect grasping and mediate thus the knowledge of true being' (*CQ*, 1938, 51, n. 3). Bailey's solution is that the phenomena 'contain the data for the true knowledge of the realities', which the mind reaches 'by inference' (*Atomists*, 183, 184). How atoms in motion can account for discursive thinking, indirect grasping and mediation, or how inference is to be explained materialistically, are questions that they do not mention. Yet I am sure that, in intention at least, the materialistic explanation was not abandoned at the level of thought. Bailey is especially puzzling. We have seen his lucid explanation of how thought occurs by direct impingement of single atoms on the concentration of soul-atoms which is the mind (p. 453 above). Yet when he comes to theory of knowledge, he quotes

[1] Aristotle (*De sens.* 442b10) holds it against Democritus that he treats 'common sensibles' (such as Aristotle believed to be the objects of more than one sense) as special ones. He mentions size, shape, roughness and smoothness, and sharpness and bluntness in solid bodies. All these, unlike colour, flavour, etc., are common to the world of appearances and the atoms themselves.

the view of Brandis that 'Democritus thought that the mind had direct cognizance of the atoms: far too minute to stir the senses, yet individual atoms might stir the subtle combination of pure soul-atoms and so be known, as the objects of sense are by the senses', and then adds: 'but for such an idea there is no particle of evidence'. Is it not evidence for that when we are told that thought, like sensation, is corporeal? How else could it happen? Bailey further objects that even if the atoms could be known in this way, the void could not, for it cannot 'move' anything; but if one knows where atoms are, surely one knows *eo ipso* where they are not. If a few drops of acid fall on my hand, each producing a burning sensation, they make me aware of where they are not as much as of where they are.

Certainly Democritus said (passage (viii)) that though the mind thought ill of the senses because in themselves they did not reflect reality, yet it took its evidence from them. Some process of inference is indicated, as it is also in his approval of the dictum that phenomena are a window on the unseen. Through them, if we do not stop there, we can become aware of the nature of the invisible realities.[1] Since it was impossible anyway that such a crude and elementary materialism should explain a mental process like inference, it is probably at this point that it cannot stand being pressed too hard. At any rate certain finer films of atoms pass right through the sense-organs or other 'passages' in the body and impinge on the collection of pure soul-atoms which form the mind, thus enabling it to be directly aware of the atoms themselves. Our picture of reality is built up by combining both modes of *gnosis*. Perhaps we might not even be able to interpret the message of the microscopic atoms striking on the mind if we had not experienced their properties of size, shape, hardness, etc., writ large in the phenomenal world. Moreover changes in the atomic composition of object and percipient cause changes in the sensation produced by

[1] As George Herbert wrote:

> A man that looks on glasse
> On it may stay his eye,
> Or if he pleaseth, through it passe
> And then the heav'n espie.

If the glass through which we look is the sensible world, then with 'heav'n' we have Platonism. Substitute 'atoms and void' and it is Democritean. If the word were 'real', it would fit either philosophy.

their interaction. Conversely therefore the mutability and relativity of sensations, though throwing up a barrage of falsehood in the shape of impressions of colours, sounds and tastes, can come to be seen as evidence of changes in atomic composition. The remarkable statement that eyes and ears, after receiving the atomic films, pass them on to be dispersed throughout the body may just possibly be relevant to how this is done.

Something like this is perhaps what Bailey and others have meant by 'inference'. Whatever it is called, it must be susceptible of explanation in material terms. We have not the evidence to say exactly how it happened, and we may well suspect that if we had we should find it unsatisfactory. One cannot see for instance how intellectual activity could avoid playing the same purely passive and receptive role as sensation. But this after all was a problem that still remained to worry Aristotl^ (*De an.* 3.4). Whatever the missing links, we may be sure of this: 'Leucippus and Democritus say that sensation and thought take place by the impact of images from outside. No one experiences *either* without the impact of an image'.[1]

(14) *Biology, physiology, medicine*

From the titles of the books ascribed to him, and the nature of the scraps of information reported from them, Democritus's biological work must have rivalled Aristotle's in comprehensiveness and attention to detail. But it is lost, and all that we find in later writers can do little more than tantalize. In the apocryphal story of his meeting with Hippocrates,[2] the great physician found him sitting under a plane tree surrounded by the bodies of animals which he had been dissecting (Hippocr. IX, 350 L.), and there is every reason to believe that this glimpse of him as a practical scientist is founded on fact, though at the same time he was by no means immune from the Greek love of theorizing. This as well as the thoroughness of his treatment is exemplified by the remarkable description (reproduced by Aelian, *Nat. an.* 12.18–20;

---

[1] Aët. 4.8.10 (DK, 67 A 30, quoted on p. 451 above). But the conjecture of Kirk (KR, 422) is also worth investigation, that 'in the case of thought one might suppose that self-motion by the kinetic spherical atoms is also possible, to account for apparently spontaneous thoughts'.

[2] An actual meeting between the two great contemporaries is not impossible. Hippocrates knew Abdera well, if he is the author of any of the Hippocratic treatises which give details of cases treated there. (Even addresses are occasionally included.) Examples are: *Epidemics*, 3, vol. III, 120, 130, 136 Littré; 4, vol. v, 176, 194; 5, vol. v, 258; 6, vol. v, 534; 7, vol. v, 460, 462 (four cases). Book 3, like book 1, is an impressive case-book which is with good reason attributed to the master himself.

DK, 68 A 153–5)[1] of the growth of horns in deer and cattle. It is full of physiological detail to explain the first growth, shedding and growth of new horns, the difference between the horns of whole and castrated bulls, and the reason why some cattle are hornless. In general terms the material of the horns is a flow of moisture to the spot, drawn from the animal's nourishment through a network of veins or channels, penetrating the bone covering the head, which is thin and membranous, and hardened by contact with the cold air outside. Their successful growth depends therefore on the suitability of the channels, the porosity of the top of the skull, and more accidental features like the breadth of the forehead. The shadow of the general atomic theory is seen in the idea that the top of the skull is *araion*, meaning that the interstices of void between the atoms are comparatively large, and in the emphasis on flow through passages which must be of appropriate size.

Isolated fragments about lions and owls suggest an affinity of nature between them. Lions are born and sleep with the eyes open, and contain much heat, which is why they fear fire. Owls too are born with the eyes open. The reason is the amount of fire in the eyes, which also gives them their night-vision. Spiders spin their threads from inside their bodies like an excretion, a statement which the author of the *Historia Animalium* somewhat unwisely challenges.[2] Fish live on a minute quantity of fresh water contained in the sea.[3] Theophrastus records a remark of Democritus about the amphibious habits of certain fish.[4] He classified animals as sanguineous and non-sanguineous, and believed that the latter had entrails too small to be seen.[5]

---

[1] On the genuineness of the quotations in Aelian see Wellmann, *Archeion*, 1929, 320.

[2] Lions, schol. on *Il.* 11.554 (A156), owls *Etym. Genuin. s.v.* γλαῦξ (but Aelian says that according to Democritus the lion μόνον τῶν ζῴων is born with the eyes open; see A157 for both). For spiders, [Aristotle], *HA*, 623a31. (Book 9 of the *HA*, from which this comes, is generally thought to be a Peripatetic compilation, perhaps of the third century B.C., from Aristotle, Theophrastus and Eudemus. See Regenbogen in *RE*, Suppl. VII, 1432 ff.)

[3] This belief was common among Greek naturalists, being held already by Empedocles (p. 199 above; the reference to Democritus comes in the same passage), and later by Aristotle and Theophrastus.

[4] Theophr. Π. Ἰχθύων, 12 (II, 217 Wimmer), DK, 68 A 155 b. See Löwenheim, *Wiss. Demokrits*, 162 f. (But ὀρυκτά does not mean fossils, but fish that dig themselves into the mud. Cf. [Arist.] *Mir. ausc.* 835 b 16.)

[5] Arist. *PA*, 665 a 30. (For the possibility that Democritus originated the classification see Löwenheim, *op. cit.* 165.) The σπλάγχνα belong to the same world of ἄδηλα as the atoms (p. 462, n. 1 above).

Biology

The fullest information about the biology of Democritus, much of it from Aristotle and Aelian, concerns his views on reproduction and embryology. The vehicle of life is *pneuma*, and the generative power of semen is due (as for Diogenes, p. 378 above) to the element of breath in it (Aët. 5.4.3, A 140). It is collected from every part of the body,[1] but bones, flesh, and sinews are mentioned as the most important parts (*ibid.* 3.6, A 141). This seems to depend on ancient lore rather than independent investigation, when one reflects that it is precisely these three that in the *Odyssey* (11.219) are said to be lacking to the shades in the underworld. Democritus sided with Alcmaeon and Empedocles against Anaxagoras and Diogenes in holding that both parents contributed seed (Arist. *GA*, 764a6). Differentiation of sex takes place in the womb, but depends on whether the mother's or the father's seed preponderates (as in Alcmaeon, A 14), not (as in Empedocles) on temperature nor (as in Anaxagoras) on the distinction between right- and left-hand sides.

On the order of formation of the embryo, others had argued somewhat abstractly that the 'most important part' must come first, and supposed it to be head or heart according to their relative estimates of these organs; Democritus more practically supposed it to be the umbilical cord, which had to be there first to provide an anchorage for the foetus as it grew.[2] After this the external parts take shape before the inner, an opinion which earned him a rebuke from Aristotle (*GA*, 740a13). They are specified later by Censorinus as head and belly, with the atomistic but not obviously relevant comment that these have most void (6.1, A 145).

---

[1] For a detailed account of ancient Greek theories of reproduction and heredity (including those of the Hippocratic writers), and their influence, the interested reader may be referred to Erna Lesky, *Die Zeugungs- und Vererbungslehre der Antike und ihr Nachwirken* (1950). So far as the origin of the semen is concerned, she distinguishes three main types (p. 4):

(1) The 'encephalo-myelogenic' theory, deriving the semen from the brain and marrow (first appearing in Alcmaeon; see also p. 356 above).

(2) The 'pangenesis' theory, deriving it from all parts of the body (Democritus, and after him tending to replace no. 1).

(3) The 'haematogenous', deriving it from the blood. This can be traced back to the fifth century in Parmenides fr. 18 and Diog. Apoll. A 24, but its development is due to Aristotle.

The pangenesis theory (so called because Darwin himself drew attention to the similarity between his own and the ancient) appears to have been an original contribution of Democritus. Lesky discusses it on pp. 70–6.

[2] Plut. *Am. prol.* 495e, Democritus fr. 148. Aristotle said the same, calling the cord a root (*GA*, 745b25). Democritus also uses a vegetable metaphor, calling it a stalk for the coming fruit as well as an anchor, and perhaps this analogy helped to mislead them both, as Platt suggests in the Oxford translation of Aristotle.

Democritus subscribed to the interesting theory which we have already met in Diogenes and Hippon (pp. 378, 357 above), that the embryo is nourished in the womb by suckling. This is why babies know how to apply their mouths to the breast as soon as they are born: there are nipples and mouths even in the womb. Zeller noted that this theory indicated research on the lower animals, for the cotyledons, or fleshy outgrowths, which gave rise to the belief, are found in other mammals but not in man.[1] It occurs also in the Hippocratic *De carnibus* (ch. 6, VIII, 592 L.), where the embryo is said to suck both nourishment and breath through the mouth, and the same justification for the belief is mentioned, namely, that without this pre-natal experience it could not take to the breast immediately after birth.[2] Miscarriages, said Democritus, occur more frequently in warm climates than cold, because warmth dilates the womb and loosens the foetus. Animals which produce several offspring at a birth have 'many wombs and places which receive the sperm'. Not all are filled at one copulation.[3] Monstrous births he attributed to superfoetation causing the parts to grow together and become confused.[4] The sterility of mules results from their being a creation not of nature but of human artifice, by a kind of

[1] For Democritus see Aët. 5.16.1 (A 144). This I think is sufficient warrant for including him among those whom Aristotle had in mind when he wrote in *GA* (746a19) about those who believe that infants in the womb suck nourishment through a small fleshy growth. The Shorter Oxford Dictionary defines a cotyledon (the actual word κοτυληδόνες is used with reference to Diogenes but not Democritus) as 'one of the separate patches of villi on the foetal chorion of ruminants'. The alternative theory, that nourishment was absorbed through the umbilical cord, was held by Empedocles and Anaxagoras (DK, 31 A 79 and 59 A 110). See also ZN, 1112, n. 1, Wellmann, *FGÄ*, 1.95. Aristotle gives as the reason why Democritus thought the embryo was retained in the womb 'that its parts may be formed according to the parts of the mother', and contrasts this with what he believes to be the true reason, namely, the absorption of nourishment. But this is probably a misunderstanding, as Cherniss explains (*ACP*, 288, n. 255).

[2] The theory may go back to Alcmaeon: see Rufus *ap.* Oribas. 3.156, DK 24 A 17. Influence of Democritus on the Hippocratic writings is disputed. W. C. Greene affirms it in *Moira*, 268, but refers also to the negative remarks of Jaeger, *Diokles*, 54, n. 1. Cf. also n. 1 on next page.

[3] Miscarriages, Ael. *Nat. an.* 12.17 (A 152), multiple births *ibid.* 16 (A 151). The Hippocratic *De nat. pueri*, 31 (VII, 540 L., also in A 151) adds that each foetus is 'in a recess and membrane in the womb', and mentions the same examples (pig and dog) as Aelian cites from Democritus. If this suggests direct influence (Wellmann, *Archeion*, 1929, 305), one should notice also that the Hippocratic treatise speaks of their producing two or more offspring 'from a single copulation'.

[4] Arist. *GA*, 769b30. The production of τέρατα was a subject which greatly interested Aristotle. In general terms he explained it as a failure on the part of the active element (the semen) to overcome defects in the material (provided by the female parent). Among the Presocratics opinions are recorded only for Empedocles and Democritus, of whom the former appears to have suggested a number of alternative possibilities (Aët. 5.8.1; DK, 31 A 81).

adultery. As an effect of their origin from disparate species, their genital 'passages' (*poroi*) are malformed.[1]

Plants are to all intents and purposes animals, save that they are rooted in the earth. The dubious authority of the treatise *De plantis* links Democritus with Anaxagoras and Empedocles in the belief that they have the power of thought. (Cf. p. 316 above.) The extent of his botanical interest is illustrated by his detailed explanation (reported by Theophrastus) of why plants with straight stems bud, fruit and die more quickly than those which grow crookedly.[2]

Democritus's works included a book of medical instruction, one on diet (or regimen), and one on prognosis, but we have little direct information about his teaching on therapy and the maintenance of health. Nevertheless as J. Schumacher has pointed out, there are certain indications, in what we have already seen, of the sort of line that he would take.[3] We know of the importance of breathing, the

---

[1] Arist. *GA*, 747 a 29; Ael. 12.16 (A 151). A few points from Hippocr. *De genit.* and *De nat. pueri* covering the same ground as the above paragraphs may be of interest for comparison. Seed comes from the whole body (*Gen.* chh. 1 and 3), but is gathered especially from the brain and marrow (ch. 1; cf. Democr. fr. 1 τῆς δὲ ψυχῆς οἱ περὶ τὸν μυελὸν δεσμοί, which is closely followed by Plato, *Tim.* 73 b, 81 d). Seed is emitted by female as well as male (ch. 4). Sex of infant depends on whether male or female seed predominates, and semen of both men and women contain *both*. Female-producing seed is 'weaker' than male, but the weaker can overcome the stronger if present in larger quantity (chh. 6–7). Resemblance to one or other parent in individual features is determined by whether the father's or the mother's seed proceeding from that particular part of the body is stronger and more effective (ch. 8). The navel is the channel both of respiration and of growth (*NP*, ch. 15). The growth and formation of the embryo are due to breath (ch. 17, ἡ δὲ σάρξ αὐξομένη ὑπὸ τοῦ πνεύματος ἀρθροῦται) and proceeds on the principle of like to like. This is illustrated by an experiment with earth, sand and lead filings in a bladder which bears out Democritus's remarks about the behaviour of different grains in a sieve. The author concludes by emphasizing the natural similarity between men and 'the things that grow out of the earth' (ch. 27). For further details see Wellmann in *Archeion*, 1929.

[2] Plants as ζῷα ἔγγεια (with Anaxagoras and Plato), Plut. *Qu. Phys.* 911 d (DK, 59 A 116). In this at least it seems the Epicureans did not tamely follow: 'The Stoics and Epicureans say that plants are not alive (ἔμψυχα), for soul was sometimes a principle of impulse and desire, sometimes also of thought, but plants are activated mechanically, not by soul' (Aët. 5.26.3). A cardinal point of Epicureanism is involved here, for Epicurus was determined to take account of freewill, and thought that all his predecessors had neglected the distinction between what had it and what had not. For the attribution of intelligence to plants see *De plantis*, 815 b 16 (DK, 31 A 70). The *De plantis* as we have it is a poor Latin translation of a lost Arabic version of the lost Greek original of a work once attributed to Aristotle but now to Nicolaus of Damascus (first century B.C.). For straight- and crooked-growing plants, Theophr. *CP*, 2.11.7 (A 162).

[3] *Ant. Medizin*, 144 ff. The story that, when at the point of death, he kept himself alive for three days by inhaling the steam from hot, fresh bread may well be a reflexion of something in his teaching. (It occurs in D.L. 9.43, which is now supported by a fuller version in *Anon. Lond.* col. 37, lines 34 ff.) That animals could be nourished by smells was a Pythagorean belief (vol. 1, 307, n. 2).

efficiency of which depends on the structure of the body. The healthy condition of the eye and ear is described in some detail. The general principle seems to be that there should be enough void between the atoms, and channels of the right formation, to draw in atoms from outside, whether singly or as films or 'images', and give them freedom to move and be effective. What is said about eyes and ears suggests that one impediment to this is excessive dampness. The healthy state is described generally, in terms suggestive of Alcmaeon or the Pythagoreans, as a correct blending of elements and properties in the body. Thought itself depends on this, and is affected by excessive heat or cold.

The so-called ethical fragments also have some light to throw here. Like all the best ancient medical writers, Democritus attaches more importance to a good regimen than to medicine, to prevention than to cure. Health, he says (fr. 234), is in men's own hands: they destroy it through intemperate desires. (It is perhaps relevant here that he likened the sexual orgasm to a mild fit of epilepsy.)[1] Harmony and measure in the body are inseparable from the same qualities in the spirit and life in general. In a remarkable fragment (159), he imagines the body arraigning the soul as responsible for its pains and troubles, and says that it should win its case, for it is the soul that ruins it by neglect, intemperance and love of pleasure. Conversely the right state of the body leads to that spiritual serenity and happiness the attainment of which is man's chief end. All this is in entire accord with atomic theory, which teaches that the soul itself is material and that all experience, both bodily and spiritual, results from the entry of atom-complexes into the organism with beneficial or disturbing effects.[2]

In general, what we know of Democritus's work on the biological sciences does not suggest great originality, though it must never be forgotten how miserably scanty is our information and how much detailed description is lost. Existing views were however adapted to expression in terms of atomic theory. Naturally this is not always

---

[1] Or apoplexy. See fr. 32 with the variants in DK's note.

[2] Democritus may also have followed the common belief of his time in commending the healing effect of music. Aulus Gellius (4. 13) claims to have found in a book of his the statement that correct and skilful playing of the pipe can be a remedy for snakebite and many other pathological conditions. Diels rejected the passage as belonging to the thaumaturgical writings of Bolus, but see Delatte, *Conceptions*, 74–6. The philosophy of Democritus certainly found a place for some things which we should call superstitions (§17 below).

prominent, but it appears in the emphasis on the correct degree of 'density' or 'rarity', that is, the proportion of solid to void, in various parts of the organism, and in the importance of suitable *poroi*.

(15) *Man and the cosmos: the origin of life*

It is usually accepted that Democritus was the first known Greek to apply to man the term *microcosm* (*mikros kosmos*, i.e. little world-order; the word *kosmos* has by now undoubtedly acquired the meaning 'world', while still emphasizing the element of system and order which distinguishes it from pre-cosmic chaos). This is a term which, with its Latin equivalent *minor mundus*, became common in some Hellenistic and Graeco-Roman circles, particularly those connected with mystical religion of Neopythagorean or Gnostic type. Its use continued so that Francis Bacon could write that it was 'tritum in scholis hominem minorem esse mundum'.[1] It would certainly be interesting to trace the phrase back to fifth-century atomism, apart from which the only pre-Hellenistic example is Aristotle's application of it to animals in general.[2] If we do so, however, we must admit that it has come down to us with no context whatsoever. The sole source is a Christian Neoplatonist of the sixth century, David the Armenian, and he introduces it (in the words 'even so in man, who according to Democritus is a little world') into a comparison which is obviously Platonic.[3] Hence although much has been written about its implications, it remains largely speculative.[4] Man and world are built out of the same elements, atoms and void, following the same laws. Even the soul-atoms exist outside the human organism, and are breathed in along with the air. This however serves only to remind us that even if Democritus coined the phrase, the idea of an intimate relationship between macrocosm and microcosm was far older. The breathing-in of soul from the universe, the kinship of organic and inorganic nature, the association of human goodness and

---

[1] Some examples are in Lobeck, *Aglaoph.* 921 ff. and Bouché-Leclerq, *L'Astrol. Grecque*, 77, n. 1.

[2] *Phys.* 252 b 26 εἰ γὰρ ἐν μικρῷ κόσμῳ γίγνεται, καὶ ἐν μεγάλῳ. The argument is that it might be thought as reasonable for the whole cosmos to have been at one time at rest and later in motion as it is for an animal to rouse itself from rest to motion. This is certainly not an analogy of which Democritus would have approved.

[3] David, *Prol.* 38.14 (Democr. fr. 34). It rests on the tripartite nature of both man and the cosmos, each containing a ruling, a ruled, and a ruled-plus-ruling part.

[4] See most recently Kerschensteiner, *Kosmos*, 173 f., with her references.

natural bounty in myths of the Golden Age, the emphasis on the identity of elements in ourselves and the universe, the ordering of the whole world on psychological principles of desire and aversion—some or all of these ideas can be traced in Hesiod, in Anaximenes, in the Pythagoreans, in Empedocles or Diogenes of Apollonia. Perhaps their survival in Democritus is most marked in the universal law of like tending to like, with its illustration from the world of living creatures, and we have also noted that Leucippus's account of cosmogony was not free from the traditional language of organic growth (pp. 408, 409 above); but none of these features originates with the atomists, and the most striking thing about their achievement is the extent to which they freed themselves from the anthropomorphic conception of the universe with which the microcosmic theory is most naturally linked. The special type of rounded atoms that in conjunction with the human frame go to form soul and mind may float about the world with others, but this does not make the world a living, still less a thinking, organism. Here is no 'holy mind, darting through the whole cosmos with swift thoughts' (Empedocles fr. 134), no 'world a living creature with soul and reason' as depicted in Plato's *Timaeus* (30b). Soul and mind are epiphenomena. They were not there in the beginning, and played no part in the ordering of the world.[1]

On the origin of mankind, the only information directly attributed to Democritus (none is assigned to Leucippus) is that it arose from water and mud, that the first men came out of the earth, and that like other animals they owed their origin to 'life-giving moisture'.[2] It is probable that he also held the theory of fermentation of the earth's surface and the production of bubble-like membranes, inside which, as in wombs, the first living creatures grew. This theory, which is certainly Presocratic, has been discussed in connexion with Empedocles (p. 210 above), and was adopted with so much of the earlier atomism by Epicurus. In all this Democritus seems to have had little original to offer. The idea that life arose from mud and warmth met us over a hundred years earlier in Anaximander and again in Anaxagoras; Empedocles wrote

---

[1] Aët. 2.3.2 (67 A 22) Λεύκιππος δὲ καὶ Δημόκριτος καὶ Ἐπίκουρος οὔτ' ἔμψυχον οὔτε προνοίᾳ διοικεῖσθαι [sc. τὸν κόσμον], φύσει δέ τινι ἀλόγῳ, ἐκ τῶν ἀτόμων συνεστῶτα. Cf. the emergence of men from the earth 'nullo auctore nullaque ratione' (Lactantius, *Inst. div.* 7.7.9, 68 A 139).

[2] See the passages from Censorinus, Aëtius and Lactantius collected in DK, 68 A 139.

of the first living creatures springing out of the earth under the action of heat, and Xenophanes and Archelaus held similar views, which are indeed only rationalizations of older popular notions. (See p. 315 with n. 4 above.)

(16) *Culture, language and the arts*

In contrast to poetic and religious ideas of a 'golden age' in the past, the fifth century saw the rise of more realistic evolutionary theories of human culture and society. All the epithets in Hobbes's description of man's life in his natural state—'solitary, poor, nasty, brutish and short'—can be paralleled in these ancient accounts of his earliest condition. Whether or not a religious cloak was thrown over the narrative by a rather perfunctory reference to Prometheus or some other super-human power as having bestowed on men the wit to improve their lives, it was by stern necessity and native intelligence that progress was achieved. The first men lived like animals, and not even gregarious animals. With no organization, each sought his own food and his own cave. Lacking all technical skill, they were without houses or clothes, domestic animals, agriculture, cookery or metals. Many were the victims of wild beasts or disease, until the need for survival compelled them to band together, and after many failures due to their wild and selfish nature, the rudiments of social life came into existence. Gradually this developed into the higher culture of the *polis*, and the arts and graces of civilized life began to take their place alongside the purely practical skills. This evolutionary view of culture as the daughter of necessity is to be found, identical in outline and in many of the details, in Aeschylus, Euripides, Critias, Protagoras, the Hippocratic *On Ancient Medicine*,[1] and the evidently fifth-century source of the pre-history in Diodorus 1.8. It is therefore difficult to trace its origin to any particular thinker.[2] The substance of the chapter in Diodorus has been thought to have originated with Democritus, but must have been current earlier. Nevertheless, though Democritus cannot have been the author of the view, it can scarcely be doubted that he adhered to it. It is entirely in

---

[1] A recent study of *VM* by Hans Herter, *Die kulturhist. Theorie d. hipp. Schrift u. d. alten Medizin* (*Maia*, 1963), is sensible and cautious about its relation to Democritus.

[2] See Guthrie, *In the Beginning*, chh. 4–6, especially ch. 5 and the beginning of ch. 6, and the references on p. 141, n. 9. Fuller treatment of the evolutionary theories of human society will be more appropriate to the next volume of this work.

keeping with his secular and materialistic outlook, and the supposition is borne out by his remarks on music (fr. 144) as recorded by Philodemus: 'Democritus, who was not only the most scientific of the ancients but in industry also second to none of whom we have knowledge, says that music is a fairly recent art. The reason he gives is that it was not evolved[1] by necessity but is the product of an already existing abundance.' The same outlook is reflected in his belief that in some of the most important arts men have been the pupils of animals. Observation of the spider gave us the idea of weaving and mending, from the swallow we acquired the notion of housebuilding, and by imitation of the birds we learned to sing (fr. 154).

An interesting detail of the evolutionary view of society, to which Democritus contributed, was its theory of the origin of language. As we learn from Plato's *Cratylus*, two rival views of this were current. According to one, words had a natural rightness based on an affinity with the character of what they stood for. This idea, so difficult to defend on any rational basis, was pretty clearly a survival of the belief in a magical connexion between names and objects. In contrast to this, it was being argued by the fifth century that words were sounds attached quite arbitrarily to things or notions by human agency as the necessity arose for a means of communication more comprehensive and subtle than the grunts or cries of animals or birds. Language is an artificial product in the evolutionary account of Plato's *Protagoras* (322a),[2] and the Diodoran history puts it as follows (1.8.3–4). When men banded together as a protection from the beasts,

at first they uttered confused sounds devoid of significance, then gradually began to articulate words, and agreeing among themselves on expressions for every object, created a recognized mode of communication about everything. Similar groups of men collected all over the inhabited world, so that all did not have a language that sounded the same, for each group composed its words as they chanced to come. That is why there exist languages of the most diverse character.

---

[1] ἀποκρῖναι. The word is reminiscent of Anaxagoras, as Vlastos (*Philos. Rev.* 1946, 54) and Lämmli (*Chaos zum Kosmos*, n. 673) have noted; but it is scarcely so 'auffällig' and 'unverständlich' as the latter supposes.

[2] I do not agree with the remark of Hoffman (approved by Untersteiner, *Sophists*, 74, n. 47) which connects the origin of language with θεία μοῖρα. The gods are part of the myth with which Protagoras the agnostic is deliberately clothing his rationalistic views (320c). Cf. my *In the Beginning*, 88f. The operative word here is τέχνη.

That Democritus should hold a similar view was to be expected, and is confirmed by such information as we have. Though it comes from the Neoplatonists many centuries later, there is no need to defend an account which accords so well with the atomists' general outlook. Proclus in his commentary on the *Cratylus* (p. 5.25 Pasquali, Democr. fr. 26) says that Democritus took the standpoint of Hermogenes in the dialogue, that names are not natural but conventional, and adduced four arguments in support of the belief that they cannot be essentially and naturally connected with their objects: (1) different things are sometimes called by the same name; (2) different names are applied to one and the same thing; (3) the name of a thing or a person is sometimes changed at will; (4) it is possible to think of parallel notions for one of which a word exists whereas for the other it does not. The argument appears to be that if a word were an essential part of the nature of that which it stands for, there would have to be a word for everything. To illustrate this, he used (according to Proclus) the rather strange example of derivatives: connected with thought there is a verb to think, but connected with justice there is no parallel verb (though, he presumably meant, there is a corresponding action, which ought similarly to have attached to it a single word or name).

The other reference is a little more puzzling. In Plato's *Philebus* (12c), Socrates confesses to a great fear in uttering the names of the gods. Commenting on this, Olympiodorus asks what can be the reason for it (p. 242 Stallbaum, Democr. fr. 142). 'Is it because what has belonged to something for a long time has become sacred to that to which it belongs, and it is unreasonable to disturb what is fixed; or because names are naturally adapted to their objects as is argued in the *Cratylus*; or because, as Democritus has it, even the names are "images in sound" of the gods?'[1] This cryptic phrase is cited with no further explanation

---

[1] It is of course possible for ἀγάλματα to mean adornments, honours, or gifts pleasing to the gods, and it would make sense to say that the names men assign to the gods are given in their honour. It seems certain however that images or representations are meant here, especially when we compare two other passages not expressly referred to Democritus. There is the sentence from Hierocles quoted by DK under the same fr. 142 where it is said (with particular reference to the name of Zeus) that those who first assigned names acted as ἀγαλματοποιοί in making them representations (εἰκόνες) of the functions (δυνάμεις) of their objects; and secondly the designation of names as ἀγάλματα in the sense of images in Proclus (quoted under Democr. fr. 26).

or comment. In itself it might be thought to imply the supposition of a natural connexion between names and objects, were it not that Olympiodorus explicitly distinguishes it from that, and since we have already seen Democritus cited as an upholder of the contrary view we may assume that he is right. Any interpretation must accord with Democritus's view of the gods, which we have not yet considered. Briefly, they are, like everything else in our experience, the result of material 'images', or films of atoms, striking upon our bodies and arousing certain sensations by the movements and changes which they set up in us. They are therefore as subjective as any other sights, sounds, or other sensa. Now the names of gods arouse associations and call up our notion of them in the imagination: for a man who fears Zeus, the utterance of his name may itself induce fear. In this way divine names would themselves be 'images' of the gods, i.e. images of images, twice removed from reality. If all the objects of experience have themselves only a subjective existence, their names must be even further removed from the reality that is atoms and void.[1] A similar view may be reflected in the saying attributed to Democritus that 'a word is a shadow of a deed' (or 'of reality'), cited by Plutarch as a warning against using bad language. A close connexion between the two is implied,[2] but the general atomic theory makes it inevitable that a word is far removed from reality.[3]

Democritus wrote a whole series of works on music, literature and literary style. The titles include treatises on rhythm and melody, on the

---

[1] Like time, if what I have said about it is correct (pp. 429 f. above).

[2] Fr. 145, from Plut. *De puer. educ.* 81a. The context shows that Plutarch did not understand this as meaning 'logos is *but* the shadow of the deed' (as Vlastos, *Ph. R.* 1946, 60; my italics), but as emphasizing the connexion between the two: bad talk is to be avoided because words shadow forth deeds.

[3] After all this it must be emphasized how little can be concluded with certainty from Olympiodorus, who not only lived a millennium later but is making a casual and passing reference with his mind on something else.

It is probable (many would say certain) from a passage like Arist. *Metaph.* 985 b 4 ff. that the atomists explicitly drew the analogy between letters, syllables and words on the one hand and atoms, atom-complexes, and physical wholes on the other. Frank (*Plato u. d. sog. Pyth.* 170) draws far-reaching conclusions from this about the relation between language and reality. Others too have had much more to say about Democritus's theory of language than is ventured here. For references see Alfieri's notes on frr. 26 and 142 (*Atomisti*, 210–12, 237f.) and Spoerri, *Späthell. Berichte*, 134–43. Note especially Steinthal, *Gesch. d. Sprachwiss. b. d. Gr. u. Röm.* I and Diels in *N. Jbb.* 1910.

life of the soul is made calm and stable, undisturbed by fear, superstition or any other emotion. He calls it also well-being, and by many other
names.[1]

Among these names were the one which Epicurus took over, *ataraxia*
(meaning freedom from disturbance), and *athambia* or imperturb-
ability,[2] and in fr. 31 Clement says that Democritus compared the
purging of emotion from the soul by wisdom to the healing of the body
by medicine. The word *pathos* used here, which in a psychological
context means emotion or passion,[3] covers a very wide field, for it connotes any way in which a subject is changed, wrought upon or affected.
So sensation is for Democritus a *pathos* of the perceiving subject when
disturbed by a rain of atoms, and it differs with the individual because
each individual's constitution differs according to *pathe* and age.[4] The
various senses can hardly have been dissociated in his mind, and the
aim in life is evidently to avoid all possible disturbance of any kind,
mental or emotional disturbance being of course as much a material
phenomenon as any other. The feelings, it is true, have their usefulness,
for if the obscure Diotimus is to be trusted here, we should let them be
our guide in what is to be sought and what avoided;[5] but we use them
only in order that, by choosing what suits us best, we may keep
emotional disturbance to the minimum. This involves taking the least
possible action either in public affairs or privately, and always keeping
well within one's powers (fr. 3).

Essential to contentment are *harmonia*, moderation and observance
of measure. It consists in the ability to distinguish and discriminate

[1] Cf. also Cic. *Fin.* 5.29, 87–8: 'Even if Democritus supposed happiness to consist in the
knowledge of nature (*rerum cognitione*), nevertheless he designed that his scientific study should
procure him peace of mind. That is his conception of the *summum bonum*, which he calls εὐθυμία
and often ἀθαμβία, that is, a mind free from fear. Yet though he put it excellently, it was not fully
worked out, for indeed he said very little about virtue, and that not clearly expressed. It was later
that these investigations began to be pursued, at Athens, first by Socrates.'

[2] A 167, 169 and frr. 4, 215.

[3] Vlastos (*Ph. Rev.* 1945, 579, n. 7) calls this the 'Aristotelian' sense, and takes the word here
as merely the equivalent of νόσος. This would rob the aphorism of much of its point. At the
least one must suppose that Democritus chose the more general term because both senses were
present to his mind.

[4] Theophr. *Sens.* 60, 63, 64. See p. 438 above.

[5] Sext. *Math.* 7.140. See p. 459 above. With this should be connected fr. 4 (188), where it
is said that enjoyment and its opposite are the sign of what is advantageous or the reverse. The
treatment of this fragment by D. McGibbon in *Phronesis*, 1960, suffers in my opinion from making
no distinction between τέρψις and ἡδονή. Cf. Alfieri, *Atomisti*, 254, n. 640.

between pleasures, than which, said Democritus, nothing is better or more advantageous for a man (Stobaeus, A 167; cf. fr. 233). It is secured by moderation in enjoyment and a balanced life: pleasures should be neither lacking nor excessive (fr. 191). Self-control is praised in several fragments (208, 210, 211, 214, 294). It increases pleasure (211), and the rarity of pleasures enhances their enjoyment (232). The need for discrimination in their choice also recurs in the fragments (71, 74, 207). One of the maxims in Stobaeus even says that to achieve contentment a man should not find his pleasure in mortal things.[1] The philosophy of contentment is evidently no vulgar hedonism: rather it foreshadows the 'art of measurement' in pleasure of which Socrates makes himself the champion in Plato's *Protagoras*. This at least finds no contradiction in the many maxims ascribed to Democritus, which as we have seen are unadventurous and strongly biased in favour of prudence and the safe middle way. Like Socrates he would be entirely opposed to the unbridled ambition and greed of a Callicles, as is shown also in his exaltation of the old Hellenic virtue of *aidōs*, an inner feeling of respect for what deserves respect and revulsion from wrongdoing as such and not from fear of punishment.[2] Self-respect and shame before one's own conscience should keep one from doing a wrong even if no other man will know of it (frr. 244, 264, 84). Here he takes a firm stand against the attitude of some contemporary Sophists, like Critias who suggested that the gods were invented because fear of punishment by them was the only possible means of preventing wrongdoing in secret.[3] He also pronounced on another burning question of contemporary ethics, the part played by natural disposition and training respectively in the production of virtue. Training has the leading part,[4] but it can in fact change a man's disposition so that virtue becomes a second nature (fr. 33).

In all this Democritus shows himself to be not only the climax of the impressive line of Ionian *physici* but also a contemporary of the Sophists

---

[1] Fr. 189. If this is genuine, one can only suppose that in his ethical precepts Democritus sometimes chose to speak at the level of ordinary men, without adhering too scrupulously to the requirements of his atomic theory, according to which nothing, not even a god, was ἀθάνατον. Cf. pp. 436, 478 ff. above.

[2] For a discussion of αἰδώς see C. E. von Erffa, Αἰδώς *und verwandte Begriffe*, 1937.

[3] Critias fr. 25 DK. The problem of λάθρη ἁμαρτάνειν is also dealt with in Democritus fr. 181.

[4] Fr. 242. The same view is quoted in Stobaeus as from Critias (fr. 9 DK).

and an active participant in the controversies about human nature and conduct which occupied the centre of the philosophical stage, especially at Athens, in the middle and later decades of the fifth century. This emerges also from the fragments dealing with political thought and public affairs, which were none the less worthy of his attention because 'contentment' demanded that we should be involved in them as little as possible. In fifth-century Greece they could leave no one unaffected, but at least he can plead that intestine strife is an unmitigated evil (249), and only by a spirit of internal harmony can a city achieve anything in peace or war (250). In a remarkable passage (255) he says that when the upper classes are generous, helpful and kind to the poor, the resulting compassion, solidarity, comradeship, mutual assistance and harmony are of incalculable benefit. He is a democrat, for whom poverty in a free democracy is better than prosperity under autocratic rule (251). Good government is all in all (252), and the political art should be thoroughly mastered (157). A bad ruler should be blamed, but a good one deserves no special praise, since he is only carrying out the duty for which he was elected.[1] His humane sentiments (could one say, like Plato's?) applied only to law-abiding citizens within one's own state. External enemies and disturbers of the peace like thieves and pirates are to be killed without compunction (259, 260).

As a child of his time Democritus had to show where he stood in the controversy of 'law' versus 'nature'. Should one bow to *nomos* (custom or convention, crystallized in law) or follow *physis*, nature, which some Sophists exalted in contrast with it? In their view the stronger had a natural right to power, and law and custom were only a device to thwart this in the interests of the weak (synonymous with inferior). In his physical theory Democritus had gone so far in this direction as to contrast *nomos* with reality. Our sensations existed only by *nomos* (conventionally, or in general belief), whereas in reality there were only atoms and void (fr. 9, p. 440 above). But in practical life (as by now will be expected) he upheld it, in the narrower sense of law. 'It is proper to be obedient to law, to the ruler, and to the wiser' (47).

---

[1] Fr. 265. There is an individual tone about this which inclines one to suppose it genuine, but if so, then the Calliclean remark in fr. 267, φύσει τὸ ἄρχειν οἰκήιον τῷ κρέσσονι (cf. Plato, *Gorg.* 483 d), must either be wrongly attributed or else said by Democritus polemically with κρέσσων used in the sense of morally superior (like κρείσσων ἐπ᾽ ἀρετήν in fr. 181).

'The "contented" man is inclined to what is lawful and just' (174). 'The restraint exercised by the laws on individual freedom is solely to prevent men from injuring one another' (245). 'The aim of the law is to benefit human life, but it can only do so when men are willing to accept its benefits: it reveals its excellence to those who obey' (248). Law then, though good, is not all-powerful, for one cannot make men virtuous by force, but only by persuasion. 'By encouragement and persuasive words one will prove a more powerful advocate of virtue than by law and compulsion; for he who is kept from wrong by law is likely to sin in secret, but he who is brought to duty by conviction is unlikely to err either in secret or openly. Wherefore the man who acts rightly from intelligence and knowledge becomes both courageous and right-minded' (181).[1] The high status of *nomos* comes out especially in one of the exhortations not to be tempted to do wrong by the thought that no one will discover it. The quality of self-respect which makes this impossible 'should be established as a *nomos* (law) in the soul' (fr. 264). Here the *psyche* is the centre of moral and rational being as it is in Socrates, and *nomos* is far removed from the sense of mere convention or subjective belief in which, in the atomic philosophy of nature, it is contrasted with reality.[2]

A case for the integration of Democritus's physical and ethical theory was put forward by O. Gilbert in 1911, but not very successfully. More effective have been the recent arguments of von Fritz and Vlastos.[3] Here we must be brief. We know that sensation and even thought depend on a physical alteration caused by the movement and rearrangement of atoms. Since the soul is itself an atomic compound,

[1] The duty of the lawgiver to use persuasion rather than threats is similarly emphasized by Plato in the *Laws* (890b–d).

[2] The Christian Epiphanius (fourth century), in his refutation of heresies, ascribes to Democritus what seems an extreme antinomian position (3.2.9, DK 68 A 166): 'He said that the laws were an evil device, and that the wise man must not submit to them, but live in freedom.' This is a complete misunderstanding (cf. ZN, 1149, n. 4; Alfieri, *Atomisti*, 177, n. 452; *At. Id.* 203, n. 1), which could perhaps have had its origin in Democritus's denial of an absolute validity to law and his insistence that it cannot prevent secret wrongdoing, for which πειθώ and αἰδώς are the only remedy. The νόμος τῇ ψυχῇ καθεστώς (fr. 264) is certainly different from law in its commonly accepted sense. See also Langerbeck, Δόξις, p. 55.

[3] Gilbert, *Gr. Religionsphil.* 457–78; von Fritz, *Philos. und sprachl. Ausdr.* 32ff.; Vlastos in *Ph. Rev.* 1945 and 1946. Cf. also Alfieri, *Atom. Id.* 196f.

it would be only consistent to suppose that character is moulded in the same way, and there is something in the language of Democritus to suggest that it is. Compounds of the word *rhythmos*, which in his terminology meant 'shape' (p. 393 above), are used in ethical contexts, just as in the field of knowledge opinion was described as 'reshaping' (p. 458). His comment on the current question of the relationship between natural disposition and teaching is worded thus: 'Nature and teaching are similar: teaching re-forms a man, and by re-forming creates his nature.'[1] Fools are 'shaped' by the gifts of fortune, but understanding men by those of wisdom.[2] Vlastos also makes a point of the fact that words related to 'turning' (*trope*), used by Democritus for the position of atoms, are also applied to moral qualities.[3] However, the strongest evidence for the theories of von Fritz and Vlastos is in fr. 191, where moderate pleasures and a balanced life are said to be necessary for contentment because excess or defect of pleasure 'causes change and brings about great movements in the soul; and souls that are moved over large intervals are neither stable nor contented'. The language here, as von Fritz says, can hardly be metaphorical. Disturbance and scattering of the soul-atoms are prejudicial to peace of mind.[4] Together this evidence is sufficient to show that even when writing of conduct and the *telos* of life, Democritus did not always forget his universal materialism. But it does not suffice to explain how far he went, or how successful he was, in attempting a systematic integration of the two.

(20) *Conclusion*

Our account of Leucippus and Democritus has tried to explain their thought in the light of the assumptions of their own time and the philosophical problems that faced them. This is also the best basis for

[1] Fr. 33: ἡ φύσις καὶ ἡ διδαχὴ παραπλήσιόν ἐστι. καὶ γὰρ ἡ διδαχὴ μεταρυσμοῖ τὸν ἄνθρωπον, μεταρυσμοῦσα δὲ φυσιοποιεῖ. Only the Greek can fully bring out the parallel with physical terminology. Cf. ἀνάγκη τὰ σχήματα μεταρρυθμίζεσθαι in A 132.

[2] Fr. 197 (ῥυσμοῦνται).

[3] *Ph. Rev.* 1946, 55, n. 10. He quotes two fragments, 57 and 61. But in 61 the word is τρόπος, which was so familiar to everyone in the sense of habits or character that it is absurd to suppose that in using it Democritus would have his technical use of τροπή in mind. In 57 the phrase is ἤθεος εὐτροπίη. Vlastos also sees the last of the three atomic differentiae, διαθιγή, reflected in the phrase γνώμης κακοθιγίη (fr. 223). But this conjectural reading is by no means certain.

[4] Von Fritz, *op. cit.* 35; Vlastos, *Ph. Rev.* 1945, 582–4. With μεταπίπτει in this fr. may be compared the instability of the object of our knowledge, μεταπῖπτον κατά τε σώματος διαθήκην καὶ τῶν ἐπεισιόντων καὶ τῶν ἀντιστηριζόντων (fr. 9). On this verb see Dyroff, *Demokritstudien*, 84, n. 2.

any comparison with later developments of the atomic theory of matter. To make such a comparison adequately would call for a more than superficial understanding of physics down to the present day, and a lengthy treatment of changing theories through the centuries.[1] For Newton and the classical physics of the nineteenth century, atoms were still basically what they were for Democritus: ultimate units of matter which were hard, impenetrable, ponderable, immutable. But already the inadequacy of these units by themselves, with the sole additional assumption of void or 'not-being', to explain the complexity of phenomena was apparent. For Democritus action at a distance was impossible, and everything must be accounted for by the actual impact, entanglement and separation of atoms of different shapes. The hypothesis displayed both courage and ingenuity, but in fact could explain no more than the simplest physical processes. The complexities of chemical change, and the higher forms of organization and directive activity culminating in life and consciousness, proved to demand more subtle processes and the introduction of forces capable of acting over greater or smaller distances. From Newton onwards scientists have spoken in terms of fields of force—gravitational, electric, magnetic and others—involving the concepts of continuity and action at a distance, both of which were strictly forbidden to the atomists by the terms in which their own philosophical problems were set. Even so, the atomic structure of matter itself was basically unaltered; the forces acting on it, though their precise nature raised difficulties, could still be regarded as distinct from the matter acted on. It is the virtual abolition of this distinction in recent years, the change in the status of microphysical entities from permanent particles to what some would prefer to call events,[2] that has made the concepts of modern physics so fundamentally different from those of Democritus. It should however be mentioned, before leaving the subject, that the Democritean was not the only form of atomism bequeathed to us by Greek philosophy. According to

[1] I cannot claim wide reading on these subjects, or the ability to understand them fully; but writings which I have found illuminating are Toulmin and Goodfield's *Architecture of Matter* (with its especially useful bibliographies), van Melsen's *From Atomos to Atom*, von Weizsäcker's *World View of Physics*, and various writings of Werner Heisenberg (*Philosophical Problems of Nuclear Science, The Physicist's Conception of Nature*, and the symposium *On Modern Physics* which he shared with Born, Schrödinger and Auger).

[2] E.g. M. Čapek in *J. of Philos.* 1960, 292.

Heisenberg at least, it is the more mathematical atomism of Plato's *Timaeus* that comes nearest to modern conceptions.

It is not only the classical scholar who is impressed with the importance of seeing ancient atomism in the context of its time. Among modern scientists and philosophers of science, von Weizsäcker emphasizes the origin of atomism in the Eleatic denial of becoming and change; Toulmin gives as the reason for its limitations the metaphysical problems about being and not-being which its authors had to solve (and adds that science has broken away from the dilemma only at the cost of postponing the metaphysical questions); and Popper sees the basic problem of the Eleatic school, and so of Democritus, as that of the rational understanding of change, which 'still remains the fundamental problem of Natural Philosophy'.[1] One may mention in conclusion some of the philosophical problems which the atomists either raised for the first time, or at least brought into sharp focus and made inescapable. It is in raising and formulating questions, rather than in providing definitive answers, that the fruitfulness of sixth- and fifth-century speculation is chiefly to be found.

The atoms, it is clear, are an intellectual hypothesis to explain phenomena. This immediately raises a question in a philosopher's mind. Are they only physically, empirically imperceptible because of their small size, or are they imperceptible absolutely and in theory, being no more than constructions of the intellect? Such theoretical constructions have been seen at various periods to be valuable instruments of scientific advance,[2] down to the mathematical 'world-image' of the twentieth-century physicist. This, said Planck, is 'merely an intellectual structure. To a certain extent it is arbitrary.' It is 'due to our imagination and is of a provisional and changeable character...an artificial human product'.[3] Yet by its employment we attain a deeper understanding of the physical world itself. In an interesting discussion, Dr Toulmin notes in Democritus a certain ambiguity in the status of the

---

[1] Von Weizsäcker, *World View*, 38 f., *Relevance of Science*, 61 f.; Toulmin, *Architecture of Matter*, 72; Popper, *Conj. and Ref.* 79–81.

[2] They can also provide protection against the opposition of an established orthodoxy, like Osiander's instrumentalist interpretation of the Copernican theory in his preface to the *De revolutionibus* (quoted by Popper, *op. cit.* 98).

[3] *Philos. of Physics*, 50, 68, 69.

32-2

atoms. 'Sometimes he speaks as if only their minute size prevented us from seeing or feeling them. At others, he argues that they both *do* and *must* escape our senses.' I do not agree that the sentence 'Man is separated from reality' (fr. 6, p. 458 above) necessarily implies the absolute or theoretical imperceptibility of the atoms, but the repeated statement in our authorities that the atoms have no sensible qualities may be thought to say the same thing. (See especially p. 393 with n. 4 above.) Toulmin's conclusion is that Democritus exploited both interpretations, as Eudoxus may have done with the hypothesis of celestial spheres in astronomy.[1] My own impression is that Democritus was not so conscious of the problem as these words imply. Perhaps it could hardly arise until Plato and Aristotle had made explicit the distinction between sensible and intelligible existence. (Compare what is said about Democritus's attitude to phenomena on p. 456 above.) In any case it can hardly be right to say that, besides being too small to be seen, his atoms 'only existed in a manner of speaking, since one could discover what was *really* going on in the world only by hypothesis and rational inference'. This is not the logic of Democritus, who had learned his lesson from the Eleatics: what is reached by rational inference is the *only* thing that has absolute and unqualified existence. At the same time it belonged to the physical—that is, material—world, since for him there was no other.

Though Anaxagoras had put forward the notion of the infinitely small (p. 289 above), it is probably true that it was Leucippus and Democritus 'who made the question of the infinite divisibility of matter a basic question of philosophy'.[2] They excited the rivalry of atomic and continuum theories which has persisted to the present day.[3] It was not long before the Stoics put forward the opposite view in what has been claimed as 'the first consistent and elaborate continuum theory of matter',[4] and continuum theory was to be the successful rival of

[1] Toulmin, *op. cit.* 58 f. On Eudoxus see also Popper, *op. cit.* 99, n. 6.

[2] Von Weizsäcker, *World View*, 38.

[3] See Toulmin, *op. cit.*, 'Continuum theories of matter' in index, and his conclusion on p. 302: 'On the everyday level, atomism and continuum theory began as rivals; at the molecular level, they became partners with divided responsibilities; at the electronic level, they have become merged together into a single composite theory.'

[4] Sambursky, *Physics of Stoics*, 44. See also his 'Atomism versus Continuum Theory in Ancient Greece', in *Scientia*, 1961.

atomic for many centuries. Again, their explicit refusal of existence to anything but what was solid and impenetrable, anything but 'matter' in its most uncompromising form, brought philosophers for the first time face to face with the problems raised by an avowedly materialistic philosophy. Henceforth they had to make the choice whether to be materialistic or not, and justify it with argument. The ambiguous status, in this respect, of mind in Anaxagoras was no longer a possibility. With characteristic intellectual courage Leucippus and Democritus tried to reduce even life, consciousness and thought to the reciprocal action of atoms in contact with each other. They failed,[1] but by showing how far one could go even with such primitive concepts as theirs, they encouraged the faith of all who in later ages have been attracted by the notion of man as a machine: might he not be simply a more complicated and highly developed machine than the intellectual and experimental resources of the ancient atomists allowed them to suppose? The mind–matter dualism of a Descartes would have seemed to them a betrayal of principle, that same principle which was reaffirmed by Julien de la Mettrie in the eighteenth century in the words: 'Let us then conclude boldly that man is a machine, and that the whole universe consists only of a single substance [Matter] subjected to different modifications.'[2] Related to this is the choice between mechanism and teleology. Is function determined by structure or structure by function? Has matter formed itself unaided into organisms of an almost incredible complexity, delicacy and adaptability to purpose, or has this order and efficacy been imposed from outside by a rational agent working to a plan? To put it another way, should the animate world be modelled on the inanimate, or should it be the other way round? Hylozoism had not really posed the question, nor was it settled by traditional Greek religion as it is by Christianity. Anaxagoras and more particularly Diogenes of Apollonia inclined towards the ordering of matter by mind, but it was Democritus who first compelled philosophers to take sides by his detailed exposition of a system in which intelligence, direction and purpose were epi-

---

[1] This was perhaps inevitable. 'There is something in the internal logic of a *purely* atomistic theory which necessarily debars it from solving the problems of organization and directed activity' (Toulmin, *op. cit.* 64).

[2] Quoted by Toulmin, *op. cit.* 166. On Descartes and La Mettrie see also the article by K. Gunderson in *Philosophy*, 1964.

phenomena emerging at a late stage from nothing but the undesigned clash and recoil of individually inanimate particles. Now it stood forth starkly and could no longer be ignored. The reaction was swift. In the pages of his younger contemporary Plato, though the name of Democritus is never mentioned, one can sense the shock of hostility which he and those who thought like him had aroused. Democritus and Plato fought the first round in a contest which still continues and can never be decided by reason and observation alone.

Is reality to be discovered by deductive theory or sensible observation? Or rather, what is the relative importance to be attached to each in the search for it? No one but Parmenides had had the audacity to rely wholly on theory in flat contradiction of sensible experience, and even he, when he had stated the 'truth', felt compelled (from whatever motives) to append a long description of the origin and structure of the 'false', phenomenal world. To this problem of scientific method Democritus made a permanent contribution by his distinction between the two modes of cognition. Phenomena and reality are so related that the shifting panorama of the former is an impression made on our senses by the permanent realities of which both our own bodies and the external world are composed. Consequently the principle is established that the investigator must start from phenomena, and though reality lies beyond them and is reached by theory, the only theory admissible is one which does not contradict, but explains them:[1] 'Phenomena are the sight of the unseen.' Connected with this is the first statement of the distinction between what were later to be known as 'primary' and 'secondary' qualities and for Democritus were the object of 'legitimate' and 'bastard' knowledge respectively. This is essentially the distinction whose revival is often credited to Locke, though it is made in the clearest possible terms by Galileo,[2] and which Berkeley and Hume rejected in favour of the more sceptical conclusion that the so-called primary qualities are just as subjective as the secondary. Once again the first step in an age-long controversy was taken by the atomists of the fifth century B.C.

[1] This point is well expressed by Popper (*op. cit.* 82), who adds: 'This philosophy has remained fundamental to the whole development of physics, and has continued to conflict with all "relativistic" and "positivistic" tendencies.'

[2] See the quotation in Toulmin, *op. cit.* 175.

APPENDIX

INDIVISIBILITY AND THE ATOMS

The question whether the atoms of Leucippus and Democritus are only physically indivisible (a-tomic), because of such attributes as solidity and impenetrability, or also logically and mathematically indivisible, has been under lively discussion in recent times. The discussion continues. Professor Gregory Vlastos, in particular, is engaged on a thorough re-examination of the evidence, from which he concludes that the atoms of Democritus are indivisible for physical reasons, but infinitely divisible as portions of the three-dimensional extensive continuum, i.e. if regarded mathematically. The evidence is complicated and sometimes conflicting, and I make no claim to be saying the last word on it. What follows must be read with this proviso.

In the text I have emphasized what was for the Abderites the primary condition that their atoms had to satisfy, namely the Eleatic (and especially Parmenidean) canons of unity. What is one must be free from any possibility of change, not susceptible to addition or subtraction, a plenum, continuous and indivisible. It is a single whole, without parts, on the primitive logical ground that one and many are contradictory attributes which cannot apply to the same thing. Thus whether or not these arguments would satisfy a more mature or mathematically-minded thinker, the atoms were for Leucippus and Democritus without parts, logically as well as physically indivisible, although each was a physical body possessed of a certain magnitude. The infinite divisibility of matter was inconceivable.

The most important evidence is in Aristotle, *GC*, 316 a 14 ff., Democritus's 'point-for-point' reply to the Eleatics.[1] If body is divisible 'through and through' (πάντη), suppose it to be so divided. What is left? A magnitude? No, for if so, it can be further divided. Infinite divisibility

---

[1] So Popper, *Conj. and Ref.* 83; that it does in fact reproduce Democritus's arguments has been frequently shown, first by Hammer-Jensen, *op. cit.* below, 211 ff. Cf. also Alfieri, *Atom. Id.* 57, Luria, *op. cit.* below, 129 f., 135. Doubts are expressed by Mau, *op. cit.* below, 25 f.

therefore implies that magnitudes can come from non-magnitudes (ἐκ μὴ μεγεθῶν μέγεθος εἶναι 316 b 5), which is absurd. (Democritus, we notice, drew from infinite divisibility the same conclusion which Anaxagoras thought would follow from a limit of divisibility, p. 289, n. 2 above.) Moreover Aristotle, who did believe in infinite divisibility, speaks of Democritus's contrary view as 'necessarily in conflict with mathematical science' (*De caelo*, 303 a 20, cf. 271 b 10).

For a fuller treatment of this question, see S. Luria, *Die Infinitesimal-theorie der antiken Atomisten* (*Qu. u. Stud.* 1932, esp. pp. 119–29) and J. Mau, *Problem des Infinitesimalen* (1954, 2nd ed. 1957). The Demo-critean arguments in Aristotle were discussed earlier by I. Hammer-Jensen, *D. und Platon* (*Arch. f. Gesch. d. Phil.* 1909–10). Luria's exposition is brilliant and indispensable, yet the conclusion of his final section, though argued with his usual acumen, cannot be accepted. He supposes that there were two kinds of atom. The one, out of which the physical world is built up, is physically indivisible because of hardness, solidity and so forth, but actually has parts and is therefore mathe-matically divisible. The other is mathematically indivisible because without parts (ἀμερής). 'Atoms' of the first kind (one would surely have to put the word between quotation marks) are divisible into those of the second. This, as Luria agrees, involves assuming a state of things of which neither Aristotle himself nor any later commentators had any apprehension. Even more important is it, I should say, that on this hypothesis the atoms on whose characteristics Leucippus and Demo-critus relied for their proof that a physical universe could be accounted for without contravening the logic of Parmenides, would utterly fail to satisfy that logic.[1]

Luria's final thesis has been denied by Mau (*Problem*, 24–7), who however surprisingly fails to mention Luria's first and most striking piece of evidence.[2] Commenting on Aristotle's criticism that Leucip-

---

[1] It might be thought that they were paying attention here rather to Melissus. The atoms had a certain bulk, and Melissus had said (fr. 9): εἰ ἔχοι πάχος [sc. τὸ ὄν] ἔχοι ἂν μόρια. But we have seen already that it was Parmenides rather than his followers whom they respected. They could not meet Melissus by supposing the atoms to have parts, for then these parts would have to be without magnitude and once again one would have μέγεθος ἐκ μὴ μεγεθῶν.

[2] Presumably he felt excused from doing so on the grounds that 'wenn wir in dieser Frage von Aristoteles abweichen, dann wagen wir uns auf das Gebiet der reinen Konjektur' (p. 24), which at least has the virtue of courage.

Appendix

pus and Democritus neglected to explain the cause and nature of motion, Alexander of Aphrodisias says (*Met.* 35.26ff.):

οὐδὲ γὰρ τὸ πόθεν ἡ βαρύτης ἐν ταῖς ἀτόμοις λέγουσι· τὰ γὰρ ἀμερῆ τὰ ἐπινοούμενα ταῖς ἀτόμοις καὶ μέρη ὄντα αὐτῶν ἀβαρῆ φασιν εἶναι· ἐκ δὲ ἀβαρῶν συγκειμένων πῶς ἂν βάρος γένηται;

Neither do they explain weight in the atoms, for they say that the partless entities which are assumed for the atoms and are parts of them are without weight. Yet how could weight be derived from a combination of entities without weight?

Our lack of the atomists' own writings, and dependence in part on commentators who lived from 500 to 1000 or more years later, must inevitably lead sometimes to almost insoluble difficulties. From what we have already seen, I do not think this can be accepted as a historical statement. Nor can it be supported from the μόρια μὲν ἔχειν of Simplicius, *Phys.* 82.1, since Simplicius himself contradicts this by the ἀμερές of 925.15. (See below for these passages.) The impossibility of producing a weight from weightless parts is advanced by Aristotle against the Pythagoreans (*Metaph.* 1090a30) and Plato (*De caelo*, 299b15), but never against the atomists. In spite of his general good sense, it looks as if Alexander had confused these different (though also in some ways similar) theories of the structure of reality, and our suspicion is confirmed by his immediately following words: 'This is discussed more fully in the third book of the *De caelo*', where in fact Aristotle is criticizing Plato.[1]

Some see a difference between Leucippus and Democritus in the reasons which they alleged for the indivisibility of the atoms. Alfieri (*Atom. Id.* 66) thinks it probable (in spite of Simpl. *Phys.* 925.13, DK 67 A 13: Leucippus and Democritus attributed their indivisibility to impassivity, smallness and lack of parts) that Leucippus alleged only smallness and lack of parts, impassivity (ἀπάθεια) being added by Democritus. Kirk says the same (KR, 408), though in the sole passage which he quotes (from Galen) one would think that οἱ περὶ Λεύκιππον, contrasted as it is with οἱ περὶ Ἐπίκουρον, is poor evidence for separating Leucippus from Democritus. (The view goes back to von Arnim, and has been refuted by Luria, *op. cit.* 125.) Bailey (*Atomists*, 78f.) attributes all three properties to Leucippus, though ἀπάθεια was

[1] Attention was already drawn to this reference by Zeller, ZN, 1068, n. 1.

'elaborated on' by Democritus. Here as always, the touchstone must be the necessity which Leucippus felt to pay heed to Eleatic logic. ἀπάθεια is such an essential characteristic of the One of Parmenides that he is most unlikely to have overlooked it. At Simpl. *Cael.* 242.18 (DK, 67 A 14) and *Phys.* 82.2 (not in DK) it is said to be a necessary consequence of solidity. (So also D.L. 9.44 and Plut. *Adv. Col.* 1111 a, 68 A 57. The testimony obviously comes from Theophrastus, who calls the atom ἀπαθές in *Caus. Plant.* 6.7.2, 68 A 132.) Thus all the Eleatic properties of immutability, continuity, indivisibility and 'fulness' appear closely linked in the atom.

One would like to agree with Mau when he says (*Problem*, 19) that from what we know of Democritus he did not, *any more than his predecessor*, argue the indestructibility of the atoms from their smallness and lack of parts, but only from their solidity and lack of internal void. There does however seem to be evidence that Leucippus thought of smallness as contributing both to the indivisibility and to the general ἀπάθεια of the atoms. Indeed, if one were to suppose any difference between the two, it might lie in this, that Democritus saw the weakness in the argument from smallness and lack of parts. (It was open to Zeno's objection that the atoms would then have no extension at all, and again, so far as size is concerned, to an argument given by Philoponus, *GC*, 175.7, that if the atoms were only indivisible because of their small size, they would not be truly—φύσει—atoms. After all, he says, even those who do not believe in atoms do not carry out division to infinity. They realize that smallness must bring actual division to a halt, but believe that no body is by its nature indivisible: all are potentially divisible to infinity.) Simplicius at *Phys.* 81.34 enumerates three ways in which something may be indivisible. The second and third are: '(2) that which in its own nature cannot be divided, like the point and the unit, (3) that which has indeed parts and magnitude but is impassible owing to solidity and compactness, *like each of the atoms of Democritus.*' Nevertheless in view of the frequency with which both authors of the atomic theory are named together, and the uncertainty whether a mention of Democritus alone includes what he learned from Leucippus, I do not myself think that any of these complicated arguments from isolated sources are very profitable. Simplicius himself, at *Phys.* 925.13 (DK, 67 A 13), cites Democritus as well as

Appendix

Leucippus for the σμικρὸν καὶ ἀμερές of the atoms. Either he was confused, or in the general, exhaustive statement of all conceivable kinds of indivisibility he was *interpreting* the atoms of Democritus as they must appear to a post-Aristoteiian philosopher for whom everything that has magnitude must have parts.[1]

In concluding that for Democritus at least the atoms were both physically and mathematically indivisible, I have not been uninfluenced by the general impression, which has been left on me by the experience of living with his remains for a year or more, of his strongly individual philosophical character. He appears as an atomist through and through, with all the exaggerated faith of a pioneer in the new theory, and it is improbable that he would admit mathematical considerations as an exception to the physical and metaphysical reasons which caused him to postulate atomic magnitudes. He had a mind which naturally saw things in concrete terms, and would not wish to admit any distinction between physical and mathematical modes of being. His apparent disregard of the mathematical science of his time (of which he was certainly not ignorant) was due not so much to more primitive thinking as to his out-and-out materialism. At this period of philosophy the overriding questions were ontological, and the mathematical views of philosophers were not independent of their answers to the great ontological questions. His main concern is with the problem of reconciling the phenomenal world with Parmenidean canons of Being, and his conclusion is that Being—all that is—must be divisible but not infinitely divisible. On this contention his whole philosophy rests. 'The statement that atoms are indivisible is an ontological proposition.'[2] If infinitely divisible magnitudes are admitted in any sense whatever, the atomic philosophy of Being falls apart, since there is no class of mathematical 'beings' distinct from physical. He had learned from Parmenides the lesson of the Pythagorean fallacy. Mathematics could only be an object of 'genuine' as opposed to 'bastard' cognition, and this, we may be sure, reveals nothing but the atomic structure of reality.

---

[1] It occurs to me as a possibility that Simplicius might have misunderstood Aristotle's words at *Phys.* 203 b 1, μεγέθει κατὰ μόρια καὶ σχήματι διαφέρον, as referring to the atoms singly instead of to their common substance which is 'divided quantitatively' into parts which *are* the atoms. His μόρια μὲν ἔχειν καὶ μέγεθος could be an echo of this passage.

[2] Von Weizsäcker, *Relevance of Science*, 62.

BIBLIOGRAPHY

The following list contains full particulars of books or articles mentioned (often with shortened titles) in the text or notes. In addition, a few titles have been included which may be useful for reference although there has not been occasion to mention them in the course of the work.

Source-collections (other than those of individual philosophers) precede the general list. (On the sources of our knowledge of early Greek philosophy see pp. xv–xvi.)

The Greek commentators on Aristotle (most frequently Simplicius and Alexander of Aphrodisias) are referred to in the text by page and line in the appropriate volume of the Berlin Academy's edition (*Commentaria in Aristotelem Graeca*, various dates).

COHEN, M. R. and DRABKIN, I. E. *A Source-book in Greek Science*. New York, 1948 (2nd printing, Cambridge (Mass.), 1958).

DE VOGEL, C. J. *Greek Philosophy: a collection of texts with notes and explanations*. 3 vols., Leiden, 1950–9.

DIELS, H. *Doxographi Graeci*. Berlin, 1879.

DIELS, H. and KRANZ, W. *Die Fragmente der Vorsokratiker* (Greek and German). 6th ed., 3 vols., Berlin, 1951–2 (or later editions; the pagination remains the same).

FREEMAN, K. *Ancilla to the Presocratic Philosophers* (translation of the texts in Diels–Kranz). Oxford (Blackwell), 1948.

KERN, O. *Orphicorum Fragmenta*. Berlin, 1922.

KIRK, G. S. and RAVEN, J. E. *The Presocratic Philosophers*. Cambridge, 1957 (selected texts with translation and commentary).

RITTER, H. and PRELLER, L. *Historia Philosophiae Graecae*. 9th ed., Gotha, 1913 (selection of texts with Latin notes).

WELLMANN, M. *Fragmentsammlung der griechischen Ärzte*, Band I: *Die Fragmente der sikelischen Ärzte Akron, Philistion und des Diokles von Karystos*. Berlin, 1901.

ADAM, J. 'The Doctrine of the Celestial Origin of the Soul from Pindar to Plato', *Cambridge Praelections*, Cambridge, 1906, 27–67.

ALBERTELLI, P. *Gli Eleati: testimonianze e frammenti*. Bari, 1939.

ALFIERI, V. E. *Gli Atomisti: frammenti e testimonianze*. Bari, 1936.

ALFIERI, V. E. *Atomos Idea: l'origine del concetto dell'atomo nel pensiero greco*. Florence, 1953.

ALFIERI, V. E. 'Per la cronologia della scuola di Abdera', *Estudios . . . Mondolfo*, fasc. 1, Tucumán, 1957, pp. 149–67. This appeared also, under the title 'Caratterizzazione e cronologia della scuola di Abdera', as ch. 2 of *Atomos Idea*, Florence, 1953. And a note on p. vii of that work states that it had already been published in substantially the same form in *Riv. crit. di Storia della filos.* 1952.

Bibliography

ALFIERI, V. E. 'L'atomo come principio intelligibile', *Epicurea in memoriam Hectoris Bignone*. Genoa, 1959, 61–8.

ALLAN, D. J. 'The Problem of Cratylus', *AJP*, 1952, 271–87.

ANDRADE, E. N. DA C. *Sir Isaac Newton*. London, 1954.

APELT, O. 'Melissus bei pseudo-Aristoteles', *Jahrbücher für classische Philologie*, 1886, 729–66.

ARNIM, H. VON. 'Die Weltperioden bei Empedokles', *Festschrift Gomperz*, Vienna, 1902, 16–27.

ARUNDEL, M. R. 'Empedocles fr. 35, 12–15', *CR*, 1962, 109–11.

BAEUMKER, C. *Das Problem der Materie in der griechischen Philosophie*. Münster, 1890.

BAILEY, C. *The Greek Atomists and Epicurus*. Oxford, 1928.

BAMBROUGH, J. R. 'Universals and Family Resemblances', *Proceedings of the Aristotelian Society*, 1960–1, 207–22.

BARRON, J. P. 'The Sixth-Century Tyranny at Samos', *CQ*, 1964, 210–29.

BAUER, J. B. 'Μονίη: Empedokles B. 24.4 und 28.3', *Hermes*, 1961, 367–9.

BAYLIS, C. A. 'A Criticism of Lovejoy's Case for Epistemological Dualism', *Philosophy and Phenomenological Research*, 33 (1962–3), 527–37.

BEARE, J. I. *Greek Theories of Elementary Cognition*. Oxford, 1906.

BEAUFRET, J. *Le Poème de Parménide*. Paris, 1955.

BERNAYS, J. *Gesammelte Abhandlungen*, herausgegeben von H. Usener, vol. 1, Berlin, 1885.

BICKNELL, P. J. 'The Fourth Paradox of Zeno (Ar. *Phys.* 293b33–240a18)', *Acta Classica* (Cape Town), 1961, 39–45.

BIDEZ, J. *La Biographie d'Empédocle*. Ghent, 1894.

BIGNONE, E. *Empedocle. Studio critico, traduzione e commento delle testimonianze e dei frammenti*. Turin, 1916.

BLOCH, K. 'Über die Ontologie des Parmenides', *Classica et Medievalia*, 1953, 1–29.

BOLLACK, J. 'Sur deux fragments de Parménide', *REG*, 1957, 56–71.

BOOTH, N. B. 'Were Zenos arguments directed against the Pythagoreans?', *Phronesis*, 1957, 90–103.

BOOTH, N. B. 'Were Zeno's arguments a reply to attacks upon Parmenides?', *Phronesis*, 1957, 1–9.

BOOTH, N. B. 'Zeno's Paradoxes', *JHS*, 1957, ii, 187–201.

BOOTH, N. B. 'Did Melissus believe in incorporeal being?', *AJP*, 1958, 61–5.

BOOTH, N. B. 'Empedocles' Account of Breathing', *JHS*, 1960, 10–15.

BORGEAUD, W. 'Un cas bizarre de tmèse chez Parménide', *Museum Helveticum*, 1955, 277.

BOUCHÉ-LECLERCQ, A. *L'Astrologie Grecque*. Paris, 1899.

BOWRA, C. M. 'The Proem of Parmenides', *CP*, 1937, 97–112.

BRIEGER, A. *Die Urbewegung der Atome bei Leukippos und Demokritos*. Halle, 1884.

BRIEGER, A. 'Demokritos' angebliche Leugnung der Sinneswahrheit', *Hermes*, 1902, 56–83.

Bibliography

BRIEGER, A. 'Die Urbewegung der demokriteischen Atome', *Philologus*, 1904, 584–96.

BROCHARD, V. *Etudes de philosophie ancienne et de philosophie moderne*. Paris, 1926. I (pp. 3–14), 'Les arguments de Zénon d'Élée contre le mouvement'. II (pp. 15–22), 'Les prétendus sophismes de Zénon d'Élée'.

BURKERT, W. *Weisheit und Wissenschaft: Studien zu Pythagoras, Philolaos und Platon*. Nurnberg, 1962.

BURKERT, W. 'Iranisches bei Anaximandros', *Rheinisches Museum*, 1963, 97–134.

BURNET, J. *Greek Philosophy: Part I, Thales to Plato* (all published). London, 1924.

BURNET, J. *Early Greek Philosophy*. 4th ed., London, 1930.

CAJORI, F. 'The History of Zeno's Arguments on Motion', *American Mathematical Monthly*, 1915.

CALOGERO, G. *Studi sul Eleatismo*. Rome, 1932.

CALOGERO, G. 'Parmenides e la genesi della logica classica', *Annali della Scuola Normale Superiore di Pisa*, 1936, 143–85.

CAPEK, M. 'The Theory of Eternal Recurrence', *Journal of Philosophy*, 1960, 289–96.

CAPELLE, W. 'Anaxagoras', *Neue Jahrbücher für das klassische Altertum*, 1919, 81–102 and 169–98.

CAPELLE, W. 'Farbenbezeichnungen bei Theophrast', *Rheinisches Museum*, 1958, 1–51.

CARDINI, M. TIMPANARO. 'Respirazione e la clessidra', *Parola del Passato*, 1957, 250–70.

CARDINI, M. TIMPANARO. 'La clessidra di Empedocle e l'esperienza di Torricelli', *Convegno di Studi Torricelliani*, Faenza, 1958, 151–6.

CARDINI, M. TIMPANARO. 'La zoogonia di Empedocle e la critica aristotelica', *Physis*, 1960, 5–13.

CASSIRER, H. *Aristoteles' Schrift 'Von der Seele' und ihre Stellung innerhalb der aristotelischen Philosophie*. Tübingen, 1932.

CATAUDELLA, Q. 'Empedoclea', *Rivista di filologia*, 1960, 124–32.

CHADWICK, N. K. *Poetry and Prophecy*. Cambridge, 1942.

CHALMERS, W. R. 'Parmenides and the Beliefs of Mortals', *Phronesis*, 1960, 5–22.

CHAPPELL, V. C. 'Time and Zeno's Arrow', *Journal of Philosophy*, 1962, 197–213.

CHERNISS, H. *Aristotle's Criticism of Presocratic Philosophy*. Baltimore, 1935.

CHERNISS, H. 'Aristotle, *Metaphysics* 987 A 32–B 7', *AJP*, 1955, 184–6.

CLASSEN, C. J. 'The Study of Language amongst Socrates' Contemporaries', *Proceedings of the African Classical Associations*, 1959, 33–49.

CLEVE, F. M. *The Philosophy of Anaxagoras*. New York, 1949.

CORNFORD, F. M. 'Mystery Religions and Pre-Socratic Philosophy', *Cambridge Ancient History* IV, 1926, 522–78.

CORNFORD, F. M. 'Anaxagoras' Theory of Matter', *CQ*, 1930, 14–30 and 83–95.

CORNFORD, F. M. 'Parmenides' Two Ways', *CQ*, 1933, 97–111.

CORNFORD, F. M. *Plato's Theory of Knowledge*. London, 1935 (repr. 1949).

Bibliography

CORNFORD, F. M. 'The Invention of Space', *Essays in Honour of Gilbert Murray*. London, 1936, 215–35.

CORNFORD, F. M. 'Innumerable Worlds in Presocratic Cosmogony', *CQ*, 1934, 1–16.

CORNFORD, F. M. *Plato's Cosmology*. London, 1937 (repr. 1948).

CORNFORD, F. M. *Plato and Parmenides*. London, 1939 (repr. 1950).

CORNFORD, F. M. *Principium Sapientiae: the origins of Greek philosophical thought*. Cambridge, 1952.

CORNFORD, F. M. *Before and After Socrates*. Cambridge, 1932 (repr. 1950).

COVOTTI, A. 'Melissi Samii reliquiae', *Studi italiani di filogia classica*, 1898, 213–27.

COXON, A. H. 'The Philosophy of Parmenides', *CQ*, 1934, 134–44.

CROISSANT, J. 'La δόξα de Parménide', *Mélanges Desrousseaux*, 1937, 99–104.

DAHLMANN, H. J. *De philosophorum graecorum sententiis ad loquellae originem pertinentibus capita duo*. Diss. Leipzig, 1928.

DAVISON, J. A. 'Protagoras, Democritus, and Anaxagoras', *CQ*, 1953, 33–45.

DEICHGRÄBER, K. *Hippocrates über Entstehung und Aufbau des menschlichen Körpers*. Leipzig, 1935.

DEICHGRÄBER, K. 'Parmenides' Auffahrt zur Göttin des Rechts: Untersuchung zum Prooimion seines Lehrgedichtes', *Abhandlungen der Akademie Mainz, Geistes– und sozialwissenschaftliche Klasse*, 1958, no. 11, Wiesbaden, 1959.

DELATTE, A. *Les Conceptions de l'enthousiasme chez les philosophes présocratiques*. Paris, 1934.

DE SANTILLANA, G. 'Prologue to Parmenides', University of Cincinnati, 1964.

DIEHL, E. *Anthologia Lyrica Graeca*, 3rd ed., fasc. 1, Leipzig, 1949. (Published after Diehl's death by R. Beutler.)

DIELS, H. 'Gorgias und Empedokles', *Sitzungsberichte der preussischen Akademie* (SBB), 1884, 343–68.

DIELS, H. 'Leukippos und Diogenes von Apollonia', *Rheinisches Museum*, 1887, 1–14.

DIELS, H. 'Über die Excerpte von Menons Iatrika in dem Londoner Papyrus 137', *Hermes*, 1893, 407–34.

DIELS, H. *Parmenides' Lehrgedicht, griechisch und deutsch*. Berlin, 1897.

DIELS, H. 'Über die Gedichte des Empedokles', *Sitzungsberichte der preussischen Akademie* (SBB), 1898, 396–415.

DIELS, H. 'Die Anfänge der Philologie bei den Griechen', *Neue Jahrbücher für das klassische Altertum*, 1910, 1–25.

DIÈS, A. *Le Cycle mystique*. Paris, 1909.

DIETERICH, A. *Kleine Schriften*. Leipzig and Berlin, 1890.

DIETERICH, A. *Nekyia. Beiträge zur Erklärung der neuentdeckten Petrusapokalypse*. Leipzig, 1893.

DILLER, H. ὄψις ἀδήλων τὰ φαινόμενα, *Hermes*, 1932, 14–42.

DILLER, H. 'Die philosophiegeschichtliche Stellung des Diogenes von Apollonia', *Hermes*, 1941, 359–81.

DODDS, E. R. *The Greeks and the Irrational*. California Univ. Press, 1951.

Bibliography

DREYER, A. *History of the Planetary Systems from Thales to Kepler*. Cambridge, 1906.

DÜMMLER, F. *Akademika: Beiträge zur Literaturgeschichte der sokratischen Schulen*. Giessen, 1889.

DYROFF, A. *Demokritstudien*. Munich, 1899.

EISLER, R. 'Babylonische Astrologenausdrücke bei Demokritos', *Archiv für Geschichte der Philosophie*, 1918, 52–4.

ELIADE, M. *Shamanism: Archaic Techniques of Ecstasy*. English ed., revised. London, 1964.

ERFFA, C. E. VON. Αἰδώς *und verwandte Begriffe von Homer bis Demokritos*. Diss. Leipzig, 1937. (Philologus, *Suppl.* 30, 2.)

FARRINGTON, B. *Greek Science*. London (Penguin Books), 2 vols., 1944 (repr. 1949).

FRANCOTTE, A. 'Les disertes juments de Parménide', *Phronesis*, 1958, 83–94.

FRANK, E. *Plato und die sogenannten Pythagoreer*. Halle, 1923.

FRÄNKEL, H. 'Homerische Wörter', *Antidoron (Festschrift Wackernagel)*, Göttingen, 1923, 274–82.

FRÄNKEL, H. 'Zeno of Elea's Attacks on Plurality', *AJP*, 1942, I. 1–25, II. 193–206. (Revised version in German in *Wege und Formen*, 198–236.)

FREDRICH, K. *Hippokratische Untersuchungen*. Berlin, 1899.

FREEMAN, E. A. *A History of Sicily from the Earliest Times*. 4 vols., Oxford, 1891–4.

FREGE, G. 'About the Law of Inertia', translated by R. Rand, *Synthèse*, 1961, 350–63.

FRENKIAN, A. 'Theophrast, *De Sensu*, Kap. 10', *Philologus*, 1963, 313.

FRITZ, K. VON. *Pythagorean Politics in South Italy: an analysis of the sources*. New York, 1940.

FRITZ, K. VON. 'νοῦς, νοεῖν and their derivatives in Homer', *CP*, 1943, 79–93.

FRITZ, K. VON. *Philosophie und sprachliche Ausdruck bei Demokritos, Platon und Aristoteles*. New York, n.d. (1939).

FRITZ, K. VON. 'Pythagoras', *RE* XXIV (1963), 171–209.

FUCHS, W. 'Zu den Metopen des Heraion von Selinus', *Mitteilungen des Deutschen Archäologischen Instituts (Römische Abteilung)*, 1956, 102–21.

FURLEY, D. J. 'Empedocles and the Clepsydra', *JHS*, 1957 (i), 31–4.

GADAMER, H.-G. 'Retraktationen zum Lehrgedicht des Parmenides', *Varia Variorum (Festschrift* for Reinhardt). Munster/Cologne, 1952, 58–68.

GAYE, R. K. 'On Aristotle *Physics* Z ix 239b33–240a18. (Zeno's Fourth Argument against Motion.)', *Journal of Philology*, 1908, 95–116.

GERSHENSON, D. E. and GREENBERG, D. A. 'Melissus of Samos in a New Light: Aristotle's *Physics* 186a10–16', *Phronesis*, 1961, 1–9.

GIGON, O. 'Zu Anaxagoras', *Philologus* 91 (1936–7), 1–41.

GILBERT, O. *Die meteorologischen Theorien des griechischen Altertums*. Leipzig, 1907.

Bibliography

GILBERT, O. 'Ionier und Eleaten', *Rheinisches Museum*, 1909, 185–201.

GILBERT, O. *Griechische Religionsphilosophie*. Leipzig, 1911.

GOMPERZ, H. "Ασώματος', *Hermes*, 1932, 155–67.

GOMPERZ, T. *Greek Thinkers: a history of ancient philosophy*. 4 vols., London, 1901–12 (vol. I transl. L. Magnus, vols. II–IV transl. G. G. Berry).

GOODFIELD, J. *See* TOULMIN, S.

GOODWIN, W. W. *Syntax of Moods and Tenses of the Greek Verb*. London, 1897.

GRAHAM, J. W. *See* ROBINSON, D. M.

GREENBERG, D. A. *See* GERSHENSON, D. E.

GREENE, W. C. *Moira: fate, good and evil in Greek thought*. Harvard Univ. Press, 1944. Repr. New York and Evanston, 1963.

GRONINGEN, B. A. VAN. 'Trois notes sur Empédocle', *Mnemosyne*, 1956, 221–4.

GRUBE, G. M. A. *Plato's Thought*. London, 1935 (repr. 1958).

GRUPPE, O. *Die rhapsodische Theogonie und ihre Bedeutung innerhalb der orphischen Litteratur. XVII. Supplementband des Jahrbuchs für classische Philologie*, 1890.

GUNDERSON, K. 'Descartes, La Mettrie, Language and Machines', *Philosophy*, 1964, 193–222.

GUTHRIE, W. K. C. *The Greeks and their Gods*. London, 1950/54.

GUTHRIE, W. K. C. *Orpheus and Greek Religion*, corrected ed., London, 1952.

GUTHRIE, W. K. C. 'The Presocratic World-Picture', *Harvard Theological Review*, 1952, 87–104.

GUTHRIE, W. K. C. 'Aristotle as a Historian of Philosophy', *JHS*, 1957 (i), 35–41.

GUTHRIE, W. K. C. *In the Beginning: some Greek views on the origins of life and the early state of man*. Methuen, 1957.

GUTHRIE, W. K. C. Review of Spoerri, *Späthellenistische Berichte*, *Göttingische Gelehrte Anzeigen*, 1963, 69–73.

HAAS, A. E. 'Antike Lichttheorien', *Archiv für Geschichte der Philosophie*, 1907, 345–86.

HAMLYN, D. W. *Sensation and Perception*. London, 1957.

HAMMER-JENSEN, I. 'Demokritos und Platon', *Archiv für Geschichte der Philosophie*, 1910, 92–105 and 211–29.

HAMMER-JENSEN, I. 'Pseudo-Demokrit', *RE Suppl.* IV (1924), 219–23.

HASSE, H. and SCHOLZ, H. *Die Grundlagenkrisis der griechischen Mathematik*. Berlin, 1928.

HAVELOCK, E. A. 'Parmenides and Odysseus', *HSCP*, 1958, 133–43.

HAVELOCK, E. A. *Preface to Plato*. Oxford (Blackwell), 1963.

HEAD, B. V. *Coins of Ancient Sicily*. London, 1903.

HEAD, B. V. *Historia Numorum, a Manual of Greek Numismatics*, new and enlarged edition. Oxford, 1911.

HEAD, B. V. (based on the work of). *A Guide to the Principal Coins of the Greeks, from c. 700 B.C. to A.D. 260*. London (British Museum), 1932.

HEATH, T. L. *Aristarchus of Samos, the Ancient Copernicus: a history of Greek astronomy to Aristarchus together with Aristarchus's treatise on the sizes and distances of the sun and moon*. Oxford, 1913.

Bibliography

HEATH, T. L. *A History of Greek Mathematics.* 2 vols., Oxford, 1921.

HEATH, T. L. *Mathematics in Aristotle.* Oxford, 1949.

HEIDEL, W. A. 'The Pythagoreans and Greek Mathematics', *AJP*, 1940, 1–33.

HEIDEL, W. A. 'περὶ φύσεως: a study of the conception of nature among the Pre-Socratics', *Proceedings of the American Academy*, 1910, 77–133.

HEIDEL, W. A. 'On certain fragments of the Pre-Socratics', *Proceedings of the American Academy of Arts and Sciences*, 1913, 681–734.

HEIDEL, W. A. *The Frame of the Ancient Greek Maps, with a Discussion of the Discovery of the Sphericity of the Earth.* New York, 1937. (American Geographical Society, Research Series, no. 20.)

HEINIMANN, F. *Nomos und Physis.* Basel, 1945.

HEISENBERG, W. *Philosophical Problems of Nuclear Science*, transl. Hayes. London, 1952.

HEISENBERG, W. *The Physicist's Conception of Nature*, transl. A. J. Pomerans. London, 1958.

HEISENBERG, W. (With Born, Schrödinger, Auger.) *On Modern Physics*, transl. Goodman and Binns. London, 1961.

HERTER, H. 'Die kulturhistorische Theorie der hippokratischen Schrift von der alten Medizin', *Maia*, 1963, 464–83.

HÖLSCHER, U. 'Grammatisches zu Parmenides', *Hermes*, 1956, 385–97.

HORNE, R. A. 'Atomism in Ancient Greece and India', *Ambix*, 1960, 98–110.

HÜFFMEIER, F. 'Teleologische Weltbetrachtung bei Diogenes von Apollonia?', *Philologus*, 1963, 131–8.

JACOBY, F. *Apollodors Chronik, Sammlung der Fragmente.* Berlin, 1902.

JACOBY, F. 'Some Remarks on Ion of Chios', *CQ*, 1947, 1–17.

JAEGER, W. *Paideia: the ideals of Greek culture*, transl. G. Highet. 3 vols., Oxford, 1939–45 (vol. 1, 2nd ed.).

JAEGER, W. *The Theology of the Early Greek Philosophers.* Oxford, 1947.

JAEGER, W. *Diokles von Karystos: die griechische Medizin und die Schule des Aristoteles.* Berlin, 1938.

JAEGER, W. *Aristotle, Fundamentals of the History of his Development.* 2nd ed., Oxford, 1948.

JAMESON, G. J. '"Well-rounded Truth" and Circular Thought in Parmenides', *Phronesis*, 1958, 15–30.

JONES, W. H. S. *The Medical Writings of Anonymus Londinensis.* Cambridge, 1947..

KAHN, C. H. 'Anaximander and the Arguments concerning the ἄπειρον at *Phys.* 203b14–15', *Festschrift Ernst Kapp*, Hamburg, 1958, 19–29.

KAHN, C. H. 'Religion and Natural Philosophy in Empedocles' Doctrine of the Soul', *Archiv für Geschichte der Philosophie*, 1960, 3–35.

KAPP, E. Review of Langerbeck's Δόξις ἐπιρρυσμίη in *Gnomon*, 1936, 65–77 and 158–69.

KARSTEN, S. *Empedoclis Agrigentini carminum reliquiae.* Amsterdam, 1838.

KARSTEN, S. *Parmenidis Eleatae carminis reliquiae.* Amsterdam, 1835.

Bibliography

KERN, O. *De Orphei Pherecydis Epimenidis theogoniis quaestiones criticae*. Berlin, 1888.

KERN, O. *Die Religion der Griechen*. Berlin, I. Band, 1926, II. Band, 1935.

KERSCHENSTEINER, J. 'Zu Leukippos A I', *Hermes*, 1959, 441–8.

KERSCHENSTEINER, J. *Kosmos: quellenkritische Untersuchungen zu den Vorsokratikern*. Munich, 1962.

KIRK, G. S. 'The Problem of Cratylus', *AJP*, 1951, 225–53.

KIRK, G. S. and STOKES, M. C. 'Parmenides' Refutation of Motion', *Phronesis*, 1960, 1–4.

KNATZ, F. 'Empedoclea', *Schedae...Usener...oblatae*, Bonn, 1891, 1–9.

KNIGHT, T. S. 'Parmenides and the Void', *Philosophy and Phenomenological Research*, 19 (1958–9), 524–8.

KRAMER, S. N. (ed.). *Mythologies of the Ancient World*. Chicago, 1961.

KRANZ, W. 'Empedocles und die Atomistik', *Hermes*, 1912, 18–42.

KRANZ, W. 'Die ältesten Farbenlehren der Griechen', *Hermes*, 1912, 126–40.

KRANZ, W. 'Über Aufbau und Bedeutung des parmenideischen Gedichts', *Sitzungsberichte des königlichen preussischen Akademie der Wissenschaften*, 1916, 1158–76.

KRANZ, W. 'Vorsokratisches I und II', *Hermes*, 1934, 114–19 and 226–8.

KRANZ, W. 'Die Katharmoi und die Physika des Empedokles', *Hermes*, 1935, 111–19.

KRANZ, W. 'Kosmos und Mensch in der Vorstellung frühen Griechentums', *Nachrichten von der Gesellschaft der Wissenschaften zu Göttingen*, Ph.-hist. Kl., 1938, 121–61.

KRANZ, W. 'Kosmos als philosophischer Begriff frühgriechischer Zeit', *Philologus*, 1938, 430–48.

KRANZ, W. *Empedokles: antike Gestalt und romantische Neuschöpfung*. Zürich, 1949.

KRANZ, W. 'Zwei kosmologische Fragen', *Rheinisches Museum*, 1957, 114–29.

KRANZ, W. 'Die Sonne als Titan', *Philologus*, 1961, 290–5.

'KÜHNER–GERTH.' R. Kühner, *Ausführliche Grammatik der griechischen Sprache*, 3rd ed. by F. Blass and B. Gerth. Two parts in 4 vols., 1890–1904.

KULLMANN, W. 'Zeno und die Lehre des Parmenides', *Hermes*, 1958, 157–72.

LÄMMLI, F. *Vom Chaos zum Kosmos: zur Geschichte einer Idee*. Basel, 1962.

LAN, C. E. 'Die ὁδὸς πολύφημος der parmenideischen Wahrheit', *Hermes*, 1960, 376–9.

LANGERBECK, H. Δόξις ἐπιρρυσμίη: *Studien zu Demokrits Ethik und Erkenntnislehre*. Berlin, 1935.

LAST, H. 'Empedocles and his Clepsydra Again', *CQ*, 1924, 169–73.

LAUE, H. *De Democriti fragmentis ethicis*. Göttingen, 1921.

LEE, H. D. P. *Zeno of Elea*. Cambridge, 1936.

LEON, P. 'The Homoeomeries of Anaxagoras', *CQ*, 1927, 133–41.

LESKY, E. *Die Zeugungs- und Vererbungslehren der Antike und ihr Nachwirken*. *Akademie der Wissenschaften und der Literatur in Mainz, Abhandlungen der geistes- und sozialwissenschaftlichen Klasse*, Wiesbaden, 1950, no. 19, 1225–1425.

Bibliography

Lexikon des frühgriechischen Epos, unter Leitung von Prof. Dr. B. SNELL und Dr. U. FLEISCHER. Verantwörtlicher Redaktor Prof. Dr. J. H. METTE. Göttingen (in progress).

LIEPMANN, H. C. *Mechanik der Leukippisch-Demokriteischen Atome.* Leipzig, 1886.

LLOYD, G. E. R. 'Right and Left in Greek Philosophy', *JHS*, 1962, 56–66.

LLOYD, G. E. R. 'Who is attacked in *On Ancient Medicine?*', *Phronesis*, 1963, 108–26.

LOBECK, C. A. *Aglaophamus sive de theologiae mysticae Graecorum causis.* 2 vols., Koenigsberg, 1829.

LOENEN, J. H. M. M. *Parmenides, Melissus, Gorgias. A Reinterpretation of Eleatic Philosophy.* Assen, 1959.

LOEW, E. 'Die Ausdrücke φρονεῖν und νοεῖν bei den Vorsokratikern: I. Bei Heraklit und bei Parmenides', *Philologische Wochenschrift*, 1929, 426–9.

LOMMATZSCH, S. *Die Weisheit des Empedokles.* Berlin, 1830.

LONG, A. A. 'The Principles of Parmenides' Cosmogony', *Phronesis*, 1963, 90–107.

LONG, H. S. 'The Unity of Empedocles' Thought', *AJP*, 1949, 142–58.

LOVEJOY, A. O. 'The meaning of φύσις in the Greek physiologers', *Philosophical Review*, 1909, 369–83.

LÖWENHEIM, L. *Die Wissenschaft Demokrits und ihr Einfluss auf die moderne Wissenschaft.* Berlin, 1914.

LURIA, S. 'Die Infinitesimaltheorie der antiken Atomisten', *Quellen und Studien zur Geschichte der Mathematik*, Abteilung B, Band 2, Heft 2, 1932, 106–85.

LURIA, S. *Anfänge griechischen Denkens.* Berlin, 1963.

MAASS, E. *Orpheus: Untersuchungen zur griechischen römischen altchristlichen Jenseitsdichtung und Religion.* Munich, 1895.

McDIARMID, J. B. 'Theophrastus on the Presocratic Causes', *Harvard Studies in Classical Philology*, 1953, 1–156.

McDIARMID, J. B. 'Phantoms in Democritean Terminology', *Hermes*, 1958, 291–8.

McDIARMID, J. B. 'Theophrastus *De sensibus* 61–62: Democritus' Theory of Weight', *CP*, 1960, 28–30.

McGIBBON, D. 'Pleasure as the "criterion" in Democritus', *Phronesis*, 1960, 75–7.

MANSFELD, J. *Die Offenbarung des Parmenides und die menschliche Welt.* Assen, 1964.

MATHEWSON, R. 'Aristotle and Anaxagoras: an examination of F. M. Cornford's interpretation', *CQ*, 1958, 67–81.

MATSON, W. I. 'Democritus, Fragment 156', *CQ*, 1963, 26–9.

MAU, J. *Zum Problem des Infinitesimalen bei den antiken Atomisten.* Berlin, 2nd ed., 1957.

MELSEN, A. G. VAN. *From Atomos to Atom: the History of the Concept Atom,* transl. H. J. Koren. Pittsburgh, 1952.

MENSCHING, E. *Favorinus von Arelate: der erste Teil der Fragmente.* Berlin, 1963.

MERKELBACH, R. 'Eine orphische Unterweltsbeschreibung auf Papyrus', *Museum Helveticum*, 1951, 1–11.

MEULI, K. 'Scythica', *Hermes*, 1935, 121–76.

Bibliography

MILLER, H. W. 'The Concept of the Divine in *De Morbo Sacro*', *TAPA*, 1953, 1–15.

MILLERD, C. E. *On the Interpretation of Empedocles*. Chicago, 1908.

MINAR, E. L. Jr. 'Parmenides and the World of Seeming', *AJP*, 1949, 41–53.

MINAR, E. L. Jr. 'Cosmic Periods in the Philosophy of Empedocles', *Phronesis*, 1963, 127–45.

MONDOLFO, R. *See also* ZELLER–MONDOLFO.

MONDOLFO, R. *L'Infinito nel pensiero dei Greci*. Florence, 1934; 2nd enlarged edition, under the title *L'Infinito nel pensiero dell'antichità classica*, 1956.

MONTERO, F. 'El pensar en la doctrina de Parmenides', *Rivista di Filosofia*, 1958, 349–61.

MOORE, C. A. *See* RADHAKRISHNAN, S.

MOORHOUSE, A. C. 'Δέν in Classical Greek', *CQ*, 1962, 235–8.

MOORHOUSE, A. C. 'The Origin and Use of ὁ, ἡ, τὸ δεῖνα', *CQ*, 1963, 19–25.

MORRISON, J. S. 'The Place of Protagoras in Athenian Public Life', *CQ*, 1941, 1–16.

MORRISON, J. S. 'Parmenides and Er', *JHS*, 1955, 59–68.

MUGLER, C. 'Sur quelques fragments d'Empédocle', *Revue de Philologie*, 1951, 33–65.

MUGLER, C. *Devenir cyclique et pluralité des mondes*. Paris, 1953.

MUGLER, C. 'Le problème d'Anaxagore', *REG*, 1956, 314–76.

MUGLER, C. 'Sur l'histoire de quelques définitions de la géométrie grecque et les rapports entre la géométrie et l'optique', *L'Antiquité Classique*, 1958, 76–91.

MUGLER, C. 'Les théories de la vie et la conscience chez Démocrite', *Revue de Philologie*, 1959, 8–38.

MUGLER, C. 'L'invisibilité des atomes', *REG*, 1963, 397–403.

MUNDING, H. 'Zur Beweisführung des Empedokles', *Hermes*, 1954, 129–45.

NATORP, P. 'Diogenes und Leukippos', *Rheinisches Museum*, 1887, 374–86.

NATORP, P. *Die Ethika des Demokritos: Text und Untersuchung*. Marburg, 1893.

NEEDHAM, J. *Science and Civilisation in China*. Cambridge, 1954–. (In progress.)

NELSON, J. O. 'Zeno's Paradoxes on Motion', *Review of Metaphysics*, 16 (1962–3), 486–90.

NICOL, A. T. (Mrs MARKWICK). 'Indivisible Lines', *CQ*, 1936, 120–6.

NILSSON, M. P. *Griechische Feste von religiöser Bedeutung mit Ausschluss der attischen*. Leipzig, 1906.

O'BRIEN, D. 'Empedocles, fr. 35, 14–15', *CR*, 1965, 1–4.

ONIANS, R. B. *Origins of European Thought*. Cambridge, 1951.

OWEN, G. E. L. 'Zeno and the Mathematicians', *Proceedings of the Aristotelian Society*, 1957–8, 199–222.

OWEN, G. E. L. 'Eleatic Questions', *CQ*, 1960, 84–102.

PANETH, F. A. 'The Epistemological Status of the Chemical Concept of Element', Part II, *British Journal for the Philosophy of Science*, 13 (1962–3), 144–60.

PANZERBIETER, F. *Beiträge zur Kritik und Erläuterung des Empedokles*. Weinigen, 1844.

PATIN, A. 'Parmenides im Kampf gegen Heraklit', *Jahrbücher für classische Philologie*, 25. Supplementband, 1889, 489–660.

Bibliography

PECK, A. L. 'Anaxagoras: Predication as a Problem in Physics', *CQ*, 1931, 27–37 and 112–20.

PFLIGERSDORFFER, G. *Studien zu Poseidonios.* Vienna, 1959. (*Sitzungsberichte der österreichischen Akademie*, 232.5.)

PFUHL, E. *Malerei und Zeichnung der Griechen.* 2 vols., Munich, 1923.

PHILIP, J. A. 'Parmenides' Theory of Knowledge', *Phoenix*, 1958, 63–6.

PHILIPPSON, R. Review of Dahlmann, *De philosophorum graecorum sententiis ad loquellae originem pertinentibus*, in *Philologische Wochenschrift*, 1929, 666–76.

PHILIPPSON, R. Review of Bailey, *The Greek Atomists and Epicurus*, in *Gnomon*, 1930, 460–73.

PLANCK, M. *The Philosophy of Physics.* London, 1936.

POHLENZ, M. 'Nomos und Physis', *Hermes*, 1953, 418–38.

POHLENZ, M. *Hippokrates und die Begründung der wissenschaftlichen Medizin.* Berlin, 1938.

POPPER, K. R. 'The Nature of Philosophical Problems and their Roots in Science', *British Journal for the Philosophy of Science* (1952–3), 124–56.

POPPER, K. R. *Conjectures and Refutations: the Growth of Scientific Knowledge.* London, 1963.

POWELL, J. U. 'The Simile of the Clepsydra in Empedocles', *CQ*, 1923, 172–4.

PRANTL, C. *Aristoteles über die Farben, erläutert durch eine Übersicht der Farbenlehre der Alten.* Munich, 1849.

PRITCHETT, W. R. 'The Attic Stelai, Part II', *Hesperia*, 1956, 178–317.

QUAN, S. 'The Solution of the Achilles Paradox', *Review of Metaphysics*, 16 (1962–3), 473–85.

RADHAKRISHNAN, S. and MOORE, C. A. *A Source Book in Indian Philosophy.* Princeton and Oxford, 1956.

RADLOFF, W. *Aus Sibirien: lose Blätter aus dem Tagebuch eines reisenden Linguisten.* Leipzig, 1885. (The chapter on 'Das Schamanentum und sein Kultus' was also printed separately.)

RANULF, S. *Der eleatische Satz vom Widerspruch.* Copenhagen, 1924.

RATHMANN, W. *Quaestiones Pythagoreae Orphicae Empedocleae.* Diss. Halle, 1933.

RAVEN, J. E. *Pythagoreans and Eleatics.* Cambridge, 1948.

RAVEN, J. E. 'The Basis of Anaxagoras's Cosmogony', *CQ*, 1954, 123–37.

REESOR, M. E. 'The Meaning of Anaxagoras', *CP*, 1960, 1–8.

REESOR, M. E. 'The Problem of Anaxagoras', *CP*, 1963, 29–33.

REICH, K. 'Anaximander und Parmenides', *Marburger Winckelmann-Programm*, 1950–1, 13–16.

REICH, K. 'Parmenides und die Pythagoreer', *Hermes*, 1954, 287–94.

REICHE, H. A. T. *Empedocles' Mixture, Eudoxan Astronomy, and Aristotle's Connate Pneuma.* Amsterdam, 1960.

REINHARDT, K. 'Hekataios von Abdera und Demokrit', *Hermes*, 1912, 492–513.

REINHARDT, K. *Poseidonios.* Munich, 1921.

REINHARDT, K. 'Empedokles, Orphiker und Physiker', *CP*, 1950, 172–7.

Bibliography

REINHARDT, K. *Parmenides und die Geschichte der griechischen Philosophie*. 2nd ed., Frankfurt-a.-M., 1959. (1st ed., Bonn, 1916.)

RENAN, E. *Mélanges d'histoire et de voyages*. Paris, 1878.

RIEZLER, K. *Parmenides*. Frankfurt, 1934.

RITCHIE, A. D. 'Why Achilles does not fail to catch the tortoise', *Mind*, 1946, 310.

ROBIN, L. *Greek Thought*, transl. M. R. Dobie. London, 1928.

ROBINSON, D. M. *Excavations at Olynthus, Part X, Metal and Minor Miscellaneous Finds*. Baltimore, 1941.

ROBINSON, D. M. and GRAHAM, J. W. *Excavations at Olynthus, Part VIII, The Hellenic House*. Baltimore, 1938.

ROHDE, E. *Psyche: The cult of souls and belief in immortality among the Greeks*, transl. W. B. Hillis. London, 1925.

ROSCHER, W. H. *Ausführliches Lexikon der griechischen und römischen Mythologie*. 6 vols. with 4 supplements, Leipzig, 1884–1937.

ROSCHER, W. H. *Die hippokratische Schrift von der Siebenzahl in ihrer vierfachen Überlieferung*, Paderborn, 1913.

ROSE, H. J. 'The Ancient Grief. A study of Pindar, Fr. 133 (Bergk)', *Greek Poetry and Life*, Oxford, 1936, 79–96.

ROSE, H. J. 'The Grief of Persephone', *Harvard Theological Review*, 1943, 247–50.

ROSS, W. D. Aristotle's *Physics* (ed.). Oxford, 1936. (Pp. 71–85, 'The Paradoxes of Zeno'.)

ROSTAGNI, A. *Il verbo di Pitagora*. Turin, 1924.

RUSSELL, B. *Our Knowledge of the External World*. London, 2nd ed., 1926.

SAMBURSKY, S. *The Physical World of the Greeks*. London, 1956.

SAMBURSKY, S. *Physics of the Stoics*. London, 1959.

SAMBURSKY, S. 'Conceptual Developments in Greek Atomism', *Archives internationales d'Histoire des Sciences*, 1959, 251–61.

SAMBURSKY, S. 'Atomism versus Continuum Theory in Ancient Greece', *Scientia*, 1961, 376–81.

SCHMID, W. 'Der Ausgang der altionischen Naturphilosophie: die Atomistik', ch. VIII of Schmid–Stählin, *Geschichte der griechischen Literatur*, I. Teil, 5. Band, 2. Hälfte, 2. Abschnitt, Munich, 1948, pp. 224–349.

SCHOLZ, H. *See* HASSE, H.

SCHOTTLAENDER, R. 'Drei vorsokratische Topoi', *Hermes*, 1927, 435–46.

SCHRAMM, M. *Die Bedeutung der Bewegungslehre des Aristoteles für seine beiden Lösungen der zenonischen Paradoxie*. Frankfurt-a. M., 1962. (See criticisms by P. Merlan in *Isis*, 1963, 299f. and D. W. Hamlyn in *CR*, 1963, 287f.)

SCHULTZ, W. *Farbenempfindungssystem der Hellenen*. Leipzig, 1904.

SCHUMACHER, J. *Antike Medizin: die naturphilosophischen Grundlagen der Medizin in der griechischen Antike*. Berlin, 2nd ed., 1963.

SCHWABL, H. 'Sein und Doxa bei Parmenides', *Wiener Studien*, 1953, 50–75.

SCHWABL, H. 'Forschungsbericht, Parmenides, I. 1939–1955', *Anzeiger für die Altertumswissenschaft*, 1956, 129–56. (Also 'Nachtrag zu Parmenides', 214–24.)

Bibliography

SCHWABL, H. 'Zur "Theogonie" bei Parmenides und Empedokles', *Wiener Studien*, 1957, 278–89.

SCHWABL, H. 'Hesiod und Parmenides: zur Formung des parmenideischen Prooimions', *Rheinisches Museum*, 1963, 134–42.

SIEGEL, R. E. 'The Paradoxes of Zeno: some similarities between ancient Greek and modern thought', *Janus*, 1959, 24–47.

SIEGEL, R. E. 'Parmenides and the Void', *Philosophy and Phenomenological Research*, 22 (1961–2), 264–6. (Reply to T. S. Knight, *q.v.*)

SNELL, B. *The Discovery of the Mind: the Greek Origins of European Thought*. Oxford (Blackwell), 1953. (A third ed. in German, published in 1955, contains several additional chapters.)

SOLMSEN, F. Review of Fränkel, *Parmenidesstudien*, *Gnomon*, 1931, 474–81.

SOLMSEN, F. 'Aristotle and Presocratic Cosmogony', *HSCP*, 63 (1958), 265–82.

SOLMSEN, F. *Aristotle's System of the Physical World*. Cornell Univ. Press, 1960.

SOLMSEN, F. 'Anaxagoras B 19', *Hermes*, 1963, 251–2.

SOLMSEN, F. 'Nature as Craftsman in Greek Thought', *JHI*, 1963, 473–96.

SOUILHÉ, J. 'L'énigme d'Empédocle', *Archives de Philosophie*, 1932, 337–59.

SPENGEL, L. *Eudemi Rhodii fragmenta quae supersunt*. London and Edinburgh, 1866.

SPOERRI, W. *Späthellenistische Berichte über Welt, Kultur und Götter: Untersuchungen zu Diodor von Sizilien*. Basel, 1959.

SPRAGUE, R. K. 'Parmenides: a suggested rearrangement of fragments in the "Way of Truth"', *CP*, 1955, 124–6.

STEIN, E. *Empedoclis Agrigentini Fragmenta*. Bonn, 1852.

STEINTHAL, H. *Geschichte der Sprachwissenschaft bei den Griechen und Römern* I. 2nd ed., Berlin, 1890.

STELLA, L. A. 'Intorno alla cronologia di Democrito', *Rivista di filologia e d'istruzione classica*, 1942, 21–46.

STELLA, L. A. 'Valore e posizione dell'etica di Democrito', *Sophia*, 1942, 207–58.

STEWART, Z. 'Democritus and the Cynics', *HSCP*, 63 (1958), 179–91.

STOKES, M. C. 'Parmenides, fr. 16', *CR*, 1961, 193 f.

STOKES, M. C. *See* KIRK, G. S.

STRANG, C. 'The Physical Theory of Anaxagoras', *Archiv für Geschichte der Philosophie*, 1963, 101–18.

STRATTON, G. M. *Theophrastus and the Greek Physiological Psychology before Aristotle*. London, 1917.

TANNERY, P. *Pour l'histoire de la science hellène*. 2nd ed. by A. Diès, Paris, 1930.

TANNERY, P. *La géométrie grecque*. Paris, 1883.

TAYLOR, A. E. 'On the Date of the Trial of Anaxagoras', *CQ*, 1917, 81–7.

TAYLOR, A. E. *A Commentary on Plato's* Timaeus. Oxford, 1928.

TAYLOR, A. E. *The Parmenides of Plato translated into English*. Oxford, 1934. (Appendix A: 'On the Work of Zeno.')

THEILER, W. *Zur Geschichte der teleologischen Naturbetrachtung bis auf Aristoteles*. Zürich and Leipzig, 1925.

THIELE, G. 'Zu den vier Elementen des Empedokles', *Hermes*, 1897, 68–78.

Bibliography

TOPITSCH, E. 'Die platonisch-aristotelischen Seelenlehren in weltanschauungs-kritischer Beleuchtung', *Sitzungsberichte der Akademie in Wien*, Phil.-Hist. Kl.', 1959, no. 4.

TOULMIN, S. and GOODFIELD, J. *The Architecture of Matter*. London, 1962.

TUGWELL, S. 'The Way of Truth', *CQ*, 1964, 36–41.

'UEBERWEG–PRAECHTER.' Ueberweg, F. *Grundriss der Geschichte der Philosophie*, ed. K. Praechter. 13th ed., Basel, 1953 (photographic reprint of 12th ed., 1923).

UNTERSTEINER, M. *Parmenide: Studio critico, frammenti, testimonianze, commento*. Turin, 1925.

UNTERSTEINER, M. *The Sophists*, transl. K. Freeman. Oxford (Blackwell), 1954.

UNTERSTEINER, M. *Parmenide: testimonianze e frammenti. Introduzione, traduzione e commento*. Florence, 1958.

UNTERSTEINER, M. *Zenone: testimonianze e frammenti*. Florence, 1963.

USENER, H. *Epicurea*. Leipzig, 1887.

USHENKO, A. 'Zeno's Paradoxes', *Mind*, 1946, 151–65.

VERDENIUS, W. J. *Parmenides, some Comments on his Poem*. Groningen, 1942.

VERDENIUS, W. J. 'Notes on the Presocratics', *Mnemosyne*, 1947, 271–89, and 1948, 8–14.

VERDENIUS, W. J. 'Empedocles' Doctrine of Sight', *Studia... Vollgraff...oblata*, Amsterdam, 1958, 155–64.

VERDENIUS, W. J. 'Parmenides B2. 3', *Mnemosyne*, 1962, 237.

VERDENIUS, W. J. and WASZINK, J. H. *Aristotle on Coming-to-be and Passing-away*. Leiden, 1946.

VLASTOS, G. 'Ethics and Physics in Democritus', *Philosophical Review*, 1945, 578–92, and 1946, 53–64.

VLASTOS, G. 'Parmenides' Theory of Knowledge', *TAPA*, 1946, 66–77.

VLASTOS, G. 'The Physical Theory of Anaxagoras', *Philosophical Review*, 1950, 31–57.

VLASTOS, G. Review of Cleve, *The Philosophy of Anaxagoras*, *Philosophical Review*, 1950, 124–6.

VLASTOS, G. 'Theology and Philosophy in Early Greek Thought', *Philosophical Quarterly*, 1952, 97–123.

VLASTOS, G. Review of Zafiropoulo, *L'École Éléate*, *Gnomon*, 1953, 166–9.

VLASTOS, G. Review of Kirk and Raven, in *Philosophical Review*, 1959, 532–5.

VLASTOS, G. Review of Fränkel's 'Wege und Formen', *Gnomon*, 1959, 193–204.

VOS, H. 'Die Bahnen von Nacht und Tag', *Mnemosyne*, 1963, 18–34.

WAERDEN, B. L. VAN DER. 'Zenon und die Grundlagenkrise der griechischen Mathematik', *Mathematische Annalen*, 1941, 141–61.

WAERDEN, B. L. VAN DER. *Science Awakening*. Groningen, 1954.

WASSERSTEIN, A. 'A Note on Fr. 12 of Anaxagoras', *CR*, 1960, 4–5.

WASSERSTEIN, A. Review of Sambursky's *Physics of the Stoics*, in *JHS*, 1963, 186–90.

WASZINK, J. H. *See* VERDENIUS, W. J.

Bibliography

WEHRLI, F. *Die Schule des Aristoteles: Texte und Kommentar* (Basel), Heft I: Dikaiarchos, 1944; Heft II: Aristoxenos, 1945; Heft V: Straton von Lampsakos, 1950; Heft VII: Herakleides Pontikos, 1953; Heft VIII: Eudemos von Rhodos, 1955.

WEISS, H. 'Democritus' Theory of Cognition', *CQ*, 1938, 47–56.

WEIZSÄCKER, C. F. VON. *The World-View of Physics*, 1952 (transl. by Marjorie Grene from 4th German ed., 1949).

WEIZSÄCKER, C. F. VON. *The Relevance of Science: Creation and Cosmogony.* London, 1964.

WELLMANN, M. 'Die Georgika des Demokritos', *Abhandlungen der preussischen Akademie*, 1921, no. 4.

WELLMANN, M. 'Die Φυσικά des Bolos Demokritos und der Magier Anaxilaos aus Larissa', *Abhandlungen der Preussischen Akademie*, 1928, no. 7.

WELLMANN, M. 'Spuren Demokrits von Abdera im Corpus Hippocraticum', *Archeion*, 1929, 297–330.

WEST, M. L. 'Anaxagoras and the Meteorite of 467 B.C.', *Journal of the British Astronomical Association*, 1960, 368–9.

WEYGOLDT, G. P. 'Zu Diogenes von Apollonia', *Archiv für Geschichte der Philosophie*, 1888, 161–71.

WHEWELL, W. *The Philosophy of the Inductive Sciences*, 2nd ed., 2 vols., London, 1847.

WIGHTMAN, W. P. D. *The Growth of Scientific Ideas.* Edinburgh, 1950.

WILAMOWITZ, U. VON. *Platon.* 2 vols., Berlin, 1920.

WILAMOWITZ, U. VON. 'Die Καθαρμοί des Empedokles', *Sitzungsberichte der preussischen Akademie* (SBB), 1929, 626–61.

WILAMOWITZ, U. VON. *Der Glaube der Hellenen.* 2 vols., Berlin, 1931–2.

WILLERDING, F. *Studia Hippocratica.* Göttingen, 1914.

WILLEY, B. *The Seventeenth-Century Background.* London, 1942.

WISDOM, J. O. 'Why Achilles does not fail to catch the tortoise', *Mind*, 1941, 58–73.

WOODBURY, L. 'Parmenides on Names', *HSCP* 63 (1958–9), 145–60.

ZAFIROPOULO, J. *Anaxagore de Clazomène.* I. *Le mythe grec traditionnel de Thalès à Platon.* II. *Théorie et fragments.* Paris, 1948. (*See also* its reviews by Heinimann in *Gnomon*, 1952, 271ff., Minar in *AJP*, 1953, 205–7, Valentin in *REG*, 1953, 438–40.)

ZAFIROPOULO, J. *L'École Éléate: Parménide–Zénon–Mélissos.* Paris, 1950. (*See also* its reviews by Vlastos in *Gnomon*, 1953, 166, and Verdenius in *Mnemosyne*, 1952, 157.)

ZAFIROPOULO, J. *Empédocle d'Agrigente.* Paris, 1953. (*See also* its review by J. Tate in *CR*, 1955, 48–50.)

'ZELLER–MONDOLFO.' *La Filosofia dei Greci.* Part I, vol. I, Florence, 3rd ed., 1951; vol. II, 2nd ed., 1950; vol. IV, 1961. (Zeller's work translated and enlarged by R. Mondolfo.)

'ZELLER–NESTLE.' E. Zeller, *Die Philosophie der Griechen*, 1. Teil, 1. Hälfte (7th ed., 1923) and 2. Hälfte (6th ed., 1920), edited by W. Nestle (Leipzig).

ZIMMER, H. *Philosophies of India.* London, 1951.

INDEXES

I. INDEX OF PASSAGES QUOTED
OR REFERRED TO

Index of passages quoted or referred to

Index of passages quoted or referred to

Index of passages quoted or referred to

Index of passages quoted or referred to

Index of passages quoted or referred to

531   34-2

Index of passages quoted or referred to

Index of passages quoted or referred to

Index of passages quoted or referred to

II. GENERAL INDEX

Bold figures denote a main or more important entry. The entries for modern scholars are often selective, and as a rule no entry is made where the text has no more than a reference.

Abaris, 11, 437
Abdera, 465 n. 2; School of, 382 n. 1
Achilles, 35; horses of, 7, 10 n. 2; and the tortoise, 92 f.
Acragas, 129 ff., 190 n. 3
Acron, pupil of Empedocles, 217
Adam, J. (quoted), 19
Aegospotami, fall of meteorite at, 266, 302 ff.; battle of, 302 n. 3
Aenesidemus, 430 n. 1
aer (ἀήρ), 185, 187, 195, 196, 197, 294 f., 295 n. 3. *See also* air
Aeschylus, on Nile floods, 311 with n. 2; on evolution of civilisation, 473
Agatharchus, 270, 271 n. 1
Aidoneus, as Empedoclean element, 141, 144, 145, 146
Air, corporeal nature of, 'proved' by Empedocles, 224; in Anaximenes, 225; supports the earth, 310, 371, 372 n. 1, 380; not an element for Anaxagoras, 282, 295, 315; identified with Mind by Archelaus, 341; by Diogenes of Apollonia, 369; as primary substance, 354, (Idaeus) 359, (Diogenes) 364 ff.; and fire as primary substances (Oenopides), 360; as principle of life, 369, 373 f., 434 n. 2; hence semen contains *pneuma*, 467; surrounding the cosmos, 371; as God and mind in Greek literature, 379 f. See also *aer*, *aither*
aistheton, 25 f.
Aithalides, 11, 12
aither, 190 f., 225, 262, 310; home of *nous* in Euripides, 18; as sky-father, 59; = air in Empedocles, 145, 185, 187; equated with Zeus, 145; in Anaxagoras (= fire), 273 n. 4, 295 f., 302, 303; divine, 262, 315 n. 4
alchemy, 148 n. 1
Alcmaeon, 19 n. 2, 47, 139, 142 n. 2, 237, 239, 325, 356 with notes, 434
Alfieri, V. E., 382 n. 1, 385 n. 1, 399 n. 1 505
Ameinias, Pythagorean philosopher, 3
Ananke, *see* Necessity
Anaxagoras, 1, 59, 78, 105 n. 1, 114, 116, 143, 174, 222 n. 1, 262 n. 1, **266–338**

relation to Empedocles (chronological), 128 n. 4, 241, 266, 275 n. 1; (in doctrine), 271 f., 282, 293, 295
reaction to Zeno, 281, 289; and other Eleatics, 271, 296 n. 1, 301
secular outlook, 266, 267, 272, 320
date, 266, 322 f.
life, 266 ff., 322 f.; friendship with Pericles, 268, 323; prosecution for impiety, exile and death, 268, 322 f.; school of, at Lampsacus, 268 f., 269 n. 1; representations of, on coins, 269 n. 1
survival of his treatise, 269; wrote on perspective: speculations of E. Frank on this, 270 f.
no becoming and perishing, only mixture and separation, 271
Mind, 272 ff.; as separate motive cause, 182, 274; non-teleological, 274 f.; characteristics of, 276; mixed with no thing, 276; whether entirely incorporeal, 276 ff.; special relation to living creatures, 278 f.; cause of good according to Aristotle, 279; summing-up, 279
theory of matter, 279 ff.; as answer to Eleatics, 281; every natural substance is real, 272, 281; 'a portion of everything in everything', 282, 285; reason for this, 286 f.; homoeomers in Aristotle and Anaxagoras, 282 f., 292 f., 325 f.; the opposites, 284; are substances not qualities, 285, 288 n. 1; the problem of nutrition, 287 f.; infinite divisibility and the infinitely small, 289 (but cf. 298 n. 2); as many substances in the large as the small, but not in equal portions in each, 290 f.; all things still together, 291 f.; did he posit elements at all?, 292 ff.
the original state: all things together, 292, 297 f.; and motionless, 278, 294; rotation and growth of the cosmos, 296 f.; the 'seeds', 298 ff.; stages of cosmogony, 301 f.; origin of heavenly bodies, 302 f.
cosmology, 304 ff.; inclination of pole, 305; shape of cosmos, 305; moon, 66, 198,

General index

General index

General index

corpses, retain some power of perception (Parmenides), 69, 73, 435 n. 2; (Democritus), 435

Cos, see medicine

cosmogony, denied by Parmenides, 28 f., 30, 33, 38; incompatible with monism, 53 f.; in Parmenides, 57 ff.; Pythagorean, 63, 296; always proceeds from mixture to separation, 173 with nn. 2 and 4; in Empedocles, 185 ff.; in Diodorus, 188; in Anaxagoras, 294 ff.; in Archelaus, 342 f.; in Diogenes of Apollonia, 370; in atomists, 406 ff.

cosmology, of Parmenides, 57 ff.; of Empedocles, 190 ff.; of Anaxagoras, 304 ff.; of Diogenes of Apollonia, 370; of the atomists, 419 ff.

not divorced from study of animal and human life, 350 f.

cosmos, impossible according to Parmenides, 32; word used for middle region of sky (Pythagoreans), 60; does not include all matter (Empedocles), 180; compared to an egg, 190 f. with n. 5, 408 n. 1; size of (Empedocles), 191; right and left sides to, 191 with n. 2; unique in Anaxagoras, 313 ff.; purpose of studying (Pythagoreans), 346; breathes (Diogenes and Pythagoreans), 371; skin of, 410 f.; is living and intelligent (Plato), 472. See also *kosmos*, pole

cotyledons, 378, 468 with n. 1

Covotti, A., 113 n. 1

Coxon, A. H., 50

Cratinus, 354

Cratylus, 358 f.

Critias, 350, 473, 494

Croton, 132 (see also medicine)

crystalline heaven, see sky

cycle, of births (see also transmigration), 251 ff.; of worlds (Empedocles), 167 ff.

daimon, 253; title of Love and Strife in Empedocles, 203; souls as incarnate *daimones* (Empedocles), 245, 258, 263 ff.; *daimones* in Hesiod, 264

darkness, as a substance, 195

Darwin, Charles, 203, 467 n. 1

Davison, J. A., 322 n. 2, 323

day, house and gates of Night and Day, 8, 9, 51, 72; growing shorter (Empedocles), 186; atomists' conception of day and night, 429 f.

death, explanation of, in Empedocles, 226; in

Anaxagoras, 317 with n. 1; in Democritus, 434 f.; moment of death uncertain (Democritus), 435; resuscitation of the apparently dead, 134, 437 f. See also corpses

Deichgräber, K., 54 n. 2

deification, 133 f., 134 n. 1. See also apotheosis

Delatte, A., 125, 227 n. 3, 478 n. 1

Demeter, 130

Demetrius (Cynic), 489 n. 3

Democrates, 489

Democritus, 1, 33, 65, 114, 225, 321, 349 f., 352, 353, **386–9** and ch. VIII *passim* visit to Athens, 349 with n. 2; wrote against Protagoras, 350, 386 n. 2, 485 f.; on perspective, 270, 271 n. 1, 446; on the next world, 436 ff.; writings in general, 436, 469 date and life, travels, contacts, 386 f.; postponed death by inhaling steam, 469 n. 3; reputed magical powers, 387 n. 2, 389

density and rarity, denied by Melissus, 104, 112, 115

Descartes, R., 20, 147 n. 1, 157, 278 n. 1, 440 n. 3, 501

Deucalion, 207, 358

dialectic, technique invented by Zeno, 82 f.

Diels, H., 3 n. 1, 4 n. 1, 9, 11, 20 n. 1, 31, 50, 123 n. 1; on Empedocles, 124, 126

Diès, A., 50, 259

Dieterich, A., 10 n. 3

Diller, H., 368 n. 1

Diocles, 217, 378 n. 2

Diodorus Cronus, 91 n. 1

Diodorus Siculus, cosmogony, zoogony and prehistory in, 59, 210 with n. 1, 343 n. 3, 389 n. 1, 473

Diogenes of Apollonia, 111, 115, 119, 120, 349, 352, 353, **362–81**; date and life, 362 f.; writings, 363 f.; return to monism: air as *arché*, 364 ff.; answer to pluralists, 367; to Eleatics, 367 f.; acceptance of void, 367 f.; chronological relation to Melissus, 368 n. 1; cosmology and meteorology, 370 f.; magnetism, 372 f.; life and intelligence, 374 f.; sensation, 375 f.; brain, 375, 376 f.; blood, 377; physiology, reproduction, 378; influence of, 379 ff.

Dionysus, 126, 253 n. 1, 258, 262

Diopeithes, decree of, 268, 323

Diotimus, 459

divinity, invisible and intangible (Empedocles), 256; assimilation to (Empedocles), 256; of souls in Empedocles, 251, 258, 262, 263 ff. See also god

541

divisibility, infinite, 88, 92, 93, 455, 485 n. 1; (in Anaxagoras), 289, 298 n. 2; of the elements in Empedocles, 148, 158

Dodds, E. R., 11 n. 1, 13, 125

dreams, atomic explanation of, 482

dualism, essential to cosmogony (Parmenides), 53 f.; of mind and matter in Anaxagoras, 321

Dyroff, A., 382 n. 2

ear, 238 f., 375

earth
  as passive element, 58 f.
  as mother of life, 59, 63, 64, 70, 207, 209, 218 n. 5, 315, 343; milky fluid from, 343 with n. 3
  as planet (Philolaus), 63
  associated with Justice, 64
  shape of, in Parmenides, 64 f.; in Empedocles, 198; flat in Anaxagoras, 310; and Leucippus, 422; concave (Archelaus), 342; (Democritus), 422
  division into zones, 65
  is compacted air (Parmenides), 66
  drying-up of, 188
  reason for central position (Empedocles), 198; (Anaximander), 424
  rides on air (Anaxagoras), 310; (Archelaus), 341; (atomists), 424
  porosity of, 310
  isolated inhabited hollows in, 314
  floats on water, 357
  motion of, 422 f.

earthquakes, cause of (Anaxagoras), 310 f.; (Aristotle), 311 n. 1; (Democritus), 424

eclecticism, 253 f., 371

eclipses, 421 n. 3 (Leucippus)
  of sun, explanation of by Empedocles, 196 f.; correct explanation by Anaxagoras, 307 f.
  of moon, explanation of by Anaxagoras, 306 f.

ecliptic, obliquity of, 360

effluences, theory of in Empedocles, 151; role in sensation (Empedocles), 231 ff.; in magnetism, 232, 373, 426; in vision and hearing (atomists), 442 f., 448

egg, cosmos compared to, 190, 408 n. 1

ekstasis, 126

Elea, 2

Eleatic School, 1 ff.; Aristotle's criticism of, 112; relation to Ionians, 119 f.; two possible responses to, 121; response to, of Empedocles, 138 ff.; of Anaxagoras, 271, 281, 296 n. 1, 301; of the atomists, 389 ff.,

398, 455 f., 499. *See also* Parmenides, Zeno, Melissus

element, concept of, discovered by Parmenides?, 54 n. 2; by Empedocles, 142; meaning, 147

elements, four mentioned by Melissus, 105
  in Empedocles (*see also* Empedocles), 116; proportions of in organic compounds, 210 ff.; order of in animal bodies, 217; role in sensation, 229; spirits' journey through, 252, 254
  when first distinguished, 141 f.
  mutually transformable in Plato and Aristotle, 143
  fifth element, 263
  in Anaxagoras, the homoeomers according to Aristotle, 282, 283 n. 4; but in fact no truly elemental bodies, 292 ff.
  in the atomists, 413 f.

Eleusinia, 10 n. 3

embryology, 79; of Empedocles, 218 f.; of Diogenes of Apollonia, 378; of Democritus, 467 f.

embryos nourished by sucking (Hippon), 357; (Diogenes of Apollonia), 378; (Democritus), 468; (Hippocratic), 469 n. 1

Empedocles, 1, 59, 63, 66, 67, 78, 114, **122–265**, 349, 353; book on, by Zeno, 81; opposed by Melissus, 104, 105, 115 f.; complex character of, 123, 132 ff.; his two poems contrasted, 124 ff., 137 f.; religion and science in, 125 f.
  date, 128; relation to Parmenides, 128 n. 4, 138 ff.; political activity, 131, 247; visit to Thurii, 131; death, 131; medical interests, 132 f., 216 f.; technical achievements and miracles, 133 f.; writings, 134 f.; technical similes, 135 f., 188, 199, 200 n. 1, 226, 235; method of composition, 136 f., 154 f.
  on limitations of senses, 138 f.
  denial of void, 139; of becoming and perishing, 139 f.
  monism abandoned, 140; the four roots (elements), 141 ff.; their divinity, 143 ff., 254; activated by desire and aversion, 157, 167, 172, 178 n. 3, 231; names of, 144 ff.; immutability of, 146 f.; motion of, 164 f.
  mingling and separation replace becoming and perishing, 148; particulate structure of matter, 149 ff.; its relation to atomism, 150, 152

General index

General index

pole, celestial, inclination of, 191 f., 305 with n. 2, 342

Polybus, 101 n. 2

Popper, K. R., 147 n. 1, 499, 502 n. 1, 503 n. 1

pores, 223; in Empedocles, 150 f., 218; role in sensation (Empedocles), 231 ff.; (atomists), 442 f., 448; in magnetism, 232, 373, 426

Poseidon, 141, 248, 249

possession, divine, 227

Presocratic philosophers, methods of study of, 122; scope of the term, xi, 345 with n. 1

prester, 312, 425

Prodicus, 347, 349

Prometheus, 18 n. 2, 70, 188, 473

prophecy, 227, 482

proportion, in combinations of elements (Empedocles), 211 f.; whether confined to organic substances, 213 ff.

Protagoras, 81, 129, 131, 340, 347, 351, 473; opposed by Democritus, 350; reputed pupil of Democritus, 386 n. 2; subjectivism of, 350, 455; on tangents, 485 f.

psyche, 226, 263, 316; localized in breast (Parmenides), 67, 69; identified with brain (Hippon), 356; two main functions of, 373; in Diogenes of Apollonia, 373 f.; in the atomists, relation to fire, 430 ff.; Socrates's conception of, 496. *See also* Mind

purification, means of, 244 f.

putrefaction, origin of life from, 212 n. 4

Pythagoras, 12, 23 n. 2, 65, 66, 129, 247 n. 3, 251 with n. 3, 308 n. 4, 324, 349 n., 450

Pythagoreanism, 5, 37, 114, 117, 118, 130, 132, 197; void in, 33, 48, 397; opposed by Parmenides, 30, 48 f., 53; his debt to it, 76; divisions of the sky in, 60; cosmologies of, 63; contrasted with atomic, 427; on the sun, 360; astronomy of, 420 n. 2; table of opposites in, 58, 77; attacked by Zeno?, 83–5, 89, 90, 91, 96; relation to Melissus, 115; emphasis on mathematics, 122, 321; secrecy in, 137; the four elements in, 141; theory of vision, 234; assimilation to the divine, 256; taught that moon is inhabited, 308 n. 4; religion and science in, 321 f.; purpose of studying cosmos, 346; relation to atomism, 389, 391; conception of time, 428; on nourishment by smells, 469 n. 3

qualities, conceived as active powers, 57, 286 n. 1; qualities and substances, 284, 291 n. 1

rainbow, in Anaxagoras and Empedocles, 312

ratios, of elements in compounds (Empedocles), 211 ff.

Raven, J. E., 14, 49, 84, 110 n. 2, 111 n. 1, 116 n. 4, 284, 289 n. 3, 290 n. 1, 298

reason, contrasted with senses by Parmenides, 25, 32. See also *logos*, mind, *nous*

reflexion, in Empedocles, 193, 238 f.; as explanation of vision (atomists), 442 f. *See also* mirrors

Reich, K., 5 n. 1

Reiche, H. A. T., 160 n. 2, 219 n. 4, 223 n. 3, 227 n. 1, 259

reincarnation, *see* transmigration

Reinhardt, K., 23, 27, 28, 50, **76**, 102 n. 2, 127 n. 2, 142 n. 2

relativity, of sensation and judgment, 353 f.; (Diogenes of Apollonia), 377 with n. 3, 381; (Protagoras), 350, 455; (atomists), 438 f., 440, 452

religion, and science in Greek antiquity, 125 f., 321 f. *See also* chthonian religion, divinity, god, and names of individual gods

Renan, E., 123

reproduction, account of in Empedocles, 217 ff.; in Anaxagoras, 317; in Hippon, 356 n. 1; in Diogenes of Apollonia, 378; in Democritus, 467 f.

respiration, of newborn infant, 219 f., 378 with n. 2; explanation of by Empedocles, 220 ff.; by Plato, 223; of fish (Anaxagoras), 317; (Diogenes of Apollonia), 379; all substances breathe (Diogenes), 372; role of void in (Diogenes), 379; life maintained by (atomists), 434

Rhodes, *see* medicine

right and left, distinguished in the cosmos, 191 with n. 2; significance of in embryology and correspondence with male and female (Parmenides), 78; (Empedocles), 218 n. 3; (Anaxagoras), 317 with n. 2

rivers, how formed (Anaxagoras), 311

rocks, origin of (Empedocles), 189

Rohde, E., on Empedocles, 102

Ross, Sir David, 97 n. 2, 222

Rostagni, A., 67, 139 n. 2, 141 n. 2, 251 n. 3

roundness, significance of in Greek thought, 47

Russell, Bertrand, 71 n. 2, 84

Sainte-Beuve, 18 n. 1

salt, extraction of, in Sicily, 190. *See also* sea

Sambursky, S., 366 n. 1, 397 with n. 2, 440 n. 2

Sandbach, F. H., 246 n. 3

Santillana, G. de, 31, 50, 64 n. 2

General index

553

III. INDEX OF GREEK WORDS

Greek words transliterated in the text will be found in the general index.